Lecture Notes in Computer Science 3222

Commenced Publication in 1973
Founding and Former Series Editors:
Gerhard Goos, Juris Hartmanis, and Jan van Leeuwen

Hai Jin   Guang R. Gao
Zhiwei Xu   Hao Chen (Eds.)

Network and Parallel Computing

IFIP International Conference, NPC 2004
Wuhan, China, October 18-20, 2004
Proceedings

 Springer

Volume Editors

Hai Jin
Hao Chen
Huazhong University of Science and Technology
Cluster and Grid Computing Lab
430074, Wuhan, China
E-mail: {hjin, haochen}@hust.edu.cn

Guang R. Gao
University of Delaware
Computer Architecture and Parallel System Laboratory
140 Evans Hall, Newark, DE 19716, USA
E-mail: ggao@capsl.udel.edu

Zhiwei Xu
Chinese Academy of Sciences
Institute of Computing Technology,
P.O. Box 2704, Beijing, 100080, China
E-mail: zxu@ict.ac.cn

Library of Congress Control Number: 2004112954

CR Subject Classification (1998): C.2, F.2, D.2, H.4, H.5, D.4, K.6

ISSN 0302-9743
ISBN 3-540-23388-1 Springer Berlin Heidelberg New York

Springer is a part of Springer Science+Business Media

springeronline.com

© IFIP International Federation for Information Processing 2004
Printed in Germany

Typesetting: Camera-ready by author, data conversion by Boller Mediendesign
Printed on acid-free paper   SPIN: 11318729   06/3142   5 4 3 2 1 0

We are deeply grateful to the program committee members. The large number of submissions received and the diversified topics and coverage of the topics made this review process a particularly challenging one. Also, the program committee was working under a very tight schedule. We wish to thank the program committee vice-chairs Victor K. Prasanna, Albert Y. Zomaya, and Hai Jin for their assistance in organizing the NPC 2004 program and the paper selection guidelines. Without the solid work and dedication of the program committee members, the success of this program would not have been possible.

We appreciate the contribution of Hai Jin and his local team at the Huazhong University of Science and Technology, Wuhan — in particular, the local chair Song Wu and Web chair Li Qi — who organized and handled the conference website for paper submissions and the review process, the organization of the final program, the design and maintenance of the NPC 2004 conference websites, the solicitation of sponsorships and support, and numerous other matters related to the local arrangements of the conference. We are deeply impressed by the efficiency, professionalism, and dedication of their work.

We also appreciate other support we received at the Institute of Computing Technology (ICT), Beijing, and the University of Delaware. In particular, we wish to acknowledge the assistance from Zhenge Qiu and Jiang Yi at ICT, and Yingping Zhang and Yanwei Niu at the University of Delaware.

July 2004

H.J. Siegel, Guojie Li
Kemal Ebcioglu,
Guang R. Gao, Zhiwei Xu

Preface

This proceedings contains the papers presented at the 2004 IFIP International Conference on Network and Parallel Computing (NPC 2004), held at Wuhan, China, from October 18 to 20, 2004. The goal of the conference was to establish an international forum for engineers and scientists to present their ideas and experiences in network and parallel computing.

A total of 338 submissions were received in response to the call for papers. These papers were from Australia, Brazil, Canada, China, Finland, France, Germany, Hong Kong, India, Iran, Italy, Japan, Korea, Luxemburg, Malaysia, Norway, Spain, Sweden, Taiwan, UK, and USA. Each submission was sent to at least three reviewers. Each paper was judged according to its originality, innovation, readability, and relevance to the expected audience. Based on the reviews received, a total of 69 papers were accepted to be included in the proceedings. Among the 69 papers, 46 were accepted as full papers and were presented at the conference. We also accepted 23 papers as short papers; each of these papers was given an opportunity to have a brief presentation at the conference, followed by discussions in a poster session. Thus, due to the limited scope and time of the conference and the high number of submissions received, only 20% of the total submissions were included in the final program.

In addition to the contributed papers, the NPC 2004 program featured several keynote speakers: Kai Hwang from the University of Southern California, Jos Fortes from the University of Florida, Thomas Sterling from the California Institute of Technology, Bob Kuhn from Intel, and Elmootazbellah Elnozahy from the IBM Austin Research Center. In addition, there was an invited session with several invited talks. The keynote and invited speakers were selected due to their significant contributions and reputations in the field.

Also associated with NPC 2004 were a tutorial session and two workshops, the Workshop on Building Intelligent Sensor Networks, and the Workshop on Multimedia Modeling and the Security in the Next Generation Network Information Systems.

The IFIP NPC 2004 conference emerged from initial email exchanges between Kemal Ebcioglu, Guojie Li, and Guang R. Gao in 2002, with the vision toward establishing a new, truly international conference for fostering research and collaboration in parallel computing. We are happy to see that the NPC conference, with its eminent team of organizers, and its high-quality technical program, is well on its way to becoming a flagship conference of IFIP.

We wish to thank the contributions of the other members of the organizing committee. We acknowledge the solid work by Nelson Amaral for his dedication in organizing the tutorial and workshop sessions. We thank the publicity co-chairs Cho-Li Wang and Chris Jesshope for their hard work in publicizing the NPC 2004 information under a very tight schedule constraint.

Conference Committees

General Co-Chairs

H.J. Siegel (Colorado State University, USA)
Guojie Li (Institute of Computing Technology, CAS, China)

Steering Committee Chair

Kemal Ebcioglu (IBM T.J. Watson Research Center, USA)

Program Co-Chairs

Guangrong Gao (University of Delaware, USA)
Zhiwei Xu (Institute of Computing Technology, CAS, China)

Program Vice-Chairs

Victor K. Prasanna (University of Southern California, USA)
Albert Y. Zomaya (University of Sydney, Australia)
Hai Jin (Huazhong University of Science and Technology, China)

Publicity Co-Chairs

Cho-Li Wang (The University of Hong Kong, Hong Kong)
Chris Jesshope (The University of Hull, UK)

Workshop/Tutorial Chair

Jose N. Amaral (University of Alberta, Canada)

Local Arrangement Chair

Song Wu (Huazhong University of Science and Technology, China)

Publication Chair

Hao Chen (Huazhong University of Science and Technology, China)

Steering Committee Members

Jack Dongarra (University of Tennessee, USA)
Guangrong Gao (University of Delaware, USA)
Jean-Luc Gaudiot (University of California, Irvine, USA)
Guojie Li (The Institute of Computing Technology, CAS, China)
Yoichi Muraoka (Waseda University, Japan)
Daniel Reed (University of North Carolina, USA)

Program Committee Members

Ishfaq Ahmad (University of Texas at Arlington, USA)
Shoukat Ali (University of Missouri-Rolla, USA)
Makoto Amamiya (Kyushu University, Japan)
David Bader (University of New Mexico, USA)
Luc Bouge (IRISA/ENS Cachan, France)
Pascal Bouvry (University of Luxembourg, Luxembourg)
Ralph Castain (Los Alamos National Laboratory, USA)
Guoliang Chen (University of Science and Technology of China, China)
Xueqi Cheng (Institute of Computing Technology, CAS, China)
Jong-Deok Choi (IBM T. J. Watson Research Center, USA)
Alain Darte (CNRS, ENS-Lyon, France)
Chen Ding (University of Rochester, USA)
Jianping Fan (Institute of Computing Technology, CAS, China)
Xiaobing Feng (Institute of Computing Technology, CAS, China)
Guangrong Gao (University of Delaware, USA)
Jean-Luc Gaudiot (University of California, Irvine, USA)
Minyi Guo (University of Aizu, Japan)
Mary Hall (University of Southern California, USA)
Yanbo Han (Institute of Computing Technology, CAS, China)
Salim Hariri (University of Arizona, USA)
Kai Hwang (University of Southern California, USA)
Anura Jayasumana (Colorado State Univeristy, USA)
Chris R. Jesshope (The University of Hull, UK)
Hai Jin (Huazhong University of Science and Technology, China)
Ricky Kwok (The University of Hong Kong, Hong Kong)
Francis Lau (The University of Hong Kong, Hong Kong)
Chuang Lin (Tsinghua University, China)
Soo-Mook Moon (Seoul National University, Korea)
John Morrison (University College Cork, Ireland)
Lionel Ni (Hong Kong University of Science and Technology, Hong Kong)
Stephan Olariu (Old Dominion University, USA)
Yi Pan (Georgia State University, USA)
Depei Qian (Xi'an Jiaotong University, China)
Daniel A. Reed (University of North Carolina at Chapel Hill, USA)

Wolfgang Rehm (Chemnitz University of Technology , Germany)
Jose Rolim (University of Geneva, Switzerland)
Arnold Rosenberg (University of Massachusetts at Amherst, USA)
Sartaj Sahni (University of Florida, USA)
Selvakennedy Selvadurai (University of Sydney, Australia)
Franciszek Seredynski (Polish Academy of Sciences, Poland)
Hong Shen (Japan Advanced Institute of Science and Technology, Japan)
Xiaowei Shen (IBM T. J. Watson Research Center, USA)
Gabby Silberman (IBM Centers for Advanced Studies, USA)
Per Stenstrom (Chalmers University of Technology, Sweden)
Ivan Stojmenovic (University of Ottawa, Canada)
Ninghui Sun (Institute of Computing Technology, CAS, China)
El-Ghazali Talbi (University of Lille, France)
Domenico Talia (University of Calabria, Italy)
Mitchell D. Theys (University of Illinois at Chicago, USA)
Xinmin Tian (Intel Corporation, USA)
Dean Tullsen (University of California, San Diego, USA)
Cho-Li Wang (The University of Hong Kong, Hong Kong)
Weng-Fai Wong (National University of Singapore, Singapore)
Zhiwei Xu (Institute of Computing Technology, CAS, China)
Qing Yang (University of Rhode Island, USA)
Yuanyuan Yang (State University of New York at Stony Brook, USA)
Xiaodong Zhang (College of William and Mary, USA)
Weimin Zheng (Tsinghua University, China)
Bingbing Zhou (University of Sydney, Australia)
Chuanqi Zhu (Fudan University, China)

Reviewers

Nova Ahmed	Lichun Bao	Jose G Castanos
Sahra Ali	Leung Benny	Karam S. Chatha
Sahra Sedigh-Ali	Janaka Balasooriya	Mei Chao
Gautam Altekar	Bharat Bhargava	Ajay Chankramath
Gulsah Altun	Noah Beck	Chun Chen
Alain Andrieux	Stanislav Belenki	Li Chen
Joerg Anders	Aart Bik	Weisong Chen
Kostas Anagnostakis	Mats Bjorkman	Shigang Chen
Chuck Anderson	Michael Buettner	Fei Chen
Boon S Ang	Ranjita Bhagwan	Weisong Chen
Oscar AU	Azzedine Boucherche	Huaping Chen
Mohammad Banikazemi	Tracy Braun	Mingyu Chen
Faisal Bashir	RajKumar Buyya	Songqing Chen
Robert Baumgartl	Hailong Cai	Xiaowu Chen
Florin Baboescu	Jose Castanos	Mingyu Cheng
HyoKyung Bahn	Mario Cannataro	S.C.Cheung

Steve Chiu
Derek Chiou
Chung-Ping Chung
Guojing Cong
Carmela Comito
Antonio Congiusta
Groire Danoy
Sajal Das
David Daniel
Zampunieris Denis
Inanc Dogru
Shoubin Dong
Alin Dobra
Alban Douillet
Liu Donghua
Pasqua D'Ambra
Patrick Duessel
Zhihui Du
Colin Egan
Thomas Engel
Behdis Eslamnour
Jianxi Fan
Yanfei Fan
Weijian Fang
Tang Feng
Hannes Frey
Giancarlo Fortino
Gianluigi Folino
Li Gang
He Ge
Min Gao
Kanad Ghose
Andreas Goerdt
Kartik Gopalan
Yili Gong
Li Guo
Ning Gu
Yu Haiyan
Joachim Hammer
Shaohua Han
Wang Hao
Xubin He
Luc Hogie
Philip Healy
Dan Hong

Jochen Hollman
Jingcao Hu
Mingchang Hu
Ziang Hu
Yu Huashan
Chao Huang
Junwei Huang
Praveena Jayanthi
Mathieu Jan
Chris Jermaine
Ma Jie
Song Jiang
Hong Jiang
Weihua Jiang
Sunil John
Dongsoo Kang
Jaeyeon Kang
Winfried Kalfa
Mihailo Kaplarevic
Robel Y. Kahsay
Ajay K Katangur
Anne-Marie Kermarrec
Mujtaba Khambatti
Hye-Young Kim
Jin-Soo Kim
Geunhyung Kim
Suhyun Kim
Chung-Ta King
Jim Klosowski
Robert S. Klosiewicz
Dimitrij Krepis
Ajay Kshemkalyani
Matthias Kuehnemann
Tyrone Kwok
Gisik Kwon
Ashfaq Khokhar
Chen-Chi Kuo
Wing Cheong Lau
Hanno Lefmann
Pierre Leone
Andrew Leung
Brian Levine
Myung J. Lee
Yoon-Ju Lee
Kang-Won Lee

Jaemok Lee
Myung J. Lee
Victor Lee
Yuanzhen Li
Xiang-Yang Li
Wei Li
Minglu Li
Xiaofei Liao
Shao Liang
Xiaohui Lin
Chen Lin
Donghua Liu
limin Liu
Xingwu Liu
Hong Liu
Xiang Lian
Weifa Liang
Xiaobin Lin
Jonathan Liu
King-Shan Lui
Chen Liu
Tao Liu
Yunhao Liu
Hui Liu
Wei Liu
Zhongzhi Luan
Bjorn Landfeldt
Chi Ma
Jian Ma
Ming Ma
Praveen Madiraju
M. Maheswaran
Joseph Manzano
Jan-Willem Maessen
W.H. Mangione-Smith
Alper Mizrak
Andres Marquez
Robert Marcus
Nordine Melab
Dan Meng
Frank Mietke
Carlo Mastroianni
Sastien Monnet
Yanwei Niu
Padraig O'Dowd

Adarsh Patil
Christian Perez
Francesco Pupo
Andrea Pugliese
A.E. Papathanasiou
Chong-Dae Park
Myong-Soon Park
Chanik Park
Tania Perez
Keith Power
Juhua Pu
Michael Powell
Olivier Powell
Ding Qiang
Sanjay Ranka
M.M. Rashid
Sriram Ramanujam
Thomas Rauber
Niranjan Regatta
FengYuan Ren
Albert Reuther
Scott Rixner
Krzysztof Rzadca
Ram Rajamony
Won Woo Ro
Jamie Ross
Steffen Rothkugel
Hongbo Rong
William Saylor
Siddhartha Saha
Subhradyuti Sarkar
Jennifer Schopf
Li Shang
Basit Shafiq
Zhiyuan Shao
Alex Shafarenko
Sveta Shasharina
Gang Shi
Bill Scherer
Chistoph Schommer
John Seng
Xiaojun Shen
Bartlomiej Sieka
Ulrich Sorger
Ernesto Su

Yuzhong Sun
Justin Song
Junehwa Song
Jon A. Solworth
Julio Solano
Hu Songlin
Giandomenico Spezzano
Xipeng Shen
Guangzhong Sun
Pierre Sens
Claude Tadonki
Mario Trams
Alex Tudor
Nathan Tuck
Sven Trautmann
Anthony Tam
Spyros Tragoudas
Tqwang
Paolo Trunfio
Theo Ungerer
Thiemo Voigt
Cheuksan Edward Wang
Ye Wang
Rui Wang
Tianqi Wang
Cheung Wang
Guojun Wang
Chen Wang
Nanbor Wang
Jiang Wei
Adam Wierzbicki
Haiping Wu
Zhaohui Wu
Haiping Wu
Junmin Wu
Qin Wang
Peng Wang
Lijuan Xiao
Nong Xiao
Gui Xie
Yinlong Xu
Yun Xu
Guoliang Xue
Mi Yan
Weidong Yang

XiaoJun Yang
Qiang Yang
Guangwen Yang
Ruoyun Yang
Baoliu Ye
Weilie Yi
Guo Yi
Kyueun Yi
Hao Yin
Chen Yu
Yueqiang
Heon Young Yeom
Li Yue
Maciej Zawodniok
Li Zha
Chengliang Zhang
Weihua Zhang
Michael Zhang
Yongdong Zhang
Michael Zhang
Xiaolan
Dawei Xu
Zhang
Yuan Zhang
Ming Zhang
Xiaomin Zhang
Yuanyuan Zhang
Xiaolei Zhang
Xinming Zhang
Qilong Zheng
Shen Zheng
Yifeng Zhu
Jiahua Zhu
Yutao Zhong
Ming Zhong
Jiling Zhong
Wei Zhong
Yongkang Zhu
Wenzhang Zhu
Weirong Zhu
Yanmin Zhu
Wenzhang Zhu
Zoltan Zsska
Thierry Zwissig

Table of Contents

Secure Grid Computing with Trusted Resources and Internet
Datamining 1
Kai Hwang

Towards Memory Oriented Scalable Computer Architecture and High
Efficiency Petaflops Computing 2
Thomas Sterling

In-VIGO: Making the Grid Virtually Yours 3
José Fortes

Productivity in HPC Clusters 4
Bob Kuhn

Whole-Stack Analysis and Optimization of Commercial Workloads on
Server Systems 5
*C. Richard Attanasio, Jong-Deok Choi, Niteesh Dubey, K. Ekanadham,
Manish Gupta, Tatsushi Inagaki, Kazuaki Ishizaki, Joefon Jann,
Robert D. Johnson, Toshio Nakatani, Il Park, Pratap Pattnaik,
Mauricio Serrano, Stephen E. Smith, Ian Steiner, Yefim Shuf*

Session 1: Grid Computing

Fuzzy Trust Integration for Security Enforcement in Grid Computing.... 9
Shanshan Song, Kai Hwang, Mikin Macwan

Atomic Commitment in Grid Database Systems 22
Sushant Goel, Hema Sharda, David Taniar

A Data Grid Security System Based on Shared Context............... 30
Nong Xiao, Xiaonian Wu, Wei Fu, Xiangli Qu

A Study on Performance Monitoring Techniques for Traditional Parallel
Systems and Grid 38
Sarbani Roy, Nandini Mukherjee

A Workflow-Based Grid Portal for Problem Solving Environment 47
Yong-Won Kwon, So-Hyun Ryu, Jin-Sung Park, Chang-Sung Jeong

A Real-Time Transaction Approach for Grid Services: A Model and
Algorithms 57
Feilong Tang, Minglu Li, Joshua Zhexue Huang, Lei Cao, Yi Wang

QoS Quorum-Constrained Resource Management in Wireless Grid 65
Chan-Hyun Youn, Byungsang Kim, Dong Su Nam, Eung-Suk An,
Bong-Hwan Lee, Eun Bo Shim, Gari Clifford

A Data-Aware Resource Broker for Data Grids 73
Huy Le, Paul Coddington, Andrew L. Wendelborn

Managing Service-Oriented Grids: Experiences from VEGA System
Software 83
YuZhong Sun, Haiyan Yu, JiPing Cai, Li Zha, Yili Gong

An Efficient Parallel Loop Self-scheduling on Grid Environments 92
Chao-Tung Yang, Kuan-Wei Cheng, Kuan-Ching Li

ALiCE: A Scalable Runtime Infrastructure for High Performance Grid
Computing 101
Yong-Meng Teo, Xianbing Wang

Mapping Publishing and Mapping Adaptation in the Middleware of
Railway Information Grid System 110
Ganmei You, Huaming Liao, Yuzhong Sun

A Heuristic Algorithm for the Job Shop Scheduling Problem 118
Ai-Hua Yin

Coordinating Distributed Resources for Complex Scientific Computation . 129
Huashan Yu, Zhuoqun Xu, Wenkui Ding

Efficiently Rationing Resources for Grid and P2P Computing 133
Ming Chen, Yongwei Wu, Guangwen Yang, Xuezheng Liu

Grid Resource Discovery Model Based on the Hierarchical Architecture
and P2P Overlay Network 137
Fei Liu, Fanyuan Ma, Shui Yu, Minglu Li

Collaborative Process Execution for Service Composition with
StarWebService 141
Bixin Liu, YuFeng Wang, Bin Zhou, Yan Jia

Session 2: Peer-to-Peer Computing

Efficient Gnutella-like P2P Overlay Construction 146
Yunhao Liu, Li Xiao, Lionel M. Ni, Baijian Yang

Lookup-Ring: Building Efficient Lookups for High Dynamic
Peer-to-Peer Overlays 154
Xuezheng Liu, Guangwen Yang, Jinfeng Hu, Ming Chen, Yongwei Wu

Layer Allocation Algorithms in Layered Peer-to-Peer Streaming 167
Yajie Liu, Wenhua Dou, Zhifeng Liu

Build a Distributed Repository for Web Service Discovery Based on
Peer-to-Peer Network 175
Yin Li, Futai Zou, Fanyuan Ma, Minglu Li

Performance Improvement of Hint-Based Locating & Routing
Mechanism in P2P File-Sharing Systems 183
Hairong Jin, Shanping Li, Gang Peng, Tianchi Ma

Session 3: Web Techniques

Cache Design for Transcoding Proxy Caching 187
Keqiu Li, Hong Shen, Keishi Tajima

Content Aggregation Middleware (CAM) for Fast Development of High
Performance Web Syndication Services 195
Su Myeon Kim, Jinwon Lee, SungJae Jo, Junehwa Song

Domain-Based Proxy for Efficient Location Tracking of Mobile Agents ... 205
Sanghoon Song, Taekyoung Kwon

Session 4: Cluster Computing

Inhambu: Data Mining Using Idle Cycles in Clusters of PCs 213
*Hermes Senger, Eduardo R. Hruschka, Fabrício A.B. Silva,
Liria M. Sato, Calebe P. Bianchini, Marcelo D. Esperidião*

Request Distribution for Fairness with a New Load-Update Mechanism
in Web Server Cluster 221
MinHwan Ok, Myong-soon Park

Profile Oriented User Distributions in Enterprise Systems with
Clustering 230
Ping-Yu Hsu, Ping-Ho Ting

CBBS: A Content-Based Bandwidth Smoothing Scheme for Clustered
Video Servers 238
Dafu Deng, Hai Jin, Xiaofei Liao, Hao Chen

SuperNBD: An Efficient Network Storage Software for Cluster 244
Rongfeng Tang, Dan Meng, Jin Xiong

I/O Response Time in a Fault-Tolerant Parallel Virtual File System 248
Dan Feng, Hong Jiang, Yifeng Zhu

SARCNFS: Self-Adaptive Redundancy Clustered NAS File System 252
Cai Bin, Changsheng Xie, Ren Jin, FaLing Yi

Research and Implementation of a Snapshot Facility Suitable for
Soft-Failure Recovery 256
Yong Feng, Yan-yuan Zhang, Rui-yong Jia

Session 5: Parallel Programming and Environment

GOOMPI: A Generic Object Oriented Message Passing Interface........ 261
Zhen Yao, Qi-long Zheng, Guo-liang Chen

Simulating Complex Dynamical Systems in a Distributed Programming
Environment 272
E.V. Krishnamurthy, Vikram Krishnamurthy

Design and Implementation of a Remote Debugger for Concurrent
Debugging of Multiple Processes in Embedded Linux Systems 280
Jung-hee Kim, Hyun-chul Sim, Yong-hyeog Kang, Young Ik Eom

Session 6: Network Architecture

Performance Evaluation of Hypercubes in the Presence of Multiple
Time-Scale Correlated Traffic..................................... 284
Geyong Min, Mohamed Ould-Khaoua

Leader Election in Hyper-Butterfly Graphs......................... 292
Wei Shi, Pradip K. Srimani

A New Approach to Local Route Recovery for Multihop TCP in
Ad Hoc Wireless Networks 300
Zhi Li, Yu-Kwong Kwok

Graph-Theoretic Analysis of Kautz Topology and DHT Schemes 308
Dongsheng Li, Xicheng Lu, Jinshu Su

A Parameterized Model of TCP Slow Start......................... 316
Xiaoheng Deng, Zhigang Chen, Lianming Zhang

SMM: A Truthful Mechanism for Maximum Lifetime Routing in
Wireless Ad Hoc Networks 325
Qing Zhang, Huiqiong Chen, Weiwei Sun, Bole Shi

A Dioid Linear Algebra Approach to Study a Class of Continuous Petri
Nets.. 333
Duan Zhang, Huaping Dai, Youxian Sun

A Fully Adaptive Fault-Tolerant Routing Methodology Based on
Intermediate Nodes 341
*Nils Agne Nordbotten, Maria Engracia Gómez, Jose Flich,
Pedro López, Antonio Robles, Tor Skeie, Olav Lysne, José Duato*

Extended DBP for (m,k)-Firm Based QoS 357
Jiming Chen, Zhi Wang, Yeqiong Song, Youxian Sun

Weighted Fair Scheduling Algorithm for QoS of Input-Queued Switches .. 366
Sang-Ho Lee, Dong-Ryeol Shin, Hee Yong Youn

A Scalable Distributed Architecture for Multi-party Conferencing
Using SIP 374
Young-Hoon Cho, Moon-Sang Jeong, Jong-Tae Park

DC-mesh: A Contracted High-Dimensional Mesh for Dynamic Clustering. 382
Masaru Takesue

The Effect of Adaptivity on the Performance of the OTIS-Hypercube
Under Different Traffic Patterns 390
H.H. Najaf-abadi, H. Sarbazi-Azad

An Empirical Autocorrelation Form for Modeling LRD Traffic Series 399
Ming Li, Jingao Liu, Dongyang Long

Statistical Error Analysis on Recording LRD Traffic Time Series 403
Ming Li

Load Balancing Routing in Low-Cost Parallel QoS Sensitive Network
Architecture.. 407
Furong Wang, Ye Wu

Session 7: Network Security

Reversible Cellular Automata Based Encryption 411
Marcin Seredynski, Krzysztof Pienkosz, Pascal Bouvry

Ontology Based Cooperative Intrusion Detection System 419
Yanxiang He, Wei Chen, Min Yang, Wenling Peng

Adding Security to Network Via Network Processors 427
Hao Yin, Zhangxi Tan, Chuang Lin, Guangxi Zhu

A Method to Obtain Signatures from Honeypots Data 435
Chi-Hung Chi, Ming Li, Dongxi Liu

A Framework for Adaptive Anomaly Detection Based on Support
Vector Data Description 443
Min Yang, HuanGuo Zhang, JianMing Fu, Fei Yan

Design and Analysis of Improved GSM Authentication Protocol for
Roaming Users 451
GeneBeck Hahn, Taekyoung Kwon, Sinkyu Kim, JooSeok Song

A Novel Intrusion Detection Method 459
ShengYi Jiang, QingHua Li, Hui Wang

Session 8: Network Storage

An Implementation of Storage-Based Synchronous Remote Mirroring
for SANs... 463
Ji-wu Shu, Rui Yan, Dongchan Wen, Weimin Zheng

A Network Bandwidth Computation Technique for IP Storage with
QoS Guarantees 473
Young Jin Nam, Junkil Ryu, Chanik Park, Jong Suk Ahn

Paramecium: Assembling Raw Nodes into Composite Cells 481
Ming Chen, Guangwen Yang, Yongwei Wu, Xuezheng Liu

The Flexible Replication Method in an Object-Oriented Data Storage
System 485
Youhui Zhang, Jinfeng Hu, Weimin Zheng

Enlarge Bandwidth of Multimedia Server with Network Attached
Storage System 489
Dan Feng, Yuhui Deng, Ke Zhou, Fang Wang

The NDMP-Plus Prototype Design and Implementation for Network
Based Data Management 493
Kai Ouyang, Jingli Zhou, Tao Xia, Shengsheng Yu

Session 9: Multimedia Service

Further Optimized Parallel Algorithm of Watershed Segmentation
Based on Boundary Components Graph 498
Haifang Zhou, Xuejun Yang, Yu Tang, Nong Xiao

The Transmitted Strategy of Proxy Cache Based on Segmented Video ... 502
Zhiwen Xu, Xiaoxin Guo, Yunjie Pang, Zhengxuan Wang

The Strategy of Batch Using Dynamic Cache for Streaming Media 508
Zhiwen Xu, Xiaoxin Guo, Yunjie Pang, Zhengxuan Wang

New Regions of Interest Image Coding Using Up-Down Bitplanes Shift
for Network Applications 513
Li-bao Zhang, Ke Wang

Workshop1: Building Intelligent Sensor Networks

Bridging the Gap Between Micro and Nanotechnology: Using
Lab-on-a-Chip to Enable Nanosensors for Genomics, Proteomics, and
Diagnostic Screening 517
Jonathan M. Cooper, Erik A. Johannessen, David R.S. Cumming

The Development of Biosensors and Biochips in IECAS 522
Xinxia Cai, Dafu Cui

Open Issues on Intelligent Sensor Networks 526
Yiqiang Chen, Wen Gao, Junfa Liu

Enabling Anytime Anywhere Wireless Sensor Networks 527
John Crawford

A Query-Aware Routing Algorithm in Sensor Networks 528
Jinbao Li, Jianzhong Li, Shengfei Shi

Sensor Network Optimization by a Novel Genetic Algorithm 536
Hui Wang, Anna L. Buczak, Hong Jin, Hongan Wang, Baosen Li

Online Mining in Sensor Networks 544
Xiuli Ma, Dongqing Yang, Shiwei Tang, Qiong Luo, Dehui Zhang,
Shuangfeng Li

The HKUST Frog Pond - A Case Study of Sensory Data Analysis 551
Wenwei Xue, Bingsheng He, Hejun Wu, Qiong Luo

BLOSSOMS: A CAS/HKUST Joint Project to Build Lightweight
Optimized Sensor Systems on a Massive Scale 559
Wen Gao, Lionel Ni, Zhiwei Xu

A Pervasive Sensor Node Architecture 565
Li Cui, Fei Wang, Haiyong Luo, Hailing Ju, Tianpu Li

Cabot: On the Ontology for the Middleware Support of Context-Aware
Pervasive Applications 568
Chang Xu, Shing-Chi Cheung, Cindy Lo, K.C. Leung, Jun Wei

Accurate Emulation of Wireless Sensor Networks 576
Hejun Wu, Qiong Luo, Pei Zheng, Bingsheng He, Lionel M. Ni

LEAPS: A Location Estimation and Action Prediction System in a
Wireless LAN Environment 584
Qiang Yang, Yiqiang Chen, Jie Yin, Xiaoyong Chai

Reliable Splitted Multipath Routing for Wireless Sensor Network 592
Jian Wu, Stefan Dulman, Paul Havinga

Reliable Data Aggregation for Real-Time Queries in Wireless Sensor
Systems 601
Kam-Yiu Lam, Henry C.W. Pang, Snag H. Son, BiYu Liang

Workshop2: Multimedia Modeling and the Security in the Next Generation Network Information Systems

The Design of a DRM System Using PKI and a Licensing Agent 611
KeunWang Lee, JaePyo Park, KwangHyoung Lee, JongHee Lee, HeeSook Kim

Multimedia Synchronization for Handoff Control with MPEG in All-IP
Mobile Networks 618
Gi-Sung Lee, Hong-jin Kim, Il-Sun Hwang

Fuzzy Logic Adaptive Mobile Location Estimation 626
Jongchan Lee, Seung-Jae Yoo, Dong Chun Lee

A Host Protection Framework Against Unauthorized Access for
Ensuring Network Survivability 635
Hyuncheol Kim, Sunghae Kim, Seongjin Ahn, Jinwook Chung

A Design and Implementation of Network Traffic Monitoring System
for PC-room Management 644
Yonghak Ahn, Oksam Chae

A Vulnerability Assessment Tool Based on OVAL in Linux System 653
Youngmi Kwon, Hui Jae Lee, Geuk Lee

Performance Analysis of Delay Estimation Models for Signalized
Intersection Networks 661
Hyung Jin Kim, Bongsoo Son, Soobeom Lee

Network Intrusion Protection System Using Rule-Based DB and RBAC
Policy 670
Min Wook Kil, Si Jung Kim, Youngmi Kwon, Geuk Lee

Effective FM Bandwidth Estimate Scheme with the DARC in
Broadcasting Networks 676
Sang Woon Lee, Kyoo Jin Han, Keum Chan Whang

Enhanced Algorithm of TCP Performance on Handover in Wireless
Internet Networks 684
Dong Chun Lee, Hong-Jin Kim, JaeYoung Koh

Author Index 691

Secure Grid Computing with Trusted Resources and Internet Datamining

Kai Hwang

University of Southern California
Los Angeles, CA. 90089 USA

Abstract. Internet-based Grid computing is emerging as one of the most promising technologies that may change the world. Dr. Hwang and his research team at the University of Southern California (USC) are working on self-defense tools to protect Grid resources from cyber attacks or malicious intrusions, automatically. This project builds an automated intrusion response and trust management system to facilitate authentication, authorization, and security binding in using metacomputing Grids or peer-to-peer web services. The trusted GridSec infrastructure supports Internet traffic datamining, encrypted tunneling, optimized resource allocations, network flood control and anomaly detection, etc. The USC team is developing a NetShield library to protect Grid resources. This new security system adjusts itself dynamically with changing threat patterns and network traffic conditions. This project promotes the acceptance of Grid computing through international collaborations with the research groups in INRIA, France, Chinese Academy of Sciences, and Melbourne University. The fortified Grid infrastructure will benefit securitysensitive allocations in digital government, electronic commerce, anti-terrorism activities, and cyberspace crime control. The broader impacts of this ITR project are far reaching in an era of growing demand of Internet, Web and Grid services

H. Jin et al. (Eds.): NPC 2004, LNCS 3222, pp. 1-1, 2004.
© IFIP International Federation for Information Processing 2004

Towards Memory Oriented Scalable Computer Architecture and High Efficiency Petaflops Computing

Thomas Sterling

Center for Advanced Computing Research
California Institute of Technology

Abstract. The separation of processor logic and main memory is an artifact of the disparities of the original technologies from which each was fabricated more than fifty years ago as captured by the "von Neumann architecture". Appropriately, this separation is designated as "the von Neumann bottleneck". In recent years, the underlying technology constraint for the isolation of main memory from processing logic has been eliminated with the implementation of semiconductor fabrication foundries that permit the merger of both DRAM bit cells and CMOS logic on the same silicon dies. New classes of computer architecture are enabled by this opportunity including: 1) *system on a chip* where a conventional processor core with its layers of cache are connected to a block of DRAM on the same chip, 2) *SMP on a chip* where multiple conventional processor cores are combined on the same chip through a coherent cache structure, usually sharing the L3 cache implemented in DRAM, and 3) *processor in memory* where custom processing logic is positioned directly at the memory row buffer in a tightly integrated structure to exploit the short access latency and wide row of bits (typically 2K) for high memory bandwidth. This last, PIM, can take on remarkable physical structures and logical constructs and is the focus of the NASA Gilgamesh project to define and prototype a new class of PIM-based computer architecture that will enable a new scalable model of execution. The MIND processor architecture is the core of the Gilgamesh system that incorporates a distributed shared memory management scheme including in-memory virtual to physical address translation, a lightweight *parcels* message-driven mechanism for invoking remote transaction processing, multithreaded single cycle instruction issue for local resource management, graceful degradation for fault tolerance, and pinned threads for real time response. The MIND architecture for Gilgamesh is being developed in support of "sea of PIMs" systems for both ground based Petaflops scale computers and scalable space borne computing for long term autonomous missions. One of its specific applications is in the domain of symbolic computing for knowledge management, learning, reasoning, and planning in a goal directed programming environment. This presentation will describe the MIND architecture being developed through the Gilgamesh project and its relation to the Cray Cascade Petaflops computer being developed for 2010 deployment under DARPA sponsorship.

H. Jin et al. (Eds.): NPC 2004, LNCS 3222, pp. 2-2, 2004.
© IFIP International Federation for Information Processing 2004

In-VIGO: Making the Grid Virtually Yours

José Fortes

Department of Electrical and Computer Engineering, University of Florida

Abstract. Internet-based Grid computing is emerging as one of the most promising technologies that may change the world. Dr. Hwang and his research team at the University of Southern California (USC) are working on self-defense tools to protect Grid resources from cyber attacks or malicious intrusions, automatically. This project builds an automated intrusion response and trust management system to facilitate authentication, authorization, and security binding in using metacomputing Grids or peer-to-peer web services. The trusted GridSec infrastructure supports Internet traffic datamining, encrypted tunneling, optimized resource allocations, network flood control and anomaly detection, etc. The USC team is developing a NetShield library to protect Grid resources. This new security system adjusts itself dynamically with changing threat patterns and network traffic conditions. This project promotes the acceptance of Grid computing through international collaborations with the research groups in INRIA, France, Chinese Academy of Sciences, and Melbourne University. The fortified Grid infrastructure will benefit security-sensitive allocations in digital government, electronic commerce, anti-terrorism activities, and cyberspace crime control. The broader impacts of this ITR project are far reaching in an era of growing demand of Internet, Web and Grid services.

H. Jin et al. (Eds.): NPC 2004, LNCS 3222, pp. 3-3, 2004.

Productivity in HPC Clusters

Bob Kuhn

Intel Corp.
bob.kuhn@intel.com

Abstract. This presentation discusses HPC productivity in terms of: (1) effective architectures, (2) parallel programming models, and (3) applications development tools. The demands placed on HPC by owners and users of systems ranging from public research laboratories to private scientific and engineering companies enrich the topic with many competing technologies and approaches. Rather than expecting to eliminate each other in the short run, these HPC competitors should be learning from one another in order to stay in the race. Here we examine how these competing forces form the engine of improvement for overall HPC cost/effectiveness. First, what will the effective architectures be? Moore's law is likely to still hold at the processor level over the next few years. Those words are, of course, typical from a semiconductor manufacturer. More important for this conference, our roadmap projects that it will accelerate over the next couple of years due to Chip Multi Processors, CMPs. It has also been observed that cluster size has been growing at the same rate. Few people really know how successful the Grid and Utility Computing will be, but virtual organizations may add another level of parallelism to the problem solving process. Second, on parallel programming models, hybrid parallelism, i.e. parallelism at multiple levels with multiple programming models, will be used in many applications. Hybrid parallelism may emerge because application speedup at each level can be multiplied by future architectures. But, these applications can also adapt best to the wide variety of data and problems. Robustness of this type is needed to avoid high software costs of converting or incrementally tuning existing program. This leads to OpenMP, MPI, and Grid programming model investments. Third, application tools are needed for programmer productivity. Frankly, integrated programming environments have not made much headway in HPC. Tools for debugging and performance analysis still define the basic needs. The term debugging is used advised because there are limits to the scalability of debuggers in the amount of code and number of processors even today. How can we breakthrough? Maybe through automated tools for finding bugs at the threading and process level? Performance analysis capability similarly will be exceeded by the growth of hardware parallelism, unless progress is made.

H. Jin et al. (Eds.): NPC 2004, LNCS 3222, pp. 4-4, 2004.
© IFIP International Federation for Information Processing 2004

Whole-Stack Analysis and Optimization of Commercial Workloads on Server Systems

C.R. Attanasio[1], Jong-Deok Choi[1]*, Niteesh Dubey[1], K. Ekanadham[1], Manish Gupta[1], Tatsushi Inagaki[2], Kazuaki Ishizaki[2], Joefon Jann[1], Robert D. Johnson[1], Toshio Nakatani[2], Il Park[1], Pratap Pattnaik[1], Mauricio Serrano[1], Stephen E Smith[1], Ian Steiner[1]**, and Yefim Shuf[1]

[1] IBM T.J. Watson Research Center
{dicka, jdchoi, niteesh, eknath, mgupa, joefon, robertdj, ilpark, pratap, mserrano, stesmith, isteine, yefim}@us.ibm.com
[2] IBM Tokyo Research Laboratory
{e29253, ishizaki, nakatani}@jp.ibm.com

Abstract. The evolution of the Web as an enabling tool for e-business introduces a challenge to understanding the execution behavior of large-scale middleware systems, such as J2EE [2], and their commercial workloads. This paper presents a brief description of the whole-stack analysis and optimization system – being developed at IBM Research – for commercial workloads on Websphere Application Server (WAS) [5] – IBM's implementation of J2EE – running on IBM's pSeries [4] and zSeries[3] server systems.

1 Introduction

Understanding the execution behavior of a software or hardware system is crucial for improving its execution performance (i.e., optimization or performance tuning). The evolution of the Web as an enabling tool for e-business introduces a challenge to understanding the execution behavior of large-scale middleware systems, such as J2EE [2], and their applications.

J2EE is a collection of Java interfaces and classes for business applications. J2EE implementations provide a container that hosts Enterprise JavaBeans (EJBs), from which J2EE applications are constructed. The J2EE container is like an operating system for EJBs, providing services such as database access and messaging, as well as managing resources like threads and memory.

J2EE is a Java application running on a Java Virtual Machine (JVM). The JVM in turn is like an operating system for J2EE and its applications, providing services such as synchronizations and memory management. JVM, typically written in C or C++, is an application of the underlying operating system,

---

* Contact author
** Also at Univ. of Illinois at Urbana-Champaign

H. Jin et al. (Eds.): NPC 2004, LNCS 3222, pp. 5–8, 2004.
© IFIP International Federation for Information Processing 2004

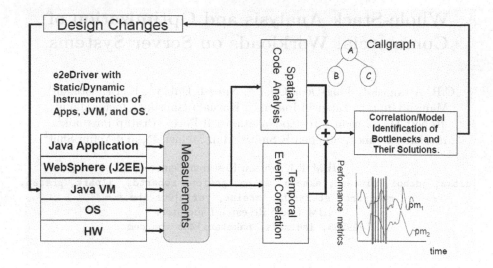

Fig. 1. Performance Analysis and Optimization Methodology

which itself is a client of the underlying hardware. The complicated interactions between the various layers of the software stack, from the J2EE applications to J2EE to JVM and to the operating system, and the underlying hardware layer, is a major source of the challenge to understanding and optimizing the performance of large-scale middleware systems and their applications.

This paper presents a brief description of the whole-stack analysis and optimization system – being developed at IBM Research – for commercial workloads on Websphere Application Server (WAS) running on IBM's pSeries [4] and zSeries[3] server systems. WAS is IBM's implementation of the J2EE middleware.

2   Whole-Stack Analysis and Optimization System

Figure 1 shows the performance analysis and optimization methodology of the system. The methodology provides means for:

1. instrumenting the software layers to collect statistics about software events at source level,
2. instrumenting hardware to collect statistics about various hardware events, and more importantly
3. correlating these two so that one can see the hardware events that correspond to a software event, and vice versa.

This enables the detection of hot-spots at either level and initiate generation of corresponding events at the other level.

The system employs static and dynamic instrumentation of the whole software stack, and generates trace of various software and hardware runtime events

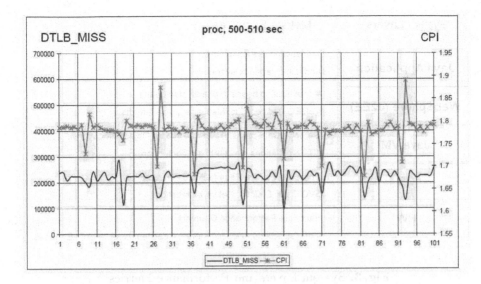

Fig. 2. Correlation between Data TLB (DTLB) Misses and CPI

both for online reduction and offline evaluation. Two major analyses are then applied to the trace: the *spatial code analysis* and the *temporal event correlation*.

The spatial code analysis identifies the static code body whose execution behavior is of interest; it identifies methods or basic blocks in a method that incur high execution overhead. A major tool of this analysis is the static and dynamic call graph and the call tree. The temporal event correlation correlates runtime events and performance metrics from the software and the hardware layers that are of interests; it identifies the relationship among various runtime events, such as Java garbage collection or thread synchronizations, and performance metrics such as *cycles per instruction* (CPI). Figure 2 shows an example performance metric trace that exhibits the correlation between CPI and the data TLB misses. The trace is generated by IBM's *hardware performance monitor (hpm)* tool kits [1]. Figure 3 shows the system layers, and examples of the performance metrics available for each layer.

The results from the spatial code analysis and the temporal event correlation are combined to identify static code bodies responsible for relatively poor performance, and potential remedies for unsatisfactory performance. Based on these findings, the system is redesigned and modified, and the cycle of performance analysis and optimization repeats until the performance becomes satisfactory.

3   Conclusion

We have presented a brief description of the whole-stack analysis and optimization system, being developed at IBM Research, for commercial workloads on

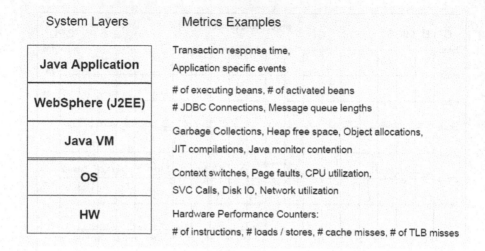

System Layers   Metrics Examples

Java Application
Transaction response time,
Application specific events

WebSphere (J2EE)
# of executing beans, # of activated beans
JDBC Connections, Message queue lengths

Java VM
Garbage Collections, Heap free space, Object allocations,
JIT compilations, Java monitor contention

OS
Context switches, Page faults, CPU utilization,
SVC Calls, Disk IO, Network utilization

HW
Hardware Performance Counters:
# of instructions, # loads / stores, # cache misses, # of TLB misses

Fig. 3. System Layers and Performance Metrics

Websphere Application Server (WAS) running on IBM's pSeries [4] and zSeries[3] server systems. Based on the analysis results we have obtained so far, we are currently experimenting with several optimizations at the various software stack layers, from WAS to the operating system, and also at the hardware. We will publish the results of these optimizations in the future.

References

[1] HPM Tool Kit. http://www.alphaworks.ibm.com/tech/hpmtoolkit.
[2] Java 2 Platform, Enterprise Edition (J2EE). http://java.sun.com/j2ee.
[3] Mainframe servers: zSeries. http://www-1.ibm.com/servers/eserver/zseries.
[4] IBM pSeries Information Center. http://publib16.boulder.ibm.com/pseries/en_US/infocenter/base.
[5] WebSphere Application Server. http://www.ibm.com/websphere.

Fuzzy Trust Integration for Security Enforcement in Grid Computing*

Shanshan Song, Kai Hwang, and Mikin Macwan

Internet and Grid Computing Laboratory
University of Southern California, Los Angeles, CA. 90089 USA
{shanshas, kaihwang}@usc.edu

Abstract. How to build the mutual trust among Grid resources sites is crucial to secure distributed Grid applications. We suggest enhancing the trust index of resource sites by upgrading their intrusion defense capabilities and checking the success rate of jobs running on the platforms. We propose a new *fuzzy-logic trust model* for securing Grid resources. Grid security is enforced through trust update, propagation, and integration across sites. Fuzzy trust integration reduces platform vulnerability and guides the defense deployment across Grid sites. We developed a SeGO scheduler for trusted Grid resource allocation.

The SeGO scheduler optimizes the aggregate computing power with security assurance under fixed budget constraints. The effectiveness of the scheme was verified by simulation experiments. Our results show up to 90% enhancement in site security. Compared with no trust integration, our scheme leads to 114% improvement in *Grid performance/cost ratio*. The *job drop rate* reduces by 75%. The *utilization of Grid resources* increased to 92.6% as more jobs are submitted. These results demonstrate significant performance gains through optimized resource allocation and aggressive security reinforcement.

1. Introduction

In Grid computing systems [2], user programs containing malicious codes may endanger the Grid resources used. Shared Grid resources once infected may damage the user applications running on the Grid platforms [8]. We address these issues by allocating Grid resources with security assurance. The assurance is achieved by hardware, software, and system upgrades to avoid application disasters in an open Grid environment.

Mutual trust must be established between all participating resource sites. Like human relationship, trust is often expressed by linguistics terms rather numerically. Fuzzy logic is very suitable to quantify trust among peer groups. The fuzzy theory [10] has not been explored much in network security control. To our best knowledge, only Manchala has suggested a fuzzy trust model for securing E-commerce [12].

---

* The work was presented in the IFIP *International Symposium on Network and Parallel Computing* (NPC-2004), Wuhan, China, October 18-22, 2004. This research was supported by NSF/ITR Grant ACI-0325409 to the University of Southern California.

H. Jin et al. (Eds.): NPC 2004, LNCS 3222, pp. 9-21, 2004.

Azzedin and Maheswaran [3] and Liu and Shen [11] have developed some security-aware models between resource providers and consumers. Globus GSI uses public key certificates and proxies for trust propagation [7]. We use fuzzy inferences to consolidate security enforcement measures in trusted Grid computing.

Our trust assessment involves the measurement of dependability, security, reliability and performability. Trust level is updated after the Grid successfully executed user jobs. Butt and Fortes, et al [3] protect Grid resources from distrusted applications. We choose a reverse approach by assuring security in the resource pool. Figure 1 shows the interaction between two Grid Resource sites.

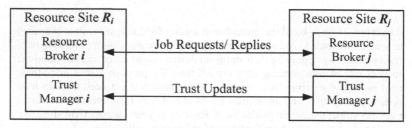

Fig. 1. Securing Grid resources with trust integration and resource brokerage

We propose a *Secure Grid Outsourcing* (SeGO) scheduler to outsource jobs to multiple resources. We aim at maximizing the computing power under security scrutiny and cost minimization. In this paper, we report simulation results on the SeGO performance by executing 300 jobs on six Grid resource sites. Other studies on Grid resource allocation can be found in [2], [4], [6], [14].

The remaining sections are organized as follows. In Section 2, we present our distributed security architecture at USC GridSec project. Section 3 introduces the fuzzy logic for trust management. Section 4 describes the process of fuzzy trust integration. Section 5 introduces the optimized resource allocation scheme. All experimental results are reported in Section 6. Finally, we summarize the research findings and make suggestions for further work.

2. GridSec Project for Trusted Grid Computing

As shown in Fig.1, the GridSec (*Grid Security*) project at USC builds security infrastructure and self-defense toolkits over multiple Grid resource sites. The security functionalities are monitored and coordinated by a *security manager* in each site. All security managers work together to enforce the central security policy. The security managers overlook all resources under their jurisdiction [9]. The GridSec architecture supports scalability, high-security, and system availability in trusted Grid computing. Our purpose is to design for scalability and security assurance at the same time.

Virtual Private Networks (VPNs) are built for Grid trust management among private networks through a public network. We establish only a minimum number of encrypted channels in the VPN. The VPN has a number of advantages over the use of PKI in Grid computing. Using encrypted channels in a Grid reduces or eliminates the overheads in frequent authentication; trust propagation, key management, and authorization in most Grid operations [14]. VPN achieves single sign-on easily without using public-key certificates. VPN also reduces the packet exchanges among Grid sites. No certificate authority is needed in VPN-based Grid architecture, once the tunnels are established. The design is aimed at optimizing Grid resources under the constraints of limited computing power, security assurance, and Grid service budget.

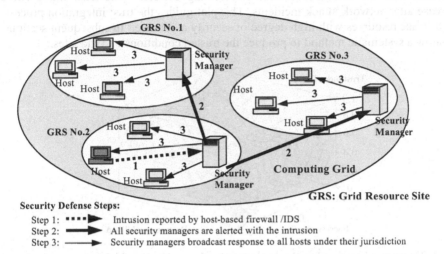

Security Defense Steps:

Step 1:	▪▪▪▪▶	Intrusion reported by host-based firewall /IDS
Step 2:	▬▬▶	All security managers are alerted with the intrusion
Step 3:	───▶	Security managers broadcast response to all hosts under their jurisdiction

Fig. 2. USC GridSec Project: A distributed Grid security architecture, built with encrypted tunnels, micro firewalls, and hybrid intrusion detection systems, coordinated by cooperative security managers at scattered resource sites

A self-defense software library, called *NetShield*, is under development in the GridSec project. This package supports fine-grain access control with automatic intrusion prevention, detection, and responses [9, 13]. This system is based on dynamic security policies, adaptive cryptographic engines, privacy protection, and VPN tunneling. Dynamic security demands the adaptability in making policy changes at run time. Three steps are shown in Fig.2 for intrusion detection, alert broadcast, and coordinated intrusion responses.

3. Fuzzy Logic for Trust Management

The trust relationships among Grid sites are hard to assess due to uncertainties involved. Two advantages of using fuzzy-logic to quantify trust in Grid applications are: (1) Fuzzy inference is capable of quantifying imprecise data or uncertainty in measuring the security index of resource sites. (2) Different membership functions and inference rules could be developed for different Grid applications, without changing the fuzzy inference engine.

We close up the security gap by mapping only secure resources to Grid applications. Security holes may appear as OS blind spots, software bugs, privacy traps, and hardware weakness in resource sites. These holes may weaken the trust index value. In our scheme, the *trust index* Γ (or t_{ij}) is determined by job *success rate* Φ and self-*defense capability* Δ of each resource pair.

In Fig.3, we plot the variation of the *trust index* of a resource site, as the *job success rate* and site *self-defense capability* are enhanced from low to high values. These two attributes enhance each other on many computer platforms. The trust index increases with the increase of both contributing factors.   The trust index could decrease after network attack incidents. This plot guides the trust integration process. We allocate resources with high degree of security assurance. In subsequent sections, we show a systematic method to produce the trusted conditions on Grid sites.

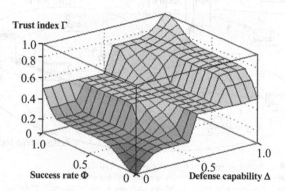

Fig. 3. Variation of trust index Γ with respect to the variations of job success rate Φ and intrusion defense capability Δ at each resource site

Essentially, previous job execution experiences determine the trustworthiness of the peer machines. In the initialization of the trust index of a new resource site, the reported job success rate and intrusion defense capability are used to generate an initial trust value. The trust index is then updated periodically with the site operations, until the site is removed from the Grid domain.

We treat these security attributes as fuzzy variables, characterized by the membership functions in Fig.4. In Fuzzy logic, the *membership function* $\mu(x)$ for a fuzzy element x specifies its degree of membership in a fuzzy set. It maps element x into the interval [0, 1], while 1 for full membership and 0 for no membership. Fuzzy logic can handle imprecise data or uncertainty in the *trust index* of a resource site.

Figure 4(a) shows "high" membership function for trust index Γ. A resource site with 0.75 trust index is considered *high* trust. Figure 4(b) shows five membership functions corresponding to *very low, low, medium, high*, and *very high* degree of trustworthiness. Figure 4(c) shows the cases of three ascending degrees of the self-defense capability. Figure 4(d) shows five levels of job success rate. The inference rules are subject to designer's choice.

Fuzzy inference is a process to assess the trust index in five steps: (1) Register the initial values of the success rate Φ and defense capability Δ. (2) Use the membership functions to generate membership degrees for Φ and Δ. (3) Apply the fuzzy rule set to map the input space (Φ - Δ space) onto the output space (Γ space) through fuzzy 'AND' and 'IMPLY' operations. (4) Aggregate the outputs from each rules, and (5)

Derive the trust index through a *defuzzification process*. The details of these five steps can be found in *Fuzzy Engineering* by Kosko [10].

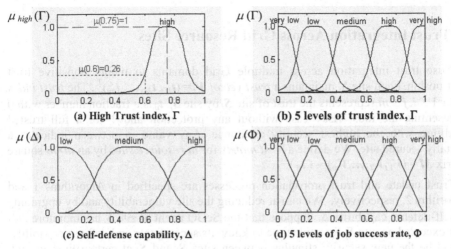

(a) High Trust index, Γ

(b) 5 levels of trust index, Γ

(c) Self-defense capability, Δ

(d) 5 levels of job success rate, Φ

Fig. 4. Membership functions for different levels of the trust index Γ, job success rate Φ, and site defense capability Δ

Figure 5 shows the trust inference process using the membership functions in Fig.4. We consider initial values: $\Phi = 0.84$ and $\Delta = 0.26$, obtained from previous Grid application experiences. Two example *fuzzy inference rules* are given below for use in the inference process shown in Fig.5.

Rule 1:   If Φ is very high and Δ is medium, then Γ is high.
Rule 2:   If Φ is high and Δ is low, then Γ is medium.

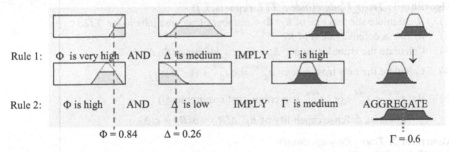

Rule 1:   Φ is very high AND   Δ is medium   IMPLY   Γ is high

Rule 2:   Φ is high   AND   Δ is low   IMPLY   Γ is medium   AGGREGATE

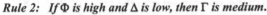

$\Phi = 0.84$ $\Delta = 0.26$ $\Gamma = 0.6$

Fig. 5. Fuzzy logic inference between job success rate Φ and self-defense capability Δ to induce the trust index Γ of a resource site

All selected rules are inferred in parallel. Initially, the membership is determined by assessing all terms in the premise. The fuzzy operator 'AND' is applied to determine the support degree of the rules. The AND results are aggregated together. The final trust index $\Gamma = 0.6$ is generated by defuzzifying the aggregation. The "AGGREGATE" superimposes two curves to produce the membership function for Γ.

There are many other fuzzy inference rules that can be designed using various conditional combinations of the fuzzy variables, Φ and Δ.

4. Trust Integration Across Grid Resource Sites

We use trust integration across multiple Grid domains to model transitive trust relationship. Each site S_j maintains a *trust vector* $V_j = (t_{1j}, t_{2j}, ..., t_{mj})^T$. The *trust index* t_{ij} for $1 \le i, j \le m$ represents the trust of site S_i by site S_j. t_{ij} is a fraction number with 0 representing the most risky case without any protection and 1 for a full trusted condition with the highest security assurance. Any value in between indicates a partially secured site. We define a *trust matrix* for m *resource sites* by an $m \times m$ square matrix $M = (V_1, V_2, ..., V_m) = (t_{ij})$.

Trust update and trust propagation processes are specified in Algorithms 1 and Algorithm 2, respectively. We aim at reducing the site vulnerability and by upgrading its self-defense capability Δ. Suppose that the SeGO agent of site S_i has monitored all jobs executed on site S_j for some time to know its success rate and defense capability. Let s_{ij} be the new security stimulus between sites S_i and S_j at certain time instant. Equation (1) calculates the new trust index from the old value and present stimulus.

$$t_{ij}^{new} = \alpha\, t_{ij}^{old} + (1-\alpha)\, s_{ij} \qquad (1)$$

The weighting factor α is a random variable in the range (0, 1). For security-critical applications, the trust index should change timely to reflect new situation, thus a small α is adopted such as $\alpha < 0.3$. But for low security applications, a large α is adopted with $\alpha > 0.9$. In general situations, one can set α in the range of (0.7, 0.8).

Algorithm 1: *Trust_Update(index_TTL reports, i, j)*
(1) R_i calculate success rate of R_j: Φ = number of success jobs/$index\_TTL$;
(2) R_i assess defense rate Δ of R_j;
(3)   Calculate the stimulus value: S_{ij} = Fuzzy_inference(Φ, Δ);
(4)   Calculate the new trust index: $t_{ij}^{new} = \alpha t_{ij}^{old} + (1-\alpha)s_{ij}$;

(5)   if $((t_{ij}^{new} < t_{ij}^{old})$ or $(t_{ij}^{new} <$ average trust requirement))

   Enhance defense capability of R_j, $\Delta(R_j) = \Delta(R_j) + \varepsilon(\Delta)$.

Algorithm 2: *Trust_Propagation(i)*
(1) R_i broadcasts V_i;
(2)   for $j = 1$ to i-1, i+1 to M
(3) $V_j^{new} = (m-1/m)V_j^{old} + V_i/m$.

We introduce two simulation terms: the trust *index_TTL* and trust *vector_TTL*, to measure user applications submitted to each site. When site S_j accumulates *index_TTL* job reports from site S_i, it updates the trust index t_{ij} using Eq.(1). With fuzzy trust quantification, the stimulus value s_{ij} is determined first. Then the new trust index t_{ij} is updated, accordingly. If the trust index decreases or it is lower than the average, the defense capability Δ of S_j is forced to increase by an amount ε characterized in Eq.(2).

$$\Delta(S_j) = \Delta(S_j) + \varepsilon(\Delta) \qquad (2)$$

In Eq. (2), the increment $\varepsilon(\Delta)$ is a function of the current Δ value. If current Δ is high, ε should be set with a small increment. If Δ is low, ε should be larger. The site that has low Δ should catch up faster this way. The ultimate purpose of trust integration is to enhance the trust index or security level at weak resource sites. Trust integration leads to normalization and equalization of trust indices at all sites. The trust vectors are broadcasted periodically. When a site S_j has accumulated *vector_TTL* of job execution reports, it broadcasts its trust vector to other sites. With m sites, the contribution from each site is roughly $1/m$. Algorithm 2 is used to calculate the new trust vector for site S_i by each resource site S_j for $j = 1,2,\ldots, m$.

5. Optimization of Trusted Resource Allocation

Based on the fuzzy trust model, we present below in Algorithm 3 the SeGO scheduler for optimized Grid resource allocation. The SeGO scheduler was developed under the following assumptions: (1) non-preemptive job scheduling, (2) divisible workload across Grid sites, and (3) space sharing in a batch mode over multiple jobs. Our SeGO scheduler is specified with a nonlinear programming model [5].

Algorithm 3: *SeGO (R_j, Job = (W, D, T, B))*

Input: Submit *Job* = (W, D, T, B) to resource site R_j at time τ, R_j requests
              resources from all m sites.

Output: Workload distribution ($W_1, W_2, \ldots, W_m$) and estimated execution time
              L for *Job* based on allocation $X = (x_1, x_2, \ldots, x_m)$ generated.

(1) R_j sends requests to obtain available resources information from all sites;
(2)   **for** $i = 1$ **to** m
(3)   **if** $(t_{ij} < T)$ $x_i = 0$.
(4)   **end for**
(5)   Estimate execution time $L = D - \tau$;
(6)   Generate the allocation vector $X = (x_1, x_2, \ldots, x_m)$, which maximize

$$E = \sum_{i=1}^{m} x_i P_i L t_{ij} \Big/ \sum_{i=1}^{m} x_i P_i L C_i \text{, subject to the following constraints}$$

$$\sum_{i=1}^{m} x_i P_i L \geq W \text{, } \sum_{i=1}^{m} x_i P_i L C_i \leq B \text{, and } 0 \leq x_i \leq 1;$$

(7)   **for** $i = 1$ **to** m $W_i = x_i P_i L$;
(8)   **return** ($W_1, W_2, \ldots, W_m, L$) with allocation $X = (x_1, x_2, \ldots, x_m)$.

A job is submitted with the descriptor *Job* = (W, D, T, B), representing the *workload, execution deadline, minimum trust,* and *budget limit.* A job is required to complete execution before the posted deadline. Denote the current time instant by τ. This is the start time of a job execution. The *estimated job execution time* is denoted by $L = D - \tau$. Let x_i be the percentage of the peak power P_i allocated to the job J. The product x_iP_i represents the actual power allocated. We define $W_i = x_iP_iL$ as the *workload* to be executed at site R_i for the job J.

The input to Algorithm 3 is the successive job descriptions including the site and the time when job is submitted. After passing a qualification test, step (2)-(4), the unqualified sites are filtered out. The estimated execution time L is registered first. Then, the *resource allocation vector* $X = (x_1, x_2,..., x_m)$ is generated by optimizing the objective function or the *trusted performance/cost ratio E*, defined below.

The numerator is the *aggregate computing power*, weighted by the trust index t_{ij} and allocated from m Grid sites. The denominator is the *total Grid service charge* for executing the job. The terms P_i and C_i are the computing power and service charge at site R_i. The SeGO solution is obtained with a nonlinear programming solver, subject to the constraints listed in step 6.

$$E = \sum_{i=1}^{m} W_i t_{ij} \bigg/ \sum_{i=1}^{m} W_i C_i = \sum_{i=1}^{m} x_i P_i L t_{ij} \bigg/ \sum_{i=1}^{m} x_i P_i L C_i \tag{3}$$

Algorithm 4 specifies the trust integration process, in which n jobs are mapped to m sites. The trust vectors are propagated and integrated periodically. If a job is submitted to R_j, this site is responsible to dispatch workload to all sites and monitors the job execution. Once a job is finished, the occupied resources are released for other jobs. User applications can resubmit their jobs, if the earlier execution was unsuccessful. The trust integration process includes trust update (Algorithm 1), trust propagation (Algorithm 2), and SeGO optimization (Algorithm 3). The inputs to this algorithm are jobs submitted at all sites. The output is the trusted resource allocation and the updated trust vectors.

Algorithm 4: Trust integration for optimized resource allocation
Input: n jobs submitted at m resource sites.
Output: Resource allocation for jobs and updated trust vectors for all sites.
(1)   **Do until** (all submitted jobs are executed)
(2)   **if** (τ = arrival time of current $Job = (W, D, T, B)$)
(3) Job is put in the job queue of R_j;
(4) $(W_1, W_2, ..., W_m, L) \leftarrow SeGO (R_j, Job)$;
(5)   **for** $i = 1$ **to** m resource reservation, i.e., $P_i = P_i - W_i/L$;
(6)   **end if**
(7)   **if** (R_j gets the previous $Job = (W, D, T, B)$ report at time τ)
(8)   **for** $i = 1$ **to** m
(9)   resource release, i.e., $P_i = P_i + W_i/L$;
(10)   **if** (R_j accumulates *index_TTL* job reports from R_i)
(11)   *Trust_Update* (*index_TTL* reports, i, j);
(12)   **if** (R_j accumulates execution reports for *vector_TTL* jobs)
(13)   *Trust_Propagation* (j);
(14)   **end for**
(15)   **end if**
(16) **end do**

6. Simulation Results on Trusted Grid Resource Allocation

We have developed a discrete-event simulator at USC to simulate the trust integration and resource optimization processes. We simulated $n = 300$ jobs running on $m = 6$ Grid resource sites. Each resource site is configured with computing power, which is set between 1 Tflop/s and 5 Tflop/s, randomly. Each site is configured with a site reliability and intrusion defense capability in the range (0, 1).

Jobs are mapped evenly across sites, and all job arrivals are modeled by a Poisson distribution with an inter-arrival time of 10 minutes. The job workload demand varies between 4 Tflop to 50 Tflop. The deadline varies between 4 minutes and 20 minutes after the job is submitted. The minimum trust is set in the range (0.4, 0.7) randomly. Both the resource unit service charge and user application budget limitations are set between \$180K/Tflop and \$320K/Tflop, randomly.

Figure 6 depicts the variation of the trust index values at 6 resource sites, R_1 through R_6. The intial trust index values at step 0 vary from 0.07 to 0.77 for sites R_1 through R_6 along the Y-axis. The x-axis represents the trust integration step taken during simulation runs. The average trust index at each site increases steadily after each step. Through the process, all trust indices grow to the range (0.7, 0.93) at step 5.

In the best case, the lowest index value of 0.07 at site R_1 increases to 0.7 in 5 steps. This corresponds to a security enhancement of 90% = (0.7 - 0.07)/0.7 for site R_1. In the worst case for site R_6, the trust index is upgraded from 0.7 to 0.93 in 5 steps. There is a normalization effect of the trust integration process, which brings the security levels of all sites to almost the same high level.

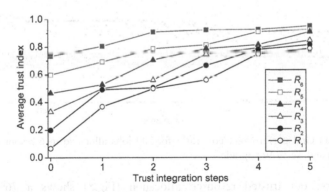

Fig. 6. Variation of the trust indices of six resource sites after five trust integration steps

We present in Fig.7 and Fig.8 two scatter plots of the *performance/cost ratio*. The two scatter plots result from running the SeGO simulation under different trust management polices. Each triangle represents the performance/cost ratio of one job. Both figures plot the Grid performance under limited budget with initial trust values ranging from 0.07 to 0.77 given at step 0 in Fig.6.

Figure 7 depicts performance/cost ratio E of 300 jobs with fixed trust, meaning no security upgrade over the resource sites. Figure 8 plots E with trust integration to upgrade the defense capabilities at six resource sites. We observed two job groups in these plots. One group consists of those dropped jobs due to short of resources before the deadline expired. Those jobs are represented with $E = 0$ along the X-axis. The second job group contains the successful executed jobs. There are 76 dropped jobs in Fig.7 and 18 dropped jobs in Fig.8 out of 300 jobs simulated. This translates to a *job drop rate* of 76/300 = 25.3% in Fig.7 and 18/300 = 6% in Fig.8.

In Fig.7, the E-plot for successful jobs varies from 1.67 to 2.71 Tflop/\$1M with an average $E = 2.27$ Tflop/\$1M. In Fig.8, the successful jobs achieve $E = 1.67$ to 3.57 Tflop/\$1M with an average $E = 2.92$ Tflop/\$1M. Overall, the scatter plot in Fig.7 shows almost no increasing trend as more jobs are submitted. However, the E-plot in Fig.8 increases steadily as more jobs are submitted. Considering the last 50 jobs, we achieved $E = 2.94$ to 3.57 Tfop/\$1M in Fig.8. We observe an *improvement factor* by 114% = (3.57-1.67)/1.67 for the best-case scenario.

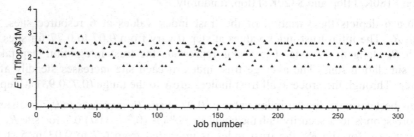

Fig. 7. Grid performance/cost ratio for 300 jobs allocated to six resource sites with fixed trust index and no site security reinforcement

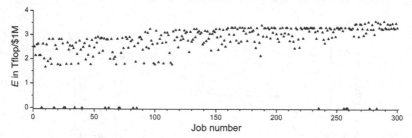

Fig. 8. Improved Grid performance/cost ratio for 300 jobs allocated to 6 resource sites after trust integration and security upgrade

In summary, our trusted resource allocation (Fig.8) shows a 76% - 114% improvement in *Grid performance/cost ratio E*. The *job drop rate* is reduced by (76-18)/76 = 75% in favor of trust integration solution. On the average E, a performance gain of 28% = (2.92-2.27)/2.27 was resulted from trusted resource allocation. As a matter of fact, the trust-integration process is at work very early on. After the submission of the first 15 jobs, the E starts to climb, and achieves more than 3.0 Tflop/\$1M at the 100th job. The results clearly demonstrate the effectiveness of trust integration. Trusted Grid sites accommodated 94% = 1 - 6% of 300 user jobs.

Utilization rate is defined as percentage of allocated resources among all available resources. The utilization rate for resources with fixed trust values remains at the constant level at 40% during the simulation runs. The utilization rate for resources with integrated trust values varies from a low of 48.1% to a high of 92.6%. The utilization of Grid resources increases with more jobs submitted. These results demonstrate significant gain in Grid performance through optimized resource allocation and aggressive security reinforcement by trust integration.

Table 1. Utilization of Grid Resources at Six Sites for the Execution of 300 Jobs

Grid resource utilization rate	Job Number					
	1 - 50	51 - 100	101 - 150	151 - 200	201 - 250	251 - 300
With fixed trust	39.4%	45.1%	43.0%	34.9%	45.1%	38.4%
With trust integration	48.1%	78.0%	65.4%	84.2%	92.6%	82.9%

7. Conclusions and Suggestions for Further Research

This work offers the first step towards trusted Grid computing. In several recent reports from USC Internet and Grid Computing Laboratory, one can find comprehensive treatment of the GridSec architecture [9], Internet traffic datamining for automated intrusion detection [13], and trusted Grid resource allocation [14]. We summarize below research findings and make a few suggestions for further research.

- Fuzzy trust integration reduces platform vulnerability and guides the defense deployment across Grid sites. Our VPN-supported trust integration is meant to enforce security in Grids beyond the use of PKI services [2, 9, 14]. Comprehensive simulation results were reported in [14] to prove the effectiveness of the SeGO scheduler for trusted resource allocation in computational Grids.

- Self-defense toolkits are needed to secure Grid computing [9]. We have suggested the use of distributed firewalls, packet filters, virtual private networks, and intrusion detection systems at Grid sites. A new anomaly-based, intrusion detection system was developed with datamining of frequent traffic episodes in TCP, UDP, and ICMP connections as reported in [13].

- Regarding future research directions, we suggest to integrate the SeGO scheduler with other Grid job/resource management toolkits such the Globus/GRAM, AppLex, and NimRod/G [2, 4]. Grid security policies and Grid operating systems are needed to establish truly secure Grid computing environment [15].

References

1. F. Azzedin and M. Maheswaran, "Towards Trust-Aware Resource Management in Grid Computing Systems", *Proc. of Int'l Symp. on Cluster Computing and the Grid*, 2002.
2. F. Berman, G. Fox, and T. Hey, (Editors), *Grid Computing: Making The Global Infrastructure a Reality*, John Wiley & Sons, 2003.

3. Butt, S. Adabala, N. Kapadia, R. Figueiredo, and J. Fortes, "Fine-Grain Access Control for Securing Shared Resources in Computational Grids", *Proceedings of Int'l Parallel and Distributed Processing Symposium*, April 2002.
4. R. Buyya, M. Murshed and D. Abramson. "A Deadline and Budge Constrained Cost-Time Optimization Algorithm for Scheduling Task Farming Applications on Global Grids", *Int'l Conf. on Parallel and Distributed Processing Techniques and Applications*, 2002.
5. R. Byrd, M. E. Hribar, and J. Nocedal. "An Interior Point Method for Large Scale Nonlinear Programming", *SIAM Journal on Optimization*, Vol. 9, 1999, pp. 877-900.
6. K. Czajkowski, I. Foster, and C. Kesselman, "Resource Co-Allocation in Computational Grids", *Proc. of the 8th IEEE Int'l Symp. on High Perf. Distributed Computing*, 1999.
7. Foster, C. Kesselman, G. Tsudik, and S. Tuecke, "A Security Architecture for Computational Grids", *Proc. of ACM Conf. on Computer and Comm. Security*, 1997.
8. M. Humphrey and M. Thompson, "Security Implications of Typical Grid Computing Usage Scenarios", *Proceedings of Int'l Symposium on High Performance Distributed Computing* (HPDC), San Francisco, CA. Aug. 7-9, 2001.
9. Hwang, et al, "The GridSec and Netshield Architecture for Securing Grid and Distributed Computing", *Technical Report 2004-15*, USC Internet and Grid Computing Lab, 2004.
10. B. Kosko, Fuzzy Engineering, Prentice Hall, 1997.
11. H. Liu and J. Shen, "A Mission-Aware Trust Model for Grid Computing Systems", *Int'l Workshop on Grid and Cooperative Computing*, Sanya, China, Dec. 26, 2002.
12. Manchala, "E-Commerce Trust Metrics and Models", *IEEE Internet Computing*, March 2000, pp. 36-44.
13. M. Qin and K. Hwang, "Anomaly Intrusion Detection by Internet Datamining of Traffic Episodes", *Technical Report No. 2004-6*, USC Internet and Grid Computing Lab, also submitted to *ACM Trans. on Information and System Security* (TISSec), March 2004.
14. S. Song and K. Hwang, " Security Binding for Trusted Resource Allocation in Computational Grids", *Technical Report 2004-8*, USC Internet and Grid Computing Lab, also submitted to *IEEE Trans. on Parallel and Distributed Systems*, May 2004.
15. Z. Xu, W. Li, H. Fu, and Z. Zeng," The Vega Grid Project in China", Institute of Computing Technology, Chinese Academy of Sciences, Beijing, China, April 2003. http://link.springer.de/link/service/series/0558/papers/2436/24360228.pdf

Biographical Sketches

Shanshan Song received her BS degree in Computer Science from a special class for gifted young in the University of Science and Technology of China, Hefei, in 2001, and the MS degree in Computer Science from University of Southern California (USC) in 2003. Currently, She is pursuing the Ph.D. degree in Department of Computer Science at USC. Her research interest lies primarily in the area of network security and dynamic resource allocation for computational Grids. She can be reached at shanshas@usc.edu.

Kai Hwang is a Professor and Director of Internet and Grid Computing Laboratory at the University of Southern California. He received the Ph.D. from the University of California, Berkeley. An IEEE Fellow, he specializes in computer architecture, parallel processing, Internet and wireless security, cluster and Grid computing systems. Presently, he leads a NSF-supported ITR Grid security project at USC. The GridSec group develops security-binding techniques for trusted outsourcing in Grid computing. They build self-defense software toolkits for protecting Grid and distributed computing resources. Dr. Hwang can be reached at kaihwang@usc.edu or through the URL: http://GridSec.usc.edu/Hwang.html

Mikin Macwan received the B.E. degree from Pune University, India in 1999, and the M.S. degree in Computer Science from Texas A&M University - College Station, in 2001. After working as a Software Engineer at Sun Microsystems, CA (2001 - 2002), he joined the Computer Science Program at USC. He is now pursuing the Ph.D. degree at USC. His primary areas of research are Network Security and Intrusion Detection and Response Systems. He can be reached at macwan@usc.edu.

Atomic Commitment in Grid Database Systems

Sushant Goel[1], Hema Sharda[1], and David Taniar[2]

[1] School of Electrical and Computer Systems Engineering, Royal Melbourne Institute of
Technology, Australia
s2013070@student.rmit.edu.au
hema.sharda@rmit.edu.au
[2] School of Business Systems, Monash University, Australia
David.Taniar@infotech.monash.edu.au

Abstract. Atomic Commitment Protocol (ACP) is an important part for any distributed transaction. ACPs have been proposed for homogeneous and heterogeneous distributed database management systems (DBMS). ACPs designed for these DBMS do not meet the requirement of Grid databases. Homogeneous DBMS are synchronous and tightly coupled while heterogeneous DBMS, like multidatabase systems, requires a top layer of multidatabase management system to manage distributed transactions. These ACPs either become too restrictive or need some changes in participating DBMS, which may not be acceptable in Grid Environment. In this paper we identify requirements for Grid database systems and then propose an ACP for grid databases, *Grid-Atomic Commitment Protocol (Grid-ACP)*.

1 Introduction

Atomic commitment is one of the important requirements for transactions executing in distributed environments. Among Atomicity, Consistency, Isolation and Durability (ACID) [4] properties of a transaction, Atomic Commitment Protocols (ACP) preserves the atomicity of transaction running in distributed environment. *Two-phase Commit* (2PC) and its variants are widely accepted as ACP for transactions running in distributed data repositories [2,3,14]. These data repositories are considered to be homogeneous, tightly integrated and synchronous.

Grid infrastructure [7,8], a new and evolving computing infrastructure promises to support collaborative, autonomously evolved, heterogeneous, data intensive applications. Grid databases would access distributed resources in general and distributed data repositories in particular. Thus, protocols developed for homogeneous distributed architecture will not work in the Grid infrastructure. Hence classical approaches of data management need to be revisited to address challenges of grid databases.

Transaction management is critical in any data based application, be it simple file management system or structured Database Management Systems (DBMS). Transaction management is responsible to manage concurrency control and reliability protocols. Many applications will not need transactional support, i.e. ACID properties, while executing on Grids e.g. Business Activities [12]. Our earlier work

H. Jin et al. (Eds.): NPC 2004, LNCS 3222, pp. 22-29, 2004.
© IFIP International Federation for Information Processing 2004

was focused on concurrency control in Grid environment [17]. In this paper we particularly focus on ACP in Grid environment.

Grid databases [1,2] are expected to store large data from scientific experimentations viz. astronomical analysis, high-energy physics [16], weather forecasting, earth movement etc. These experiments generate huge volume of data daily. Particle physics experiments, e.g. *Babar*, may need to store up to 500 GB of data each day and is arguably world's largest database that stores approx. 895 TB of data as of today (Mar '04) [15]. Wider research community is interested in generic data collected at various data collecting sites [1,10,13,15]. Distributed access to data raises many issues like security, integrity constraints, manageability, accounting, replication etc. But, here we will be mainly concerned with managing the transaction in Grids and its requirement of atomic commitment. In this paper distributed database is used in a broader sense to cover distributed/federated/multidatabase systems, since all these accesses data located at physically distributed sites, unless otherwise stated.

The remainder of the paper is organized as follows. Section 2 explains the background work in distributed DBMS. Section-3 explains the working model and identifies the problem in applying existing ACP in the Grid model. We propose the Grid-ACP to meet Grid requirement for ACPs in section-4 along with proof of correctness of the protocol. Section-5 concludes the work and explains future work.

2 Background

Atomic commitment is an important requirement of transactions running in distributed environment. All cohort of distributed transaction should either commit or abort to maintain the *atomicity* property of the transaction and thus consequently maintain the correctness of stored data. We broadly classify distributed DB systems in two categories: (a) Homogeneous and (b) Heterogeneous distributed DBMS. Detailed classification can be found in [14].

2.1 Homogeneous Distributed Database

2PC [4] is the simplest and most popular ACP proposed in the literature to achieve atomicity in homogeneous DBMS [3,14]. We briefly discuss 2PC from the literature to help our further discussion. The site where the transaction originates acts as *coordinator* for that transaction; all other sites where data is accessed are *participants*. 2PC works as follows [4]:

The coordinator sends *vote_request* to all the participating sites. After receiving a request the site responds by sending its vote, *yes* or *no*. If the participant voted *yes*, it enters in *prepared* (or *ready*) state and waits for final decision from the coordinator. If the vote was *no*, the participant can abort its part of the transaction. After collecting all the votes, if all of them including the coordinator's vote are *yes* then the coordinator decides to *commit* and send the message accordingly to all the sites. Even if, one of the votes is *no* the coordinator decides to abort the whole transaction. After receiving *commit* or *abort* decision from the coordinator, the participant commits or aborts accordingly from prepared state. While the participant is in prepared state it is *uncertain* of the final decision from the coordinator. Hence 2PC is called as a *blocking protocol*.

2.2 Heterogeneous Distributed Database

Multidatabase systems assume heterogeneous environment [5,9] for transaction execution. They typically execute a top layer of multidatabase management system for transaction management. These systems are designed for certain application specific requirements and mostly for short and synchronous transactions. Due to high autonomy (design and execution) requirements in multidatabase systems, the ACPs are not designed for replicated data. Thus these protocols are not suitable for Grid environment. In literature [9] following major strategies are discussed for atomic commitment of distributed transaction in heterogeneous database environment: (1) Redo (2) Retry (3) Compensate.

Since all sites may not support prepare-to-commit state and thus even if global transaction decides to commit, some local sub-transaction may decide to abort while others may decide to commit. Hence, transactions that decided to abort must *redo* the write operation, and commit, to reach consistent global decision [9]. Another approach to deal with above problem is the *retry* approach, as discussed in [9]. In retry approach, the whole subtransaction is retried rather than *redo*ing only the write operations. Inherent limitation of this approach is that the subtransaction must be *retriable*. A subtransaction is retriable only if the top layer of multidatabase system has saved the execution state of the aborted subtransaction. If the global decision is to abort and any local subtransaction has already committed, then *compensating* transactions can be executed [9]. Compensating transactions also need to access information stored in global DBMSs.

3 Grid Database Model and Problem Identification

In this section we first discuss the general model and terminology that we use in our study. Then we discuss the problem in implementing standard ACPs in this model.

3.1 Model

The Grid middleware will join geographically separate computing and data resources. Concept of virtual organization (VO) [7] has been coined for integrating organizations over network. Grid infrastructure is expected to support and make use of *web-services* for specialized purposes. We focus on the collaborative, data intensive work that need to access data from geographically separated sites. The general model is shown below:

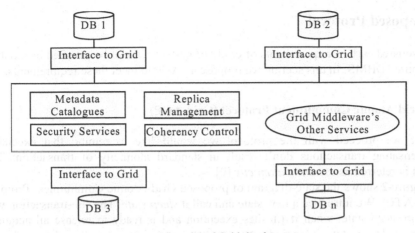

Fig. 1. General model of Grid database system

All individual database systems are autonomously evolved and hence heterogeneous in nature. These database systems may join and leave the Grid as per their convenience. A transaction is termed as global transaction if it originates at any site and need to access data from other sites, in other terms if the transaction has to access data from more than one site it is a global transaction. The division of the global transaction at individual sites are called subtransactions.

3.2 Problem Identification

2PC is the most widely accepted ACP in distributed databases. 2PC is a consensus-based protocol that asks all the participating sites to vote whether *subtransactions* running at that site can *commit*. After collecting and analyzing all votes, the coordinator decides the fortune of the distributed transaction. It involves two phases, *voting phase* and *decision phase*, of communication messages before terminating the transaction atomically, hence the name *two-phase commit*.

Many variations and optimizations have been proposed to increase the performance of 2PC. But, homogeneity between sites is the basic assumption behind the originally proposed 2PC for distributed databases. Multi/federated database systems are heterogeneous but the nature of transactions and applications these heterogeneous database systems are studied, designed and optimized are much different than their counterparts in Grid databases, e.g. for short, synchronized, non-collaborative transactions, to name few of them. These systems have a leverage of a top level layer, known as multidatabase management system that assists in making decision but Grids may not enjoy this facility due to distributed nature of database systems. Multidatabase employs redo, retry and compensate approach for ACP. These requirements may not be implemented in absence of top-layer management system and at the same time may be too restrictive [6]. Grid databases need to operate in a loosely coupled *service-oriented* architecture. Apart from data consistency perspective Grid databases will be expected to access data from via WWW [11,12]. Most of the distributed DBMSs are not designed to operate in WWW environment.

4 Proposed Protocol

As discussed earlier, requirements of Grid DB systems cannot be satisfied by existing distributed DBMS. In this section we propose an ACP to meet these requirements.

4.1 Grid Atomic Commitment Protocol (Grid-ACP)

Before we proceed with the protocol we would like to remind that executing compensating transactions don't result in standard atomicity of transaction. The notion is referred as *semantic atomicity* [9].

Figure-2 shows the state diagram of proposed Grid-Atomic Commitment Protocol (Grid-ATC). We introduce a new state and call it *sleep state*. The sub-transaction will enter in *sleep* state, when it finishes execution and is ready to release all acquired resources. *Sleep* state is an indication to transaction managers that the local sub-transaction of global transaction has committed. But it is still waiting for decision from the originator of the transaction. If any of the other participating sites aborts the subtransaction, the coordinator informs all the *sleep*ing sites to *compensate* the changes made by the transaction.

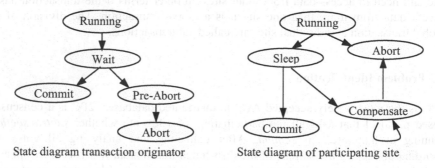

State diagram transaction originator   State diagram of participating site

Fig. 2. State diagram of Grid-ATC

The Grid-ATC algorithm is explained as follows:

1. The transaction originator splits the transaction based on the information at *Grid-middleware service* and submits to participating database systems.
2. Respecting the autonomy of participating sites, they execute their portion of sub-transaction and goes to *sleep* state, after logging all the necessary compensating information in the stable storage. The site then informs the outcome of the sub-transaction execution to the originator.
3. The originator, after collecting response from all participants, then decides whether to commit or to abort. If all participants decided to go in sleep state the decision is to commit else the decision is to abort. If the decision is to abort, message is sent only to those participants who are in sleep state. If the decision is to commit, it is sent to all participants.
4a. If the local site decided to commit and is in sleep state and the global decision is also to commit, the transaction can directly go to commit state. As everything went as expected by the local site.

Grid-ACP: Originator's Algorithm

```
submit sub-transactions to participants;
wait for response from all participants;
if all response to sleep then begin
      write commit record in log;
      send global_commit to all participants;
end if
else begin
      write abort record in log;
      send global_abort to participants who decided to commit
      wait for response from these participants;
end
return
```

Grid-ACP: Participant's Algorithm

```
received sub-transaction from originator
if participant decides to commit then begin
      write sleep in log
      send commit decision to originator
      wait for decision from originator
      if decision is commit then
          write commit in log
      end if
end if
else if decision is abort then begin
      start compensating transaction for this transaction
line 10:   if compensating transaction aborts then begin
          restart compensating transaction until it commits
          write commit for compensating transaction
      end if
      else
          write commit for compensating transaction
      end
end if
else if participant decides to abort then begin
      write abort in log
      send abort decision to originator
end if
return
```

4b. If the local site decided to commit and is in sleep state but the global decision is to abort the transaction, then the local transaction must be aborted. But as mentioned earlier when the local site enters the sleep state it releases all locks on data items as well as all acquired resources. This makes abortion of transaction impossible. Hence, a compensating transaction must be executed to revert all the changes, using *compensation rules*, to restore the semantics of database before executing the original subtransaction, thus achieving *semantic atomicity*. If the compensating transaction fails, it is resubmitted. We are not defining the compensation rules as they are out of scope of the paper.

Maintaining autonomy of local sites is primary in Grid environment. Considering that, different sites may employ different protocols for serializability as well. Some sites may employ *locking protocols* while others may employ *timestamping* or *optimistic* concurrency control strategy at local sites. Thus, in presence of such an autonomous and heterogeneous environment in Grids and absence of a top-layer management system it may be impossible to avoid cascading aborts. The proposed *sleep* state restricts the number of cascading aborts. We would also like to highlight that the *sleep* state does not interfere with the autonomy of the local sites. Implementing this state does not need any modification in local *transaction manager* module. Whenever the site decides to join the Grid, the *sleep* state may be defined in the interface and hence no changes are required in any local modules.

We briefly discuss the time and message complexity of the proposed algorithm. Grid-ACP needs 2 rounds (*time complexity*) of message under normal conditions: (1) after the local sites decide to commit/abort (2) the decision from the originator. Maximum number of messages required is $2n$ (*message complexity*) to reach a consistent decision under normal conditions i.e. without failure. Where n is the number of participants in ACP. Considering that originator sends the final decision to all the sites, the number of messages in each round is n.

4.2 Correctness of Proposed Protocol

We show the correctness of our ACP by following lemma:

Lemma 1: All participating sites reach the same final decision.

Proof: We prove this lemma in two parts, part-I for consistent commit and part-II for consistent abort.

Part I: In this part we show that when the global decision is to commit, all participant commits. From step-2 of the algorithm it is clear that the participants execute autonomously. If local decision is to commit, the information is logged in the stable storage and the subtransaction goes in *sleep* state after sending a message to the originator. If the originator of the transaction finds all commit decision in response, it sends the final *commit* to all participants. In this case the participant is not required to do any action as all resources were already released when the participant entered the *sleep* state. Participant just has to mark the migration of state from *sleep* to *commit*.

Part II: The participants have to do more to achieve this part. In this part we show that if the global decision is abort all participants decides to abort. All participants that decided to commit now receives abort decision from the originator. Those participants decided to abort have already decided to abort unilaterally. Those subtransactions that decided to commit, have already released locks on data items and cannot be aborted. Hence, compensating transactions are constructed using the *event-condition-action* or the *compensation rules*. These compensating transactions are then executed to achieve the semantic atomicity (step-4b of the algorithm). To achieve semantic atomicity the compensating transaction must commit. If the compensating transaction aborts for some reason it is re-executed until it commits. The compensating transaction has to eventually commit, as it is a logical inverse of a committed transaction. This is shown in the state diagram by self-referring compensate state and *line-10* of the participant's algorithm. Though the compensating transaction commits, the semantic of the subtransaction is abort. Thus all participants terminate with consistent decision.   ∎

5 Conclusion

We have seen that ACP proposed or homogeneous DBMS e.g. 2PC is not suitable for autonomously evolved heterogeneous Grid databases. Strategies for traditional heterogeneous DBMS like multidatabase management system are too restrictive and need a global management system. We have proposed an ACP to meet Grid database requirements that uses *sleep* state for participating sites. The proposed *sleep* state will also help in putting a cap on the number of aborting transactions. We also demonstrated correctness of the proposed protocol. In future we intend to quantify and optimize the capping values of the protocol.

References

[1] A. Chervenak, I. Foster, C. Kesselman, C. Salisbury, S. Tuecke, "The Data Grid: Towards an architecture for the Distributed Management and Analysis of Large Scientific Datasets", *Journal of Network and Computer Applications*, vol. 23, pp 187-200, '01

[2] H. Stockinger, "Distributed Database Management Systems and the Data Grid", *18th IEEE Symposium on Mass Storage Systems* '01.

[3] T,Ozsu, P.Valduriez, "*Distributed and Parallel Database Systems*", *ACM Computing Surveys*, vol.28, no.1, pp 125-128, March '96.

[4] P. A. Bernstein, V. Hadzilacos, N. Goodman, *Concurrency Control and Recovery in Database Systems*, Addision-Wesley, 1987.

[5] K. Barker, "Transaction Management on Multidatabase Systems", PhD thesis, Department of Computer Science, The university of Alberta, Canada, 1990.

[6] P. Muth, T. C. Rakow, "Atomic Commitment for Integrated Database Systems", *Proceedings of IEEE, 7th Intl. Conference on Data Engineering*, pp 296-304, 1991.

[7] I. Foster, C. Kesselman, S.Tuecke, "The Anatomy of the Grid", *International Journal of Supercomputer Applications*, vol. 15, no. 3, 2001.

[8] I. Foster, C. Kesselman, J. M. Nick, S.Tuecke, "The Physiology of the Grid", http://www.globus.org/research/papers/ogsa.pdf.

[9] Y. Breitbart, H. Garcia-Molina, and A. Silberschatz. "*Overview of multidatabase transaction management*". VLDB Journal, vol. 1, no. 2, pp.181-240, 1992.

[10] P. Watson, "*Databases and the Grid*", Technical Report, CS-TR-755, Uiversity of New Castle, 2002

[11] IBM, Microsoft, BEA, "*Web Services Coordination*" ftp://www6.software.ibm.com/software/developer/library/ws-coordination.pdf, Sept. 2003.

[12] IBM, Microsoft, BEA, "*Web Services Transaction*" http://www.ibm.com/developerworks/library/ws-transpec/, August 2002.

[13] M. P. Atkinson, V. Dialani, L. Guy, I. Narang, N. W. Paton, D. Pearson, T. Storey, P. Watson, "Grid Database Access and Integration: Requirements and Functionalities" *Global Grid Forum, DAIS-Working Group*, Informational Document, 2003.

[14] M.T. Ozsu and P. Valduriez, editors. *Principles of Distributed Database Systems* (Second Edition). Prentice-Hall, 1999.

[15] Baber Home Page, http://www.slac.stanford.edu/BFROOT/

[16] http://www.griphyn.org/

[17] S. Goel, H. Sharda, D. Taniar, "Preserving Data Consistency in Grid Databases with Multiple Transactions", *2nd International Workshop on Grid and Cooperative Computing (GCC '03), Lecture Notes in Computer Science*, Springer-Verlag, China, Dec. 2003.

A Data Grid Security System Based on Shared Context*

Nong Xiao, Xiaonian Wu, Wei Fu, Xiangli Qu

School of Computer Science, National University of Defense Technology,
410073 Changsha, China
xiao-n@vip.sina.com

Abstract. Data grid system supports uniform and secure access of heterogene-ous distributed data resources across a range of administrative domains, each with its own local security policy. The security challenge has been a focus in a data grid environment. This paper mainly presents GridDaEn's security mecha-nisms. In addition to the basic authentication and authorization functionality, it provides an integrated security strategy featured by shared context-based secure channel building to leverage security processing efficiency so as to improve in-teraction performance occurring among multiple domains in GridDaEn. Mean-while, by means of proxy credential single-sign-on across multiple domains can be achieved. Experiments show that this approach can guarantee system secu-rity and reliability with great performance enhancement.

1 Introduction

Data grid system integrates and manages heterogeneous distributed data resources across a range of administrative domains, each with its own local security policy. The system implies a major security challenge while providing conveniences.

GridDaEn[1](Grid Data Engine) is a data grid middleware, it is implemented by NUDT (National University of Defense Technology). The system is faced with some noted security problems in data grid circumstances such as integration, interoperabil-ity and trust problems, which greatly complicate system security mechanisms. Ac-cording to our grid application backgrounds, we adopt GSI[2](Globus Security Infra-structure) as a basic framework and improve it with the introduction of shared context. GridDaEn's security mechanism is built in combination with PKI[3] (Public Key Infrastructure), with the following features included:

- Supporting mutual authentication and communication confidentiality;
- Supporting a fine-grained RBAC authorization mechanism;
- Supporting single sign-on;
- Supporting shared context-based secure channel building to improve per-formance.

* This paper was supported by the National 863 High Technology Plan of China under the grant No. 2002AA131010, and the National Natural Science Foundation of China under the grant No. 60203016.

H. Jin et al. (Eds.): NPC 2004, LNCS 3222, pp. 30-37, 2004.

The rest of the paper is organized as follows: Section 2 presents a brief introduction of GridDaEn system. Section 3 describes the structure and features of GridDaEn security system in detail. Section 4 shows the implementation. Section 5 exhibits the performance improvement by comparing the time overheads in building secure channels with two different approaches. Section 6 introduces some related work on grid security. Finally, in Sections 7 we present our conclusions and future work.

2 GridDaEn System Overview

2.1 GridDaEn Structure Model

GridDaEn (Grid Data Engine) system is a Data Grid middleware, which can integrate various kinds of file systems and provides uniform seamless access to distributed datasets. GridDaEn consists of four major components: Client tools, Security and System manager, DRB (Data Request Broker) servers, and MDIS (Metadata Information Service), as is illustrated in figure 1.

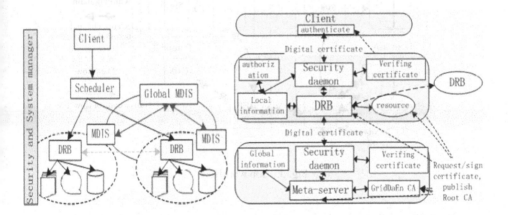

Fig. 1. The structure of GridDaEn   **Fig. 2.** GridDaEn structure with security mechanism

There are more than one administrative domains in GridDaEn. In each domain, there is a DRB server, which performs actual data operations on local storage resources in responding to requests from users and applications. MDIS, which provides metadata service for each DRB server, is organized into a distributed structure, including several local metadata servers and a global metadata server. Security information such as authorization information is partly stored in MDIS.

2.2   A Job-Flow Across Multi-domains in GridDaEn

In order to illustrate the mechanisms implemented in GridDaEn, first, we will analyze a typical job flow scenario across multiple domains in GridDaEn, as is demonstrated in Figure 3.

- A user contacts DRB A, and submits a job to DRB A
- DRB A contacts its MDIS M, in cooperation with which it checks the user's rights
- DRB A locates the required data. If it is located in the local domain, DRB A will contacts site S where the data resides, and then obtain data from site S. Otherwise, DRB A will inquire of MDIS M about where the data resides, then find its broker, for example, DRB B
- DRB A then contacts DRB B, and delivers the original job to DRB B
- DRB B contacts its MDIS N, checks the user's rights, and then locates the Resource site T
- DRB B contacts site T, and obtains the required data
- DRB B returns the data to the user via DRB A

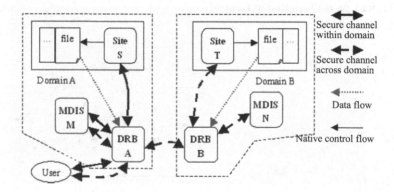

Fig. 3.   Job workflow

3   GridDaEn Security Mechanisms

3.1   GridDaEn Security Structure

As is mentioned before, it is necessary to provide many security functionalities such as authentication, authorization, and communication confidentiality to guarantee security in GridDaEn. To meet the security requirements raised in GridDaEn, such functionalities as GridDaEn CA (Certificate Authority), mutual authentication, authorization, communication confidentiality etc. are mainly provided. Meanwhile, single sign-on is realized by means of proxy credentials. The security structure of GridDaEn is illustrated in Figure 2.

In Figure 2, there is a CA located at the site where GridDaEn Global MDIS resides. GridDaEn entities, such as users, DRBs, MDISes and resource sites, should request and obtain a digital certificate to identify themselves from CA.

3.2 Features of GridDaEn Security System

As can be seen from Figure 3 in Section 2.2, for security guarantee, any two participants should do mutual authentication to build a secure channel before the job can start. It is clear that, if the required data is within DRB A's domain, the system must build three secure channels (as denoted by the solid lines). Otherwise, five channels (as denoted by the dashed lines) must be built. If the job is somehow more complex, the amount of secure channels will be even larger. As a result, a large amount of time is consumed in building so many secure channels. For performance considerations, it is necessary to minimize the number of secure channels. Therefore, shared context-based secure channels are introduced to be a solution. Besides this distinct feature, other security mechanisms, such as single sign-on, RBAC authorization and so on, are also well-supported.

3.2.1 Shared Context-Based Secure Channels

From the above analyses, we can infer that the performance of secure channels will greatly affect the performance of the whole system. Our solution is what we called a context mechanism, similar to a connection pool, which reduces the overheads (caused by security authentication) by sharing or reusing context. Such context is built by the secure channel between any two participants in GridDaEn. When a DRB is started, it will automatically start a mutual authentication process with an MDIS to build secure channels. After that, the information associated with this process will be saved in a *context*, which has many properties and methods, as is sketched in figure 4. Notice that, for the dynamic and changeable nature of grid environment, each context should have a lifetime field to specify its validity period. Within the specified lifetime, all the data transferred between this DRB and its MDIS will be encrypted and passed by this context, and the access rights is also authorized by the identity recorded in the context. When a user wants to access some data resided in a site, a context between this user and the DRB for this site will also be established.

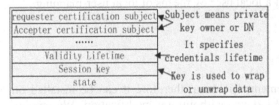

Fig. 4. The properties of a context

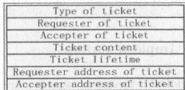

Fig. 5. A context table entry

Actually, different users cannot share the contexts between users and DRBs, that is mutual authentication must be performed again when a user wants to contact another DRB. However, those contexts between DRB and MDIS, or between DRB and resource sites, or one DRB and another DRB, can be easily shared or reused by others. Therefore, overheads will be lowered and performance will be improved..

However, how to use and manage these contexts can be a troublesome problem. Here we adopt the idea of route table. Once the system builds a context, it will be classified by its creator and saved into a table with its lifetime. The address information of the two participants is used to index this table. Figure 5 gives an example of a context table's entries. Therefore, the subsequent requests can quickly find a context and greatly accelerate its authorization process.

3.2.2 Single Sign-On and Authorization

Combined with user's proxy credentials, GridDaEn implements single sign-on. Before a user authenticates with a DRB, he will generate a proxy credential by his digital certificate. Then he authenticates himself to the DRB by this proxy. Afterwards, the proxy will execute all the activities that the user wants to do at all the sites, in complete representative of his identity.

For authorization in GridDaEn security system, we borrow some ideas from RBAC. The basic concept of RBAC[4] is that users should be assigned some roles associated with specific permissions, and users' permissions are the combination of these roles. Here we also try to introduce this flexible and effective approach into our authorization mechanism.

We have developed several tools for permission definition, role definition, and user definition. First, we define several elementary permissions for resources in our authorization mechanism. Then we define roles for each domain separately, assigning corresponding permissions to them. Note that, these roles only work in their own domains. Finally, we create grid users and assign roles to users according to some policy. If a user is assigned roles of a domain, he can perform the corresponding privileges in this domain. However, without roles of that domain, he cannot do anything. Thus, it can obtain fine-grained authorization. In order to simply authorization operations, we also introduce the notion of group, to which roles can be assigned. A user belonging to a group will inherit all the roles assigned to the group automatically. All authorization information is saved in MDIS. If authenticated, a user will be checked whether or not he possesses the specific privileges to complete his job. After that, the job will be run in identity of a local user by means of local user-mapping.

4 Implementation

GridDaEn security system is implemented in Java, therefore it can be installed on various platforms such as Linux, Windows, without any modification. We employ some functionalities of Java CoG Kit[5], such as authentication, proxy credentials generation, on which some improvement is made to meet our specific requirements.

We provide GridDaEn CA to suit for our purpose, which responds to certification requests from GridDaEn entities, also depicted in figure 2. Two participants authenticate each other using their own digital certificates. Another important module is to issue proxy certificate for each client, by means of which single sign-on can be achieved. Of course, direct authentication can also be made by digital certificate to get higher security privilege. After authentication between any two participants, all the transferred data would be encrypted by their context to guarantee communication confidentiality. And all interfaces and APIs are standard, supported by GSS-APIs(Generic Security Service Application Program Interface).

Based on the above security functionalities, we build a context table to save contexts built after authenticated. Also it records lifetime and other information about contexts. Figure 6 illustrates a Sequence Diagram using case view, which describes how to build and share a context across multiple domains in GridDaEn. As is depicted, the context between DRB A and MDIS is built when client 1 contacts DRB A and submits job to DRB A, and it is used to process jobs from client 1, such as 5 and 6. Also it is used to process jobs from client 2, such as 14 and 15 within its lifetime. Other contexts are similar as above.

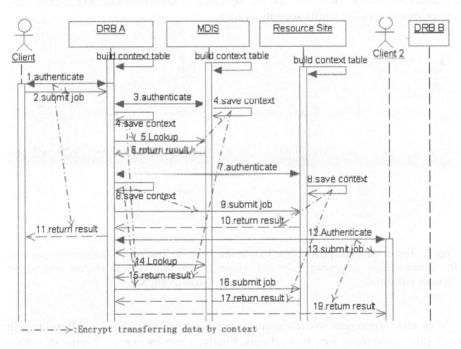

Fig. 6. A Sequence Diagram describing how to build and share context

By adopting PKI model, our security system can integrate with existing systems and technologies, and it can be deployed on all kinds of platforms or hosting environments, with distributed structure support. Meanwhile, digital certificates signed by GridDaEn CA can help to establish trust relationships among multiple domains in GridDaEn by mutual authentication.

5 Performance

For the main concern of security efficiency in our system, we have carried out some experiments to test its performance. The test environment is built with a 10Mbps hub and four machines. The client is running on an Intel machine with 2.4GHz CPU, 512MB of main memory, 40GB Seagate IDE disk and Windows 2000 operation system. A resource site is running on a machine as above. A DRB is running on a Pentium IV machine with 2.4GHz CPU, 512MB of main memory, 40GB Seagate IDE disk and Red Hat Linux release 8.0 operation systems. An MDIS is running on a machine same as the machine running the DRB.

In one experiment, a client sends a request to DRB, reading a file from some site. Firstly, one test for mutual authentication is made, secondly, another test processing a job request for security authentication and encrypting transferred data is carried out. Time consumed in both are illustrated in Figure 7. Note that, MDIS and Resource-Site authenticate with DRB separately, and DRB authenticates with Client in addition. As can be seen from figure 7, time consumed in authentication takes a large percentage in the whole security processing (including authentication, data encryption/decryption etc.), Therefore, the performance of authentication will greatly affect the performance of the whole security system.

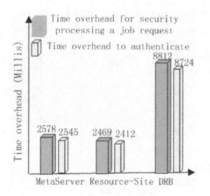
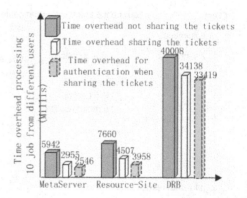

Fig. 7. Test results comparing time overheads for authentication processing only and whole security processing

Fig. 8. Test results comparing time overheads with shared context and without shared context

In another experiment, we test security overhead in DRB, MDIS and Resource-Site when processing many jobs from clients. Firstly, a test for many job requests without shared contexts is made, and secondly, we test these jobs with shared contexts. Figure 8 illustrates the time overheads of both. Note that, with shared contexts, MDIS and Resource-Site authenticate with DRB once respectively, but DRB must authenticate with Clients each time.

From the above figures, we can see that shared contexts can improve the efficiency of the security system to a large amount.

6 Related Work

GSI is a component of the Globus Toolkit[3, 6] that has become the de-facto standard for Grid security. GSI employs PKI[4], which communicates by SSL (Secure Socket Layer), provides mutual authentication and communication confidentiality using public key cryptography and digital certification, and extends to support single sign-on. But authorization is too coarse-grained by a girdmap file.

To summarize, although existing distributed security technologies can solve relating problems faced in its domains, and provide some solutions, but which cannot adequately address the issues in our data grid environment.

7 Conclusion

In this paper, we present a new security mechanism implemented in GridDaEn system: the shared context-based security mechanism. The main contribution is that it can offer security guarantee while meeting the stringent performance requirements for GridDaEn. Currently, we are preparing for publishing the next version of this security system and totally integrating it into GridDaEn.

References

1. Nong xiao,wei fu,bin huang,xicheng lu,: Design and Implementation of data grid system GridDaEn, Computer Nation Conference of China (CNCC),2003.11
2. Luis Ferreira,Viktors Berstis,Jonathan Armstrong,et al,: Introduction to Grid Computing with Globus, http://www.ibm.com/redbooks, 2002, page 51-81
3. Internet X.509 Public Key Infrastructure: Certificate and Certificate Revocation List (CRL) Profile. http://www.ietf.org/rfc/rfc3280.txt, 2002
4. DAVID F.FERRAIOLO,RAVI SANDHU,SERBAN GAVRILA,et al,: Proposed NIST Standard for Role-Based Access Control, ACM Transactions on Information and System Security, Vol. 4, No. 3, August 2001, Pages 224-274.
5. Gregor von Laszewski,Ian Foster,Jarek Gawor,and Peter Lane,: A Java Commodity Grid Kit, Concurrency and Computation: Practice and Experience, vol.13, no.8-9, pp.643-662, 2001.
6. I. Foster, C. Kesselman, G. Tsudik, and and S. Tuecke,: A Security Architecture for Computational Grids, 5th ACM Conf, on Computer and Communication Security, 1997.

A Study on Performance Monitoring Techniques for Traditional Parallel Systems and Grid

Sarbani Roy (nee Ghosh) [1] and Nandini Mukherjee [2]

[1] Department of Computer Science and Engineering,
St. Thomas College of Engineering and Technology,
West Bengal University of Technology, Kolkata 700 023, India
sarbani_roy77@yahoo.co.in
[2] Department of Computer Science and Engineering,
Jadavpur University, Kolkata 700 032, India
nmukherjee@vsnl.com

Abstract: During the last decade, much research has been done to evolve cost-effective techniques for performance monitoring and analysis of applications running on conventional parallel systems. With the advent of technology, new Grid-based systems emerged by the end of the last decade, and received attention as useful environments for high-performance computing. The requirements for discovering new techniques for monitoring the Grid have also come to the front. The objective of this paper is to study the techniques used by tools targeting traditional parallel systems and highlight the requirements and techniques used for Grid monitoring. We present case studies of some representative tools to get an understanding of both paradigms.

1. Introduction

Computer scientists and researchers have a long-time target to develop effective methods and tools for performance analysis of compute-intensive applications and providing support for automatic parallelisation and performance tuning. In other words, performance engineering of such applications in a cost-effective manner has been a major focus of the researchers during the last decade. Many tools for measuring or predicting performance of serial / parallel programs have been developed. These tools were designed with diverse objectives, targeted different parallel architectures and adopted various techniques for collection and analysis of performance data. The scope of these tools comprises instrumentation, measurement (monitoring), data reduction and correlation, analysis and presentation and finally, in some cases, optimisation.

The second half of the last decade however witnessed radical changes in technology. Clusters of workstations / personal computers / SMPs offered an attractive alternative to traditional supercomputers, as well as MPPs. With the advent of Internet technology, we then entered the era of Grid Computing. Introduction of this new paradigm in the world of high performance computing has forced the computer scientists to look into the performance-engineering problem with an entirely different

H. Jin et al. (Eds.): NPC 2004, LNCS 3222, pp. 38–46, 2004.

view. The term Grid indicates an execution environment in which high speed networks are used to connect supercomputers, clusters of workstations, databases, scientific instruments located at geographically distributed sites. Monitoring such an environment for executing compute-intensive applications and performance engineering these applications is one of the central tasks of Grid computing research. Performance monitoring of Grid and Grid applications, by its very own nature, differs from the underlying principles of traditional performance analysis tools. The heterogeneous nature of computational resources, potentially unreliable networks connecting these resources and different administrative management domains pose the biggest challenge to the performance monitoring / engineering community in Computer Science research.

The objective of this paper is to study the main trends of traditional performance analysis tools and Grid monitoring tools, to compare the techniques used by them, to focus on the major issues of Grid monitoring and applicability of various techniques for monitoring the applications and resources in Grid environment. Traditional performance analysis tools are discussed in Section 2 based on some case studies. The paper then summarises the properties of Grid and compares with conventional distributed systems. It also highlights the main issues that need to be tackled while designing a Grid monitoring system (Section 3). Case studies on representative Grid monitoring tools are furnished in Section 4 followed by a discussion on various aspects of Grid monitoring. Section 5 presents related work and Section 6 concludes.

2. Performance Monitoring and Analysis for Traditional Parallel Systems

This section focuses on the performance monitoring and analysis techniques adapted for use on traditional parallel systems. We present case studies on two performance analysis tools with an emphasis on their important features.

2.1 SCALEA

SCALEA is a performance analysis tool developed at the University of Vienna [17]. It provides support for automatic instrumentation of parallel programs, measurement, analysis and visualization of their performance data. The tool has been used to analyse and to guide the application development by selectively computing a variety of important performance metrics, by detecting performance bottlenecks, and by relating performance information back to the input program.

The components of *SCALEA* include *SCALEA Instrumentation System (SIS)*, *SCALEA Runtime System*, *SCALEA Performance Data Repository*, and *SCALEA Performance Analysis and Visualization System*. Each of these components can also be used as a separate tool. The *SCALEA Instrumentation system (SIS)* enables the user to select code regions of interest and automatically inserts monitoring code to collect all relevant performance information during an execution of the program. An execution of a program on a given target architecture is referred to as an experiment. Unlike most performance tools, *SCALEA* supports analysis of performance data obtained from individual experiments, as well as from multiple experiments. All the important information about performance experiments including source code, machine information and performance results are stored in a data repository. *SCALEA* focuses on four major categories of temporal overheads including data movement, synchronization, control of parallelism, and additional computation. The classification of overheads in *SCALEA* is hierarchical.

2.2 Paradyn

Paradyn, from the Computer Sciences Department of University of Wisconsin, Madison, is a tool for measuring and understanding the performance of serial, parallel and distributed programs [8]. It consists of a data collection facility (the Data Manager), an automated bottleneck search tool (the Performance Consultant), a data visualization interface (the Visualization Manager), and a User Interface Manager. The central part of the tool is a multi-threaded process and communication between threads is defined by a set of interfaces constructed to allow any module to request a service of any other module.

The performance consultant module of *Paradyn* automates the search for a predefined set of performance bottlenecks based on a well-defined model, called the W^3 search model. It attempts to find the answer of three questions: firstly why is the application performing poorly, secondly where is the performance problem located, and finally when does the problem occur. *Paradyn* uses *dynamic instrumentation* to instrument only those parts of the program relevant for finding the current performance problem. Dynamic instrumentation defers instrumenting the program until it is executed and dynamically inserts, alters and deletes instrumentation during program execution. What data to be collected is also decided during the execution of the program under the guidance of the Performance Consultant.

2.3 Discussion

In this section, we summarise the salient features of performance analysis tools discussed above. Although these tools are only representatives of the vast number of performance analysis tools available for traditional parallel architectures, the following discussion will give some idea about the techniques adopted by majority of them.

☐ The important **components** of performance analysis tools are (a) tools for instrumentation and data collection, (b) tools for analysing and identification of performance problems, and (c) tools for visualisation.
☐ Monitoring data is **collected** through source code instrumentation and trace libraries are used for recording monitoring events. For example, *SCALEA* uses SISPROFILING, and PAPI (does profiling using timers, counters, and hardware parameters) libraries.

☐ **Source code instrumentation** is generally guided by the user (in an interactive manner). Modern tools employ dynamic instrumentation techniques to dynamically change the focus and performance bottlenecks are identified during run-time.

☐ The tools are designed to work on divers **hardware platforms.** For example, the platform dependent part of *Paradyn* is available for SPARC, x86 and PowerPCs.

☐ One requirement of these tools is to support different **programming paradigms**. *SCALEA*, for example, supports performance analysis of HPF, OpenMP and MPI codes.

☐ Each tool defines their own **data storage formats**, thus limiting the portability of monitoring data.

3. High Performance Computing and Grids

Grids are persistent environments that enable software applications to integrate computational and information resources, instruments and other types of resources managed by diverse organizations in widespread locations. Computational resources on a Grid together can solve very large problems requiring more resources than is available on a single machine. Thus harnessing the power of these distributed computational resources "computational power grids" may be created for high performance computing. This concept is often referred to as a "Computational Grid".

Grids are usually viewed as the successors of distributed computing environments; although from the user's point of view conventional distributed systems and Grids are intrinsically semantically different. The resources in a Grid are typically heterogeneous in nature with fast internal message passing or shared memory [1]. A relatively slow wide area network externally connects the individual resources.

3.1 Performance Analysis in Grid Environment

Grid performance analysis is distinctively different from the performance analysis for traditional parallel architectures. The fundamental and ultimate goal of parallel processing is speeding up the computation, i.e. executing the same task in shorter time. In a Grid environment, however, speed of the computation is not the only issue. Mapping application processes to the resources in order to fulfill the requirement of the application in terms of power, capacity, quality and availability forms the basis of Grid performance evaluation. The huge amount of monitoring data generated in a Grid environment are used to perform fault detection, diagnosis and scheduling in addition to performance analysis, prediction and tuning [2]. The dynamic nature of Grid makes most parallel and distributed programming paradigms unsuitable and the existing parallel programming and performance analysis tools and techniques are not always appropriate for coping with such an environment.

The important elements that make performance analysis for Grids different from the performance analysis for SMPs or MPPs may be summarised as below [10]:

☐ **Lack of prior knowledge about the execution environment:** The execution environment in a Grid is not known beforehand and also the environment may vary from one execution to another execution and even during the same execution of an application.

☐ **Need for real-time performance analysis:** Due to the dynamic nature of a Grid-based environment, offline analysis is often unsuitable. Sometimes it becomes necessary to predict the behaviour of an application based on some known characteristics of the environment. However, in the absence of precise knowledge about the future shape of the Grid, this prediction-based analysis is also of little use.

☐ **Difficulty in performance tuning of applications:** It may not be possible to exactly repeat an execution of a given application in a dynamic Grid environment. Therefore, performance tuning and optimisation of the application is difficult.

☐ **Emergence of new performance problems:** The very different nature of a Grid infrastructure gives rise to new performance problems that must be identified and tackled by the performance analysis tool.

☐ **Requirement of new performance metrics:** Usual performance metrics used by traditional performance analysis tools are inappropriate and therefore new performance metrics must be defined.

☐ **Overheads due to Grid management services:** Grid information services, resource management and security policies in a Grid environment add additional overhead to the execution of an application.

Global Grid Forum proposed a Grid Monitoring Service Architecture [6, 15] which is sufficiently general and may be adapted in variety of computational environments including Grid, clusters and large compute farms. The essential components of the architecture as described in [6] are as follows:

☐ *Sensors:* for generation of time-stamped performance monitoring events for hosts, network processes and applications. Error conditions can also be monitored by the sensors.

☐ *Sensor Manager:* responsible for starting and stopping the sensors.

☐ *Event Consumers:* request data from sensors.

☐ *Directory Service:* for publication of the location of all sensors and other event suppliers.

☐ *Event Suppliers or Producers:* for keeping the sensor directory up-to-date and listening to data requests from event consumers.

☐ *Event archive:* for archiving the data that may be used later for historical analysis.

In the next Section we present case studies on two Grid monitoring tools and highlight their important characteristics.

4. Performance Monitoring and Analysis Tools for Grid

Currently available Grid Monitoring Tools may be classified into two main categories: Grid infrastructure monitoring tools and Grid application monitoring tools. Although the primary focus of majority of the tools is on monitoring and analysis of

Grid infrastructure, many tools are nowadays concentrating on a unified approach. In the following sections, we present brief overviews of three such tools. It must be noted that there is no specific motive behind the selection of these three tools apart from rendering some basic idea about the requirements of Grid monitoring tools and their major components. A detail survey of existing performance monitoring and evaluation tools may be found in [5] which has an objective of creating a directory of tools for enabling the researchers to find relevant properties, similarities and differences of these tools.

4.1 SCALEA-G

SCALEA-G [18], developed at the University of Vienna is the next generation of the *SCALEA* System. SCALEA-G is a unified system developed for monitoring Grid infrastructure based on the concept of Grid Monitoring Architecture (GMA) [15] and at the same time for performance analysis of Grid applications [6]. SCALEA-G is implemented as a set of Grid services based on the Open Grid Service architecture (OGSA) [4]. OGSA-compliant grid services are deployed for online monitoring and performance analysis of a variety of computational resources, networks, and applications.

The major services of SCALEA-G are: (a) *Directory Service* for publishing and searching information about producers and consumers of performance data, (b) *Archival Service* to store monitored data and performance results, (c) *Sensor Manager Service* to manage sensors. Sensors are used to collect monitoring data for performance analysis. Two types of sensors are used: *system sensors* (for monitoring Grid infrastructure) and *application sensors* (to measure the execution behaviour of Grid applications). XML schemas are used to describe each kind of monitoring data and any client can access the data by submitting Xpath / Xquery-based requests. The interactions between sensors and Sensor Manager Services also take place through the exchange of XML messages.

SCALEA-G supports both source code and dynamic instrumentation for profiling and monitoring events of Grid Applications. The source code instrumentation service of SCALEA-G is based on *SCALEA* Instrumentation System [17]. Dynamic instrumentation (based on Dyninst from [3]) is accomplished by using a *Mutator Service* that controls the instrumentation of application process on the host where the process is running. An XML-based Instrumentation Request Language (IRL) has also been developed for interaction with the client.

4.2 GrADS and Autopilot

Researchers from different universities led by a team at Rice University are working in the GrADS project [12] that aims at providing a framework for development and performance tuning of Grid applications. As a part of this project, a *Program Execution Framework* is being developed [7] to support resource allocation and reallocation based on performance monitoring of resources and applications. A performance model is used to predict the expected behaviour of an application and actual behaviour is captured during its execution from the analysis of measured performance data. If there is a disagreement between the expected behaviour and observed behaviour, actions like replacement or alteration of resources or redistribution of the application tasks are performed.

The monitoring infrastructure of GrADS is based on Autopilot, which monitors and controls applications, as well as resources. The Autopilot toolkit supports adaptive resource management for dynamic applications. Autopilot integrates dynamic performance instrumentation and on-the-fly performance-data reduction with configurable, malleable resource management algorithms and a real-time adaptive control mechanism. Thus, it becomes possible to automatically choose and configure resource management policies based on application request patterns and system performance [13]. Autopilot provides a flexible set of performance sensors, decision procedures, and policy actuators to accomplish adaptive control of applications and resources. The policy implementation mechanism of the tool is based on fuzzy logic.

4.3 Discussion

The Section describes some representative tools for Grid monitoring and performance tuning of Grid Applications. It is evident that on a large, complex and widely distributed system similar to Grid, post-mortem performance analysis is of no use. Thus, all tools perform real-time analysis and some use these analysis data for automatic performance tuning of applications. The essential ingredients of real-time analysis are

☐ *dynamic instrumentation and data collection mechanism* (as performance problems must be identified during run-time),

☐ *data reduction* (as the amount of monitoring data is large and movement of this amount of data through the network is undesirable),

☐ *low-cost data capturing mechanism* (as overhead due to instrumentation and profiling may contribute to the application performance), and

☐ *adaptability to heterogeneous environment* (for the heterogeneous nature of Grid, the components along with the communicating messages and data must have minimum dependence on the hardware platform, operating system and programming languages and paradigms).

The basis of most monitoring tools is the general Grid Monitoring Architecture proposed by the Global Grid Forum. However, when the tools extend their functionality to incorporate real-time performance analysis and tuning, they have to confront with complex issues like fault diagnosis and application remapping.

Many of the already existing libraries and performance monitoring tools for traditional parallel systems form parts of the Grid monitoring tools. For example, SCALEA-G uses the instrumentation system of *SCALEA* [17] and Dyninst [3] and one of the current foci of GrADS project is to incorporate the instrumentation of SvPablo [14].

5. Related Work

Performance tools for conventional parallel systems are in use for quite some time. Therefore, many researchers have already studied, discussed and compared these tools. Some of the recent studies focus on the survey of Grid monitoring tools [2, 5]. In particular, [5] provides a directory of recently available tools along with a comparative analysis of them.

The objective of this paper is not to prepare a survey report, nor does it aim at the comparative analysis of performance tools. The main intention is to study the requirements for Grid monitoring tools in comparison to the standard performance monitoring and analysis techniques applicable to conventional parallel architectures.

6. Conclusion

This paper discussed and highlighted different monitoring techniques for traditional parallel architectures and Grids. The observations that surfaced in this paper grow an understanding of the recent road-map of performance engineering tools for developing high performance applications targeting modern systems. In addition, a direction for new generation tools is also set up.

References

1. R.J. Allan, J.M. Brooke and F. Costen and M.westhead, *Grid based high Performance Computing*, Technical Report of the UKHEC Collaboration, June 2000.
2. Z. Balaton, P. Kacsuk, N. Podhorszki and F. Vajda, *Comparison of Representative Grid Monitoring Tools*, Report of the Laboratory of Parallel and Distributed Systems, Computer and Automation Research Institute of the Hungarian Academy of Sciences, 2000.
3. *Dyninst: An Application Program Interface (API) for Runtime Code Generation*, http://www.dyninst.org.
4. I. Foster, C. Kesselman, J. M. Nick, S. Tuecke, *Grid Services for Distributed System Integration*, IEEE Computer, Pages 37-46, June 2002.
5. M. Gerndt et al, .*Perforrmance tools for the Grid: State of the Art and Future- APART White Paper*, http://www.fz-juelich.de/apart.
6. Grid Performance Working Group, Global Grid Forum, *White Paper: A Grid Monitoring Service Architecture*.
7. Ken Kennedy et al, *Toward a Framework for Preparing and Executing Adaptive Grid Programs*, Proceedings of the International Parallel and Distributed Processing Symposium Workshop (IPDPS NGS), IEEE Computer Society Press, April 2002.
8. B. P. Miller et al, *The Paradyn Parallel Performance Measurement Tools*, IEEE Computer 28(11), (November 1995). Special issue on performance evaluation tools for parallel and distributed computer systems.
9. Norbert Padhorszki and Peter Kacsuk, *Presentation and analysis of Grid Performance Data*, Proceedings of EuroPar-2003, Klagenfurt, Austria, 2003.

10. Z. Nemeth, *Performance Evaluation on Grids: Directions, Issues, and Open Problems*, Report of the Laboratory of Parallel and Distributed Systems, Computer and Automation Research Institute of the Hungarian Academy of Sciences, 2002
11. *Paradyn Parallel Performance Tools*. http://www.cs.wisc.edu/paradyn/
12. D. Reed, C. Mendes and S. Whitmore, *GrADS Contract Monitoring*, Pablo Group, University of Illinois, http:// www- pablo. cs. uiuc. edu
13. R. L. Ribler, H. Simitci, D. A. Reed, *The Autopilot Performance-Directed Adaptive Control System*, Future Generation Computer Systems, 18[1], Pages 175-187, September 2001.
14. L. D. Rose and D. Reed, *SvPablo: A Multi-Language Architecture-Independent Performance Analysis System*, Proceedings of the 1999 International Conference on Parallel Processing, p.311, September 1999
15. B.Tierney, *A Grid Monitoring Architecture*, http://www-didc.lbl.gov/GGF-PERF/GMA-WG/papers/GWD-GP-16-2.pdf.
16. B. Tierney, B. Crowley, D. Gunter, M. Holding, J. Lee, M. Thompson, *A Monitoring Sensor Management System for Grid Environments*, Proceedings of the IEEE High Performance Distributed Computing conference, August 2000.
17. Hong-Linh Truong and Thomas Fahringer, *SCALEA: A Performance Analysis Tool for Parallel Programs*. Concurrency and Computation: Practice and Experience, 15(11-12): Pages 1001-1025, 2003.
18. Hong-Linh Truong and Thomas Fahringer, *SCALEA-G: a Unified Monitoring and Performance Analysis System for the Grid*, 2nd European Across Grids Conference, Cyprus, January 2004.

A Workflow-Based Grid Portal for Problem Solving Environment*

Yong-Won Kwon, So-Hyun Ryu, Jin-Sung Park, and Chang-Sung Jeong

Department of Electronics Engineering Graduate School, Korea University
5-ka, Anam-dong, Sungbuk-ku, Seoul, Korea
{luco|messias|honong13}@snoopy.korea.ac.kr, csjeong@charlie.korea.ac.kr
Tel: 82-2-3290-3229, Fax: 82-2-926-7621

Abstract. In this paper, we present a Workflow-based grId portal for problem Solving Environment(WISE) which has been developed by integrating workflow, Grid and web technology to provide an enhanced powerful approach for problem solving environment. Workflow technology supports coordinated execution of multiple application tasks on Grid resources by enabling users to describe a workflow by composing many existing applications and new functions, and provides an easy powerful tool to create new Grid applications. We propose new Grid portal to allow us to use Grid resources with improved workflow patterns to represent various parallelisms inherent in parallel and distributed Grid applications and present Grid Workflow Description Language(GWDL) to specify our new workflow patterns. Also, We shall show that the MVC(Model View Control) design pattern and multi-layer architecture provides modularity and extensibility to WISE by separating the application engine control and presentation from the application logic for Grid services, and the Grid portal service from Grid service interface.

1 Introduction

For the success of Grid computing, an easy powerful PSE, which provides computing resources and high quality apparatus to solve complex problems of science and engineering technology, are needed. In internet and distributed computing, there are useful technologies for PSE, which have evolved in parallel. Web technology has emerged with revolutionary effects on how we access and process information. Grid computing enables us to use a large or nationwide network of resource as a single unified computing resource[1]. So, clear steps must be taken to integrate Grid and Web technologies to develop a enhanced powerful tool for PSE. Workflow technology is very useful because it enables us to describe a process of work by composing of multiple application tasks on multiple distributed Grid resources. It allows users to easily develop new applications by composing services and expressing their interaction. In [11,12,15,13,16,14,17,18,19], several

---

* This work has been supported by a Korea University Grant, KIPA-Information Technology Research Center, University research program by Ministry of Information & Communication, and Brain Korea 21 projects in 2004.

H. Jin et al. (Eds.): NPC 2004, LNCS 3222, pp. 47–56, 2004.
© IFIP International Federation for Information Processing 2004

researches about previous workflow management systems for Grid computing were published, and have been studied. However, their workflow models have too simple workflow patterns like sequence, parallel constructs like AND-split/merge, conditional constructs like XOR-split, and iteration constructs to implement parallel and distributed Grid applications efficiently.

In this paper, we present a Workflow-based grId portal for problem Solving Environment(WISE) which has been developed by integrating workflow, Grid and web technology to provide an enhanced powerful approach for problem solving environment. Workflow technology supports coordinated execution of multiple application tasks on Grid resources by enabling users to describe a workflow by composing many existing applications or new functions, and provides an easy powerful tool to create new grid applications. we show our advanced workflow pattern and description language. Our new Grid portal allows us to use Grid resources with improved workflow patterns to represent various parallelisms inherent in parallel and distributed Grid applications. Also, we are concerned about the design and implementation of Grid portal architecture enhanced with softwares to allows users to transparently access remote heterogeneous resources through Grid services. We shall show that the MVC(Model View Control) design pattern and multi-layer architecture provides modularity and extensibility by separating the application engine control and presentation from the application logic, and the Grid portal service from Grid service interface.

The outline of our paper is as follows: In section 2, we describe the basic concepts of Grid and workflow technology, together with their related works. In section 3, we present our new workflow pattern and workflow description language. In section 4, we illustrate the architecture of WISE, and describe the detailed services. In section 5, we explain the implementation of WISE. In section 6, we give conclusion.

2   Related Work

2.1   Grid User, PSE, and Grid Portal

A Grid user does not want to be bothered with details of its underlying infrastructure but is really only interested in execution of application and acquisition of correct results in a timely fashion. Therefore, a Grid environment should provide access to the available resources in a seamless manner such that the differences between platforms, network protocols, and administrative boundaries become completely transparent, thus providing one virtual homogeneous environment. Grid requires several design features: a wide range of services on heterogeneous systems, information-rich environment on dynamic Grid, single sign-on, and use of standards and the existing applications. Globus toolkit establishes a software framework for common services of Grid infrastructure by providing a meta computer toolkit such as Meta Directory Service, Globus Security Infrastructure, and Resource Allocation Manager[2,3]. However, it is responsibility of application users to devise methods and approaches for utilizing Grid services.

PSE is a useful tool for solving problems from a specific domain. Traditionally, it was developed as client-side tools. Recently, a web-based Grid portals have been developed to launch and manage jobs on the Grid, via Web, and allow users to program and execute distributed Grid applications by a conventional Web browser. Webflow is a pioneering computing web portal work, where http server is used as computing server proxy using CGI technology[4]. GridPort[5] allows developers to connect Web-based interfaces with the computational Grid behind the scenes through Globus Toolkit[2] and Web technologies such as CGI and Perl. Hotpage user portal is designed to be a single point-of-access to all Grid resources with informational and interactive services by using GridPort. Astrophysics Simulation Collaboratory (ASC) portal is designed for the study of physically complex astrophysical phenomena[6]. It use Globus and Cactus as a core computational tool.

2.2 Workflow Patterns

In Grid computing, workflow is a process that consists of activities and inter-actions between them. An activity is a basic unit of work: a grid service or an application executed on Grid. In [11,12,13], the existing workflow patterns are introduced for describing the only control flow. Most of them are basic patterns such as sequence, simple parallel constructs like AND-Split/Join, conditional constructs like XOR-Split/Join, OR-Split/Join, iteration construct. Other patterns such as N out of M join, deferred choice, and arbitrary cycle are presented in [11,15]. These are insufficient to express parallel applications. Triana [13,14] presents link elements for data flow and simple control flow patterns such as a pair of AND-Split and AND-Join, a pair of IF-Split and If-Join, and Count Loop and While Loop. The Grid Services Flow Language(GSFL) [16] is an XML based language that allows the specification of workflow descriptions in the OGSA framework. It also use simple link elements. GridAnt [18] is a client side workflow tool based on java Apache Ant. It describes parallelism by specifying dependencies between tasks. The myGrid workflow [19] provides a graphical tool and workflow enactor, but in terms of the parallel control flow, they support only simple parallelism like the above workflow models and languages.

3   Grid Workflow Description

3.1   New Advanced Workflow Patterns

We need new advanced workflow patterns for Grid applications to describe various parallelism such as pipeline, data parallelism, and many synchronizing constructs and to prevent incomprehensible workflow description. Complex workflow can be made by simple link patterns, but it is difficult. Moreover, any control flow produced by composing sequence and arbitrary cycle may generate ambiguity which is a state to be too complex and difficult to comprehend correct meaning. Therefore, to describe a precise workflow easily and fast, the structured patterns with clear context is more efficient than the non-structured ones

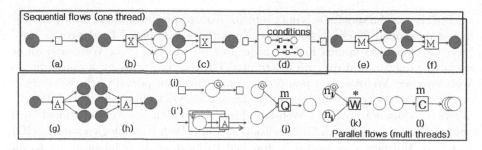

Fig. 1. Advanced basic control patterns: (a) Sequence (b) XOR-Split (c) XOR-Join (d) Loop (e) Multi-Split (f) Multi-Join (g) AND-Split (h) AND-Join (i) AND-Loop symbol (i') AND-Loop description (j) Queue (k) Wait (l) Node copy

made by any compositions of sequences and arbitrary cycles. The details of our workflow model are published in [20]

In figure 1 we show our basic patterns with three groups. In sequential flow, there are four types: sequence for sequential control flow, XOR-Split for conditional execution, XOR-Join for conditional selection among many executed activities, and Loop for repetition. In mixed flow, there are two patterns: Multi-Split for multiple conditional execution, and Multi-Join for multiple conditional selection. Parallel flow includes AND-Split for parallel execution, AND-Join for blocked synchronization, AND-Loop, Queue, Wait, and Node copy. Whenever an iteration of AND-Loop is complete, two control flows occur to two directions like figure 1 (i'): the one for repetition and the other for next sequential activities. The circular-arrow in figure 1 (i) is the graphic notation of AND-Loop. AND-Loop can send many flows to a next node N continuously. If N is bottleneck, activities that send flows to N may stop or be processed slowly. A pattern is needed to prevent this situation. In queue pattern, all input control flows are stored in queue and transferred whenever the next node is idle. In node copy pattern, a node is copied up to the limited number of times. An idle node is selected and executed in parallel whenever a input control flow occurs. This pattern can increases computing power and may solve the above bottleneck problem. In wait pattern, wait node blocks until some or all input control flows are received. For example, in figure 1 (k) wait node blocks until all control flows generated by AND-Loop n_1 and node n_i are received. The symbol '*' means all.

3.2 Grid Workflow Description Language

We define the Grid Workflow Description Language (GWDL) which is an XML based language that specifies our workflow model using XML Schemas. The GWDL architecture consists of dataDefine, resourceDefine, activityDefine, and flowDefine elements. DataDefine lists user data types that are used to describe input/ouput data of an activity node. ResourceDefine describes host address

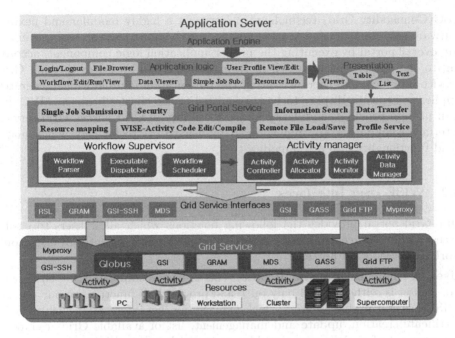

Fig. 2. The Overall Architecture of WISE

or resource specification for executing an activity. ActivityDefine lists activities which are executions of executable files or requests to running services on Grid resources. It describes function, names and types of input/output data. FlowDefine defines activity node elements which have an activity and a resource specification, and both of control and data flows which describe the interaction of activity nodes. It has basic control flow elements for representing our new workflow patterns in section 3.1. We also define three elements for control flow: <sequence>, <parallel>, and <loop>. Activity nodes in sequence element and parallel element are connected sequentially and executed concurrently respectively. Loop element iterates the sub-workflow. It has a 'pipeline' attribute which indicates AND-Loop. Also, in flowDefine elements, there are data elements for describing data flow, which has source, destination, and variable name.

4   WISE Architecture

4.1   Overall Architecture

Our Grid portal has a 3-tier architecture which consists of clients, web application server, and a network of computing resources like figure 2. Web application server in the middle tier is augmented with Grid-enabling software to provide accesses to Grid services and resources. It is designed as a multilayered structure which exploits MVC(Model-View-Controller) design pattern and

CoG(Commodity Grid) technology to construct a highly modular and flexible software environment. Application engine in web server controls and organizes the overall portal by executing the proper application logic component, according to the client request, which in turn carry out Grid services through Grid service interface, and then activating the presentation module which generates application specific display to be transmitted to the client's browser. MVC design pattern provides modularity and extensibility of Grid portal. Grid service interface components are implemented by using CoG technology which maps Grid functionality into a commodity tool.

4.2   WISE User Interfaces

Our Grid portal provides the following functions which allow users to easily access Grid resources and make new Grid applications efficiently by using our workflow-based Grid portal.

User Authentication and Profile: This is basic components for Grid portal. A user is authenticated only once and provided all functions of our portal. WISE has user profile function which manages his/her information such as Grid certificate creation, update and management, list of available Grid resources, management of environment variables on many distributed host, request of resource authorization to its manager and email address.

Remote File Browser: This is file management functions such as file directory browsing of remote hosts, creation, delete, editing, upload from local file system, download to the local, file transfer between two remote hosts by GridFTP, and edit/save of remote file. By this basic and powerful function for remote file management, User can modify and move remote files, configuration/parameter files of application, and so on.

Graphic Workflow Editor: This editor is for creating a GWDL file. User can describe a workflow by graphical tool or text-based XML editor. First activities and its input/output data are defined. Second, User describes the interaction between them by making a workflow with them. User can specify the host to execute an activity, or yield the choice of host to workflow execution function.

Our workflow system provides not only an executable file execution but also WISE-activity which interacts workflow supervisor tightly and can send data to another WISE-activity with socket. Workflow supervisor monitors the state of WISE-activity and controls its execution and data transfer through socket. User can program and compile WISE-activity codes with this workflow editor after define its name and input/output data in GWDL. User will use WISE-activities to implement new Grid applications or monitoring programs to report input, output, and state of an executed legacy application efficiently.

Workflow Execution: After edit a GWDL file, we run it with this function. This shows the state of executed workflow graphically. The execution of an activity, state of input/output data transfer, values of some variables in workflow, and standard output/error of an running activity are displayed. If user specifies the requirement for the host to run an activity, workflow supervisor will selects an idle host by using resource mapping portal service.

Data Viewer: User can select a data file through file browser and see it with a data viewer which is associated with the data type. User can add new data viewer that is implemented by java or Microsoft COM to our Grid portal.

Resource Information: Resource Information function enables us to find data and status about Grid resources such as CPU, memory, file system, network, os, and software through MDS.

Simple Job Submission: User can send a request to run single executable file to a remote host and see the text type standard output of it.

4.3   Grid Portal Service

The Grid portal services forms the foundation of WISE, and are used directly by the application logic and presentation activated by the application engine. Each application logic and presentation has one-to-one correspondence with a user request from GUI on client side for solving a specific application problem on remote resources. In this subsection, we describe how various Grid portal services complete their missions by executing Grid services through the Grid service interface components.

Single Job Submission: Job submission service can be executed in two modes. In user mode, user can prepare a job specification using RSL component, and job submission service executes the jobs in the remote resources as specified in RSL by using GRAM component. In automatic mode, job submission service finds a computing resources from resource mapping service.

Information Service: Information service provides static and dynamic information on resources by querying and formatting results obtained from the MDS component in Grid service interface layer. It supports querying the MDS for hardware information such as CPU type, number of CPUs, CPU load and queue information that can be used by the user to make more efficient job scheduling decisions.

Data Transfer Service: Data transfer provides file transfer capabilities between client and target machine, or between third-party resources as well as file browsing to facilitate the transfer of programs or data files for remote execution and data retrieval by using GridFTP in Grid service interface layer.

Security: Security service simplifies the authentication task by exploiting GSI of Globus which provides a secure method of accessing remote resources by enabling a secure, single sign-on capability, while preserving site control over access control policies and local security infrastructure.

User Profile Service: User profile allows user to keep track of past jobs submitted and results obtained by maintaining the user history, and in addition enables the customization of a particular set of resources by users to provide additional application specific information for a particular class of users. Also sending an email, and management of user certificate are provided.

Workflow Supervisor: Workflow supervisor consists of three parts: parser, scheduler, and dispatcher. First, a GWDL file is inserted into workflow parser. The parser parses it and sends the activity node information into scheduler. Second, despatcher acquires data about executable files of activities and distributes the executables to Grid resources. Third, Scheduler runs the input GWDL file with the activity node information. It sends requests of activity execution to activity manager, monitors the information of activities, and controls activities. If no host name for an activity node, it get a host from resource mapping service.

Activity Manager: Activity manager controls an execution of activities with Globus GRAM service, acquires the state of activities, and manages input/output data of activities with GridFTP service. Also it controls and monitors WISE-activity directly with socket for state acquisition and data transfer.

WISE-Activity Editing/Complile: First, user describe the name, and input/output data of WISE-activity in a GWDL file, and then workflow editor generates the template codes for WISE-activity from content of the GWDL. Second, User can program logic of WISE-activity and compile the codes. This service provides two functions: making template codes and compiling user codes.

Resource Mapping: This service finds computing resources to which a user can submit jobs by using MDS component, and return idle resources according to the user requirements such as memory size, CPU performance, and etc.

4.4   Grid Service Interface

Grid service interface defines classes that provide access to basic Grid services and enhanced services suitable for PSE, and encapsulates the functionality for Grid services offered in Globus toolkit by using CoG.

RSL component provides methods for specifying resource requirements in Resource Specification Language(RSL) expressions. GRAM component provides methods which allows users to submit jobs on remote machines as specified in RSL, monitor job status and cancel jobs. GridFTP[8] component provides file transfer on Grid. GASS component supports the access of remote file system on Grid. MDS component allows users to easily access MDS service in Globus. MyProxy is a secure online certificate repository for allowing users to store certificates and then to retrieve them at a later time. User can acquire Globus proxy with ID and password from MyProxy server.

5   Implementation

WISE deploys Apache web server, a free, open source web server that support SSL. WISE was developed under the open source Tomcat java servlet container which is freely and widely available and implemented by usig java language, JSP, Java Beans, and java servlet. Grid service interfaces are implemented in Java packages that provide the interface to the low level Grid services by using Java CoG kit[10]. WISE provides users with various interactive operations : login/out, job submission, MDS query, GridFTP, file browsing, user profile, workflow editing and running. They support transparent access to heterogeneous resources by providing a unified and consistent window to Grid by allowing users to allocate the target resources needed to solve a specific problem, edit and transfer programs or data files to the target machines for remote execution and data retrieval, select and submit the application jobs automatically, query the information on the dynamic state of hardware and software on Grid for the more efficient job scheduling decisions as well as private user profile. In addition, WISE also provides a easy-to-use user interface for using workflow-based parallel programming environment on Grid, by supporting graphical workflow editor, resource finding, authentication, execution, monitoring, and steering. Therefore, Grid portal provides a transparent mapping between user interface and remote resources, hiding the complexity of the heterogeneous backend underlying systems.

6   Conclusion

Commodity distributed computing technology in Web enables the rapid construction of sophisticated client-server applications, while Grid technology provides advanced network services for large-scale, wide area, multi-institutional environments and applications that require the coordinated use of multiple resource. In this paper, we present a web-based Grid Portal which bridge these two worlds on internet in order to enable the development of advanced applications that can benefit from both Grid services and commodity web environments. Also We provide new workflow patterns and GWDL which can overcome the limitations of the previous approaches by providing several powerful workflow patterns used efficiently to represent parallelisms inherent in parallel and distributed applications. To describe a workflow of grid application without ambiguity, we have proposed formally new advanced basic patterns such as And-Loop, queue, wait, node copy and etc by classifying them into three categories; sequential, parallel, and mixed flow. Our workflow-based Grid portal have been designed to provide a powerful problem solving environment by supporting a unified and consistent window to Grid which enables a substantial increases in user ability to solve problems that depend on use of large-scale heterogeneous resources. It provides users with a uniform and easy to use GUI for various interactive operations for PSE such as login/out, job submission, information search, file browsing, file transfer, and user profile, and especially supports interfaces for using workflow-based parallel programming environment on Grid, by supporting graphical workflow editor, resource finding, authentication, execution, monitoring, and steering. We have proposed a multi-layer architecture which can provide modularity and extensibility by each layer interacting with each other using the uniform interfaces. Also, we have shown that MVC design pattern provides flexibility and modularity by separating the application engine control and presentation from the application logic for Grid services, and that commodity-to-Grid technology for Grid service interface supports various platforms and environments by mapping Grid functionality into a commodity distributed computing components. As a future work, we are extending our Grid portal which enables the automatic conversion of a given problem into optimized parallel programming models by supporting more specific coarse-grained parallel programming models in our system.

References

1. I. Foster, C. Kesselman, S. Tuecke, "The Anatomy of the Grid: Enabling Scalable Virtual Organizations," International J. Supercomputer Applications, 15(3), 2001.
2. Globus Toolkit, http://www.globus.org
3. I. Foster, and C. Kesselman, "The Globus Project: A Status Report," Heterogeneous Computing Workshop, pp. 4-18, 1998.
4. W. F. Erol Akarsn, G. C. Fox and T. H. Haupt, "Webflow High-level Programming Environment and Visual Authoring Toolkit for High Performance distributed Computing, In Proceedings of Supercomputing '98, 1998.
5. S. M. Mary thomas, and J. Boisseau, "Development of Web Toolkits for computational Science Portals: The NPACI Hot page," In Proceedings of HPDC 9, pp. 308-309, Aug. 2000.
6. Astrophysics Simulation collaboratory: ASC Grid Portal, http://www. ascportal.org.
7. K. Czajkowski, S. Fitzgerald, I. Foster, C. Kesselman, "Grid Information Services for Distributed Resource Sharing," Proceedings of the Tenth IEEE International Symposium on High-Performance Distributed Computing (HPDC-10), IEEE Press, August 2001.
8. W. Allcock, J. Bester, J. Bresnahan, A. Chervenak, L. Liming, S. Meder, S. Tuecke, "GridFTP Protocol Specification," GGF GridFTP Working Group Document, September 2002.
9. K. Czajkowski, I. Foster, and C. Kesselman, "Resource Co-Allocation in Computational Grids," Proceedings of the Eighth IEEE International Symposium on High Performance Distributed Computing (HPDC-8), pp. 219-228, 1999.
10. G. V. Laszewski, I. foster, J. Gawor and P. Lane,"A Java Commodity Grid Kit." concurrency and computation: Practice and Experience, pp. 645-662.
11. B. Kiepuszewski, Expressiveness and suitability of languages for control flow modelling in workflows, http://tmitwww.tm.tue.nl/research/patterns/download/phd_bartek.pdf
12. W.M.P. van der Aalst, A.H.M, Hofstede, B. Kiepusziewski, A.P. Barros. (2003). Workflow Patterns, Distributed and Parallel Databases, Jule 2003, pp. 5-51
13. Junwei C., Stephen A. J., Subhash S., and Grahan R. N., GridFlow: Workflow Management for Grid Computing, Proc. 3rd IEEE/ACM Int. symp. on cluster Computing and the Grid, 2003
14. Triana Workflow, http://www.gridlab.org/WorkPackages/wp-3/D3.3.pdf
15. Dan C. M., A Grid Workflow Management Architecture, http://www.cs.ucf.edu/ dcm/GWfA.pdf
16. Sriram K., Patrick W., Gregor von L., GSFL:A Workflow Framework for Grid Services http://www-unix.globus.org/cog/projects/workflow/gsfl-paper.pdf
17. Hugh P. B., Grid Workflow http://vir.sandia.gov/ hpbiven/ggf/draft-bivens-gridworkflow.pdf
18. GridAnt, 2003, http://www-unix.globus.org/cog/projects/gridant/
19. myGrid workflow, 2003, http://www.mygrid.org.uk/myGrid/
20. Kwon Y. W., Ryu S. H., Jeong C. S. and Park H. W., XML-Based Workflow Description Language for Grid Applications, LNCS 3043, ICCSA 2004. pp. 319-327

A Real-Time Transaction Approach for Grid Services: A Model and Algorithms

Feilong Tang[1], Minglu Li[1], Joshua Zhexue Huang[2], Lei Cao[1], and Yi Wang[1]

[1] Department of Computer Science and Engineering,
Shanghai Jiao Tong University, Shanghai 200030, China
{tang-fl,li-ml}@cs.sjtu.edu.cn
[2] E-Business Technology Institute, The University of Hong Kong, China
jhuang@eti.hku.hk

Abstract. Because transactions in Grid applications often have deadlines, effectively processing real-time transactions in Grid services presents a challenging task. Although real-time transaction techniques have been well studied in databases, they can not be directly applied to the Grid applications due to the characteristics of Grid services. In this paper[3], we propose an effective model and corresponding coordination algorithms to handle real-time transactions for Grid services. The model can intelligently discover required Grid services to process specified subtransactions at runtime, and invoke the algorithms to coordinate these services to satisfy the transactional and real-time requirements, without users involvement in the complex process. We use a Petri net to validate the model and algorithms.

1 Introduction

One objective of developing a service Grid is to provide users with transparent services and hide the complex process from them. The technology for processing a real-time transaction is a key to determine whether the service Grid can be widely accepted in commercial use because many Grid applications have time restrictions and transactional requirements. The real-time transaction for Grid services [1] differs from conventional real-time database transactions because (a) Grid services are loosely coupled, and (b) Grid services can dynamically join and leave the Grid. Therefore, it is important to investigate the real-time transaction technology in the Grid service environment.

The deadline of a real-time transaction specifies the time by which the transaction must complete or else undesirable results may occur. Based on the strictness of deadlines, real-time transactions for Grid services can be classified into three types, similar to those in the traditional distributed systems [2].

- Hard real-time transaction. This is the strictest real-time transaction. If these transactions miss their deadlines, there are catastrophic consequences.

---

[3] This paper is supported by 973 project of China(No.2002CB312002), and grand project of the Science and Technology Commission of Shanghai Municipality(No.03dz15027).

– Firm real-time transaction. It is of no value to complete a firm real-time transaction after its deadline but catastrophic results will not occur if a firm real-time transaction misses its deadline.
– Soft real-time transaction. Satisfaction of the deadline is primarily the performance goal. Unlike a firm real-time transaction, however, there still are some benefits for completing a soft real-time transaction after its deadline.

In this paper, we focus on the soft and firm real-time transactions. Our motivation is to provide a model, with the key component of the real-time transaction service (GridRTS) so application programmers can use GridRTS to easily materialize real-time applications.

2   Related Work

To process a transaction in a distributed environment, a common agreement is generally achieved by negotiations between a coordinator and the participants. DTP(Distributed Transaction Processing)[3] is a widely accepted model in distributed transaction processing. It defines three kinds of roles (Application Program, Transaction Manager and Resource Manager) and two kinds of interfaces (TX interface between Application Program and Transaction Manager, and XA interface between Transaction Manager and Resource Manager). However, DTP does not support the real-time transaction.

The real-time transaction schemes have heavily been researched in the database area. Abbott [4] presented a new group of algorithms for scheduling real-time transactions that produce serializable schedules. A model was proposed for scheduling transactions with deadlines on a single processor disk resident database system. The scheduling algorithms have four components: a policy for managing overloads, a policy for assigning priorities to tasks, a concurrency control mechanism, and a policy for scheduling I/O requests. Some real-time transaction scheduling algotirhms were proposed in [5], which employ a hybrid approach, i.e., a combination of both pessimistic and optimistic approaches. These protocols make use of a new conflict resolution scheme called dynamic adjustment of serialization order, which supports priority-driven scheduling, and avoids unnecessary aborts.

This paper extends these previous results to the Grid service environment by providing the GridRTS with a set of interfaces for Grid application programmers.

3   Real-Time Transaction Model

The real-time transaction model we present here is based on the Globus Toolkit 3. The core component GridRTS, as shown in Fig. 1, consists of the following:

– Service Discovery. It discovers the required Grid services that can complete the sub-tasks for a real-time transaction.

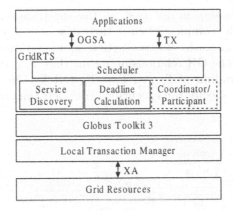

Fig. 1. The real-time Grid transaction model

- Deadline Calculation. It calculates deadlines of (sub)transactions to coordinate these activities.
- Coordinator or Participant. It is dynamically created by the scheduler of GridRTS and lives until the end of a global transaction. The scheduler of GridRTS creates a coordinator or a participant when it receives a request to initiate a global transaction or perform a sub-transaction.
- Scheduler. It takes charge of scheduling above modules.
- Interfaces. The OGSA interfaces are responsible for service management such as creating a transient Grid service instance while the TX interfaces are used to manage transactions.

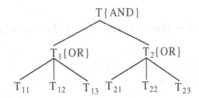

Fig. 2. A simple real-time Grid transaction

Definition 1. A real-time transaction is a 6-tuple={T, D, S, R, DL, P}, where T is the set of sub-transactions and each sub-transaction T_i is completed by several alternative functional services; D is the set of data operated by the real-time transaction; S is the state set; R is the set of relationships between (sub)transactions, defined as R={AND, OR, Before, After}; DL is the set of deadlines; and P is the priority set.

The AND relationship means that all the sub-transactions T_i of a global transaction T must be completed before their deadlines $d(T_i)$, i.e., $T=T_1$ AND T_2 AND... AND T_m. Each sub-transaction T_i is performed by n alternative functional services. The OR relationship means that T_i is completed if any T_{ij} finishes before the deadline of T_i, i.e., $T_i = T_{i1}$ OR T_{i2} OR ... OR T_{in} (see Fig. 2). Before and After specify the execution order between sub-transactions.

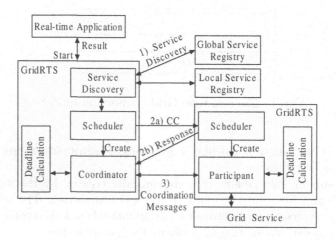

Fig. 3. The execution flow of the real-time Grid transaction.

4   Coordination of the Real-Time Grid Transaction

4.1   The Process of the Real-Time Grid Transaction

In the Grid service environment, a typical real-time transaction includes the following steps, as shown in Fig. 3.

- Step 1: GridRTS initiates a global transaction on behalf of a real-time Grid application, discovers and selects required Grid services to serve as participants, using the service discovery module as described in [6].
- Step 2: The scheduler creates a coordinator and broadcasts the Coordination-Context (CC) messages to all selected remote participants, that are created locally and return Response messages to the coordinator.
- Step 3: The created coordinator and participants interact to control the transaction execution, including the correct completion and failure recovery. The detail is described in the following subsection.

4.2   Coordination Algorithms

As described above, a sub-transaction is completed by a set of alternative functional services from an alternative functional service group (AFSG). The members of the AFSG execute the same sub-task in parallel. If one member of the AFSG can complete successfully and reports a Committable message, the AFSG is considered committable and other members are aborted.

In the preparation phase, each alternative functional service executes a specified sub-task in its private work area (PWA). On receipt of the Abort message, the service rollbacks the operations taken previously, by releasing the PWA. In the commit phase, the Commit message notifies the participants that have reported Committable messages to the coordinator. These participants are called committable participants and actually commit sub-transactions (see Fig. 4).

Algorithm of Coordinator
Input: service references of all functional
  alternative services S_i and d(T)
Output: result of T or failure
{
  for all S_i in all AFSGs
    send Prepare messages to them;
  end for
  while (t≤ d(T)){
    wait and record incoming messages;
    for each AFSG
      if (receive a Committable)
        send Abort to others in this AFSG;
    end for
    if (all AFSGs receive Committable)
      send Commit to committable
        Participants;
    else
      send Rollback to them;
} }

Algorithm of Participant
Input: d(T_i)
Output: result of T_i or failure
{ while (t≤ d(T_i)) {
    wait & record incoming messages;
    if (receive a Prepare){
      execute sub-task in PWA;
      if (successfully)
        report Committable;
      else { report Uncommittable;
        rollback; } }
    Case (receive a message)
    Commit: {
      actually commit sub-transaction;
      send Committed; }
    Abort:
      rollback and send Aborted;
    Rollback:
      rollback and send Rollbacked;
    EndCase } }

(a) Coordinator algorithm   (b) Participant algorithm

Fig. 4. Coordination algorithms of the real-time Grid transaction

Fig. 5 illustrates the state transformation diagram of the real-time Grid transaction. The solid rectangles indicate the states of both the coordinator and participants. The Dashed rectangle denotes the state of participants. The transaction enters Prepared state only when the coordinator receives a Committable message from each AFSG before the deadline d(T). Otherwise, the coordinator sends Rollback messages to undo the effect produced by the previous operations.

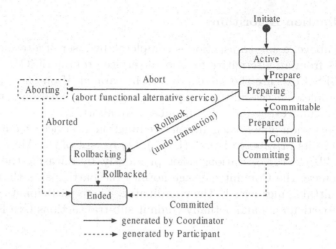

Fig. 5. The state transformation diagram of the real-time Grid transaction

5   Algorithm Validation

5.1   Modeling Algorithms with Petri Net

A Petri net is an abstract and formal modelling tool. It models systems' events, conditions and the relationships among them. The occurrence of these events may change the state of the system, causing some previous conditions to cease holding and other conditions to begin to hold [8]. In this work we model the coordination algorithms with a Petri net to verify their correctness. In the model, the transitions indicate actions taken by participants, and the places represent the states of the coordinator and/or participants or the receipt of the coordination messages from the coordinator.

Assume that a real-time Grid transaction consists of two sub-transactions and each sub-transaction is completed by two Grid services. We use P_{I1}, P_{I2} and P_{II1}, P_{II2} to represent the first and second AFSGs respectively. Without losing the generality, we let P_{I1} and P_{II1} first return Committable messages and finally commit while P_{I2} and P_{II2} are aborted. The Petri Net model RTPNM of this real-time transaction is depicted in Fig.6, where P_{I1} and P_{II1} are illustrated by S_1, and P_{I2} and P_{II2} by S_2. The weights of the arcs indicate the number of changed tokens whenever a firing happens (i.e. added or removed).

5.2   Analysis of the RTPNM

Let $M=(M_1, M_2, \ldots, M_{13})$ be a marking, where M_i is the number of tokens in place S_i. The RTPNM has two initial markings:

- $M_{0s}=(2,2,4,0,0,2,0,0,0,2,0,0,0)$, when P_{I1} and P_{II1} commit while P_{I2} and P_{II2} are aborted, and

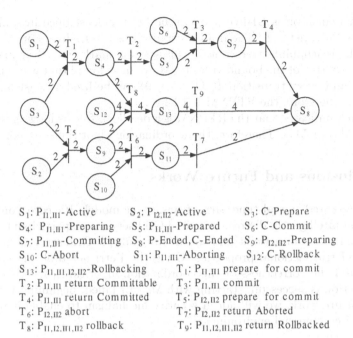

S₁: $P_{II,III}$-Active   S₂: $P_{I2,II2}$-Active   S₃: C-Prepare
S₄: $P_{II,III}$-Preparing   S₅: $P_{II,III}$-Prepared   S₆: C-Commit
S₇: $P_{II,III}$-Committing   S₈: P-Ended,C-Ended   S₉: $P_{I2,II2}$-Preparing
S₁₀: C-Abort   S₁₁: $P_{II,III}$-Aborting   S₁₂: C-Rollback
S₁₃: $P_{II,III,I2,II2}$-Rollbacking   T₁: $P_{II,III}$ prepare for commit
T₂: $P_{II,III}$ return Committable   T₃: $P_{II,III}$ commit
T₄: $P_{II,III}$ return Committed   T₅: $P_{I2,II2}$ prepare for commit
T₆: $P_{I2,II2}$ abort   T₇: $P_{I2,II2}$ return Aborted
T₈: $P_{II,I2,III,II2}$ rollback   T₉: $P_{II,I2,III,II2}$ return Rollbacked

Fig. 6. The Petri net model of the real-time Grid transaction(RTPNM)

– M_{0f}=(2,2,4,0,0,0,0,0,0,0,0,4,0), when at least one AFSG can not prepare for
commit, resulting in all four services are rolled back.

The Petri net model can analyze the behavioral properties, which depend on
the initial marking, including reachability, boundedness, liveness, coverability,
reversibility, persistence and so on. For a bounded Petri net, however, the coverability tree is called the reachability tree and all above problems can be solved
by the reachability tree [7]. Peterson [8] also pointed out that in Petri nets, many
questions can often be reduced to the reachability problem. In this paper, we
focus on the boundedness and reachability using the reachability tree, which is
not illustrated here because it is too large. By analysis of the reachability tree
of the RTPNM, we can draw following conclusions.
Theorem 1. RTPNM is bounded.
Proof: A Petri net (N, M_0) is said to be k-bounded or simply bounded if
the number of tokens in each place does not exceed a finite number k for any
marking reachable from the initial marking, i.e., $M_i \leq k$ for every place S_i and
every marking $M \in R(M_0)$[7], where M_0 is an initial marking and $R(M_0)$ is the set
of all possible markings reachable from the M_0. By inspection of the reachability
tree of the RTPNM, we have found that ω (represent an arbitrarily large value)
does not occur anywhere, and the number of tokens in each place is no more
than 4. Therefore, the RTPNM is bounded and k is 4.
Theorem 2. RTPNM is L1-live.

Proof: A transition is L1-live if it can be fired at least once in some firing sequences. A Petri net is L1-live if all its transitions are L1-live. For a bounded Petri net, the reachability tree contains all possible markings. After inspecting the reachability tree of the bounded RTPNM, we have found that every marking is reachable and every transition T_i $(1 \leq i \leq 9)$ can be fired at least once from M_{0s} or M_{0f}. Therefore, the RTPNM is L1-live.

Theorem 2 indicates that the RTPNM is a deadlock-free as long as the firing starts with M_{0s} or M_{0f}. Therefore, the coordination algorithms are correct.

6   Conclusions and Future Works

We have presented a real-time Grid transaction model. Its core component GridRTS can intelligently discover required Grid services as participants to perform specified sub-transactions, and coordinate multiple Grid services to achieve real-time and transactional properties. Using the Petri net tool, moreover, we have validated the correctness of the coordination algorithms, whether a real-time transaction is successful, starting with M_{0s}, or failed, beginning with M_{0f}.

In our future work, we will add a security mechanism to enable it to adapt to the actual commercial environment.

References

1. I. Foster, C. Kesselman, J. M. Nick and S. Tuecke. The Physiology of the Grid-An Open Grid Services Architecture for Distributed Systems Integration. June, 2002. http://www.globus.org/research/papers/ogsa.pdf.
2. E. Kayan, O . Ulusoy. Real-Time Transaction Management in Mobile Computing Systems. Proceedings of the Sixth International Conference on Database Systems for Advanced Applications. April, 1999, pp. 127-134.
3. I. C. Jeong and Y. C. Lew, DCE (Distributed Computing Environment) based DTP (Distributed Transaction Processing). Proceedings of the 12th International Conference on Information Networking. January, 1998.
4. R. K. Abbott. Scheduling Real-Time Transactions: A Performance valuation. ACM Transactions on Database Systems, Vol 17. No. 3, 1992, pp. 513-560.
5. S. H. Son and J. Lee. A New Approach to Real-Time Transaction Scheduling. Proceedings of Fourth Euromicro workshop on Real-Time Systems, June , 1992, pp. 177-182.
6. F. L. Tang, M. L Li, J. Cao et al. GSPD: A Middleware That Supports Publication and Discovery of Grid Services. Proceedings of the Second International Workshop on Grid and Cooperative Computing. December, 2003, pp. 738-745.
7. T. Murata. Petri Nets: Properties, Analysis and Applications. Proceedings of the IEEE, Vol 77, No. 4, 1989, pp. 541-580.
8. J. L. Peterson. Petri Nets. Computing Surveys, Vol. 9, No. 3, September, 1977, pp. 223-252.

QoS Quorum-Constrained Resource Management in Wireless Grid

Chan-Hyun Youn[1], Byungsang Kim[1], Dong Su Nam[1], Eung-Suk An[1],
Bong-Hwan Lee[2], Eun Bo Shim[3], and Gari Clifford[4]

[1] School of Engineering, Information and Communications University
119 MunjiRo, Yousong-gu, Daejeon 305-732, Korea
{chyoun, bskim, dsnam, sunyan}@icu.ac.kr
[2] Dept. of Information and Communications Engineering, Daejeon University
96-3 Yongun-dong, Dong-gu, Daejeon 300-716, Korea
blee@dju.ac.kr
[3] Dept. of Mechanical Engineering, Kwangwon National University
192-1 Hyoja 2-dong, Chunchon 200-701, Kwangwon-do, Korea
ebshim@kangwon.ac.kr
[4] Harvard-MIT Division of Health Science Technology, MIT
Cambridge, MA 02139, USA
gari@mit.edu

Abstract. In wireless Grid computing environment, end-to-end Quality
of Service (QoS) could be very complex, and this highlights the increasing requirement for the management of QoS itself. Policy quorum-based
management offers a more flexible, customizable management solution
that allows controlled elements to be configured or scheduled on the fly,
for a specific requirement tailored for a customer. This paper presents a
QoS guaranteed management scheme, Policy Quorum Resource Management (PQRM), which facilitates the reliable scheduling of the wireless
Grid system with dynamic resource management architecture aimed at
fulfilling the QoS requirements. Experimental results show the proposed
PQRM with resource reconfiguration scheme improves both performance
and stability, which is suitable for a wireless Grid services.

1 Introduction

Grid computing provides widespread dynamic, flexible and coordinated sharing
of geographically distributed heterogeneous networked resources among dynamic
user groups. Wireless communications is a rapidly evolving and promising sector
of the communications arena, and even in a challenging time for the telecommunications industry, represents a significant development opportunity for companies
and organizations in creating a global market. The increasing reliance on wireless networks for information exchange makes it critical to maintain reliable and
secure communications even in the instances of a component failure or security
breach. In wireless networks, mobile application systems continuously join and
leave the network and change locations with the resulting mobility impacting

H. Jin et al. (Eds.): NPC 2004, LNCS 3222, pp. 65–72, 2004.
© IFIP International Federation for Information Processing 2004

the degree of survivability, security and reliability of the communication. Our research focuses on policy based dynamic resource allocation and management for Quality of Service (QoS) guaranteed applications in a wireless Grid [1], [2].

Our resource management policy will need to effectively map the pre-defined QoS requirements to the actual resources on the wireless network. Ideally some of these QoS requirements will be defined at the local system level to minimize protocols utilized at the middleware system, however, we need to address the problem of combining different kinds of QoS from the multiple resources available in the Grid and among multiple Grids. We present a dynamic resource management architecture aimed at the fulfillment of the above requirements in wireless Grid services. We discuss the efficiency of the proposed reconfiguration policy on the experimental Grid testbed. We imagine that these kinds of reliable, secure and QoS guaranteed Grid services would be required for future mobile health care applications.

2   The Management for Cardiovascular Simulator in Wireless Grid

A general architecture for future wireless access networks involves a hybrid of technologies. Advances in patient care monitoring have allowed physicians to track an Intensive Care Unit patient's physiological state more closely and with greater accuracy. Modern computerized clinical information systems can take information from multiple data sources and store it in a central location. The Multi-parameter Intelligent Monitoring for Intensive Care (MIMIC) II database [3] takes advantage of the data collection systems installed at a partner hospital to collect large numbers of real patient records. The MIMIC II Relational Database Management System (RDBMS) is used to administer this database and create table definitions. Data such as nursing notes, medications, fluid input and output, updates to patient charts, lab results, CareVue data etc., can be downloaded from the hospital's Infrastructure Support Mart (ISM) and entered into the MIMIC II database. Waveforms such as electrocardiograms (ECGs), blood pressure, and pulse oximetry are stored in a separate waveform collection system in a separate database at the hospital, which is the waveform counterpart to MIMIC II.

Fig. 1 represents a computational physiological scenario using a wireless Grid. Cardiovascular (CV) data measured at home are transferred to a "patient monitoring manager" to assess those data. In this manager server, the monitored data is compared with the pathological data set stored in the MIMIC II database of PhysioNet [4]. If the signal is determined to be indicative of a pathological state, the cardiovascular information is used to determine the parameters of a CV model. CV hemodynamic variables under a specific physiological hypothesis are simulated and compared with the abnormal signal. In this simulation stage, Grid computing is utilized to speed up the analysis.

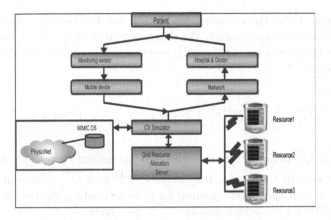

Fig. 1. Data flow for a mobile patient monitoring application using a CV simulation distributed on the wireless Grid interacting with a CV database

3   Quorum-Based Resource Management Model

3.1   Definition of Quorum Model

Most Grid applications specify the type of required resources such as various types of processing, storage, and communication requirements among such elements. To guarantee the QoS in user's application, the Grid manager should assign the resources to each application. The Quorum based management system will define the QoS vector to each application from the profile at input. We define two items; the one is system QoS vector and the other is network QoS vector. Each service requester must specify its QoS requirements for the Quorum Manager (QM) in terms of the minimum QoS properties for both the node system and network resources. We define the resource Quorum QR that represents current status of the resource. Each resource has its resource status vector which is represented both invariable and variable description [5]. System resource can take the processor specification or memory size as invariable description and processor utilization or available memory space as variable description and end-to-end available bandwidth, delay, data loss rate as variable specification.

$$Q_R = \left\{ \langle \overrightarrow{\theta_i}, \overrightarrow{\theta_{jk}} \rangle | i, j, k = 1, \ldots, n \right\}, \tag{1}$$

where $\overrightarrow{\theta_i}$ denotes the current available resource level of the system resource i and $\overrightarrow{\theta_{jk}}$ represents the current available resource level of the network between system resource j and k.

We assume the system has to admit and allocate resources for the set $A = \{a^1, \ldots, a^k, \ldots, a^m\}$ of applications. An application also represented by undirected graph with tasks and their communication relation. A required QoS level represents the vector of the resource description and has the range between minimum and maximum requirement. We denote them with q and Q, respectively. We define the QoS-Quorum, Q_A, which represents the required quality level for an application set A.

$$Q_A = \left\{ \left\langle \left[\vec{q}_i^{\,k}, \vec{Q}_i^{\,k} \right], \left[\vec{q}_{ij}^{\,kl}, \vec{Q}_{ij}^{\,kl} \right] \right\rangle \mid i \neq j, i, j = 1, \ldots, \mu, k \neq l, k, l = 1, \ldots, m \right\}, \tag{2}$$

where $\vec{q}_i^{\,k}$ and $\vec{Q}_i^{\,k}$ denote the minimum and maximum QoS level required for task k on the system resource i, respectively. $\vec{q}_{ij}^{\,kl}$ and $\vec{Q}_{ij}^{\,kl}$ represent the minimum and maximum QoS level required for communicating the task k in system resource i and task l in system resource j, respectively.

A resource universe $R = \{r_1, \ldots, r_n\}$ assumes a collection of resources that can be taken in the administration domain. A resource, $r = < S, N >$, can be represented as undirected graph with system, S and their communication networks, N. To get the reliability in resource management, we define available resource Quorum, Q_{AR}, which is a selected resource set which satisfying the QoS requirement from SLAs.

$$Q_{AR} = \{ \langle S_i, N_{ij} \rangle \subseteq R \mid \vec{q}_i^{\,k} \leq \vec{\theta}_i \leq \vec{Q}_i^{\,k}, \vec{q}_{ij}^{\,kl} \leq \vec{\theta}_{ij} \leq \vec{Q}_{ij}^{\,kl} \}, \tag{3}$$

where $i, j = 1, \ldots, n' \leq \mu$ and $k, l = 1, \ldots, m$. Q_{AR} is a set that satisfies a desired minimum QoS level of application. An available resource Quorum set is obtained from the policy module in the resource allocation server.

3.2   Resource Configuration for Resource Scheduling

The Resource configuration for scheduling, $F(A, Q_{AR}\}$, is the mapping function;

$$F(A, Q_{AR}) = \{ \langle S_i^k, N_{ij}^{kl} \rangle \} = \{ \langle V^k, E^{kl} \rangle \xrightarrow{Q} \langle S_i, N_{ij} \rangle \}, \tag{4}$$

where $i, j = 1, \ldots, n' \leq u$ and $k, l = 1, \ldots, m$.

$S_i^k(\vec{\theta}_s)$ or $S_i^k(\vec{\theta}_n)$ is identified the resource topology from status of reflecting the resource quality. We intend to estimate current resource utilization of each application activity. Assuming that application represents its previous execution progress as an event, we can predict the current resource allocation sensitivity for the target application. On the network performance vector, end-to-end resource performance, such as bandwidth, delay, or data loss rate is peer-to-peer value. If a Grid resource management system should measure all the peer systems, it surely faces scalability problem and unrealistic. Thus, usually, in the initial step of the resource allocation, resource allocation and policy server generate the available resource Quorum in the network established by the resource brokers and each peer.

4 Policy Quorum Based Resource Management in Wireless Grids

In order to address the resource allocation problem, we propose a Policy Quorum-based Resource Management (PQRM) System that provides a reliable resource scheduling scheme in wireless Grid. A PQRM shown in Fig. 2 has the layered architecture involving a session admission controller with an application profile, and requested applications as inputs [6], [7].

The Session Admission Controller (SAC) gives inform to Quorum Manager (QM). The QM inspects available resources that satisfy minimum QoS requirements through MDS(Monitoring and Discovery Service). The Monitoring Manager (MM) obtains the information of Grid resources from the agent that queries the resources. The SLA is an important work for the SAC, which interacts with users and their requirement such as time or cost deadlines.

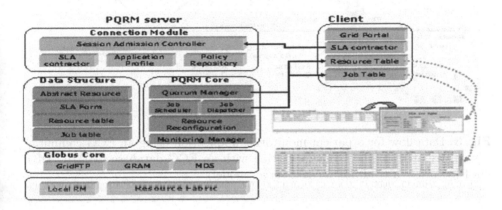

Fig. 2. Operational architecture of the PQRM system

We can obtain the initial resource configuration set as mapping from sub-jobs to available resource Quorum set: the initial resource configuration will satisfy the QoS requirement because it is subset of the Q_{AR} which is the set of establishment from the user's SLA. Failure of system or admission of the other application in the resource has influence on the variable QoS vector. Temporal instants Ti's are event generation points of each application. In general, in order to measure the application performance, instrumentation technique is a useful method that recognizes the application behavior.

5 Experimental Results and Discussions

Fig. 3 represents a computational physiological scenario using Grid computing. In this figure, the human ECG is monitored and transmitted to the PhysioNet server. The monitored data is then delivered to a simulator via a mobile computer, where the system compares it with the pathological data set stored in MIMIC [3]. In case of an abnormal signal, identified through a nodal fit to data in MIMIC, the algorithm may provide pertinent advice to the monitored subject. The information can then be delivered to a medical doctor. Furthermore, personally optimized medication information can also be delivered to the patient client.

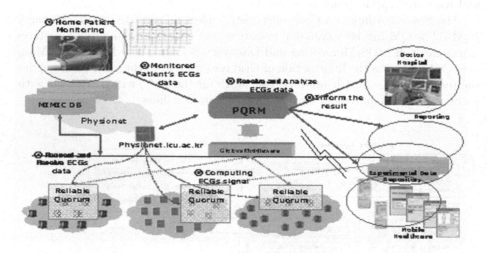

Fig. 3. Data flow for a patient monitoring application using an ECG computation distributed on the Grid interacting with an ECG database (MIMIC DB) via PhysioNet (a traditional client-server model)

In a wireless Grid infrastructure, all computation needed to simulate the monitored ECG signal will be executed on the available resources provided by a PQRM system. For real-time processing, it is necessary to identify the resources available in the Grid infrastructure. In particular, in order to ascertain the reliability of the wireless environment, policy based Quorum will be considered in the context of resource management. If a user wishes to access his/her daily biometrics from a Grid server, it is necessary for some computational resources to remain online regardless of its location with respect to the VOs. The systems used in this experiment are eight in total, which consist of six systems in Korea and a PhysioNet server at MIT in the US. We assume that each user jobs J1, J2, J3, J4, J5 and J6 starts at time instants, T1, T2, T3, T4, T5, and T6, respectively. Each job is executed independently at each node. Each job is composed of 4 sub-jobs. Each sub-job calculates the entropy of the ECG signal that is transmitted from users. To identify the mobility-based resource management, we identified two types of experiments, e.g. a case of no resource reconfiguration after initial configuration and a case of resource reconfiguration. In case of no reconfiguration approach, the jobs were executed with resource topology determined at S1. The initial Quorum Set is {S1, S2, S3, S4, S5, S6}. A non-reconfiguration method executes jobs sequentially at the system S1 and resource reconfiguration method performs at each temporal instant Ti, such as Quorum S1={(J1, T1), (J2, T2), (J3, T3), (J4, T4), (J5, T5), (J6, T6)}. On the other hand, user's mobility will invoke a policy-Quorum management module in PQRM to reconfigure the resource to guarantee the initial SLAs. A reconfiguration algorithm may change the current Quorum set through reshuffling the resources topology. Fig. 5 shows that the resource reconfiguration was triggered at T4. After triggering the resource reconfiguration, newly generated resource Quorum and resource re-allocation will be determined with S1 = {J1, J2, J3, J6}, S7 = {J4, J5} at T4. The S8 is added in new resource quorum and J4 and J5 are moved from system S1 to S8. Fig. 4 represents resource status after reconfiguration. Fig. 5 depicts the performance comparison of the average execution time with and without a Resource Reconfiguration (RR) policy. Quorum management policy with resource configuration (in the bottom two bars) shows more stable execution time than with no reconfiguration management scheme.

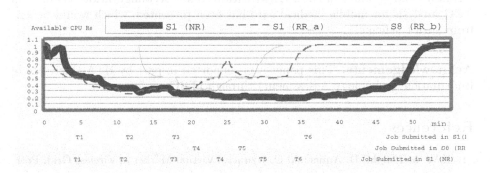

Fig. 4. Comparison of resource status (available CPU ratio) in S1 and S8 after reconfiguration at T4 (NR: No reconfiguration policy, RR: Resource Reconfiguration policy)

6   Conclusions

End-to-end QoS can be very complex in the wireless Grid computing environment. Policy based management offers a more flexible, customizable management solution that allows controlled elements to be configured or scheduled on the fly, for a specific requirement tailored for a customer. The proposed Quorum based resource management policy is suitable to effectively map the pre-defined QoS requirements to the actual resources on the wireless network. This paper has presented a QoS guaranteed management scheme that facilitates the reliable scheduling of the wireless Grid system with dynamic resource management

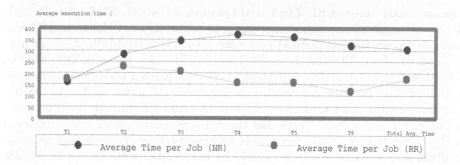

Fig. 5. Performance comparison of execution time with and without policy of resource reconfiguration (NR: No reconfiguration policy, RR: Resource Reconfiguration policy)

architecture aimed at fulfilling the QoS requirements. We have discussed the performance and stability of the PQRM with resource reconfiguration scheme. An ECG analysis for mobile medical care has been presented, which would benefit from such a scheme.

Acknowledgements. This paper was supported in part by IITA (Institute of Information Technology Assessment) through ITRC project.

References

1. L.W. McKnight, D. Anius and O. Uzuner, "Virtual Market in wireless Grid: Peering policy prospects", *TPRC2002 Research conference on Communication, Information and Internet Policy*, 2002.
2. F. Berman, G.C. Fox, A.J.G. Hey, *Grid Computing*, Wiley, 2003.
3. M. Saeed, C. Lieu, G. Raber, R.G. Mark, "MIMIC II: A massive temporal ICU patient database to support research in intelligent patient monitoring", *Computers in Cardiology*, pp641-644, 2002.
4. A. Golberger, L. Amaral, L. Glass, J.M. Hausdorff et al, "PhysioBank, PhysioToolkit, and PhysioNet :Component of a New Research Resource for Complex Physiologic Signals," *Circulation* 101 (23), June,2000.
5. L.J. Franken, B.R. Haverkort, The performability manager, *IEEE Network*, pp.24-32, Jan/Feb. 1994.
6. I. Cardei, S. Varadarajan, M. Pavan, M. Cardei, M. Min, "Resource Management for Ad-hoc wireless networks with cluster organization", *Journal of Cluster Computing in the Internet*, Kluwer Academic Publishers, Jan. 2004.
7. R.J. Alali, O.F. Rana, D.W. Walker, "G-QoSM: Grid Service Discovery Using QoS Properties", *Computing and Informatics Journal*, Vo. 21, pp.363-382, 2002.

A Data-Aware Resource Broker for Data Grids

Huy Le, Paul Coddington, and Andrew L. Wendelborn

School of Computer Science, University of Adelaide
Adelaide, SA 5005, Australia
{paulc,andrew}@cs.adelaide.edu.au

Abstract. The success of grid computing depends on the existence of grid middleware that provides core services such as security, data management, resource information, and resource brokering and scheduling. Current general-purpose grid resource brokers deal only with computation requirements of applications, which is a limitation for data grids that enable processing of large scientific data sets. In this paper, a new data-aware resource brokering scheme, which factors both computational and data transfer requirements into its cost models, has been implemented and tested. The experiments reported in this paper clearly demonstrate that both factors should be considered in order to efficiently schedule data intensive tasks.

1 Introduction

The term grid computing is typically used to refer to a networked virtual computing environment which extends across geographical and organisational boundaries [1, 2]. It allows a group of individuals and/or institutions, a "virtual organisation", to share resources. Resources that can be shared include computing cycles, data storage, software, and special scientific equipment. The heterogenous and dynamic nature of the grid environment makes the task of developing grid applications extremely challenging. Thus, the success of grid computing will depend on the existence of high-level frameworks or middleware to abstract over the complexity of the underlying environment, and facilitate the design, development and efficient execution of grid applications.

Broadly speaking, such a framework will have components for: high-level description of the stages of processing needed to produce desired results from available data; decomposition of that processing into tasks, or jobs, that can be deployed on grid resources; a *resource broker* mechanism for matching the requirements of these jobs with the resources available and scheduling their execution; and mechanisms for deploying jobs onto chosen resources.

In this paper, we investigate resource management and scheduling issues associated with the resource broker component, which is responsible for matching resource requirements of jobs with actual available and suitable grid resources.

Clearly, the resource broker must have ready access to up-to-date information about the grid in which to initiate a process of *resource discovery* to firstly find a set of candidate resources, and a mechanism for determining the most suitable

H. Jin et al. (Eds.): NPC 2004, LNCS 3222, pp. 73–82, 2004.

of these candidates. A resource broker takes into account relevant properties of a given resource, typically computational properties such as processor speed, amount of memory, and processor architecture. Other properties that may be considered by a resource broker for data grids are communication bandwidth and data storage. Information is provided by information services such as the Metadata Directory Service (MDS) and Replica Catalog of the Globus Toolkit [3] and the Network Weather Service (NWS) [4].

A resource broker that uses primarily computational properties in its decision making we refer to as *compute-centric*, and one using principally data-oriented properties as *data-centric*. A compute-centric strategy is appropriate when jobs are primarily computationally intensive. A data-centric strategy may be appropriate when using a massive data set, with better performance achieved by moving code to data.

Our interest here is in general data grids, in which both computation and data are important. Many interesting applications involve geographically dispersed analysis of large repositories of measured or computed data. For example, the Belle experiment [5], at the KEK particle accelerator in Japan, is a large world-wide collaboration. It generates terabytes of experimental and simulation data, with significant data transfer costs. Computation is also important, as researchers conduct simulations and analysis. Here, the broker should make better choices by using a strategy accounting for costs of both data transfer and computation. Studies by Ranganathan and Foster [6] support this view.

However, current general-purpose grid resource brokers are compute-centric. Batch queuing systems such as PBS, LSF, Sun Grid Engine and Condor were originally developed to manage job scheduling on parallel computers or local-area networks of workstations, and therefore ignored the cost of data movement. These systems have been extended to manage job scheduling in wide-area computational grids, but still do not consider data transfer costs in their scheduling models. The Nimrod project [7] offers a novel approach to scheduling, based on an economic model that assigns costs to resource usage [8], allowing users to trade-off execution time against resource costs, but data transfer is not considered by the scheduler.

The AppLeS (Application Level Scheduling) project [9] approaches the scheduling problem at the application level, dynamically generating a schedule based on application-specific performance criteria. Data properties can be used, but scheduling logic is embedded within the application itself, an approach not easily re-targeted for different applications or execution environments [10]. Our work aims to create a generic resource broker for any grid application.

After the work reported in this paper had been completed, similar work on data-aware resource brokers was published. The approach of the Gridbus Broker [11] is that when a job is being scheduled, if there is a choice of compute nodes of similar capability, the scheduler will choose the one with the highest bandwidth connection to a copy of the input data. Version 1.1 of the JOSH system [12] for Sun Grid Engine also takes into account data transfer in its scheduling decisions.

The primary objective of this investigation is to show that application performance can be improved by making scheduling decisions that take into account not just the computational performance of resources, but also data transfer factors. To this end, we discuss the design, implementation, measurement and evaluation of a new, data-aware resource broker.

2   The Data-Aware Resource Broker

The Data-Aware Resource Broker (DARB) is a generic resource broker, designed specifically with the needs of data-intensive applications in mind. DARB undertakes resource discovery, that is, finding resources in the grid environment that match the needs of the application; and resource selection, that is, choosing between alternative data, software and hardware resources.

For this investigation, DARB was implemented in Java within the Gridbus framework [13]. Gridbus is an extension of Nimrod/G [7], which supports execution of parameter sweep experiments over global grids. Such studies are ideal for the grid, since they consist of a large number of independent jobs operating on different input data. Nimrod/G and Gridbus provide a simple declarative parametric modelling language and GUI tools for specifying simulation parameters. A job is generated for each member of the cross product of these parameters. The system manages the distribution of the various jobs to resources and organises the aggregation of results.

2.1   Architecture and Implementation

Our experimental framework comprises three key components, shown in Figure 1.

1. The Job Submission Component provides a mechanism for users to submit applications for execution.
2. The Scheduling Framework is the resource broker component, responsible for allocating the user-submitted jobs to available resources in an efficient manner.
3. The Job Dispatching Component interfaces with the underlying grid middleware, dispatching and monitoring jobs.

Here we focus on the scheduling framework, which we have implemented using DARB. For these experiments, we use the job submission and dispatching modules provided by Gridbus. DARB interfaces with the Gridbus system, however it is important to note that the DARB resource broker is generic, and can be "plugged in" to other grid environments.

DARB consists of three modules:

1. The Grid Information Module regularly queries the MDS and NWS for state information of the grid nodes and network links. This information is used to build a model of the current grid environment, representing the grid as a graph structure in which grid nodes are represented by vertices and communication links by edges.

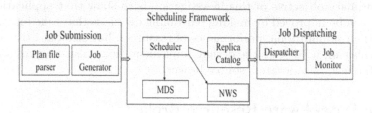

Fig. 1. System Architecture

2. The Replica Catalog Module provides a convenient interface for accessing information on file locations using the Globus Replica Catalog. It is used to support data-aware scheduling.
3. The Scheduler Module uses information from the Grid Information and Replica Catalog modules to map jobs (generated by the Initializer Module) to appropriate grid nodes (using the Dispatcher Module).

To form a complete system, these modules are used in conjunction with Initializer, Dispatcher and Job Monitor modules provided by the Gridbus system.

2.2   The Scheduler Module

The data grid environment which the DARB targets consists of distributed sites that have both data stores and computational capabilities. Input data sets for applications are replicated among these sites. The Globus Replica Catalog provides a mapping between the logical name of a data set and its physical locations. Each site in the environment may have different computational capabilities and data stores, which will change over time. In such an environment, it is vital for a resource broker to be provided with information about these characteristics, so it can and factor them into an appropriate performance model.

In the Scheduler module, MDS and NWS information from the Grid Information module is used to determine the current state of the grid environment. The Replica Catalog is used to determine the locations of a data file requested by an application. In order to arrive at a schedule for an application, DARB takes into account the machine architecture, clock speed, and number of CPUs; the CPU load; the network bandwidth; the size of the input data (obtained from the Replica Catalog); and the amount of computation involved.

The total time to execute a job on a particular compute node comprises of two components: data transfer time and computation time. If the compute node already has the input file, data transfer time will be zero. Otherwise, the time to transfer the input file is calculated using the bandwidth forecast obtained from the NWS. Experiments have shown that latency is negligible for the transfer of large data files, and as such, the latency forecast from NWS is not factored into the calculation. We use an estimate, based on input data size and bandwidth information (from the Grid Information Module), of expected transfer time.

A correction is applied in the calculation of the transfer time, since our experiments showed that the NWS tends to return bandwidth forecasts that are less than the actual value. As noted by Primet et al. [14], NWS transfers small amounts of data (default 64KB) which leads to very short transfer time on fast networks. Thus, any error in the time determination, due to the TCP slow start mechanism or other factors, will strongly influence measured bandwidth values. Primet et al. suggested the complementary use of additional tools to conduct less frequent probe experiments using larger amounts of data. An alternative approach is taken in DARB, which relies on measurements of data transfer times from the execution of previously submitted jobs.

The expected computation time is taken from a user-supplied estimate of job execution time on a given architecture, adjusted by the current load on a candidate node, and the number of CPUs at that node. In parameter sweep applications, the user estimate could be refined based on measured times for previous executions of the same program, however this has not yet been implemented.

2.3   The Scheduling Algorithm

Parameter sweep applications involve N independent jobs (each with the same task specification, but a different input file) on M distributed nodes, where N is typically much larger than M. In order to efficiently map these jobs to the nodes, it is important to consider both availability of computational resources and location of required data. A balance needs to be reached between minimizing computation and data transfer times. In general, if computational resources are available, it is preferable to execute the jobs where data already exists in order to minimize network traffic. However, when nodes containing data are busy and there are idle nodes elsewhere, the cost of data transfer may be outweighed by the increase in job throughput if the jobs are rescheduled to the free nodes.

Initially, the Data-Aware Resource Broker attempts to allocate the jobs to the nodes that already contain the input data. The available CPU value of each node is monitored to ensure that they are not overloaded with jobs. This process continues until it is no longer optimal in terms of overall throughput for the nodes containing the data to execute the jobs. This occurs when there are idle nodes and the expected execution time on one of those nodes is less than the expected execution time on the node containing the data. If this is the case, the resource broker retrieves the list of nodes that are available and calculates the expected completion time for the particular job on each node. The expected execution time of a job on a particular node is calculated via the following steps:

1. retrieve the list of nodes containing the input file required by the job;
2. select, from the above list, the best node in terms of bandwidth to the node that the job is to be executed on;
3. calculate the expected execution time, by adding expected execution and transfer times.

The job is rescheduled to the node that gives the best expected execution time.

3   Experimental Evaluation

This section presents the results of some initial experiments to evaluate the performance of the Data-Aware Resource Broker, and compare it with the standard compute-centric and data-centric resource broker strategies. The experiments are based on the requirements of the Belle data grid, but would be common to many scientific applications.

It is assumed that there are a large number of data files distributed across the nodes of the grid, and a researcher wants to run a data processing program on each of a specified subset of these data files. The researcher may even want to run many instances of the program for each data file, using different input parameters. It is assumed that all required jobs can be run independently, and the researcher's goal is to minimize the total turnaround time in executing all of these jobs. The resource broker should therefore schedule the jobs to the available nodes so that the job throughput is maximized. Hence, performance is measured in terms of total elapsed (wall clock) time to execute a specified set of jobs.

In some cases the data files to be processed may be distributed fairly regularly across nodes in the grid, for example in the Belle data grid these could be the output of Monte Carlo simulations of the Belle experiment, which are generated on each of the nodes and might be stored on the node on which they were generated. In other situations the distribution of the data among grid nodes may be highly irregular, for example data from a physics experiment such as Belle may be stored on a single server at the experiment's location, with replicas of the data located at a relatively small number of other nodes.

The experiments were performed on the Australian Belle Data Grid testbed composed of five compute server nodes located at the the University of Melbourne, the University of Sydney, the University of Adelaide, and the Australia National University in Canberra. Two machines were located in Melbourne, the rest were hundreds of kilometers apart. All of the servers used Intel processors running Linux, with a single 2.8 GHz Xeon processor at Adelaide and Sydney, dual 2.8 GHz Xeons at Melbourne and Canberra, and a single 2 GHz Pentium 4 processor at Melbourne. The average network bandwidth between the different machines varied considerably, from about 2 Mbits/sec (Adelaide to Canberra) to 15 Mbits/sec (Sydney to Canberra) for machines in different cities, and around 60 Mbits/sec between the two Melbourne nodes. We implemented a single clique containing all the nodes of our testbed for the purpose of running NWS sensors.

A simulated application, called DataSim, was developed for initial testing of DARB. It is a simple program which reads from an input file, performs some computation, and writes to an output file. The program does not require all the input to be available when it starts. Computation can proceed as soon as there is a specified amount of input to be processed, i.e. it can support data streaming. Several factors are customisable via its arguments, including the compute/input ratio (how much computation is performed per input element); the output/input ratio (how much output is written per input element); and whether input and output are streamed.

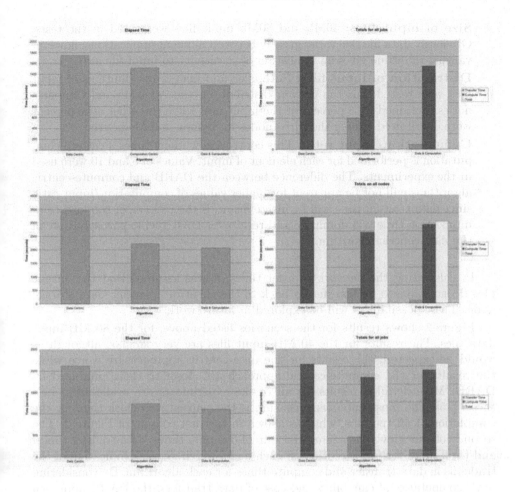

Fig. 2. Total execution times for all 40 runs of the DataSim application with 80 MB input files using compute-centric, data-centric or data-aware resource brokers. The first column gives the total elapsed wall clock time, while the second column is the aggregated time for computation and communication summed over all nodes. Results for even distribution of files are shown in the first row (compute/input ratio of 5) and second row (compute/input ratio of 10). The third row gives results for uneven distribution with compute/input ratio of 10.

Each experiment consisted of 40 runs of the test application for a particular set of parameters, with four runs for each of 10 different input files that were distributed across all five nodes in the grid testbed. This was repeated 10 times for each experimental scenario, to get an average result. The following parameters were varied in the different scenarios:

- **Size of input files:** 40Mb and 80Mb input files were used in the tests. Obviously data file size varies greatly between different applications, however varying the value gives an indication of sensitivity to input file sizes.
- **Distribution of input files:** Both even and uneven distributions of input files were tested. For the uneven distribution, the Adelaide and Canberra nodes contained 60% percent of the input files while the other 40% percent were distributed among the three nodes in Sydney and Melbourne.
- **Computation/Input ratio:** This controls how many times a certain computation is performed for each element of input. Values of 5 and 10 were used in the experiments. The difference between the DARB and compute-centric algorithms will not be apparent for higher values of computation/input ratio since data transfer time will be insignificant. If the ratio is set too low, communication time will dominate and results for DARB will approach those of the data-centric algorithm.

In calculating the network transfer times, it was assumed that the output files do not have to be transferred back to the client or a specific data storage node. These possibilities will be explored in future work.

Figure 2 shows results for the scenarios listed above, for the 80 MB input data files. The results for the 40 MB input files are very similar, although as would be expected, the results for the data-centric approach are worse while the results for the compute-centric approach are closer to those produced by DARB. More detailed results for all of the experiments are available in Le's thesis [15]. The most important measure is the elapsed wall clock time for the completion of all the jobs, which is shown in the first column of Figure 2. The second column shows the aggregated sum of compute times, data transfer times, and total times for job execution on each node, which gives an indication of the tradeoffs in data transfer and compute times for each algorithm. By considering both computational capability and cost of data transfers, the DARB approach gave the lowest total elapsed time in all the experiments.

As expected, the data-centric approach did better when the input file sizes were larger and/or the computation/input ratio was lower. By always scheduling jobs to nodes which already contain the data, the data-centric algorithm left many of the more computationally powerful nodes idle while the slowest node was completing its allocation of jobs. This led to significantly poorer job throughput.

The compute-centric approach did better when the input file sizes were smaller and/or the computation/input ratio was higher. Even in the cases when the compute-centric approach did almost as well as DARB for total execution time, the total data transfer time for the compute-centric algorithm was several times higher than that for the DARB algorithm. In situations where network costs are based on traffic volume, this could add significantly to the monetary cost of the computations. This can also lead to network congestion, and it was noted in some experiments that the large amount of network traffic caused certain connections to become bottlenecks, leading to significant variation in performance in the compute-centric algorithm.

In the case where the data is irregularly distributed, the data-centric approach does relatively worse. This is a problem since the data-centric model is perhaps most likely be used in situations with a relatively small number of servers having copies of very large data sets with large data transfer costs.

4 Conclusion

We have described the design, implementation and evaluation of DARB, a data-aware resource broker designed to efficiently handle the allocation of jobs to available resources in a data grid environment. Information from NWS and the Globus MDS and Replica Catalog are used to predict likely computation and data transfer times for each job, which are then used to generate a schedule for the jobs that tries to maximize throughput.

The initial experiments reported here showed that DARB outperformed algorithms based only on computational requirements or data location, and hence it is necessary to take both into account for efficient job execution on a data grid. DARB also resulted in significantly reduced network traffic compared to a standard compute-centric approach.

This Gridbus Broker [11] has an advantage over DARB, since it does not require accurate estimates of the compute time or the data transfer time. However where such estimates are available, we would expect DARB to perform better, since the Gridbus Broker would not handle the situation where a slower node might be a better option due to much faster data communication times.

The performance of DARB has so far only been tested using a small number of experimental scenarios on a small grid testbed using a simulated program. In future work, further experimentation using DataSim will investigate a wider range of input file sizes and computation/input ratios, different numbers of data files, multiple input files, and a variety of distributions and replications of data files. DARB will also be evaluated on a larger and more heterogenous grid testbed, and using a variety of real data grid applications.

Currently DARB assumes that output files remain where they are computed. However, outputs are often needed elsewhere, such as the client, or a data repository. DARB can easily be extended to take into account transfer of output files, but only if the size of these files is known beforehand. This could be specified by the user, or estimated based on previous runs.

Currently the performance of the DARB is dependent on the accuracy of the user's estimate of computation time for different architectures and and clock speeds. A better approach would be to keep a profile of past execution times for each node, which could easily be done in an environment for parameter sweep applications, such as Nimrod/G or Gridbus.

Acknowledgements

Four of the machines used for the experimental evaluation of DARB were generously provided by IBM. We are very grateful to the Gridbus group, especially

Srikumar Venugopal and Rajkumar Buyya, for help with Gridbus and discussions on scheduling, and also the Belle Data Grid group, particularly Lyle Winton, for help with Globus problems and general grid issues.

References

[1] Foster, I., Kesselman, C., eds.: The Grid: Blueprint for a Future Computing Infrastructure. Morgan-Kaufmann (1999)

[2] Foster, I.: The Anatomy of the Grid: Enabling Scalable Virtual Organizations. International Journal of Supercomputer Applications (2001)

[3] Foster, I., Kesselman, C.: Globus: A Metacomputing Infrastructure Toolkit. Intl. Journal of Supercomputer Applications **11** (1997)

[4] Wolski, R., Spring, N., Hayes, J.: The Network Weather Service: A distributed resource performance forecasting service for metacomputing. Journal of Future Generation Computing Systems **15** (1999) 757–768

[5] KEK: The Belle experiment. http://belle.kek.jp/ (2003)

[6] Ranganathan, K., Foster, I.: Decoupling computation and data scheduling in distributed data intensive applications. In: Proc. of 11th IEEE Int. Symposium on High Performance Distributed Computing (HPDC-11), Edinburgh (2002)

[7] Abramson, D., Giddy, J., Kotler, L.: High-performance parametric modelling with Nimrod/G: Killer application for the Global Grid? In: Proc. of IPDPS 2000, Cancun, Mexico (2000)

[8] Buyya, R., Abramson, D., Giddy, J.: An economy driven resource management architecture for global computational power grids. In: Proc. of Int. Conf. on Parallel and Distributed Processing Techniques and Applications (PDPTA 2000), Las Vegas (2000)

[9] Berman, F., et al.: Adaptive computing on the grid using AppLeS. IEEE Transactions on Parallel and Distributed Systems **14** (2003) 369–382

[10] Su, A., Berman, F., Wolski, R., Strout, M.: Using AppLeS to schedule simple SARA on the computational grid. International Journal of High Performance Computing Applications **13** (1999) 253–262

[11] Venugopal, S., Buyya, R., Winton, L.: A grid service broker for scheduling distributed data-oriented applications on global grids. Technical Report GRIDS-TR-2004-1, Grid Computing and Distributed Systems Laboratory, University of Melbourne (2004) http://www.gridbus.org/techreports.html.

[12] Sun Data and Compute Grids Project: JOb Scheduling Hierarchically (JOSH). http://gridengine.sunsource.net/project/gridengine/josh.html (2003)

[13] Buyya, R.: The Gridbus Project. http://www.gridbus.org/ (2003)

[14] Primet, P., Harakaly, R., Bonnassieux, F.: Experiments of network throughput measurement and forecasting using the Network Weather Service. In: Proc. of 2nd IEEE/ACM Int. Symposium on Cluster Computing and the Grid (CCGRID'02), Berlin (2002)

[15] Le, H.: The Data-Aware Resource Broker: A resource management scheme for data intensive applications. Technical Report DHPC-140, Distributed and High-Performance Computing Group, University of Adelaide (2003) http://www.dhpc.adelaide.edu.au/reports/140/abs-140.html.

Managing Service-Oriented Grids: Experiences from VEGA System Software

YuZhong Sun, Haiyan Yu, JiPing Cai, Li Zha, Yili Gong

Institute of Computing Technology, Chinese Academy of Sciences, Beijing 100080, China
yuzhongsun@ict.ac.cn

Abstract. Recent work towards a standard based, service oriented Grid represents the convergence of distributed computing technologies from e-Science and e-Commerce communities. A global service management system in such context is required to achieve efficient resource sharing and collaborative service provisioning. This paper presents VEGA system software, a novel grid platform that combines experiences from operating system design and current IP networks. VEGA is distinguished by its two design principles: a) ease of use. By service virtualization, VEGA provides users such a location-independent way to access services that grid applications could transparently benefit from systematic load balancing and error recovery. b) ease of deployment. The architecture of VEGA is fully decentralized without sacrificing efficiency, thanks to the mechanism of resource routing. The concept of grid adapters is developed to make joining and accessing the Grid a 'plug-and-play' process. VEGA has been implemented on Web Service platforms and all its components are OGSI-compliant services. To evaluate the overhead and performance of VEGA, we conducted experiments of two categories of benchmark set in a real size Grid environment. The results have shown that VEGA provides an efficient service discovery and selection framework with a reasonable overhead.

1 Introduction

The Grid has been demonstrated as an efficient approach for providing computational services for various scientific applications [2]. Recently, common demands from the e-Commerce and e-Science communities have forced the convergence of technologies between these two fields. The move towards service-oriented Grids, exemplified by Open Grid Services Architecture [6] .

In a service-oriented architecture (SOA)[7], a management system in charge of service provisioning plays a crucial role in mediating provider-consumer interactions. Challenges for managing a service Grid originate from the nature of the Grid: the diversity of resources and the dynamic behavior of resources.

As the Grid is an open society of resources and users from different application domains, it is not applicable to predefine the unique criteria for classifying resources and all user requirements. Service publishing and matching protocols could be ad hoc or domain specific, making the global service discovery and scheduling more difficult to implement. Resources are often autonomous, which results in their volatile

H. Jin et al. (Eds.): NPC 2004, LNCS 3222, pp. 83-91, 2004.

behaviors. For example, a resource may join or leave the grid at any time without notifying the management system. This makes managing and searching for available resources increasingly complex.

The objective of this paper is to present VEGA [5] (acronym for Versatile services, Enabling intelligence, Global uniformity, and Autonomous control) as a novel approach to deal with these problems. VEGA aims at developing key techniques that are essential for building grid platforms and applications. VEGA has been applied in building a national-wide grid testbed called Chinese National Grid (CNGrid), which targets putting high performance computers in China together to provide a virtual super computing environment.

The rest of the paper is organized as follows. The section 2 introduces the related work. The designing principles of VEGA are depicted in Section 3. The Section 4 describes the architecture. The Evaluation of Grid router is given in Section 5. The Section 6 shows the evaluation of VEGA. The conclusion is depicted in the Section 7.

2 Related Works

A number of research efforts target the management of services for dynamic, heterogeneous computing environment. In web service architecture, meta-information of services are maintained by a centralized repository like UDDI. Services published onto UDDI are location-dependant and dynamic information cannot be reflected.

MDS in Globus has realized a globally uniform naming of distributed resources. In the MDS architecture, information is organized in the strict tree-like topology. The directory service used in MDS is LDAP, which is designed for reading rather than writing. While in grid environments resource may change frequently over time, which could result in a writing bottleneck.

In ICENI, ontology information is annotated with the description of service interfaces, which facilitates the automatic matching and orchestration of services at a semantic level. It leverages Jini technology for dynamic service discovery and publishing with the help of a registry service similar to UDDI.

P2P networks rely on routing techniques for locating resources. In early systems, message flooding is used in which queries are propagated along a dynamically changing path. Unfortunately, you cannot ensure two same queries return the same result set. In later semi-structured systems like CAN, distributed hash table (DHT) algorithm is used for locating a resource within limited hops.

3 Design Principles of VEGA System Software

3.1 Virtualization and Ease of Use

From the users' point of view, resource management should be completely transparent. It is the responsibility of the management system to translate abstract resource requirements into a set of actual resources.

To obtain the full physical resource independent properties in VEGA, we adopt the conception of virtual services and physical services with the Grid Service Space (GSS) model. In this model, we present Virtual Service Space (VSS) and Physical Service Space (PSS) with coessential mapping, scheduling mapping and translating mapping.

In the GSS model, a virtual service is an abstract representation of one or many physical services that have common interfaces. A virtual service can only be mapped to one physical service at one time point. This mapping process is called resource scheduling or resource binding. A programmer can refer to a virtual service by a location-transparent name and hence the application can obtain several benefits such as load balancing (by choosing alternative physical services with lower load), fault tolerance (by switching to a new physical service in response to service failure), locality of service access (by locating a nearer physical service), etc.

3.2 Decentralization and Ease of Deployment

A centralized resource management system is conceptually able to produce very efficient schedules. For the Grid, it is not practicable to build such a centralized entity as resources are owned by various administrative organizations. Conversely, a decentralized structure composed of many management points does scale well with increasing size of the Grid[1][3].

There are two fundamental methods to accomplish resource joining: 1) deploy the service onto a hosting environment and start it 2) register the resource's meta information to the information service so as to make it open to grid users. Normally, node administrators manually do these registering works. However, the Grid may accommodate huge amount of resources varying over time. Manually handling joining and leaving process of those resources could be impossible.

Enlighten by IP network, we designed counterparts of routers and network adapters in a network system, which facilitate automating the discovering, publishing and deployment of resources in a grid environment [4]. In [4], we propose a Routing-Transferring resource discovery model, which includes three basic roles: the resource requester, the resource router and the resource provider. The provider sends its recourse information to a router, which maintains this information in routing tables. When a router receives a resource request form a requester, it checks the routing tables to choose a router for it and transfer it to another router or provider.

4 Architecture

4.1 Layered Logical Overview

Scalability and ease of deployment are two driving forces of our architecture design. We proposed three key components in VEGA: Grid Operating Systems (GOS), Grid Routers (GR) and Grid Adapters (GA). Their responsibilities are similar to the counterparts of operating systems, IP routers and network adapters in present network systems, respectively.

VEGA is conformed to the OGSA framework. Currently VEGA was implemented based on Globus Toolkit 3, which is used to encapsulate the physical services and physical resources. A Grid Application accesses to virtual services the Grid provides by Vega Grid operating system (GOS) which call the Vega Grid router to discover the Grid or web services. Figure 4.1 shows the layered architecture of VEGA.

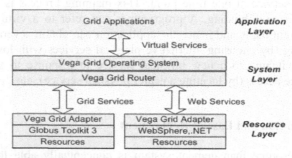

Figure 4.1. The layered architecture of VEGA.

At the resource layer, the distributed resources are encapsulated as grid services or web services hosting by various application servers such as GT3 container and .NET. Like a network adapter, a GA is enabling software for connecting a node machine to the Grid, making services hosted by the node machine known to the nearby GR.

The system layer comprises two components. The interconnection of GRs constitutes an overlay network that provides underlying information service for resource mapping. GRs are capable of routing resource requests to appropriate matching nodes. GOS could aggregate encapsulated physical services together and provide a virtual view for application developers.

At the application layer, developers can use the APIs, utilities and developing environments provided by Vega GOS to build virtual service based applications.

GOS is the kernel of the entire VEGA architecture. It is comprised of job broker service, resource management service, file service, system monitor service, GSML server, and user & CA virtual interface service.

4.2 Runtime Architecture

Figure 4.2 illustrates a runtime architecture of VEGA and information flows when deploying grid resources, locating grid resources as well as using grid resources. Two categories of grid nodes are shown in the figure, one equipped with GA (left outline rectangle) and the other without (right outline rectangle).

A complete service access process from the Grid client-side consists of the following steps: Grid clients submit abstract resource requests to the GOS, then GOS forward the requests to any one GR. The response data will contain a candidate set of physical services. By certain resource selection algorithms, GOS selects one appropriate service from the candidates and deliver subsequent invocations from the client to it. The invocation requests and responses are passed through GOS with the exception of large bulks of data transferring or other situations where performance becomes critical.

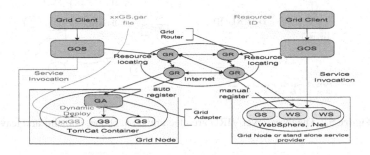

Figure 4.2 A Runtime Architecture of VEGA system software

5 Evaluation of Grid Routers

Grid routers are the backbone of VEGA system, which are transfer stations for resource request. We propose a Routing-Transferring resource discovery model,more details can be get in section 3.2. Figure 5.1 illustrates how a request mr is transferred from router R0 to R2 and eventually U0 finds the resource r which is located on the provider P1.

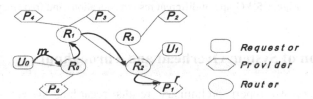

Figure 5.1 The routing-transferring model and the process of locating resource

In [9], based on the router architecture, we propose a three-level fully decentralized and dynamic VEGA Infrastructure for Resource Discovery (VIRD) shown in Figure 5.2. The top level is a backbone consisting of Border Grid Resource Name Servers (BGRNS); the second level is made up of several domains and each domain consists of Grid Resource Name Servers (GRNS); and the third level is leaf layer that include all clients and resource providers. A client can query its designated GRNS in two ways, recursive or iterative, and the server will answer the request by its knowledge about the grid.

We present a resource naming scheme and a link state like algorithm for resource information propagation. The VIRD architecture allows every server has its own data organization, searching and choosing policies.

The analysis shows that the resource discovery time is dependent on topology and distribution of resources. When topology is definite, the performance is determined by resource frequency and location. The result shows that high frequency and even distribution can reduce the resource discovery time greatly.

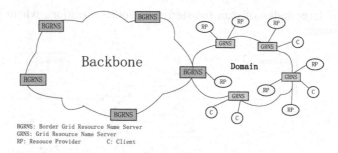

Figure 5.2 The three-level VIRD architecture: a backbone, domains and leaves.

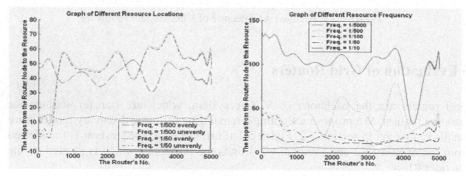

Figure 5.3 Graph of different resource locations and frequency

6 Evaluation of System Overhead and Throughput

In this section, we report preliminary results regarding system overhead and throughput of VEGA. The overhead derives from three aspects: a) The XML-based SOAP protocol overhead. b) key components of VEGA are secure GT3 services that require overhead c) VEGA is written in JAVA. The overall performance is sometimes unstable due to the JVM scheduling mechanisms such as auto garbage collection.

The experiments were done over a non-dedicated network of PC servers in the Institute of Computing Technology (ICT) and National Research Center for Intelligent Computing Systems (NCIC) of China. For simplicity, we deployed one GOS at ICT, two resource routers both at ICT and NCIC. Resource routers connect dozens of nodes mainly PC servers with dual 1800Mhz AMD Athlon processors.

We use two categories of applications as the benchmark set. One is a simple echo application whose execution time on a single machine is so trivial that it can be used to measure the overall system overhead. Another is the notable biology software named BLAST, which is used to measure system throughput.

We divide stages of a job execution into three phases: initialization, execution and ending. The initialization phase starts when the job has just been submitted; it ends when the job's status becomes submitted. The initialization time represents the overhead of a middle management system. The execution phase is the real execution time of the job. In the ending phase, temporary data or garbage is collected.

Figure 6.1 have shown the affect of different scheduling strategies on the execution time of jobs, and the system overhead. A series of identical job requests are orderly submitted to GOS. The execution time of using load balancing scheduling outperforms using round robin. We observe that with the job index increases, the execution time reduce smoothly. The reason is that since we repeatedly submit the same job, system cache in components takes effect so less time was consumed. It is also showed that the system overhead is relatively large, about 2 and 4 seconds, respectively. This is because the timer on the client side updates each 2 seconds.

Figure 6.1 Execution time of Blast with 1 second execution time and one job per time.

Figure 6.2 illustrates the different initialization and ending times for two scheduling strategies, load balance and round-robin. The experiments show the performance of Round-Robin is much better than load-balance. The reason is the load-balance has to poll all the possible sites for online load information. This proves that the Round-Robin outperforms the load-balance in scalability. Another noticeable point is that the stability of Round-Robin is much better than load-balance. The reason is the overhead to poll a site for online load information varies dynamically over time regarding to the system and network situations.

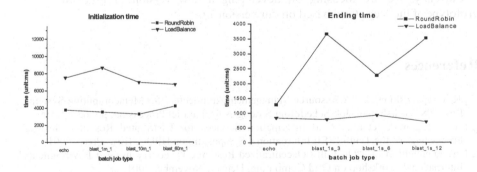

Figure 6.2 Initialization time and ending time of different jobs

Regarding of so many computers in a Grid environment, we should apply as simple load balance algorithms such as Round-Robin as possible. However, Figure 6.3 illustrates that when the scale of Grid is not very much, a job with long enough execution time may suffer the same in the load balance as in the Round-robin in a small or middle scale. According to our experiments, we can suppose randomly selected site algorithm may be as efficient and scalable as Round-Robin. In the future, we should test this kind of load balance strategy.

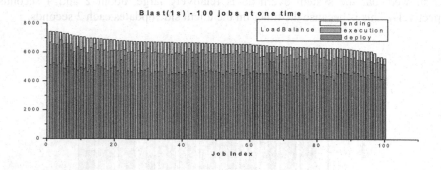

Figure 6.3 Run 100 jobs in parallel on a grid comprised of two servers.

7 Summary

In this paper, we have reviewed the challenging issues on grid service management, descript design principles of VEGA and introduce its architecture. Finally, we give an evaluation of VEGA, including routers, system overhead and throughput.

VEGA combines experiences from operating system design and current IP networks. It is distinguished by its two design principles: a) ease of use, providing users with a location-independent way to access services. b) ease of deployment. The architecture of VEGA is fully decentralized without sacrificing efficiency.

Currently, we are focusing on developing a new version of proof-of-concept prototype of the Vega Grid based on our version 1.0.

References

[1] K. Czajkowski et al., "A Resource Management Architecture for Metacomputing Systems", Proc. '98 Workshop on Job Scheduling Strategies for Parallel Processing, pp. 62-82, 1998.
[2] K. Czajkowski et al., "Grid Information Services for Distributed Resource Sharing", Proceedings of the Tenth IEEE International Symposium on HPDC, IEEE Press, 2001.
[3] A. Iamnitchi et al., "On Fully Decentralized Resource Discovery in Grid Environments", International Workshop on Grid Computing, Denver, November 2001.
[4] W. Li et al., "Grid Resource Discovery Based on a Routing-Transferring Model", 3rd International Workshop on Grid Computing (Grid 2002), pp. 145-156, November 2002.

[5] Z. Xu et al, "Mathematics Education over Internet Based on Vega Grid Technology", Journal of Distance Education Technologies, vol. 1:3, pp. 1-13, July 2003.

[6] I. Foster, et al, "The Physiology of the Grid: An Open Grid Services Architecture for Distributed Systems Integration," Open Grid Service Infrastructure WG, GGF, 2002.

[7] Randall Perrey, Mark Lycett, "Service-Oriented Architecture," 2003 Symposium on Applications and the Internet Workshops (SAINT'03 Workshops), 2003.

[8] Wei Li, Zhiwei Xu, Li Cha, Haiyan Yu, Jie Qiu, Yanzhe Zhang, "A Service Management Scheme for Grid Systems," GCC2003, 2003.

[9] Yili Gong, Fangpeng Dong, Wei Li, Zhiwei Xu, "A Dynamic Resource Discovery Framework in Distributed Environments," GCC2002, 2002

An Efficient Parallel Loop Self-scheduling on Grid Environments

Chao-Tung Yang[1], Kuan-Wei Cheng[1], and Kuan-Ching Li[2]

[1]High Performance Computing Laboratory
Dept. of Computer Science and Information Engineering
Tunghai University
Taichung, 407 Taiwan, R.O.C.
ctyang@mail.thu.edu.tw
[2]Parallel and Distributed Processing Center
Dept. of Computer Science and Information Management
Providence University
Shalu, Taichung, 433 Taiwan, R.O.C.
kuancli@pu.edu.tw

Abstract. The approaches to deal with scheduling and load balancing on PC-based cluster systems are famous and well-known. Self-scheduling schemes, which are suitable for parallel loops with independent iterations on cluster computer system, they have been designed in the past. In this paper, we propose a new scheme that can adjust the scheduling parameter dynamically on an extremely heterogeneous PC-based cluster and grid computing environments in order to improve system performance. A grid computing environment consists of multiple PC-based clusters is constructed using Globus Toolkit and SUN Grid Engine middleware. The experimental results show that our scheduling can result in higher performance than other similar schemes.

Keywords. Parallel loops, Self-scheduling, PC-based clusters, Grid Computing

1. Introduction

Parallel computers are increasingly widespread, and nowadays, many of these parallel computers are no longer shared-memory multiprocessors, but follow the distributed memory model due to scalability factor. These systems consist of homogeneous workstations, where all these workstations have processors, memory and cache memory with exactly identical specifications. Nowadays, more and more systems are composed of homogeneous and clustered together with a number of heterogeneous workstations, where they may have similar or different architectures, speed, and operating systems. For this reason, first of all we have to do is to distinguish whether the target system is homogeneous or heterogeneous. Therefore, we define a frame of relativity to decide the cluster system to two typical cases comparatively, say relatively homogeneous and relatively heterogeneous.

After the system architecture is clear, the next starting point is the task analysis. As we know, the major source of program parallelization is loop. If the loop iterations

H. Jin et al. (Eds.): NPC 2004, LNCS 3222, pp. 92-100, 2004.

can be distributed to different processors as evenly as possible, the parallelism within loop iterations can be exploited. Loops can be roughly divided into four kinds, as shown in Figure 1: uniform workload, increasing workload, decreasing workload, and random workload loops. They are the most common ones in programs, and should cover most case. In a relatively homogeneous case, workload can be partitioned proportionally by computing power respectively to each working computer, but in relatively heterogeneous case, this method will not work. The self-scheduling scheme works well not only in moderate heterogeneous cluster environments but also in extremely heterogeneous environment where the performance difference between the fastest computer and the slowest computer is large.

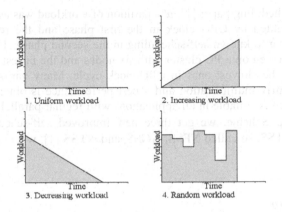

Figure 1. Four kinds of loop style

In this paper, we revise known loop self-scheduling schemes to fit both homogeneous and heterogeneous PC clusters environment. The HINT Performance Analyzer [2] is given for a help to distinguish whether the target system is relatively homogeneous or relatively heterogeneous. Afterwards we partition loop iteration styles by four different ways according to the cluster system typical cases for achieving good performance in any possible executive environment. In this paper, we propose a new scheme that can adjust the scheduling parameter dynamically on an extremely heterogeneous PC-based cluster and grid computing environments in order to improve system performance. A grid computing environment consists of multiple PC-based clusters is constructed using Globus Toolkit and SUN Grid Engine middleware. The experimental results show that our scheduling can result in higher performance than other similar schemes.

2. Background

2.1. Self-scheduling

Self-scheduling is a large class of adaptive/dynamic centralized loop scheduling schemes. In a common self-scheduling scheme, p denotes the number of processors,

N denotes the total iteration and f() is a function to produce the chunk-size at each step. At the *i-th* scheduling step, the master computes the chunk-size C_i and the remaining number of tasks R_i,

$$R_0=N, \qquad C_i=f(i,p), \qquad R_i=R_{i-1}-C_i$$

where f() possibly has more parameters than just i and p, such as R_{i-1}. The master assigns C_i tasks to an idle slave and the load imbalancing will depend on the execution time gap between t_j, for $j=1, \cdots, p$ [7].

2.2. The α Self-scheduling Scheme

In the previous scheduling paper [1], a% partition of workload was according to their performance weighted by CPU clock in the first phase and the rest $(100-a)$% of workload according to known self-scheduling in the second phase. The experimental results were conducted on a PC cluster with six nodes and the fastest computer is 7.5 times faster than the slowest ones in CPU-clock cycle. Many various a values are applied to the matrix multiplication and a best performance is obtained with $a=75$. Thus, our approach is suitable in all applications with regular parallel loops. Through α Self-Scheduling Scheme, we get three new improved self-scheduling schemes; From FSS, GSS, TSS, so called **NFSS**, **NGSS**, and **NTSS** [1], where N means "new" here.

3. Methodology

The adjustment of scheduling parameters dynamically and fit multiform system architectures to accomplish our system has been implemented. Later, we combined Grid computing technology, the HINT Performance Analyzer, our α self-scheduling scheme, and the dynamic adjustment of scheduling parameters into a whole new approach.

3.1. System Definition

System definition is the first step in our approach. The HINT Performance Analyzer [2] is given for helping us to distinguish whether the target system is relatively homogeneous or relatively heterogeneous. We gather CPU performance capabilities, amounts of memory, cache sizes, and basic system performance by HINT. An updatable library, called System Information Array (**SIA**), is build to record the collection of the information. Define the two Cluster System Typical Cases as follows:

Gather CPU Information, $P_1, P_2 \ldots P_n$,

Assume P_1 is the node that has the worst performance (working ability) of all.

Say, $P_n = r^n P_1$

Partition α % of workload according to their performance weighted by CPU clock and the rest (100- α)% of workload according to known self-scheduling scheme.

(1) Define *Heterogeneous Ratio* (**HR**), HR= $\dfrac{P_1}{P_n} \approx \dfrac{MinQUIPS}{MaxQUIPS} \approx \dfrac{1}{r^n}$ < α '/ 100,

where α ' is the temporary value of α .

(2) Case 1: If α ' < HR, then we say the target system is relatively heterogeneous case.

Case 2: If α ' > HR, then we say the target system is relatively homogeneous case.

(3) If the target system is relatively heterogeneous system, we start the α self-scheduling scheme with α = α ' %

If the target system is relatively homogeneous, then we run the HINT benchmark to build (and update) the SIA, and start the α self-scheduling scheme with α =100 %

There is still a point for attention: not always update the SIA before each time of job submission, only when the system has one or more new nodes added, SIA-update will be needed and α will be properly adjusted.

3.2. Loop Styles Analysis

For the programs with regular loops, intuitively, we may want to partition problem size according to their CPU clock in heterogeneous environment. However, the CPU clock is not the only factor which affects computer performance. Many other factors also have dramatic influences in this aspect, such as the amount of memory available, the cost of memory accesses, and the communication medium between processors, etc [5]. Using this intuitive approach, the result will be degraded if the performance prediction is inaccurate. A computer with largest inaccurate prediction will be the last one to finish the assigned job.

Loops can be roughly divided into four kinds, as shown in figure 1: uniform workload, increasing workload, decreasing workload, and random workload loops. They are the most common ones in programs, and should cover most cases. These four kinds can be classified two types: regular and irregular. The first kind is regular and the last three ones are irregular. Different loops may need to be handled in different ways in order to get the best performance. Since workload is predictable in regular loops, it is not necessary to process load balancing at beginning.

We propose to partition problem size in two stages. At first stage, partition α% of total workload according to their performance weighted by CPU clock. In the way, the communication between master and slaves can be reduced efficiently. At second stage, partition following (100-α) % of total workload according to known self-scheduling scheme. In the way, load balancing can be archived. This approach can be suitable for all regular loops. An appropriate α value will lead to good performance.

Furthermore, dynamic load balancing approach should not be aware of the run-time behavior of the applications before execution. But in *GSS* and *TSS*, to achieve good performance, computer performance of each computer in the cluster has to be in order in extreme heterogeneous environment, which is not very applicable. With our schemes, this trouble will not exist. In this paper, the terminology "*FSS*-80" stand for "α=80, and remainder iterations use *FSS* to partition" and so on.

Example 1

Suppose that there is a cluster consisting of five slaves. Each of computing nodes has CPU clock of 200MHz, 200MHz, 233MHz, 533MHz, and 1.5GHz, respectively. Table 1 shows the different chunk sizes for a problem with the number of iteration *I*=2048 in this cluster. The number of scheduling steps is parenthesized.

Table 1. Sample partition size of Example 1

GSS	410, 328, 262, 210, 168, 134, 108, 86, 69, 55, 44, 35, 28, 23, 18, 14, 12, 9, 7, 6, 5, 4, 3, 2, 2, 2, 1, 1, 1, 1 (N=30)
GSS-80	923, 328, 144, 123, 121, 82, 66, 53, 42, 34, 27, 21, 17, 14, 11, 9, 7, 6, 4, 4, 3, 2, 2, 1, 1, 1, 1, 1 (N=28)
FSS	205, 205, 205, 205, 205, 103, 103, 103, 103, 103, 51, 51, 51, 51, 51, 26, 26, 26, 26, 26, 13, 13, 13, 13, 13, 6, 6, 6, 6, 6, 3, 3, 3, 3, 3, 2, 2, 2, 2, 2, 1, 1, 1 (N=43)
FSS-80	923, 328, 144, 123, 121, 41, 41, 41, 41, 41, 21, 21, 21, 21, 21, 10, 10, 10, 10, 10, 5, 5, 5, 5, 5, 3, 3, 3, 3, 3, 1, 1, 1, 1, 1, 1, 1, 1, 1, 1 (N=39)
TSS	204, 194, 184, 174, 164, 154, 144, 134, 124, 114, 104, 94, 84, 74, 64, 38 (N=16)
TSS-80	923, 328, 144, 123, 121, 40, 38, 36, 34, 32, 30, 28, 26, 24, 22, 20, 18, 16, 14, 12, 10, 8, 1 (N=23)

To model our approach, we use following terminology:
- *T* is the total workload of all iterations in a loop.
- *W* is the α% of total workload.
- *b* is the fewest workload in an increasing/decreasing workload loop. It can be the workload of the first iteration (in an increasing workload loop) or the workload of the last iteration (in a decreasing workload loop).
- *h* is the different of workload between consequence iterations. *h* is a positive integer.
- *x* is the iteration number on which the α % accumulating workload is reached. *x* is positive real.

3.3. System Modeling

In our new parallel loop self-scheduling scheme, the HINT Performance Analyzer help us to decide the cluster system for two typical cases comparatively, and the next we must have proper reaction and appropriate self scheduling scheme processed on which system architecture and loop style are changeable. Parallel loop style analysis is essential since parallel loops can be roughly divided into four kinds, as shown in Figure 1: uniform workload, increasing workload, decreasing workload, and random workload loops. They should be the most common ones in programs, and should cover most cases. Moreover, we implement the adjustment of scheduling parameters dynamically to fit multiform system architectures, and message passing interface (MPI) directives parallelizing code segment to be executed by multiple CPUs which is so called cluster. In the loop parallelism region, our self-scheduling scheme must be hand inserted into source code in the region where the largest possible loops that may be parallelized. An example of how our new self-scheduling scheme works is shown in Figure 2.

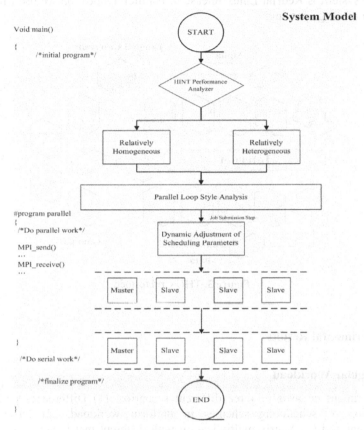

Figure 2. System model.

4. Experimental Results

4.1. Hardware and Software Configuration

Our Grid architecture is implemented on top of Globus Toolkit, name grid-cluster. It is built three PC clusters to form a computational grid environment (Figure 3).

- Alpha site: Four PCs, each PC has two AMD Athlon MP2000 processors, 512MB DDRAM and Intel PRO100VE NIC.
- Beta site: Four PCs, each PC has one Intel Celeron 1.7GHz processor, 256MB DDRAM, and 3Com 3c9051 NIC.
- Gamma site: Four PCs, each PC has two Intel P3 866 MHz processors, 256MB SDRAM and 3Com 3c9051 NIC.

SGE QMaster daemon is run on the master node of each PC cluster, and SGE execute daemon is run to manage and monitor incoming job and Globus Toolkit v2.4. Each slave node is running SGE execute daemon to execute income job only. The operating system is RedHat Linux release 9. Parallel application we use MPICH-G2 v1.2.5 for message passing.

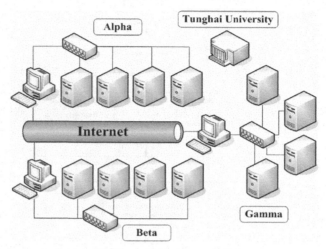

Figure 3. THU Grid testbed

4.2. Experimental Results

4.2.1. Regular Workload

The experiment consists of three different scenarios: (1) Differences performance presentation of scheduling schemes in uniform workload. (2) Different grid environment and (3) Matrix multiplication with different matrix sizes. At first step, we run a MPI program on different grid system to evaluate the system performance. Second step, we connect these grid systems together to form a grid environment (In our testbed is grid Alpha, Beta and Gamma) Then, running the same MPI program to evaluate the system performance. Third step, through the different system topologies, we connect the system characteristics together for a performance analysis. Finally, we run the same MPI program to evaluate the system performance of different system architectures. Our new scheme can guarantee whether what kind of parallel loop scheduling situation happen, they can be properly well-arranged in our approach and achieved better performance than other scheme developed before, all of the performance analysis are presented in Figures 4, 5, and 6.

Figures 4, 5, and 6 note that our approach connects these grid systems together to form a grid environment (In our testbed is grid Alpha, Beta and Gamma) Then, running the same MPI program to evaluate the system performance and implements FSS, GSS, and TSS group approach. In previous methods, NFSS, NTSS, and NGSS get worse performance than new scheme with dynamic parameterization and systematic adjustment automatically.

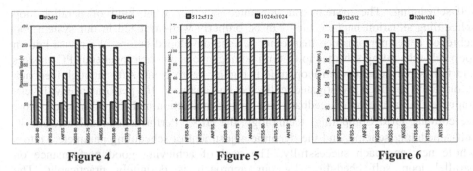

| Figure 4 | Figure 5 | Figure 6 |

Figure 4. A chart of execution time of different sizes of matrix multiplication by grid $\alpha + \beta + \gamma$.

Figure 5. A chart of execution time of different sizes of matrix multiplication by grid β.

Figure 6. A chart of execution time of different sizes of matrix multiplication by grid $\beta + \gamma$.

4.2.2. Irregular Workload

The experiment consists of three scenarios: Differences performance presentation of scheduling schemes in (1) Increasing workload. (2) Decreasing workload and (3) Random workload. Fig 7, 8, 9, note that execution time of simulated increasing, random, and decreasing workload loop by various self-scheduling approaches grid $\alpha + \beta + \gamma$.

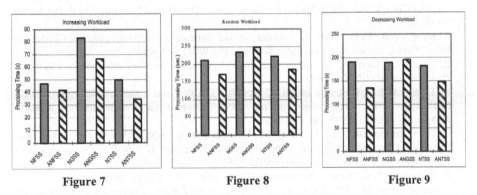

| Figure 7 | Figure 8 | Figure 9 |

Figure 7. A chart of execution time of simulated increasing workload loop by various self-scheduling approaches grid $\alpha + \beta + \gamma$.

Figure 8. A chart of execution time of simulated random workload loop by various self-scheduling approaches grid $\alpha + \beta + \gamma$.

Figure 9. A chart of execution time of simulated decreasing workload loop by various self-scheduling approaches grid $\alpha + \beta + \gamma$.

5. Conclusion and Future Work

In this paper, we can find that Grid Computing technology certainly can bring more computing performance than the traditional PC Cluster or SMP system. Moreover, we try to draw up and integrate a nice and complete system implemented on parallel loop self-scheduling. The system can guarantee whether what kind of parallel loop scheduling situation happen, they can be properly well-arranged in our system and achieved better performance than other scheme developed before. We revise known loop self-scheduling schemes to fit both homogeneous and heterogeneous PC clusters and Grid environment when loop style is regular or irregular. After enough feedback information has been investigated, collected, and analyzed, the performance will well-improved in each time of feedback information collection and job submission. Now we combine Grid Computing technology, the HINT Performance Analyzer, our α self-scheduling scheme, and the dynamic adjustment of scheduling parameters into a whole new approach successfully. The goal of achieving good performance on parallel loop self-scheduling by our approach is definitely practicable. The appropriate method to investigate the performance trend after the new computing nodes added and the proper way to adjust the value of α are our future work.

References

1. Chao-Tung Yang and Shun-Chyi Chang, "A Parallel Loop Self-Scheduling on Extremely Heterogeneous PC Clusters," *Lecture Notes in Computer Science*, vol. 2600, Springer-Verlag, pp. 1079-1088, P.M.A. Sloot, D. Abramson, A.V. Bogdanov, J.J. Dongarra, A.Y. Zomaya, Y.E. Gorbachev (Eds.), June 2003.
2. T. H. Tzen and L.M. Ni, "Trapezoid Self-Scheduling: A Practical Scheduling Scheme for Parallel Compilers," *IEEE Trans. on Parallel and Distributed Systems*, Vol 4, No 1, Jan. 1993, pp 87 - 98.
3. Christopher A. Bohn, Gary B. Lamont, "Load Balancing for Heterogeneous Clusters of PCs," *Future Generation Computer Systems*, 18 (2002) 389–400.
4. E. Post, H. A. Goosen, "Evaluating the Parallel Performance of a Heterogeneous System," *Proceedings of HPCAsia2001*.
5. H. Li, S. Tandri, M. Stumm and K. C. Sevcik, "Locality and Loop Scheduling on NUMA Multiprocessors," *Proceedings of the 1993 International Conference on Parallel Processing*, Vol. II, 1993, pp. 140-147.
6. A. T. Chronopoulos, R. Andonie, M. Benche and D.Grosu, "A Class of Loop Self-Scheduling for Heterogeneous Clusters," *Proceedings of the 2001 IEEE International Conference on Cluster Computing*, pp. 282-291
7. P. Tang and P. C. Yew, "Processor self-scheduling for multiple-nested parallel loops," *Proceedings of the 1986 International Conference on Parallel Processing*, 1986, pp. 528-535.
8. Yun-Woei Fann, Chao-Tung Yang, Shian-Shyong Tseng, and Chang-Jiun Tsai, "An intelligent parallel loop scheduling for multiprocessor systems," *Journal of Info. Science and Engineering - Special Issue on Parallel and Distributed Computing*, vol. 16, no. 2, pp. 169-200, March 2000.
9. S. F. Hummel, E. Schonberg, L. E. Flynn, "Factoring, a Scheme for Scheduling Parallel Loops," *Communications of the ACM*, Vol 35, No 8, Aug. 1992.
10. C. D. Polychronopoulos and D. Kuck, "Guided Self-Scheduling: a Practical Scheduling Scheme for Parallel Supercomputers," *IEEE Trans. on Computers*, Vol 36, Dec. 1987, pp 1425 - 1439.
11. I. Foster, C. Kesselman, eds., *The Grid: Blueprint for a New Computing Infrastructure*, Morgan Kaufmann; 1st edition (January 1999)
12. *A Grid-Enabled MPI: Message Passing in Heterogeneous Distributed Computing Systems.* I. Foster, N. Karonis. Proc. 1998 SC Conference, November, 1998.

ALiCE: A Scalable Runtime Infrastructure for High Performance Grid Computing

Yong-Meng Teo[1,2] and Xianbing Wang[2]

[1]Department of Computer Science, National University of Singapore, Singapore 117543
{teoym, wangxb}@comp.nus.edu.sg
[2]Singapore-Massachusetts Institute of Technology Alliance, Singapore 117576

Abstract. This paper discusses a Java-based grid computing middleware, ALiCE, to facilitate the development and deployment of generic grid applications on heterogeneous shared computing resources. The ALiCE layered grid architecture comprises of a core layer that provides the basic services for control and communication within a grid. Programming template in the extensions layer provides a distributed shared-memory programming abstraction that frees the grid application developer from the intricacies of the core layer and the underlying grid system. Performance of a distributed Data Encryption Standard (DES) key search problem on two grid configurations is discussed.

1 Introduction

Grid computing [4, 8] is an emerging technology that enables the utilization of shared resources distributed across multiple administrative domains, thereby providing dependable, consistent, pervasive, and inexpensive access to high-end computational capabilities [5] in a collaborative environment. Grids can be used to provide computational, data, application, information services, and consequently, knowledge services, to the end users, which can either be a human or a process.

Grid computing projects can be hierarchically categorized as *integrated grid systems*, *application(s)-driven* efforts and *middleware* [1]. NetSolve [3] is one example of an integrated grid system. It is a client/server application designed to solve computational science problems in a wide-area distributed environment. A NetSolve client communicates, using Matlab or the Web, with the server, which can adopt any scientific package in the computational kernel. The European DataGrid [12] is a highly distinguished instance of an application-driven grid effort. Its objective is to develop a grid dedicated to the analysis of large volumes of data obtained from scientific experiments, and to establish productive collaborations between scientific groups based in different geographical locations. Middlewares developed for grid computing include Globus [6], Legion [11]. The Globus metacomputing toolkit attempts to facilitate the construction of computational grids by providing a *metacomputing abstract machine*: a set of loosely coupled basic services that can be used to implement higher-level components and applications. Globus is realigning its toolkit with the emerging OGSA grid standard [7]. Legion is

H. Jin et al. (Eds.): NPC 2004, LNCS 3222, pp. 101–109, 2004.
© IFIP International Federation for Information Processing 2004

a metacomputing toolkit that treats all hardware and software components in the grid as objects that are able to communicate with each other through method invocations. Like Globus, Legion pledges to provide users with the vision of a single virtual machine.

This paper presents ALiCE (*Adaptive and scaLable Internet-based Computing Engine*), a grid computing *core middleware* designed for secure, reliable and efficient execution of distributed applications on any Java-compatible platform. Our main design goal is to provide developers of grid applications with a user-friendly programming environment that does away with the hassle of implementing the grid infrastructure, thus enabling them to concentrate solely on their application problems. The middleware encapsulates services for compute and data grids, resource scheduling and allocation, and facilitates application development with a straightforward programming template [15, 16].

The remainder of this paper is structured as follows. Section 2 describes the design of ALiCE including its architecture and runtime system. Section 3 discusses the ALiCE template-based distributed shared-memory programming model. Section 4 evaluates the performance of ALiCE using a key search problem. Our concluding remarks are in Section 5.

2   System Design

2.1   The Objective of ALiCE

Several projects, such as Globus and Legion, attempt to provide users with the vision of a single abstract machine for computing by the provision of core/user-level middleware encapsulating fundamental services for inter-entity communications, task scheduling and management of resources. Likewise, ALiCE is a portable middleware designed for developing and deploying general-purpose grid applications and application programming models. However, unlike Globus toolkit which is a collection of grid tools, ALiCE is a grid system.

ALiCE is designed to meet a number of design goals. ALiCE achieves *flexibility* and *scalability* through its capability to support the execution of multiple applications concurrently and the presence of multiple clients within the grid. ALiCE enables grid applications deployment on all operating systems and hardware platforms due to its implementation in the *platform independent* Java language, unlike systems such as Condor [9], which is C-based and executes only on WinNT and Unix platforms. ALiCE also offers an API to achieve *generic* runtime *infrastructure support*, allowing the deployment of any distributed application: this is a major feature a middleware has to provide, which distinguishes itself from application-driven efforts that are problem-specific, like SETI@Home [14].

2.2   Architecture

The AliCE grid architecture as shown in Figure 1 comprises of three constituent layers, *ALiCE Core*, *ALiCE Extensions* and *ALiCE Applications and Toolkits*, built upon a set of Java technologies and operating on a grid fabric. The ALiCE system is written in Java and implemented using *Java technologies* including Sun Microsystems' Jini^{TM} and JavaSpaces^{TM} [13] for resource discovery services and object communications within a grid. It also works with GigaSpaces^{TM} [10], an industrial implementation of JavaSpaces.

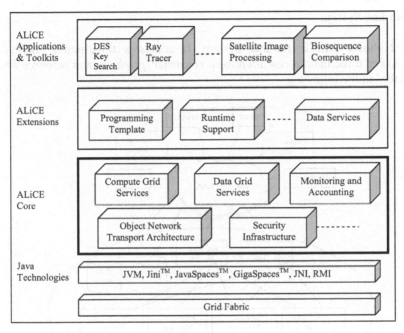

Figure 1: ALiCE Layered Grid Architecture

The *ALiCE core* layer encompasses the basic services used to develop grids. Compute Grid Services include algorithms for resource management, discovery and allocation, as well as the scheduling of compute tasks. Data Grid Services are responsible for the management of data accessed during computation, locating the target data within the grid and ensuring multiple copy updates where applicable. The security service is concerned with maintaining the confidentiality of information within each node and detecting malicious code. Object communication is performed via our Object Network Communication Architecture that coordinates the transfer of information-encapsulated objects within the grid. Besides these grid foundation services, a monitoring and accounting service is also included.

The *ALiCE extensions* layer encompasses the ALiCE runtime support infrastructure for application execution and provides the user with a distributed-shared memory programming template for developing grid applications at an abstract level. Runtime support modules are provided for difficult programming languages and machine platforms. Advanced data services are also introduced to enable users to customize the means in which their application will handle data, and this is especially useful in problems that work on uniquely formatted data, such as data retrieved from specialized databases and in the physical and life sciences. This is the layer that application developers will work with.

The *ALiCE applications and toolkits* layer encompasses the various grid applications and programming models that are developed using ALiCE programming template and it is the only layer visible to ALiCE application users.

2.3 Runtime System

Figure 2 shows ALiCE runtime system. It adopts a three-tiered architecture, comprising of three main types of entities: *consumer, producer* and *resource broker*, as described in the following:

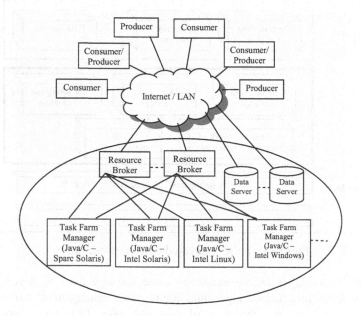

Figure 2: ALiCE Runtime System

- *Consumer*. This submits applications to the ALiCE grid system. It can be any machine within the grid running the ALiCE consumer/producer components. It is responsible for collecting results for the current application run, returned by the tasks executed at the producers, and is also the point from which new protocols and new runtime supports can be added to the grid system.
- *Resource broker*. This is the core of the grid system and deals with resource and process management. It has a *scheduler* that performs both *application* and *task* scheduling. Application scheduling helps to ensure that each ALiCE application is able to complete execution in a reasonable turnaround time, and is not constrained by the workload in the grid where multiple applications can execute concurrently. Task scheduling coordinates the dissemination of compute tasks, thereby controlling the utilization of the producers. The default task scheduling algorithm adopted in ALiCE is *eager scheduling* [2].

- **Producer.** This is run on a machine that volunteers its cycles to run ALiCE applications. It receives tasks from a resource broker in the form of serialized live objects, dynamically loads the objects and executes the encapsulated tasks. The result of each task is returned to the consumer that submitted the application. A producer and a consumer can be run concurrently on the same machine.
- **Task Farm Manager.** ALiCE applications are initiated by the Task Farm Manager and the tasks generated are then scheduled by the resource broker and executed by the producers. The task farm manager is separated from the resource broker for two principal reasons. Firstly, ALiCE supports non-Java applications that are usually platform-dependent, and the resource broker may not be situated on a suitable platform to run the task generation codes of these applications. Secondly, for reasons of security and fault tolerant the execution of alien code submitted by consumers is isolated from the resource broker.

3   Grid Programming

ALiCE adopts the *TaskGenerator-ResultCollector* programming model. This model comprises of four main components: *TaskGenerator*, *Task*, *Result* and *ResultCollector*. The consumer first submits the application to the grid system. The *TaskGenerator* running at a task farm manager machine generates a pool of *Tasks* belonging to the application. These *Tasks* are then scheduled for execution by the resource broker and the producers download the tasks from the task pool. The results of the individual executions at the producers are returned to the resource broker as *Result* object. The *ResultCollector*, initiated at the consumer to support visualization and monitoring of data collects all *Result* objects from the resource broker.

The template abstracts methods for generating tasks and retrieving results in ALiCE, leaving the programmers with only the task of filling in the task specifications. The Java classes comprising the ALiCE programming template are:

a. *TaskGenerator.* This is run on a task farm manager machine and allows tasks to be generated for scheduling by the resource broker. It provides a method process that generates tasks for the application. The programmer merely needs to specify the circumstances under which tasks are to be generated in the main method.
b. *Task.* This is run on a producer machine, and it specifies the parallel execution routine at the producer. The programmer has to fill in only the execute method with the task execution routine.
c. *Result.* This models a result object that is returned from the execution of a task. It is a generic object, and can contain as many user-specified attributes and methods, thus permitting the representation of results in the form of any data structure that are serializable.
d. *ResultCollector.* This is run on a consumer machine, and handles user data input for an application and the visualization of results thereafter. It provides a method collectResult that retrieves a *Result* object from the resource broker. The programmer has to specify the visualization components and control in the collect method.

4 Performance Evaluation

We have developed several distributed applications using ALiCE. These include life science applications such as biosequence comparison and progressive Multiple Sequence Alignment [16], satellite image processing [15], distributed equation solver, etc. In this paper, we present the results of the DES (*Data Encryption Standard*) key search [18]. DES key search is a mathematical problem, involving the use of a brute force method to identify a selected encryption key in a given key space. A DES key consists of 56 bits that are randomly generated for searching, and 8 bits for error detection. In the algorithm, a randomly selected key, K, is used to encrypt a known string into a ciphertext. To identify K, every key in the key space is used to encrypt the same known string. If the encrypted string for a certain key matches with the ciphertext, then the algorithm converges and the value of K is returned. This problem requires immense computational power as it involves exhaustive search in a potentially huge key space.

The test environment consists of a homogeneous cluster and a heterogeneous cluster with all nodes running RedHat Linux. The 64-node homogeneous cluster (*Cluster I*) consists of dual processors Intel Xeon 1.4GHz processors with 1GB of memory. The nodes are connected by a Myrinet network. The 24-node heterogeneous cluster (*Cluster II*) consists of sixteen nodes Pentium II 400MHz with 256MB of RAM, and eight nodes Pentium III 866MHz with 256MB of RAM. These nodes are connected via 100Mbps Ethernet switch.

Our performance metric is the execution time to search the *entire* key space. The sequential execution time grows exponentially with increasing key sizes. The DES key problem can be partitioned into varying number of tasks with a task size measured by the number of keys and its execution time can be estimated using the time from the sequential run. Table 1 shows the task characteristics for varying task sizes and problem sizes. The table was used to select an appropriate task size for the experiments to be carried out in the two grid configurations.

task size (keys)	32-bit Key			36-bit Key		40-bit Key	
	no. of tasks	Est. Time/Task (secs)		no. of tasks	est. time/task (secs)	no. of tasks	est. time/task (secs)
		cluster I	cluster II		cluster I		cluster I
5,000,000	859	20.8	32.9	13,744	20.8	219,902	430.3
10,000,000	429	41.1	65.4	6,872	43.4	109,951	862.4
30,000,000	143	122.9	196.6	2,291	127.8	36,650	2587.7
50,000,000	86	201.9	322.0	1,374	211.4	21,990	4314.3
100,000,000	43	395.4	641.2	687	420.1	10,995	8629.5

Table 1: Estimated Task Execution Times for Varying Task Sizes

For our experiments conducted, we selected a task size of 50 million keys per task and a problem size of 36-bit keys for Cluster I and 32-bit keys for Cluster II. Table 2 shows the results for 4 to 32 producer nodes. The execution time for key search reduces significantly with increasing number of nodes, resulting in greater speedup.

No. of Producers	Cluster I (36-bit Key)	Cluster II (32-bit Key)
1 (Est. Sequential)	78 hr 23 min	8 hr 43 min
4	23 hr 36 min	3 hr 43 min
8	11 hr 6 min	2 hr 7 min
10	8 hr 34 min	1 hr 42 min
12	7 hr 21 min	1 hr 26 min
16	5 hr 11 min	1 hr 7 min
32	2 hr 29 min	-

Table 2: Execution Time for Varying Number of Producer Nodes

We define *speedup* as T_s/T_p, where T_s is the execution time of the sequential program and T_p is the execution time of the derived parallel program on p processors. As shown in Figure 5, a speedup of approximately 32 is attained for key size 36-bits on Cluster I and 8 for 32-bits on Cluster II. We consider these results highly encouraging, although the performance of key search needs to be further evaluated with more key space sizes and nodes. The effects of using other scheduling algorithms in the resource broker must also be studied, as it may result in different overheads to the execution time.

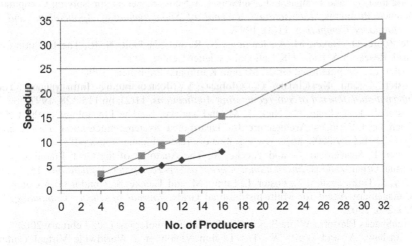

Figure 3: Speedup vs Varying Number of Producers

5 Conclusions and Further Works

We discussed the design and implementation of the Java-based ALiCE grid system. The runtime system comprises of consumers, producers and resource broker. Parallel grid applications are written using programming template that supports the distributed-shared memory programming model. We presented the performance of ALiCE using the DES key search problem. The result shows that a homogeneous cluster yields greater speedup than on a heterogeneous cluster for the same task size. A homogeneous cluster generally has a better load balance than a heterogeneous cluster which is made up of different platforms and capabilities.

Much work still needs to be done to transform ALiCE into a comprehensive grid computing infrastructure. We are in the process of integrating new resource scheduling techniques and load-balancing mechanisms into the ALiCE core layer to reduce the overhead in running applications [17]. Task migration, pre-emption and check-pointing mechanisms are being incorporated to improve the reliability and fault-tolerance ability of the system.

References

1. Baker, M., Buyya, R. and Laforenza, D., Grids and Grid Technologies for Wide-Area Distributed Computing, *International Journal of Software: Practice and Experience (SPE)*, 32(15), Wiley Press, USA, November 2002.
2. Baratloo. A, Karaul. M, Kedem. Z and Wyckoff. P, Charlotte: Metacomputing on the Web, *Proceedings of the 9th International Conference on Parallel and Distributed Computing Systems*, 1996.
3. Casanova, H. and Dongarra, J., NetSolve: A Network Server for Solving Computational Science Problems, *International Journal of Supercomputing Applications and High Performance Computing*, 11(3), 1997.
4. De Roure, D., Baker, M. A., Jennings, N. R. and Shadbolt, N. R., The Evolution of the Grid, Research Agenda, UK National eScience Center, 2002.
5. Foster, I., Computational Grids, Morgan Kaufmann Publishers, 1998.
6. Foster. I and Kesselman. C, Globus: A Metacomputing Infrastructure Toolkit, *International Journal of Supercomputing Applications*, 11(2), pp 115-128, 1997.
7. Foster, I., Kesselman, C., Nick, J. M. and Tuecke, S., The Physiology of the Grid: An Open Grid Services Architecture for Distributed Systems Integration, *Proceedings of CGF4*, February 2002, http://www.globus.org/research/papers/ogsa.pdf.
8. Foster, I., Kesselman, C. and Tuecke, S., The Anatomy of the Grid: Enabling Scalable Virtual Organizations, *International Journal of Supercomputer Applications*, 15(3), 2001.
9. Frey, J., Tannenbaum, T., Foster, I., Livny, M. and Tuecke, S., Condor-G: A Computation Management Agent for Multi-Institutional Grids, *Journal of Cluster Computing*, 5, pp. 237-246, 2002.
10. GigaSpaces Platform White Paper, GigaSpaces Technologies, Ltd., February 2002.
11. Grimshaw, A. and Wulf, W., The Legion Vision of a Worldwide Virtual Computer, *Communications of the ACM*, 40(1), January 1997.
12. Hoschek, W., Jaen-Martinez, J., Samar, A., Stockinger, H. and Stockinger, K., Data Management in an International Data Grid Project, *Proceedings of the 1st IEEE/ACM International Workshop on Grid Computing (GRID2000)*, Bangalore, India, pp. 17-20, December 2000.
13. Hupfer, S., The Nuts and Bolts of Compiling and Running JavaSpaces Programs, Java Developer Connection, Sun Microsystems, Inc., 2000.
14. SETI@Home: Search for Extraterrestrial Intelligence at Home, http://setiathome.ssl.berkeley.edu.

15. Teo., Y.M., S.C. Tay and J.P. Gozalijo, Geo-rectification of Satellite Images using Grid Computing, Proceedings of the International Parallel & Distributed Processing Symposium, IEEE Computer Society Press, Nice, France, April 2003.
16. Teo Y.M. and Ng Y.K., Progressive Multiple Biosequence Alignments on the ALiCE Grid, *Proceeding of the 6th International Conference on High Performance Computing for Computational Science,* Springer Lecture Notes in Computer Science Series, xx, Spain, June 28-30, 2004 (accepted for publication).
17. Teo Y.M., X. Wang, J.P. Gozali, A Compensation-based Scheduling Scheme for Grid Computing, *Proceedings of the 7th International Conference on High Performance Computing,* IEEE Computer Society Press, Tokyo, Japan, July 2004.
18. Wiener, M., Efficient DES Key Search, Practical Cryptography for Data Internetworks, William Stallings, IEEE Computer Society Press, pp. 31-79, 1996.

Mapping Publishing and Mapping Adaptation in the Middleware of Railway Information Grid System

Ganmei You, Huaming Liao, Yuzhong Sun

Institute of Computing Technology, Chinese Academy of Sciences, Beijing 100080
ganmeiu@ict.ac.cn

Abstract. When adopting the mediator architecture to integrate distributed, autonomous, relational model based database sources, mappings from the source schema to the global schema may become inconsistent when the relational source schema or the global schema evolves. Without mapping adaptation, users may access no data or wrong data. In the paper, we propose a novel approach the global attribute as view with constraints (GAAVC) to publish mappings, which is adaptive for the schema evolution. Also published mappings satisfy both source schema constraints and global schema constraints, which enable users to get valid data. We also put forward the GAAVC based mapping publishing algorithm and mapping adaptation algorithms. When we compare our approach with others in functionality, it outperforms. Finally the mapping adaptation tool GMPMA is introduced, which has been implemented in the middleware of railway information grid system.

1 Introduction

A serious issue in integrating distributed, autonomous, relational model based databases is the evolution of schemas. As for mediator architecture, mappings from source schemas to the global schema are used to create source views that query data from sources. When schemas change, users will get invalid data without modifying mappings. However it is time-waste and heavy work to revise mappings manually. In this paper we propose a GAAVC based mapping publishing algorithm and corresponding mapping adaptation algorithms to automatically adjust mappings.

Our main contributions are as follows. (1) We put forward the nested schema decomposition model according to which we propose the approach the global attribute as view to construct mappings. (2) We develop the GAAVC based mapping publishing approach and the corresponding algorithm. The approach is adaptive to the evolution of the source schema and the global schema. Also source views created by the mappings guarantees that data from sources is valid. (3) We develop algorithms to adjust invalid mappings automatically as schemas evolve. (4) We implement the GMPMA tool that implements the algorithms.

Section 2 introduces related work. Section 3 defines valid mappings. Section 4 gives the GAAVC approach and the mapping publishing algorithm. Section 5 introduces mapping adaptation algorithms. Section 6 compares the GAAVC approach with other approaches. Section 7 describes the architecture of GMPMA tool before section 8 concludes.

H. Jin et al. (Eds.): NPC 2004, LNCS 3222, pp. 110-117, 2004.

2 Related Works

The approach adapts to the schema evolution if only local attributes that have no invalid mappings can still be accessed as schemas evolve.

The local as view (LAV) method [1] defines the local schema as the view over the global schema. When schemas evolve, all the local attributes that are in the same schema cannot be accessed. So LAV is not adaptive to schema changes. Because source schemas match the global schema, source schema constraints are satisfied when global constraints are satisfied by views. The global as view (GAV) approach [2] defines the global schema as the view over the source schema. When schemas change, all the local attributes that are in the same view cannot be accessed. So GAV has problems when schemas change. Because the global schema matches source schemas, global schema constraints are satisfied when source constraints are satisfied by views. The global-local as view (GLAV) [3] approach is a variation of LAV. The approach has the same problem with the LAV approach. The both as view (BAV) [4] approach defines the global attribute with the view of the local schema and the local attribute with the view of the global schema. The approach is adaptive for the schema evolution. However, the view is defined manually. The approach has considered constraints of the global schema and source schemas. The correspondence view (CV) [5] approach sets up the mapping of view, other attributes of the same view cannot be accessed when schemas change. So the approach is not adaptive to the schema evolution. What is more, the approach considers foreign key constraints but not key constraints of the global schema.

3 Valid Mappings

We study relational based XML and relational schemas with key constraints and foreign key constraints in this paper. We suppose that there is at most one view for a set of elements in XML schema or tables in relational schemas.

Definition 3.1 An **attribute** is of the form <ID, label, type>.

We use Greek alphabets, α, β, $\cdots$, to represent a set of attributes.

Definition 3.2 A **schema** is of the form (< ID, label>, {attribute}, {schema}).

Definition 3.3 A **mapping of global attributes** is an expression of source views: $Mapping(\alpha_g): \alpha_g = G(V(\alpha_{S_1}), V(\alpha_{S_2}), ..., V(\alpha_{S_n})) = F(\alpha_{S_1}, \alpha_{S_2}, ..., \alpha_{S_n})$. α_g are global attributes. V is a function of attributes of one source and the $V(\alpha_{S_i})$ is the view of the source S_i (i = 1, 2, ... , n). G is a function of views of different sources. F is a composite function of G and V and F is a function of attributes of different sources. The expression is made up of union, intersection and set difference operators.

Definition 3.4 The **mapping of the global schema R** is the set of the mappings of all the attributes of the schema: $Mapping_R = \{\alpha_g = F(\alpha_{S_1}, \alpha_{S_2}, ..., \alpha_{S_n}) \mid \alpha_g \in R\}$.

The expression $\alpha \rightarrow_{KEY} \beta$ denotes that α is the key of the schema of β and $\alpha \rightarrow_{FK} \beta$ denotes that β is the foreign key of α. $Mapping_{S_1}(\alpha)$ denotes the mapping of α in source S_1.

Lemma 3.1 (Null value constraints for foreign key, briefly $\alpha \rightarrow_{FK\_NULL} \beta$) Suppose $\alpha \rightarrow_{FK} \beta$,if α =null then β =null.

Definition 3.5 Valid data are data that satisfy key constraints and null value constraints for foreign key of the global schema.

Definition 3.6 A **valid source view** is a source view that satisfies key constraints and null value constraints for foreign key of the global schema.

Definition 3.7 Valid mappings of a global schema are mappings that produce valid source views.

By valid mappings of a global schema, users can get valid data from databases.

4 The Global Attribute as View with Constraints (GAAVC) Based Mapping Publishing Approach

4.1 The Nested Schema Decomposition Model

$R (\kappa, A_1, R'(\kappa',A_1',\cdots),\cdots,A_m) = R_1(\kappa) \cup R_2(\kappa,A_1) \cup R_3(\kappa, \kappa') \cup R_4(\kappa, \kappa',A_1') \cup \cdots \cup R_n(\kappa, A_m)$, R is a nest relational schema or XML schema. R' is the sub-schema of R. κ is the key of R and κ' is the key of R'. $\kappa = (k_1, k_2,\cdots, k_n)$. $\kappa' = (k_1', k_2',\cdots, k_n')$. Atom schemas, $R_1,\cdots, R_n$, inherit foreign key constraints of R.

Lemma 4.1 In the nested schema decomposition model, the decomposition is a lossless join decomposition.

The lemma 4.1 indicates that no information will be lost after the decomposition.

4.2 The Global Attribute as View with Constraints (GAAVC) Approach

Definition 4.1 A **view key set** is the keys' union of all the schemas of the view:
$key(R_1,R_2,...,R_n) = key(R_1) \cup key (R_2) \cup \cdots \cup key(R_n)$

Lemma 4.2 The view key set is the key of the view.

Definition 4.2 Key constraints on mapping are the global schema key constraints on mapping: If $\beta_g \rightarrow_{KEY} \alpha_g$, $\beta_g = F(\beta_s)$, $\alpha_g = F(\alpha_s)$, $\beta_s = (\beta_{s_1}, \beta_{s_2},...,\beta_{s_n})$, $\alpha_s = (\alpha_{s_1}, \alpha_{s_2},..., \alpha_{s_n})$, then for any $\alpha_{s_i} \in \alpha_s$ (i =1,2,$\cdots$, m), there is a view key set β_{s_j} (1≤j≤n), $\beta_{s_j} \rightarrow_{KEY} \alpha_{s_i}$, $\beta_{s_j} \in \beta_s$, $S'_i = S_j$.

Lemma 4.3 (key constraints on null mapping) If $\beta_g \rightarrow_{KEY} \alpha_g$, Mappings($\beta_g$)= null, and the mappings of β_g and α_g satisfy key constraints on mapping, then Mappings(α_g)=null.

Lemma 4.4 (foreign key constraints on null mapping, $\beta_g \rightarrow_{FK\_NULL} \alpha_g$) if $\beta_g \rightarrow_{FK} \alpha_g$, Mapping($\beta_g$)=null, then Mapping($\alpha_g$)=null.

Definition 4.3 (the global attribute as view approach, GAAV) the GAAV approach is using source views to express each atom schema of the global schema.

Definition 4.4 (the global attribute as view with constraints (GAAVC) approach)
Given the nested schema $R(\kappa, A_1, R^1(\kappa^1, A^1{}_1,...),..., A_m)$, the mapping expression of R: $R_{mapping}=\{ \kappa = F_1(\alpha_{s_1}, \alpha_{s_2},..., \alpha_{s_n}), A_1 = F_2(A_{1,s_1}, A_{1,s_2},..., A_{1,s_n}), \kappa^1 = F_3(\alpha^1{}_{s_1}, \alpha^1{}_{s_2},..., \alpha^1{}_{s_n}), A^1{}_1 = F_4(A^1{}_{s_1}, A^1{}_{s_2},..., A^1{}_{s_n}),..., A_m = F_k(A_{m,s_1}, A_{m,s_2},..., A_{m,s_n})\}$, mappings are constructed according to the following rules:

1) According to the nested schema decomposition model, the approach constructs mappings between atom schemas and source schemas, which are equal to mappings between the original global schema and source schemas
2) Mappings of atom schemas satisfy key constraints on mapping.
3) Mappings of atom schemas satisfy foreign key constraints on null mapping.
4) The mapping expression of an atom schema is the expression of the attribute in deepest schema, while operands are all the attributes of the atom schema.

Theorem 4.1 Mappings that created by the GAAVC approach are valid mappings.

4.3 Mapping Expressions

Mappings of atom schemas of the global schema are expressed as follows:

The key mapping expression: <addKey, <global key>, expression (<<source attributes>, source view constraints>)>

The non-primary attribute mapping expression: <addAttribute, <global key, global non-primary attribute>, expression (<<source attributes>, source view constraints>)>.

The GAAVC approach adapts to schema evolutions because attributes that have no invalid mapping can still be accessed when schemas change.

Lemma 4.5 Given $\kappa \rightarrow_{KEY} A$, source view constraints of $R(\kappa)$ and $R(\kappa, A)$ are the same.

4.4 The GAAVC Based Mapping Publishing Algorithm

Given a global schema, source schemas and a set of mappings between the global schema and source schemas, we set up mappings according to GAAVC approach.

Step 1: verify if mappings satisfy key constraints on mapping. If not, exit.

Step 2: get M the minimal cover of global functional dependencies.

Step 3: get ordered partitions of M so that β and α are in the same partition and β is before α if $\beta \rightarrow_{KEY} \alpha$ or $\beta \rightarrow_{FK} \alpha$.

Step 4: build mapping expressions of attributes of each ordered partition in sequence. The mapping expression of α is built only if for any attributes β, $\beta \rightarrow_{KEY} \alpha$ or $\beta \rightarrow_{FK} \alpha$, Mapping($\beta$)$\neq$null.

Step 2 gets rid of redundant functional dependencies of global schema and step 3 makes partitions to decrease searching times.

5 Mapping Adaptations

When a schema changes, we should adjust mappings to ensure them valid. Adding attributes has no influence on mappings. When renaming a schema or an attribute, we only review all the mapping expressions to change the name.

5.1 Deleting an Attribute or Deleting the Mapping of an Attribute

The step 2, 3, 7 and 8 in the following algorithm ensure key constraints on mapping. The step 4, 5,11, and 12 ensure foreign key constraints on null mapping.

```
deleteAttribute( α_k ){
if α_k is a global attribute, that is α_g                        1
  for each mapping expression E that contains α_g              2
    delete E                                                   3
    for each attribute set λ, Mapping( λ )≠null,
    κ →_FK λ, κ is the key of E                                4
      deleteAttribute( λ )                                     5
if α_k is an attribute of source S, that is α_s               6
  for each mapping expression E that contains α_s             7
    delete E the mapping of source S                          8
    if the global attributes β of E is key                    9
      if no mapping expression contains β                     10
        for each attribute set λ, Mapping( λ )≠null
        and β →_FK λ )                                        11
          deleteAttribute( λ )    }                           12
```

5.2 Deleting a Foreign Key Constraint

Step 2 and step 3 in the following algorithm ensure key constraints on mapping, while step 5 and step 6 ensure foreign key constraints on null mapping.

```
deleteForeignKey ( α →_FK β ){
if α and β are attributes of source S                         1
  for each mapping expression E that contains α →_FK β        2
    delete the mapping of E in source S                       3
```

```
    if the global attributes β in E are the primary

    key and no mapping expression contains β              4

        for each global attribute set λ,

        Mapping(λ)≠null and β →_FK λ                       5

        deleteAttribute(λ)  }                              6
```

5.3 Adding a Foreign Key Constraint

When adding a source foreign key constraint, the existing mappings are still valid. When adding a global foreign key constraint, step 3 and step 4 in the following algorithm ensure foreign key constraints on null mapping.

```
addForeignKey (α →_FK β){                                  1

if α and β are global attributes                           2

    if Mapping(β)≠null and Mapping(α)=null                 3

    deleteAttribute (β) }                                  4
```

5.4 Adding a Source Mapping

The foreign key constraints on null mapping are ensured by step 1, step 2 and step 3.

```
AddSourceMapping(Mapping_s(α_m)= F(α_s)){

    for each global attributes λ, λ →_FK α_m               1

    if Mapping(λ) = null                                   2

        exit                                               3

    if the mapping of α_m satisfy key constraints

    on mapping when adding Mapping_s(α_m)= F(α_s)          4

    add the mapping Mapping_s(α_m)= F(α_s) }               5
```

5.5 Deleting a Source Mapping

Step 2 ensures key constraints on mapping. Step 4, 5 and 6 ensure foreign key constraints on null mapping.

```
deleteSourceMapping(Mapping_s(α_m)= F(α_s)){

    for each mapping expression E that contains α_m        1

        delete the mapping of E in source S                2
```

```
if α  is a set of attributes of key κ                          3
     m
  if Mapping(κ) = null                                          4
     for each attributes λ,Mapping(λ)≠null and κ →   λ  5
                                                    FK
        deleteAttribute(λ)   }                                  6
```

6 Comparisons

Table 1. Mapping publishing approaches comparisons

Publishing methods / Comparisons	LAV	GAV	GLAV	BAV	CV	GAAVC
Be adaptive to schema evolution	No	No	No	Yes	No	Yes
Consider key and foreign key constraints	Yes	Yes	Yes	Yes	Only foreign key constraints	Yes
Adjust mappings manually	No	No	No	Yes	No	No

The detailed discussion is in related works. From the table 1, it can be seen that our GAAVC approach outperforms.

7 Architecture of the GAAVC Based Mapping Publishing and Mapping Adaptation (GMPMA) Tool

We implement the GAAVC based mapping publishing algorithm and mapping adaptation algorithms using the GMPMA tool. Figure 1 shows the architecture of the GMPMA tool. With the graphical user interface or the monitor, schema evolutions are detected. Then the mapping publishing and mapping adaptation engine constructs mappings or adjusts mappings. The architecture has been implemented in the middleware of the railway information grid system.

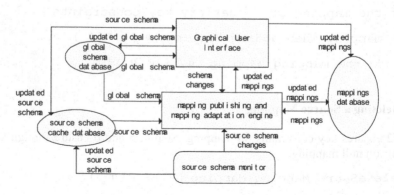

Fig. 1. The GMPMA Architecture

8 Conclusions

To ensure users to get valid data when schemas evolve, we propose the GAAVC based mapping publishing algorithm and mapping adaptation algorithms and implement them in the GMPMA tool in the middleware of railway information grid system. Our approach is unique in many ways: 1) The GAAVC approach constructs the mappings that adapt to the schema evolution. 2) Our mappings enable users to get valid data. 3) We consider mappings from one computation expression of some source attributes to one global attribute. How to make adaptation to schema evolutions of object-oriented databases is our future work.

References

1. T. Kirk, A.Y. Levy, and Y. Sagiv. The information manifold. In: Proc of the AAAI Spring Symposium on Information Gathering From Heterogeneous, Distributed Environments. AAAI press, 1995, 85~91.
2. H. Garcia-Molina, Y. Papakonstantinou, D. Quass, A. Rajararnan, Y. Sagiv, J. Ullman, V. Vassalos, and J. Widom. The TSIMMIS Approach to Mediation: Data Models and Languages. Journal of Intelligent Information Systems, 1997,8(2): 117~132.
3. M. Friedman, A. Y. Levy, and T. D. Millstein. Navigational Plans For Data Integration. In: Proc of the Sixteenth National Conference on Artificial Intelligence and Eleventh conference on Innovative Applications of Artificial Intelligence. AAAI Press / The MIT Press, 1999, 67~73.
4. P. McBrien , A. Poulovassilis. Data integration by Bi-directional Schema Transformation Rules. In: Proc of the 19th International Conference on Data Engineering. Morgan Kaufmann, 2003, 227~238.
5. Y. Velegrakis, R. J. Miller, L. Popa. Mapping Adaptation under Evolving Schemas. In International Conference of Very Large Databases (VLDB), September 2003, pp. 584-595.

A Heuristic Algorithm for the Job Shop Scheduling Problem

Ai-Hua Yin

UFsoft School of Software Jiangxi University of Finance and Economics, Nanchang 330013,
Jiangxi China
Aihuayin@mail.china.com

Abstract. The job shop scheduling problem that is concerned with minimizing makespan is discussed. A new heuristic algorithm that embeds an improved shifting bottleneck procedure into the Tabu Search (TS) technique is presented. This algorithm is different from the previous procedures, because the improved shifting bottleneck procedure is a new procedure for the problem, and the two remarkable strategies of intensification and diversification of TS are modified. In addition, a new kind of neighborhood structure is defined and the method for local search is different from the previous.

This algorithm has been tested on many common problem benchmarks with various sizes and levels of hardness and compared with several other algorithms. Computational experiments show that this algorithm is one of the most effective and efficient algorithms for the problem. Especially, it obtains a lower upbound for an instance with size of 50 jobs and 20 machines within a short period.

1. Introduction

The job shop scheduling problem with which we are concerned consists in scheduling a set of jobs on a set of machines for the objective of minimizing the make-span, i.e., the maximum of completion time needed for finishing all the jobs. Any scheduling is subject to the constrains that each job has a fixed processing order through the machines and each machine can process at most one job at a time.

The job shop scheduling problem is NP-hard in a strong sense and even is one of the hardest combinational optimization problems [5]. It is well known that only small size instances can be solved with a reasonable computational time by exact algorithms, however, for large size instances, some encouraging results have been recently obtained with heuristic algorithms that are based on local search method [1,8,14]. Generally, Starting from an initial feasible solution, a local search method iteratively selects a proper solution from the neighborhood. As the observation of Van Laarhoven et al. [17] and Nowicki et al. [18], both the choice of a good-initial solution and the neighborhood structure are important aspects of algorithm's performance.

This paper is a further research based on our recent work, and a heuristic algorithm that is based on a Tabu Search (TS) technology and on the improved shifting

H. Jin et al. (Eds.): NPC 2004, LNCS 3222, pp. 118-128, 2004.
© IFIP International Federation for Information Processing 2004

bottleneck procedure (ISB) [9] is presented. Here, ISB is used to find a good-initial solution, and the local re-optimization procedure of ISB is used to direct the local search of TS from a region to some different one in the solution space. In the local search procedure of TS, we define a new kind of neighborhood structure that is different from the previous. These two points make certain of the efficiency and effectiveness of our algorithm.

In this paper, the job shop scheduling problem is formalized in terms of a mathematical model and is represented on a disjunctive graph. Then, the TS technique with two strategies of intensification and diversification are analyzed, and the new heuristic algorithm, denote TSISB, is described. Finally, computational results on several test problems instances are shown, and the algorithm is compared with some typical algorithms for the problem.

2. The Problem Definition

Let $J = \{1, 2, ..., n\}$ be a set of jobs, $M = \{1, 2, ..., m\}$ be a set of machines and $V = \{0, 1, 2, ..., N, \#\}$ be a set of operations. Each job consists of a sequence of operations each of which has to be processed on a given machine for a given time. Here, 0 and # represent the dummy *start* and *finish* operations, respectively. A schedule is an allocation of each operation to the time (start time) from which it is processed. In other words, it is an allocation of processing order of the operations on the machines. The problem is to find a schedule that minimizes the make-span, which is subject to constraints: (i) the precedence of operations on each job must be respected; (ii) once a machine starts to process an operation it can not be interrupted and each machine can process at most one operation at a time. Let A denote the set of pair of adjacent operations constrained by the precedence relations as in (i); V_k denote the set of operations that are processed by the machine k ($k \in M$); $E_k \subset V_k \times V_k$ be the set of pairs of operations which therefore have to be sequenced as specified in (ii); d_i and t_i be the process-time (fixed) and the start time (variable) of the operation i ($i \in V$), respectively. The process-times of both 0 and # are zero, i.e. $d_0 = d_\# = 0$. Now, the problem can be stated as following mathematic model:

$$\min t_\#$$
$$t_i \geq 0 \qquad\qquad i \in V$$
$$t_j - t_i \geq d_i \qquad\qquad (i, j) \in A \qquad\qquad (1)$$
$$t_j - t_i \geq d_i \vee t_i - t_j \geq d_j \qquad\qquad (i, j) \in E_k, k \in M$$

The first set of constraints means that $t = 0$ is the start time of the system, and the next two represent the constraints (i) and (ii), respectively, where "$\vee$" means "or". Any solution of (1) is called a schedule, a feasible solution of the problem.

It is useful to represent this problem on a disjunctive graph $G := (V, A, E)$ [4], where V is the set of nodes, A is the set of ordinary (conjunctive) arcs and E is the set of disjunctive arcs. The node, the directed arc and the disjunctive pair-arc of G correspond to operation, precedence relation of two adjacent operations of a job and the pair-operation that are processed by the same machine, respectively. So, $E = \cup E_k$

($k \in M$), where E_k is the subset of disjunctive pair-arc corresponding to the pair-operation that are processed by the machine k. The weight (length) of each arc (i, j) is d_i that infers the process time of operation i, where $i \in V$, $(i, j) \in A \cup E$ and operation i is processed right before operation j.

Fig.1. is the disjunctive graph for an instance with $n = 3$, $m = 3$, and $N = 8$. The number of each conjunctive arc is the weight (length) of the arc and the weight of each disjunctive arc is removed.

A subset of E_k ($k \in M$) is called a selection S_k that contains just one arc of each disjunctive pair-arc of E_k, and S_k is acyclic if it doesn't contain any cycle. According to Adams [2], a feasible processing order of the operations on the machine k is equivalent to the only one acyclic selection S_k, and, to determine a processing order of the operations on a machine is to sequence this machine. So, to sequence machine k is to find an acyclic selection S_k of E_k.

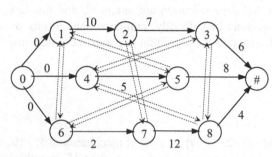

Fig. 1. Disjunctive graph of an instance

Let M_0 be the set of the machines that have been sequenced, so, a partial selection S is the union of selections S_k, one of each E_k ($k \in M_0$). It is easy to understand that each S gives rise to a directed graph $D_S = (V, A \cup S)$. If D_S is acyclic, then S is acyclic, however, the converse is not true [2]. A complete selection S (i.e. $M_0 = M$) that generates an acyclic directed graph D_S defines a schedule, and it is a feasible solution of the job shop scheduling problem. To solve the problem is to find a complete selection S^* that gives rise to an acyclic D_{S^*} and minimizes the length of the longest (critical) path in D_{S^*}.

Let $G_k = (V_k, E_k)$, any acyclic selection S_k in E_k corresponds to the only one Hamilton path (denote H_k) of G_k, and the inverse is also true [2]. In this paper, the acyclic S_k, $S = \cup S_k$ ($k \in M_0$) and $D_S = (V, A \cup S)$ are replaced by the H_k, $H = \cup H_k$ ($k \in M_0$) and $D_H = (V, A \cup H)$, respectively.

For a feasible solution (a schedule) D_H, the swap of two adjacent operations processed by the same machine on the critical path may improve the solution [17], which is usually a base to define the neighborhood for local search. For this reason, the critical path is decomposed into a series of *critical blocks* ($B_1, B_2, \ldots, B_r$) [13]. Each block

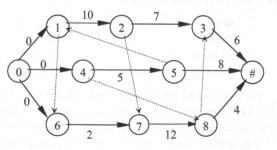

Fig. 2. A feasible solution of above instance

contains the operations processed on one machine, and any two operations, in the block B_i and B_{i+1} ($1 \leq i < r$), respectively, are processed by different machines.

Fig.2. shows a feasible solution via a digraph D_H, $H=$ ((5,1), (1,6))$\cup$((2,7))$\cup$ ((4,8), (8,3)). A critical path $P(0, \#)$ in this D_H is (0,4,5,1,6,7,8,3,#) with $r=4$, $B_1=(4)$, $B_2=(5,1,6)$, $B_3=(7)$ and $B_4=(8,3)$ and length of 47.

3. The Algorithm

Both the technique TS and the procedure ISB are the cornerstone of the new algorithm TSISB. In this section these two techniques are describes in details.

3.1 The Tabu Search

The Tabu Search technique proposed and formalized by Glover [10,11] is a meta-heuristic algorithm that is used to get optimal or near-optimal solution of combinational optimization problems. This method is based on an iterative procedure of neighborhood search, to find a member θ^* in a certain finite set Ω of feasible solutions, where θ^* minimizes some objective function $C(\bullet)$.

Neighborhood search methods are iterative procedures in which a neighborhood $N(\theta)$ must be predefined for each solution $\theta \in \Omega$, and each neighbor of θ is defined by some modifications of θ it-self. The next solution θ' to θ (one of the neighbors of θ) is searched among $N(\theta)$, and a step from θ to the θ' is usually called a *move*. Starting from a current feasible solution θ^c, all the neighbors in $N(\theta^c)$ are examined and the solution θ' with usually the best value of the objective function is chosen as the next solution, θ': $C(\theta') \leq C(\theta'')(\theta', \theta'' \in N(\theta))$. It is just the greedy scheme that is easy to get stuck of local optima. So, the strategy that the movement from θ^c to $\theta' \in N(\theta^c)$ is allowed even if $C(\theta') > C(\theta^c)$ helps the search escape from the trap of local optima. This strategy is one of the important characters of TS technology.

With TS scheme, the cycling, i.e. the search return to the solution that has been visited, may be met. To prevent this cycling, a structure called *Tabu list L* with length l is introduced in order to prevent the search from returning to a solution visited within the last l iterations. In general, the TS process stops when the $C(\theta)$ is close enough to the lower bound of $C(\bullet)$, or, when no improvement occurs over the best solution within a given number of iterations or the time-limit runs out.

3.2 Neighborhood Structure

It is known that there is no any fork on the searching track of TS. To this end, there must be more information to direct the exploration. In fact, there are *short-term* and *long-term* information concerned with the exploration process. This systematic use of the information is the essential feature of TS. The approach uses this strategy not only to avoid cycling but also to explore new directions in the neighborhood. The short-term information represented by the *Tabu list*, is based on the last l iterations and will partly prevent cycling. The long-term information contains C^*, the best value of $C(\bullet)$ found by TS so far.

The exploration process in Ω is described in terms of *move*. For each solution θ $\in\Omega$, let $M(\theta)$ denotes the set of *moves* that can be applied to θ, and let a next solution of θ be $w = \theta \oplus v$, then the neighborhood of θ can be denoted as $N(\theta) = \{w \mid \exists v \in M(\theta), w = \theta \oplus v\}$. In general, the *move* is reversible, i.e. for each v there exits a move v^{-1} such that $(\theta \oplus v) \oplus v^{-1} = \theta$. So, instead of storing the information of complete solution, the *Tabu list* stores only the *move* it-self or the reverse of it associated with the *move* actually performed. Unfortunately, the restrictions of the *Tabu list* sometimes are so strong that they prevent getting a very good solution. This short-come can be overcome by using a sort of long-term information, *aspiration criterion* that allows the algorithm to choose a move from those forbidden moves, i.e. *tabu moves*. A *tabu move* applied to a solution θ is promising if it gives a solution better than the best one so far found.

The neighborhood structure used in our algorithm is described as following. In the next content, we denote the job-predecessor and job-successor of an operation w by $p(w)$ and $s(w)$, respectively. As a matter of fact, if $p(w)$ or $s(w)$ exists, then $(p(w), w)$ or $(w, s(w))$ belong to A. For a feasible solution D_H, denote $L(w, u)$ as the longest path from w to u in D_H, and $P(0, \#)$ as a critical path of D_H. Let $(w, h_1, h_2, \ldots, h_k)$ be a critical block of $P(0, \#)$, and $p(w)$ be in $P(0, \#)$. For any $h_i (i = 1, 2, \ldots, k)$, if there is

$$L(0,w) \geq L(0, p(h_i)) \tag{2}$$

then a *backward move* on w and h_i, i.e., let operation h_i be processed right before the operation w, will yield a new feasible solution [9]. This new solution is looked as one of neighbors of D_H. Also, let $(h_1, h_2, \ldots, h_l, u)$ be another critical block of $P(0, \#)$, and $s(u)$ be in $P(0, \#)$. For any $h_j (j = 1, 2, \ldots, l)$, if there is

$$L(0, s(h_j)) \geq L(0, u) \tag{3}$$

then a *forward move* on h_j and u, i.e., let operation h_j be processed right after the operation u, will yield a new feasible solution[9]. This new solution is looked as one of the neighbors of D_H, too. For all critical blocks of $P(0, \#)$, we test them by use of the inequalities (2) and (3) to generate all neighbors of D_H. It has been proved that swap w and h_1 or h_l and u must lead feasible neighbor of D_H, so the two inequalities are ignored in our algorithm.

Based on these two kinds of *moves*, the neighborhood of D_H consists of all those neighbors of it. Furthermore, this new kind neighborhood structure is different from all those used by previous authors, such as Larrhoven et al.[15], Nowicki et al.[16] and Pezzella et al.[17]. Compared with our neighbor- hood, those of Larrhoven and Pezzella are larger, which slows down the local search, and that of Nowicki is smaller, which usually limits the local search in a quite narrow area of the solution space. Balas takes use of a kind of neighborhood structure similar to ours, which gets a balance between the search speed and search space [5]. However, we reduce the computational cost in each step greatly.

Now, let θ^* be the best solution so far and I be the iteration counter, the TS procedure is described as follows:

Step1. Choose an initial solution θ, set $\theta^* = \theta$, $I=0$;

Step2. $I = I+1$, and generates the subset $N^\#$ of $N(\theta)$ such that either the applied move does not belong to the Tabu list or at least one of the aspiration criterions satisfied;

Step3. Choose a best solution $\theta \in N^\#$ according to the objective function $C(\bullet)$ of the problem;

Step4. If $C(\theta) < C(\theta^*)$, then set $\theta^* = \theta$. Update the tabu list and the aspiration criterion;

Step5. If stopping criterion is met, then stop. Otherwise, go to **Step 2.**.

Where, Steps2, 3, 4 consists of the local search procedure of TS. Some of the stopping rules are as follows: □ $N(\theta)=\phi$; □ I is larger than the maximum number of iterations or the number of iterations is larger than a specific number since the last improvement of the best solution and □ the optimal or near-optimal solution is found.

3.3 Initial Solution and Tabu List

In most of the algorithm associated with TS technology, a good initial solution is fundamental for the computational performance of the algorithm. ISB is an affective algorithm for the job shop scheduling problem. This choice generation of the initial feasible solution allows our algorithm to obtain quite good solutions in comparable computational time or the same solution in shorter computational time.

The improved shifting bottleneck procedure is based on the famous SB that is proposed by Adams[2], and it solves one machine problem by DS (Schrage algorithm with disturbance). The main steps of ISB is as following:

Step1. Identify the bottleneck machine and sequence it with DS;

Step2. Re-optimize the machines of M_0 with DS in turn (at most 3 times), while keep the others fixed. If $M_0 = M$, stop. Otherwise, go to **Step1**.

The procedure iterates over each machine and finishes when no improvement is found. At the last step, after the last machine has been sequenced, the procedure continues to local re-optimization until there is no improvement for the full cycle.

In the acyclic digraph D_H, let $r_i = L(0, i)$, $q_i = L(i, \#) - d_i$, DS is given as following:

Step1. Set $t = \min\{r_i; i \in V_k\}$, $R = V_k$;

Step2. If $r_i > t$, then $u_i = q_i - \delta(r_i - t)$, otherwise $u_i = q_i$, $i \in R$;

Step3. Choose an operation from R, say j, with the greatest u_j, and if there are ties, break them by giving preference to the greatest q_j, and if there are ties still, break them by giving preference to the greatest d_j, and if there are ties other still, break them by choosing randomly. Set $t_j = \max\{r_j, t\}$, $R \Leftarrow R \setminus \{j\}$;

Step4. If $R = \phi$, stop. Otherwise, set $t = \max\{t_j + d_j, \min\{r_i; i \in R\}\}$, go to **Step 2.**.

Where δ is the disturbance coefficient with value of $\lceil 3\sqrt{n}/2 \rceil$, and n is the number of nodes in V_k. It is easy to know that the complexity of DS is $O(n^2)$.

As a matter of fact, the tabu list L is one of the components of the neighborhood structure of TS, and the value of the length l is an important parameter. Nowocki implements a fixed value of $l = 8$ [16], and Pezzella adopts a variable value of l from $2n/3$ to $2n$ [17]. Since any implementation of TS is problem oriented and needs particular definitions of values of tuning parameters such as l and level of aspiration [17], l is a semi-variable value of $\lfloor (n+m)/2 \rfloor$ in our experiments. Because of concerning with n and m, this is a new way to determine the value of l. In TSISB, the way of updating the *Tabu list* is not the same as that of Nowocki's procedure. Especially, when $N^{\#}=\phi$, but $N(\theta^c) \neq \phi$, TSISB selects the oldest *tabu move* while not repeating the latest *tabu move*.

3.4 The Intensification and Diversification

Recently, TS is improved by *aspiration criteria, intensification* and *diversification* [12], which is to improve the effectiveness and efficiency of TS. However, our strategies of *intensification* and *diversification* are different from those of other authors.

Intensification strategy is to make the algorithm search around some smart solutions. TSISB implements this strategy not by back jumping scheme in the procedure of Nowocki et al. but by setting a quite large value of the up-bound of iterations. This up-bound is denoted as *Maxiter*. TSISB does not change the local search strategy of TS until it does not improve the best solution obtained so far within *Maxiter* iterations. Usually, the larger the *Maxiter* is the better the quality of solutions is. However, a larger *Maxiter* needs more computating time and the quality of solutions may not be improved indefinitely. In one word, the *intensification* procedure is just the local search procedure of TS, Steps 2,3,4 as described in §3.2.

On the other hand, *diversification* strategy is to make the algorithm search in different regions of the solution space, and these regions are far from each other. According to the literatures, the enough large number of iterations is used to differ these regions from each other [12]. To direct the search to different regions, TSISB implements the local re-optimization procedure of ISB after *Maxiter* steps of the local search of TS are implemented. This local re-optimization is the procedure of Step2 in ISB, where $M_0=M$, and it does not stop until there is no improvement during a full cycle. In fact, from a feasible solution, the re-optimization procedure is also a local search procedure whose neighborhood consists of the swap of any two operations processed by the same machine[5]. It is clear that the local re-optimization procedure with a low complexity is very different from the local search procedure of TS, which makes our *diversification* efficient and effective. In other words, once this strategy is implemented, usually the local search can really arrive at a new region. Further more, this *diversification* is different from those in literatures [3,6,7,17], one important reason is that the constraint of *tabu list* is ignored while implementing this *diversification* procedure. To get good solutions in a moderate period, the time of implementing diversification strategy is less than *Maxt*.

Let T denotes the time that this strategy is implemented, the main steps of TSISB is described as follows:

Step1. Get initial solution θ by ISB, and set $\theta^*= \theta, I=0$ and $T=0$;

Step2. $I=I+1$, and generates the subset $N^{\#}$ of $N(\theta)$ such that either the applied move does not belong to the tabu list or at least one of the aspiration criterions satisfied;

Step3. Choose a best solution $\theta \in N^{\#}$ according to the objective function $C(\bullet)$ of the problem;

Step4. If $C(\theta)<C(\theta^*)$, then set $\theta= \theta^*$. Update the Tabu list and the aspiration criterion;

Step5. If θ^* is optimal or equal to the lower bound, then stop. If $C(\theta) < C(\theta^*)$, set I = 0, and go to **Step2.**;

Step6. If $I <$ *Maxiter*, go to **Step2.** . Otherwise, $T = T + 1$ and implement the re-optimization procedure;

Step7. If $T <$ *Maxt*, set $I = 0$ and go to **Step2.**, Otherwise, stop.

4. Computational Results

TSISB is implemented in C language on personal computer Pentium 166MHz. The algorithm has been tested on 88 problem instances of various sizes and hardness level provided by OR-Library (http:// mscmga. Ms.ic.ac.uk/info.html) classed as following:

(a) Three instances FT6, FT10, FT20 due to Fisher and Thompson with $n \times m$=6×6, 10×10, 20×5, and five instances ABZ5-9 due to Adams et al. with two $n \times m$=10×10 and three $n \times m$=20×15.

(b) Eighty instances of eight different sizes ($n \times m$ = 15×15, 20×15, 20×20, 30×15, 30×20, 50×15, 50×20, 100×20) denoted as TD1-80. This class contains "partially hard " cases selected by Tailard among a large number of randomly generated instances [18]. The optimal solution is known only for 33 out of 80 instances.

TSISB is compared with all latest procedures for which we can find results (make-span, CPU time) in the literatures. The following notations are for those procedures: NS(3) gives the outcome of over three runs stand for the tabu search procedure of Nowicki and Smutniki; TD stands for the taboo search procedure of Taillard [18]. TSSB stands for a Tabu search procedure of Pezzella and Merelli [17]. SB-GLS1, SB-RGLS5,10 stand for three of the twelve guided local search procedures of Balas and Vazacopoulos[5]; and BV-*best* stands for the best solution of these 12 procedures.

Table 1. Comparison with TSSB on instances (a)

Problem	n	m	OPT (UB LB)	TSISB UB	RE	Time	TSSB UB	RE	Time
FT6	6	6	55	55	0.00	-	55	0.00	-
FT10	10	10	930	930	0.00	200	930	0.00	80
FT20	20	5	1165	1165	0.00	73.2	1165	0.00	115
ABZ5	10	10	1234	1234	0.00	9.0	1234	0.00	75
ABZ6	10	10	943	943	0.00	231	943	0.00	80
ABZ7	20	15	656	665	1.37	2028	666	1.52	200
ABZ8	20	15	(645 669)	671	4.03	2196	678	5.12	205
ABZ9	20	15	(661 679)	686	3.64	2724	693	4.84	195
MRE					1.13			1.44	

The best lower bound (LB) for the problem is taken from [17]. The relative error RE (%) is calculated for each procedure and each instance, i.e. the percentage by which the solution obtained is above the LB, 100((UB-LB)/LB), and MRE means the mean relative error. The Time stands for computer independent CPU times that are based on Dongarra [7], as interpreted by Vaessens et al. [19].In our experiments, when $m \leq 15$ or $m > 15$, the parameters Maxiter gets the value 8000 and 12000 respectively; when $m \leq 10$, $m = 15$ or $m > 15$, Maxt gets the values 5, 10 and 15 respectively. The optimal solution and the lower bound for the stop criteria are equal to the LB.

Table1 compares TSISB with TSSB on instances (a). This class of instances includes the notorious FT10 (10×10) due to Fisher and Thompson , and it takes TSISB a quite reasonable period to obtain its optimal solution. Both of these algorithms find the optimal solution of five instances except three hard instances ABZ7,8,9, and the optimal solutions of ABZ8,9 are not known yet. Because the parameter Maxt is set as 10, TSISB makes greater efforts than TSSB to compute the three instances ABZ7-9, however, the MER of TSISB is smaller than that of TSSB.

Table 2. Comparison with other 7 algorithms on the instances of TD1-50

Problem Class	n	m	TD	NS(3)	SB-GLS1	SB-RGLS5	SB-RGLS10	BV-*best*	TSSB	TSISB
TD1-10	15	15	1.60	2.41	2.24	1.32	1.25	1.16	1.45	1.32
			–	(203)	(57)	–	–	(1498)	(2175)	(1097)
TD11-20	20	15	4.52	5.46	6.18	4.17	4.00	3.67	4.13	4.04
			–	(271)	(113)	–	–	(4559)	(2526)	(2232)
TD21-30	20	20	6.67	7.95	8.12	6.70	6.56	6.10	6.52	6.38
			–	(361)	(165)	–	–	(6850)	(34910)	(6644)
TD31-40	30	15	2.43	3.05	3.53	1.49	1.30	0.79	1.92	1.34
			–	(407)	(175)	–	–	(8491)	(14133)	(4101)
TD41-50	30	20	6.32	8.34	8.50	5.86	5.73	5.20	6.04	5.70
			–	(542)	(421)	–	–	(16018)	(11512)	(17784)
MRE			4.31	5.44	5.71	3.91	3.77	2.65	4.01	3.76

The average computing time for each class is in the parenthesis, – means not reported

Next, the 80 instances TD1-80 are computed. Among these instances, about 30 are easy because the number of jobs are several times that of machines [5], and the other 50 ones TD1-50 are hard not only because the number of their jobs and machines are almost same but also because their quite large sizes. The number of operations of these 50 instances is between 225 and 600, and these instances are divided into 5 classes according their sizes. Table2 gives the MRE for each of the class and the MRE of all these instances. Three of the 8 algorithms did not report their computing time. Not only on the MRE but also on the computing time, TSISB has the best performance, especially when the number of machines is equal to 20. It is contribute to several factors, such as, the producer for the initial solution, the *diversification* strategy and the new neighborhood in our algorithm.

TSISB has got the 28 optimal solutions out of the 30 easy instances except for TD62 and TD67 ($n \times m = 50 \times 20$) whose optimal solutions are not found yet. However, it obtains the best solutions of these two instances with the make-span of 2826 and 2879, respectively. Furthermore, the value of 2879 is the lowest up-bound so far of instance TD62 whose computing time is 8334 seconds, and the average computing time of TSISB on the 30 instances are much less than that of both TSSB and BV-*best*. In details, the average computing time for these three classes instances is TD51-60: 70.6 seconds; TD61-70: 2296 seconds and TD71-80: 186 seconds.

5. Conclusion

The new heuristic algorithm TSISB that is based on the TS technique and the improved shifting bottleneck procedure turns out to be effective and efficient. It gets initial solution with a new procedure ISB. TSISB implements TS procedure in a very nature way and improves the *intensification* and *diversification* strategies of TS by using both the local search procedure of TS and the local re-optimization procedure of ISB in turn. In the local search procedure of TS, TSISB adopts new neighborhood structures and executes the parameters δ, l, *Maxite* and *Maxt* in a simple manner.

The computational experiments show that TSISB is better than TSSB. TSISB performs better than SB-RGLS5,10 on the instances TD1-80. Especially, within a moderate period, TSISB has found a lower up-bound than them for the instance TD62 with a quite large size of $n \times m - 50 \times 20$. It can conclude that TSISB is robust, effective and efficient algorithm for its performance on the 88 benchmarks. Further more, other local search procedure and parallel algorithm can benefit from the way of implementing of *diversification* strategy in TSISB.

6. Reference

1. Aarts, E., LenstraJ, K.: Local Search and Combinational Optimization. Wiley, New York (1997)
2. Adams, J., Balas, E., Zawack, D.: The Shifting Bottleneck Procedure for Job Shop Scheduling. Management Sci. 3 (1988) 391-401
3. Applegate, D., Cook, W.: A Computational Study of Job-shop Scheduling. ORSA J. Computing. 2 (1991) 149-156
4. Balas, E.: Machine Sequencing via Disjunctive Graphs: An Implicit Enumeration Algorithm. Oper. Res. 17 (1969) 941-957
5. Balas, E., Vazacopoulos, A.: Guided Local Search with Shifting Bottleneck for Job Shop Scheduling. Management Sci. 2 (1998) 262-275

6. Dell'Amico, M., Trubian, M.: Applying Tabu-search to the Job-shop Scheduling Problem, Ann. Oper. Res. 4 (1993) 231-252

7. Dongarra, J. J.: Performance of Various Computers Using Standard Liner Equations Software. Report CS-89-85, Computer Science Department, University of Tennessee, Knoxville TN (1993)

8. French, S.: Sequencing and Scheduling: An Introduction to the Mathematics of the Job Shop. Wiley, New York (1982) 31-157

9. Huang, W.q., Yin, A.H.: An Improved Shifting Bottleneck Procedure for the Job Shop Scheduling Problem. Computers and Operations Research. 12 (2004) 2093-2110

10. Glover, F.: Tabu Search—Part I. ORSA J. Computing. 3 (1989) 190-206

11. Glover, F.: Tabu Search—Part II. ORSA J. Computing. 1 (1990) 4-32

12. Glover, F., Laguna, M.: Tabu Search. Kluwer Academic Publishers Boston (1997)

13. Grabowski, J., Nowicki, E., Zdrzalaka, S.: A Block Approach for Single Machine Scheduling with Release Dates and Due Dates. European J. of Oper. Res. 1 (1986) 278-285

14. Hertz, A., Taillard, E., De Werra, D.: Local Search in Combinatorial Optimization. In: Aarts, E., Lenstra, J. (eds.): Tabu Search. vol. 5. Wiley, New York (1977) 121-136

15. Van Laarhoven, P. J. M., Aarts, E. H. L., Lenstra, J. K.: Job Shop Scheduling by Simulated Annealing. Oper. Res. 2 (1992) 113-125

16. Nowicki, E., Smutnicki, C.: A Fast Taboo Search Algorithm for the Job Shop Scheduling Problem. Management Sci. 6 (1996) 797-813

17. Pezzella, F., Merelli, E.: A Tabu Search Method Guided by Shifting Bottleneck for the Job Shop Scheduling Problem. European J. of Oper. Res. 2 (2000) 297-310

18. Taillard, E.: Benchmarks for Basic Scheduling Problems. European J. Operational Res. 4 (1993) 278-285

19. Vaessens, R. J. M., Aarts, E. H. L., Lenstra, J. K.: Job Shop Sheduling by Local Sarch. Memorandum COSOR 94-05. Eindhoven University of Technology, Department of Mathematics and Computing Science. Eindhoven The Netherlands (1994)

Aihua Yin: Ph.D.. UFsoft School of Software Jiangxi University of Finance and Economics. Research interests are in intelligent computing, combinatorial optimization, operational research, covering problem and SAT problem.

Coordinating Distributed Resources for Complex Scientific Computation[1]

Huashan Yu, Zhuoqun Xu, Wenkui Ding

School of Electronic Engineering and Computer Science, Peking University, Beijing, 100871, P.R. China
yuhs@ailab.pku.edu.cn, zqxu@pku.edu.cn, ding@ailab.pku.edu.cn

Abstract. There exist a large number of computational resources in the domain of scientific and engineering computation. They are distributed, heterogeneous and often too restricted in computability for oneself to satisfy the requirement of modern scientific problems. To address this challenge, this paper proposes a component-based architecture for managing and accessing legacy applications on the computational grid. It automatically schedules legacies with domain expertise, and coordinates them to serve large-scale scientific computation. A prototype has been implemented to evaluate the architecture.

1 Introduction

It is well known that there exist a large number of legacy applications in almost every scientific and engineering domain. They are unchangeable and too valuable to be given up. Each alone is very restricted in computability, due to both the target platform's limitation and the programming complexity. However, some of them are complementary in function and resolvable problem characteristics, and others are compatible. It is doubtless that their aggregation is almost powerful enough to solve every problem reliably and efficiently. The idea of coordinating these legacy applications and their target platforms with Grid technologies [1, 2] to solve large-scale and complex scientific problems is straightforward, and the advantages are obvious. However, despite the technical advances of Grid computing in recent years, this kind of coordinative computing remains a grand challenge.

We have attempted to devise an application framework *AOD* for coordinating and scheduling distributed legacy applications on the computational grid, so as to with. It is component-based and built on top of OGSA [2], supporting distributed but complementary legacies to be selected dynamically for solving large-scale complex scientific problems in a cooperative way. Our ultimate goal is to equip the computational grid with the mechanisms for coordinating and scheduling legacies automatically, and hence to create an on-demand computing environment. In this environment, legacies are augmented with domain expertise and abstracted as consistent services for performing specific computation on the computational grid.

---

[1] This work was supported by National Natural Science Foundation of China (No. 60303001, No.60173004)

H. Jin et al. (Eds.): NPC 2004, LNCS 3222, pp. 129-132, 2004.

Every service is automatically implemented with a collection of complementary and competitive legacies. These services are self-optimizing, self-healing and adaptive to problem characteristics. A grid application is a set services connected with each other by directed edges, and AOD provides the mechanisms for executing it on the computational grid.

The next section presents an approach for automatically managing and accessing legacy applications on the computational grid, and discusses the mechanisms for coordinating them to solve large-scale scientific problems. Section 3 introduces a prototype of AOD. Related works are overviewed in section 4, followed by a conclusion of this paper.

2 A Grid Environment for Large-Scale Scientific Computation

To manage and access legacy applications on the computational grid, we have proposed the concept of *grid-programming component* that provides an approach for incorporating domain expertise into the grid environment. A *grid-programming component* (GP component) is an autonomic and extensible entity exiting on the computational grid, aggregating a collection of legacies augmented with necessary domain expertise, and providing a set of functions for developing grid applications. Every function implies some kind of computation with its domain-customized interface, and is automatically implemented with the legacies. They are self-healing for failures occurred on the computational grid, self-optimizing according to problem characteristics and dynamic statuses of grid resources. We call every function as an *on-demand computing service* (OD service) of the grid-programming component.

Every GP component uses a generic configuration framework to specify its underlying computational resources and the augmented expertise. When it is registered, the configuration is interpreted by AOD to configure and implement its OD services on the computational grid. The configuration declares a list of IO ports and OD services as the GP component's interface. The IO ports are used by the OD services to input and output their arguments. Every port input or output one type of data objects in files, and specifies every transferred file's syntax and semantic in domain terms. Generally, an OD service has more than one candidate implementation. Every candidate is provided by some local platform independently, involving one or more legacies installed on the platform. Different candidates may differ in efficiency and resolvable problem characteristics. The configuration not only specifies an executing scheme of every candidate's underlying resources, but also details three kinds of domain expertise for dynamically selecting candidate. One is the annotation of every candidate's applicability to problem characteristics. The second is the methods for querying dynamic statuses of every candidate's underlying resources. And the third is the methods for detecting automatically a problem's characteristics from its data. With the expertise and the support of Grid middleware like Globus Toolkit [3], an OD service dynamically selects one optimal candidate to execute and complete the desired computation when it is invoked.

Based on the concept of GP component, AOD provides a Grid environment for combining distributed legacy resources dynamically to serve large-scale scientific computation. Every legacy in AOD is encapsulated in some GP component. In grid applications, a complex problem is divided into several concurrent and relatively simple sub-problems, and every sub-problem is specified with a reference to some OD service. These references are connected with directed edges to specify the problem domain's concurrency. When the application is submitted to run, AOD will automatically create a formal sub-problem description for every reference, according to the application's arguments and the connected edges. The referred OD services are invoked concurrently, and each is provided a formal sub-problem description. AOD is also responsible for transferring data objects and communicating messages for the invoked OD services on the computational grid.

AOD consists of **repository**, **scheduler** and **broker**, and is built on top of Grid middleware for OGSA. The repository is responsible for configuring and managing all registered GP components and their OD services on the computational grid. It also provides an environment for every OD service to select and schedule its underlying computational resources. An OD service's behaviors on any underlying host are conducted by the local broker instance. The scheduler automatically invokes and synchronizes concurrent OD services when an application is executing.

3 Implementation and Experiment

Based on Globus Toolkit, we have implemented a prototype for AOD. In this prototype, the scheduler, the repository and every broker instance exchange have been assigned a local TCP/IP port respectively, in order to receive messages real-time messages with GlobusIO, so as to invoke OD services, perform computation and synchronize concurrent OD services. The local broker instances on every host are managed with GRAM. When an OD service is invoked, its arguments are transferred on the computational grid with GridFTP. The prototype provides three XML schemas for programmers. The first schema is for domain experts to define FC descriptors. The second one is for developing the configurations of GP components, and the last one is for developing grid applications. We also have developed a tool for running grid applications with Internet browsers.

Table 1. Experimental Result of a Demonstrative Example

GP component	computing host	working directory	Start time	End time
prePrc	162.105.203.100	/home/chen/lyan/test1/	16:43:41	16:45:39
voiFilt	162.105.203.100	/home/chen/lyan/part1/	16:45:47	16:46:58
qCom	162.105.203.38	/home/aitest/oil/part2/	16:45:47	16:48:16
Synth	162.105.80.17	/home/globus/lyan/test2/	16:48:31	16:55:26

Table 1 is the experimental result of a demonstrative example performed on the prototype. The example consists of four GP components *prePrc*, *voiFilt*, *qCom* and *Synth*, performing some kind of simplified pre-stack migration for oil-prospecting data processing. Every GP component provides one OD service with the corresponding legacy application and several additional executables. *prePrc* accepts the primal sampling data, and its result is passed to *voiFilt* and *qCom* respectively. *Synth* creates the final result by synthesizing the results of *voiFilt* and *qCom*. The experimental sampling data is about 2 GB, consisting of two binary data files.

4   Related Works and Conclusion

In recent years, the challenge of developing grid applications has been investigated extensively. The OGSA is the first effort to standardize Grid functionality and produce a Grid programming model consistent with trends in the commercial sector. It integrates Grid and Web services concepts and technologies. In this architecture, resources are encapsulated to be Grid services [2, 4] with standard interfaces and behaviors. XCAT [5, 6] and ICENI [7] attempt to build an application component framework on top of OGSA for distributed computation, and support grid applications that require the collaboration of different Grid services. Neither OGSA nor XCAT takes account of complementary or competitive resources in resource scheduling. ICENI seeks to annotate the programmatic interfaces of Grid services using WEB Ontology Language, allowing syntactically different but semantically equivalent services to be autonomously adapted and substituted.

AOD provides the mechanism for scheduling complementary and competitive resources universally, according to problem characteristics and dynamic resource statuses. It abstracts distributed and heterogeneous computational resources to be services that are self-healing for failures occurred on the computational grid and adaptive to both problem characteristics and dynamic statuses of computational resources, and supports multiple services to serve complex scientific problems collaboratively. This kind of resource managing strategy not only improves the dependability and efficiency of grid computing, but also simplifies the complexity of developing grid applications. We are going to replace current candidate implementations of OD services with Grid/Web services, so as to simplify the complexity of developing GP components.

References

1. I. Foster, C. Kesselman, S. Tuecke. The Anatomy of the Grid: Enabling Scalable Virtual Organizations. International J. Supercomputer Applications, 15(3), 2001.
2. I. Foster, C. Kesselman, J. Nick, S. Tuecke. The Physiology of the Grid: An Open Grid Services Architecture for Distributed Systems Integration. Open Grid Service Infrastructure WG, Global Grid Forum, June 22, 2002.
3. Globus Toolkit. http://www.globus.org/toolkit/default.asp
4. S. Tuecke, K. Czajkowski, I. Foster, J. Frey, S. Graham, C. Kesselman, T. Maguire, T. Sandholm, P. Vanderbilt, D. Snelling. Open Grid Services Infrastructure (OGSI) Version 1.0. Global Grid Forum Draft Recommendation, 6/27/2003
5. Dennis Gannon, Sriram Krishnan, Liang Fang, Gopi Kandaswamy, Yogesh Simmhan, and Aleksander Slominski. On Building Parallel and Grid Applications: Component Technology and Distributed Services. http://extreme.indiana.edu/labpubs.html
6. Sriram Krishnan and Dennis Gannon. XCAT3: A Framework for CCA Components as OGSA Services. In Accepted for publication to HIPS 2004, 9th International Workshop on High-Level Parallel Programming Models and Supportive Environments. IEEE Computer Society Press, 2004. http://extreme.indiana.edu/labpubs.html
7. J. Hau, W. Lee, and Steven Newhouse, Autonomic Service Adaptation using Ontological Annotation. In 4th International Workshop on Grid Computing, Grid 2003, Phoenix, USA, Nov. 2003.

Efficiently Rationing Resources for Grid and P2P Computing*

Ming Chen, Yongwei Wu, Guangwen Yang, and Xuezheng Liu

Dept. of Computer Science and Technology, Tsinghua University
cm01@mails.tsinghua.edu.cn, wuyw@tsinghua.edu.cn,
ygw@mail.tsinghua.edu.cn, xuezhengliu00@mails.tsinghua.edu.cn

1 Introduction

As Grid and P2P computing become more and more popular, many schedule algorithms based on economics rather than traditional pure computing theory have been proposed. Such algorithms mainly concern balancing resource supply and resource demand via economic measures. As we know, fairness and efficiency are two conflicting goals. In this paper, we argue that overbooking resources can greatly improve usage rates of resources and simultaneously reduce responsive time of tasks by shortening schedule time especially under extreme overload, while maintaining schedule principles. This is accomplished by scheduling more eligible tasks above resource capacity in advance, therefore overbooking the resource. We verify our claim on Grid Market[1].

2 Enhance Grid Market with Overbooking

2.1 Grid Market[1]

There are two types of participants in the market: resource suppliers and resource consumers. Suppliers compete to sell resources while consumers contend to buy resources. There exists a market transaction center where all orders from suppliers and consumers are matched based on order type and match algorithm. Running pricing algorithms, software agents on behalf of suppliers and consumers automatically post orders.

Resource market periodically uses price-driven continuous double auction process to match consumers' bid orders (buy orders) and suppliers' ask orders (sell orders). Bid orders and ask orders can be submitted at anytime during the trading duration. At the end of a match period, if there are open bids and asks that match or are compatible in terms of price and requirements, a trade is executed. Bids are ranked from highest to lowest according to bid prices while asks are sorted from lowest price to highest price. The match process starts from

* This project is supported by the National Natural Science Foundation of China under Grant No. 60373004, No. 60373005, and No. 60273007, and by the National High Technology Development Program of China under Grant No. 2002AA104580

H. Jin et al. (Eds.): NPC 2004, LNCS 3222, pp. 133–136, 2004.

the beginning of ranked bids and asks. If prices are equal, match priorities are based on the principle of time first and quantity first.

Grid Market proposed two pricing algorithms: consumer pricing algorithm and supplier pricing algorithm. The consumer pricing function is: $P_{bid}(t) = \alpha + \beta \Delta t$, where α, denoting base price, and β, expressing price elasticity, are consumer-specific coefficients and t is the time parameter. The supplier function is: $P_{asked}(t) = \alpha - \beta \Delta t$, where α, denoting base price, and β, expressing price elasticity, are supplier-specific coefficients and t is the time factor. These two functions automatically make temporal differences between bid prices and ask prices to converge to clear the market.

2.2   Overbooking

Consider such a scenario in a basic Grid Market. A resource is released by a consumer and is open to compete by potential consumers. If the resource's sell price is higher than any buy prices posted by consumers, the resource is inevitably idle until ask price and bid price gravitate towards each other and meet or cross finally. The wasted negotiation time may be negligible in most light-loaded cases, but it may cause severe service bottleneck in heavy load situation. And the existing of idle time decreases resource utility rates and prolongs task's responsive time, which is the sum of negotiation time and service time.

As a widely used technology, overbooking can improve resource utility rates. The basic idea of overbooking goes as follows. A resource can be assigned loads more than its stated capacity temporarily and, using priority-based algorithm, serves them at its best. So, the resource works in high gear and no resource is squandered. Nevertheless, in the long-term the resource's capability should not be overwhelmed by average loads to maintain service quality.

Therefore, we introduce overbooking into Grid Market. A resource keeps a waiting queue in which successfully bidders for it are lined up. A new winning consumer will be queued in when a consumer frees the entire/partial resource. The length of waiting queue depends on three parameters. The first is the match interval. A relative short waiting queue is enough to preserve utility usage rates for frequenter matches relative to service time, which can effectively shorten necessitated negotiation time. The second is the number of a resource's servants, which determines the number of consumers that can simultaneously served by the resource. The number of candidates in the queue must be as many as, or more than the number of servants of corresponding resource. Otherwise, until succeeding consumers successfully win out, fractional resource released by served consumers may be unoccupied. The third is the ratio of negotiation time to service time. The higher the ratio is, the longer the waiting queue should be to ensure the pipeline's feeding. While service time is relatively fixed, negotiation time relies on several factors in market wide scope: consumers' starting prices, elasticities, and ceilings, and suppliers' starting prices, elasticities, and floors. In common practices, we expect that the ratio of the waiting queue's length to the number of servants of a resource should predominately account for the efficiencies and we take 1/1, say the length of the queue is equal to the number of corresponding servants, as a rough estimation for the suitable length. Adaptation policy can be applied here.

3 Analysis and Simulation

3.1 Analysis

The system is modelled as a M/M/N queuing network[6]. Task streams of all consumers are bound into a single task stream as system input stream. We employs below equations[6] to theoretically analyze the resource utilization rate and responsive time of our system: $\rho = \frac{\lambda N_{consumers}}{\mu N_{suppliers}}$, where $N_{consumers}$ and $N_{suppliers}$ are the number of consumers and suppliers separatively and ρ is the system resource usage rate. $K = (\sum_{i=0}^{N-1} \frac{(N\rho)^i}{i!})/(\sum_{i=0}^{N} \frac{(N\rho)^i}{i!})$, $C = \frac{1-K}{1-\rho K}$. System responsive time is: $T_{rst} = \frac{C}{N}\frac{\mu}{(1-\rho)} + 1/\mu$.

3.2 Simulation

We use a event-driven prototype to explore the schedule efficiency of this algorithm in aspects of task responsive time and resource utilization rate varying elasticity coefficients, which should be the primary determinant factor in common settings (Figure 1 and Figure 2). To emphasize the algorithm's performance in bad settings, we set match interval to 2 time units, which greatly protracts the negotiation duration.

First, we can see from figures that our schedule algorithm is highly efficient: the theoretical curves (plotted according to ρ and T_{rst} respectively) are almost approximated by experiment curves when system's load is not high. Second, without overbooking, time burden due to *bargaining* between consumers and suppliers increases sharply as system approaches saturation and the degree of increased burden is negatively related to elasticity coefficients. The reason behind it is straightforward: bargaining time costs are neglectable relative to *'long'* arrival interval when system load is light, but it does matter in high load cases. These costs reduce resource utilization rates and increase responsive time. Third, overbooking greatly improves the algorithm's performance especially in high load environment. With the help of overbooking, responsive time curve and utility utilization rate curve all draw near their theoretical curves respectively. Finally, the heavier the time burden incurred by participants' parameters is, the more efficient the overbooking is.

4 Related Work

Spawn[2] employs Vickrey Auction[3]—second-price sealed auction—to allocate resources among bidders. Bidders receive periodical funding and use balance of fund to bid for hierarchical resources. Task-farming master program spans and

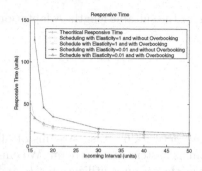

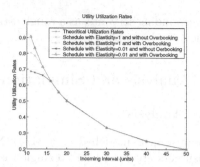

Fig. 1. Responsive Time (1 consumer vs. 1 supplier): $\alpha_{consumer} = 1$, $\alpha_{supplier} = 10$; $Ceiling_{consumer} = 7$, $Floor_{supplier} = 4$; $\mu = 1/10$

Fig. 2. Usage Rates (1 consumer vs. 1 supplier): $\alpha_{consumer} = 1$, $\alpha_{supplier} = 10$; $Ceiling_{consumer} = 7$, $Floor_{supplier} = 4$; $\mu = 1/10$

withdraws subtasks depending on its relative balance to its counterparts. Monte Carlo simulation applications are its main targets. Rexec/Anemone[4] implements proportional resource sharing in clusters. Users assign utility value to their applications and system allocates resources proportionally. Cost requirement is not its consideration. In JaWS (Java Web-computing System)[5], machines are assigned to applications via auction process in which highest bidder wins out. These above solutions don't make use of continuous double auction.

5   Conclusion

With the pervasion of Grid and P2P computing, arises a critical problem, efficiently and fairly allocating resources especially under extreme overload. In this paper, we contend that overbooking resources can greatly improve usage rates without disobeying algorithm-specific scheduling principle. Simulation results conducted on Grid Market enhanced by overbooking testify these claims.

References

1. Ming Chen, Guangwen Yang, Xuezheng Liu, *Gridmarket: A Practical, Efficient Market Balancing Resource for Grid and P2P Computing*, Grid and Cooperative Computing 2003, Shanghai, 2003.
2. Hogg, B. Huberman, J. Kephart, and W. Stornetta, *Spawn: A Distributed Computational Economy*, IEEE Transactions on Software Engineering, February 1992.
3. W. Vickrey, *Counter-speculation, auctions, and competitive sealed tenders*, Journal of Finance, Vol. 16, No. 1, pp. 9-37, March 1961.
4. B. Chun and D. Culler, *Market-based proportional resource sharing for clusters*, Technical Report CSD-1092, University of California, Berkeley, USA, Jan. 2000.
5. S. Lalis and A. Karipidis, *An Open Market-Based Framework for Distributed Computing over the Internet*, Proceedings of the First IEEE/ACM International Workshop on Grid Computing (GRID 2000), Dec. 17, 2000, Bangalore, India.
6. Hock N C. *Queuing Modelling Fundamentals*, John Wiley & Sons Ltd., 1997

Grid Resource Discovery Model Based on the Hierarchical Architecture and P2P Overlay Network

Fei Liu, Fanyuan Ma, Shui Yu, and Minglu Li

Department of Computer Science and Engineering, Shanghai Jiaotong University,
Shanghai, P. R. China, 200030
{liufei001, fyma, yushui, mlli} @sjtu.edu.cn

Abstract. The Grid technology enables large-scale sharing and coordinated use of networked resources. The kernel of computational Grid is resource sharing and cooperating in wide area. In order to obtain better resource sharing and cooperating, discovering resource must be efficient. In this paper, we propose a Grid resource discovery model that utilizes the flat and fully decentralized P2P overlay networks and hierarchical architecture to yield good scalability and route performance. Our model adapts efficiently when individual node joins, leaves or fails. Both the theoretical analysis and the experimental results show that our model is efficient, robust and easy to implement.

1 Introduction

The kernel of computational Grid is resource sharing and cooperating in wide area. We propose a grid resource discovery model that utilizes the flat decentralized P2P overlay networks. P2P overlay networks, such as Chord [1], CAN [2] and Tapestry [3], are always used in file-sharing systems in which the discovery result has to perfectly mach the request. But resource discovery in Grid are in the absence of a naming scheme. GRIP [4] is used to access information about resource providers, while the GRRP [4] is used to notify register nodes services of the availability of this information. To deal with the problem we combine P2P and hierarchical architecture in our model. In our model nodes in Grid can be classified into two types. Register nodes are those that do not provide any resource but only manage the nodes that provide resource. This mode apply P2P architecture to register nodes, which makes the framework of register better scalable than traditional register architecture such as centralized register, hierarchical register etc. Resource nodes are the other nodes that provide resource and take on a little manage work.

2 Constructing Register and Resource Provider P2P Network

The scalability of centralized architecture is bad because the register node is its bottleneck. So in our model, we combine P2P overlay network and hierarchical architectures. There are two P2P overlay networks. One is register P2P overlay

H. Jin et al. (Eds.): NPC 2004, LNCS 3222, pp. 137-140, 2004.

network that consists of register nodes the other is resource provider P2P overlay network that is constructed by resource provider nodes. We assume that IP is the identifier of node. We can regard IP as a point in a virtual 4-dimensional Cartesian coordinate space which is defined as $S_a=\{(0,0,0,0),(255,255,255,255)\}$. We assume the 4 axes of S_a are x, y, z, w. The first register node $R1$ holds space S_a. When the second register node $R2$ joins, S_a is divided into two parts averagely. One parts is controlled by $R1$ and the other is held by $R2$. The central point of the space controlled by $R1$ is closer to $R1$ than the other space. $R1$ records the IP of $R2$ and space controlled by $R2$ and $R2$ records IP of $R1$ and space controlled by $R2$. In this way the neighbor relationship between $R1$ and $R2$ sets up. After the register overlay network contains m node $[R1, R2,..., Rm]$, the $(m+1)^{th}$ register node joins which will split the space controlled by node Rn $\{1<=n<=m\}$ which IP is closest to IP of $Rm+1$ into two parts.

We assume $P1$ is a resource provider node that IP is (162.146.201.148) and it knows the register node $R1$ (28.18.36.112). Then $P1$ sends its GRIP data to $R1$. $R1$ checks IP of $P1$ and its space then transfer the GRIP data of $P1$ to its neighbor. The neighbor of $R1$ does the same as $R1$ and Finally the GRIP data is received by $R2$. After $R2$ receives the GRIP data, it records the static resource and only dynamic resource types and sends the feedback to $P1$. Owning to the dynamic resource changes over time, if $R2$ holds the dynamic resource, it has to refresh dynamic resource periodically which consume much $R2$ resource and result in low scalable performance. So we only store dynamic resource types in register nodes. The feedback contains the IP of $R2$, space controlled by $P1$ (in 4-dimensional Cartesian coordinate space), spaces controlled by $P1$'s neighbors and static resource and dynamic resource types of $P1$'s neighbors. If there is no neighbor of $P1$, $P1$ will hold the space controlled by $R2$. Then $P1$ sends its GRIP data to its neighbors and its neighbors record the dynamic resource of $P1$. $P1$ will send message to its neighbors to refresh the record of its dynamic resource periodically. Thus there are at most 9 nodes know the dynamic resource of $P1$. Here $P1$ registers successfully and $P1$ join the resource provider P2P overlay network. In this way, we can construct the resource provider P2P overlay network.

3 The Process of Resource Discovery

If a client c knows any node in Grid, it can get at least one register node from that node. Then c sends request to register node $R1$ to obtain some resource. After receiving the request $R1$ checks the space controlled by it whether contains the resource c requesting. If the space contains the static resource c asking for, $R1$ tells c that the static resource is found and sends the location of the resource to c. Otherwise $R1$ transfers the request to its neighbors and waits for the response. If one of its neighbor has that resource, $R1$ select the neighbor and sends its IP to c, then c resends request to the selected neighbor of $R1$ to ask for resource. If all the neighbors of $R1$ have not the resource, $R1$ extends the search extent to make more register nodes check its resource until at least one register node Rn finds the resource and resource provider node Pn which belongs to the space controlled by Rn can provide the resource.

If *R1* has the dynamic resource *c* asking for, it randomly select a resource provider *P1* which provides the resource and maximum of the resource is not smaller than *c* requesting, then *R1* sends the IP of *P1* to *c*. After *c* receives the feedback, it sends message to *P1* to check the current load of the resource. If the free resource matches the request of *c*, *P1* accepts the request of *c* and allocate the free resource to *c*. Otherwise *P1* use experience-based+random algorithm to transfers the request of *c* to its neighbor (Fig. 1-a). The experience-based+random is as follows: nodes learn from experience by recording the requests answered by other nodes. A request is forwarded to the peer that answered similar requests previously. If no relevant experience exists, the request is forwarded to a randomly chosen node. If *R1* has not the dynamic resource *c* asking for, it do the same as the static resource discovery to find a register node *Rn* which contain the dynamic resource and the maximum of the resource is not smaller than *c* requesting (Fig. 1-b).

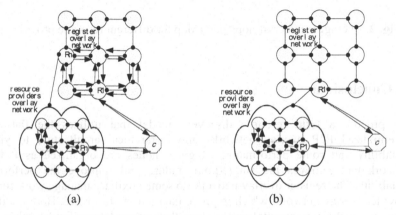

(a)   (b)

Fig. 1. The process of dynamic resource discovery

4 Experimental Results

In our experiment, we use GT-ITM models to obtain 2 groups of nodes. One group contains 5000 nodes that are used as resource providers and the other group contains 100 nodes that are regarded as registers. 20 kinds of static resources and 50 kinds of dynamic resources are in our simulator. Each kind of static resource has 10 instances and every kind of dynamic resource has 10 instances too. These resources are allocated randomly for resource providers.

In our experiment, we investigate the influence of the number of nodes to the number of hops. We activate 1000, 2000, 3000, 4000, 5000 resource providers respectively. We randomly select 40 resource providers as client to send requests. The 40 resource providers are divided into 4 groups. Fig. 2 shows that the number of hops increases slightly with the number of the computing nodes increasing. However there is still some slight disobedience in the curve because the resource which client search may be in its local node or neighbor or some near nodes. The four curves are very similar that shows our model has fine stability.

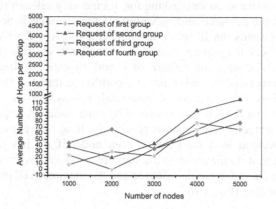

Fig. 2. Average number of hops per group for different resource provider numbers

5 Conclusions

We propose a Grid resource discovery model that utilizes the flat and fully decentralized P2P overlay networks and hierarchical architecture to yield good scalability and route performance. Register nodes are organized as P2P overlay network that removes the single-point failure and improve the performance of scalability. The register overlay network do some auxiliary manage work for resource provider overlay network, which improve the route performance. Both the theoretical analysis and the experimental results show that our model is efficient, robust and easy to implement.

Acknowledgements. This paper is supported by 973 project (No.2002CB312002) of China, and grand project of the Science and Technology Commission of Shanghai Municipality (No. 03dz15027 and No. 03dz15028)..

References

1. Ratnasamy, S.m Francis, P.m Handley, M.m Kapp, R.m And Shenker, S. A scalable content addressable network. In ACM SIGCOMM (2001)
2. Stoica, I., Morris, R., Karger, D.m Kaashoek, M., and Balakrishnan, H. Chord: A scalable peer-to-peer lookup service for internet applications. In ACM SIGCOMM (2001)
3. Zhao, B.m Kubiatowicz, J.m And Joseph, A. Tapestry: An infrastructure for fault-resilient wide-area location and routing. Tech. Rep. UCB//CSD-01-1141, U.C. Berkeley, 2001
4. K. Czajkowski, S. Fitzgerald, I. Foster, C. Kesselman: Grid Information Services for Distributed Resource Sharing. Proc. Of the 10th IEEE int'l Symp. On high Performance Distributed Compting (2001)

Collaborative Process Execution for Service Composition with StarWebService

Bixin Liu, YuFeng Wang, Bin Zhou, and Yan Jia

National University of Defense Technology, ChangSha, China
{bxliu, yfwang, binzhou, yanjia}@nudt.edu.cn

Abstract. This paper gives a brief introduction to a collaborative process execution mechanism for service composition implemented in StarWebService system. The main idea is to partition the global process model of composite service into local process models for each participant, so as to enable distributed control and direct data exchange between participants. It is a novel solution to the issues of scalability and autonomy of centralized execution.

1   Introduction

With the growing trend of service oriented computing, composition of web services has received much interest to support dynamic inter-enterprise application integration. Many research plans and projects [1,2,3] are established on this attractive theme.

A main approach to realize service composition is to orchestrate the constituent services according to a high-level business process model. Current strategies mainly follow the work of workflow technology and propose centralized composition engine to execute the process model [1]. However we believe that service composition targets at large scale information systems in open environments, which demands that execution efficiency will not decrease with the increase of participant services, exchanged data volumes and concurrent requests. A centralize engine will have inherent limits in scalability. Moreover, centralization conflicts the autonomy of business partners and prevents them from accommodating to exceptions in an autonomous manner.

In this paper, we present the collaborative process execution mechanism provided by StarWebService that allows a composite service to be carried out on multiple nodes. By virtue of distributed scheduling control and direct communications, better scalability can be achieved, as well as autonomy of participating services.

2   StarWebService Overview

StarWebService is a research project of StarMiddleware Group [5] which provides a service-oriented integration infrastructure for enterprise applications. It bridges the gap between traditional middleware technologies and web services seamlessly, and enables flexible and scalable inter-enterprise integrations by composing services into high level business process.

H. Jin et al. (Eds.): NPC 2004, LNCS 3222, pp. 141-145, 2004.

Primary components of StarWebService system include: the web service runtime environment based on Bus-Container-Service architecture; bi-directional application gateways for exporting various middleware-based enterprise resources (like CORBA objects, EJBs) as web services, as well as importing web services as specific middleware resources; and collaborative service composition engine for cross-organizational integrations. The first two are abridged from this paper for space limit.

3   Collaborative Process Execution

The overall concept is a strategy of "divide and collaborate". Process model of a composite service is partitioned into several fragments and deployed to several peer composition engines. At run time, those engines collaborate with each other and schedule the composite service in a decentralized manner.

3.1   Global Process Model Vs. Local Process Model

Generally speaking, the process model of composite service captures control flows and data flows among activities which map to invocations on different constituent services. It is a logical centralized view of the contract between participants (including all the constituent services and the composite service itself). So we call it *global process model* (GPM) for the composite service.

Ideas of partitioning business process to enable distributed execution have been proposed in [2,3]. But they divide the process model into fragments consisting of only one activity (task), and then distribute them over a set of selected nodes responsible for carrying them out. However, we argue that a business process usually involves complex conversations within participants who carry out more than one activity. So we adopt a relative course-grained policy and group all the activities and interactions with respect to one participant together. It's also presented as a process but only consists of activities that are assigned to specific participant. We call it *local process model (LPM) for the participant* in the composition. A composition involving N constituent services can be decomposed into N+1 LPMs.

Compared with GPM, LPM only concerns the behavior of a specific participant in the context of a composition, such as whom it speaks with, when to perform its operations, and how to exchange messages. The logic relations among activities in LPMs accord with those in GPM. In fact, a LPM can be understood as the projection of GPM on a specific participant.

Algorithm can be developed to deduce LPMs from GPM. Its main idea is to partition activities into several subsets in terms of their performers and then to relate them by analyzing their causal and data dependencies in GPM. Explicit activities are added to represent communications between LPMs if two activities are data-dependent in GPM but belong to different LPMs. Sec. 4 will give an example of GPM and generated LPMs. Details of the algorithm will be presents in other papers.

3.2   Service Composition Engine

The service composition engine in StarWebService consists of the following parts:
  – *Partition module* implements the algorithm that divides the GPM of a composite service into LPMs for its participants.
  – *Deploy module* distributes a process model to composition engine in a target node and deploys it in the service runtime environment for execution.
  – *Execution module* manages the execution of processes by event-driven mechanism and maintains contexts for process instances.
Note that deployed processes are wrapped as services with published WSDL documents and can be invoked through SOAP messages. Furthermore, the partition module and the deploy module are also implemented as special services deployed in the system to enable communication between composition engines.

3.3   Collaborative Execution with StarWebService

Instead of executing GPM in a centralized engine, composite service execution with StarWebService involves multiple nodes which respectively execute a LPM for the composition. The whole procedure can be illustrated as two phrases.
In the prepare phrase, GPM of the composite service is pre-processed by the partition module and LPMs for every participant are generated. After the concrete constituent service providers for each participant are decided, their deploy modules are invoked to transmit and deploy LPMs to their composition engine. LPM for the composite service itself is deployed at the node that wishes to host it, which is called *master node*, others *participant nodes*. Now it's ready for execution.
The master node reacts on the customs' requests and initiates the composite service. Execution module in the master node then load its LPM and schedules activities defined in. In most cases, the master node does few things but invokes participants' local processes and then waits for their termination. Sometimes callback interfaces are necessary. For the participant nodes, their LPMs are activated as response to invocations from the master node. Actions taken on both master and participant nodes and communications among them are strictly conducted by their LPMs, which assures compatible behaviors with each other. Thus, each of the involved engines schedules a part of activities in the composition and collaborates with each other through peer-to-peer communication.

4   An Example

We refer to the purchase order process example in BPEL4WS specification [4] to demonstrate our idea. It is composed of invoice service (IS), shipper service (SS) and production scheduling service (PSS), with GPM depicted in the left of Fig1. LPMs for 4 participants in the composition are shown in the right. Take the LPM of the shipper for instance. It specifies the activities happened on the shipper site. It requests the shipper information to decide the shipper after the order arrives. Then it notifies the invoice service of shipping information in parallel with logistics arrangement. At last the shipping schedule is sent to the production scheduling service to end the process.

Both the GPM and LPM can be specified with existing business process modeling languages. BPEL4WS is adopted by StarWebService for process definition and engine implementation. Fig 2 shows part of BPEL definition for the shipper's LPM.

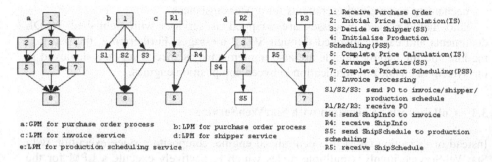

1: Receive Purchase Order
2: Initial Price Calculation(IS)
3: Decide on Shipper(SS)
4: Initialize Production Scheduling(PSS)
5: Complete Price Calculation(IS)
6: Arrange Logistics(SS)
7: Complete Product Scheduling(PSS)
8: Invoice Processing
S1/S2/S3: send PO to invoice/shipper/ production schedule
R1/R2/R3: receive PO
S4: send ShipInfo to invoice
R4: receive ShipInfo
S5: send ShipSchedule to production scheduling
R5: receive ShipSchedule

a:GPM for purchase order process   b:LPM for purchase order process
c:LPM for invoice service   d:LPM for shipper service
e:LPM for production scheduling service

Fig. 1. GPM and LPMs of the purchase order process

```
< sequence>                                    inputContainer="shippingInfo"/>
  < receive partner= "purchaseOrderProcess"   < sequence>
     portType= "purchaseOrderprocessPT "        < recieve partner= "shippingProvider"
     operation= "sendPO "  container= "PO ">       portType= "invoiceProcessPT "
  < assign> ...< /assign>                          operation= "sendSchedule"
  < invoke  partner= "shippingProvider"           container= "shippingSchedule"/>
     portType= "shippingPT "                     < invoke
     operation= "requestShipping"                   partner= "productionScheduleProcess">
     inputContainer= "shippingRequest"              portType= "productionScheduleProcessPT ">
     outputContainer= "shippingInfo">               operation= "sendShippingShedule"
  < flow >                                          container= "shippingSchedule"/>
     < invoke partner= "invoiceProcess"          < /sequence>
        portType= "invoiceProcessPT "          < /flow >
        operation= "sendShippingPrice"       < /sequence>
```

Fig. 2. Part of BPEL4WS definition for the shipper's LPM

5   Conclusions

We propose a collaborative process execution mechanism for service composition in this paper. By distributing the control to multiple nodes and enabling direct communication between distributed composition engines, it provides a novel solution to scalable and autonomous inter-enterprise integration.

Reference

1. Senthilanand Chandrasekaran, John A. Miller, etc. "Composition, Performance Analysis and Simulation of Web services". *Electronic Markets Volumn13(2)*, Nov.2003
2. Roger Weber, Christoph Schuler, Patrick Neukomm, etc.. "Web Service Composition with O'Grape and Osiris". In Proc. of 29th VLDB Conference, Berlin, Germany, 2003
3. Boualem Benatallah, Marlon Dumas, etc. "Declarative Composition and Peer-to-Peer Provisioning of Dynamic Web Services". Proceedings of ICDE02, 2002
4. BPEL4WS specification 1.0 http://www.ibm.com/,2002
5. StarMiddleware Group, http://www.starmiddleware.net

Efficient Gnutella-like P2P Overlay Construction

Yunhao Liu[1], Li Xiao[2], Lionel M. Ni[1] and Baijian Yang[3]

[1] Department of Computer Science, Hong Kong University of Science and Technology,
Kowloon, Hong Kong, China
ni@cs.ust.hk
[2] Department of Computer Science and Engineering, Michigan State University, East Lansing,
MI 48824, USA
lxiao@cse.msu.edu
[3] Department of Industry and Technology, Ball State University, Muncie, IN 47306, USA
byang@bsu.edu

Abstract. Without assuming any knowledge of the underlying physical topology, the conventional P2P mechanisms are designed to randomly choose logical neighbors, causing a serious topology mismatch problem between the P2P overlay network and the underlying physical network. This mismatch problem incurs a great stress in the Internet infrastructure and adversely restraints the performance gains from the various search or routing techniques. In order to alleviate the mismatch problem, reduce the unnecessary traffic and response time, we propose two schemes, namely, location-aware topology matching (LTM) and scalable bipartite overlay (SBO) techniques. Both LTM and SBO achieve the above goals without bringing any noticeable extra overheads. More-over, both techniques are scalable because the P2P over-lay networks are constructed in a fully distributed manner where global knowledge of the network is not necessary. This paper demonstrates the effectiveness of LTM and SBO, and compares the performance of these two approaches through simulation studies.

1 Introduction

As an emerging model of communication and computation, peer-to-peer systems are currently under intensive study [6, 10, 12, 15, 16]. This paper focuses on unstructured P2P systems, such as Gnutella [2] and KaZaA [4], since they are most commonly used in today's Internet. File placement is random in these systems, which has no correlation with the network topology. The typical search mechanism adopted will blindly "flood" a query to the network among peers (such as in Gnutella) or among super nodes (such as in KaZaA). The query is broadcasted and relayed until a certain criterion is satisfied. If an inquired peer can provide the requested object, a response message will be sent back to the source peer along the inverse of the query path. The flood mechanism ensures that the query messages can reach as many peers as possible within a short period of time in a P2P overlay network.

Studies in [15] and [14] have indicated that P2P systems, such as FastTrack (including KaZaA and Grokster) [1], Gnutella, and DirectConnect, contribute the largest portion of the Internet traffic. Among those P2P traffic, a considerable portion of the

H. Jin et al. (Eds.): NPC 2004, LNCS 3222, pp. 146-153, 2004.

load is caused by the inefficient overlay topology and the blind flooding, which also makes the unstructured P2P systems far from being scalable [13].

Aiming at alleviating the mismatch problem, reducing the unnecessary traffic, and addressing the limits of existing solutions, we propose location-aware topology matching (LTM) and scalable bipartite overlay (SBO) scheme. In LTM, each peer issues a detector in a small region so that the peers receiving the detector can record relative delay information. Based on the delay information, a receiver can detect and cut most of the inefficient and redundant logical links, and add closer nodes as its direct neighbors. SBO takes another approach where Gnutella-like peer-to-peer over-lays are optimized by disconnecting redundant connections and choosing physically closer nodes as logical neighbors. Our simulation studies reveal that the total traffic and response time of the queries can be significantly reduced by both LTM and SBO without shrinking the search scope.

The rest of the paper is organized as follows. Section 2 introduces related work. Section 3 discusses unnecessary traffic and topology mismatch problems. Section 4 outlines the designs of LTM and SBO schemes. Simulation and performance evalua-tion of the LTM and SBO are presented in Section 5, and we conclude our work in Section 7.

2 Related Work

Many efforts have been made to avoid the large volume of unnecessary traffic in-curred by the flooding-based search in decentralized unstructured P2P systems. In general, three types of approaches have been proposed to improve search efficiency in unstructured P2P systems: forwarding-based, cache-based and overlay optimiza-tion. The above three different approaches are not exclusive and can be integrated to achieve better results.

In forwarding-based approaches, instead of passing on the query messages to all but incoming logical neighbors, a peer selects a subset of its neighbors to relay the query. The second approach is cache-based search, which includes data index cach-ing and content caching. Centralized P2P systems provide centralized index servers to keep indices of shared files of all peers. KaZaA utilizes cooperative super peers, each of which is an index server of a subset of peers. Some systems distribute the function of keeping indices to all peers [11].

The third search strategy is overlay topology optimization, which inspires the work we are presenting in this paper. End system multicast, Narada, proposed in [7], con-structs shortest-path-spanning trees on top of a rich connected graph. Each tree rooted at the corresponding source employs the well-known DVMRP routing algorithm. Narada has proven to be a sound overlay system when the number of participants is not significant. However, because its system overheads are exponential to the size of the multicast group, it is not suitable for the P2P system, which is normally very dy-namic and involves a good many nodes crossing a wide area of networks. Recently, researchers in [17] have proposed to measure the latency between each peer to multi-ple stable Internet servers called "landmarks". The measured latency can then be served to determine the distance between peers. This measurement is conducted in a global P2P domain. In contrast, we choose a completely distributed approach where distance measurement is managed in many small regions. As a result, our schemes can significantly reduce the network traffic while retaining high accuracy.

3 Unnecessary Traffic and Topology Mismatch

In a P2P system, all participating peers form a P2P network over a physical network. Maintaining and searching operations of a Gnutella peer are described in [3]. When joining a P2P network, a new peer-node gets the IP addresses of a list of existing peers from a bootstrapping node. It then attempts to connect itself to these peers as their neighbors. Once the new peer gets connected with a P2P network, it will periodically *ping* the network connections to obtain the IP addresses of some other peers in the network. Unfortunately, the join mechanism specified in a P2P network, the dynamics of peer memberships, and the nature of flooding would end up with a mismatched overlay network structure and thus incur a large amount of unnecessary traffic [12].

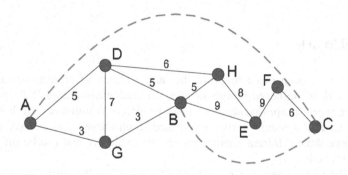

Fig. 1. An example of topology mismatch problem

An example of topology mismatch is illustrated in Fig. 1, where solid lines represent the underlying physical connections and dotted lines denote the overlay connections in a Gnutella-like P2P system. For a query message sent along the overlay path A→C→B, node B is visited twice. Although B is a peering node, B is first visited as a non-peering node when A tries to reach C. Because of the mismatch problem, the same message may traverse the same physical links, such as BE, EF and FC in Fig. 1, multiple times, causing a large amount of unnecessary traffic and increasing the P2P users' query search latency as well.

To quantitatively evaluate how serious the topology mismatch problem is in Gnutella-like networks, we simulate 1,000,000 queries on different Gnutella-like topologies with average number of neighbors being 4, 6, 8 and 10. In this simulation, we track the response of each query message to check if the response comes back along a mismatched path. We count a path as a mismatched path if a peering node on the path has been visited more than once. Result shows more than 70% of the paths are suffered from the topology mismatch problem.

We also have the following observations from the simulation. First, a query may be flooded to multiple paths that are merged to the same peer. Second, two neighboring peers may forward the same query message to each other before they receive it from the other one. In both cases, redundant query messages are generated even among logical links.

Existing studies on overlay optimization connect physically closer nodes as overlay neighbors using different techniques. However, these kinds of approaches may destroy the connectivity of the overlay and thus create many isolated islands in the P2P system. Therefore they are not feasible in unstructured P2P systems.

4 LTM and SBO

Optimizing inefficient overlay topologies can fundamentally improve P2P search efficiency. In this section, we present our solutions, LTM and SBO.

4.1 LTM

If the system can detect and disconnect the low productive logical connections and switch the connection of AC to AB as shown in Fig. 1, the total network traffic could be significantly reduced without shrinking the search scope of queries. This is the basic principle of our proposed location-aware topology matching technique[8]. Location-aware topology matching consists of three operations: TTL2 detector flooding, low productive connection cutting, and source peer probing.

Based on Gnutella 0.6 P2P protocol, we design a new message type called *TTL2-detector*. In addition to the Gnutella's unified 23-byte header for all message types, a TTL2-detector message has a message body in two formats. The short format is used in the source peer, which contains the source peer's IP address and the timestamp to flood the detector. The long format is used in a one-hop peer that is a direct neighbor of the source peer, which includes four fields: *Source IP Address, Source Timestamp, TTL1 IP Address, TTL1 Timestamp*. The first two fields contain the source IP address and the source timestamp obtained from the source peer. The last two fields are the IP address of the source peer's direct neighbor who forwards the detector and the timestamp when forward it. In the message header, the initial TTL value is 2. The payload type of the detector can be defined as 0x82.

Each peer floods a TTL2-detector periodically. We use $d(i, S, v)$ to denote the TTL2-detector who has the message ID of i with TTL value of v and is initiated by S. We use $N(S)$ to denote the set of direct logical neighbors of S, and use $N^2(S)$ to denote the set of peers being two hops away from S. A TTL2-detector can only reach peers in $N(S)$ and $N^2(S)$. We use network delay between two nodes as a metric for measuring the cost between nodes. The clocks in all peers can be synchronized by current techniques in an acceptable accuracy[1]. By using the TTL2-detector message, a peer can compute the cost of the paths to a source peer, and optimizes the topology by conducting low production cutting and source peer probing operations.

4.2 SBO

Instead of flooding queries to all neighbors, SBO employs an efficient strategy to select query forwarding path and logical neighbors [9]. The topology construction and optimization of SBO consist of four phases: bootstrapping a new peer, neighbor distance probing and reporting, forwarding connections computing, and direct neighbor replacement.

Phase 1: bootstrapping a new peer. When a new peer is joining the P2P system, it will randomly take an initial color: red or white. A peer should keep its color until it leaves, and again randomly select a color when it rejoins the system. Thus, each peer has a color associated with it, and all peers are separated into two groups, red and white. In SBO, a bootstrap host will provide the joining peer a list of active peers with color information. The joining peer then tries to create connections to the different color peers in the list. In such a way, all the peers form a bipartite overlay, in which a red peer will only have white peers as its direct neighbors, and vice versa.

Phase 2: neighbor distance probing and reporting by white peers. We use network delay between two peers as a metric for measuring the traffic cost between peers. We modify the Limewire implementation of Gnutella 0.6 P2P protocol [3] by adding one routing message type for a peer to probe the link cost to its neighbors. Each white peer broadcast this message only to its immediate logical neighbors, forms a neighbor cost table, and sends this table to all its red neighbors.

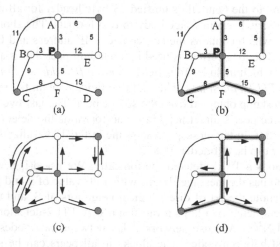

Fig. 2. An example of SBO operations

---

[1] Current implementation of NTP version 4.1.1 in public domain can reach the synchronization accuracy down to 7.5 milliseconds [5]. Another approach is to use distance to measure the communication cost, such as the number of hops weighted by individual channel bandwidth.

Phase 3: forwarding connections computing by red peers. Based on the obtained neighbor cost tables, a minimum spanning tree (MST) can be built by each red peer, such as P in fig. 2-(b). Since a red peer builds a MST in a two-hop diameter, a white peer does not need to build a MST. The thick lines in the MST are selected as for-warding connections (FC), while the thin lines are non-forwarding connections (NFC). Queries are forwarded only along the FCs.

Phase 4: direct neighbor replacement by white peers. After phase 3 where a MST within two hops distance is constructed, a red peer P is able to send its queries to all the peers within this range. Some white peers become non-forwarding neighbors, such as E in Fig. 2. In this case, for peer E, P is no longer its neighbor. In the phase of direct neighbor replacement, a non-forwarding neighbor, E, will try to find another red peer being two hops away from P to replace P as its new neighbor.

5   Performance Evaluation

To evaluate the effectiveness of LTM and SBO, we generate both physical network topologies and logical topologies in our simulation. The physical topology should represent the real topology with Internet characteristics. The logical topology represents the overlay P2P topology built on top of the physical topology. All P2P nodes are in a subset of nodes in the physical topology.

In our first simulation, we study the effectiveness of LTM and SBO in a static P2P environment where the 8,000 peers do not join and leave the system. Figures 3 and 4 show the traffic cost reduction of LTM and SBO, respectively. In these figures, the curve of 'c_n-neigh' shows the average traffic cost caused by a query to cover the whole network and the average number of logical neighbors is denoted as c_n. We can see that the traffic cost decreases when LTM and SBO are conducted multiple times. They both reach a threshold after several steps of optimization. LTM may reduce traffic cost by around 80-85% while SBO reduces traffic cost between 85% and 90%. However, LTM converges in around 2-3 steps while SBO needs 4-5 steps. The simulation results in Fig. 5 and Fig. 6 show that LTM reduces response time by more than 60% in 3 steps but SBO needs 8 steps to reduce 60% of the response time in a static environment.

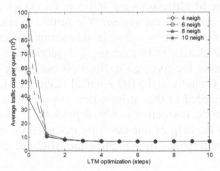

Fig. 3. Traffic reduction vs. optimization step in LTM

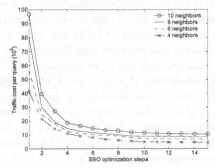

Fig. 4. Traffic reduction vs. optimization step in SBO

152   Y. Liu et al.

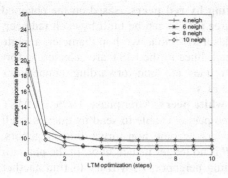

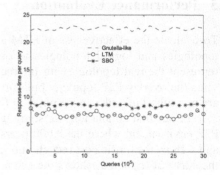

Fig. 5. Average Response time vs. opt. step in LTM

Fig. 6. Average Response time vs. opt. step in SBO

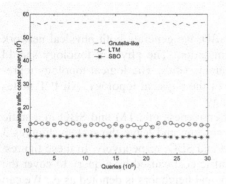

Fig. 7. Average traffic cost comparison of LTM and SBO in a dynamic P2P environment

Fig. 8. Average response time comparison of LTM and SBO in a dynamic P2P environment

P2P networks are highly dynamic with peers joining and leaving frequently. The observations in [15] have shown that over 20% of the logical connections in a P2P last 1 minute or less, and around 60% of the IP addresses keep active in FastTrack for no more than 10 minutes each time after they join the system. We further evaluate the effectiveness of LTM and SBO in dynamic P2P systems. In this simulation, we assume that peer average lifetime in a P2P system is 10 minutes; 0.3 queries are issued by each peer per minute. Fig. 7 shows the average traffic cost per query of Gnutella-like P2P systems, LTM enabled Gnutella and SBO enabled Gnutella. Here the traffic cost includes all the overhead needed in the optimization steps. SBO and LTM drop the average cost by 85% and 80%, respectively. Fig. 8 plots the average query response time of each system. With the help of our carefully designed the optimization algorithms, the LTM reduces the response time to 30% and SBO decrease the response time to 35%.

6 Conclusion

We have evaluated our proposed LTM and SBO overlay topology match algorithms in static as well as dynamic environments. Both schemes are fully distributed and scalable in that each peer can conduct the algorithm independently without requesting any global knowledge. The other strength of LTM and SBO is that they are complementary to cache-based and forwarding-based approaches so that further improvements can be made when deployed together. LTM shows its advantages in convergent speed but slightly creates more overhead than SBO. It also demands synchronized time among peers, which implies that an additional overhead is needed to run a clock synchronization protocol, such as NTP.

References

[1] Fasttrack, http://www.fasttrack.nu
[2] Gnutella, http://gnutella.wego.com/
[3] The Gnutella protocol specification 0.6, http://rfc-gnutella.sourceforge.net
[4] KaZaA, http://www.kazaa.com
[5] NTP: The Network Time Protocol, http://www.ntp.org/
[6] Y. Chawathe, S. Ratnasamy, L. Breslau, N. Lanham, and S. Shenker, "Making Gnutella-like P2P Systems Scalable," *Proceedings of ACM SIGCOMM*, 2003.
[7] Y. Chu, S. G. Rao, and H. Zhang, "A Case for End System Multicast," *Proceedings of ACM SIGMETRICS*, 2000.
[8] Y. Liu, X. Liu, L. Xiao, L. M. Ni, and X. Zhang, "Location-Aware Topology Matching in Unstructured P2P Systems," *Proceedings of IEEE INFOCOM*, 2004.
[9] Y. Liu, L. Xiao, and L. M. Ni, "Building a Scalable Bipartite P2P Overlay Network," *Proceedings of 18th International Parallel and Distributed Processing Symposium (IPDPS)*, 2004.
[10] Y. Liu, Z. Zhuang, L. Xiao, and L. M. Ni, "A Distributed Approach to Solving Overlay Mismatch Problem," *Proceedings of the 24th International Conference on Distributed Computing Systems (ICDCS)*, 2004.
[11] D. A. Menasce and L. Kanchanapalli, "Probabilistic Scalable P2P Resource Location Services," *ACM SIGMETRICS Performance Evaluation Review*, vol. 30, pp. 48-58, 2002.
[12] M. Ripeanu, A. Iamnitchi, and I. Foster, "Mapping the Gnutella Network," *IEEE Internet Computing*, 2002.
[13] Ritter, Why Gnutella Can't Scale. No, Really, http://www.tch.org/gnutella.html
[14] S. Saroiu, K. P.Gummadi, R. J. Dunn, S. D. Gribble, and H. M. Levy, "An Analysis of Internet Content Delivery Systems," *Proceedings of the 5th Symposium on Operating Systems Design and Implementation*, 2002.
[15] S. Sen and J. Wang, "Analyzing Peer-to-peer Traffic Across Large Networks," *Proceedings of ACM SIGCOMM Internet Measurement Workshop*, 2002.
[16] C. Wang, L. Xiao, Y. Liu, and P. Zheng, "Distributed Caching and Adaptive Search in Multilayer P2P Networks," *Proceedings of the 24th International Conference on Distributed Computing Systems (ICDCS)*, 2004.
[17] Z. Xu, C. Tang, and Z. Zhang, "Building Topology-aware Overlays Using Global Soft-state," *Proceedings of the 23rd International Conference on Distributed Computing Systems (ICDCS)*, 2003.

Lookup-Ring: Building Efficient Lookups for High Dynamic Peer-to-Peer Overlays[1]

Xuezheng Liu, Guangwen Yang, Jinfeng Hu, Ming Chen, Yongwei Wu

Department of Computer Science and Techonology
Tsinghua University, Beijing P.R.China
{liuxuezheng00,hujinfeng00,cm01}@mails.tsinghua.edu.cn,
{ygw,wuyw}@tsinghua.edu.cn

Abstract. This paper is motivated by the problem of poor searching efficiency in decentralized peer-to-peer file-sharing systems. We solve the searching problem by considering and modeling the basic trade-off between forwarding queries among peers and maintaining lookup tables in peers, so that we can utilize optimized lookup table scale to minimize bandwidth consumption, and to greatly improve the searching performance under arbitrary system parameters and resource constraints (mainly the available bandwidth). Based on the model, we design a decentralized peer-to-peer searching strategy, namely the Lookup-ring, which provides very efficient keyword searching in high dynamic peer-to-peer environments. The simulation results show that Lookup-ring can easily support a large-scale system with more than 10^6 participating peers at a very small cost in each peer.

1. Introduction

The searching efficiency is a crucial factor for peer-to-peer (P2P) file-sharing systems (Napster [1], Gnutella [2], Kazaa [3]). Although centralized indexing is efficient (e.g. Napster, [1]), it has inherent defects [6] that research communities and internet users turn to decentralized systems, in which searching is performed cooperatively by forwarding queries among peers and use peers' lookup tables (containing replication of items' metadata) to find results (e.g. Gnutella [2], KaZaA [3]). Notable advancements [3, 4, 5, 6, 11, 13] have been made on decentralized searching to improve the performance, however, searching (especially searching by keywords) in decentralized P2P system still remains challenging.

Different from existing approaches which take into account either metadata replication [5, 6, 11, 13] or enhanced queries forwarding [4], in this paper we solve the problem of decentralized searching by simultaneously considering metadata replication and queries, and utilizing optimized lookup tables to minimize bandwidth consumption and greatly improve searching performance. Our concept is as follows: putting more metadata (e.g. file indices) in peers' lookup tables makes queries be resolved more quickly and reduces bandwidth costs on query forwarding; however,

---

[1] Supported by NSFC under Grant No. 60373004, No. 60373005, and 973 project numbered 2003CB3169007

H. Jin et al. (Eds.): NPC 2004, LNCS 3222, pp. 154-166, 2004.

more indices imply that system variations (peers' joining or departure) will cause more corresponding updates for expired metadata and increase bandwidth costs on metadata maintenance. So, there is a basic trade-off between queries and metadata maintenance, and we model this trade-off to find the optimized scales of peers' lookup tables, so as to minimize total bandwidth consumption or maximize searching performance under given environment parameters. In Section II, we propose the model to estimate optimized lookup table scales, and find that both bandwidth consumption and average searching hops can be reduced to $O(N^{1/2})$ (N is the number of peers) in comparison with the $O(N)$ complexity in conventional random walk strategy [5]. Based on the model, we propose a decentralized P2P file-sharing system, the *Lookup-ring*, which implements a general searching strategy with nearly optimal performance under arbitrary system parameters (system scale, magnitude of shared files and frequency for users issuing queries, etc) and resource constraints (mainly the bandwidth constraint in peers). In current Internet environment, Lookup-ring can easily afford a system with more than 10^6 peers where most searching queries are resolved within a few hops.

The rest of paper is organized as follows. Section II gives the model. Section III presents details of Lookup-ring design. Section IV presents performance evaluation. Section V discusses related works and Section VI concludes the paper.

2. Model for Bandwidth and Trade-Off

In this section, we propose an analytic model to estimate bandwidth consumption and describe the trade-off between querying and metadata maintenance. We first define notations in the model (see Table.1). We consider a system consisting of N peers (N is around 10^6) and sharing U unique files (we don't count file replicas in U), denoted by $f_1, f_2, ...f_U$. Each unique file may have some replicas shared by users who download the file. We use r_i to denote the number of f_i's replicas, and TR to denotes the total replica number ($TR = r_1+r_2+...+r_U$). For system variations, the peers' average session time is denoted by $T_{session}$. Based on measurement works [7, 8] we have referenced values of these system parameters, as listed in the Table.1 (these values are only used for reference in the model, not necessary).

Considering that there are totally k_i indices of file f_i in all peers' lookup tables (for $i=1...U$), we call k_i as f_i's "*indexing factor*". The search process is a sequence of probes: when a peer is probed, it attempts to match the query on its local file indices; we assume the searching is perfect and strict, i.e. a query for file f_i can always and only be resolved by a probe to peer containing an index to f_i. For random search process, the *search size* (number of probed peers) for resolving a query of f_i is a random variable, with the expectation equal to N / k_i [13, 4].

Now we present the model. First we estimate bandwidth costs for querying. Unique files have their respective popularities modeled by *query distribution*. Let $q = < q_1, q_2, ...q_U >$ be a vector of probability that sum to 1, where q_i is the probability that a query is for file f_i. Therefore, q is the query distribution [13, 4]. Considering there are totally Q queries submitted per second, the totally bandwidth for querying is:

$$BW_{query} = \sum_{i=1}^{U} Q \cdot q_i \cdot (\frac{N}{k_i}-1) \cdot m_q \tag{1}$$

where m_q is the average size of querying message (bits), and $(N / k_i\text{-}1)$ is the expectation of hops to resolve a query for f_i.

Table 1. Notation and Model Parameters.

Parameter	Meanings	Referenced value
N	Number of peers in the system	10^6
U	Number of unique files	$10 \cdot N = 10^7$
$f_1, f_2, ... f_U$	Unique files shared in the system	
r_i	Number of f_i's replicas	Zipf
TR	Total replica number. $TR = \sum_{i=1}^{U} r_i$	$200 \cdot N = 2 \cdot 10^8$
Q	Number of queries per second	$1/60 \cdot N$
$T_{session}$	Average peers' session time (on-line time)	1 hour
λ_{peer}	Poisson parameter for peer variations	$1/3600$
V_{peer}	Number of peer variatons per second for both join and departure	$\lambda_{peer} \cdot N$
V_{file}	Number of file varations per second for both adding and removing files	$1.74 \times 10^{-3} N$
k_i	Number of indices of f_i	
$q = <q_1, ... q_U>$	Query rate distribution. $\sum_{i=1}^{U} q_i = 1$	$q_i \propto r_i$
m_q, m_p	Average message size for querying and updating expired index	0.5KByte
R_{msg}	For redundant messging: peer receives one updating message for R_{msg} times.	

Second, we estimate the maintenance costs. When replica variation occurs, we need to update the affected indices in lookup tables. So, the bandwidth costs is made up of the following parts: BW_{peer_depart} for updating expired indices pointing to a leaving peer; BW_{peer_join} for a joining peer downloading its lookup tables from others; and BW_{file} for updating lookup tables due to file variations (both sharing new files and removing shared files). We use V_{peer} and V_{file} to denote the variation frequency (time per second) for peer and file respectively. Peer variation are usually modeled with Poisson distribution with parameter $\lambda_{peer} = 1/T_{session}$ [14, 19], and we have $V_{peer} = \lambda_{peer} \cdot N$ for both joins and departures. For V_{file}, in [7] we know the largest number of successful downloaded files per peer per day is no more than 75 files (a very large number), and thus $V_{file} \approx 2 \cdot 75/(24 \times 3600) \cdot N$ for both new downloaded files and removed files. (The model describes stationary system behavior, so we assume number of new files to be approximate equal to deleted files in certain duration.)

Now we calculate maintenance costs. A failure of file replica invalidates all indices pointing to it. These "expired" indices should be updated sooner or later; otherwise the total number of valid indices will decrease. We suppose the indexing assignment has no preference for replicas with higher availability. Thus, for a unique file f_i with r_i replicas and totally k_i indices, one replica failure will averagely cause k_i/r_i expired indices. For BW_{peer_depart}, seeing that departure of a peer P causes failures of all its replicas, for file f_i with r_i replicas the probability that a departing peer P contains f_i is r_i/N. So the expectation of expired indices caused by a peer departure is:

$$\text{expired number} = \sum_{i=1}^{U} \frac{r_i}{N} \cdot \frac{k_i}{r_i} = \sum_{i=1}^{U} \frac{k_i}{N} \tag{2}$$

So, bandwidth consumption for maintaining them is:

$$BW_{\text{peer\_depart}} = \sum_{i=1}^{U} \frac{k_i}{N} \cdot V_{peer} \cdot R_{msg} \cdot m_p \tag{3}$$

where m_p is the average size of updating message. In (3) we use R_{msg} to denote the *redundancy factor of messages*, which indicates that in order to updating a single index, a peer will averagely receive R_{msg} times of the corresponding updating message, each of which has complete updating information (this is defined for non-acknowledged messages. For acknowledged message transmission, R_{msg} is defined as the double value of non-acknowledged case). The R_{msg} is a system parameter to characterize updating algorithm in specific system. To make update tolerant to message lost, some algorithms utilize redundant messaging where peers may receive the same message more than once. In the model we use R_{msg} to reflect this manner.

A peer loses its lookup table after departure, and should download entire table in join time. The average number of indices in lookup table is $\sum_{i=1}^{U} k_i / N$, So:

$$BW_{\text{peer\_join}} = \sum_{i=1}^{U} \frac{k_i}{N} \cdot V_{peer} \cdot m_p \tag{4}$$

For file variations, from above analysis a variation of f_i may generate $k_i/r_i \cdot R_{msg} \cdot m_p$ bandwidth cost for updating indices, so totally bandwidth is:

$$BW_{\text{file}} = V_{file} \cdot R_{msg} \cdot m_p \cdot \sum_{i=1}^{U} \frac{k_i}{r_i} \cdot \frac{r_i}{TR} \tag{5}$$

where TR is total replica number (see Table.1), and the number of variations for f_i is assumed to be proportional to f_i's replicas' number r_i (i.e. number of peers containing f_i). Thus, summate all these cost and we will have the estimation of total bandwidth consumption, as follows:

$$BW_{\text{total}} = BW_{\text{query}} + BW_{\text{peer\_depart}} + BW_{\text{peer\_join}} + BW_{\text{file}} \tag{6}$$

Notice that $\{k_i\}$ are independent, and we can minimize each term of the summation in (6) by choosing the best k_i. The optimized choices of k_i for minimum BW_{total} is:

$$k_i^* = N \cdot \sqrt{\frac{Q}{V_{peer} + R_{msg} \cdot (V_{peer} + N/TR \cdot V_{file})} \cdot \frac{m_q}{m_p} \cdot q_i} = N \cdot \theta \sqrt{q_i} \tag{7}$$

subject to $k_i^* \leq N$ (recall that k_i is the indexing factor of file f_i), where θ is a system parameter independent to i. The minimum BW_{total} is:

$$BW_{\text{total}}^* = BW_{\text{total}}\big|_{k_i = k_i^*, i=1 \cdots U} = \frac{2m_q Q}{\theta} \sum_{i=1}^{U} \sqrt{q_i} \leq \frac{2m_q Q}{\theta} \sqrt{U} \tag{8}$$

where we used Cauchy inequality to the summation. So, the average bandwidth cost in each peer based on k_i^* is:

$$bw_{\text{per peer}} = \frac{BW_{\text{total}}^*}{N} \leq \frac{2m_q}{\theta} \frac{Q}{N} \sqrt{\frac{U}{N}} \cdot \sqrt{N} \quad (9)$$

From (7) the optimized k_i is proportional to the querying rate $q_i^{1/2}$ for each file f_i. It is clear that k_i is a trade-off between querying and maintaining the system, since the numerator $Q \cdot m_q \cdot q_i$ and denominator $(V_{peer}+R_{msg}\cdot(V_{peer}+N/TR\cdot V_{file}))\cdot m_p$ represent cost for queries and maintenance respectively. In (9) we have average bandwidth cost per peer. The Q/N is the number of queries each peer submits to system per second (e.g. 1/60). U/N is also a stationary environment parameter (e.g. 10~20 based on [8]). So, the bandwidth cost per peer is $O(N^{1/2})$ in optimization. Because of the square root, the scalability of system with optimized indexing factor is fairly good. Using practical parameter values in (9), we find the random searching strategy becomes surprisingly powerful under optimized indexing factors (i.e. optimized lookup table scale). For example, for $N=10^6$ peers with only 1 hour session time, using $R_{msg}=5$ (very redundant messaging) and other reference values in Table.1, the optimized strategy can support the heavy queries where each peer submit a query per minute, within only 15Kbps bandwidth per peer (both upstream and downstream). This is a very low bandwidth cost that modem connections can easily afford, and we can even reduce it with more efficient messaging (lower R_{msg}). For comparison, based on report in year 2001 [18], in Gnutella each peer consumes more than 150 Kbps bandwidth both upstream and downstream.

The model illustrates theoretical lower bound of peer consumptions for constructing a lookup system based on random searching process. It shows that with appropriate lookup scales and updating mechanism, a uniform system (i.e. no supernodes) with simple unbiased search is capable to support very large systems. In the following sections we give practical design derived from the model.

3. Design of Lookup-Ring

This section presents design of Lookup-ring Lookup-ring is derived from the model to achieve optimized performance, in which indexing factors is calculated based on equation (7). Lookup-ring is built on top of most structured P2P infrastructures, e.g. Chord, Pastry [9] and SkipNet [20]. In this paper we illustrate how it works on top of Pastry and SkipNet as example. For details of their structures, please refer to [9, 20].

3.1 Indexing Factor and File Levels

Assuming we know the query rate distribution $<q_1,q_2,...q_U>$ (due to limited space, we do not provide estimation of q_i, but only point out it is reasonable to assume q_i to be proportional to replica number r_i), we can obtain best indexing factor k_i^* with (7). We first quantify k_i^* into discrete levels, and files whose k_i^* belong to the same level have the same actual (quantified) indexing factor k_i. The indexing factor is quantified into m levels with radix 2, i.e. we use a set of m kinds of indexing factor values $M=\{N, 2^{-1}\cdot N, 2^{-2}\cdot N, ...,2^{-(m-1)}\cdot N\}$ for all indices. For f_i with k_i^*, the actual indexing factor k_i should be the closest $2^{-j}\cdot N$ in M to k_i^*, and we call f_i as a "j-level" file.

3.2 PeerId, FileId, and Peer Groups

In Lookup-ring, each peer is assigned with a unique and uniformly distributed peerId. We also generate a uniformly distributed fileId for each *unique* file by hash functions. We use peerId to partition peers into groups, and fileId to match unique files with groups.

Peers are partitioned into hierarchical groups as follows. All peers with the same j-bit prefixes in peerIds are united into a j-level group, for $j=0,1,...(m-1)$. A j-level group is denoted by the j-bit common prefix of containing peers. The prefix of a group is also called the group's *groupId*. For example, 010-group is a 3-level group with groupId "010", which consists of all peers with the same 3-bit prefix "010". Due to uniformity of peerIds, a j-level group has approximately $2^{-j} \cdot N$ peers.

Each j-level unique file is matched to one j-level group whose groupId equals to j-bit prefix of the file's fileId. If a file is matched to a group, all peers belong to the group should contain the file's index in their lookup tables. Thus, a peer P with peerId id_P contains indices of all j-level files with fileIds sharing id_P's j-bit prefix, for $j=0$, 1, ..., m, and a j-level file is indexed by approximately $2^{-j} \cdot N$ peers, as our original purpose. Consequently, any query for a j-level file can be resolved by traversing all j-level groups, i.e. forwarding query to 2^j peers with different j-bit peerId prefixes. If doing so, we also obtain all unique files with file level less than j. Therefore, we can resolve any query by traveling $2^{-(m-1)} \cdot N$ peers with different $(m-1)$-bit prefixes.

Since Lookup-ring is built on top of structured P2P infrastructure, the peer partitioning ought to be consonant with underlying peer organization, and peerId should have ability to partition peer into groups in DHT organization. If Lookup-ring is built on Pastry, we use Pastry's nodeId as peerId in Lookup-ring, because in Pastry's organization the nodeIds plays the role of partitioning nodes into prefex-based groups.[2] The peer groups and file levels are shown in Fig.1.

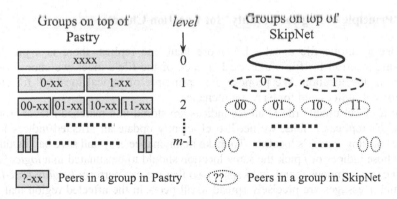

Fig. 1. Partition on top of Pastry and SkipNet.

---

[2] Other P2P infrastructures (e.g. chord) also have similar nodeId playing the partitioning role. For SkipNet, note that it is a "bi-id" system whose NameId indicates proximity between nodes while NumericId partition nodes into hierarchical rings. So, we use SkipNet's NumericId as the peerId in Lookup-ring.

3.3 Searching in Lookup-Ring

Lookup-ring provides searching by keywords and substrings. Each unique file is associated with a "label" for searching, e.g. the filename. Each file index defines a match between a unique file's label and location of *one of* the file's replicas. Thus, a file index contains the file label, IP of location. We also store the file's fileId and location's peerId in the index. For 20~30-byte file label, we need only about 64-byte file index. Based on the model, each peer of a 10^6-peered system needs to contain about 10^4 indices, and the lookup table size is no more than 1Mbyte.

Lookup-ring has a "*prefix-traversing*" searching strategy. Consider a query q submitted in peer P_0. We first check P_0's lookup table to see whether q could be resolved locally. Here we obtain all 0-level results of q. If q is satisfied (i.e. get enough results) we stop searching, otherwise q is forwarded to a peer P_1 which has a different 1-bit prefix with P_0. From both P_0 and P_1 we can find all 1-level results of q, because P_0 and P_1 represent all 1-level groups. If still unresolved, we keep up this prefix-traversing. In general, before the j-th step q has been forwarded to $2^{(j-1)}$ peers $\{P_0, P_1, ...P_{2^{\wedge}(j-1)-1}\}$ with the peerIds covering all $(j-1)$-bit prefixes. In the j-th step we forward q to another $2^{(j-1)}$ peers namely $P_{2^{\wedge}(j-1)},...P_{2^{\wedge}j-1}$, so that j-bit peerId prefixes of all searched peers $\{P_0, P_1, ...P_{2^{\wedge}j-1}\}$ have covered all the j-bit prefixes. After that, we have traversed all groups with no more than j levels and found all results whose levels are no more than j. The searching process stops either query is resolved or we reach the last level ((m-1)-level) when all unique files' indices has been searched.

Due to the consistency of Lookup-ring' peerId with underlying DHT, it is very easy to perform prefix-traversing searching, because it is a natural property of most DHTs to perform such prefix-traversing [16]. Therefore, searching in Lookup-ring is very efficient without redundant query forwarding.

3.4 "Principle of Logical Locality" for Location Choices

Because a unique file usually has more than one replica, there is a problem for choosing location for file's indices. For each of the file's index we choose *only one* replica as the location. We propose our "principle of logical locality" for choosing locations of indices and for easy maintenance.

For a j-level unique file f_i, all f_i's indices are stored in a matched j-level group g. If one of f_i's replicas P fails, we need to efficiently update all affected indices in g, i.e. indices picking P as f_i's location. To make maintenance easy and save bandwidth, peers in g whose indices of f pick the same location should to be situated in a *logical locality* in g (i.e. a continuous region is id-space), so that we can perform *locality-based update* in which messages are precisely spread to all peers in the affected region that exactly "need" the update, while other peers will not receive the message. For this purpose, we use "*principle of logical locality*" to choose location for each index, i.e., *when chooses the location for an index of a unique file, a peer should always pick the logically "closest" replica of that file*. In other words, location in peer's index should always be the living replica which is current the closest one to the peer in logical distance. The goal of maintenance is to keep this invariance after system variations.

Similar to the peerId, here the "locality" should also be consonant with underlying peer organization to facilitate updating algorithm. In Pastry, both locality and peer portioning is based on Pastry's nodeId. Thus, we ask each Lookup-ring peer to choose the replica whose peerId is currently the closest one. Obviously this design fits all fundamental considerations of our design, e.g., locality-based updating, since peers choosing the same location of a file are logically adjacent in DHT's id-space. However, from Fig.1 and Fig.2 the replica locations being chosen in a certain group are not uniformly distributed, since peerIds in a group have a common prefix and do not fill in peerId-space where replicas' peerIds scatter themselves. So, we can extend this approach to get better uniformity of choosing locations (this extension is not necessary to Lookup-rings). We first map peerIds of replicas into the group with linear transformation before using principle of locality. For a j-level file f matched to a j-level group g with j-bit groupId id_g, we map all peerIds of f's replicas into g by right-shifting them by j-bits and add j-bit prefix id_g. After this linear transformation, replicas' mapped peerIds are uniformly distributed in g while also keep their primary order. Then, peer in g picks the replica of f whose mapped peerId is the closest one. Fig.2 shows this mapping, and in Fig.2 the I, II, and III are the three sections in the group (i.e. locality) which consist of peers choosing replica a, b, and c as the location of index, respectively. When variation occurs (e.g. b suddenly fails), peers in section II should be updated with new replica locations. Based on the principle, section II is then divided into I' and III' which should update their locations with a and c, and be merged into I and III, respectively. The boundaries of I' and III' can be determined only with peerId of a, b and c (the boundary between I' and III' has the equivalent distance to peerId(a) and peerId(c)). So, after b's failure we have the following update strategy: b's neighbor replica a and c find b's failure (how they find the failure is explained in Section 3.5), send their locations and boundaries of I' and III' to two certain peers in I' and III' correspondingly (the dashed lines in Fig.2), and these peers spread received messages in I' and III' for updating all other peers in the either locality. When b joins there's a similar process: b calculates section II's boundaries from a's and c's locality and spread updating message in II.[3]

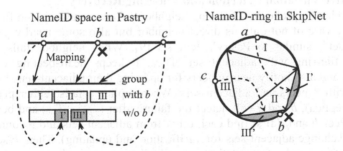

Fig. 2. Principle of locality in Lookup-ring, and the updates of indices after variation

---

[3] In SkipNet the logical locality is defined by NameId rather than NumericId, because in each SkinNet-ring the sequence and neighborhood of peers are indicated by NameId. So, on top of SkipNet we use NameIds of replicas to determine the sections and guide location choosing. Fig.2 shows one group (i.e. a SkipNet-ring) and its sections based on replicas' NameIds.

3.5 Maintaining Lookup-Ring

For maintenance, we should actively detect variations and update affected indices. We construct *file-ring* in Lookup-ring, where all replicas of a unique file connect to form a ring structure and keep connections with heart-beating messages, so that variations can be soon detected. After that, the detector generates an appropriate update immediately.

3.5.1 File-Rings

A file-ring is shown in Fig.3. Consider a certain unique file f_i with r replicas stored in r peers. These peers are connected into a ring structure (file-ring), ordered with logical locality in DHT, namely $P_1, P_2, \ldots P_r$ (logical locality is defined in last Section). Peers participating in a file-ring should hold the links to its two neighbors (predecessor and successor in ring) and send "heart-beating" messages to them every T_{probe} of time to maintain connectivity. A peer may participate in many file-rings according to its shared unique files.

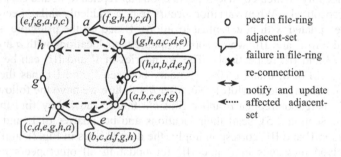

Fig. 3. Maintaining file-ring connectivity

3.5.2 Active Variation Detection and File-Ring Recovery

Peers periodically probe their file-ring neighbors. To reconnect broken file-ring, peers should be aware of not only its direct neighbor but also some nearby peers, namely "adjacent-set", similar to Pastry's leaf set [9]. When neighbor fails, a peer can reconnect file-ring with adjacent set. Then, it keeps heart-beating with its new neighbors, and also notify nearby peers for updating their adjacent-sets. Fig.3 shows a file-ring with 8 peers and adjacent-sets. When replica c fails (either peer failure or dropping replica), b and d will detect the failure after $(T_{probe}+T_{out})$ and begin to repair file-ring. Peer b and d first find each other from adjacent-sets and reconnect file-ring (b and d exchange adjacent-sets for verification and updating). Then, b sends its new adjacent-set to a and h for updating expired adjacent-sets in them, and d also updates e's and f's adjacent-sets. For replica c joining file-ring, a similar procedure is performed that b and d receive the joining request, break their interconnection and turn to keep the connection with c, and notify a, h and e, f for updating adjacent-sets.

We set the T_{probe} as 60 seconds and keep 16 peers in the adjacent-set. For variation, each detector notifies 7 peers in its side, with an acknowledged messaging.

3.5.3   Updating Lookup Tables After System Variations

Replicas in file-ring are ranged by logical locality; therefore the two detectors of replica failure are exactly the two replicas whose locations should be used to update expired indices. Thus, in Fig.2 peer a and c will detect b's failure within $(T_{probe}+T_{out})$ due to file-ring heartbeat messaging. After that, a and c calculate their respective updating sections (i.e. I' and III'), and each of them immediately sends an update message to *one peer* in corresponding section for maintaining lookup tables, via underlying P2P routing. The update message contains the new location of replica (a or c), the fileId of the unique file, and boundaries of section inside of which the message should be spread. The peer receiving the updating message then spreads it to entire updating section in the file's group, by way of message broadcasting algorithm in the underlying structured peer organization.

In detail, most DHTs can perform *locality-based message broadcasting* as a basic service, i.e. broadcasting messages to all peers in a consecutive section based on its logical locality in a partitioned group [16]. Lookup-ring utilizes DHT-based broadcasting for spreading its update messages, following the algorithm proposed in [16]. On top of Pastry (and Chord, etc), we can derive from the routing tables a spanning tree for an arbitrary nodeId section (rooted by any peer in the section). Via broadcasting the first peer can spread the update information to all other M peers in the section through exactly $(M-1)$ messages [16]. This broadcast has no message redundancy that each peer receives the needed message exactly once. So, the R_{msg} in the model (see Section.2) should be 1. To further guarantee the update, we use confirmed messaging that all updating messages should be acknowledged. If an acknowledgement is not received within a timeout period the message is retransmitted. Therefore, considering both acknowledgement and redundancy during broadcast, the message redundancy factor R_{msg} in our model should be 2 for Pastry.[4]

4.   Performance Evaluation

We perform our evaluation of Lookup-ring with simulations. We run our simulator on Linux running on Pentium IV CPU with 2G memory, which can support more 10^4 simulated peers. We construct and evaluate Lookup-ring on top of SkipNet. We implement SkipNet based on [20], using basic type of SkipNet with only R-table and density parameter k equal to 2. For shared files, the unique file number is 10 times of the peer number and the total file number is 200 times of peer number, derived from [8, 7]. The simulation has two aspects. First we examined feasibility and efficiency of Lookup-ring by simulating environments with different peer numbers and peer availabilities, in order to see bandwidth cost in each peer to support a heavy query load (one query per peer per minute). Second, we compared Lookup-ring with random walks searching [5] in order to see how much improvement we have gained. We are mostly concerned about the following two metrics: the average search size (in hop number), and the maximum query workload under a fixed bandwidth. The former indicates how quickly a query is resolved, and the latter shows system scalability.

---

[4] On top of SkipNet there's a slight difference that the derived spanning tree has some redundancy, where each peer will averagely receive an updating message for 1.5 times, and R_{msg} should be 3 for confirmed messaging. Here we omit the discussions and readers can refer to [12] for details.

Fig.4.a shows the messages and bandwidth consumptions for each peer in supporting one query per peer per minute, under different peer availability ($T_{session}$) and system scale (number of total peers). If m_q and m_q is both 1Kbit message on average, the values in y-axis of Fig.4.a is also the needed bandwidth for each peer. We can see the trend of bandwidth consumptions when enlarge system scale, which is roughly in proportion with the *square root* of peer number, e.g. when expand peer number for 10 times from 10^3 to 10^4, the bandwidth increase from 0.36 to 1.42 Kbps (i.e. 3.9 times, nearly $10^{1/2}$) for 1.5 hours online time ($T_{session}$=5400s). From this trend, we can deduce that for 10^6 peers, the bandwidth is nearly 10 times of the case with 10^4 peers, i.e. nearly 16Kbps for $T_{session}$=3600s and 12Kbps for $T_{session}$=7200s, in both upstream and downstream. This result shows very good scalability for large systems.

Fig.4.b is the average search size of Lookup-ring and random walk. The results demonstrate the improvement of search size in our strategy. In 10^4 peers, the search size is only 1/40 of random walk. This outperforming becomes more remarkable when peer number N grows, since we have $O(N^{1/2})$ search size while random walk is nearly $O(N)$.

Fig.4.c is the comparison of maximum supported query workload under different bandwidth. We compare Lookup-ring with random walk in system of 5000 and 10000 peers (T_{sesson}=3600s), with 1Kbit querying messages. From the results we also see that Lookup-ring greatly overcome the Gnutella-like system, esp. when system scale grows. The reason is because by using adaptive indices, we significantly save query hops and simultaneously constrain the maintenance cost to a low level.

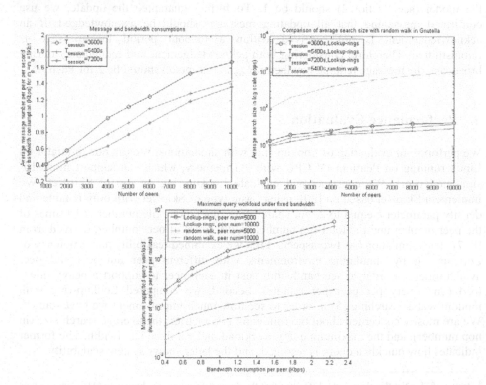

Fig. 4. Performance evaluation. a) up-left. b) up-right. c). bottom.

5. Related Works

To improve searching efficiency, researches try to exploit all aspects of typical query-based decentralized searching. In strategy of forwarding queries, [5] propose to replace flooding-based query-forwarding with random walks, so that network traffic is reduced. [4] further exploit data correlations and user interests to guide forwarding directions and improve searching performance. Instead of [4], Lookup-ring doesn't need specific data correlations, and thus is suitable for more applications. In the aspect of local lookup tables, results caching [11] and supernode [3] are employed. [13] suggests replicating files in accordance with their query rates, so that the expectation of searching size is optimized. In comparison, Lookup-ring has fully controlled and optimized caching (the indices), and doesn't need supernode. Recently, researchers present to employ biased overlay topology towards peers with larger lookup tables, and Gia in [6] is an integrative design combining many above features. For DHT-based approaches, most DHTs support only precise search with precise resource ID, while the others have very limited capability in keyword search [6, 17]. Lookup-ring uses DHT as underlying organization for system maintenance, and the efficient keyword search is built on a higher level.

6. Conclusions

Our contribution is in the following aspects. First, we propose an analytic model to describe trade-off between query and maintenance, based on which the optimized lookup table scales can be estimated. Second, we design a efficient decentralized P2P searching strategy, where there are no supernodes and all peers are utilized uniformly. Third, we demonstrate the maximum query load and system scale that an unbiased decentralized P2P system can support. We show that unbiased decentralized P2P system can achieve a heave query load in a large-scale system, with low peer costs.

Reference

[1]   Napster, the napster homepage. In http://www.napster.com/
[2]   Gnutella, In http://www.gnutella.com
[3]   KaZaA, file sharing network. In http://www.kazaa.com
[4]   E. Cohen, A. Fiat, and H. Kaplan. Associative Search in Peer to Peer Networks: Harnessing Latent Semantics. In Proceedings of the IEEE INFOCOM'03 Conference. 2003
[5]   Q, Lv, P. Cao, E. Cohen, K. Li, S. Shenker. Search and Replication in Unstructured Peer-to-Peer Networks . In Proceedings of 16th ACM International Conference on Supercomputing (ICS'02), 2002.
[6]   Y. Chawathe, S. Ratnasamy, L. Breslau, N Lanham, S. Shenker. Making Gnutella-like P2P Systems Scalable, In Proceeding of ACM Sigcomm'03
[7]   S. Saroiu, P. K. Gummadi, S. D. Gribble. A Measurement Study of Peer-to-Peer File Sharing Systems. In Proceedings of Multimedia Computing and Networking 2002 (MMCN'02), CA, Jan. 2002.

[8] J. Chu, K. Labonte, and B. Levine. Availability and locality measurements of peer-to-peer file systems. In Proceedings of ITCom: Scalability and Traffic Control in IP Networks, July 2002.

[9] A. Rowstron and P. Druschel. Pastry: Scalable, decentralized object location, and routing for large-scale peer-to-peer systems. In IFIP/ACM Middleware, Nov. 2001.

[10] J. Wang. Gnutella bandwidth usage. Nov. 2001. https://resnet.utexas.edu/trouble/p2p-gnutella.html.

[11] B. Bhattacharjee, et al. Efficient Peer-To-Peer Searches Using Result-Caching, In IPTPS'03

[12] X. Z Liu, J. F. Hu, D. X. Wang. Lookup-Rings: Building Efficient Lookups for High Dynamic Peer-to-peer Overlays. In http://166.111.68.162/granary/index.htm

[13] E. Cohen and S. Shenker. Replication strategies in unstructured Peer-to-Peer networks. In Proceedings of the ACM SIGCOMM'02 Conference. 2002

[14] A. Gupta, B. Liskov, R. Rodrigues. One Hop Lookups for Peer-to-Peer Overlays. In HotOS IX, 2003

[15] I. Gupta, K. Birman, P. Linga, A. Demers, and R. van R. Kelips: Building an efficient and stable P2P DHT through increased memory and background overhead. In IPTPS, 2003.

[16] S El-Ansary, L Alima, P. Brand, S. Haridi: Efficient broadcast in structured P2P networks. In IPTPS'03.

[17] M. Harren, J. M. Hellerstein, R. Huebsch. Complex queries in DHT-based P2P Networks. In IPTPS'01.

[18] J. Wang. Gnutella bandwidth usage. Nov. 2001. https://resnet.utexas.edu/trouble/p2p-gnutella.html.

[19] Z. Ge, D. R. Figueiredo, S. Jaiswal, J. Kurose, D. Towsley. Modeling Peer-Peer File Sharing Systems. In Proceedings of IEEE INFOCOM'03, 2003

[20] N. J. A. Harvey, M. B. Jones, S. Saroiu, M. Theimer, and A. Wolman. SkipNet: A Scalable Overlay Network with Practical Locality Properties. In Proceedings of 4th USITS, Mar. 2003.

Layer Allocation Algorithms in Layered Peer-to-Peer Streaming

Yajie Liu, Wenhua Dou, and Zhifeng Liu

School of Computer Science,
National University of Defense Technology, ChangSha, 410073, China
liu_lyj@hotmail.com

Abstract. In layered peer-to-peer streaming, as the bandwidth and data availability (number of layers received) of each peer node are constrained and heterogeneous, the media server can still become overloaded, and the streaming qualities of the receiving nodes may also be constrained for the limited number of supplying peers. This paper identifies these issues and presents two layer allocation algorithms, which aim at the two scenarios of the available bandwidth between the media server and the receiving node, to reach either or two of the goals: 1) minimize the resource consumption of the media server, 2) maximize the streaming qualities of the receiving nodes. Simulation results demonstrate the efficiencies of the proposed algorithms.

1 Introductions

Peer-to-peer streaming is cost-effective for it can capitalize the resources of peer nodes to provide service to other receivers. In general, there exist three properties on peers: 1) peer's outbound bandwidth or the bandwidth it willing to contribute is limited, there always need multiple supplying peers cooperate to serve a requesting node, 2) different peer nodes can receive and process different levels of streaming qualities, which means their data availabilities as supplying peers are also heterogeneous and constrained, 3) peers' inbound and outbound bandwidths are also heterogeneous. Layered peer-to-peer streaming has the potential to address the issues of heterogeneities, but under it there also exist some factors such as the available outbound bandwidths of peers are less than their inbound bandwidths, the number of supplying peers is limited to the receiver sometimes, the data availabilities(number of layers received) are constrained and so on, these factors can lead two results, 1) the media streaming server can still become overloaded when the system is in large scale, 2) the receiver's streaming quality may also be constrained with limited heterogeneous supplying nodes.

We identify these issues and present a layer allocation framework which contains two layer allocation algorithms. Concerning the available bandwidth between the media server and a receiver, there exist two scenarios, 1) sufficient available bandwidth, which means all the expected layers of the receiver can be solely provided by the media server, and a layer allocation algorithm is presented to minimize the resource consumption of the media server while satisfying the streaming quality of the receiver, 2) insufficient available bandwidth,

H. Jin et al. (Eds.): NPC 2004, LNCS 3222, pp. 167–174, 2004.

which means the receiver's expected layers can not solely be provided by the media server, and another layer allocation algorithm is presented to maximize the streaming quality of the receiver. Either of the algorithms is executed on the receiver side, and we only focus on the situation that a receiver has one or more candidate supplying peer nodes besides the media server, otherwise the receiver's streaming quality will only be determined by the available bandwidth between the server and the receiver, here we don't discuss it for the simplicity. In addition, we suppose that each peer node can cache all the layers that it has received and each receiving node can identify the available bandwidths between it and the candidate supplier nodes, and these available bandwidths keep unchanged without the failures of the supplier nodes.

There has been related work on layered peer-to-peer streaming. For example, [1] proposed a framework for quality adaptive playback of layered media streaming, the data allocation granularity of it was based on data packets, and ours is based on layers. To our knowledge, the most closely related work is [2], and the main differences between it and this paper include, 1) this paper presents an improved layer allocation algorithmin compares to [2], in the scenario of sufficient and with the assumption that the layer rates are heterogeneous; 2) in addition, this paper discusses and formalizes the problem in the scenario of insufficient which is not mentioned in [2], and present a heuristic layer allocation algorithm.

2   System Model and Layer Allocation Algorithms

Let p denote a receiving node, p_0 denote the media server, $l_1, l_2, \ldots, l_l$ denote the layers of the stream that p will request, with l_1 as the base layer and others as the enhancement layers, these layers are accumulative, i.e., l_i can be only decoded if layers l_1 through l_{i-1} are available. Let r_i denote the streaming rate of l_i and the layer rates are heterogeneous, $L = \{l_1, l_2, \ldots, l_m\}$ $(m \le l)$ denote the expected layer set that p expects to receive according to its inbound bandwidth and the layer rates. Let $P = \{p_1, p_2, \ldots, p_n\}$ denote the candidate supplying peer node set of p, $b(p_j, p)\,(0 \le j \le n)$ denote the available bandwidth between p_j and p, a_i denote the number of layers that p_i has cached, $x_{i,j}$ denote whether l_i will be provided by p_j, if will then assigned to 1 otherwise assigned to 0. Let $L(p_j)$ denote a subset of L where the layers are provided by p_j.

2.1   The Scenario of Sufficient

In this scenario, the goal of the layer allocation problem is to maximally save the resource consumption of the server. We can formalize this problem as follows:

$$Maximiz \sum_{i=1}^{m} \sum_{j=1}^{n} x_{i,j} * r_j \qquad (1)$$

$$Subject\ to \sum_{j=0}^{n} x_{i,j} = 1, \quad i = 1, 2, \ldots, m \qquad (2)$$

$$\sum_{i=1}^{m} x_{i,j} r_i \leq b(p_j, p), \quad j = 1, 2, \ldots, n \tag{3}$$

$$x_{i,j} * i \leq a_j \, . \ i = 1, 2, \ldots, m, \quad j = 1, 2, \ldots, n \tag{4}$$

Formulation (1) indicates that the goal is to maximally allocate the expected layers to the peer set P. Equation (2) indicates each layer can only be allocated to a candidate supplier. Inequation (3) indicates the sum rate of the layers that allocated to a peer node can not exceed the available bandwidth between the peer node and p. Inequality (4) indicates the layers that a peer can provide can not exceed what it has cached.

From the formulations (1)-(4) we can see that this optimal allocation problem belongs to the integer programming (IP) problems, it is NP-Hard for these constraints especially each variable $x_{i,j}$ must be 0 or 1. Here we present an approximation algorithm for this problem which includes three steps: 1) relax the integrality of each $x_{i,j}$, and thus make the IP problem become a linear programming (LP) problem, 2) solve the LP problem by a maximum flow algorithm on a constructed directed graph, 3) adjust the flow value on the graph until each $x_{i,j}$ becomes 0 or 1. Next we will describe this approximation algorithm in details.

We first relax the integrality of each variable $x_{i,j}$ and make this optimization problem become a LP problem. As the dimension of the matrix that corresponding to the LP problem's constraints is large, here we don't try to solve it using the traditional simplex or dual-simplex algorithms, but convert it to a maximum flow problem on a directed graph $G(V, E)$. $G(V, E)$ is constructed as follows: the vertex set $V = L \cup P \cup \{s, t\}$ where s is the source, t is the sink, L and P keep the meanings mentioned above; for each l_i, direct an arc from s to l_i, its capacity is assigned r_i; for each l_i and each p_j, if p_j has cached l_i and $b(p_j, p)$ is not less than r_i, then direct an arc $e(l_i, p_j)$ with capacity r_i from l_i to p_j; for each p_j, direct an arc form p_j to t, its capacity is assigned $b(p_j, p)$. From $G(V, E)$'s construction, we can conclude that the maximum sum rate of the layers that allocated to the peers in P can not exceed the maximum flow value through $G(V, E)$.

Definition 1. *To any arc $e(l_i, p_j)$ that belongs to $\{e(l_i, p_j) | 1 \leq i \leq m, \ 1 \leq j \leq n\}$ of $G(V, E)$, if the flow value on $e(l_i, p_j)$ equals to r_i or 0, then call this arc an integral arc, otherwise a fractional arc.*

After constructing the directed graph, the next step of the algorithm is to calculate the maximum flow on $G(V, E)$, here we use the classical algorithm *MPM* [3] to calculate the maximum flow and let $w(l_i, p_j)$ denote the flow value on $e(l_i, p_j)$. After this calculation each variable $x_{i,j}$ is assigned to $w(l_i, p_j)/r_i$. If $x_{i,j}$ equals to 1, then add l_i to the set $L(p_j)$. If each arc of $\{e(l_i, p_j) | 1 \leq i \leq m, \ 1 \leq j \leq n\}$ is integral at this time, then end this algorithm for it has got an optimal allocation result; otherwise further adjust the flow on $G(V, E)$ as follows.

Construct a edge-induced subgraph $G(V', E')$ of $G(V, E)$, $G(V', E')$ is induced by those fractional arcs from the arc set $\{e(l_i, p_j) | 1 \leq i \leq m, \ 1 \leq j \leq n\}$ of $G(V, E)$, all parameters on these arcs are kept unchanged in the construction.

Definition 2. *To any vertex that belonging to P of $G(V', E')$, if a vertex's in-degree equals to 1, then call this vertex a singleton vertex.*

Repeat the following substeps until all the arcs of $G(V', E')$ are removed: if there does not exist any singleton vertex, then adjust the flow according to the rounding rule 1, else adjust the flow according to the rounding rule 2.

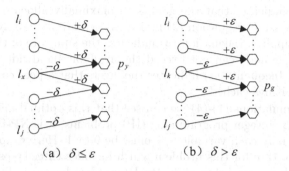

(a) $\delta \leq \varepsilon$ (b) $\delta > \varepsilon$

Fig. 1. The flow adjustment on $G(V', E')$

Rounding rule 1: Ignore the edge directions of $G(V', E')$ and find a longest path on $G(V', E')$. As at this time there does not exist any singleton vertex, the two end vertices of the longest path must belong to L, otherwise leads a contradiction. Suppose the two end vertices of the longest path are l_i and l_j, denote the longest path as $l_i \sim l_j$. Let δ denote the minimum flow value of all the arcs comprised in $l_i \sim l_j$, $e(l_x, p_y)$ denote the arc whose flow value equals to δ on $l_i \sim l_j$. Let ε denote the minimum remaining capacity of all the arcs comprised in $l_i \sim l_j$, and $e(l_k, p_g)$ denote the arc whose remaining capacity equals to ε on $l_i \sim l_j$. Execute either the following branches on $l_i \sim l_j$: (i) If $\delta \leq \varepsilon$, adjust the flow as illustrated in Fig.1(a), we can see that the flow value on the arc $e(l_x, p_y)$ will become zero, which means at least an arc $(e(l_x, p_y))$ will become an integral arc after this type adjustment; (ii) if $\delta > \varepsilon$, adjust the flow as illustrated in Fig.1(b), we can see that the flow value on the arc $e(l_k, p_g)$ will equal to its capacity, which means at least an arc $(e(l_k, p_g))$ will become an integral arc after this type adjustment. At last remove some arcs of $G(V', E')$ as follows: to each arc (suppose $e(l_u, p_v)$) of the path $l_i \sim l_j$, if its flow value equals to zero, then remove it from $G(V', E')$; if its flow value equals to its capacity, then add l_u to $L(p_v)$, remove all the arcs that associated with l_u. We can see after the above adjustments, the flow value through each $p_j (1 \leq j \leq n)$ keeps unchanged, the flow value on each arc does not exceed its capacity.

Rounding rule 2: Select a existent singleton vertex on $G(V', E')$, suppose it is p_j. p_j's single neighbor vertex must belong to L, suppose it is l_i. Remove all arcs that associated with l_i, add l_i to $L(p_j)$, construct a subset of $L(p_j)$ that the layer's sum rate of this subset does not exceed the available bandwidth $b(p_j, p)$ but is nearest to $b(p_j, p)$, substitute this subset for $L(p_j)$.

The maximum flow on $G(V, E)$ can be computed in $0(|V|^3)$ time. At least an arc will be removed in either the rounding rules, and there at most exist

$m * n$ arcs on $G(V', E')$, so this layer allocation algorithm is a polynomial time algorithm.

2.2 The Scenario of Insufficient

In this scenario, as the receiving node's expected layers can not solely be supplied by the media server, the goal of the layer allocation algorithm is to maximize the streaming quality of the receiving node. Considering that a layer l_i can only be decoded if layers l_1 through l_{i-1} are available, we first define a special layer subset of L before formalize the allocation goal of this scenario.

Definition 3. *Suppose S is a subset of L, we call S a prefixed-subset of L if and only if the following condition satisfied: if layer $l_i(1 \le i \le m)$ belongs to S, then all the layer(s) $\{l_j | 1 \le j < i\}$ must also belong to S.*

Suppose S is a prefixed-subset of L to be constructed, the allocation goal can be formalized as

$$Maximize\ |S| \tag{5}$$

$$Subject\ to\ \sum_{j=0}^{n} x_{i,j} = 1,\ i : l_i \in S \tag{6}$$

$$\sum_{i:l_i \in S} x_{i,j} r_i \le b(p_j, p),\ j = 0, 2, \ldots, n \tag{7}$$

$$x_{i,j} * i \le a_j\ .\ i = 1, 2, \ldots, m,\quad j = 1, 2, \ldots, n \tag{8}$$

Formulation (5) indicates the goal is to maximize the size of S, which means to maximize the receiver's streaming quality by optimally allocating layers to the candidate supplying node set $P \cup \{p_0\}$. Equation (6) indicates each layer in S must be allocated to a node of $P \cup \{p_0\}$. The meanings of the formulation (7) and (8) are similar to the meanings of the formulation (3) and (4).

Theorem 1. *The optimal layer allocation problem in the scenario of insufficient is NP-Hard.*

Proof: Consider a decision problem that corresponds to the optimal layer allocation problem in the scenario of insufficient. Regard any prefixed-subset $L' = \{l_1, l_2, ..., l_k\}(k \le m)$ of L as an item set, each item l_i is associated with a size r_i; regard the candidate supplier set $P \cup \{p_0\}$ as a bin set, each bin $p_j(0 \le j \le n)$ is associated with a capacity $b(p_j, p)$; for the simplicity let $a_1 = a_2 = ... = a_n = m$ which means any item is allowed to be placed into any bin. Then the decision problem can be described as: if all the items of L' can be put into the bin set $P \cup \{p_0\}$ while the sum size of the item(s) that placed into each bin does not exceed the bin's capacity. As the 3-partition problem can be regarded as a special case of this decision problem and the 3-partition problem is NP-Complete [6], so the above decision problem is NP-Complete, and the corresponding optimal layer allocation problem is NP-Hard.

Here we propose an heuristic algorithm (Fig.2) for this optimization problem, its main idea is to allocate the layers from the base layer to the enhancement layers in turn and allocate each layer to a best suitable supplier. The algorithm's complexity is $0(mn)$.

1. let $U \leftarrow \Phi$, $L(p_j) \leftarrow \Phi$ $(0 \leq j \leq n)$;
2. for $i \leftarrow 1$ to m do
3.   for $j \leftarrow 0$ to n do
4.   if $a_j \geq i$ and $b(p_j,p) \geq r_i$ then $U \leftarrow U + \{p_j\}$;
5.   end for
6.   if $|U| = 0$ then
7.   return $i - 1$ and exit; /* $i - 1$ is the number of allocated layers */
8.   if $|U| = 1$ then /* suppose U equals to $\{p_j\}$*/
9. $L(p_j) \leftarrow L(p_j) + \{l_i\}$, $b(p_j,p) \leftarrow b(p_j,p) - r_i$;
10.   if $|U| > 1$ then
11.   select the supplier(s) that with the least available bandwidth to p ;
12.   if multiple such suppliers exist, then
13.   select a supplier which cached the least number of the layers;
14.   if the selected supplier is p_j then
15. $L(p_j) \leftarrow L(p_j) + \{l_i\}$, $b(p_j,p) \leftarrow b(p_j,p) - r_i$;
16.   let $U \leftarrow \Phi$;
17. end for

Fig. 2. The heuristic algorithm to maximize a receiver's streaming quality

2.3   Fault-Tolerance Mechanism

Node departures can happen frequently in peer-to-peer community. Our fault-tolerance mechanism that adapts to this can be described as follows: when a receiving node detects that a supplying node has ceased to provide the media data, it sends a request to the media server and tries to get the missing layers from it; if the receiving node's request can be satisfied by the media server, then it will get the missing layers from the media server; otherwise, on the side of the receiving node the algorithm that described in Section 2.2 will be executed to reallocate the layers to the candidate suppliers thus try to maximize the receiving node's streaming quality.

3   Simulation Results

In this section, we present simulation results to evaluate the performance of the proposed algorithms. A 6-layered encoding mode whose layer rates are from 64kbps to 192kbps and a 10-layered encoding mode whose layers rates are from 64kbps to 128kbps are used in the simulation, both with the sum rate 768kbps (denoted as R_0). The topology used in the simulation has three levels: the first two levels are generated using the GT-ITM Generator [5] which contain 400 routers, and 1000 host nodes are attached to the stub routers as the lowest level. The media server is attached to a transit router. The link bandwidths of the first level are assigned 100M, and are chosen in the range [1M, 10M] of the second level. The available inbound bandwidths of nodes are distributed in the range [128K, 1M], the outbound bandwidth that each node willing to contribute is distributed in the range $[0.1R_0, 0.6R_0]$ which reflects the diversity in the P2P community [4].

As [2] had proposed a greedy layer allocation algorithm which had the similar goal and assumptions to the algorithm presented in Section 2.1, and in the simulation we will compare the performance of the two algorithms, and name the algorithm in [2] as $GEBALAM$(GrEed Based Approximation Layer Allocation algorithM) and ours as $FABALAM$ (Flow Adjustment Based Approximation Layer Allocation algorithM) in the simulation.

A experiment is simulated as follows with first setting a lower-limit: each node joins the system by submitting a request to the server in random order; the server constructs a candidate supplying peer set P as a response to a request that received according the statuses of peers that have joined, each peer in P can at least supply a expected layer of the requesting node; if the size of P is larger than the lower-limit setting, then P and p_0 will be returned to the requesting node, and either of the algorithms presented in this paper will be executed on the requesting node side according to either the scenarios; otherwise only p_0 is returned and the requesting node will begin to get data from p_0; each node will become a peer node when it begins to receive the media data; after all nodes have joined the system, we repeat the above procedure but substitute the algorithm $GEBALAM$ for $FABALAM$. Each experiment is performed 10 times, and the simulation results are averaged over all results.

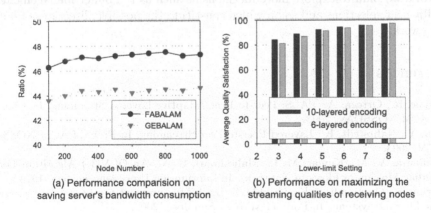

(a) Performance comparision on saving server's bandwidth consumption

(b) Performance on maximizing the streaming qualities of receiving nodes

Fig. 3. Performance of the proposed algorithms

Fig.3(a) shows the performance comparison results on saving the server's bandwidth consumption of the two algorithms with the lower-limit 6 and the 10-

layered encoding mode. The axis x denotes the number of nodes that have joined the system. The y axis denotes the ratio of the server's bandwidth consumption to the sum of the bandwidths that consumed by the joined nodes. It shows that our proposed algorithm can save more bandwidth consumption (2%~3%) of the media server than the corresponding greedy algorithm proposed in [2].

Define a metric *streaming quality satisfaction* as the ratio of the sum rate of the layers that a node actually receives to the sum rate of its expected layers. We select these allocation samples in each experiment where the available bandwidth between a receiving node and the media server is insufficient and let the average streaming quality satisfaction of all the samples to denote the performance of the algorithm that presented in Section 2.2. From Fig.3(b) it can be seen that the streaming qualities of these receiving nodes keep at high levels, furthermore, the larger the lower-limit setting, the higher the steaming qualities, this is because the more the number of candidate supplying peer nodes, the more likely it is that a receiving node can receive more expected layers.

4   Conclusions

This paper presented a layer allocation framework for layered peer-to-peer streaming. Considering the constraints of the supplying peer nodes and the increasing trend of the server's bandwidth consumption, this framework comprised two algorithms according to the different scenarios of the available bandwidth between the media server and a receiving node to reach either or two of the goals: 1) minimize the resource consumption of the media server, 2) maximize the receiving node's streaming quality. Simulation studies show the efficiency of the layer allocation framework. Our fault-tolerance mechanism is the initial result of the work, we plan to explore more mechanisms such as the buffer management, standby peer selections and so on which constitute the possible directions of our future work.

References

1. Rejaie, R., Ortega, A.: PALS: Peer-to-Peer Adaptive Layered Streaming. In Proc. of ACM NOSSDAV, 2003.
2. Cui, Y., Nahrstedt, K.: Layered Peer-to-Peer Streaming. In Proc. of ACM NOSS-DAV, 2003.
3. Malhotra, V. M., Kumar, M. P., Maheshwari, S. N.: An O(|V|3) Algorithm For Finding Maximum Flows in Networks. In Information Processing Letters, 1978.
4. Saroiu, S., Gummadi, P. K., Gribble, S. D.: A Measurement Study of Peer-to-Peer File Sharing Systems. In Porc. of MMCN, San Jose, 2002.
5. Calvert, K., Doar, M., Zegura, E.: Modeling Internet Topology. In IEEE Communication Magazine, pages 35:160-163, 1997.
6. Garey, M., Johnson, D.: Computers and Intractability: A Guide to the Theory of NP-Completeness. 1979.

Build a Distributed Repository for Web Service Discovery Based on Peer-to-Peer Network[1]

Yin Li, Futai Zou, Fanyuan Ma, Minglu Li

The Department of Computer Science and Engineering,
Shanghai Jiaotong University, Shanghai, China, 200030
{liyin, zoufutai, ma-fy, li-ml}@cs.sjtu.edu.cn

Abstract. While Web Services already provide distributed operation execution, the registration and discovery with UDDI is still based on a centralized repository. In this paper we propose a distributed XML repository, based on a Peer-to-Peer infrastructure called pXRepository for Web Service discovery. In pXRepository, the service descriptions are managed in a completely decentralized way. Moreover, since the basic Peer-to-Peer routing algorithm cannot be applied directly in the service discovery process, we extend the basic Peer-to-Peer routing algorithm with XML support, which enables pXRepository to support XPath-based composite queries. Experimental results show that pXRepository has good robustness and scalability.

1. Introduction

Web services are much more loosely coupled than traditional distributed applications. Current Web Service discovery employs a centralized repository such as UDDI[1], which leads to a single point of failure and performance bottleneck. The repository is critical to the ultimate utility of the Web Services and must support scalable, flexible and robust discovery mechanisms. Since Web services are widely deployed on a huge amount of machines across the Internet, it is highly demanded to manage these Web Services based on a decentralized repository.

Peer-to-peer, as a complete distributed computing model, could supply a good scheme to build the decentralized repository for the Web Service discovery. Existing Peer-to-Peer systems such as CFS[3] and PAST[4] seek to take advantage of the rapid growth of resources to provide inexpensive, highly available storage without centralized servers. However, because Web Services utilize XML-based open standard, such as WSDL for service definition and SOAP for service invocation, directly importing these systems by treating XML documents as common files will make Web Service discovery inefficient. INS/Twine[5] seems to provide a good solution for building the Peer-to-Peer XML repository. However, INS/Twine does not provide a solution to provide XPath-like query.

---

[1] This paper is supported by 973 project (No.2002CB312002)of China, and grand project of the Science and Technology Commission of Shanghai Municipality (No. 03dz15027 and No. 03dz15028).

H. Jin et al. (Eds.): NPC 2004, LNCS 3222, pp. 175-182, 2004.

We designed a decentralize XML repository for Web service discovery based on structured Peer-to-Peer network named pXRepository (Peer-to-Peer XML Repository). Unlike Twine, as We allow index keys to be tree-structured or non-prefix sub-keys. For improved scalability, index entries are further organized hierarchically. We have extended the Peer-to-Peer routing algorithm based on Chord[2] for supporting XPath composite query in pXRepository. We name this algorithm eXChord (extended XML based Chord). Experimental results have shown that pXRepository has good scalability and robustness.

2. System Overview

pXRepository is a Peer-to-Peer XML storage facility. Each peer in pXRepository acts as a service peer (SP for simplicity), which not only provides Web service access, but also acts as a peer in the Peer-to-Peer XML storage overlay network. The architecture of the service peer in pXRepository is shown in Fig. 1.

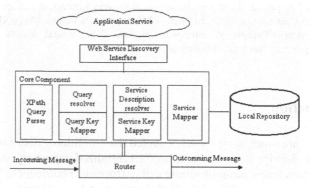

Fig. 1. The architecture of the service peer

In pXRepository, XPath[6] is used as query language for retrieving XML documents stored over the Peer-to-Peer storage network. Each SP consists of three active components called the Web Service Discovery Interface, the core component and the router, and a passive component called the local repository. Web Service Discovery Interface provides access interface to publish or locate Web services and also exposes itself as a Web service. The service description resolver is responsible for extracting key nodes from a description. Each key node extracted from the description is independently passed to the service key mapper component, together with service description or query. The service key mapper is responsible for associating HID(Hash ID) with each key node. It does this by hashing the key node. More details are given in section 3. The Query Resolver and the Query Key Mapper work almost the same way as the Service Description Resolver and the Service Key Mapper do except that the Query Resolver generates query string based on the parsing tree, which is produced by XPath parser. Service mapper is responsible for mapping HIDs to service descriptions and will return the results to the application services through the Web service discovery interface. Local repository keeps the Web service interface, service descriptions and HIDs that SP is responsible for. The router routes query requests and returns routing results.

In pXRepository, we organize every service peer in a structured Peer-to-Peer overlay network. Because Chord has the features of simplicity, provable correctness, and provable performance compared with other lookup protocols, we use Chord protocol to organize the SP's routing table.

3. Web Service Discovery in pXRepository

Service locating algorithm specifies how to route the query to the service peer who satisfies the service request. In pXRepository, the service request is expressed in XPath. However, the routing algorithm, Chord, in underlying Peer-to-Peer overlay network only supports exact-match. We extend the Chord algorithm to support XPath based match. The extended Chord algorithm is called eXChord.

In pXRepository, WSDL is used to describe the Web service interface, and the service description metadata is generated based on the content of WSDL document and the description that the user inputs before publishing. An example of Web service description metadata is shown in Fig.2.

```
<services><service>
 <name>ListPriceService</name>
 <documentation>List the product price</documentation>
 <location>http://services.companya.com/product/
ListProductService.wsdl</location></service>
 <service><name>OrderService</name>
 <documentation>Make order to product</documentation>
 <location>http://services.companya.com/product/
OrderService.wsdl</location></service></services>
 <description><company>CompanyA</company>
<industry>Manufactory</industry><region>China</region>
<keyword>Automobile Price Order</keyword>
<comments>......</comments>
 </description>
```

Fig. 2. An example of Web service description metadata in pXRepository

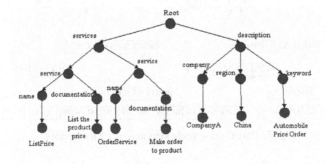

Fig. 3. A sample NVTree converted from service description shown in Fig. 2.

To publish the Web Services, the Web Service description metadata will be first converted to a canonical form: a node-value tree (NVTree). Fig.3 shows an example of the NVTree converted from the Web Service description shown in Fig. 2.

pXRepository extracts each node from the NVTree. Fig.4 shows the concatenating strings produced from the left sub-tree in Fig.3. Each node in Fig.4 is associated with a string called node key (denoted by S1,S2,...). The node key is concatenated by the child node keys and its self's node value with a slash(/) between them. If the node has multiple child nodes, each child node key is enclosed by a bracket and concatenated in left-to-right order. The concatenating process is a recursive step in post tree scanning order. The right sub-tree in Fig.3 is produced in the same way.

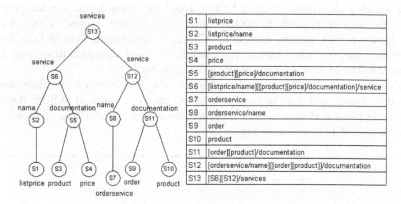

S1	listprice
S2	listprice/name
S3	product
S4	price
S5	[product][price]/documentation
S6	[listprice/name][[product][price]/documentation]/service
S7	orderservice
S8	orderservice/name
S9	order
S10	product
S11	[order][product]/documentation
S12	[orderservice/name][[order][product]]/documentation
S13	[S6][S12]/services

Fig. 4. Splitting a NVTree into service description key strings

Each node key is passed to the hash function to produce a HID, which will be used as a key to insert into the underlying Peer-to-Peer overlay network. In pXRepository, the hierarchical relationship of the nodes in NVTree will be preserved as shown in Fig.5. Each element in Fig.5 resides in a specific service peer in pXRepository correspond to the hash value of its node key (denoted as h(S1), h(S2),...).

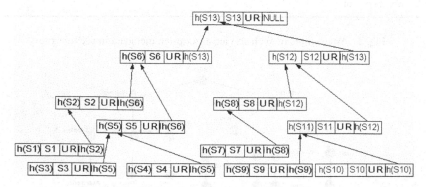

Fig. 5. Distributing node keys across pXRepository

Before presenting pXRepository service publishing and locating algorithm which is named as eXChord, we first introduce some definitions:

Definition 1. Let SD stands for a Web Service description document, then Ü(SD) stands for the URI of the document, Γ (SD) represents the NVTree of SD, and N (SD) stands for the set of NVTree nodes, where N (SD)=$\{N_1, N_2, ..., N_m\}$.

Definition 2. Let N stands for a NVTree node, then P (N) stands for its parent node and K (N) represents the node key.

The pseudocode of eXChord service description publishing algorithm is given in Fig.6. Function Publish is run on peer n, take a service description (SD) as input and publishes the SD into the Peer-to-Peer overlay network.

```
1    n.Publish(SD){
2       key=hash(Ü(SD)); n`=n.Route(key); // Chord routing algorittm
3       n`.Insert(key, SD); Compute N (SD)={N₁, N₂,...,Nₘ };
4       for each Nᵢ in N (SD){
5          nodekey= K (Nᵢ);   parentkey= K ( P (Nᵢ));
6          n.Distribute(nodekey, parentkey,SD); }
7       }
8    n.Distribute(nk, pk, SD){
9       id = hash(nk);  n`=n.Route(id);
10      n`.Insert(id, nk, Ü(SD), hash(pk));
11   }
```

Fig. 6. The pseudocode of eXChord service description publishing algorithm

```
1    Let R= Φ  // R is the result set of the query
2    n.Locate(QD){
3       Compute N (QD)={N₁, N₂,...,Nₘ };
4       for each Nᵢ in N (QD){
5          key=hash( K (Nᵢ));  n`=n.Route(key);
6          NV= n`.get(key); /*NV represents the set of nodes having the
                  node key value of K (Nᵢ) */
7          for each NVᵢ in NV {
8             SD= n`.Match(NVᵢ, QD); /*Macth is a recursive process finding
                       matching document set*/
9             if SD !=NULL then     R=R∪SD;}
10         }
11      }
12   n.Match(N, QD){
13      status = IsMatch(N, QD );/*status can be Yes, No, or Not Sure*/
14      if status=Yes then
15         return SD; // SD is the service description document that matches QD
16      elseif status=No then    return NULL;
17      else{
18         key=hash( K ( P (N))); // get parent node key hash value
19         n`=n.Route(key);   NV= n`.get(key);
20         for each NVᵢ in NV{
21            SD= n`.Match(NVᵢ, QD);
22            if SD !=NULL then    R=R∪SD;}
23      }
24   }
```

Fig. 7. The pseudocode of eXChord service locating algorithm.

To search for a Web Service, the client must specify the query requirement, which is expressed in XPath language. pXRepository supports composite XPath queries, and each XPath query only contains text matching constraints. An XPath query can be converted to a tree called XPTree. Because each node key in NVTree preserves the sub-tree structure information, the Web Service searching process can be a sub-tree matching problem.

To present the Web Service locating algorithm, we first introduce some definitions:

Definition 3. Let QD stands for a XPath query, then Γ (QD) represents the XPTree of QD, and N (QD) stands for the set of leaf nodes, where N (QD)=$\{N_1, N_2, ..., N_m\}$.

Definition 4. Let N stands for a XPTree node, then K (N) represents the value of the node.

The pseudocode of eXChord service locating algorithm is given in Fig.7. Function Locate is run on peer n, take query requirement QD as its input and searches the Peer-to-Peer overlay network for the services that satisfy its requirements.

4. Evaluation and Experimental Results

In this section, we evaluate pXRepository by simulation and compare pXRepository with centralized service management approach such as UDDI. We compared latency, space overhead, load, and robustness of pXRepository with UDDI.

We use the Georgia Tech Internetwork Topological Models (GT-ITM)[7] to generate the network topologies used in our simulations. We use the "transit-stub" model to obtain topologies that more closely resemble the Internet hierarchy than pure random graph. An Internetwork with 600 routers and 28800 service peers (node for simplicity) are used in our experiment.

4.1 Latency

We evaluate the latency metric in the number of the hops in the network. Fig.8 shows the effect of number of nodes on latency. Since the routing table of pXRepository is same as that of Chord, which has the logarithmic relationship between logical hops and number of the nodes. If the average latency of single logical hop is κ, thus, latency of pXRepository $Latency_{pXRepository} = \kappa \times \log(N_H)$.

Experimental results further show that the latency of UDDI is roughly 80. This is because the logical hops of UDDI is 2, and has nothing to do with N_H. Although latency of pXRepository is higher than that of UDDI, pXRepository has lower space overhead, lower load, and good robustness (refers to 4.2, 4.3, 4.4).

4.2 Space Overhead

In order to analyze conveniently, we first give a definition and two assumptions:

Definition 5. The memory size of routing ID and corresponding IP is called memory unit, size of which is σ.

Assumption 1. Node ID and Web service description ID are distributed uniformly in ID space, and there are n service peers in the system, each peer publishes m service description documents in average. For each service description, s keys will be generated by extracting the concatenating strings from the service description.

Assumption 2. The average overhead of each service description item is $k \times \sigma$. Overhead of pXRepository is:

$$Space_{pXRepository} = \log(n) \times \sigma + m \times s \times k \times \sigma \tag{1}$$

Since UDDI maintains all information in central repository, overhead of UDDI is:

$$Space_{UDDI} = n \times m \times k \times \sigma \tag{2}$$

For $m = 80$, $k = 2$, $s=10$ and $\sigma = 200$, the effect of number of nodes N_H on space overhead is shown in Fig.9. Experimental results in Fig.9 reveal that the space overhead of pXRepository is much better than that of UDDI.

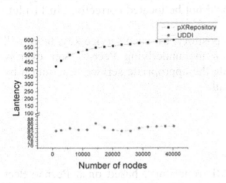

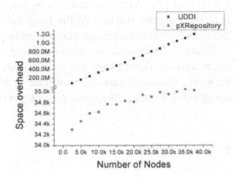

Fig. 8. Effect of number of nodes on latency

Fig. 9. Effect of number of nodes on Space overhead

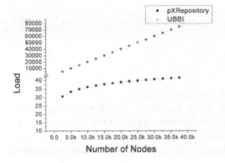

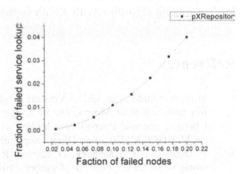

Fig. 10. Load of pXRepository and UDDI

Fig. 11. The effect of node failure

4.3 Load

Load is an important metric to evaluate Web service management approach. This paper uses the number of messages in and out of the node as a metric to evaluate the load. We assume that each service lookup query will generate 3 keys in average, and each key will be used to locate the service. Fig.10 shows the comparisons in loads between pXRepository and UDDI. The load of UDDI increases linearly with the number of nodes, however, the load of pXRepository and the number of nodes is in logarithmic relationship.

4.4 Robustness

In this experiment, we consider 28800 nodes with each node distribute 10 pieces of service descriptions, and each service description will generate 10 keys. We also assume that each service query requirement issued by client user will generate 2 keys covered by the service description keys. Then we randomly select a fraction of the nodes that fail. After the failures occur, we wait for the network to stabilizing, and then measure the fraction of the keys that could not be located correctly. Fig.11 plots the effect of node failure on service lookup.

Since in eXChord algorithm used in pXRepository, for each service key, there will be a service description copy distributed in the underlying Peer-to-Peer overlay network, the client can still continue to locate the appropriate service description by using other keys in case some service peers fail.

5. Conclusions

In this paper, we propose a distributed XML repository, based on a Peer-to-Peer infrastructure called pXRepository for Web Service discovery. In pXRepository, the Web service descriptions are managed in a totally distributed way, which avoids single point of failure and can be scalable and robust. We also extend the basic Peer-to-Peer routing algorithm with XPath support.

References

1.   http://www.uddi.org/, UDDI Version 3.0, Published Specification.
2.   Ion Stoica, Robert Morris, David Karger, M. Frans Kaashoek, and Hari Balakrishnan. Chord: a scalable Peer-to-Peer lookup service for Internet applications. Proceedings of ACM SIGCOMM`01, San Diego, September 2001.
3.   F. Dabek, M. F. Kaashoek, D. Karger, R. Morris, and I. Stoica. Wide-area cooperative storage with CFS. SOSP '01, October 2001.
4.   P. Druschel and A. Rowstron. PAST: A large-scale persistent Peer-to-Peer storage utility. In Proc. HOTOS Conf., 2001.
5.   M. Balazinska, H. Balakrishnan, and D. Karger, "INS/Twine: A scalable Peer-to-Peer architecture for intentional resource discovery," in Proceedings of the International Conference on Pervasive Computing, August 2002.
6.   W3C. XML Path Language (XPath) 1.0. http://www.w3.org/TR/xpath, November 1999.
7.   Zegura, E. w., Calvert. k., and Bhattacharjee, S. How to model an Internetwork. In Proceed-ings of IEEE INFOCOM (1996).

Performance Improvement of Hint-Based Locating & Routing Mechanism in P2P File-Sharing Systems[1]

Hairong Jin, Shanping Li, Gang Peng, and Tianchi Ma

College of Computer Science, Zhejiang University, Hangzhou, P.R.China 310027
hrjin@eyou.com, shan@cs.zju.edu.cn, e_pglmary@hotmail.com,
mtc@cad.zju.edu.cn

Abstract. Hint-based Locating & Routing Mechanism (HBLR) derives from the locating & routing mechanism in Freenet. HBLR uses file location hint to enhance the performance of file searching and downloading. In comparison with its ancestor, HBLR saves storage space and reduces file request latency. However, because of the inherent fallibility of hint, employing location hint naively for file locating in P2P file-sharing system will lead to under-expectant performance. In this paper, hint's uncertainty and related bad results are analyzed. According to the causation, pertinent countermeasures including credible hint, master-copy transfer, and file existence pre-detection are proposed. Simulation shows the performance of HBLR is improved by adopting the proposed policies.

1 Introduction

The Hint-based Locating & Routing Mechanism (HBLR) [3] is based on the *document routing model* [1] in Freenet [2]. It processes file location hints searching instead of direct file searching and distributes file location hints instead of files themselves. Comparing to Freenet, HBLR has two obvious advantages: disk space saving on peers, and file transfer time reducing by downloading file from the selected peer.

However, distributing hints instead of files also has its drawbacks. Following are several problems accompanied with proposed solutions:

1. Stale hint set. If all hints that a requestor receives are stale, the request will fail undoubtedly. However, the file may exist on some peers, most probably on the file's publisher. So, employing the publisher as a credible file holder, and keeping the corresponding hint on peers can provide at least one downloading source.

2. Credible file holder absence. If a publisher encounters space shortage, it may delete previously published files. Moving the file to another peer, and maintaining necessary links between the old and new holders can resolve the problem.

3. Repetitious downloading attempts. If the hints pointing to some relatively better positions are all stale, the requestor will fail to download several times until a correct hint related position in its turn. It's inefficient and a file existence pre-detection mechanism is needed.

---

[1] The Project Supported by Zhejiang Provincial Natural Science Foundation of China (No.602032)

H. Jin et al. (Eds.): NPC 2004, LNCS 3222, pp. 183-186, 2004.

The rest of this paper is organized as follows: Section 2 describes the proposed mechanisms. Section 3 gives simulation and discussion. Section 4 gives some related work. Finally, the author's work is summarized at Section 5.

2 Improving Hints' Accuracy in HBLR

The searching and distribution methods for file in Freenet and for hint in HBLR are equal. Therewith, their searching success ratios are almost equal too. If the hint's accuracy can be ensured, HBLR's performance can be improved.

2.1 Credible Hint and Master-Copy

For a given file, if (1) there is a credible file holder, (2) hint about this holder is kept on all the peers, which have the hint entries about the given file, and (3) the hint about the credible holder will always be transferred to the requestor, then HBLR's request success ratio can be improved to Freenet's level.

A publisher, which provides the file for share, will keep the file as long as possible. So, the publisher is a quite credible holder, condition (1) can be satisfied. In *finite-hint* [3] solution, every hint items are transferred back naturally. In *full-hint* [3] solution, as long as a special policy is adopted, assuring the publisher related hint to be transferred back, condition (3) can be satisfied. A peer in HBLR obtains hints during three procedures: (a) Publishing; (b) Hints transferring in request; (c) Updating after file downloading. No matter in which way, so long as condition (3) is satisfied, the holder related hint could always be kept. So, condition (2) can be satisfied.

We call the publisher *credible holder*, and the publisher related hint *credible hint*. The copy of a file on its publisher is called *master-copy*.

2.2 Master-Copy Transfer

The file's publisher is a quite credible holder, but not a completely credible holder. When it encounters space shortage, it may delete a previously published file. The publisher should transfer the master-copy to a neighbor peer. The criteria in target peer selection include free space and communication latency. The publisher also remains a link pointing to the new holder for master-copy access. The new holder is also enabled to transfer the file while facing space shortage.

2.3 File Existence Pre-Detection

After receiving hints, the requestor selects a best peer for downloading. But, if the file on the best peer was deleted, the downloading attempt fails, and reselecting is needed. Though with credible hint and master-copy transferring mechanism, the file will be obtained in the end, repetitious attempts are inefficient. File existence pre-detection should be involved in the selection step, and file existence becomes a precondition.

3 Simulations

The success ratio, space usage, and average file service time were concerned in simulations. 100 peers and 4000 different files were involved. The files' average size was variable and each peer contributed 800Mbytes storage space to Freenet or HBLR.

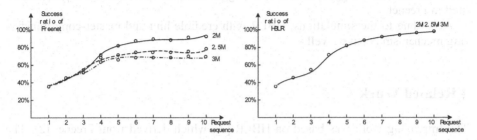

Fig. 1. Success ratio of file requests

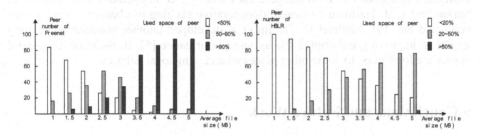

Fig. 2. Space usage

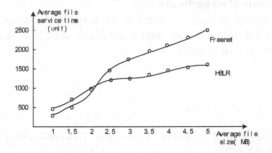

Fig. 3. File service time

Success ratios of requests were compared. The two systems both processed ten continuous request sequences, each containing 1000 requests. The files' average size was adjusted among 2M/2.5M/3Mbytes. As Fig.1 shows, HBLR achieved approximate success ratio to Freenet. When file size became bigger, HBLR's success ratio exceeded that of Freenet in latter sequences. The cause was that Freenet deleted some cached copies for providing space to the new coming, thus reduced copy distribution.

Space usage was seriously concerned. The simulation process included 3000 file requests. The files' average size was adjusted from 1Mbytes to 5Mbytes. As Fig.2 shows, Freenet used much more space than HBLR, especially with bigger files.

As Fig.3 shows, HBLR paid out for its relatively complex operation, its performance of average file service time was below Freenet with smaller files. But it did better when files were bigger. Because the bigger the files were the less copies distributed in Freenet.

According to the simulations, HBLR with credible hint and master-copy transferring mechanism behaved well.

4 Related Work

The improving work was based on HBLR [3], which derived from Freenet [2]. The basic locating models in the systems are all document routing model [1].

Cooperation is an essential character and requirement in P2P. Other cooperative systems' experience can be referenced for building P2P cooperative mechanisms. P. Sarkar and J. H. Hartman proposed a cooperative caching mechanism, using master copy and hint [4]. Michael D. Dahlin et al developed another cooperative caching model to improving distributed file system performance [5]. In their models, useful copies are forwarded to some other places when facing local deletion.

5 Conclusions and Future Work

In this paper, credible hint and master-copy transferring mechanism were imported to resolve hint uncertainty problem in HBLR. These new elements performed energetically in HBLR, improved its performance.

HBLR is an ongoing project and some work needs to be done in the future. The credible hint is a minimum step for improving hint's accuracy. Advanced hint management mechanism is still needed.

Reference

1. Dejan S. Milojicic et al. Peer-to-Peer Computing. Hewlett-Packard Internal Document, HPL-2002-57. March 2002.
2. Ian Clarke et al. Freenet: A Distributed Anonymous Information Storage and Retrieval System. Lecture Notes in Computer Science. 2000.
3. Hairong Jin, Shanping Li, Tianchi Ma, and Liang Qian. A Hint-based Locating & Routing Mechanism in Peer-to-Peer File Sharing Systems. GCC2003, December 2003.
4. Prasenjit Sarkar and John H. Hartman. Hint-Based Cooperative Caching. ACM Transactions on Computer Systems, Vol. 18, No. 4, Pages 387–419. Nov. 2000.
5. Michael D. Dahlin et al. Cooperative Caching: Using Remote Client Memory to Improve File System Performance. The First Symposium on Operating Systems Design and Implementation, 1994.

Cache Design for Transcoding Proxy Caching

Keqiu Li, Hong Shen, and Keishi Tajima

Graduate School of Information Science
Japan Advanced Institute of Science and Technology
1-1 Tatsunokuchi, Ishikawa, 923-1292, Japan

Abstract. As audio and video applications have proliferated on the
Internet, transcoding proxy caching is attracting an increasing amount
of attention, especially in the environment of mobile appliances. Since
cache replacement and consistency algorithms are two factors that play
a central role in the functionality of transcoding proxy caching, it is
of particular practical necessity to involve them into transcoding cache
design. In this paper, we propose an original cache maintenance algorithm, which integrates both cache replacement and consistence algorithms. Our algorithm also explicitly reveals the new emerging factors
in the transcoding proxy. Specifically, we formulate a generalized cost
saving function to evaluate the profit of caching a multimedia object.
Our algorithm evicts the objects based on the generalized cost saving
to fetch each object into the cache. Consequently, the objects with less
generalized cost saving are to be removed from the cache. On the other
hand, our algorithm also considers the validation and write rates of the
objects, which is of considerable importance for a cache maintenance
algorithm. Finally, we evaluate our algorithm on different performance
metrics through extensive simulation experiments. The implementation
results show that our algorithm outperforms comparison algorithms in
terms of the performance metrics considered.

Key words: Transcoding proxy caching, cache maintenance, Cache replacement,
cache consistency, World Wide Web.

1 Introduction

With the explosive growth of the World Wide Web, proxy caching has become
an important technique to improve network performance [15,16]. Due to the
limited cache space, it is impossible to store all the web objects in the cache.
As a result, cache replacement algorithms [10,14,16] are used to determine a
suitable subset of web objects to be removed from the cache to make room
for a new web object. However, the improvement of network performance, such
as access latency reduction achieved by caching web objects, does not come
completely for free. In particular, maintaining the content consistence with the
primary servers generates extra requests. Many proxy cache implementations
depend on a consistency algorithm to ensure a suitable form of consistency for the

H. Jin et al. (Eds.): NPC 2004, LNCS 3222, pp. 187–194, 2004.

cached documents. Cache consistency algorithms [1,3,11] are used to guarantee the consistency of the cache web objects.

Transcoding is used to transform a multimedia object from one form to another, frequently trading off object fidelity for size for prevailing the operating environment. Since the transcoding proxy plays an important role in the functionality of caching, transcoding proxy caching is attracting more and more attention [4,7,9,12]. However, due to the new emerging factors in the environment of transcoding proxies, existing cache replacement and consistency algorithms cannot be simply applied to solve the same problems for transcoding proxy caching. In [5], the authors presented several examples to explain the influence of these factors and explored the aggregate effect for efficient cache replacement in transcoding proxies. However, they considered only the problem of cache replacement and have not involved any issues on cache consistence. We argue that cache consistence has great influence on cache design. Consequently, it is of particular practical necessity to address the problem of cache maintenance by including both the cache replacement and consistence algorithms and the new emerging factors in the transcoding proxy. In this paper, we propose an original cache maintenance algorithm for transcoding proxy caching, which integrates both the cache replacement and consistence algorithms. Specifically, we formulate a generalized cost saving function to evaluate the profit of caching a multimedia object. Our algorithm evicts the objects based on the generalized cost saving to fetch each object into the cache. Consequently, the objects with less generalized cost saving are to be removed from the cache. On the other hand, our algorithm also considers the validation and write rates of the objects, which is of considerable importance for a cache maintenance algorithm. We evaluate our algorithm on different performance metrics through extensive simulation experiments and compare our algorithm with other algorithms proposed in the literature.

The remainder of this paper is structured as follow: We present a cache maintenance algorithm in transcoding proxies in Section 2. The simulation and performance evaluation are described in Section 3 and Section 4, respectively. Section 5 summarizes our work and concludes the paper.

2   A Cache Maintenance Algorithm in Transcoding Caching

The relationship among different versions of a multimedia objects can be expressed by a weighted transcoding graph [5]. Let $o_{i,j}$ denote version j of object i. $\omega(i,j)$ is the transcoding cost from version i to version j. The reference rates to different versions of objects, denoted by $f_{i,j}$, are assumed to be statistically independent, where $f_{i,j}$ is the mean reference rate to version j of object i. $\lambda_{i,j}$ is the read cost of version j of object i from the server, $\mu_{i,j}$ is the write cost of version j of object i, $\eta_{i,j}$ is the cost of validating the consistency of version j of object i, and $p_{i,j}$ is the probability of invalidating version j of object i cached.

First we calculate the cost saving from caching only one version of an object in the transcoding cache (no other versions are cached). From the standpoint of clients, an optimal cache replacement algorithm should maximize the cost saving from caching multiple copies of objects by considering both the read cost and the write cost. Thus, the individual cost saving of caching only $o_{i,j}$ is defined as follows.

Definition 1. $CS(o_{i,j})$ *is a function for calculating the individual cost saving of caching* $o_{i,j}$, *while no other versions of object i are cached.*

$$CS(o_{i,j}) = \sum_{x \in D(j)} \lambda_{i,x}(d_{i,x} + \omega(1,x) - \omega(j,x) - \eta_{i,j} - p_{i,j}d_{i,x}) - \mu_{i,j}d_{i,j} \quad (1)$$

where $D(j)$ is the set of versions that can be transcoded from version j.

In Equation (1), $d_{i,x}$ is the cost of reading or writing $o_{i,x}$ from the server and $\omega(1,x)$ is the cost of transcoding from the original version to version x if $o_{i,j}$ is not cached. On the other hand, $\omega_{j,x}$ is the cost of transcoding from version j to version x, $\lambda_{i,x}$ is the read rate of $o_{i,x}$ from the client, and $\mu_{i,j}$ is the write rate of $o_{i,j}$ from the server if $o_{i,j}$ is cached.

As a matter of fact, there may be many versions of an object that can be cached at the same time if this is valuable. In the following we discuss the aggregate cost saving of caching multiple versions of an object. The aggregate cost saving of caching multiple versions of an object at the same time can be defined as below.

Definition 2. $CS(o_{i,j_1}, o_{i,j_2}, \cdots, o_{i,j_k})$ *is a function for calculating the aggregate cost saving of caching* o_{i,j_1}, o_{i,j_2}, $\cdots$, o_{i,j_k}.

$$CS(o_{i,j_1}, o_{i,j_2}, \cdots, o_{i,j_k}) = \sum_{y \in \{j_1, j_2, \cdots, j_k\}} (\sum_{x \in D(y)} \lambda_{i,x}(d_{i,x} \\ + \omega(1,x) - \omega(y,x) - \eta_{i,y} - p_{i,y}d_{i,x}) - \mu_{i,y}d_{i,y}) \quad (2)$$

Now we define the marginal cost saving of caching a version of object i if there is at least one version cached.

Definition 3. $CS(o_{i,j}|o_{i,j_1}, o_{i,j_2}, \cdots, o_{i,j_k})$ *is a function for calculating the marginal cost saving of caching* $o_{i,j}$, *given that* o_{i,j_1}, o_{i,j_2}, $\cdots$, o_{i,j_k} *are already cached, where* $j \neq j_1, j_2, \cdots, j_k$.

$$CS(o_{i,j}|o_{i,j_1}, o_{i,j_2}, \cdots, o_{i,j_k}) = \\ CS(o_{i,j}, o_{i,j_1}, o_{i,j_2}, \cdots, o_{i,j_k}) - CS(o_{i,j_1}, o_{i,j_2}, \cdots, o_{i,j_k}) \quad (3)$$

If we use $s_{i,j}$ to denote the size of $o_{i,j}$, then we formulate the generalized cost saving function as follows:

$$CS^G(o_{i,j}) = \begin{cases} \frac{CS(o_{i,j})}{s_{i,j}} & \text{if no other versions are cached} \\ \frac{CS(o_{i,j}|o_{i,j_1}, o_{i,j_2}, \cdots, o_{i,j_k})}{s_{i,j}} & \text{if } o_{i,j_1}, o_{i,j_2}, \cdots, o_{i,j_k} \text{ are cached} \end{cases} \quad (4)$$

It is easy to see that the generalized cost saving function is further normalized by the size of $o_{i,j}$ to reflect the object size factor. The rationale behind this normalization is to order the objects by the ratio of cost saving to object size. The generalized cost saving function defined in Equation (4) explicitly takes into consideration the new emerging factors in transcoding caching and the aggregate effect of cache multiple versions of an object. Importantly, it takes into account not only the read cost but also the write cost.

Based on this function, we propose our cache replacement scheme as follows. Suppose the size of a new object to be cached is s, then we should find a subset of objects $O^* = \{o_{f_1,g_1}, o_{f_2,g_2}, \cdots, o_{f_l,g_l}\} \subseteq O$ that satisfies the following conditions. Here $O = \{o_{1,1}, o_{1,2}, \cdots, o_{1,l_1}, o_{2,1}, o_{2,2}, \cdots, o_{2,l_2}, \cdots, o_{m,1}, o_{m,2}, \cdots, o_{m,l_m}\}$ is the set of objects cached.

(1)
$$\sum_{o_{f,g} \in O^*} o_{f,g} \leq s$$

(2)
$$\sum_{o_{f,g} \in O^*} CS^G(o_{f,g}) \leq \sum_{o_{f,g} \in O'} CS^G(o_{f,g}), \; \forall \; O' \subseteq O \text{ that satisfies (1)}$$

Obviously, (1) is to make enough room for the new object, and (2) is to evict those objects whose total cost saving is minimized.

With the two conditions above, we can devise the pseudocode of our scheme as follows.

Algorithm GCS $(C, S_c, S_u, o_{i,j})$
```
1        add o_{i,j} into C
2        recalulate the generalized cost saving of each version of object i
3        BuildHeap(C)
4        while S_u − S_c < s do
5            Remove the first object from C
6               S_u = S_u − s_{f,g}
7            recalulate the generalized cost saving of each version of object i
8            BuildHeap(C)
```

In Algorithm GCS, C is used to hold the cached objects, S_c is the cache capacity, S_u is the cache capacity used, and $o_{i,j}$ is the object to be cached. For this algorithm, we can see that the most important thing is to find the objects with minimal cost saving.

It can be shown that the time complexity of Algorithm GCS is $O(S^2 log(S))$, where S is the number of different objects cached. However, from the algorithm we know that we have to search the entire cache for the other versions of the object and then recalculate the generalized cost saving for them whenever we insert or evict an object into or from the cache. Such operations are, in general, very costly. Here we apply the data structure proposed in [5] to facilitate such operations.

In the actual implementation, the parameters for computing the generalized cost saving are usually not constant. To realize our algorithm, these parameters may have to be relaxed. Here, we adopt a "sliding window" technique [15] which has been widely applied. It combines both the history data and the current value to estimate the parameters. Specially, the parameters are estimated as follow.

$$d_{i,j} = \alpha \cdot d_{i,j}^{new} + (1 - \alpha) \cdot d_{i,j}^{old}$$
$$\lambda_{i,j} = \frac{K_1}{t_{i,j} - t_{i,j}^{K_1}}$$
$$\mu_{i,j} = \frac{K_2}{s_{i,j} - s_{i,j}^{K_2}}$$

where $d_{i,j}^{new}$ is the newly measured cost of reading or writing $o_{i,j}$ from the client or the server and $d_{i,j}^{old}$ is the measured cost of reading or writing $o_{i,j}$ from the client or the server last time; $t_{i,j}$ is the time when the new request to $o_{i,j}$ is received from the client and $t_{i,j}^{K_1}$ is the time when the last K request is received from the client; $s_{i,j}$ is the time when the new update to $o_{i,j}$ is sent from the server and $s_{i,j}^{K_2}$ is the time when the last K update is sent from the server. $\eta_{i,j}$ is considered as a constant since it just sends an invalidation message to the server for all the documents. We estimate $p_{i,j}$ by $\frac{\lambda_{i,j}}{\lambda_{i,j} + \mu_{i,j}}$.

3   Simulation Model

In the simulation, to generate the workload of clients' requests, we model a single server that maintains a collection of m multimedia objects[1]. The object popularity followed a Zipf-like distribution [2]. Specifically, the popularity of the ith video was proportional to $1/i^\alpha$. The default values of m and α were set to be 1000 and 0.75 respectively. The sizes of the videos followed a heavy tailed distribution with the mean value of $12K$ Bytes [13]. The clients are divided five classes. Without loss of generality, we assume that the sizes of the five versions of each video to be 100 percent, 80 percent, 60 percent, 40 percent, and 20 percent of the original video size. The access probabilities of the clients are described as a vector of $< 0.2, 0.15, 0.3, 0.2, 0.15 >$. The transcoding relationship of the six versions is shown in Figure 1.

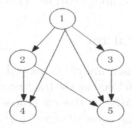

Fig. 1. Transcoding Graph for Simulation

Regarding the transcoding rate, we set it to be $20K$ bytes per second. The delays of fetching the videos from the server are given by an exponential distri-

---

[1] In the simulation, the multimedia objects are assumed to be videos.

bution. We assume that there is no correlation between the video size and the delay of fetching it from the server. This is justified by Shim et al. in [15].

The synthetic workloads are generated according to the recent results on the web workload characterization [6,8,13]. Table 1 lists the parameters and their values used in the simulation.

Table 1. Parameters Used in Our Simulation

Parameter	Value
Number of Nodes	10000
Delay of Fetching Objects	Exponential Distribution $p(x) = \theta^{-1}e^{-x/\theta}$ $(\theta = 0.45\ Sec)$
Number of Multimedia Objects	1000 objects
Web Object Size Distribution	Pareto Distribution $p(x) = \frac{ab^a}{a-1}$ $(a = 1.1, b = 8596)$
Web Object Access Frequency	Zipf-Like Distribution $\frac{1}{i^\alpha}$ $(i = 0.7)$
Average Request Rate Per Node	$U(1,9)$ requests per second
Transcoding Rate	$20KB/Sec$

We compare our scheme with the following algorithms. (1) Least Recently Used (LRU) evicts the web object which was requested the least recently. The requested object is stored at each node through which the object passes. The cache purges one or more least recently requested objects to accommodate the new object if there is not enough room for it. (2) Least Normalized Cost Replacement $(LNC - R)$ [14] is an algorithm that approximates the optimal cache replacement algorithm. (3) Aggregate Effect (AE) [5] is an algorithm that explores the aggregate effect of caching multiple versions of an object in the cache.

4   Performance Evaluation

The primary cache performance metric employed in the simulation is delay-saving ratio (DSR), which is defined as the fraction of communication and server delays which is saved by satisfying the references from the cache instead of the server. We also use average access latency (AST), object hit ratio (OHR) as secondary performance metrics. Here OHR is defined as the ratio of the number of requests satisfied by the caches as a whole to the total number of requests. We use staleness ratio (SR) as the primary consistency metric. The staleness ratio is defined as a fraction of cache hits which return stale objects. Here "stale" means that the time that an object was brought to the cache is less than the last-modified timestamp corresponding to the request. In the following figures LRU, $LNC - R$, and AE denote the results for the three algorithms, and

$CERWC$ shows the results for the model of coordinated en-route web caching in transcoding proxies, as proposed in Section 2.

In the experiments, we compare the performance of different models across a wide range of cache sizes, from 0.04 percent to 15.0 percent. The first experiment investigates DSR as a function of the relative cache size at each node and Figure 2(A) shows the simulation results. MA gives on average 13.3% improvement over LRU and and 5.3% over $LNC - R$. The maximal improvement over LRU and $LNC - R$ is 17.2% and 8.2% for cache size 0.5% and 2.0% respectively. On average, The DSR of MA is only 1.0% below that of AE. In the worst case, the DSR of MA is only 1.38% that of AE for cache size 10%.

Figure 2(B) shows the results of OHR as a function of the relative cache size for different models. Although MA is not designed to maximize the object hot ratio, it still provides an improvement over LRU and $LNC - R$. In particular, the average improvement is 29.6% over LRU and 22.5% over $LNC - R$. The object hit ratio provides even closer to the hit ratio of AE; on average, 1.1% and no more than 2.39% below the object hit ratio of AE.

In addition to improving performance of the cache, the MA algorithm also significantly improves irs consistence. On average, MA achieves a staleness ratio which is by factor of 3.2 better than that of AE, in the worst case it improves SR of AE by factor of 1.9 when the cache size is 0.5%. MA also improves SR over LRU and $LNC - R$. On average, MA achieves a staleness ratio which is 50.8% better than that of LRU and 50.1% better than that of $NC - R$. In the worst case, it improves SR of LRU by 10.2% when the cache size is 0.5% and improves SR of $LNC - R$ by 8% when the cache size is 2.0%. The staleness ratio comparison of the four algorithms can be found in Figure 2(C).

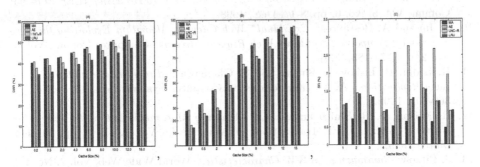

Fig. 2. Experiments for $DSR, OSR, and SR$

5   Conclusions

In this paper, we proposed a maintenance algorithm for transcoding proxy caching, which combined both cache replacement and cache consistence. The simulation indicated that our algorithm could significantly improve the staleness ratio, while keeping the cache performance within acceptable loss. This greatly benefit the cache design for transcoding proxy caching.

References

1. M. Bhide, P. Deolasee, A. Katkar, and A. Panchbudhe. *Adaptive Push-Pull: Disseminating Dynamic Web data.* IEEE Transactions on Computers, Vol. 51, No. 6, pp. 652-667, June, 2002.
2. L. Breslau, P. Cao, L. Fan, G. Phillips, and S. Shenker. *Web Caching and Zip-like Distributions: Evidence and Implications.* Proc. IEEE INFOCOM'99, pp. 126-134, 1999.
3. P. Cao and C. Liu. *Maintaining String Cache Consistency in the World Wide Web.* IEEE Transactions on Computers, Vol. 47, No. 4, pp. 445-457, April, 1998.
4. C. Chandra and C. S. Ellis. *JPEG Compression Metric as a Quality-Aware Image Transcoding.* Proc. USENIX Second Symposium Intenet Technology and Systems, pp. 81-92, 1999.
5. C. Chang and M. Chen. *On Exploring Aggregate Effect for Efficient Cache Replacement in Transcoding Proxies.* IEEE Transactions on Parallel and Distributed Systems, Vol. 14, No. 6, pp. 611-624, June, 2003.
6. C. Cunha, A. Bestavros, and M. Crovella. *Characteriatics of WWWW Client-Based Traces.* Technical Report TR-95-010, Boston University, April, 1995.
7. R. Floyd and B. Housel. *Mobile Web Access Using Network Web Express.* IEEE Personal Comm., Vol. 5, No. 5, pp. 47-52, Dec., 1998.
8. S. Glassman. *A Caching Relay for the World Wide Web.* Computer Network and ISDN Systems, Vol 27, No. 2, pp, 165-173, 1994.
9. R. Han, P. Bhagwat, R. LaMaire, T. Mummert, V. Perret, and J. Rubas. *Dynamic Adaption in an Image Transcoding Proxy for Mobile Web Browsing.* IEEE Personal Comm., Vol. 5, No. 6, pp. 8-17, Dec., 1998.
10. S. Jin and A. Bestavros. *Greeddual* Web Caching Algorithm Exploiting the Two Sources of Temporal Locality in Web Request Streams.* Computer Comm., Vol. 4, No. 2, pp. 174-183, 2001.
11. R. Ladin, B. Liskov, L. Shrira, and S. Ghemawat. *Providing Availability Using Lazy Replication.* ACM Transactions on Conputer Systems, Vol. 10, No. 4, pp. 360-391, 1992.
12. R. Mohan, J. R. Smith and C. Li. *Adapting Multimedia Internet Content for Univeral Access.* IEEE Transactions on Multimedia, Vol. 1, No. 1, pp. 104-114, March 1999.
13. J. Pitkow. *Summary of WWW Characteristics.* World Wide Web, Vol. 2, No. 1-2, pp. 3-13, 1999.
14. P. Scheuermann, J. Shim, and R. Vingralek. *A Case for Delay-Conscious Caching of Web Documents.* Computer Network and ISDN Systems, Vol 29, No. 8-13, pp. 997-1005, 1997.
15. J. Shim, P. Scheuermann, and R. Vingralek. *Proxy Cache Algorithms: Design, Implementation, and Performance.* IEEE Transactions on Knowledge and Data Engineering, Vol 11, No. 4, pp. 549-562, 1999.
16. R. P. Wooster and M. Abrams. *Proxy Caching that Estimates Page Load Delays.* Computer Networks and ISDN Systems, Vol 29, Nos. 8-13, pp. 977-986, 1997.

Content Aggregation Middleware (CAM) for Fast Development of High Performance Web Syndication Services

Su Myeon Kim, Jinwon Lee, SungJae Jo and Junehwa Song

Dept. of EECS., Korea Advanced Institute of Science and Technology,
371-1 Guseong-Dong, Yuseong-Gu, Daejon, 305-701, Korea
{smkim, jcircle, stanleylab, junesong}@nclab.kaist.ac.kr

Abstract. The rapid expansion of the Internet accompanies a serious side effect. Since there are too many information providers, it is very difficult to obtain the contents best fitting to customers' needs. Web Syndication Services (WSS) are emerging as solutions to the information flooding problem. However, even with its practical importance, WSS has not been much studied yet. In this paper, we propose the Content Aggregation Middleware (CAM). It provides a WSS with a content gathering substratum effective in gathering and processing data from many different source sites. Using the CAM, WSS provider can build up a new service without involving the details of complicated content aggregation procedures, and thus concentrate on developing the service logic. We describe the design, implementation, and performance of the CAM.

1 Introduction

The Internet has been growing exponentially for the past decades, and has already become the major source of information. The estimated number of Internet hosts reached 72 million in February 2000, and is expected to reach 1 billion by 2008[1]. However, such a rapid expansion accompanies a serious side effect. Although users can easily access the Internet, it is very difficult to obtain the contents best fitting to their needs since there are too many information providers (Web hosts). This problem is usually called information flooding.

Various Web Syndication Services (WSS) (See Figure 1) are emerging as solutions to the information flooding problem. WSS is a new kind of Internet service which spans over distributed Web sites. It provides value-added information by processing (e.g., integrating, comparing, filtering, etc) contents gathered from other Web sites. Price comparison service such as Shopping.com [2] and travel consolidator service like Expedia.com [3] can be considered as examples of the WSSs. To ordinary clients who are not familiar with a specific domain, a WSS targeting the domain would be of a great help to overcome the information flooding.

Providing a WSS is technically challenging. It is much more complicated than providing an ordinary service. However, even with its practical importance, WSS has not been much studied yet. A system providing a WSS can be seen into two parts; the

H. Jin et al. (Eds.): NPC 2004, LNCS 3222, pp. 195-204, 2004.

WSS service logic and the content aggregation subsystem. The content aggregation is the common core of many WSS's while the service logic is service specific and differs from service to service. It receives requests from clients and interacts with source sites to process the requests. In this paper, we propose the Content Aggregation Middleware (CAM). The CAM is an efficient content aggregation system designed to be a base for many WSS's. Using the CAM, a service provider can easily develop and deploy a high performance WSS system supporting a large number of clients and source sites.

We identify several requirements for a WSS site. First, a WSS site should support a high level of performance. The performance requirement in a WSS site is a lot higher than in ordinary Web sites. It should manage much larger number of requests from clients spread over the Internet. Additionally, it should handle a huge number of source sites and interactions with them. Second, it should support high dynamics of Internet environment. In a fully Internet-connected environment, real world events can be quickly reflected and propagated to systems. Once generated, the information will go through frequent changes. Third, a WSS site should deal with many source sites, which are highly heterogeneous.

The CAM has been designed to meet the above requirements of a WSS site. It provides a WSS with a content gathering substratum effective in gathering and processing data from many different source sites. Using the CAM, WSS provider can build up a new service without involving the details of complicated content aggregation procedures, and thus concentrate on developing the service logic. The CAM simplifies the complex procedure of interacting with content providers through a formalized service contract (SC). Also, it effectively masks the high level of heterogeneity among different source sites. In addition, it is a high performance system much relaxing the burden of performance concerns in system development. Below, we describe the novel characteristics of the proposed content aggregation system.

First, the CAM is a source data caching system along with basic data processing capabilities. It caches data in the form of source data, e.g., the unit of database fields as stored in content providers' databases. For value-added service, fine-grained control on the cached contents gathered is required. Source data caching makes such fine-grained control possible. For data processing, basic functions such as content conversion, filtering, and query processing, are provided.

Second, it is a high performance system. As mentioned, a WSS should handle a high rate of requests from lots of clients. In addition, it should be capable of managing a lot of interactions with source sites to keep the freshness of cached data. With a source data caching, keeping cached data up-to-date can be done efficiently. Also, to manage a large volume of data efficiently, it uses main memory as a primary storage.

Third, the CAM is equipped with real-time update capability. To keep the freshness of cached contents, any modification on the data at source sites is propagated to the CAM as soon as possible. The update mechanism is based on server invalidation scheme; upon modification, the source site initiates invalidation and modification of the cached data in the CAM. In this way, the delay to the data update can be shortened.

Fourth, a wrapper is used to deal with the heterogeneity of the source sites. The CAM gathers contents from many different source sites. So, handling the different sites in a uniform way is critical to the CAM system. By deploying a wrapper module to each source server, the CAM can handle different source sites in a uniform way.

In this paper, we present the design and implementation of the CAM. We also show some measurement results to demonstrate the performance of the system. The current version of our system is designed for WSS interacting with typical Web sites. Thus, Web sites adopting new technologies such as XML and Web Services, are not considered in this paper. We believe that such emerging Web technologies can be easily incorporated to our system.

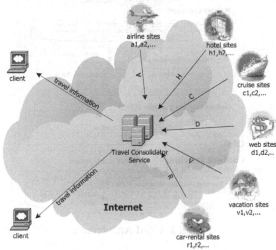

Fig. 1. An Example of Web Syndication Services – Travel Consolidator Service

This paper is organized as follows. The CAM architecture is described in Section 2. A few challenging issues are discussed in Section 3. In Section 4, system performance is discussed. We discuss related work in Section 5. Finally, we conclude our work in Section 6.

2 Content Aggregation Middleware (CAM) Architecture

A WSS can be constructed with a front-end WSS logic and a back-end CAM (See Fig. 2). The WSS logic implements service specific application logic. It is usually implemented as Web applications using JSP, Servlet, etc. It interacts with clients via Web server or application server to receive requests and deliver results. It also interacts with the CAM to request or to receive data required to construct result pages.

The CAM has a modular structure, which consists of four components: Content Provider Wrapper (CPW), Content Provider Manager (CPM), Memory Cache Manager (MCM), and Memory Cache (MC). CPW runs on content provider sites and enables the CAM to access different content providers in an identical way. The other components are on the WSS site. CPM communicates with content providers and receives contents. MCM manages MC, which stores and manages the retrieved data.

2.1 Processing Flow

The CAM mainly deals with two kinds of requests: content update request and content access request. The request processing flows are shown in Fig. 2.

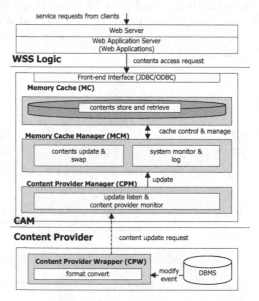

Fig. 2. CAM Architecture

The update process is initiated when data is modified in the content provider's database. The content provider detects and notifies the update event, including table ID, field names, and modified values, to CPW. CPW receives the notification message. Then, it converts the data according to the converting information and sends the converted result to CPM. CPM receives the update message and forwards it to MCM. Finally, MCM replaces the data in the MC with the new data in the update message.

The content access process is initiated when clients request a service. Web applications implementing WSS logic retrieve data from MC and generate a service result. The Web applications access MC via a popular database interface such as JDBC or ODBC

2.2 Deployment of WSS and the CAM

In order to start a WSS with the CAM, content providers as well as the WSS provider need to participate in service deployment process. First, both the WSS provider and participating content providers should agree on how to interact with each other. Second, content providers need to install and configure a CPW. We use Service Contract (SC) to simplify the configuration process. The SC represents a collection of well-defined and externally visible rules which both human and machine can understand [4]. It is used as an enforcement mechanism for proper interactions between the CAM and content providers. The structure of the SC is shown in Fig. 3.

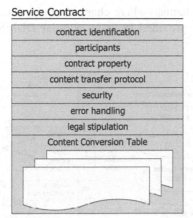

Fig. 3. Structure of the Service Contract

After the SC is filled up and a CPW is installed in a content provider server, the content provider and the CAM configure their systems according to the SC. Since the SC contains the specification for all the interaction rules, the configuration is simply done by feeding the SC into the systems. At the content provider site, the CPW first parses the SC and then sets up related components such as the communication interfaces.The CAM also parses the SC. Then, it notifies CPM's monitoring module and update-listening module of the new content provider. If needed, it also forwards configuration information such as valid actions, protocols, and addresses, to each module. Based on this information, the modules prepare themselves for the new content provider. Note that, in the proposed architecture, the re-configuration is easily done dynamically by feeding a new SC into the CAM and the contracted content provider.

3   Design Challenges

3.1   Instant Update Mechanism

It is important to keep the data in the CAM up-to-date. Thus, any modifications of contents in the content provider's database should be promptly reflected to those in the CAM. In addition, the update mechanism should be efficient since a high number of update requests are expected.

The update scheme is based on server-push. The content provider server instantly identifies any modification in the database, and initiates an update in the CAM by sending out an invalidation message. Thus, an update is propagated to the CAM with very small delay. When sending an invalidation message, we piggyback the message with the modified field and value. Thus, an update can be completed with one message.

The instant identification of content modification is done based on a trigger mechanism in the content provider's database. Using a trigger mechanism, the update process can be done very efficiently. It is so since fine grained invalidation is possible due to the use of the mechanism where changes can be detected in the unit of a field. Trigger mechanisms are provided in many popular DBMS's such as Oracle, DB2, and MySql .

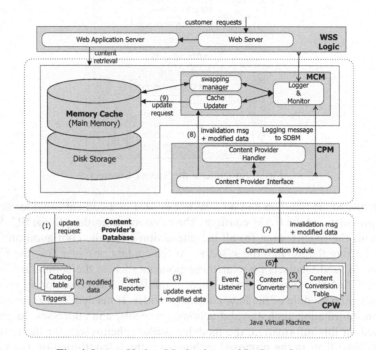

Fig. 4. Instant Update Mechanism and Its Procedure

Currently, time-to-live (TTL) based schemes are most popularly used as a cache consistency mechanism in the Internet [8]. However, TTL-based schemes are not proper for the CAM since they cannot quickly propagate updates to a cache. Prompt propagation of updates may be achieved if a cache frequently polls changes in servers in a very small interval. However, this will incur excessive overhead to the cache. On the contrary, server-push style approaches can more quickly reflect changes in original data.

Fig. 4 shows the detailed structure of CPW and the whole update process from database modification at content provider server to actual update at the CAM. When an update occurs at the content provider's database (1), the trigger routine activates a trigger, here we named it as Event Reporter. (2). The Event Reporter sends the modified information to CPW (3). The update information is received by the Event Listener module in CPW. Then, Content Converter converts the schema and format of the received information (4) by referring to Content Conversion Table, if needed (5). The Content Converter makes an update message with the converted information (6). Then, the Communication Module sends the message to the CAM (7). As soon as CPM receives the update message, it forwards the message to MCM (8). Lastly, MCM constructs a proper query message based on the received message and commits the update transaction on MC, logging this event if required (9).

3.2 Template-Based, Safe Wrapper Mechanism

In CPW design, safety should be importantly considered since it runs in foreign (i.e., content providers) servers. It may access confidential data, crash, or generate an error disturbing the server system.

For safety, we propose a dynamically customizable wrapper. In our approach, a generic wrapper template is composed and used for every content provider. Since there is only one template, certifying the safety of the wrapper becomes easy. For instance, the safety can be certified by the third part agency. Once certified, the safety of the wrapper is assured for every content provider. Each wrapper instance is generated from the template along with an SC. The instance will act as specified in the SC. Note that the SC is signed by the WSS provider as well as the content provider.

We implement the wrapper using Java. Java-based implementation is advantageous in several ways. First, the module can be installed in any computing environment running Java Virtual Machine (JVM). Second, faults in a wrapper module do not affect the reliability of a content provider system. Faults in the wrapper module propagate only to the virtual machine. Third, by using the powerful access control mechanism of JAVA, content providers can prevent a wrapper from accessing their resources.

4 Performance Evaluation

The performance of the CAM prototype is evaluated using a prototype. For high performance, the CAM prototype was implemented mostly in C++ on Linux platform. Most of the MCM's functions, including system monitoring and logging, have been implemented. In the current prototype, the number of requests for each content object and that of messages from each content provider are monitored and logged. The current version of MC has been implemented by customizing the third party main memory database, "Altibase" [9]. This helps us quickly implement the prototype. To help content providers set up database triggers, we plan to provide templates and samples of the triggers for different DBMS's. For the time being, those for the Oracle DBMS are provided

4.1 Experimental Environment

We assume that the CAM is deployed on a single node. The performance will increase when the CAM is deployed on multiple nodes. For the simplicity of measurement, clients and content providers are connected to the CAM via 100M local area networks. Each node has a Pentium III 1Ghz CPU and 512MB main memory except the node for the CAM which has 2GB main memory. Red Hat Linux 7.2 is used as the operating system, and Sun JAVA 1.3 is used as the JVM. Apache 1.3.20 and Tomcat 3.2.3 is used for the Web server and the application server, respectively. In the rest of this section, we assume that all the cached contents fit in the main memory.

4.2 Workload and Measures

The performance of the CAM prototype is evaluated via three different measures: (1) browse, (2) update, (3) mixed throughputs. The browse throughput is measured when requests are only from clients, while the update throughput is measured when requests are only from content providers. The mixed throughput is measured when the two types of requests are issued.

To measure the performance of browse request processing, we use a transactional Web benchmark: TPC Benchmark™ W (TPC-W) [13]. It is commonly used to measure the performance of a database-backed web serving system. We slightly modified the TPC-W benchmark. Originally, there are two kinds of interactions in the TPC-W specification: browsing and ordering. We use only browse interactions in our experiment since the browsing interaction is composed of database retrieval operations. Note that *database scale factor* is used to specify the scale of the measured web serving system. To measure the update throughput, we made our own utility called update request generator. It generates and sends multiple update requests simultaneously, emulating the situation where several content providers update their contents at the same time.

4.3 Performance Evaluation

We measure the throughput and response time when database scale is 10k or 100k. Fig. 5 shows the throughput of five browsing interactions. Throughput is represented in WIPS - the number of interactions processed per second. The total WIPS, i.e., the summation of the WIPS for five interactions, is 77 and 8 when database scale is 10k or 100k, respectively. The response time measured from the same experiments shows that all requests are processed in 0.23 and 1 second when database scale is 10k or 100k, respectively.

Fig. 6 (a) shows the throughputs as the number of threads in the update request generator increases from one to ten; the number of threads represents the number of content providers sending updates simultaneously. We run the experiments when the update message size is 64 and 256 bytes. Although the update size would be arbitrary, we assume that the sizes of frequently changed database fields are not large. The number 64 is chosen since it is the smallest power of two larger than 38, which is the maximum digit of numeric variable in Oracle database. Similarly, 256 is the closest number to 255 which is the default size of char type in Oracle. The figure shows that the CAM processes about 400 requests per second. The number of active content providers or update message size has a negligible effect on the performance.

To measure the mixed throughput, we kept sending a fixed number of update requests per second via the update request generator, and then measured the browse throughput via TCP-W. Fig. 6 (b) shows the results. For simplicity, the throughput is represented as the total WIPS. Note that from the previous experiments, the browse only throughput, i.e., browse throughput without any update, is 77 and the update only throughput is 411.

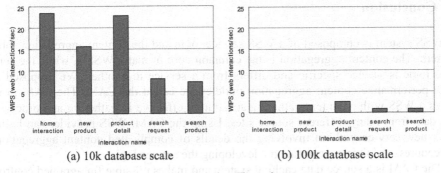

(a) 10k database scale   (b) 100k database scale

Fig. 5. Browsing Throughput

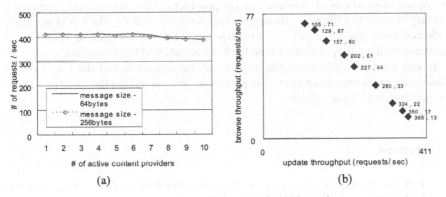

(a)   (b)

Fig. 6. (a) Update Throughput, (b) Mixed Throughput

5 Related Work

Content aggregation tools such as Agentware [10], Active Data Exchange [11], and Enterprise Content Management Suite [12] help to retrieve and aggregate contents from multiple information sources. However, those tools are for an intra-organizational use, while the CAM is designed for inter-organizational use.

Recently, a number of researches have proposed techniques for dynamic data caching [5, 6, 7]. These techniques have been proposed mainly as the scalability solution for ordinary Web services, noting that the generation of dynamic data becomes a major bottleneck. The CAM is different in that it focuses on the provision of a WSS, which is a new type of cross-organizational data services, based on the cached information. The CAM is also different from others in that other caches can be considered as reverse proxies that are used within the contexts of specific servers, whereas the CAM is closer to a proxy that operates along with a number of content providers.

6 Conclusion

A WSS system is composed of a WSS service logic and the content aggregation subsystem. The content aggregation is the common core of many WSS's, while the service logic is service specific and differs from a service to another. We proposed a high performance content aggregation middleware called the CAM. The CAM provides a WSS with a content gathering substratum effective in gathering and processing data from many different source sites. Using the CAM, WSS provider can build up a new service without involving the details of complicated content aggregation procedures, and thus concentrate on developing the service logic.

The CAM is a source data caching system and makes possible fine-grained control of gathered contents. It is a high performance system capable of handling a high rate of request from lots of clients and content providers. Also, it uses main memory as a primary storage to efficiently manage a large volume of data. The CAM is equipped with real-time update capability to keep the freshness of cached contents. It is equipped with a wrapper to deal with the heterogeneity of the source sites.

In this paper, we described the design and implementation of the CAM. We also showed the performance of the CAM prototype. We currently plan to further improve the performance of the system.

References

1.   T. Rutkowski,http://www.ngi.org/trends/TrendsPR0002.txt, Bianual strategic note, Center for Next Generation Internet, February, 2000
2.   http://www.shopping.com/, price comparison service site
3.   http://www.expedia.com/, travel consolidator service
4.   Asit Dan and Francis Parr, The Coyote approach for Network Centric Service Applications: Conversational Service Transactions, a Monitor and an Application, High Performance Transaction Processing (HPTS) Workshop, Sep, 1997
5.   Khaled Yagoub and Daniela Florescu and Cezar Cristian Andrei and Valerie Issarny, Building and Customizing Data-intensive Web Site using Weave, Proc. of the Int. Conf. on Very Large Data Bases (VLDB), Cairo, Egypt, Sep, 2000
6.   K. Selcuk Candan and Wen-Syan Li and Qiong Luo and Wang-Pin Hsiung and Divyakant Agrawal, Enabling Dynamic Content Caching for Database-Driven Web Sites, Proceedings of SIGMOD'2001,pages 532 – 543, California, USA, May, 2001
7.   Qiong Luo and Jeffrey F. Naughton, Form-based proxy caching for database-backed web sites, Proc. of the Int. Conf. on Very Large Data Bases (VLDB), Roma, Italy , Sep, 2001
8.   Balachaner Krishnamurthy and Jennifer Rexford,Web Protocols and Practice - HTTP/1.1, Networking Protocols, Caching and Traffic Measurement, Addison-Wesley, 2001
9.   http://www.altibase.com, Altibase Main Memory Database
10.   http://www.agentware.net/, AgentWare (integrating the internet) - AgentWare Syndicator
11.   http://www.activedatax.com/, Active Data Exchange - active data Syndicator
12.   http://www.reddot.com/, RedDot Solutions - Content Import Engine
13.   http://www.tpc.org/tpcw/default.asp, TPC benchmark W specification version 1.4, Feb., 2001

Domain-Based Proxy for Efficient Location Tracking of Mobile Agents

Sanghoon Song and Taekyoung Kwon

School of Computer Engineering, Sejong University, Seoul 143-747, Korea
{song,tkwon}@sejong.ac.kr

Abstract. The provision of location tracking for mobile agents is designed to deliver a message to a moving object in a network. Most tracking methods exploit relay stations that hold location information to forward messages to a target mobile agent. In this paper, we propose an efficient location tracking method for mobile agents using the domain-based proxy as a relay station. The proxy in each domain is dynamically determined when a mobile agent enters a new domain. The proposed method exploits the domain-based moving patterns of mobile agents and minimizes registration and message transfer costs in mobile agent systems.

1 Introduction

Mobile agents are software objects that can migrate across the network representing users in various tasks. The most attractive applications are e-commerce, network management, and real-time control in many distributed system areas. The code mobility provides many advantages. When the data volume in a remote host is very big, mobile agent systems can save the network bandwidth tremendously. Instead of requesting whole data through network connection, a mobile agent migrates to the target host, filters through the data locally, and brings back only the result. For real-time control of remote devices, the traditional client/server design is not a good candidate due to the irregular network delay. However, a mobile agent that has migrated to a remote system can directly control the target system in real time. Mobile agents are also useful for applications in wireless environments, such as laptops or PDAs, that can be disconnected at short notice [1,2,3].

Apart from these advantages, there are many problems to be solved. Most of the research focuses on providing system support for the security of mobile agents, reliable communication with fast moving mobile agents, and efficient location management [4,5]. The typical application of mobile agent is to bypass the communication link and to exploit local access to resources on a remote server. Thus one may argue that the communication issue is not important. However, we have several situations that require efficient communication with mobile agents. For example, a user may launch a mobile agent with some parameters directing the behavior of the agent and may want to change the parameters

H. Jin et al. (Eds.): NPC 2004, LNCS 3222, pp. 205–212, 2004.
© IFIP International Federation for Information Processing 2004

later due to changes in the context that determined their creation [4]. Mobile agent systems should have location tracking functions to transfer messages only to target agents. Whenever a mobile agent migrates to a new node, the new location information should be registered somewhere in the system.

In this paper, we propose an efficient location tracking method called Domain-Based Proxy. A domain consists of a group of hosts that are close to each other, measured by the number of hops in a network. Mobile agents can reduce the length of their migration paths by visiting the hosts in the same domain first, rather than selecting hosts randomly. The proposed method exploits the domain-based moving patterns of mobile agents and minimizes the registration and message delivery cost. We do not consider the chasing problem that occurs when mobile agents migrate so frequently that relay stations keep forwarding messages to hosts where the target agent no longer stays [4].

Section 2 explains background information in the field and motivation for this work, and section 3 explains the idea of domain-based proxy and its effectiveness in reducing the registration and message delivery costs. In section 4, we discuss simulation results with various parameters. Finally, we present our conclusions in section 5.

2   Background and Motivation

In recent years, there have been several protocols on location tracking of mobile agents. The common ground of these protocols is to have relay nodes that hold the current location of an agent and forward messages to it [5]. There are three different forms of relay nodes: a relay node that is fixed, a relay node that is movable, and a chain of relay nodes that are linked with a pointer. The relay nodes provide location transparent service to senders so that senders do not care about the current locations of agents and their movements. We assume that senders know the homes of mobile agents and the home nodes also act as relay nodes.

2.1   Home

The home node of a mobile agent carries the current location information of the agent and forwards messages from senders to the destination agent. Whenever a mobile agent migrates to a new host, it registers its current location with the home node. The protocol is simple, but the registration cost is high when the agent is far away from the home. Since there is no other relay node between the home and the destination node, the message delivery cost is low.

2.2   Pointer Chain

Each node on the migration path of a mobile agent keeps the pointer to the next node on the path. The home node becomes the first node in the pointer chain. When a mobile agent migrates between the nodes within a domain that is far away from the home, the registration cost is low compared to the Home method. However, the message delivery cost becomes very high, since messages are forwarded through all the nodes on the chain.

2.3 Mailbox

Each mobile agent has a mailbox that relays messages to it. The agent registers its current location with its mailbox whenever it moves to a new node. The mailbox decoupled from the agent can reside in different hosts and moves independently [3]. Since it is movable, the home node should have the updated location information for the mailbox. After getting the current mailbox location from the home node, the sender delivers messages to its mailbox that can relay the messages to the target agent. The method of mailbox movement has not been published yet. Without an efficient mailbox movement, the performance will be nearly the same as the Home method.

3 Domain-Based Proxy

We define the term domain as a group of hosts that are close to each other in network structure. Each host belongs to only one domain. A proxy is determined at the time of entry to a new domain. The first host that a mobile agent visits in a new domain serves as a proxy in the domain. Whenever the mobile agent moves to a host in the same domain, it registers its location with the proxy in the domain. If the mobile agent migrates to a host in another domain, the host becomes a proxy in the new domain and registers with the proxy in the previous domain. Since another mobile agent can enter the same domain by visiting a different host, there may exist several proxies in one domain. A proxy has a data structure that points to the proxy of the next domain to which the mobile agent has already migrated, or points to the host which the mobile agent is currently visiting. We can lower the registration cost if hosts in a domain are close to each other. Messages are forwarded through the proxy chain and the last proxy in the chain forwards them to the host in which the mobile agent stays.

Figure 1 shows the proxy chain after the mobile agent migrates to h_{10}. It followed the path P_1, h_2, h_3, h_4, P_2, h_6, h_7, P_3, h_9, and h_{10}. Proxy P_1, P_2, and P_3 represent the first host the mobile agent visited in each domain respectively. The solid line indicates the message-forwarding path. The message-forwarding path is relatively shorter than that in the Pointer Chain method. Assuming that the inter-domain distances are relatively far, the registration costs within a domain are lower than those between domains. Thus we can reduce the registration cost for migrations within a domain. If the domain of the current host is equal to that of the previous host, two hosts are in the same domain. Hence, the current host will register with the proxy of this domain. If the domains are different, the current host becomes the proxy of the new domain. Consequently, the proxy of the new domain will be linked to the proxy of the previous domain.

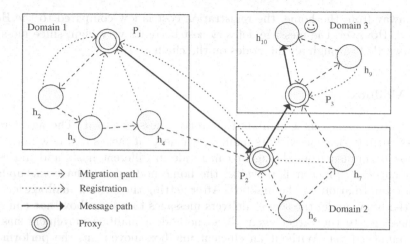

Fig. 1. Migration in the Domain-Based Proxy scheme

3.1   Compacting Proxy Chain

Messages are forwarded through the proxy chain and delivered to the host where
the target agent is. When the number of messages is high, the long proxy chain
may monopolize the overall cost by overshadowing the low registration cost.
Given the estimation of the number of messages, we can compact the proxy
chain to reduce the message delivery cost.

We define following parameters to describe compacting the proxy chain.

- N : the expected number of messages to receive
- D_0 : the distance from the home to the current node
- D_p : the distance from the home to the current node through the proxy chain
- R_0 : the registration cost at the home node
- R_p : the registration cost at the proxy node

After executing the mobile agent many times, we may predict the expected
number of messages to receive. We assume that each node knows the distance
from all other nodes including the home node. To evaluate the distance D_p from
the home to the current proxy through the proxy chain, each agent should carry
the D_{p-1}. which denotes the distance from the home to the previous proxy
through the chain. Distance D_0 and D_p can determine the registration cost R_0
and R_p respectively. With these parameters, we can estimate the registration
and message delivery costs for the cases of proxy chain compacted and proxy
chain without compacted. Since the migration within a domain does not change
the proxy, only the case of migrating to a different domain requires the following
decision on whether to compact or not.

$$N * D_p + R_p > N * D_0 + R_0$$

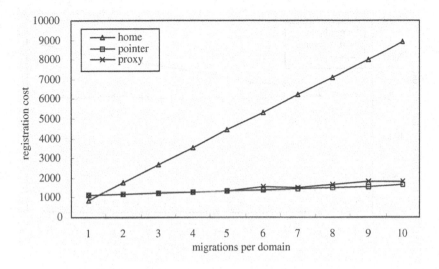

Fig. 2. Registration cost

As an extreme case, an agent may migrate through a path such that D_p equals to D_0. Since R_p is definitely smaller than R_0 for this case, keeping the proxy chain can reduce the overall costs. In most cases, the distance through the proxy chain, D_p, is larger than the direct distance, D_0, and the registration cost R_p is smaller than R_0. When no message is expected to arrive, the compaction is not necessary. However, as the expected number of messages increases, we can minimize the overall cost by compacting the proxy chain.

4   Simulation and Discussion

We assume that the network structure is in the form of a two dimensional grid and the location of each host is expressed by the coordinate (x, y) in the grid. The distance between two hosts can be calculated with the geometrical distance of two coordinates in the grid. The grid is partitioned to form domains. Each domain is also a square grid with smaller size. The costs for location registration and message delivery depend on the distance between two hosts and the data size. We assume the data size for registration is about a quarter of the data size in message delivery [5].

In the simulation, we calculate the registration and message delivery costs that occur in the host on the migration path. Starting from a randomly selected host in a domain, we continue to move to randomly selected hosts in the same domain until the number of migrations per domain is met. After completing a given number of migrations in a domain, we move to a new domain and visit hosts in the domain. Since the migration pattern can be different in various applications, the domains are selected randomly for simulation. We assume that all the hosts involved are lightly loaded and there is no additional delay in

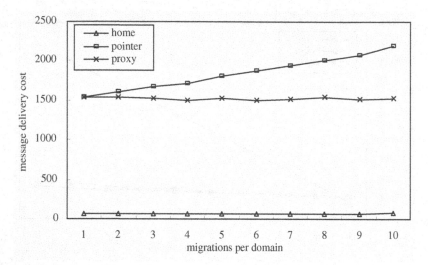

Fig. 3. Message delivery cost

processing messages. We repeat the above simulation by varying the number of migrations per domain and the number of messages.

Figure 2 represents the registration costs against the number of migrations per domain. We observe the Proxy and the Pointer Chain method outperform the Home method as the number of migrations per domain becomes larger. The reason is that the inter-domain distances are greater than the distances between hosts in a domain. When the number of migrations per domain equals one, we do not expect any performance advantage either in the Proxy or the Pointer Chain method. Since the next domain to visit is selected randomly, the distance from the visiting domain to the home node will be comparable to the average inter-domain distance.

Figure 3 shows the message delivery costs against the number of migrations per domain. Since the Pointer Chain method delivers messages through all the relay stations that are on the migration path, the message delivery cost increases linearly as the number of migrations per domain increases. However, the message delivery cost of the Proxy method remains constant because the proxy chain length does not increase even if the number of migrations per domain increases. The Home method delivers messages directly to the target agent without any relay station and the message delivery cost remains minimal.

Figure 4 shows combined costs against the number of messages with the number of migrations per domain fixed at 13. As the number of messages increases, the message delivery costs in the Proxy and the Pointer Chain method begin to dominate the registration cost and monopolize the combined cost respectively. Since the pointer chain length is longer than the proxy chain, the increase rate of the Pointer Chain method is steeper than that of the Proxy method. For the Home method, however, the registration cost still dominates the message

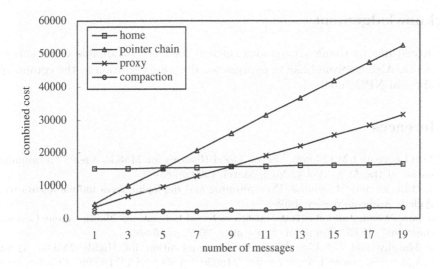

Fig. 4. Combined cost against the number of message delivery

delivery cost and the rate of increase is unnoticeable. The Compaction method demonstrates low registration cost by exploiting the domain-based proxy and keeps message delivery cost low by maintaining a short proxy chain. Random selection of domains works favorably for the Compacting method. In real-life situations, domains may be selected in a sorted order to reduce the migration path. If that is the case, we may need an elaborated compacting method to calculate the minimum path.

5   Conclusion

In this paper, we propose an efficient location tracking method for mobile agents using domain-based proxy. The domain-based proxy method can minimize registration and message delivery costs by exploiting migration patterns. The proxy is determined when a mobile agent migrates to a new domain. The first host that a mobile agent visits in a new domain serves as a proxy in the domain. In the simulation, we calculated the registration and message delivery costs by changing the parameters such as the number of migrations per domain and the number of messages. Assuming that the hosts in a domain are close to each other, we can minimize the registration cost by exploiting the proxy within the domain and minimize the message delivery cost by compacting the proxy chain. Since the domains were selected randomly in the simulation, the proposed simple compaction method is very effective in reducing the proxy chain length. In real-life situations, however, the domains may be selected in a sorted order to reduce the migration path. For a specific pattern of migration, we may need an elaborated compacting method to minimize costs.

Acknowledgement

We would like to thank anonymous referees for their invaluable comments on this work. Also we would like to express our deep appreciation to the committee members of NPC 2004.

References

1. D.B.Lange,and M.Oshima, "Seven Good Reasons for Mobile Agents ",Communication of the ACM ,Vol.42,No.3, March 1999,pp.88-89.
2. D.B.Lange and M.Oshima, Programming and deploying Java mobile agents with Aglets, Addison-Wesley, 1998
3. J.Cao, X.Feng, and S.K.Das, "Mailbox-Based Scheme for Mobile Agent Communications", IEEE Computer, September. 2002, pp. 54-60.
4. A.Murphy and G.P.Picco,"Reliable Communication for Highly Mobile Agents ",Agent Systems and Architectures/Mobile Agents (ASA/MA)'99 , October 1999, pp.141-150.
5. Jiannong Cao, Xinyu Feng, Jian Lu, Henry Chan, and Sajal K. Das, "Reliable Message Delivery for Mobile Agents: Push or Pull", ICPADS 2002, December 2002, Taiwan, ROC., pp. 314-320
6. J, Baumann and K, Rothermel, "The Shadow Approach: An Orphan Detection Protocol for Mobile Agents," , Springer-Verlag, Berlin, Germany, vol. 1477, 1998, pp. 2-13.
7. A.Pham,and A.Karmouch,"Mobile Software Agents:An Overview ", IEEE Communications magazin , Vol.36, No.7, July 1998,pp.26-37.
8. G..Kunito,Y.Okumura,K.Aizawa,and M.Hatori, "Tracking Agent:A New Way of Communication in a Multi-Agent Environment ",Proc. of IEEE 6 th Int'l Conf. on Universal Personal Comm., Vol.2, 1997, pp.903-907.
9. T.K.Shih,"Agent Communication Network -A Mobile Agent Computation Model for Internet Applications ", Proc. 1999 IEEE Int'l Symp on Computers and Communications, 1999, pp.425-431.
10. P.Francis, S.Jamin, V. Paxson, L. Zhang, D. F. Gryniewicz, and Y. Jin, "An architecture for a global Internet host distance estimation service," in Proceedings of IEEE INFOCOM '99, New York, NY, Mar. 1999.
11. N. Minar, K.H. Kramer and P. maes, "Cooperative Mobile Agents for Dynamic network Routing", in Software Agents for Future Communication Systems, Springer-Verlag, 1999. ISBN 3-540-65578-6.
12. A.Bar-Noy,I.Kessler,and M.Sidi, "Mobile Users:To Update or Not To Update?" ACM/Baltzer J.Wireless Network , Vol.1,No.2,July 1995,pp.175-195.
13. A. Fuggetta, G.P. Picco, and G. Vigna, "Understanding Code Mobility", IEEE Transactions on Software Engineering, 24(5), May 1998.
14. P.Bellavista, A.Corradi, C.Stefanelli, "Mobile Agent Middleware for Mobile Computing," IEEE Computer Vol.34, No.3. March 2001. pp. 73-81

Inhambu: Data Mining Using Idle Cycles in Clusters of PCs

Hermes Senger[1], Eduardo R. Hruschka[1], Fabrício A.B. Silva[1],
Liria M. Sato[2], Calebe P. Bianchini[2], Marcelo D. Esperidião[2]

[1] Universidade Católica de Santos (UniSantos)
R. Dr. Carvalho de Mendonça, 144
11070-906 Santos-SP, Brazil
{senger, erh, fabricio}@unisantos.br
[2] Escola Politécnica – Universidade de São Paulo
Av. Prof. Luciano Gualberto, trav 3, n. 180
05508-900 – São Paulo – SP - Brazil
{liria.sato, calebe.bianchini, marcelo.esperidiao}@poli.usp.br

Abstract. In this paper we present and evaluate Inhambu, a distributed object-oriented system that relies on dynamic monitoring to collect information about the availability of computational resources, providing the necessary support for the execution of data mining applications on clusters of PCs and workstations. We also describe a modified implementation of the data mining tool Weka, which executes the cross validation procedure in parallel with the support of Inhambu. We present preliminary tests, showing that performance gains can be obtained for computationally expensive data mining algorithms, even when running with small datasets.[1]

1 Introduction

Knowledge discovery in databases is the non-trivial process of identifying valid, novel, potentially useful, and ultimately understandable patterns in data [1]. Data Mining (DM) is a step in this process that centers on the automated learning of new facts and relationships in data, which consists of three basic steps: data preparation, information discovery and analysis of the mining algorithm output. All of these three steps exploit huge amounts of data and are computationally expensive. In this sense, several techniques have been proposed to improve the performance of DM applications, such as parallel processing [2] and implementations based on cluster of workstations [3] and computational grids [9]. These techniques can leverage the deployment of DM applications to production scales.

Building computer clusters for high performance computing has gained increasingly acceptance during the last few years. According to the November 2003's list of the top500 supercomputer sites [4], 208 were clusters, whereas only 93 clusters ap-

---

[1] This project is partially granted by CNPq (Conselho Nacional de Desenvolvimento Científico e Tecnológico, Brazil), under contract number 401439/2003-8.

H. Jin et al. (Eds.): NPC 2004, LNCS 3222, pp. 213-220, 2004.

214   H. Senger et al.

peared 12 months before. Assembling computer clusters comprised by commodity PCs or workstations is an easy roadmap to provide computational power at low cost. The effective use of clusters forcibly passes thru the availability of software tools capable to support the efficient usage of their resources. In networks of workstations or PCs, individual computers may present low indices of utilization of computational resources, so that idle resources can be used for the execution of processing and memory intensive applications. In this sense, scheduling policies should involve dynamic detection and allocation of idle resources..

In this paper, we present and evaluate Inhambu, a distributed object-oriented system that provides load monitoring and detection of idle resources in the computers that are part of the cluster. The adopted policies take into account real situations in which computers may be heterogeneous and the availability of resources may fluctuate due to presence or absence of local users. Although Inhambu can be used to provide resource management to other applications, in the context of this project it is used for supporting the execution of the Weka System [5], which is an open source software for data mining.

The remainder of this paper is organized as follows: Section 2 introduces the architecture and policies implemented by Inhambu, whereas Section 3 outlines the changes made to Weka in order to run data mining tasks in a parallel fashion. Section 4 goes on to present performance results, and Section 5 outlines some related work. Finally, Section 6 summarizes our results and outlines future work.

2 Overview of Inhambu

This section briefly describes the main components and strategies comprising our system named Inhambu, whose main components are depicted in Figure 1. Thru this architecture, Inhambu implements an extended *trading service* which can support resource management functionalities to the interaction among client/server programs written in Java. The *trader* enables server programs to publish their services, by invoking its *exportService* operation and passing service names and remote object references. Such information remains stored in the *trader*, which can be queried by client programs by means of its *importService* operation. Clients must import references to remote objects that implement the application services before they can invoke them. Clients can be either application programs, or the Weka's user interface.

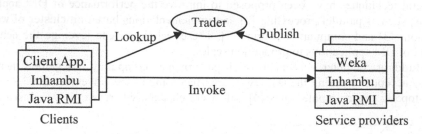

Fig. 1. The Trader Model, implemented by Inhambu.

During the execution of the import operation, a resource management policy that aims at minimizing the execution times is used. Such policy uses information about idle resources, (e.g. CPU, memory) which is periodically received from monitoring agents placed on every server computer. In summary, our policy looks for the *best computer* which implements the requested service. If such server can be found, then an object reference is returned to the requesting client. If no good server currently implements the requested service, the trader looks for another good computer to instantiate a new object that implements the service (which could be the first instance for this service type, or a new replica of existing ones). In all cases, the server selection procedure looks for the computer capable to execute the service in the shortest time, taking into account its processing power and current load. A more detailed description of the system's architecture and operation was presented in [6].

3 Parallelizing Cross Validation with Inhambu

Weka [5] is currently one of the most popular DM tools. It is an open source software developed by researchers at The University of Waikato, New Zealand, and issued under the GNU General Public License (GPL). Weka is written in Java, being currently available to Windows, MAC OS and Linux platforms. In a nutshell, Weka provides implementations of several algorithms for data mining. Its current version contains implementations of 71 algorithms for classification, 5 algorithms for clustering, 2 algorithms for association, and 12 algorithms for attribute selection. In fact, it is continually growing, incorporating more and more data mining algorithms. All these algorithms can be either applied directly to a dataset or called from Java codes.

Classification algorithms, also called classifiers, are predominant in relation to the other ones implemented in Weka. Therefore, we decided to first investigate potential benefits that Inhambu could bring in relation to the classifiers package. In this sense, the standard way of predicting the error rate of a classifier given a simple, fixed sample of data is to use stratified tenfold cross validation [5]. In the tenfold cross validation process, the dataset is divided into ten equal parts (folds) and the classifier is trained in nine parts (folds) and tested in the other one. This procedure is repeated in ten different training sets and the estimated error rate is the average in the test sets. Clearly, these experiments can be performed in a parallel way, taking advantage of Inhambu. It is important to emphasize that all classifiers implemented in Weka can benefit from such approach.

In this paper, we focus on the parallelization of the cross validation by distributing different folds to execute in different nodes of the cluster. To accomplish this, we modified the *classifiers* package. The most important class in this package is the Classifier, which defines the general structure of any scheme for classification. All classifier algorithms are implemented as subclasses of *classifier*. It contains two methods, named buildClassifier() and classifyInstance(), which must be implemented for each classifier method, so that the whole scheme redefines them according to how it builds a classifier and how it classifies data instances. The *classifier* creates a uniform interface for building and using all the classifiers methods, so that the same evaluation module can be used to evaluate the performance and accuracy of any classifier in Weka. The evaluation module is implemented by the class *Evaluation*, whose method `crossValidateModel()` implements the stratified *n-fold cross validation* procedure, in which the dataset is divided into *n* equal parts. Then, the algorithm is trained in *n-1* parts and tested in the remaining one. This procedure is repeated in *n* different training sets and the estimated error rate is the average in the test sets. Clearly, these experiments are independent and can be performed in parallel by up to *n* computers of the cluster. Although the number of folds in cross validation can be chosen by the user, the tenfold cross validation (i.e., setting *n*=10) is popularly known as a good practice among data mining practitioners and researchers. If no other value to *n* is provided by the user, Weka assumes ten (by default).

4 Performance Tests

In order to evaluate the performance of Inhambu, we have performed several simulations by means of two classifiers that are popular in the data mining community: PART and Multilayer Perceptrons. In summary, the PART classifier provides rules from pruned partial decision trees [5]. Multilayer perceptrons are feedforward neural networks that learn by means of backpropagation algorithms [10], which are gradient descent techniques with backward error (gradient) propagation. Our simulations were performed in three datasets that are benchmarks for data mining methods: Iris Plants, Wisconsin Breast Cancer, and Congressional Voting Records. These datasets are available at the UCI Machine Learning Repository [7] and describe classification problems. The Iris Plants dataset consists of three classes (Setosa, Versicolour and Virginica), each one formed by 50 examples of plants. Each plant is described by four continuous attributes (sepal and petal length and width). In the Wisconsin dataset, each object has nine ordinal attributes and an associated class label (benign or malignant). The total number of objects is 699 (458 benign and 241 malignant), of which 16 have a single missing feature. We removed those 16 objects and used the remaining ones. The Congressional Voting Records dataset includes votes for each of the U.S. House of Representatives Congressmen on 16 key votes (attributes). There are 435 instances (267 democrats, 168 republicans) and each of the 16 attributes is Boolean valued. However, there are 203 instances with missing values. These instances were removed and we employed the 232 remaining ones in our simulations.

In our simulations, we have employed Weka 3.4.1, the most recent version by the time of this writing. For remote method invocation, Inhambu currently uses the Java/RMI platform, which allows the invocation of either local or remote methods transparently. A test scenario was created that implements a *remote cross validation* service to be executed on a replicated pool of server hosts. In order to enable the cross validation to execute in parallel, we implemented a new class named *ParallelEvaluation*, which inherits the functionalities of the class *Evaluation*.. This new class creates a pool of local threads that implement the preparation of datasets, the invocation of remote cross validation services, and gathering of the results.

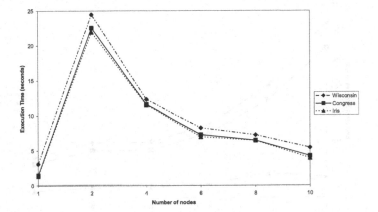

Fig. 2. The execution times for the PART algorithm.

To execute performance tests, we used a cluster composed of 16 PCs interconnected by a 100 Mbps Ethernet switch. Each cluster node is a Celeron 433 MHz single processor with 128KB of cache, 128 MB of memory, running Linux operating system and JDK 1.4.1. Initially, we executed the PART algorithm to analyze the datasets mentioned above in 1, 2, 4, 6, 8 and 10 nodes of the cluster. The *one node* test refers to a sequential execution with the original, non-modified Weka software. Each test was carried out ten times, and the average is illustrated in Figure 2. As one can see, there was no advantage in employing parallel executions to run PART in these datasets. Notice that the execution time with 2 processing nodes is around 8 times slower than local execution. This behavior is typical for PART as well as for other lightweighted classifier algorithms when small benchmark datasets are employed. It is due to the overhead of transmitting one copy of the whole dataset to ten processing nodes (for tenfold cross validation) via RMI. For each invocation, threads are created to manage the transmission process, marshalling and unmarshalling, manipulation of buffers, and so on. The overhead in this case is not paid by the short execution times (which are less than 0.2 or 0.3 seconds for this example). However, it is likely that performance gains can be obtained when applying PART to real-world datasets.

Another set of experiments was carried out in the same environment to analyze the same datasets, but using the algorithm Multilayer Perceptrons instead. The execution times for these experiments are depicted in Figure 3. In this case, the overall execution time can be reduced by a factor of 3 or 4, for a cluster with 10 processing nodes. It is important to emphasize that, in real-world data mining applications, in which huge databases are common, the performance gains are likely to be even more relevant.

In these experiments, all the computers were dedicated to execute our experiments. This measure assures the test is not influenced by other users or applications. Although in real situations the computers are not dedicated and may present fluctuating loads, Inhambu acts by selecting only those nodes which are currently idle, or present good conditions to execute tasks.

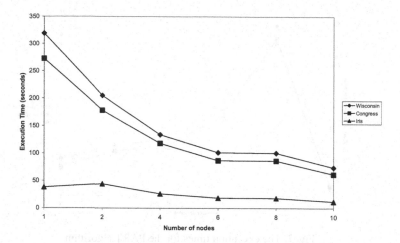

Fig. 3. The execution times for Multilayer Perceptrons.

5 Related Work

Weka-Parallel [8] is also a project that aims at providing a modified, parallel implementation of Weka. Weka-Parallel leverages parallel processing by distributing different folds of the *cross validation* to different computers of a local network. The similarities between Inhambu and Weka-Parallel are evident, since they either focus on parallelizing cross validation, and they operate on local networks of computers. However, some important differences should be highlighted here. Weka-Parallel uses *sockets* as the inter-process communication mechanism, whereas Inhambu uses RMI. The later allows Weka methods to being invoked either locally or remotely with full transparency from location details, and without the need to modify the Weka's classes. This can minimize the handy work to customize new versions of Weka to work on the top of Inhambu. In addition, Inhambu provides some important performance management functionalities, such as the capacity to deal with load fluctuations as well as the heterogeneity of the computers in the cluster. In contrast, Weka-Parallel implements a *round robin* scheduling policy, which does not consider neither the current utilization of the machines nor the differentiated processing capacities. Finally, it is worth to notice that Inhambu aims at supporting the efficient execution of a wide range of high performance applications, not restricted to Data Mining. In the context of this project, however, both Inhambu and Weka are being customized to work together.

6 Conclusion and Future Work

Data mining applications exploit huge amounts of data and are computationally expensive, demanding high quantities of computational resources such as processor cycles and main memory. Clusters comprised by commodity PCs interconnected by a local network can provide these resources at low cost for data mining practitioners. However, managing the heterogeneity and the fluctuating load of the computers in the cluster are necessary for the effective utilization of clusters of PCs. Inhambu implements mechanisms and policies that rely on dynamic monitoring to collect information about the availability of resources, providing the necessary support for the execution of data mining applications on clusters of PCs and workstations.

In this paper we describe a straightforward scheme to execute cross validation in parallel. Parallelizing cross validation is worthwhile, because it is widely used to evaluate data mining algorithms and it is the most expensive part in this process. In addition, our parallel cross validation scheme can be applied for all the 71 classification algorithms currently implemented by Weka (which implements 90 algorithms). However, deciding to use or not to use parallel processing to execute data mining applications may not be trivial. Due to loose coupling of the architecture, only the execution of sufficiently expensive tasks can be advantageous. Our experiments showed that, depending on the size of the dataset, the parallel execution of PART may not be advantageous, and suggests that it can be a typical behavior for other lightweighted algorithms like this one. However, we believe that parallel execution may be advantageous even for lightweighted algorithms, depending on the characteristics of the dataset, such as the number of instances, number and type of attributes, and the potential patterns that can be found by data mining. Our experiments also showed that more computationally expensive algorithms like the Multilayer Perceptrons always provide performance gains, even with small benchmark datasets. Besides, another common situation in data mining involves evaluating the error rate of several classifiers before choosing the best one, according to a particular application and dataset. In this situation, several cross validations could be performed in parallel, one for each classifier, increasing the degree of parallelism and potential gains.

It is worth to notice that the scheme proposed here, to execute cross validation in parallel over Inhambu, is quite straightforward and obvious. No optimization was used. However, one can notice that in parallel tenfold cross validation, the same dataset is sent up to ten different nodes. Clearly, some scheme to group tasks to execute in the same node of the cluster can reduce the transfer of datasets over the network. Such a scheme may be particularly more advantageous when several cross validation processes are managed to execute in parallel (e.g. to perform the evaluation of several classifiers in parallel). In the near future, we are going to investigate this approach, as well as its application to real-world databases, in which huge amounts of data are processed.

References

1. Fayyad, U. M., Shapiro, G. P., Smyth, P. "From Data Mining to Knowledge Discovery: An Overview". In: Advances in Knowledge Discovery and Data Mining, Fayyad, U.M., Piatetsky-Shapiro, G., Smyth, P., Uthurusamy, R., Editors, MIT Press, pp. 1-37, 1996.
2. Freitas, A.A., Lavington, S.H., *Mining Very Large Databases with Parallel Processing*, Kluwer Academic Publishers, 1998.

3. Baraglia, R. et al., Implementation Issues in the Design of I/O Intensive Data Mining Applications on Clusters of Workstations, Proc. of 3rd Workshop on High Perf. Data Mining, IPDPS'2000.
4. The TOP500 supercomputer sites list. Available online at: http://www.top500.org
5. Witten, I. H. and Frank, E. *Data Mining: Practical machine learning tools with Java implementations.*. Morgan Kaufmann, San Francisco, 2000.
6. Senger, H., Sato, L. M. Load Distribution for Heterogeneous and Non-Dedicated Clusters Based on Dynamic Monitoring and Differentiated Services. In: Proc. of the IEEE Intl. Conf. on Cluster Computing, pp. 199-206. Hong Kong. Computer Society Press, Los Alamitos, 2003.
7. Merz, C.J., Murphy, P..M., UCI Repository of Machine Learning Databases, http://www.ics.uci.edu, Irvine, CA, University of California.
8. Celis, S., Musicant, D. R. Weka-Parallel: Machine Learning in Parallel. Technical Report. Carleton College Computer Science, 2002. Available at: http://www.mathcs.carleton.edu/weka/report.pdf
9. Canataro, M., Talia, D.The Knowledge Grid,Communications of the ACM, v.46, n.1, 2003.
10. Fu, L., Neural Networks in Computer Intelligence, McGraw Hill, 1994.

Request Distribution for Fairness with a New Load-Update Mechanism in Web Server Cluster

MinHwan Ok[1], Myong-soon Park[2]

[1]Korea Railroad Research Institute
Uiwang, Gyeonggido, 437-050, Korea
panflute@korea.ac.kr
[2]Dept. of Computer Science and Engineering, Korea University
Seoul, 136-701, Korea
myongsp@ilab.korea.ac.kr

Abstract. The complexity of services and applications provided by Web sites is ever increasing as integration of traditional Web publishing sites with new paradigms, i.e., e-commerce. Each dynamic Web page is difficult to estimate its execution load even with the information from the application layer. In this paper the execution latency at Web server is exploited in order to balance loads from dynamic Web pages. With only the information such as IP address and port number for Layer-4 Web switch the proposed algorithm balances the loads with a new load-update mechanism. The mechanism uses the report packets more efficiently with the same communication cost. Moreover the proposed algorithm considers the fairness for Web clients hence the Web clients would experience higher quality of service.

1. Introduction

Web service is the most prevalent Internet service and its importance and usage gets higher as years go. For large numbers of Web client requests are headed to a popular Web site in peak times, most of the sites form multiple nodes into one Web server cluster. In these systems, any client Web request to the system is presented to a front-end server that acts as a representative for the system. This is called Web switch retains transparency of the parallel architecture for the user, guarantees backward compatibility with Internet protocols and standards, and distributes all Web client requests to the back-end Web servers. Web server cluster in this paper collectively indicates this formation of a Web switch and Web servers, as illustrated in Fig. 1. The Web switch should distribute incoming requests to Web servers in load-balanced fashion. With only the information such as IP address and port number it seems some limit exits to develop request distribution algorithm load-balancing. Moreover most of Web pages are incorporated with executing scripts such as Java, PHP and so on, load-balancing becomes much difficult with requests for those dynamic Web pages. Due to variant execution latencies of the executing scripts, load-balancing in distributing requests for dynamic Web pages need consider fairness among Web clients. In this paper we propose a request distribution algorithm with a new load-update mechanism. Although so many algorithms have been proposed, in our best knowledge, no previ-

H. Jin et al. (Eds.): NPC 2004, LNCS 3222, pp. 221-229, 2004.

ous work has suggested the load-update mechanism. In the next section the kinds of information for load-balancing is introduced and the fairness among the Web clients is described. The load-update mechanism is suggested in developing a request distribution algorithm in Section 3. The proposed algorithm is compared with the related previous works in a sense of load-update mechanism in Section 4 and the simulation results are presented in Section 5. The last section concludes with the effect of the new load-update mechanism.

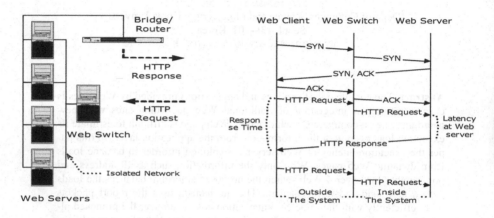

Fig. 1. Web Server Cluster with Isolated System Network

Fig. 2. Web Service Protocol of the Cluster

2. Web Switch and Request Distribution for Fairness

For the performance feature of the Web server cluster the Web switch should distribute the requests to the Web servers so the loads of Web servers are balanced in the cluster. According to the OSI protocol stack layer at which the Web switch operates, Web switches are broadly classified into Layer-4 and Layer-7 Web switches.[1] The Layer-4 Web switch has the only information related to TCP/IP layers, thus the information such as IP address and port number. The Layer-7 Web switch parses the request then gets information of up to the application layer, thus the information such as URL contents, SSL identifiers and cookies. The Layer-4 Web switch is not aware of content information whereas the Layer-7 Web switch is. As much information is supplied, the Layer-7 switch is capable for more accurate decision in distributing the requests. However the Layer-7 Web switch introduces severe processing overhead to the extent that may cause the Web switch to severely limit scalability of the Web server cluster. In [5], the peak throughput achieved by a Layer-7 Web switch is limited to 3,500 connections per second, while software based Layer-4 Web switch implemented on the same hardware is able to sustain a throughput up to 20,000 connections per second. For this reason we propose a distributing algorithm and the system organization found on the Layer-4 Web switch.

Many works on load balancing in distributing requests are conducted for the Web server cluster.[2, 3, 4] The works considers mainly the static Web pages rather than the dynamic Web pages with executing scripts. Nowadays there are much of dynamic Web pages of Java, PHP, ASP and so on. Those Web pages are difficult to estimate the load even with the information from the application layer. Although there might exist such an estimation algorithm, the Web switch cannot use highly sophisticated algorithms in distributing requests since it has to take immediate decision for hundreds or thousand of requests per second. We need a simple algorithm for this reason.

Typical service protocol of the Web server cluster is illustrated in Fig. 2. When the Web switch received the Web client request, it determines whether the request is from current connected Web client or for new connection to a Web server. In the case the request is of current connection by a hash function at Web switch, the request is relayed to the connected Web server. Otherwise, the distribution algorithm selects a Web server for new connection. After processed at the Web server the response of the request is routed to the Web client. As depicted in Fig. 2, the response time is composed of four parts;

$$t_{Response} = t_{Outside} + t_{Distribution} + t_{Inside} + t_{Processing} \tag{1}$$

$t_{Response}$ is the time elapsed after it send its request till the Web client starts receiving the Web server's response. The client request takes a half of $t_{Outside}$ to reach the Web switch, and the server response takes the other half of $t_{Outside}$ to reach the client. This is the time elapsed outside the system only. The Web switch received the request decides the Web server by the distribution algorithm or a hash function for $t_{Distribution}$. The request is then relayed to the Web server in a half of t_{Inside} and processed at the Web server for $t_{Processing}$. After processed the response takes the other half of the t_{Inside} to leave the system, in other words, to reach the bridge/router in fig.2. Among those parts, $t_{Outside}$ is dependent on the location of the Web client. Thus it is variant and unable to reduce at the system. Reducing t_{Inside} is not relevant to the distribution algorithm thus out of the scope of this paper.

To reduce $t_{Distribution}$, the latency at Web switch it is necessary a fast and simple distribution algorithm. Balancing the loads of each Web server would reduce $t_{Processing}$, the latency at Web server, although it is directly dependent on the Web server's capacity. The latency at the Web switch is common for every Web client. Thus equalizing the average of latencies at the Web servers should be fair for the Web clients with respect to the response time. For $t_{Outside}$ is variant by each Web client's distance from the system, the response times are not equal in the reality, however we appreciate it is also fair for all the clients. Therefore we use the execution latencies for comparison of each server's load to evaluate the load-balancing. Exploiting the response time is nothing new for load balancing[6], however the latency at Web server is not exactly the same with the response time. Moreover distribution algorithm we propose has a particular load-update mechanism. The new algorithm works far differently from other algorithms proposed so far.

3. Load-Balancing with a New Load-Update Mechanism

Conventionally the Web switch of the cluster gathers information of each server's load periodically. All the servers in the cluster reports their load information to the Web switch at any given rate, and the load-balancing algorithms used this *periodic load-update* mechanism. This mechanism is good for updating simultaneously actual loads of all the servers since the reporting is synchronized by all the servers. However this mechanism is not good for system scalability since the number of report packets concentrated to the Web server grows as the number of the servers increases. In this section we introduce a new load-update mechanism that the reporting is not synchronized among the servers.

The objective of load-balancing algorithm is to keep even loads among the servers. Previous studies have suggested that the run-queue length best describes a server's load, and many load-balancing algorithms have adopted this metric[9]. We focus on execution latencies thus we adopt this metric. Our basic idea is once sending equal numbers of requests to each server and then let the server having less requests report its 'lessness'.

Load-balancing Algorithm 1. *High-Communication-Cost Model*

```
For every request packet arriving at the Web switch;

1. The Web switch merely distributes the income re-
quests to servers in traditional 'Round-Robin'. Equal
numbers of requests are executing in the servers.

2. When a request finishes its execution the server
that processes the request immediately reports that one
request has finished.

3. The Web switch subtracts one from the load value of
the reported server in the Load Table.

4. IF the load values are not all equal the Web switch
finds the lowest value and sends one request to the
server,

   ELSE the Web switch sends the request in 'Round-Robin'
order.

5. Whenever the Web switch sends one request, it adds
one to the load value of the target server in the Load
Table. Continue at Line 2.
```

Line 4 of the algorithm guarantees the Web switch keep the numbers of executing requests equal among servers. This algorithm is quite simple and works nicely. There are two conditions of early finish; the execution length of the request was shorter in itself, or the request shared resources with fewer other requests, i.e. CPU. While most of other requests are in IO-phase the requests in CPU-phase gets more CPU times. Each server is processing equal number of requests at any instant, however the throughput of each server is different. Since the Web switch does not have enough time to reschedule income requests considering efficient overlap of one request's

CPU-phase and other request's IO-phase, this algorithm should show ideal load-balancing. The algorithm is compared with previous works in Section 4.

For the algorithm to work each request's finish must be immediately reported to the Web switch. We named this load-information update mechanism *Update-on-Finish*. This update is neither periodic nor synchronized among servers. If the requests received from the Web switch are n requests, the reports should be sent exactly n times. Although the 'isolated network' of the Fig. 1 could accommodate the communication for reporting, communication cost to the Web switch in this number of updates may be high. We extend the algorithm for less costly communication.

Algorithm 1 ensures all the servers keep the numbers of executing requests equal among servers. At each server, while some of requests finish the execution, new requests are arriving by Round-Robin of Algorithm 1. Thus the reporting is only necessary when the number of executing requests decreases. The Web switch distributes requests in Round-Robin or sends more requests to the server when the report comes.

Load-balancing Algorithm 2. *Lower-Communication-Cost Model*

```
For every request packet arriving at the Web switch;

1. The Web switch merely distributes the income re-
quests to servers in traditional 'Round-Robin'. Equal
numbers of requests are executing in the servers.

2. When the number of executing requests decreases the
server reports that n requests are more needed.

3. The Web switch subtracts n from the load value of
the reported server in the Load Table.

4. IF the load values are not all equal the Web switch
finds the lowest value and sends one request to the
server,

   ELSE the Web switch sends the request in 'Round-Robin'
order.

5. Whenever the Web switch sends one request, it adds
one to the load value of the target server in the Load
Table. Continue at Line 2.
```

In Algorithm 1, each server receives one more request instantly after the server reported that it has requests one less than other servers. However the Web switch is distributing requests in Round-Robin otherwise, the number of executing requests soon recovers after one request has finished. Recall that the execution lengths of requests are not same each other. Receiving the equal number of requests does not result in the equal number of executing requests.

Let Φ be the period of Round-Robin. Assume one request has finished execution at a server and the server should receive one request within $\Phi/2$ by Round-Robin. Let the server do not report, if no more requests finish within $\Phi/2$. The server counts the number of executing requests at every $\Phi/2$. Thus the server reports after one or more reports finished within the first half of Φ, and two or more requests finished within the second half of Φ. If the server counts the number of executing requests at every Φ, the line 2 of Algorithm 2 reduces the communication cost to $1/m$ when mean m execution finishes are reported in each packet.

4. Related Works and Comparison

Many experiments and simulation results have demonstrated that the Weighted Round-Robin (WRR) comprises simplicity with efficacy at best[2]. Most recent work exploited load-update mechanism is Dahlin's algorithm[7]. WRR uses periodic load-update. Once Web switch realized each server's load, it sends requests to a less loaded server with higher rate and sends requests to a more loaded server with lower rate until they reach equal loads before next load-update. Dahlin's algorithm also uses periodic load-update. The web switch realizes the differences in loads between servers by load-update. It sends requests to servers with least loads. After all other servers' loads are equalized to the most loaded server, the Web switch distributes requests in Round-Robin manner before next load-update. Now we compare the proposed algorithms to these two algorithms with respect to load-update mechanisms.

For any algorithm, higher rate of load-update achieves more balanced load distribution between servers. We define reporting cost, R, as follows;

R : the number of packets received by the Web switch for a given period

Thus reporting cost of periodic update, $R_P = n \cdot p$, where n is the number of servers and reporting are p times in the period. While exactly n report packets should be used at every reporting time in periodic update mechanism, with the same reporting cost of Update-on-Finish (in Algorithm 2), $R_U = R_P$, the server use the report packet only when the number of executing requests decreases. Whereas each server uses exactly p packets during a given period in periodic update mechanism, the Update-on-Finish mechanism (in Algorithm 2) allow more reporting for the servers that finish requests more frequently, and less reporting for the servers that finish requests less frequently with $n \cdot p$ packets. Therefore Update-on-Finish mechanism uses the report packets more efficiently with the same communication cost. In the next section we compare the proposed algorithm with the two algorithms.

5. Performance Evaluation

A simulator of Web server cluster is implemented. A Web switch and 5 Web servers constitutes the cluster. 4000 requests are processed for simulation of 10 seconds. The execution lengths of the requests range from 5 to 50 and each server processes 0.2 (in length) of a request per millisecond. The generation of execution lengths follows Pareto distribution. Pareto distribution have been found to correspond to some real world workloads such as a Web request's execution length[2]. We model the execution lengths as being generated independently and identically distributed from a distribution that follows a power law, but has an upper bound. It is characterized by three parameters: α, the exponent of the power law; k, the smallest possible observation, and p, the largest possible observation. The probability mass function of this Pareto distribution is defined as:

$$f(x) = \frac{\alpha k^{\alpha}}{1-(k/p)^{\alpha}} x^{-\alpha-1}, \; k \le x \le p. \tag{2}$$

In most cases where estimates of α were made, α tends to be close to 1, which represents very high variability in service requirements. It is known that Poisson distribution is far from realistic for request arrival through Internet. Request arrival process follows uniform distribution.

Weighted Round-Robin, Dahlin's, and Load-Balancing Algorithm 2 were simulated with the same reporting costs. The reporting costs are averaged from one hundred generations of 4000 request packets. Algorithm 2 was simulated first with one hundred generations to reckon up the number of report packets sent from the servers. Then we found equivalent update periods to the average numbers of report packets as corresponded in Table 1.

Table 1. Corresponding update periods with equal reporting costs

Number of report packets	1199	1540	2086
Update periods	42 *msec*	32.5 *msec*	24 *msec*

WRR shows 3.82 as mean execution latency of 5 servers with 1199 report packets in Fig. 3. Dahlin's shows 2.91 as mean execution latency of 5 servers with 1199 report packets in Fig. 4. Algorithm 2, the proposed load-balancing, shows 2.86 as mean execution latency of 5 servers with 1199 report packets in Fig. 5. Algorithm 2 has the lowest standard deviations(Sum of standard deviations - Dahlin's: 6.30893; Algorithm 2: 5.69997) among the three algorithms. WRR and Dahlin's performed using periodic update with the period of 42 milliseconds(equivalent to 1199 report packets). With the equal reporting cost, Algoritm 2 outperformed and the gap is ever increasing as more report packets are used. Figure 6 illustrates the effect of the update period.

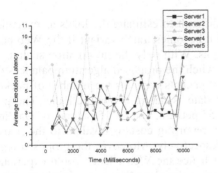

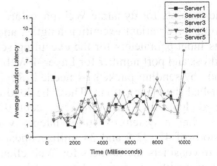

Fig. 3. Execution Latencies of Requests in WWR

Fig. 4. Execution Latencies of Requests in Dahlin's

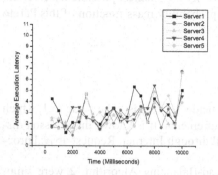

Fig. 5. Execution Latencies of Requests in Algorithm 2

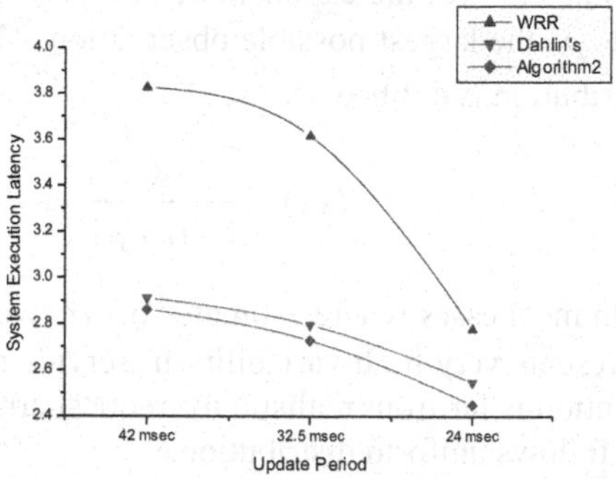

Fig. 6. Mean Execution Latency of 5 Servers, which the Web Clients Experience

The values of the figure are averaged from one hundred simulations. The mean execution latency of 5 servers, system execution latency in the figure, reduces slightly more than Dahlin's algorithm as the update period decreases. The Web switch sends reciprocally proportional numbers of packets according to each server's load for a period to balance loads of the servers until next load-update in WRR. Dahlin's balances the server loads as soon as possible with current load information, and then the next packets distributed by the Web switch are sent in Round Robin until next load-update. Since Dahlin's acquires load-balancing much earlier than WRR, the gap between the two algorithms is large. Algorithm 2 balances the loads whenever a report packet arrives, keeping request packets sent for load-balancing in the Load Table. Each server sends the request packet when it needs more request packets for a period whereas Dahlin's use report packets at mandatory update time. Thus actions for load-balancing happens more times than Dahlin's and this difference results in the gap between Dahlin's and Algorithm 2.

6. Conclusion

The requests for dynamic Web pages are difficult to estimate the loads as executing scripts have variant execution lengths, and it becomes much variant if the Web page gets input parameters for the executing scripts. With only the information such as IP address and port number for Layer-4 Web switch the proposed algorithm balances the loads by sending packets as needed. Report packets contains the number of packets finished their executions. Thus the load-update is naturally non-periodic. The proposed algorithm showed 98.32 percent, 97.57 percent, and 96.15 percent of Dahlin's algorithm in system execution latency with reporting costs equivalent to the update periods of 42, 32.5 and 24 milliseconds, respectively. Moreover the proposed algorithm considers the fairness for Web clients hence the Web clients would experience higher quality of service. Another advantage of the algorithm is its simplicity, since simpler distribution algorithm leads to higher throughput of the Web switch.

Although not resented in this paper the non-periodic load-update occurs asynchronously among servers. This reduces the communication workload for the Web switch than that of periodic update since all the report packets are not concentrated at any instant. Thus the new load-update mechanism would support higher scalability.

References

1. T. Schroeder, S. Goddard, B.Ramamurthy. "Scalable Web server clustering technologies", IEEE Network, May-June 2000, pp. 38-45
2. V. Cardellini, E. Casalicchio, M. Colajanni, P. Yu. "The state of the art in locally distributed Web-server systems", ACM Computing Surveys, 34(2), June 2002, pp. 263-311
3. M. Andreolini, M. Colajanni, R. Morselli. "Performance study of dispatching algorithms in multi-tier Web architectures", ACM SIGMETRICS Performance Evaluation Review, 30(2), September 2002, pp. 10-20
4. E. Casalicchhio, M. Colojanni. "A client-aware dispatching algorithm for Web clusters providing multiple services", 10th International World Wide Web Conference, May 2001, pp. 535-544
5. M. Aron, D. Sanders, P. Druschel, W. Zwaenepoel. "Scalable content-aware request distribution in cluster-based network servers", The 2000 USENIX Annual Technical Conference, June 2000
6. Cisco Systems Local Director. http://www.cisco.com, 2002
7. M. Dahlin. "Interpreting stale load information", IEEE Trans. Parallel and Distributed Systems, 11(10), October 2000, pp. 1033-1047
8. http://support.zeus.com/doc/tech/linux_http_benchmarking.pdf
9. T. Kunz, "The Influence of Different Work-load Descriptions on a Heuristic Load Balancing Scheme:, IEEE Trans. Software Eng., Vol. 17, No. 7, July 1991, pp. 725-230

Profile Oriented User Distributions in Enterprise Systems with Clustering*

Ping-Yu Hsu[1] and Ping-Ho Ting[1,2]

[1] Business Administration Department, National Central University, 300 JongDa Rd,
ChungLi, Taiwan 320
pyhsu@mgt.ncu.edu.tw
[2] Information Management Department, ChungChou Institute of Technology , 6,
Line 2, Sec 3, Shan-Chiao Rd.,Yuanlin Changhwa., Taiwan, 510
ding@dragon.ccut.edu.tw

Abstract. As enterprises world-wide racing to embrace real-time management to improve productivities, customer services, and flexibility, many resources have been invested in enterprise systems (ESs).All modern ESs adopt an n-tier client-server architecture that includes several application servers to hold users and applications. As in any other multi-server environments, the load distributions, and user distributions in particular, becomes a critical issue in tuning system performances.

Although n-tier architecture may involve web servers, no literatures in Distributed Web Server Architectures have considered the effects of distributing users instead of individual requests to servers. The algorithm proposed in this paper return specific suggestions, including explicit user distributions, the number of servers needed, the similarity of user requests in each server. The paper also discusses how to apply the knowledge of past patterns to allocate new users, who have no request patterns, in a hybrid dispatching program.

1 Introduction

All modern ESs share a common IT foundation, namely, the n-tier client-server architecture. The architecture has a database server in the storage layer, multiple application servers in the service layer, several web servers in the interface layer and browsers or other access devices in the presentation layer. In the architecture, programs, applications, or transactions are held and executed in the application servers. When users logging on a system, he/she either selects an application server or is being assigned to one by the system.

It is a vital issue to keep response time under control for most system administrators. When the increases of memories and CPUs reach the hardware limitation, adding more application servers to a system is a reasonable alternative. When an ES has multiple application servers, distributing users with

* This study is supported by the MOE Program for Promoting Academic Excellence of Universities:Electronic Commerce Environment, Technology Development, and Application(Project Number:91-H-FA08-1-4)

H. Jin et al. (Eds.): NPC 2004, LNCS 3222, pp. 230–237, 2004.

similar applications to the same application servers plays an important role in tuning system performance[3], as pointed out by documents of a major ES system [1, 10].

Commercial products, such as SAP R/3, equipped with a simple dispatching algorithm considers only user numbers and server response time [1]. The task of grouping users is left to system administrators [1, 10]. In addition to the rough guideline of grouping financial users into one server and logistic users into another, system administrators need specific suggestions, such as explicit user distributions, the number of servers needed, and the similarity of user requests in each server. To address the needs, the paper shows a set of algorithms to collect transaction patterns, establish pattern prediction rules, associate patterns with users, group users into clusters with patterns, select clusters to form distributions, and dispatch users with hybrid methodology that can dispatch users with or without patterns. Patterns can be collected from system logs or traces because the transactions run by each user in daily operations are specified and set in implementation phases and are seldomly changed after system going live.

2 Finding Users' Regular Transactions

To record system and user statuses, most enterprise systems include various tracing mechanisms. Among the various recordable data are user sessions and applications executed in sessions. For the purpose of the paper, these data are transformed into user profiles. A user profile is a set of {⟨ user-id, transaction-set ⟩}, where user-id is the account name of a user and transaction-set is the set of transactions accessed by the user in a session.

To compute or estimate regular transactions for each user, three steps are employed. The first one computes large itemsets with any existing set oriented pattern discovering algorithm, such as [3, 11]. In the second algorithm, each large 1-itemset is examined against each user to form users' regular transactions. For new users who do not have accumulated enough entries to computer personal regular transactions, the paper propose to predicate their regular transactions with the association rules computed with known Aprori algorithms. Assume the regular transactions is shown in Table 1.

New users do not have any records in the user profiles and do not have associated regular transactions. However, dispatching programs still need to dispatch them in run-time. Therefore, help for dispatching programs to guess the patterns of new users are in order.

If each new user provides one of the transactions she/he wishes to access after logging on, the dispatching program can check if the transaction has high association with any large itemsets. If so, the union of the large itemsets denote the user's Predicted Regular Transaction set is the third step.

---

[3] An application in an ES corresponds to an atomic and unbreakable transaction. In this paper, transactions and applications are used interchangeably.

Table 1. Regular Transactions

User-Id	Regular Transactions
1	{A, B, E, F, H}
2	{A, B, E, F, H}
3	{A, B, E, F, H}
4	{I, J, K}
5	{B, I, J, K}
6	{B, I, J, K}
7	{P, Q, R}
8	{P, Q, R}
9	{P, Q, R}
10	∅

Definition 1 *The Associated Regular Transactions of a transaction, t, under a set of large itemsets, P, a user profile, U, is*

$$AT(t) = \cup_{p \in P \ \wedge \ t \in p} CP_U(p|t) \geq confidence\ threshold,$$

where $CP_U(p|t) = \frac{|\{s|s \in U, p \in s.transaction\ set\}|}{|\{s|s \in U, t \in s.transaction\ set\}|}$

3   The Definitions of Similarity Measure, Clusters, and Distributions

Load balancing programs utilizes the benefit of multiple servers at the cost of wasting memories in keeping duplicated programs and data. In sophisticated application servers with hundreds of people on-line, the memory needed for transactions are considerable [2]. Therefore, users with similar regular transactions should be grouped into one cluster, which are then assigned to a server. This section defines the measure of similarity and proves related properties. Formal definitions of clusters and distributions are also included.

Definition 2 *A Cluster is a set of users that share similar regular transactions.*

The similarity of users in a cluster is measured by AR, Application Reusability. The AR of a transaction in a cluster is defined as the percentage of users in the cluster evoking the transaction, and the AR of a cluster is defined as the average AR of transactions in the cluster.

Definition 3

- *The Regular transactions, T, of a user, u are defined as T(u)*
- *AR of a transaction, t, in a cluster, c, is defined as*

$$R(t, c) = \frac{|\{u \mid u \in c\ and\ t \in T(u)\}|}{|c|}$$

- *The AR of a cluster, c, is defined as the average AR of regular transactions in the cluster.*

$$R(c) = \frac{\sum_{t \in T(u) \text{ and } u \in c} R(t,c)}{|\{t \mid u \in c \text{ and } c \in T(u)\}|}$$

Theorem 1 *Conditional Anti-Monotonicity of AR $R(c)$ decreases with new user added to c, if the number of transactions accessed by the new user is fewer than or equal to the average number of transactions accessed by original users.*

Proof
ommited to save space.

Therefore, $R(c)$ has the property of Conditional Anti- Monotonicity, which allows POCA to prune hapless user groups.

Definition 4

- *A cluster whose AR exceeds a given ARThreshold is called qualified cluster.*
- *A set of clusters is comprehensive under a user profile, U, if the union of the clusters includes all and only all users with regular transactions.*
- *A set of clusters is disjoined if the intersection of any two clusters in the set is empty.*
- *A set of qualified clusters is a distribution under a user profile, U, if they are comprehensive under U and disjoined.*

The clusters of $\{1, 2, 3\}$, $\{4, 5, 6\}$, and $\{7, 8, 9\}$ have ARs of 100%, 11/12, and 100%, respectively, under the running example. If the ARthreshold is set at 55% then all three are qualified clusters. The three clusters are both comprehensive and disjoined in the example, and therefore form a valid distribution.

4   Clustering and Distributing by POCA

POCA returns distributions that satisfy administrator constraints and has the fewest number of clusters, and the rules associating single transactions to predicted regular transactions. The constraints include an AR threshold, min-support, rule confidence threshold. The recommendations guarantee that when all frequent users logging on the system and accessing all regular transactions, each server still has an AR above the given AR Threshold. Information included in the recommendations are number of servers, user distribution and associate rules of predicting patterns from transactions.

POCA relies $\geq_U$, which is a chain, to hold Conditional Anti-Monotonicity and to form each user combination at most once.

Definition 5 *Let S be the set of users in a user profile, U. The order $\geq_U$ is defined on S such that for any $u_1, u_2 \in S$, $u_1 \geq_U u_2$ if*

- $T(u_1) > T(u_2)$, or
- $T(u_1) = T(u_2)$ and user-id of $u_1 \leq$ user-id of u_2.

POCA includes two major steps in computing the recommendations – computing the set of qualified clusters and selecting clusters to form server distribution. The main steps are listed as following:

Initialization: for each user with regular transactions, turns the user into a single-user cluster. These clusters form C_1, the 1-user cluster set.

Composing C_{i+1} from C_i: Conditional join C_i with C_1 to form C_{i+1}. A cluster c_i from C_i is added by one user in c_1 from C_1 if two criteria are met. The first one states that the use from c_1 has lower rank in $\geq_U$ than any user in c_i. The second criterion asserts that the new cluster has an AR value exceeding the given threshold.

Repeating Last Step Until No New Clusters are Generated: If C_{i+1} is empty then POCA has found all qualified clusters in $C_1, \ldots,$ and C_i; Otherwise, POCA has to repeat the last step.

Selecting Clusters to Form Distributions: Finding the fewest number of qualified clusters to form distributions. The algorithm includes a loop to check if i clusters can form a distribution where $1 \leq i \leq C_1$. The loop is aborted when distributions are found.

In the running example, the first cluster set is formed by turning each user into a cluster. If setting the AR threshold at 55%, C_2, the set of 2-user clusters, is equal to the join of C_1 and C_1. $C_2 = \{\{1, 2\}, \{1, 3\}, \{2, 3\}, \{5, 6\}, \{5, 4\}, \{6, 4\}$ $\{7, 8\}, \{7, 9\}, \{8, 9\}$ \}. C_3 is the conditional join of C_2 and C_1. $C_3 = \{\{1, 2, 3\}, \{4, 5, 6\}, \{7, 8, 9\}\}$. C_4 is the conditional join of C_3 and C_1. $C_4 = \{\{1, 2, 3, 7\}, \{1, 2, 3, 8\}, \{1, 2, 3, 9\}\}$. C_5 is empty since potential 5-user clusters have ARs lower than 55%.

Now that all cluster sets are ready, it is time to select clusters to form user distributions. The selection continues by examining 1-cluster distribution, 2-cluster distribution, etc. In the running example, 1-cluster and 2-cluster distributions are empty since there are no 9-user and 5-user clusters. On the other hand, 3-cluster distributions have various alternatives and are all returned to system administrators. 3-cluster distributions and corresponding ARs are listed Table 2. POCA just picks one to examine the comprehensiveness of clusters. The algorithm returns all the distributions that satisfy the requirements and let system administrators to decide which distribution he/she prefers.

Table 2. 3-Cluster Distributions and ARs

User Distributions	ARs
$\{1, 2, 3\}, \{4, 5, 6\}, \{7, 8, 9\}$	100%, 11/12, 100%
$\{1, 2, 3, 7\}, \{4, 5, 6\}, \{8, 9\}$	18/32, 11/12, 100%
$\{1, 2, 3, 8\}, \{4, 5, 6\}, \{7, 9\}$	18/32, 11/12, 100%
$\{1, 2, 3, 9\}, \{4, 5, 6\}, \{7, 8\}$	18/32, 11/12, 100%

5   An AR Based Hybrid Dispatching Approach

Each ES typically has a dispatching program listening to networks and accepts user requests. The program resides an application server, intercepts user requests, and direct them to application servers.

The distributions suggested by POCA bases on frequent patterns in user profiles. For new and infrequent users, POCA does not suggest their distributions directly but returns association rules, PR (Prediction Rules), in the output to help dispatching program make the decision. To apply the rules, a new user only needs to provide a transaction he/she plan to evoke after logging on the ES. With the association rules, a dispatching program can distribute a user according to its associated predicted regulation transactions. If the first transaction does not lead to any predicted regular transactions, then the single transaction works as the basis for dispatching.

An AR Based Hybrid dispatching algorithm distributes users while keeping the AR of each server as high as possible. In the dispatching procedure, users are distributed to a server by one of the three alternatives:

– If a regular user logging on, then send the user to the recommended server and return to listening mode.
– If an infrequent user logging on with a transaction, then find the predicted regular transactions implied by the transaction. If no entry matched then the single transaction is treated as the predicted regular transaction.
– Compute the potential new AR in each server with the addition of the user with predicted regular transactions. Assign the user to the server with the highest AR, and update the AR in the corresponding server.

The distribution in the running example has ARs of 100%, 11/12, and 100% in the three servers. If a new user with user-id 10 wishes to log on the system and submits an A as the first transaction then the user has a assumed predicted regular transaction of ABE. The ARs after adding ABE to the three servers would be 18/20, 14/24, 12/24. Therefore, the new user is distributed to the first server, and the distribution becomes {1, 2, 3, 10}, {4, 5, 6}, {7, 8, 9}.

6   Related Work

With the Internet rush, many researches have been devoted to distributing user requests with Distributed Web Server Architecture to improve the performance of web servers. Depending on the locations where request distributions happen, these researches are classified into client-based, DNS (Domain Name Server)-based, dispatcher-based, and server-based by [5, 4, 14, 15]. Since current Http protocol is stateless, each request is routed independently to a web server[4]. All of the above researches assume that requests can be independently route to different servers, where as in the application servers of ESs, requests from the same users have to be routed to the same server.

Clustering literatures are classified into partitioning clusterings and hierarchical clusterings [12, 6, 9]. If k clusters are needed, partitioning Clustering choose k centroids initially and gradually tune the constituents of each clusters or centroids with some criteria function until a locally optimized characteristic is met. Hierarchical clusterings can be further divided into agglomerative and divisive clusterings. As the name suggested, agglomerative clusterings gradually merge smaller clusters into larger clusters until k clusters are found. Divisive clustering, on the other hand, splits larger clusters into smaller clusters until k clusters are found. POCA is more close to agglomerative although it does not have predefined cluster numbers.

Most clustering algorithms employ Euclidean distances to compute similarity. The shorter the distances the similar the data points in the clusters are. However, Euclidean distances are not ideal for clustering categorical data. For example, to cluster transaction sets with Euclidean distances, each set has to be translated into a sparse binary vector. Many set oriented algorithms use Jaccard coefficient [12] and ROCK [7]. However, Jaccard coefficient and ROCK along cannot describe the number of elements in each cluster, which are important to calculate the buffer efficiency.

7   Conclusion

Managers in enterprises often add users to ESs as they extend E-business practices to various parts of corporate operations. With the addition of each user, new pressures on performances are brought upon the systems. Yet, system response time is one of the most important factors in measuring user satisfactions.

Since ESs tend to consume many memories, application servers can easily run up all memories set by hardware constraints. When this happens, next step commonly adopted in boosting performance is adding application servers to ESs. With multiple application servers in the scene, distributing users with similar application requirements to the same application servers increases buffer utilization and increase the lead time to next hardware upgrades. POCA provide suggestions of such distributions with the fewest number of clusters. Along with suggestions are Application Reusability in each server for the reference of system administrators.

Several issues require further studies, such as modeling user profiles with sequences, dynamically updating user patterns, incorporating CPU and systems loads into dispatching and distribution algorithms, and improving the efficiency of POCA.

References

[1] SAP AG. *System R/3 Technicale Consultant Training 1 - administration*, chapter R/3 WorkLoad Distribution. SAP AG, 1998.
[2] SAP AG. *System R/3 Technicale Consultant Training 3 - Perf. Tuning*, chapter R/3 Memory Management. SAP AG, 1998.

[3] R. Argawal and R. Srikant. Fast algorithms for mining associations rules. In *Proceedings of International Conference in Very Large Data Bases*, pages 487–499, 1994.

[4] H. Bryhni, E. Klovning, and O. Kure. A comparison of load balancing techniques for scalable web servers. *IEEE Network*, 14:58–64, 2000.

[5] V. Cardellini, M. Colajanni, and P.S. Yu. Dynamic load balancing on web-server systems. *IEEE Internet Computing*, 3:28–39, 1999.

[6] R. O. Duda and P. E. Hard. *Pattern Classification and Scene Analysis*. Wiley-Interscience Publication, 1973.

[7] S. Guha, R. Rastogi, and K. Shim. Rock: A robust clustering algorithm for categorical attributes. *Information Systems*, 25(5):345–366, 2000.

[8] J. Han and M. Kamber. *Data Mining: Concepts and Techniques*, chapter Mining association rules in large databases. Morgan Kaufmann Publisher, 2001.

[9] J. Han and M. Kamber. *Data Mining: Concepts and Techniques*, chapter Clustersing. Morgan Kaufmann Publisher, 2001.

[10] J.A. Hernándes. *The SAP R/3 Handbook*, chapter Distributing R/3 Systems. McGraw-Hill, 2 edition, 2000.

[11] J. Pei J. Han and Y. Yin. Mining frequent patterns without candidate generation. In *Proceedings of ACM-SIGMOD International Conference on Management of Data*, pages 1–12, 2000.

[12] A.K. Jain and R.C. Dubes. *Algorithms for Clustering Data*. Prentice Hall, 1988.

[13] P. Mohapatra and H. Chen. A framework for managing qos and improving performance of dynamic web content. In *Proceedings of Global Telecommunications Conference*, volume 4, pages 2460–2464, 2001.

[14] S. Nadimpalli and S. Majumdar. Techniques for achieving high performance web servers. In *Proceedings of International Conference on Parallel Processing*, pages 233–241, 2000.

[15] B. C-P. Ng and C-L. Wang. Document distribution algorithm for load balancing on an extensible web server architecture. In *Proceedings of International symposium on cluster computing and the Grid*, pages 140–147, 2001.

[16] J. Zhang, T. Hamalainen, J. Joutsensalo, and K. Kaario. Qos-aware load balancing algorithm for globally distributed web systems. In *Proceedings of international conferences on Info-tech and Info-net*, volume 2, pages 60–65, 2001.

CBBS: A Content-Based Bandwidth Smoothing Scheme for Clustered Video Servers*

Dafu Deng, Hai Jin, Xiaofei Liao, and Hao Chen

Cluster and Grid Computing Lab,
Huazhong University of Science and Technology, Wuhan, 430074, China,
{dfdeng,hjin,xfliao,haochen}@hust.edu.cn

Abstract. Due to the inherent bandwidth burstness, *variable-bit-rate* (VBR) encoded videos are very difficult to be effectively transmitted over clustered video servers for achieving high server bandwidth utilization and efficiency while guaranteeing QoS. Previous bandwidth smoothing schemes tend to cause long initial delay, data loss and playback jitters. In this paper, we propose a content-based bandwidth smoothing scheme, called CBBS, which first splits video objects into lots of small segments based on the complexity of picture content in different visual scenes so that one segment is exactly including one *visual scene*, and then, for each segment, a constant bit rate is allocated to transfer it. Performance evaluation based on real-life MPEG-IV traces shows that CBBS scheme can significantly improve the server bandwidth utilization and efficiency, while the initial delay and client buffer occupancy are also significantly reduced.

1 Introduction

Due to high scalability and low cost, clustered video servers [6] become inevitable to provide large capacity to serve thousands of concurrent clients. It is comprised of two parts: one RTSP server node and several RTP server nodes. The RTSP server is responsible for exchanging control messages with clients, while RTP servers are responsible for transferring video data to clients. Video objects are often divided into lots of fixed-length segments that uniformly distributed on RTP server nodes.

Usually, in order to guarantee QoS, for each stream, a bandwidth of b equaling to the peak bit rate of requested video object must be reserved in the corresponding RTP server nodes. Nevertheless, for VBR encoded video objects, the peak bit rate is far larger than the mean bit rate [8]. It indicates that the most reserved bandwidth is not used for most of the time. It tends to cause low server bandwidth utilization and better solutions are necessary.

To improve the network bandwidth utilization, previous works have proposed lots of schemes. Among them, a constant rate transmission and transporting (CRTT) scheme [3] employs *constant bit rate* (CBR) transmission of VBR video objects. It works by calculating the minimum bandwidth to prevent the client buffer underflow. Further, considering both the bandwidth and the client buffer size, it determines the amount of data

---

* This paper is supported by National 863 Hi-Tech R&D Project under grant No.2002AA1Z2102.

H. Jin et al. (Eds.): NPC 2004, LNCS 3222, pp. 238–243, 2004.

to be transmitted to the client in advance. Other schemes, such as the e-PCRTT [2], MCBA [1], DBA [8] and MVBA [4] [5], first prefetch video data until half of client buffer be filled, and then dynamically select the transmission bit rate in the "river" constructed between the maximum transmission rate that guarantees no buffer overflow and the transmission rate that guarantees no buffer underflow. Since the transmission bandwidth is dynamically changed several times, the peak bit rate is smoothed somewhat. However, for the popular client buffer configurations, it tends to result in long initial delay or large initial bandwidth requirement that prefetch video data until half of client buffer be filled.

In this paper, we focus on the pre-recorded VBR video objects and propose a content-based bandwidth smoothing scheme, called CBBS, which can significantly improve the server bandwidth utilization and efficiency while guaranteeing QoS. The following sections are organized as follows. In section 2, we describe the content-based bandwidth smoothing scheme. Section 3 estimates the performance of CBBS via real-life MPEG-IV traces. Finally, section 4 ends with conclusions and future works.

2   Content-Based Bandwidth Smoothing Scheme

The bit rate variety of VBR encoded videos is resulted from two issues. One is the picture content variety of different visual scenes, called *inter-scene* variable-bit-rate. It results in the size fluctuation of different I-frames. The other is the frame size variety in the visual scene, called *intra-scene* variable-bit-rate. Usually, in the same visual scene with same picture content, the size of I-frames are larger than that of P-frames and B-frames have smallest frame size. Tab.1 shows the quantitative analysis for different

Table 1. The quantitative analysis for different kinds of variable bit rate.

Movie	Length (frames)	Std. dev. of *inter-scene* VBR(Kb/s)	Std. dev. of *intra-scene* VBR(Kb/s)
Silence of the Lambs	89998	510.001	177.665
Mr. Bean	89998	364.201	243.740
Star Wars IV	89998	192.513	133.620
Jurassic Park	89998	490.650	241.544
Aladdin	89998	361.410	207.373
Robin Hood	89998	390.707	290.764
Sports-Soccer	89998	421.061	230.432
Sports-Formular-1	30334	373.620	223.432
News-ARD News	22498	375.941	309.414
News-ARD Talk	89998	339.640	235.097

kinds of variable bit rate based on real-life MPEG-IV video traces[1]. Since I-frames are encoded by the basic content of visual scenes. In Table 1, we assume that one visual

---

[1] The traces can be obtained from the web site: http://www-tkn.ee.tu-berlin.de/~fitzek/TRACE/pics.

scene is comprised of one *group of pictures* (GOP) and use the bit rate variety among *I*-frames to represent the variable bit rate caused by the *inter-scene*. As one can see, the bit rate variety caused by the *inter-scene* is far larger than that caused by the *intra-scene*.

Based on the above analysis, allocating a *constant bit rate* (CBR) for transferring each scene would not result in large client buffer occupancy and long initial delay since the variable quantity of the *intra-scene* VBR is relative small. Thus, we can use a splitting scheme to divide video objects according to the picture content of visual scenes and allocate constant bandwidth for transferring each segment. After bandwidth allocation, the maximum client buffer requirement to guarantee no buffer overflowing, and the segment information, such as the start playback time, the allocated bandwidth, and the IP address of the storage RTP node, are available and can be maintained on the RTSP server node. Whenever the RTSP server admits a request, for each segment of requested video object, it just needs to query the RTP node whether they have enough bandwidth to transfer in the corresponding time interval. If so, it notifies RTP server nodes to reserve the corresponding constant bandwidth. Since the reserved bandwidth is the allocated constant bandwidth not the peak bit rate, the server bandwidth utilization is improved significantly.

Let d and $p(p \geq 0)$ be the initial delay and the threshold for splitting video objects, respectively. Sequence $\{\chi_1, \chi_2, \ldots, \chi_N\}$ represents the frame size sequence of the requested video object, where χ_i represents the size of the i-th frame. We define S to be the size of first I-frame in the segment starting from time point t_s and ending at time point t_e, and define b_{min} and B_{max} to be the minimum bandwidth at which clustered video servers may transmit and the maximum buffer occupancy at client side over a given interval $[t_s, t_e]$, respectively, where the client buffer must be guaranteed no underflowing and transmission is started from initial buffer level Q.

The video splitting procedure starts a new segment if and only if the processing frame is an I-frame, and the size of this I-frame χ_k satisfies the following equation.

$$|\chi_k - S| < p \times S \tag{1}$$

For the first segment, the allocated bandwidth is set to be the mean bit rate of the first segment. i.e.

$$b_1 = \frac{\sum_{t_s^1}^{t_e^1}}{t_e^1 - t_s^1} \tag{2}$$

In order to guarantee no buffer underflow during the first segment being in playback, at the time point of each frame for the first segment, the amount of data sent must larger than or equal to the amount of data consumed. Thus, we obtain

$$d = \max\{\frac{\sum_{j=1}^{t} \chi_j}{b_1} - t_e^1\} \quad t \in \{1, 2, \ldots, t_e^1\} \tag{3}$$

For other segments, we use following equation to calculate the allocated bandwidth.

$$b_{min} = max\{\frac{\sum_{j=1}^{t} \chi_j - (\sum_{k=1}^{t_s} \chi_k + Q)}{t - t_s}\} \quad t \in \{t_s + 1, t_s + 2, \ldots, t_e\} \tag{4}$$

Once the bandwidth b_{min} has been allocated, the maximum client buffer occupancy during the processing segment being played back and the initial buffer level Q for transferring next segment can be derived as follows.

$$B_{max} = max\{t \times b_{min} + Q - \sum_{k=t_s}^{t} \chi_k\} \quad t \in \{t_s + 1, t_s + 2, \ldots, t_e\} \quad (5)$$

$$Q = b_{min} \times (t_e - t_s) - \sum_{k=ts}^{te} \chi_k \quad (6)$$

PROCEDURE FOR VIDEO SPLITTING AND BANDWIDTH ALLOCATION

INPUT: Video frame sequence $\{X_1, X_2, \ldots, X_N\}$, where N is the number of frames included in inputting video object.
OUTPUT: Initial delay, maximum client buffer occupancy and video segments with allocated bandwidth.

1. $S=X_1, Q=0, ts=1, te=1, b_1=0, d=0, b_m=0, B=0, B_{max}=0;$ $//X_1$ is the first I-frame in frame sequence.
2. FOR $(k=1;k<=N;k++)\{$
3.   IF $(S==X_1)\{$ // processing the first segment.
4.   IF $((X_k$ is not an I-frame)$||(X_k$ is an I-frame)&&$(|X_k$-S$|<pS))\{$
5. $b_1+=X_k;$
        }
6.   ELSE {
7. $b_1=b_1/k, te=k;$
8.   calculate d, using equation (3).
9. $ts=-d;$
9.   calculate Q and B_{max}, using equation (6) and (5), respectively.
10.   IF $(B<B_{max})$ $B=B_{max};$
11.   output the first segment stating from ts and ending at te, with allocated bandwidth b_1, and initial delay d;
12. $ts=k, S=X_k;$
        }
    }
13.   ELSE {   //processing other segments.
14.   IF$(X_k$ is not an$I$-frame)$||(X_k$ is an I-frame)&&$(|X_k$-S$|<pS))\{$
15.   calculate b_m, using equation (4);
        }
16.   ELSE {
17. $te=k;$
18.   calculate Q and B_{max}, using equation (6) and (5), respectively;
19.   IF $(B<B_{max})$ $B=B_{max};$
20.   output a video segment stating from ts and ending at te, with allocated bandwidth b_m.
21. $ts=k, S=X_k;$
        }
    }
}
22. output the maximum client buffer occupancy B.

Fig. 1. Pseudo-code of video splitting and bandwidth allocation algorithm.

The algorithm of video splitting scheme and bandwidth allocation scheme is presented formally in Fig.1. Notations used in this figure have been defined above.

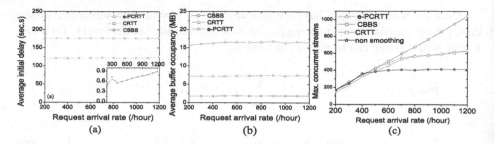

Fig. 2. Comparison of (a) the average initial delay, (b) the average buffer occupancy, and (c) the maximum concurrent streams among e-PCRTT,CRTT,and CBBS with splitting threshold $p = 0.4$.

3 Performance Evaluation

For the illustrative purpose, we evaluate the performance of the CBBS scheme by the experiment and compared it with that of the e-PCRTT and CRTT scheme. In the experiment, the clustered video servers are the prototype of Turbogrid streaming servers [2] with one RTSP server node and 8 RTP sever nodes. Each node uses 1.4GHz CPU and 100Mb/s NIC. Real-life MPEG-IV traces with different contents including *Movies, Sports, News, Talk show, several Episodes*, and *Cartoon* are splintered into lots of small segments based on the proposed video splitting scheme with threshold $p = 40\%$. The length of each video trace is 89,998 frames. All video traces are played back at a frame rate of $F = 25$ frames/s.

There are three kinds of popular clients used in our experiment-the multimedia PDA with buffer capacity 8 Mbytes, the set-top box with buffer capacity 32 Mbytes and the PC with buffer capacity 64 Mbytes. Client requests are generated using the Poisson arrival process with an interval time $1/\lambda$. The arrival rate λ is varied from 200 to 1200 per hour. Once generated, client selects a video object and sends the request to clustered video servers. If the request is admitted, the client simply playbacks the received stream until the transmission is completed.

Fig.2 plots the performance comparison among e-PCRTT, CRTT and CBBS schemes with splitting threshold $p = 0.4$, where the inner figure of part (a) is the magnification of the initial delay for CBBS with $p = 0.4$. From this figure, we can easily find that CBBS scheme significantly outperforms other two schemes. For example, the average initial delay and the average maximum buffer requirement of CBBS scheme is less than 1 second and 2MB, respectively, whereas those of the e-PCRTT scheme and the CRTT scheme needs approximately 120 seconds, 8MB and 160 seconds, 16MB, respectively. For the bandwidth utilization which can be indicated via the maximum concurrent streams supporting by the clustered video servers, CBBS scheme can support 1044 concurrent streams, while e-PCRTT and CRTT schemes can just support approximately 600 concurrent streams.

---

[2] Turbogrid streaming servers are developed by Cluster and Grid Computing Lab of Huazhong University of Science and Technology.

4   Conclusions and Future Works

In this paper, we propose a content-based bandwidth smoothing scheme, called CBBS, which can significantly improve server bandwidth utilization and efficiency while guaranteeing QoS. Unlike previous schemes, CBBS scheme first splits video objects into small segments based on the complexity of picture content in different scenes. Then, it uses constant bit rate to transfer each segment so that the *intra-scene* variable bit rate can be effectively smoothed. When admitting a request, CBBS scheme accurately judges whether the remaining bandwidth of RTP nodes is enough to transmit the stored segments in the corresponding time interval. It significantly reduces the effect of the *inter-scene* variable bit rate on the server bandwidth utilization.

On going researches include:

1. Evaluating the effect of splitting threshold p on the performance of clustered video servers and deriving the optimal p based on statistically analysis of large amount of real-life video traces;
2. Developing optimal disk retrieving models and strategies to work with the scene-based video striping scheme;
3. Designing a time-scaled resource reserving protocol to reduce the impacts of traffic burstness and improve network utilization over the Internet.

References

1. H. Chao, C. L. Hung, Y. C. Chang, and J. L. Chen, "Efficient changes and variability bandwidth allocation for VBR media streams", *International Journal of Network Management*, Vol. 12, 2002, pp. 179-185.
2. O. Hadar and R. Cohen, "PCRTT Enhancement for off-line video smoothing", *Real-Time Imaging*, Vol. 7, 2001, pp.1-14.
3. J. M. McManus and K. W. Ross, "Video on demand over ATM: Constant-rate transmission and transport", *IEEE Journal of Selected Areas in Communication*, Vol. 14, 1996, pp. 1087-1098.
4. A. R. Reibman and A. W. Berger, "Traffic descriptors for VBR video teleconferencing over ATM networks", *IEEE/ACM Transactions on Networking*, June, 1995.
5. J. D. Salehi, Z. L. Zhang, J. F. Kurose, and D. Towsley, "Supporting stored video: reducing rate variability and end-to-end resource requirements through optimal smoothing", *Proc. of ACM SIGMETRICS*, 1996.
6. C. Shahabi, R. Zimmermann, K. Fu, S. Yuen, and D. Yao, "Yima: a Second-Generation Continues Media Server", *Computer*, pp.56-64, Jun. 2002.
7. H. Zhang and E.W. Knightly, "Red-vbr: a renegotiation-based approach to support delay-sensitive vbr video", *ACM Multimedia Systems*, Vol. 5, 1997, pp. 164-176.
8. L. Zhang and H. Fu, "A novel scheme of transporting pre-stored MPEG video to support video-on-demand (VoD) services", *Computer Communications*, Vol. 23, 2000, pp.133-148.

SuperNBD: An Efficient Network Storage Software for Cluster[1]

Rongfeng Tang, Dan Meng, Jin Xiong

National Research Center for Intelligent Computing Systems
Institute of Computing Technology
Graduate School of the Chinese Academy of Sciences
{rf_tang, md, xj}@ncic.ac.cn

Abstract. Networked storage has become an increasingly common and essential component for cluster. In this environment, the network storage software through which the client nodes can directly access remote network attached storage is an important and critical requisite. There are many implementations exist with this function, such as iSCSI. However, they are not tailored for the large-scale cluster environment and cannot well satisfy its high efficiency and scalability requirements. In this paper, we present a more efficient technology for network storage in cluster and also give detailed evaluation for it through our implementation - SuperNBD.The results indicate that SuperNBD is more efficient, more scalable, and better fit for cluster environment.

1. Introduction

With the steadily increasing of data capacity produced by scientific applications and high I/O rate requirement, the networked storage has become a common but essential component of high performance cluster environment. It permits hosts to easily access remote data through network.

Most storage area networks (SAN) used to adopt Fiber Channel [1] as their private storage network, however, due to the expensive cost of the hardware, most medium and small-scale enterprises cannot afford it. Recently, with the advent of Gigabit (or even 10 Gigabit) Ethernet, the IP based storage networks (i.e. IP-SAN), which can leverage the existing LAN environment, are becoming more popular.

The network storage software for hosts to transparently access the data block on storage devices is the critical layer for network storage. iSCSI is a kind of network storage protocol currently used for IP-SAN. It encapsulates and transports the SCSI command and data across network [3], dividing the large buffer come from buffer cache of OS kernel and packetting it before sending them to the server. So every buffer transmission involves several individual messages of SCSI command and sub-buffers of data block [3]. In addition, in order to cope with the security problems when transmits across wide area network, it introduces some mechanisms which are

---

[1]This work was supported by the National High-Technology Research and Development Program of China (863 Program) under the grant No.2002AA1Z2102 and the grant No.2002AA104410

H. Jin et al. (Eds.): NPC 2004, LNCS 3222, pp. 244-247, 2004.
© IFIP International Federation for Information Processing 2004

unnecessary in a close and reliable network environment such as cluster, these mechanisms will induce more overhead and lead to decrease of performance.

We present a new compact and efficient network storage implementation technology for the cluster environment named SuperNBD. The practical experiment shows that it is well efficient and scalable.

The rest of this paper is organized as follows. In the next section we will discuss in detail about design issues and implementation of SuperNBD. In section 3 we analyze its performance and scalability, and compare these metrics with other implementations. Section 4 concludes our paper.

2. Design Issues and Implementation

SuperNBD is composed of two different parts according to their functionality: SuperNBD client and SuperNBD server; both reside at the buffer cache layer of kernel, as shown by figure 1. The SuperNBD client receives the data operation requests issued by higher layer of kernel, such as VFS and directly forwarded it to SuperNBD server. We have introduced some specialized mechanisms to improve its efficiency and scalability as follows.

Fig. 1. The overview architecture of SuperNBD

In order to increase the total data throughput of storage system, several service threads are introduced on both sides specializing in data processing, so that the data of a file distributed across multi-devices can be read and written concurrently.

Since all the blocks within a single request are corresponding to the same device in sequence, only one simple message with the information about first block's sequence number and the total block quantity need to be sent to server before data transmission, less then those of iSCSI.

During the whole process along I/O path, all data blocks requested are transferred directly from client data block cache to that of server and vice versa, eliminates any necessary of memory copy within SuperNBD.

In order to increase the write bandwidth for highly data-intensive applications we adopt a kind of asynchronous write mechanism. As one characteristic of block I/O storage, each write operation will completely overwrite the content, so it is unnecessary to read corresponding data block from disk beforehand, only allocate a block cache from main memory and directly store the data into it, thus, as to the client issues this request, the whole operation is completed promptly. The kernel will flush the entire dirty data blocks to disk when the free memory reaches a certain low watermark, so that the process of client side writing and server side real disk writing can be parallelized and greatly improve the total data writing throughput of storage I/O path.

Things are different for data reading. Most often, when clients issue read request, the file data is just on the physical storage device. The large cache that greatly contributes to high write bandwidth has little advantage here, and the read can only be handled synchronously. In order to increase the total read performance of SuperNBD, we present a kind of adaptive data block prefetching mechanism according to the locality feature of data reading on the server end. For example, assume A and B are two requests reach server side in order, but might issued by different clients, both relate with the same device. Request A read blocks with sequence number (block number) from $a0$ to an, and B from $b0$ to bm, if the value of $|b0 - an|$ are within a certain reasonable interval, it can be considered as sequential operation, and when server finishes the request B, it still keep reading next several blocks, so that the next read operation can mostly be hit on cache.

A pipeline mechanism has been introduced, which can parallelize the device reading with data transmission, two major time-consuming operations during reading process. In SuperNBD, when some of blocks are ready (hit in buffer cache or just be read from device), and others are during handling by local kernel, the ready data is firstly transferred to the clients. After finishing sending the previously ready data, most of the other blocks are ready in memory now. In this way, it can greatly reduce the response time for read request and completely exert the potential performance of hardware resource.

In addition, the feature of SuperNBD server's combining with the local buffer cache can also benefit for shared operations, i.e. multi-clients simultaneously access the same data blocks. In this situation, only one physical device operation needed for each block, so that most requests can be serviced directly from the server buffer cache. This enable SuperNBD to scale well to large number of clients.

3. Performance Comparison and Analysis

In this section, we evaluate the efficiency and scalability of SuperNBD and present performance comparison with unh-iscsi[3]. There are two sets of environments for our experiments:

（1）Set1. Consists of 33 nodes, each has four AMD opteron(tm) processor (2.2GHZ), 8GB memory, SuSE Linux 8.0 with kernel 2.4.19SMP. All nodes connected by Gigabit Ethernet. This environment is used to test efficiency and scalability of SuperNBD.

（2）Set2. Consists of 9 nodes, each with dual 2.4GHz Intel Xeon Processors , 1GB memory, Red Hat 7.2 with kernel 2.4.18-3smp. Both connected by 100bit Ethernet. This environment is used for performance comparison between SuperNBD and unh-ISCSI, for unh-iscsi cannot support x86_64 architecture.

3.1. Efficiency and Scalability Evaluation

In this test, we use one SuperNBD server and continually increments the number of clients, each read or write 1GB data with 1MB record size. Figure 2 shows SuperNBD has well efficiency and scalability and can always keep peek performance along with scale increasing. The asynchronous writing and adaptive read-ahead mechanism greatly contribute to this achievement.

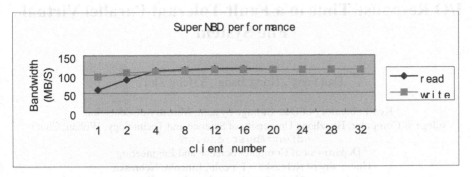

Fig. 2. Efficiency and Scalability of SuperNBD

3.2. Performance Comparison with Other Implementations

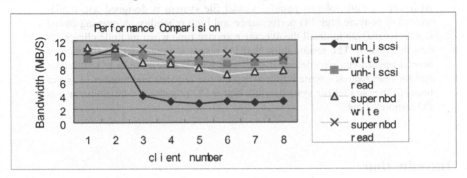

Fig. 3. Performance comparison between SuperNBD and unh-iscsi

Figure 3 shows the performance comparison between SuperNBD and unh-iscsi. SuperNBD outperforms unh-iscsi on both writing and reading, mainly due to its compact protocol and optimized implementation mentioned in section 2.

4. Conclusion and Future Work

In this paper, we present a compact but efficient technique to construct network storage for cluster and also evaluate the performance of our implementation named SuperNBD. As the result shows, SuperNBD is efficient and scalable, and better fit for the cluster environment.

References

1. Prasenjit Sarkar, Sandeep M.Uttamchandani, Kaladhar Voruganti, Storage over IP: A Performance Study. IBM research report, 12/2002
2. http://www.iol.unh.edu/
3. Julian Satran, Kalman Meth, IBM. iSCSI,draft-ietf-ips-iscsi-20. .

I/O Response Time in a Fault-Tolerant Parallel Virtual File System

Dan Feng[1], Hong Jiang[2], Yifeng Zhu[2]

[1] Key Laboratory of Data Storage System, Ministry of Education
College of Computer, Huazhong University of Science and Technology, Wuhan, China
dfeng@hust.edu.cn
[2] Department of Computer Science and Engineering
University of Nebraska – Lincoln, Lincoln, Nebraska
Jiang@csce.unl.edu

Abstract. A fault tolerant parallel virtual file system is designed and implemented to provide high I/O performance and high reliability. A queuing model is used to analyze in detail the average response time when multiple clients access the system. The results show that I/O response time is with a function of several operational parameters. It decreases with the increase in I/O buffer hit rate for read requests, write buffer size for write requests and number of server nodes in the parallel file system, while higher I/O requests arrival rate increases I/O response time.

1 Introduction

Parallel Virtual File System (PVFS) [1] is a parallel file system for Linux clusters, which stripes the data among the cluster nodes and accesses these nodes in parallel to achieve high I/O throughputs. A Cost-Effective Fault-Tolerant Parallel Virtual File System (CEFT-PVFS) [2] has been designed and implemented to meet the critical demands on reliability while still being able to deliver a considerably high throughput.

When multiple clients submit data-intensive jobs at the same time, the response time experienced by the user is an indicator of the power of the cluster. In this paper, a queuing model is used to analyze in detail the average response time when multiple clients access the fault tolerant parallel virtual file system.

2 Architecture of the Fault Tolerant Parallel Virtual File System

The diagram of the fault tolerant parallel virtual file system is shown in Fig.1. All I/O server nodes are divided into two groups, the primary one and the mirroring one. File data is striped across the primary group and duplicate on the mirroring group. When Writing, data are stored in the primary group in RAID 0 style and backed up in the mirroring group simultaneously. Data is retrieved from the nodes that have less workload between the mirrored pair to optimize the read performance.

H. Jin et al. (Eds.): NPC 2004, LNCS 3222, pp. 248–251, 2004.

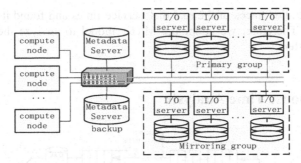

Fig.1. Diagram of the fault tolerant parallel virtual file system

3   Definitions and Notations of Disk I/O Parameters

I/O response time in the fault tolerant parallel virtual file system depends primarily on the network bandwidth, I/O buffer size and policy, and disk I/O service time. The disk I/O may become the bottleneck and it is determined by three main parameters, namely, seek time, rotational latency and transfer rate.

Definitions and notations for several relevant disk I/O parameters are given below:

C: Number of disk cylinder;

S: disk seek time, with its maximum being denoted by S_{max};

R: disk rotational latency, with the full rotation time being denoted by R_{max};

D: disk seek distance, which is a random variable in the range of $[0, C-1]$;

p_s: the probability that the seek distance is 0, $P_s = P\{D = 0\}$;

L: data striping size;

T_d: data transfer time, $T_d = L/r_d$, where r_d is disk transfer rate;

Y_r, Y_w, Y: disk read, write and whole service time, respectively.

The relationship between disk seek time and the seek distance i is given as:

$$S \approx a + b\sqrt{i} \qquad i > 0$$

where S is the seek time, a is the arm acceleration time, b is the factor of seeking track. a is the seek time between two neighboring cylinders.

The mean seek time and the second moment can be accurately approximated by[4]

$$E(S) = (1 - p_s)[a + \frac{8}{15}b\sqrt{C-1}]$$

$$E(S^2) = (1 - p_s)[a^2 + \frac{1}{3}b^2(C-1) + \frac{16}{15}ab\sqrt{C-1}]$$

When requests to a disk are independent of one another, the rotation time is assumed to be uniformly distributed in $[0, R_{max}]$, with probability density function:

$$f_R(x) = 1/R_{max} \qquad 0 \le x \le R_{max}$$

The mean rotation time and the second moment are:

$E(R) = \frac{1}{2}R_{max}$

$E(R^2) = \frac{1}{3}R_{max}^2$

The disk drive service time is $Y = S + R + T_d$.

M.Y.Kim studied traces of the real disk service times and found it to be generally distributed [5]. Therefore, we adopt the M/G/1 model to analyze the disk response time in the cluster.

4 I/O Response Time Analysis

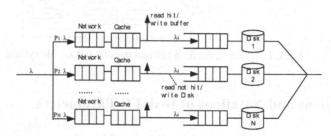

Fig.2. The Queuing Model of I/O Service

The queuing model for the system service under data-intensive load is shown in Fig.2. Part of the main memory space in a server node is used for I/O cache buffer to hide the disk I/O latency and to take advantage of data reference locality. Assume the number of I/O server nodes to be N in each group. I/O requests follow a Poisson process; with a mean arrival rate of λ. The arrival rate to the server node i is $P_i\lambda$, where P_i is the probability that the request is directed to node i. When the I/O request is a small read or write, where the data size is equal to or less than the size of a striped block, and the workload on a server node among a group is balanced, P_i is equal to 1/N. When the I/O request is a large read or write, where data is striped on all of the nodes in a group, P_i is equal to 1. So the typical range of P_i is [1/N, 1]. Let P_r and $P_w = 1 - P_r$ denote the read and write probability of a request, respectively. Assume the I/O cache buffer hit rate for read requests to be h_r and the probability of write buffer being full to be f_w. Thus, the effective arrival rate to each disk is: $\lambda_i = [P_r(1-h_r)+P_w f_w] \cdot P_i\lambda$.

Assume that the network service time and the I/O buffer service time are exponentially distributed with the average times T_{net} and T_c, respectively. Therefore, request residence time W_{net} in the network and W_{Cache} in the I/O buffer can be modeled using the M/M/1 queuing model [6]. The average residence time W_{disk} in a disk drive can be calculated according to the M/G/1 model.

The average I/O response time can be expressed as:

$$Z = W_{net} + W_{cache} + P_{disk} \cdot W_{disk}$$

$$= \frac{T_{net}}{1-P_i\lambda \cdot T_{net}} + \frac{T_c}{1-P_i\lambda \cdot T_c} + [P_r(1-h_r)+P_w f_w] \times \{\frac{\lambda_i E(Y^2)}{2[1-\lambda_i E(Y)]} + E(Y)\}$$

Where $T_{net} = L / R_{net}, T_c = L / R_{memory}$ and L is the size of data to be accessed on each I/O server node. Even though the data is striped in fixed blocks to server nodes in a RAID0 style, the blocks can be incorporated into a large block with length equal to L. R_{net} and R_{memory} is the available network bandwidth and the available memory access rate respectively.

The average I/O response time can be obtained from above formula for Z under different workload and application environments with different parameters.

5 Conclusion

The I/O response time in the fault tolerant parallel virtual file system is discussed in the paper. The analytical results show the different level of sensitivity of the average I/O response time to various system and operational parameters such as I/O buffer size, data locality, read/write probability, request data size and server group size. These results provide useful insight into the complicated relationships among different system and operational parameters, thus allowing potential optimization for system configuration and I/O performance.

6 Acknowledgment

This work was partially supported by National Science Foundation of China No.60273074, NSF grant (EPS-0091900) and Huo Yingdong Education Foundation.

References

1. P. H. Carns, W. B. Ligon III, R. B. Ross, and R. Thakur: PVFS: A Parallel File System For Linux Clusters, Proceedings of the 4th Annual Linux Showcase and Conference, Atlanta, GA (2000) 317-327
2. Yifeng Zhu, Hong Jiang, Xiao Qin, Dan Feng, David R. Swanson: Design, Implementation, and Performance Evaluation of a Cost-Effective Fault-Tolerant Parallel Virtual File System. Int. Workshop on Storage Network Architecture and Parallel I/Os, New Orleans, LA (2003)
3. Kai Hwang, Hai Jin, Edward Chow, Cho-Li Wang, and Zhiwei Xu: Designing SSI Clusters with Hierarchical Checkpointing and Single I/O Space. IEEE Concurrency, IEEE Computer Society Press, Vol.7, No.1,(1999) 60-69
4. S. Chen and D. Towsley: The Design and Evaluation of RAID 5 and Parity Striping Disk Array Architectures. Journal of Parallel and Distributed Computing, Vol. 17, (1993)
5. M.Y.Kim and A.N.Tantawi: Asynchronous Disk Interleaving: Approximating Access Delays. IEEE Trans. on Computer.(1991)
6. L.Kleinrock: Queueing System. Vol.1, John Wiley, New York (1975)

SARCNFS: Self-Adaptive Redundancy Clustered NAS File System

Cai Bin, Changsheng Xie, Ren Jin, FaLing Yi

National Storage System Laboratory, Department of Computer Science,
Huazhong University of Science and Technology. Wuhan, P.R China, 430074
hust_caibin@sohu.com

Abstract. In this paper, we describe the design and implementation of
SARCNFS File System for network-attached clustered storage system.
SARCNFS stripes the data and metadata among multiple NAS nodes, and provides file redundancy scheme and synchronization mechanism for distributed
RAID5. SARCNFS uses a self-adaptive redundancy scheme for file data accesses that uses RAID5-level for large writes, and RAID1-level for small write
so as to dynamically provide flexible switch between RAID1 and RAID5 to
provide the best performance. In addition, SARCNFS proposed a simple distributed locking mechanism that uses RAID5-level for full stripe writes, and
RAID1-level for temporary storing data from partial stripe updates. As a result,
low response latency, high performance and strong reliability are achieved.

1 Introduction

The distributed RAID concept was proposed by Stonebraker and Schloss [1]. Examples of early-distributed RAID systems include Swift/RAID [2], Petal [3] and Tertiary
Disk [4]. In distributed RAID5 implementation, there are two significant issues:
1. *Small writes accesses latency* is high because of the extra reads.
2. *Synchronization problem* is presented in cluster environment for simultaneous
writes.
    In this paper, we design and implement a file system for clustered NAS storage en-
vironment called SARCNFS that distributes user data and metadata among multiple
NAS nodes, similar to xFS [5], [6], Zebra [7], Swarm [8], Frangipani [9], and
PVFS[10]; meanwhile, we employ three redundancy schemes in SARCNFS file system: the first scheme is a striped, file-mirroring scheme like RAID1. In this scheme,
the user data are stored twice by file system; the second scheme is a RAID5-like
scheme, which uses parity-based partial redundancy; finally, we adopt a self-adaptive
scheme that uses RAID5-level for large writes, and RAID1-level for small write so as
to dynamically provide flexible switch between RAID1 and RAID5 to provide the
minimal performance degradation. In addition, we proposed a simple locking mechanism that uses RAID5-level for full stripe writes, and RAID1-level for temporary

H. Jin et al. (Eds.): NPC 2004, LNCS 3222, pp. 252-255, 2004.

storing data from partial stripe updates. Since partial stripe writes use the RAID1 scheme, we avoid the synchronization necessary in the RAID5 scheme for this access pattern to addresses the synchronization problem in distributed RAID5 environment.

2   ARCNFS Clustered NAS File System

2.1 System Architecture Overview

SARCNFS is designed as a server-less system [5], [6], in which multiple NAS nodes deal with storage of file data and manage metadata. Each SARCNFS file is striped across a set of nodes in order to facilitate parallel access. This set of modes is selected in a random way, and the data are distributed with a round-robin police using the set of nodes. The layout of SARCNFS is shown in Fig 1.

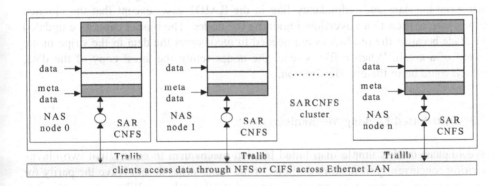

Fig. 1. Physical layout of SARCNFS in Clustered NAS Environment

The specifics of a given file distribution are described with three metadata parameters: base node number, number of nodes, and stripe size. These parameters, together with ordering of the modes for the file system, allow the file distribution to be completely located. To access SARCNFS file data, the client first obtains the metadata of the SARCNFS file on the NAS nodes, and then, the client sends requests directly to the NAS nodes storing the relevant portions of the file.

2.2 Self-Adaptive Redundancy Scheme

In RAID1 scheme implementation in SARCNFS, each NAS node stores two files per client file. One file is the data file used to store the data, just like the case in PVFS. The other file is the redundancy data file used to store redundancy. The contents of a redundancy block are identical to the contents of the corresponding data block. As a result, the RAID1 scheme in SARCNFS has ability to utilize all the available bandwidth on a read operation to provide parallel read performance. On a write, all the nodes must be written twice.

The distributed RAID5 scheme in our SARCNFS also has redundancy file on each node in addition to the data file, like the RAID1 scheme. In the distributed RAID5 scheme, however, these files contain the parity data for specific portions of the data files. On a write operation, the client checks the offset and size to judge if any stripes are about to be updated partially. There can be at most two partially updated stripes in a given write operation. The client reads the data in the partial stripes and also the corresponding parity region, and then, it computes the parity for the partial and full stripes, and writes out the new data and new parity.

In the Adaptive Redundancy scheme, the level of redundancy is selected depended on the following rule: every client write access is broken down into three portions: (1) a partial stripe write at the start (2) a portion that updates an integral number of full stripes (3) a trailing partial write. Depending on data alignment and size, portions can be empty. For the portions of the write that updates full stripes, we compute and write the parity, just like in the RAID5 case. For the portions involving partial stripe writes, we write the data and redundancy like in the RAID1 case, except that the updated blocks are written to an overflow region on the nodes. The blocks cannot be updated in place because the old blocks are needed to reconstruct the data in the stripe in the event of a crash. When a file is read, the nodes return the latest copy of the data, which could be in the overflow region.

2.3 Distributed Locking Mechanism

We implemented a simple distributed locking mechanism to ensure that two clients writing concurrently to disjoint portions of the same stripe do not leave the parity for the stripe in an inconsistent state in distributed RAID5 scheme. When a node receives a read request for a parity block, it knows that a partial stripe update is taking place. If there are no outstanding writes for the stripe, the node sets a lock to indicate that a partial stripe update in progress for that stripe. It then returns the data requested by the read. Subsequent read requests for the same parity block are put on a queue associated with the lock. When the node receives a write request for a parity block, it writes the data to the parity file, and then checks if there are any blocked read requests waiting on the block. If there are no blocked requests, it deletes the lock; otherwise it wakes up the first blocked request on the queue. The client checks the offset and size of a write to determine the number of partial stripe writes to be performed. If there are two partial stripes involved, the client serializes the reads for the parity blocks, waiting for the read for the first stripe to complete before issuing the read for the last stripe. This ordering of reads avoids deadlocks in the locking protocol.

The RAID1 scheme does not require any additional synchronization. The same is true of the Adaptive Redundancy scheme since it uses mirroring for partial stripe writes.

3 Conclusion

SARCNFS uses a self-adaptive redundancy scheme for file data access that uses a combination of RAID5 and RAID1 writes to store data. Full stripe writes use the RAID5 scheme. RAID1 is used to temporarily store data from partial stripe updates. As part of the SARCNFS implementation, we have proposed a simple locking mechanism that addresses the consistency problem of distributed implementations of RAID5 redundancy. Since partial stripe writes use the RAID1 scheme, we avoid the synchronization necessary in the RAID5 scheme for this access pattern. In addition, unlike many other clustered file system, our SARCNFS file system is not dependent on client modifications since it is full compatible with standard distributed file systems such as NFS and CIFS. As a result, SARCNFS dynamically provide the high performance, low latency and the strong reliability.

References

1. M. Stonebraker and G. Schloss.: Distributed RAID:-A New Multiple Copy Algorithm. In sixth IEEE Conference Data Engineer, IEEE Press, pages-430-437, 1990.
2. D. D. E. Long, B. Montague, and L.-F. Cabrera.: Swift/RAID: A Distributed RAID System. Computing Systems, 7(3), Summer, 1994.
3. E. K. Lee and C. A. Thekkath.: Petal: Distributed Virtual Disks. In Proceedings of the Seventh International Conference on Architectural Support for Programming Languages and Operating Systems, pages 84-92, Cambridge, MA, 1996.
4. N. Talagala, S. Asami, D. Paucrson, and K. Lutz.: Tertiary Disk: Large Scale Distributed Storage. Technical Reports, no UCB/CSD-98-989, University of California, at Berkeley, 1998.
5. T. Anderson, M. Dahlin, J. Neefe, D. Patterson, D. Roselli, and R. Young.: Serverless Network File Systems. ACM Transactions on Computer Systems, Feb. 1996.
6. T. Anderson, M. Dahlin, J. Neefe, D. patterson, D. Roselli, and R. Wang.: Serverless Network File Systems. In Proceedings of the Symposium on Operating System Principles, pages 109–126, Dec. 1995.
7. J. Hartman and J. Ousterhout.: The Zebra Striped Network File System. ACM Transactions on Computer Systems, Aug. 1995.
8. J. H. Hartman, I. Murdock, and T. Spalink.: The Swarm Scalable Storage System. Proceedings of the 19th International Conference on Distributed Computing Systems, May. 1999.
9. C. A. Thekkath, T. Mann, and E. K. Lee.: Frangipani: A Scalable Distributed File system. In Proceedings of the Symposium on Operating System Principles, pages 224-237, 1997.
10. Philip H. Carns, Walter B. Ligon III, Robert B. Ross, Rajeev Thakur.: PVFS: A Parallel File System for Linux Clusters. In Proceeding of the Extreme Linux Track: 4th USENIX Annual Linux Showcase and Conference, Oct. 2000.

Research and Implementation of a Snapshot Facility Suitable for Soft-Failure Recovery

Yong Feng, Yan-yuan Zhang, Rui-yong Jia

Computer Science & Engineering School, Northwestern Polytechnical University
710072 Xi'an, Shaanxi, China
{fengyong, zhangyy, jiary}@co-think.com

Abstract. Human error and incorrect software (a.k.a. soft-failure) are key impediments to dependability of Internet services. To address the challenge, storage providers need to provide rapid recovery techniques to retrieve data from a time-based recovery point. Motivated by it, a snapshot facility at the block level called SnapChain is introduced. Compared with former implementations, when managing different versions of snapshots, SnapChain minimizes disk space requirement and write penalty of master volume. In this paper, the metadata and the algorithms used in SnapChain will be explained.

1 Introduction

The Berkeley/Stanford ROC (Recovery-Oriented Computing) Project claims that rather than device failure (a.k.a. hard-failure), human error and incorrect software (a.k.a. soft-failure) are the largest causes of failures in Internet services [1]. To protect against soft-failure, creating point-in-time copy of data periodicity and maintaining different versions of point-in-time copies are necessary. Amazon.com, for example, is reported to create point-in-time copy of data as frequently as three times per hour [1].

Differ from the other two classes of point-in-time copies, split mirror and concurrent, snapshot requires much less storage and needs no advanced setting up prior to executing a point-in-time copy. Therefore, it is more suitable for soft-failure recovery. For snapshot facility, the expectation for continuous operation is commonplace. However, the ability to create and maintain different versions of point-in-time copies of the data efficiently, with minimal interruption and minimal overhead, is critical. This paper will only focus on the block level snapshot facilities.

Linux LVM and EVMS [2] are volume managers and support snapshot. In them, the snapshot of master volume, namely shadow volume, is achieved through a pseudo volume that contains pointers to two separate physical regions. One region is simply the unchanged blocks in the master volume. The other region, named private region, collects the original state of the master volume blocks just before they are updated, as well as any new changes made by the point-in-time consumer to the snapshot. Sun StorEdge [3] treats master volume and its related shadow volume as a volume pair. A bitmap is used to keep track of the differences of a volume pair that occur after the established point-in-time. In above implementations of snapshot, the shadow volumes of the same master volume have no relationship with each other. If they can share the

H. Jin et al. (Eds.): NPC 2004, LNCS 3222, pp. 256-260, 2004.
© IFIP International Federation for Information Processing 2004

old data just like master volume and shadow volume share unmodified contents, the mount of data, which is copied from master volume and kept in the private region of shadow volume, can be reduced. Based on such optimizations, SnapChain, the snapshot facility presented in this paper, can minimize the effort, time and incremental capacity, which are necessary to obtain point-in-time views. Especially in the environment supporting soft-failure recovery, where a master volume has a number of shadow volumes, the effects of optimizations are remarkable.

The remainder of the paper is organized as follows: The next section describes the metadata and algorithms used in SnapChain. After evaluating SnapChain in section 3, the conclusion will be drawn in the fourth section.

2   SnapChain

SnapChain is implemented in Linux, and designed to support up to 255 shadow volumes for a master volume. It uses a pool-and-pointer design, where metadata keeps the information of location and states of data chunk (a group of block) of shadow volumes. Shadow volumes of the same master volume share a large storage pool, named snapshot pool, to keep their private data. Every shadow volume owns a logic private region in snapshot pool. The snapshot pool is composed of one or multiple block devices in liner mode, and can be expanded through absorbing new devices on demand. Registering a volume in SnapChain will make it into a master volume. After registering, the content of master volume is kept untouched. Losing metadata or uninstalling SnapChain will not render data of master volume unusable.

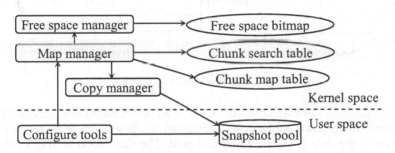

Fig. 1. Architecture of SnapChain

As Fig. 1 indicates, SnapChain has a mid-level block device driver and user space tools. The device driver can be inserted arbitrarily in a system's layered block I/O hierarchy. It consists of three components: map manager, free space manager, and copy manager. Map manager uses CMT (Chunk map table) and CST (chunk search table) to translate the virtual address of shadow volume into the corresponding physical address of master volume or snapshot pool. Free space manager uses FSB (free space bitmap) to allocate and reclaim disk space from snapshot pool for shadow volumes to store their private data. To maintain consistency of shadow volumes, copy manager controls copying data from master volume to snapshot pool. The user space tools used to configure device driver follow a set of operations.

2.1 Metadata

CMT is used to mark the current states of chunks in shadow volume and master volume. Each volume owns a CMT, and every chunk has a flag in CMT. For a chunk of master volume, the flag has two states: 0 means the chunk is not updated since the newest shadow volume is created; 1 means the chunk is updated. For a chunk of shadow volume, the flag has three states: 0 means the chunk is not stored in the private region of the shadow volume; 1 means the chunk is stored in the private region of the shadow volume and is the original state of master volume; 2 means the chunk is stored in the private region of the shadow volume and is updated by the point-in-time consumer. CST is used to map the virtual chunk of a shadow volume into the physical chunk in snapshot pool. Each shadow volume has a CST. In order to search rapidly, CST is organized into a hash table. The metadata of shadow volumes of the same master volume are chained by a bi-direction list, namely shadow volume list, in time order. The master volume keeps the head of the list. Extent (a group of chunks) is the unit during allocating disk space. In FSB, every extent of snapshot pool has one bit to record its allocation state.

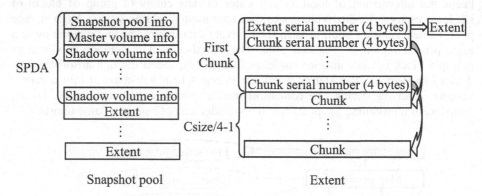

Fig. 2. Data layout in snapshot pool

It is not necessary to explicitly store CMT, CST and FSB on disk. Instead, enough information on snapshot pool can be maintained to allow them to be reconstructed. Fig. 2 shows the data layout in a snapshot pool. The first 16KB is SPDA (Snapshot Pool Descriptor Area), including snapshot pool info, master volume info, and shadow volume info. On each device of snapshot pool, SPDA is allocated for backup reasons. The remainder of snapshot pool is continuous extents. The extents are divided into several classes: free extent class and extent classes of each shadow volume. The PL method [4] is used to manage the extents. The first 4 bytes of each extent are used as a pointer to indicate the next extent of the same class. Thus the extents of the same class become a list. Shadow volume info keeps the head of the shadow volume extent list. In an extent, the first chunk, except the first 4 bytes, is used to record the serial numbers of the following chunks. The nth is the serial number of the virtual chunk, which the (n+1)th chunk in the extent corresponds to. The size of chunk (Csize) is chosen between 1KB and 8KB, and the size of extent is $(Csize^2/4)$ MB. Large chunk size can reduce the footprint of the metadata and increase the addressing range of CST. However, it may result in significant performance overhead.

2.2 Commands and Algorithms

SnapChain information can be created, displayed, and manipulated by the user space tools. The command "spcreate test_mv /dev/sda1 /dev/sda2" registers the master volume /dev/sda1 and creates its snapshot pool on /dev/sda2. The command spremove removes from the system all knowledge of the specified snapshot pool and releases the master volume from device driver. The similar commands svcreate and svdelete can be used to create and delete shadow volumes. When svcreate is executing, SnapChain stalls all incoming I/O requests for the time required to flush all outstanding writes to the master volume. When everything is synchronized on stable storage, SnapChain appends new metadata of shadow volume to shadow volumes list, and creates a new virtual block device. The command svrestore restores master volume from the specified shadow volume. SnapChain also provides to user programs an ioctl command interface and a /proc interface for device information and statistics.

The read request to master volume is directly made to master volume. When writing master volume, COFW (copy on first write) [3] is executed. Unlike former implementations, only the original date of the chunk with the CMT flag of 0 is copied to the private region of the newest shadow volume. To find the physical chunk that holds the request block of specified shadow volume, SnapChain first references CMTs of shadow volume list to locate the volume whose private region the specified chunk is stored in. It will take the following steps:
1. If the CMT chunk flag of the target shadow volume does not equal to 0, the targe shadow volume is what we want to find.
2. Otherwise, check the newer shadow volume. If the CMT chunk flag is 1, it is the volume that we want to find. If not, repeat until the volume is found. If no such shadow volume exists, the master volume is the volume that we want to find.

Then SnapChain uses CST of the found volume to get the physical address. When writing shadow volume, if the CMT flag of the target chunk is 1, the data of target chunk should be moved to elder shadow volume first. Deleting a shadow volume involves the similarly procedure. The command svrestore uses the algorithm of reading shadow volume to get the contents of the specified shadow volume, and uses the algorithm of writing master volume to update the master volume.

3   Evaluation

The goal of SnapChain is to minimize the write penalty and the capacity necessary to obtain point-in-time views. The response time and consumed capacity of SnapChain will be compared to Linux LVM. As expected, SnapChain achieves better performance and less consumed capacity.

Table 1. Consumed capacity and response time when writing to master volume.

Snapshot facility	SnapChain		Linux LVM	
Shadow volume number	4	8	4	8
Consumed Capacity (MB)	12	12	48	96
Response Time (ms)	2335	2338	5481	9767

Table 2. Response time when reading from shadow volume.

Snapshot facility	SnapChain		Linux LVM	
Shadow volume number	4	8	4	8
Response Time (ms)	180	179	178	180

The tests are run on a dual Pentium 700 MHz computer with 256 MB of RAM. NEC S2100 disk array (RAID 5) is connected directly to Emulex Lightplus 750 HBA card in the PC. The versions of Linux kernel and LVM are 2.4.20 and 2.00.07 respectively. The chunk size used by LVM and SnapChain is set to 4KB. To avoid the influence of Linux buffer cache, "raw" devices associated with the block devices are used. In the first test, the master volume has 4 shadow volumes. In the second test, it has 8 shadow volumes. Table 1 shows consumed capacity and response time, when copying 10MB data to the area of master volume, which has not been updated since the first snapshot is created. The memory consumed and response time of the SnapChain is much less than those of LVM, for only 10MB data is copied to snapshot pool in SnapChain rather than n*10MB data in LVM, where n is the number of shadow volumes. As the number of shadow volumes increased, the degree of superiority of SnapChain over LVM is increased. Table 2 shows response time, when reading 10MB data from a shadow volume. The response times of SnapChain are similar with those of LVM. Thus the optimizations do no harm to the performance of accessing shadow volume. Since restoring master volume from a specified shadow volume involves reading from shadow volume and writing to master volume, the recovery time of the SnapChain is better than that of LVM.

4   Conclusion

In this paper, we propose SnapChain – a block level snapshot facility. SnapChain enables master volume and its snapshots to share as many contents as possible. Consequently it can support more snapshots, and achieve better performance of accessing master volume, than its peers do. SnapChain supports writing request to snapshot. Besides, it can create snapshot transparent to application without disturbing current data accessing, and recovery a master volume from a specified copy-in-time in a short time. Therefore SnapChain is suitable for soft-failure recovery.

References

1. A. Brown: A Recovery-Oriented Approach to Dependable Services: Repairing Past Errors with System-Wide Undo. UC Berkeley Computer Science Division Technical Report UCB//CSD-04-1304, December 2003
2. D. Teigland, H. Mauelshagen: Volume managers in linux. Proc. the FREENIX Track of USENIX 2001 Annual Technical Conference, Boston, USA, 2001, 185-197
3. Sun Microsystems. Instant image white paper. http://www.sun.com/storage/white-papers/ii_soft_arch.pdf
4. Arun Iyengar, Shudong Jin, Jim Challenger: Techniques for efficiently allocating persistent storage, The Journal of Systems and Software 68(2), 2003, 85-102

GOOMPI: A Generic Object Oriented Message Passing Interface
Design and Implementation

Zhen Yao, Qi-long Zheng, and Guo-liang Chen

National High Performance Computing Center at Hefei
Department of Computer Science and Technology
University of Science and Technology of China
Hefei, Anhui 230027, China
yaozhen@ustc.edu qlzheng@ustc.edu.cn glchen@ustc.edu.cn

Abstract. This paper discusses the application of object-oriented and generic programming techniques in high performance parallel computing, then presents a new message-passing interface based on object-oriented and generic programming techniques — GOOMPI, describes its design and implementation issues, shows its values in designing and implementing parallel algorithms or applications based on the message-passing model through typical examples. This paper also analyzes the performance of our GOOMPI implementation.

1 Introduction

One of the most important distinction between parallel computing and normal sequential computing is the complexity and diversity of parallel computing models. From the view of programming, there are three main parallel computing models — the data-parallel model, the shared-variable model and the message-passing model [1].

The data-parallel and shared-variable models are concise and intuitive in programming, however, they often require tight-coupled parallel computers based on shared memory, e.g. parallel vector machines or SMPs, while it is difficult to implement them directly and efficiently on more popular architectures based on distributed memory, such as MPPs, COWs and SMP clusters.

The message-passing model is more intuitive and easy to implement on parallel computing environments based on distributed memory.

Typical message-passing libraries include the Parallel Virtual Machine (PVM) [2] and the Message Passing Interface (MPI) [3]. Both of them can be easily implemented in homogeneous or heterogeneous distributed environments, and so became prevailing.

Parallel programs using message-passing libraries are often able to gain a fairly more excellent performance than that using other models through elaborate handcrafted optimizations on messages sending and receiving between parallel processes.

H. Jin et al. (Eds.): NPC 2004, LNCS 3222, pp. 261–271, 2004.

However, coding a parallel program based on message-passing is more difficult than that based on data-parallel or shared-variable models. It often takes
people much time to deal with the part of a program concerning with messages.
When handling only messages of primitive data types or their arrays, the effort
is still acceptable. However, the effort becomes far more considerable and the
complexity of the message-passing part of the program increases significantly
when passing complex dynamic data structures such as binary trees, graphs,
or large sparse matrices stored in orthogonal lists. It then becomes difficult to
guarantee the correctness and efficiency of the program.

Worst of all, the complexity of the message-passing part always obscures
the structure of the algorithm and the program itself. These programs tend to
fall into implementation details and lose their abstraction and genericity. It also
causes great obstacle in reading, maintaining and extending parallel programs.

In one word, it is difficult to map a parallel algorithm into a message-passing
based parallel program rapidly and intuitively. It is the problem that the paper
tries to solve.

In the last decade, object-oriented (OO) techniques gain great success in
program and software system construction. As a complement paradigm to OO,
generic programming techniques aided with inlining and template metaprogram-
ming gain genericity and extensibility through compile time *parametric polymor-
phism*. The C++ Standard Template Library (STL) [5] is a milestone of generic
programming techniques.

Many works have been doing on applying OO and generic programming
techniques to HPC areas, such as POOMA [6], Janus [7] and HPC++ [8], etc.
The GOOMPI presented in this paper also takes advantage of those techniques,
trying to provide programmers a unified generic message-passing interface, effectively simplifying the development process of parallel programs and dramatically
improving their abstraction, genericity as well as flexibility.

The rest sections of this paper are organized as follows: in Sect. 2, a full
discussion on our GOOMPI is presented with some design policy and implementation detail; then in Sect. 3 we outline a well known matrix multiplication
example using the GOOMPI; also the performance evaluation of GOOMPI compared to normal MPI is given in Sect. 4; in the last two sections, we show some
issues about the related work and provide our conclusions on what we have
experienced.

2   The Design and Implementation of GOOMPI

2.1   The Layered Structure of GOOMPI

As an attempt of applying OO and generic programming techniques to high
performance parallel computing, we developed a generic object-oriented message-
passing library — GOOMPI. It adopts MPI, a currently widely used library in
high performance parallel computing areas, as its underlying implementation
basis. By using OO and generic programming techniques, it constructs a generic

high performance message-passing framework to effectively support the transfer of user-defined dynamic data structures of arbitrary complexity.

GOOMPI provides a complete framework for message-passing. It includes a set of well-designed interfaces and class hierarchies, and consists of two layers — the serialization layer and the message-passing layer.

The layered communication architecture of GOOMPI is depicted in Fig. 1. Further explanation is presented in the following sections.

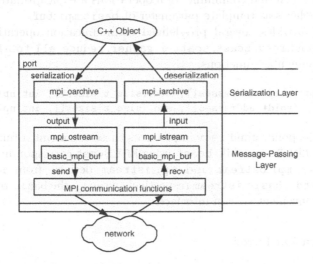

Fig. 1. Layered Communication Architecture of GOOMPI

2.2 Message-Passing Layer

The first layer of GOOMPI, the message-passing layer, uses the Iostream Library to abstract the underlying MPI communication functions and isolate its implementation details.

The iostream library is an important part of the C++ standard library. Its architecture is efficient and excellent for extension.

The iostream library also separates I/O operations into two functional layers — the formatting layer and the transferring layer. In order to effectively perform message-passing using MPI under the architecture of iostream, we write a new transferring layer by deriving a `basic_mpi_buf` class from `std::basic_streambuf`. It supports messages of both the XDR format [10] (for heterogenous environments) and native format (for homogenous environments). It follows the buffered iostream manner, and also provides optional ability to do communication without extra copies to or from buffers to make efficient large bulk of consecutive data transfer possible. Besides improved performance, it also results in more scalability. Unlike some implementations of MPI, our library supports transferring messages of *arbitrary size* due to the extensible architecture of the iostream library, and this requirement is common in scalable high performance scientific computing.

Besides standard-mode send and receive, MPI provides many other communication modes such as buffered mode, synchronous mode and ready mode, as well as nonblocking communications and a variety of collective communications (broadcast, scatter, gather, reduce, all-to-all, etc.). We choose to adopt policy-based design strategy [11] to support these variations without code duplication or loosing efficiency. Actual communication operations are encapsulated uniformly in operation policies as template parameter of basic_mpi_buf.

GOOMPI provides several pre-defined communication operation policies: send_recv, isend_recv, bcast, scatter, gather, reduce, all_to_all, etc. Each policy has two member functions:

```
void send(const void* addresses[], std::size_t sizes[], int nplayers = 2);
void recv(      void* addresses[], std::size_t sizes[], int nplayers = 2);
```

For example, policy send_recv implements these two member functions using MPI_Send and MPI_Recv, while bcast using MPI_Bcast correspondingly.

Two classes mpi_ostream and mpi_istream derived from std::basic_ostream and std::basic_istream respectively wrap up the basic_mpi_buf class to provide a convenient stream interface.

2.3 Serialization Layer

In order to support message-passing based on arbitrary data types, MPI does provide a mechanism to facilitate user-defined types by using data structures like MPI_Datatype and functions such as MPI_Address, MPI_Type_struct and MPI_Type_commit. However, it is tedious and cumbersome to use. More unfortunately, it still limited to manipulate simple Plain Old Data (POD) types such as C-style structs.

We introduce necessary serialization and deserialization of any objects. That is, when sending object of any type, the message content includes the object memory layout which is converted into a specific stream with some format; when receiving, the information extracted from the message forms a stream of that format, then a copy of the original object can be easily reconstructed.

We choose the Boost Serialization Library (BSL) [9] as the implementation basis of GOOMPI's serialization part. BSL supports noninvasive serialization. It can easily serialize primitive types as well as STL containers. BSL exploits a layered design approach, taking a stream as a parameter of its archive class to specify the actual storage and transmission of serialized objects. The archive itself only concerns with the serialization-related issues while cares nothing about how to store or transfer the serialized objects. This design makes it convenient for us to combine BSL with MPI's message-passing functionality through our MPI streams.

GOOMPI customized two high performance archive classes, mpi_oarchive and mpi_iarchive to serialize and deserialize objects of POD types as well as non-POD types (for example, which have nontrivial constructor / destructor) and transfer them through MPI streams. However, under homogenous environments, extra optimizations are provided for commonly used POD types such as C style `structs`, arrays of POD types, and even `std::vectors` with POD type elements. Especially, for large arrays and `std::vectors` of POD types, unnecessary copy operations to or from buffers are avoided. These optimizations result in high performance and little abstraction overhead of GOOMPI programs.

2.4 Stream Style User Interface

Finally, GOOMPI provides a `port` class as a *facade* [12] incorporating all the classes above, and exposes a concise iostream style interface for message-passing.

We borrow from OOMPI the notion of port. A port represents a communication channel between parallel processes. Any C++ objects with appropriate serialization support or data of primitive types can be transferred as messages through the channel.

Users of GOOMPI need not to know the internals of a port. However, one may want to customize some of the behaviors of a port before using it.

There are three aspects of port's communication behavior:

1. The communication operation of the port can be blocking or nonblocking, point-to-point or collective. It can be implemented by choosing appropriate communication policy of `basic_mpi_buf`.
2. The port can be an input-only, output-only as well as supports both input and output.
3. The port can transfer any type of data or only messages of specific data types, or in specific sequence.

Accurately, the last two aspects are *restrictions* on the behavior of a port. Restrictions do not always mean limitations. In fact, it is helpful for detecting logical errors of a program at compile time or runtime by imposing restrictions on the `port` class. In specific cases, useless functions can be removed from a port by the programmer from the beginning to eliminate the possibility of making mistakes. For example, performing an input operation on a output-only port will cause compile time error immediately.

Programmers can also choose to apply no restriction on their port classes for more functionality or just for convenience. In the latter case, they also lose the opportunity for the compiler to help detecting program errors earlier at compile time.

We use policy-based method again to design the `port` class. There are three policies correspondingly:

Operation Policy is the same as the operation policy of MPI streams and `basic_mpi_buf`. It specifies blocking or nonblocking, point-to-point or collective communication operations. The default is standard mode point-to-point operation.

Direction Policy specifies communication direction of the port to be in, out or inout. The default is inout. Attempts to communicate in invalid direction will be detected at compile time.

Message Type Policy specifies the allowed data types to be transferred by the port. The allowed types can be specified conveniently using a mechanism called *Type Patterns* which is developed by authors of this paper. (For example, pattern MyClass means the port can only transfer messages of a type named MyClass; pattern seq_type(A, B, C) guarantees the port can transfer messages of type A, B and C in sequence; while set_type(A, derived(B)) means types A or all types derived from B. Leave it blank means any type is allowed.)

The formal definition of port is as follows:

```
CommChannel        ::= port<OperationPolicy, DirectionPolicy,
                            MsgTypePolicy>
OperationPolicy  ::= P2PComm | CollectiveComm
P2PComm          ::= send_recv | isend_recv | ...
CollectiveComm   ::= bcast | scatter | gather | all_to_all | ...
DirectionPolicy  ::= inout | in | inout
MsgTypePolicy    ::= TypePattern
TypePattern      ::= TypeName | any_type | set_type(TypeList)
                     | seq_type(TypeList) | derived(TypeName) | ...
```

For example, programmers can define an output port which broadcasts messages of type Matrix like this:

```
goompi::port<bcast, out, Matrix> p(...);
```

At most time, a common port can be defined as follows, if one simply wants to use an ordinary point-to-point communication:

```
goompi::port<> p(...);
```

Such a port uses all its default polices.

2.5 Other Features of GOOMPI

Besides communication, GOOMPI also provides other useful generic components to facilitate parallel programming:

Virtual Topology of Parallel Tasks GOOMPI presents several components to support virtual topologies of parallel tasks. For example, class templates mesh_view, graph_view and tree_view represent Descartes space topologies of any finite dimensions, ordered tree and generic graph structures respectively. They all provide convenient functions to specify neighbors (such as the left, right, up and down neighbors, etc.) of each task or particular task groups (for instance a particular row, column or block of tasks). Users can also extend existing topologies or define new topologies when necessary.

Parallel I/O Real world parallel applications always have to deal with a large amount of data, for example, very large matrices or vectors. Storing and retrieving such data efficiently in parallel is a practical requirement. GOOMPI provides C++ iostream style components to support parallel I/O. Large objects can be serialized and deserialized using GOOMPI's parallel I/O streams.

3   Case Study: Implementing Cannon's Algorithm for Matrix Multiplication with GOOMPI

We choose to implement a classic parallel algorithm — the Cannon's algorithm for Matrix Multiplication [13] to illustrate the usage of GOOMPI. To represent matrix data structures, we make use of the Matrix Template Library (MTL) [20], which is an excellent C++ template library that supports a variety of matrix representations as well as many linear algebra functionality. Owe to the extensibility of generic programming, it is convenient to integrate MTL with GOOMPI to effectively divide and transfer various matrices data types.

The GOOMPI program exploits a master / worker paradigm. The master scatters matrices to all worker tasks (including itself), after SPMD style computation, the result is eventually gathered by the master. Suppose there are $P * P$ parallel tasks, torus_view<2> is used for representing the 2D-torus topology of these tasks. Source code of the master is as follows:

```
template <typename MatrixA, typename MatrixB, typename MatrixC>
void cannon(const MatrixA& A, const MatrixB& B, MatrixC& C) {
  torus_view<2> self(P, P);      // global 2D-torus view of P*P tasks
  port<scatter> q(self);
  port<gather>  r(self);

  blocked_view<MatrixA> VA(A, P, P); // create blocked views of matrices
  blocked_view<MatrixB> VB(B, P, P);
  blocked_view<MatrixC> VC(C, P, P);

  q << VA << VB;                          // scatter VA and VB

  cannon_worker<MatrixA, MatrixB, MatrixC>(); // act as a worker

  r >> VC;                                // gather the result
}
```

The following is the source code of workers:

```
template <typename MatrixA, typename MatrixB, typename MatrixC>
void cannon_worker() {
  torus_view<2> self(P, P);      // global 2D-torus view of P*P tasks
  port<scatter> q(self);
  port<gather>  r(self);
```

```
MatrixA a;                        // local submatrices of A and B
MatrixB b;

q >> a >> b;                      // receive submatrices from master

MatrixC c(a.nrows(), a.ncols());  // local result

port<isend_recv> s;               // nonblocking send to avoid deadlock

if (self.i) {                     // initial alignment
  s(self.left(self.i))  << a;
  s(self.right(self.i)) >> a;
}
if (self.j) {
  s(self.up(self.j))    << b;
  s(self.down(self.j))  >> b;
}

for (int i = 0; i < P; i++) {
  mtl::mult(a, b, c);             // c += a * b
  s(self.left())  << a;           // cyclic left shift a
  s(self.right()) >> a;
  s(self.up())    << b;           // cyclic up shift b
  s(self.down())  >> b;
}

r << c;                           // send back result to master
}
```

4   Performance Comparison of MPI and GOOMPI

We tested the performance of LAM MPI [15] and GOOMPI on a 16-node PC Cluster connected with Ethernet. The result is presented in Fig. 2.

Fig. 2 (a),(b) and (c) show that on trasferring arrays or std::vectors of primitive data types or POD structs using both point-to-point and collective communication operations (such as broadcast), there is almost no abstraction penalty. GOOMPI shows a notable performance on par with MPI. Fig. 2 (d) suggests that GOOMPI is much faster when transferring a doubly linked list.

In fact, GOOMPI is especially good at supporting any irregular dynamic data structures. In many situations where complex data structures can not be well fit into primitive types or C arrays, GOOMPI allows more natural and intuitive representations, while corresponding MPI program, is tedious and clumsy. For example, it is boring to reconstruct pointers in dynamic data structures explicitly.

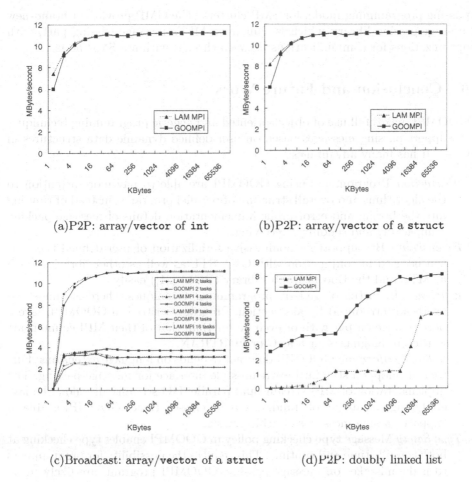

(a)P2P: array/vector of int   (b)P2P: array/vector of a struct

(c)Broadcast: array/vector of a struct   (d)P2P: doubly linked list

Fig. 2. Communication Performance Comparison of LAM MPI and GOOMPI

5   Related Work

MPI-2 [4] does have a C++ binding, unfortunately they are just simple class wrappers of MPI C functions. It does not support full object-oriented or generic programming paradigm.

A similar work to GOOMPI is the Object Oriented MPI (OOMPI). It is an object-oriented approach to MPI. It supports messages composed of user-defined types which are derived from a common base class called OOMPI_User_type, with specific data members and default constructors defined in them. This invasive approach implies that it is impractical to pass messages based on STL containers or classes from other existing libraries using OOMPI.

The Generic Message Passing Framework (GMP) [16] [17] is an attempt which follows generic programming techniques to present a single message-passing programming model for SMP clusters. The GMP provides a brand-new message-passing library which is similar to MPI's message-passing part, with optimizations for communications between threads within a SMP node.

6   Conclusion and Future Work

GOOMPI makes full use of object-oriented and generic programming techniques to support passing messages based on user-defined dynamic data structures in C++. It has many advantages:

Abstraction Programmers using GOOMPI are able to pay more attention to the algorithms and overall structure of parallel programs, instead of running into the boring and error-prone implementation details of message packing / unpacking and sending / receiving.

Extensibility By supporting noninvasive serialization of user-defined types, it can be used in conjunction with C++ STL as well as other libraries (such as MTL and the Boost Graph Library (BGL) [21]) easily.

Efficiency In virtue of generic programming techniques, there is almost no overhead introduced by abstraction. Programs written in GOOMPI have a performance on par with or even better than that of their MPI counterpart written in languages such as C or FORTRAN.

Standard Conforming GOOMPI does not depends on language extensions. Further, it adopts a standard iostream-style interface for message-passing. The implementation of MPI streams and parallel I/O streams all follow the layered design strategies of standard stream classes. Hence GOOMPI is able to support passing messages of arbitrary size.

Type Safety Message type checking policy in GOOMPI enables type checking at both compile time and runtime. This reduces the possibility for programmers to make mistakes on message-passing. GOOMPI programs are likely to be more robust and less error-prone.

With the help of GOOMPI, programmers can map parallel algorithms into high quality parallel programs intuitively, rapidly and effectively. GOOMPI is also of help in the design of parallel algorithms.

Future work includes further enhancements and optimizations of GOOMPI. We are considering about building a generic library and framework based on GOOMPI to support generic parallel and distributed data structures, and facilitate the parallelization of existing generic libraries such as MTL, Boost.uBLAS [18] and Blitz++ [19], etc.

We also prepared to integrate GOOMPI with a thread-level lightweight parallel library called Parallel Multi-Thread Library (PMT) developed by the authors to provide both a unified message-passing model as well as a unified data-parallel model for aiding parallel algorithm design and implementation on different parallel architectures.

References

1. Chen, G.: Parallel Computing — Structure, Algorithm and Programming. High Education Press. (1999) 310-318
2. PVM: Parallel Virtual Machine. http://www.csm.ornl.gov/pvm/pvm_home.html
3. Message Passing Interface Forum: MPI: a message-passing interface standard. International Journal of Supercomputer Applications, 8(3/4), (1994)
4. Message Passing Interface Forum: MPI-2: Extensions to the Message-Passing Interface. (1997)
   http://www.mpi-forum.org/docs/mpi-20-html/mpi2-report.html
5. Stepanov, A., Lee, M.: The Standard Template Library. HP Technical Report HPL-94-34. (1995)
6. POOMA. http://www.codesourcery.com/pooma/pooma
7. Gerlach, J.: Generic Programming of Parallel Applications with Janus. Parallel Processing Letters, Vol. 12, No. 2 (2002) 175-190
8. Johnson, E., Gannon, D.: HPC++: Experiments with the Parallel Standard Template Library. International Conference on Supercomputing Proceedings of the 11th international conference on Supercomputing. (1997) 124-131
9. Ramey, R.: The Boost Serialization Library. http://www.boost.org/
10. Sun Microsystems, Inc.: XDR: External Data Representation standard. RFC 1014. (1987)
11. Alexandrescu, A.: Modern C++ Design: Generic Programming and Design Patterns Applied. Addison-Wisley. (2001) 3-21
12. Gamma, E., Helm. R., Johnson, R., Vlissides, J.: Design Patterns: Elements of Reusable Object-Oriented Software. Addison-Wesley. (1994)
13. Cannon, L. E.: A Cellular Computer to Implement the Kalman Filter Algorithm. PH.D. thesis. Montana State Univ. (1969)
14. Object Oriented MPI (OOMPI). http://www.osl.iu.edu/research/oompi/
15. LAM MPI. http://www.lam-mpi.org/
16. Lee, L., Lumsdaine, A.: The Generic Message Passing Framework. Parallel and Distributed Processing Symposium, 2003. Proceedings International. (2003) 53-62
17. Lee, L.: Generic programming for high-performance scientific computing. Ph.D. thesis. University of Notre Dame. (2003) 1-78
18. Walter, J., Koch, M.: The Boost uBLAS Library. http://www.boost.org/
19. The Blitz++ Library. http://oonumerics.org/blitz/
20. Lumsdaine, A., Siek, J., Lee, L.: The Matrix Template Library.
    http://www.osl.iu.edu/research/mtl/
21. Siek, J., Lee, L., Lumsdaine, A.: The Boost Graph Library (BGL).
    http://www.boost.org/

Simulating Complex Dynamical Systems in a Distributed Programming Environment

E.V. Krishnamurthy[1] and Vikram Krishnamurthy[2]

[1]Computer Sciences Laboratory,
Australian National University, Canberra , ACT 0200, Australia
abk@discus.anu.edu.au
[2]Department of Electrical and Computer Engineering,
University of British Columbia, V6T 1Z4 Vancouver, Canada
vikramk@ece.ubc.ca

Abstract. This paper describes a rule-based generic programming and simulation paradigm, for conventional hard computing and soft and innovative computing e.g., dynamical, genetic, nature inspired self-organized criticality and swarm intelligence. The computations are interpreted as the outcome arising out of deterministic, non-deterministic or stochastic interaction among elements in a multiset object space that includes the environment. These interactions are like chemical reactions and the evolution of the multiset can mimic the evolution of the complex system. Since the reaction rules are inherently parallel, any number of actions can be performed cooperatively or competitively among the subsets of elements. This paradigm permits carrying out parts or all of the computations independently in a distributed manner on distinct processors and is eminently suitable for cluster and grid computing.

1 Introduction

Most systems we observe in nature are complex dynamical systems that consist of a large number of degrees of freedom. They may contain several inhomogeneous subsystems that are spatially and temporally structured on different scales and characterized by their own dynamics. Such complex systems often exhibit collective ("Emergence") behaviour that is difficult to model. Stochastic and chaotic dynamical systems provide an efficient methodology for modelling and simulation of complex systems by capturing the behaviour of the system at different spatial and temporal scales. The simulation based approach of a stochastic or chaotic dynamical system can be viewed as *"soft computation"*, since unlike in conventional computation where exactness is our goal, we allow for the possibility of error and randomness.

This paper describes a generic multiset programming paradigm for the simulation of complex systems. This paradigm permits us to write a generic program [2], [3] called a program shell - that implements the common control structure. It includes a few unspecified data types and procedures that vary from one application to another. Hence, this **Unified Multiset Simulation Paradigm (UMSP)** can be used for all **conventional algorithms** [15], Tabu search, Markov chain Monte Carlo (MCMC), Particle Filters [6], **Evolutionary algorithms**-classifier systems, bucket brigade learning , **Genetic algorithms and Programming** [14], **Immunocomputing**, Self-

H. Jin et al. (Eds.): NPC 2004, LNCS 3222, pp. 272-279, 2004.

organized criticality [4] and **Active Walker models** (ants with scent or multiwalker-paradigm where each walker can influence the other through a shared landscape based on probabilistic selection [9], and **Biomimicry** [16]. Also it is applicable to non-equilibrium systems using oscillatory mechanisms involving catalytic reactions - as for example of producing ATP (Adenosine triphosphate) from ATP [8].

Structure of Unified Multiset Simulation Paradigm (UMSP)
The UMSP has the following features:
(i) One or more object spaces (multisets) that contain elements whose information is structured in an appropriate way to suit the problem at hand.
(ii) A set of interaction rules that prescribes the context for the applicability of the rules to the elements of an object space. Each rule consists of a left-hand side (a pattern or attribute) of named objects and the conditions under which they interact, and a right hand side that describes the actions to be performed on the elements of the object space, if the rule becomes applicable based on some deterministic or probabilistic criteria.
(iii) A control strategy that specifies the manner in which the elements of the object space will be chosen and interaction rules will be applied, the kinetics of the rule-interference (inhibition, activation, diffusion, chemotaxis) and a way of resolving conflicts that may arise when several rules match at once.
(iv) A mechanism to evaluate the elements of the object space to determine the effectiveness of rule application (e.g., evaluating fitness for survival).

Thus, UMSP provides a stochastic frame-work of *"generate and test"* for a wide range of problems, Yao [19], and Michalewicz and Fogel [14]. Also the system structure of UMSP consisting of components and their interaction is supported by contemporary software architecture design [2].

Computational Features of UMSP
The UMSP has the following computational features:
(i) Interaction -Based: The computations are interpreted as the outcome of interacting elements of the object space that produce new elements (or same elements with modified attributes) according to specific rules. Hence the intrinsic (genotype) and acquired properties due to interaction (phenotype) can both be incorporated in the object space. Since the interaction rules are inherently parallel, any number of actions can be performed *cooperatively or competitively* among the subsets of elements, so that the new elements evolve toward an equilibrium or unstable or chaotic state.
(ii) Content-based rule activation: The next set of rules to be invoked is determined solely by the contents of the object space as in chemical reactions.
(iii) Pattern matching: Search takes place to bind the variables in such a way to satisfy the left hand side of the rule. This characteristic of pattern (or attribute) matching makes the UMSP suitable for innovative computing.
(iv) Suitable for deterministic, non-deterministic and probabilistic modes.
(v) Choice of objects, and actions: We can use strings, arrays, sets, trees and graphs, multisets, tuples, molecules, particles and even points, as the basic elements of computation and perform suitable actions on them by defining a suitable topology, geometry or a metric space.

We describe in Sections 2 and 3, the general properties of rule based paradigms. In Section 4 we give examples for UMSP. Section 5 contains the conclusion.

2 Rule -Based Programming Paradigm

Specification:
The main feature of the rule - based paradigm is the specification of the program:
G(R, A)(M) = If there exists elements a, b, c,.. in an object space M such that an interaction rule R (a, b, c,...) involving elements a , b, c is applicable then
G(R, A)((M- {a , b, c,.. }) + A(a, b , c,...)) else M.

Here M denotes the initial object space with components of appropriately chosen data type. This is a multiset or a bag in which a member can have multiple occurrences, Calude et al. [5]. The operator - denotes the removal (annihilation) of the interacted elements; it is the multiset difference; the operator + denotes the insertion (or creation) of new elements after the action A; this is multiset union of appropriately typed components. Note that R is a condition text (or interaction condition that is a boolean) that is used to check when some of the elements of the object space M can interact. The function A is the action text that describes the result of this interaction. Note that both R and A are exact and deterministic. Testing for R involves a deterministic search, and evaluation of truth or falsity of Boolean predicates. Also actions performed in A are assumed to be exact.

The function R can be interpreted as the query evaluation function in a database M and the function A can be interpreted as the updating function for a set of database instances. Hence, if one or several interaction conditions hold for several non-disjoint subsets of object space at the same time, the choice made among them can be nondeterministic or probabilistic. This leads to *competitive parallelism*. Then the actions on the chosen subset are executed atomically and committed. That is, the chosen subset undergoes an 'asynchronous atomic update'. This ensures that the process of matching and the follow-up actions satisfy the four important properties used in *Transaction Processing* [13] namely, ACID properties: Atomicity (indivisibility and either all or no actions or carried out), Consistency (before and after the execution of a transaction), Isolation (no interference among the actions), Durability (no failure). Once all the actions are carried out and committed the next set of conditions are considered. As a result of the actions followed by commitment, we derive a new database; this may satisfy new conditions of the text and the actions are repeated by initiating a new set of transactions. These set of transformations halt when there are no more transactions executable or the database does not undergo a change for two consecutive steps indicating a new consistent state of the database.

However, if the interaction condition holds for several disjoint subsets of elements in the database at the same time, the actions can take place independently and simultaneously. This leads to *cooperative parallelism*.

Deterministic and Nondeterministic Iterative Computation:
This consists of applications of rules that consume the interacting elements of the object space and produce new or modified elements in the multiset. This is essentially *Dijkstra's guarded command program*. It is well-known that the Guarded command approach serves as a universal distributed programming paradigm for all conventional algorithms with deterministic or nondeterministic components [10] So we will not elaborate on this aspect any further.

Termination: For the termination of rule application, the interaction conditions R have to be designed so that the elements in the object space can interact only if they are in opposition to the required termination condition. When the entire elements meet the termination condition, the rules are not applicable and the computation halts leaving the object space in an equilibrium state (or a fixed point).

Non–termination, instability, chaos: These cases arise when the rules continue to fire indefinitely as in chemical oscillations. Then the object space can be in a non-equilibrium state. It is also possible that the evolution leads to instability and chaos of the deterministic iterative dynamics.

For example, consider the rule-based   iterative dynamical system: For $X(0)$ in the range [-1,1], if $X(i) \geq 0$ then $G(X(i+1)) = -2X(i) +1$; else $G(x(i+1)) = 2X(i)+1$.The rules $X(i) \geq 0$ and $X(i)<0$, are mutually exclusive and non-competitive; they generate a chaotic dynamical system, unstable, having a dense orbit in [-1,1].

3 Stochastic Rule-Based Paradigm

The introduction of stochastic mechanism (randomness) in a rule-based system has several advantages:

(i) It provides ergodicity of search orbits. This property ensures that searching is done through all possible states of the solution space since there is a finite probability that an individual can reach any point in problem space with one jump.

(ii) It provides solution discovery capabilities (as in genetic programming) and enables us to seek a global optimum rather than a local optimum.

(iii) It cuts down the average running time of an otherwise worst–case running time-algorithm. We achieve this gain by producing an output having an error with a small probability.

(iv) Applicable to problems in many discipline; Genetics (genetic algorithms); Thermodynamics (simulated annealing), Statistical Mechanics (Particle transport); Complex Systems (Active -walker, Self-organization and percolation models).

The unified multiset rule-based Simulation paradigm (UMSP) is obtained from the rule based system described in Section 2, by introducing probabilities for selection to test whether one or more reaction conditions hold for several non-disjoint subsets at the same time. In this case, the choice made among these subsets is determined by a random number generator to randomly select the elements of the multiset with a probability p, test for the reaction conditions, and then perform the required actions.

UMSP is defined by the function:

PG (R (p(i), A) (M) = if there exists elements a,b,c,. .. belonging to an object space M (a multiset) such that R(a, b, c,...) then G(R,A)((M-{a, b, c,.. }) + A(a, b, c,..)) else M where   each of the possible number of subsets i that satisfy the conditions R is randomly chosen with an appropriate probability p(i) and the   corresponding text of action A   is implemented and the components of the multiset are updated appropriately. Further, if p(i) is not specified in a component program , the choice can be deterministic or nondeterministic. Thus a composite program can contain within itself the deterministic, nondeterministic and probabilistic components.

The implementation of UMSP consists of the following four basic steps:

Step 0: Initialization: Initializing the multiset representing the problem domain.

Step 1: Search: Deterministic or random searching for the candidate   elements that satisfy a given rule (interaction condition) exactly or within a probabilistic bound..

Step 2: Rule Application: Carrying out the appropriate actions on these chosen the elements as dictated by the given rule.

Step 3: Stopping: It is typical in probabilistic method, not to explicitly state a stopping criterion. A key reason for this is that the convergence theory can provide only asymptotic estimates, as the number of iterations goes to infinity. However, in practice, we need to choose a suitable stopping criterion for the given problem - otherwise, we may be wasting the resources .

In step 3, we may use various acceptance criteria; these may be involve evaluating an individual element or a selected subset or the whole object space; that is, the evaluation of the object space can take place at different levels of granularity depending upon the problem domain. Also, the acceptance criteria may be chosen dependent or independent of the number of previous trials and the choice of probabilities can remain static or can vary dynamically with each trial. Thus depending upon the evaluation granularity, acceptance criteria and the manner in which the probability assignments are made, we can devise various strategies by suitably modifying the skeletal structure of UMSP. For example one may choose to select a reaction rule from a rule-base probabilistically or vary the frequency of application of competing rules. Also one may carry out any operation probabilistically. UMSP is suitable to optimize the structure of the model used as in Genetic Programming, or optimize its parameters as in Genetic algorithms.

4   Examples for Realisation of UMSP

Practical realisation of the UMSP and application to many different types of algorithms can be achieved through a coordination programming language, Multran, using Multiset and the concept of transactions [13]. Also UMSP can be implemented in the grid and cluster-computing environment using MPI [7,17]. Due to lack of space we can give only two examples.

(i) Swarm and Ant Colony Paradigm
A swarm (flock of birds, ants, cellular automata) is a population of interacting elements that can optimize some global objective through cooperative search of space [9]. Here, individual elements in the multiset are points in space, and change over time is represented as movement of points, representing particles with velocities and the system dynamics is formulated in UMSP using the rules:
1. **Stepping rule**: The state of each individual element is updated in many dimensions, in parallel, so that the new state reflects each element's previous best success ; e.g., ,the position and momentum (velocity) of each particle.
2. **Landscaping rule**: Each element is assigned a new best value of its state that depends on its past best value and a suitable function of the best values of its interacting neighbours, with a suitably defined neighbourhood topology and geometry.
Rule 1 reflects the betterment of the individual, while rule 2 reflects the betterment of the collection of the individuals in the neighbourhood as a whole, by evaluating the relevance of each individual and providing support for its activity. These two rules permit us to model Markovian random walks which is independent of the past history of the walk and non-Markovian random walks, dependent upon past history- such as self-avoiding, self-repelling and active random-walker models. This can result in a swarm (a self - organizing system) whose global nonlinear dynamics emerges from local rules due to stochasticity or chaos introduced by the parameter variation. Also,

interesting new properties may show up- low dimensional attractors, bifurcations and chaos and various kinds of attractors having fractal dimensions presenting a swarm - like, flock-like appearances depending upon the Jacobian of the mapping; Wolfram [18].

(ii) Discrete Adaptive Stochastic Optimization

Consider the following discrete stochastic optimization problem. Let $\Theta = \{1,2,...,S\}$ denote a finite set and consider the following problem: Compute

$$\theta^* = \min_{\theta \in \Theta} E\{X_n(\theta)\}$$

where E denotes mathematical expectation and for any fixed $\theta \in \Theta$, $\{X_n(\theta)\}$ denotes a sequence of independent and identically distributed (iid) random variables that can be generated for any choice of $\theta \in \Theta$. If the density function of $X_n(\theta)$ is not known, it is not possible to analytically evaluate the above expectation and hence θ^*. In such a case, one needs to resort to simulation based stochastic approximation to compute the optimal solution θ^*.

A brute force approach of computing the optimal solution to the problem involves exhaustive enumeration over all Θ and proceeds as follows: For each $\theta \in \Theta$ generate a large number N of random samples $X_1(\theta), X_2(\theta),...X_N(\theta)$. Then compute an estimate of $E\{X_n(\theta)\}$ using the sample average (arithmetic mean)

$$G_N(\theta) = (X_1(\theta) + X_2(\theta) + ... + X_N(\theta) / N.$$

By Kolmogorov's strong law of large numbers (which is one of the most fundamental consequences of the ergodic theorem for iid processes), $G_N(\theta) \to E\{X_n(\theta)\}$ with probability one as $N \to \infty$. This and the finiteness of Θ imply that

$$\arg\max_{\theta \in \Theta} G_N(\theta) \to \arg\max_{\theta \in \Theta} E\{X_n(\theta)\} \text{ as } N \to \infty.$$

However, the above brute force procedure is inefficient – evaluating $G_N(\theta)$ at values $\theta \in \Theta$ with $\theta \neq \theta^*$ is wasted effort since it contributes nothing towards evaluating $G_N(\theta^*)$. What is required is an intelligent dynamic scheduling (search) scheme that decides at each time instant which value of θ to evaluate next, given the current estimates, in order to converge to the maximum θ^* with minimum effort.

Here we present a globally convergent discrete stochastic approximation algorithm based on the random search procedures [1,11,12,20]. The basic idea is to generate a homogeneous Markov chain taking values in Θ which spends more time at the global optimum than at any other element of Θ. This consists of the following skeletal structural steps of UMSP .

Step 0: Initialization: At time n=0, select starting point $\theta_0 \in \Theta$ randomly with uniform probability. Set $D_0 = e_{\theta_0}$, where e_i denotes the S dimensional unit vector with 1 in the i th position and zeros elsewhere. Set initial solution estimate $\hat{\theta}_0 = x_0$.

Step 1: Search (Random Sampling): At time n, sample $u_n \in \Theta - \{\theta_n\}$ with uniform distribution.
Evaluate the random sample costs $X_n(\theta_n)$ and $X_n(u_n)$.

Step 2: Rule Application: If $X_n(\theta_n) > X_n(u_n)$ then set $\theta_{n+1} = \theta_n$, else set $\theta_{n+1} = u_n$.

Update duration time vector at time n+1 as $D_{n+1} = D_n + e_{\theta_n}$

Update estimate of maximum at time n as $\hat{\theta}_n = \arg\max_{i \in \{1,2,\ldots,S\}} D_{n+1}(i)$

Step 3: Stopping: Choose stopping criteria appropriately; if not satisfied set $n \to n+1$ and go to Step 1.

Then as proved in [1], under suitable conditions (e.g., if the density function with respect to which the expected value is defined above is symmetric) the estimate $\hat{\theta}_n$ generated by the above random search stochastic approximation algorithm converges with probability one to the global optimum θ^*. It is also shown in [1], that the algorithm is attracted to the global optimum, i.e., the algorithm spends more time at the global optimum than any other candidate value. That is, for sufficiently large n, the duration time vector D_n has it maximum element at θ^*.

The above algorithm has several applications. It can be used to learn the behaviour of an ion channel (large protein molecule) in a nerve cell membrane to estimate the Nernst potential efficiently [11]. In [12,20] its recursive version optimizes the spreading code of a CDMA spread spectrum transmitter over a fading wireless channel.

5 Conclusion

The introduction of stochastic/chaotic mechanisms in a multiset chemical reaction model provides a soft-computational model to study evolutionary biological, chemical and physical systems interacting with the environment. The paradigm described here provides a new environment using a distributed architecture for swarm intelligence, membrane and bio-immunology computing, adaptive stochastic optimisation and self organized criticality. This simulation paradigm is well-suited for cluster and grid computing using MPI.

References

1.   S.Andradottir, Accelerating the convergence of random search methods for discrete stochastic optimization, ACM Transactions on Modelling and Computer Simulation, 9(4) (1999), 349-380.
2.   R.Backhouse and J.Gibbons, Generic Programming, Lecture Notes in Computer Science, Vol.2793,Springer Verlag , New York (2003)
3.   J.-P.Banatre, D.L. Me'tayer, Programming by Multiset transformation Comm. ACM, **36**, (1993) 98 -111.
4.   S.Boettcher and A. Percus, Nature's way of Optimizing, Artificial Intelligence, **119** (2000),275-286,.
5.   C.S.Calude et al., Multiset Processing, Lecture Notes in Computer Science, Vol.2235,Springer Verlag, New York (2001)
6.   A.Doucet,et al., Particle Filters for State Estimation of Jump Markov Linear Systems, IEEE Trans Signal Processing, **49**, 613-624 (2001)

7. W. Gropp, et al., *Using MPI*, M.I.T Press, Cambridge, Mass,(1992)
8. D.-Q.Jiang,et al.,Mathematical Theory of Nonequilibrium Steady states, Lecture Notes In Mathematics, Vol 1833,Springer Verlag, New York (2004)
9. J.Kennedy, and R.C.Eberhart, Swarm Intelligence,Morgan Kauffman,London (2001).
10. E.V.Krishnamurthy, Parallel Processing, Addison Wesley, Reading., Mass.,(1989)
11. V.Krishnamurthy and S.H.Chung, Adaptive Learning Algorithms for Nernst Potential and I-V curves in Nerve Cell Membrane Ion Channels modelled as Hidden Markov Models, IEEE Transactions NanoBioScience, **2** (4), 266-278 9(2003)
12. V.Krishnamurthy, et al., Adaptive Spreading Code Optimization in Multiantenna Multipath Fading Channels in CDMA, IEEE Conference on Communications, Anchorage, May 2003.
13. W.Ma et al,.,Multran - A coordination Programming Language Using Multiset and Transactions, Proc. Neural, Parallel and Scientific Computing, **1**, 301-304, Dynamic Publishers, Inc.,U.S.A.,(1995).
14. Z. Michalewicz, D.B Fogel, How to solve it : Modern Heuristics , Springer Verlag, New York (2002).
15. V.K.Murthy and E.V. Krishnamurthy, Probabilistic Parallel Programming based on Multiset transformation, Future Generation Computer Systems.11(1995)283-293.
16. K.M.Pacino, Biomimicry of bacterial foraging for distributed optimisation and control, IEEE Control System Magazine, **22**(3)(2002),52-68.
17. M.Snir et al.:MPI: The complete Reference, M.I.T.Press,Cambridge, Mass.(1995)
18. S.Wolfram: A New kind of Science, Wolfram Media Inc., Champaign, Ill (2002)
19. X.Yao, The evolution of Evolutionary computation, Lecture Notes in Artificial Intelligence, Vol.2773, 19-20 (2003).
20. G.Yin, et al. Regime Switching Stochastic Approximation Algorithms with application to adaptive discrete stochastic optimization, SIAM Journal of Optimization, to appear.

Design and Implementation of a Remote Debugger for Concurrent Debugging of Multiple Processes in Embedded Linux Systems*

Jung-hee Kim[1], Hyun-chul Sim[1], Yong-hyeog Kang[2], and Young Ik Eom[1]

[1] School of Information and Communication Eng., Sungkyunkwan University
300 cheoncheon-dong, Jangan-gu, Suwon, Gyeonggi-do 440-746, Korea
{kimjh, jlmaj, yieom}@ece.skku.ac.kr
[2] School of Business Administration, Far East University
5 San Wangjang, Gamgok, Eumseong, Chungbuk 369-851, Korea
yhkang@mail.kdu.ac.kr

Abstract. In the embedded software development environments, developers can concurrently debug a running process and its child processes only by using multiple gdbs and gdbservers. But it needs additional coding and messy works of activating additional gdb and gdbserver for each created process. In this paper, we propose an efficient mechanism for concurrent debugging of multiple remote processes in the embedded system environments by using the library wrapping mechanism without Linux kernel modification. Through the experimentation of debugging two processes communicating by an unnamed pipe in the target system, we show that our proposed debugging mechanism is easier and more efficient than preexisting mechanisms.

1 Introduction

Currently, the gdb has been popularly used as a remote debugging tool in the embedded Linux software developments. By running the gdb in the host system and the gdbserver in the target system, developers can debug a remote process running in the target system [1][2]. However, developers must insert a "sleep" function into the debugged program in order to concurrently debug a newly created child process of the current debugged process. Developers also need additional gdbserver in the target system and connect it to the blocked child process. In the host system, additional gdb is required to connect to the new gdbserver in the target system. Therefore, developers must have the same number of gdbs in the host system and gdbservers in the target system as the number of the debugged processes.

A gdbserver in the target system provides developers with the ability of debugging a process by using ptrace system call in the Linux systems. But the ptrace system call needs the parent-child relationship between a gdbserver and

---

* This work was supported by Korea Research Foundation Grant (KRF-2003-041-D20420).

H. Jin et al. (Eds.): NPC 2004, LNCS 3222, pp. 280–283, 2004.

a debugged process [3]. When a debugged process creates a new process, the parent-child relationship is not established between a gdbserver and the newly created child process. Developers need to insert the sleep code into a newly created child process code. When the newly created process is blocked by the sleep code in the target system, developers run a new gdbserver in the target system and connect it to the blocked process. Developers also run a new gdb in the host system and connect it to the new gdbserver in the target system. When two connections are established, developers can debug the newly created process in the target system by using the gdb in the host system and the gdbserver in the target system.

2   Our Proposed Mechanism

In this paper, we propose a new debugging mechanism that supports concurrent debugging of multiple remote processes by using the mgdb library and the mgdbserver. Fig. 1 shows the overview of our proposed mechanism that supports the concurrent debugging of multiple remote processes. The mgdbserver in the target system communicates with the gdb in the host system. Developers can concurrently debug multiple remote processes by selecting the process intended to debug at desired time by using the mgdbserver. Whenever a debugged process creates a new child process, the mgdbserver runs a new gdbserver in the target system and connects it to the newly created child process automatically in order to support the concurrent debugging of the newly created child process.

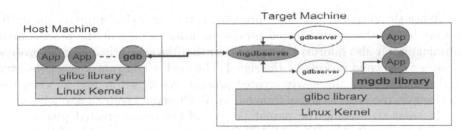

Fig. 1. Overview of our concurrent and remote debugging mechanism

In order to support concurrent debugging of multiple remote processes, the mgdbserver must know when the current debugged process invokes fork system call. In this paper, we use the mechanism of wrapping the glibc library in order to intercept the system call that a currently debugged process invokes. When the currently debugged process calls the function in the glibc library, the library wrapping scheme intercepts the function call and calls the same name function in our mgdb library. The called function in our mgdb library executes the code that is needed for debugging of multiple processes before calling the function in the glibc library that is intended to be called originally. In order to intercept system call, we use the interposition mechanism of Linux dynamic linker [4] by preloading our mgdb library before the glibc library.

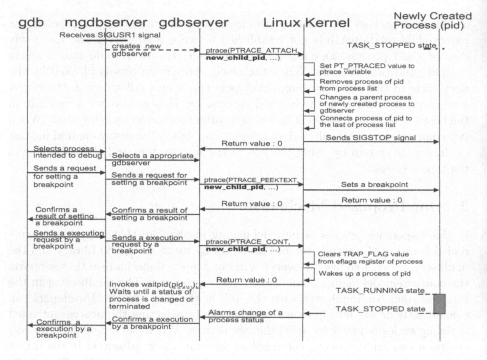

Fig. 2. Flow of debugging newly created process after mgdbserver receives signal

When the currently debugged process creates a new child process, our mgdb library blocks the newly created process in order to prevent the process from terminating. It also informs the mgdbserver that the currently debugged process creates a new child process by the signal. The mgdbserver runs a new gdbserver and connects it to the newly created process. As shown in Fig. 2, when the mgdbserver receives the signal from our mgdb library, it creates a new gdbserver.

In order to become the parent process of the newly created process, the new gdbserver sets the PT_PTRACED value to a ptrace variable of the newly created process by invoking ptrace system call. When developers want to change the currently debugged process, they can select the process to debug by using a gdb in the host system. When the new debugged process is selected by a gdb, the mgdbserver passes debugging request from the gdb to the gdbserver.

3   Experiment and Performance Analysis

The scenario used in the experiment is as follows. The parent process creates a child process and sends a string through the unnamed pipe shared by the child process. After the child process receives the string from the parent process, it rearranges the string in reverse order and sends the string to the parent process through the unnamed pipe. After the parent process receives the string, it prints the string sent by the child process.

Developers can see the debugged status information of all processes created by the currently debugged process by typing "show-remoted-debugee" at the "gdb" prompt in the host system. By selecting the process identifier number, they also can change a specific process for debugging through "change-remote-debugee" command with "pid" argument.

Table 1. Comparison of TotalView with our mgdb library and mgdbserver

	ETNUS's TotalView	Our proposed debugger
Test program image size	53658 bytes	23973 bytes
Library linking mechanism	staic	dynamic
Remote debugging	no supporting	supporting

In this experiment, we focus on the ability of our debugger tool to support concurrent and remote debugging of the parent process and the newly created child process by selecting the process intended to debug using only one gdb in the host system. As shown in Table 1, we compare our proposed scheme with ETNUS TotalView program that supports debugging of multiple processes [5]. However, the library linking mechanism in ETNUS TotalView supports only static linking, therefore the size of the debugged program in ETNUS TotalView is larger than that in our proposed scheme. ETNUS TotalView also cannot support remote debugging.

4   Conclusion

In this paper, we presented a new concurrent debugging mechanism for remote processes through the design and implementation of the mgdb library and the mgdbserver. In our proposed scheme, developers can debug all debugged processes in the target system by selecting the debugged process among them through one gdb in the host system. Compared with the preexisting mechanism, our proposed scheme provides easier and more efficient concurrent debugging for multiple remote processes in the target system.

References

1. Daniel Jacobowitz, Remoting Debugging with GDB, http://www.kegel.com/linux/gdbserver.html, 2002.
2. Richard M. Stallman, Debugging with GDB, 4th ed., Cygnus Support, 1996.
3. Uresh Vahalia, Unix Internals, Prentice Hall, 1996.
4. Sun Microsystems Inc., Linker and Libraries Guide, October, 1998.
5. Etnus, Totalview Getting Started, http://www.etnus.com/Products/TotalView/started/getting_started2.html, 2001.

Performance Evaluation of Hypercubes in the Presence of Multiple Time-Scale Correlated Traffic

Geyong Min[1] and Mohamed Ould-Khaoua[2]

[1] Department of Computing, School of Informatics, University of Bradford,
Bradford, BD7 1DP, U.K.
g.min@brad.ac.uk

[2] Department of Computing Science, University of Glasgow, Glasgow, G12 8RZ, U.K.
mohamed@dcs.gla.ac.uk

Abstract. The efficiency of a large-scale parallel computer is critically dependent on the performance of its interconnection network. Analytical modelling plays an important role towards obtaining a clear understanding of network performance under various design spaces. This paper proposes an analytical performance model for circuit-switched hypercubes in the presence of multiple time-scale correlated traffic which can appear in many parallel computation environments and has strong impact on network performance. The tractability and reasonable accuracy of the analytical model demonstrated by simulation experiments make it a practical and cost-effective evaluation tool to investigate network performance under different system configurations.

1 Introduction

Multicomputers have been widely accepted as the solution for solving grand challenge problems in high performance computing. Interconnection network [1] is a critical architectural component in multicomputer systems as any interaction between the processors ultimately depends on its effectiveness. The hypercube has been one of the popular network topologies in multicomputers owing to its desirable properties, such as regular structure, symmetry, low diameter and high connectivity to deal with fault-tolerance [2]. An n-dimensional hypercube has $N = 2^n$ nodes with 2 nodes in each dimension. Each node consists of a processing element and a router.

The switching strategy determines how data in a message traverses its route from source to destination. The circuit switching has been widely employed in computer and telecommunication systems [1]~[7]. Such a switching strategy is divided into two phases: (1) circuit establishment phase; (2) transmission phase. A dedicated path is set up prior to the transmission of data. A noticeable advantage of circuit switching is due to the fact that it does not require packetizing. Moreover, the low buffer requirement enables the construction of small, compact, and fast routers [1].

---

[1] The research was supported in part by the Nuffield Foundation through Grant NAL/00682/G, and the University of Bradford through Research Investment Fund.

H. Jin et al. (Eds.): NPC 2004, LNCS 3222, pp. 284–291, 2004.
© IFIP International Federation for Information Processing 2004

Traffic loads generated by real-world applications have very strong effects on the performance of interconnection networks. Many recent studies [8]~[10] have demonstrated that realistic traffic can reveal burstiness and correlations among inter-arrival intervals over a number of time scales. At every time scale, traffic bursts consist of bursty subperiods separated by less bursty subperiods. This fractal-like behaviour of network traffic can be much better modelled using statistically long-range dependent processes, which reveal totally different theoretical properties from the conventional Poisson process [9]. A stochastic process X with autocorrelation function $r(k)$ is long-range dependent if its autocorrelation decays hyperbolically fast, i.e. $r(k) \sim |k|^{-\beta}$, as $|k| \rightarrow \infty$ with $0 < \beta < 1$ [11]. The Hurst parameter, $H = 1 - \beta/2$ where $0.5 < H < 1$, is commonly used to measure the degree of long-range dependence.

Sahuquillo *et al.* [10] have traced some typical parallel applications and revealed that workloads generated by many scientific and engineering computations exhibit the fractal-like nature. In an effort towards providing cost-effective tools that help investigating the network performance with various design alternatives and under different traffic conditions, this paper proposes an analytical model for hypercube networks with circuit switching in the presence of multiple time-scale bursty and correlated traffic. The validity of the model is demonstrated by comparing analytical results to those obtained through simulation experiments of the actual system.

The rest of this paper is organized as follows. Section 2 presents the derivation of the analytical model. Section 3 validates the model through simulation experiments. Finally, Section 4 concludes this study.

2 Derivation of the Performance Model

The analytical model is based on the following assumptions [2], [4]~[7], [12], [13].

1) Traffic generated by each node follows an independent stochastic process with a mean arrival rate λ and autocorrelation at lag 1 $r(1) = \rho\lambda$. Traffic burstiness and correlations appear over t time scales. The autocorrelation decays hyperbolically with Hurst parameter H as the time scale increases.

2) Message destination nodes are uniformly distributed across the network nodes. Message length is M flits.

3) The local queue in the source node has infinite capacity. Each physical channel is divided into V virtual channels [1].

4) Messages are routed adaptively through the network [1, 6] using one of the available shortest paths.

Under the uniform traffic pattern, the average message distance in an n-dimensional hypercube is given by $D \cong n/2$ [2]. As the network latency consists of the time to establish a path and the time to transmit a message, it can be calculated as $T=E+D+M$ where E represents the path set-up time. Since the Laplace-Stieltjes transform (LST) of the sum of independent random variables is equal to the product of their transforms [14], the LST of T can be written as

$$T^*(s) = E^*(s)e^{-s(D+M)} \tag{1}$$

where $E^*(s)$ denotes the LST of the time to set up a path.

Following the approach proposed in Ref. [15], traffic burstiness and correlations over multiple time scales can be modelled by the superposition of L two-state Markov-Modulated Poisson Processes (MMPP) [16], typically $L=4$. We use the MMPP$^{(i)}$ with superscript i to denote the i-th MMPP ($1 \leq i \leq L$). A two-state MMPP$^{(i)}$ can be parameterised by the infinitesimal generator, $\mathbf{A}_i$, and rate matrix $\mathbf{B}_i$ as [18]

$$\mathbf{A}_i = \begin{bmatrix} -\delta_{1i} & \delta_{1i} \\ \delta_{2i} & -\delta_{2i} \end{bmatrix} \text{ and } \mathbf{B}_i = \begin{bmatrix} \lambda_{1i} & 0 \\ 0 & \lambda_{2i} \end{bmatrix} \tag{2}$$

The element δ_{1i} is the transition rate from state 1 to 2 of the MMPP$^{(i)}$ and δ_{2i} is the rate out of state 2 to 1. λ_{1i} and λ_{2i} are the traffic rate when the MMPP$^{(i)}$ is in state 1 and 2, respectively. The fitting algorithm described in Ref. [15] derives the parameters δ_{1i}, δ_{2i}, λ_{1i}, λ_{2i} for each MMPP$^{(i)}$ ($1 \leq i \leq L$) for matching the mean and autocorrelation function over different time scales. The superposition of the MMPP$^{(i)}$s ($1 \leq i \leq L$) gives rise to a new MMPP with 2^L states and its parameter matrices, $\mathbf{A}_s$ and $\mathbf{B}_s$, can be computed as (the symbol "$\oplus$" denotes the Kronecker sum [18])

$$\mathbf{A}_s = \mathbf{A}_1 \oplus \mathbf{A}_2 \oplus \cdots \oplus \mathbf{A}_L \text{ and } \mathbf{B}_s = \mathbf{B}_1 \oplus \mathbf{B}_2 \oplus \cdots \oplus \mathbf{B}_L \tag{3}$$

A message enters the network through one of the V injection virtual channels with even probability $1/V$. Given that the process resulting from the splitting of an MMPP has the same infinitesimal generator as the original MMPP [17], the infinitesimal generator $\mathbf{A}_v$ and rate matrix $\mathbf{B}_v$, of the resulting MMPP that models the traffic on an injection virtual channel in the source node are given by

$$\mathbf{A}_v = \mathbf{A}_s \text{ and } \mathbf{B}_v = \mathbf{B}_s / V \tag{4}$$

To determine the mean waiting time that a message experiences before entering the network, the injection virtual channel in the source node is modelled as an MMPP/G/1 queueing system. The mean waiting time, Ws, can be expressed as [18]

$$Ws = \frac{1}{2\mu} \left(\frac{2\mu + \lambda_v \overline{T}^{(2)} - 2\overline{T}((1-\mu)\mathbf{g} + \overline{T}\pi\mathbf{B}_v)(\mathbf{A}_v + \mathbf{e}\pi)^{-1}\widetilde{\lambda}}{1-\mu} - \lambda_v \overline{T}^{(2)} \right) \tag{5}$$

In the above equations, $\overline{T}$ and $\overline{T}^{(2)}$ denote the first two moments of the message service time and can be computed by differentiating $T^*(s)$ and setting $s=0$ [14]. $\mathbf{e}$ is a unit column vector of length 2^L. The traffic intensity $\mu = \overline{T}\lambda_v$, where λ_v is the mean traffic rate and given by $\lambda_v = \pi\widetilde{\lambda}$. $\widetilde{\lambda}$ is a column vector containing the elements on the main diagonal of $\mathbf{B}_v$, and π is the steady-state vector of the MMPP.

When a message header is blocked at an intermediate node, it experiences connection failure and will make a new attempt to establish a path from the source node. Let

Pb_i denote the probability that the header suffers blocking after making i hops. The probability of a successful connection, Ps, and a connection failure, Pf, during a single connection attempt can be written as

$$Ps = \prod_{i=0}^{D-1}(1-Pb_i) \quad \text{and} \quad Pf = 1-Ps = 1-\prod_{i=0}^{D-1}(1-Pb_i) \qquad (6)$$

A message may need a number of, say, r $(r=1,2,...,\infty)$, connection attempts in order to successfully establish a path. The traffic due to the r-th attempt of the MMPP$^{(i)}$ $(1 \le i \le L)$ can be modelled by a new two-state MMPP$^{(ir)}$ which is the resulted process from the splitting, with the probability Pf^{r-1}, of the original MMPP$^{(i)}$. The infinitesimal generator $\mathbf{A}_{ir}$ and rate matrix $\mathbf{B}_{ir}$, of the MMPP$^{(ir)}$ is given by [17]

$$\mathbf{A}_{ir} = \mathbf{A}_i \quad \text{and} \quad \mathbf{B}_{ir} = Pf^{r-1}\mathbf{B}_i \qquad (7)$$

Superposing the traffic caused by all r, $(r=1,2,...,\infty)$, connection attempts of those generated by a source node yields the *effective* traffic entering the network. Therefore, the effective traffic can be modeled by the superposition of all MMPP$^{(ir)}$'s with $(1 \le i \le L)$ and $(r=1,2,...,\infty)$. As the superposition of MMPPs gives rise again to an MMPP [18], the effective traffic from a given source node can be characterised by a new multi-state MMPP. To calculate the parameter matrices of this new MMPP, we first use a two-state MMPP$^{(1e)}$ to match the superposition of all MMPP$^{(1r)}$s with $(r=1,2,...,\infty)$ because these MMPPs model traffic burstiness and correlations over the same time scale. Using the parameter matrices of the MMPP$^{(1r)}$s with $(r=1,2,...,\infty)$ as input parameters, the method presented in Ref. [6] for superposing infinite correlated traffic streams can be used to derive the infinitesimal generator $\mathbf{A}_{1e}$ and rate matrix $\mathbf{B}_{1e}$ of the MMPP$^{(1e)}$. Similarly, we separately match the superposition of the MMPP$^{(ir)}$s with $(r=1,2,...,\infty)$ to a two-state MMPP$^{(ie)}$ with the resulting parameter matrices $\mathbf{A}_{ie}$ and $\mathbf{B}_{ie}$. We then calculate the Kronecker sum of the parameter matrices of MMPP$^{(1e)}$, MMPP$^{(2e)}$, ..., MMPP$^{(Le)}$ to parameterise the multi-state MMPP that characterises the effective traffic entering the network from a given source node. So, the infinitesimal generator $\mathbf{A}_e$ and rate matrix $\mathbf{B}_e$ of the multi-state MMPP are given by

$$\mathbf{A}_e = \mathbf{A}_{1e} \oplus \mathbf{A}_{2e} \oplus \cdots \oplus \mathbf{A}_{Le} \quad \text{and} \quad \mathbf{B}_e = \mathbf{B}_{1e} \oplus \mathbf{B}_{2e} \oplus \cdots \oplus \mathbf{B}_{Le} \qquad (8)$$

A message may encounter blocking at any of the D intermediate nodes along its path. The probability, Pf_i, that a header experiences a connection failure at a node that is i hops away from the source can be expressed as

$$Pf_i = Pb_i \prod_{j=0}^{i-1}(1-Pb_j) \qquad (9)$$

Taking into account the cases of a connection success and connection failures occurring at D possible nodes gives the average number of channels, c, traversed by a message during a single connection attempt

$$c = D \cdot Ps + \sum_{i=0}^{D-1} i \cdot Pf_i = \prod_{i=0}^{D-1} D(1 - Pb_i) + \sum_{i=0}^{D-1}\left(iPb_i \prod_{j=0}^{i-1}(1 - Pb_j)\right) \tag{10}$$

Under the uniform traffic pattern, using adaptive routing results in a balanced traffic load on all network channels. Examining Eq. (10) reveals that the average number of channels, c, traversed by a message during a single connection attempt is always less than n in an n-dimensional hypercube. This implies that the arrival traffic at a given network channel is a fraction of the effective traffic entering into the network from a source node. This fraction, f, can be estimated by

$$f = \frac{Nc}{Nn} = \frac{c}{n} \tag{11}$$

Given that the MMPP is closed under the superposition and splitting operations, we use an MMPP$^{(c)}$ to model the characteristics of the traffic on a network channel. The infinitesimal generator $\mathbf{A}_c$ and rate matrix $\mathbf{B}_c$ of the MMPP$^{(c)}$ are given by [17]

$$\mathbf{A}_c = \mathbf{A}_e \quad \text{and} \quad \mathbf{B}_c = f\mathbf{B}_e \tag{12}$$

After determining the characteristics of traffic on network channels, the joint probability $P_{(i,j)}$ that i, $(0 \le i \le V)$, virtual channels are busy and the MMPP modelling the traffic on network channels is at state j, $(1 \le j \le 2^L)$, can be calculated using a bivariate Markov chain [12]. The detailed derivation of, $P_{(i,j)}$, and calculation of the average degree of virtual channel multiplexing, $\bar{V}$, can be found in Ref. [12]. In the hypercube, a message is blocked after making i hops if all possible virtual channels at the remaining $(D-i)$ dimensions are busy. The probability, Pb_i, can be written as

$$Pb_i = \left(\sum_{j=1}^{2^L} P_{V,j} \right)^{D-i} \quad (0 \le i \le D-1) \tag{13}$$

Let E_i denote the expected time for the header to reach the destination from the current node. If the header succeeds in reserving the required virtual channel and advances to the next node, the residual expected time becomes E_{i+1}. This case occurs with probability $(1 - Pb_i)$. On the other hand, if the header encounters blocking and backtracks to the source node, the residual expected time is E_0. Therefore, E_i satisfies the following difference equations [6]

$$E_i = (1 - Pb_i)(E_{i+1} + 1) + Pb_i (E_0 + i) \quad (0 \le i \le D-1) \quad \text{and} \quad E_D = 0 \tag{14}$$

Solving the above equations yields E_0 as

$$x_i = \begin{cases} 1 & (i = 0) \\ \dfrac{x_{i-1} - Pb_i}{1 - Pb_{i-1}} & (1 \le i \le D) \end{cases} \quad \text{and} \quad y_i = \begin{cases} 0 & (i = 0) \\ \dfrac{x_{i-1} - (i-2)Pb_{i-1} - 1}{1 - Pb_{i-1}} & (1 \le i \le D) \end{cases} \tag{15}$$

$$E_0 = -\frac{y_D}{x_D} \tag{16}$$

The mean time to set up a path is given by $\overline{E} = E_0 + D$. Due to the requirement of analytic simplicity and practicality, we approximately model the distribution of the path set-up time by an exponential distribution. So $E^*(s)$ can be expressed as [14]

$$E^*(s) = \frac{\alpha}{\alpha + s} \qquad (17)$$

where α is selected to match the mean path set-up time and is given by $\alpha = 1/\overline{E}$.

The mean message latency is composed of the mean network latency and the mean waiting time at the source node. However, to model the effect of virtual channel multiplexing, the message latency has to be scaled by the average degree of virtual channel multiplexing that takes place at a given physical channel. Thus, we can write [13]

$$Latency = (\overline{T} + Ws)\overline{V} \qquad (18)$$

3 Simulation Experiments

We have developed a discrete-event simulator, operating at the flit level, in order to validate the above analytical model. Each simulation experiment was run until the network converged to its steady state. The cycle time in the simulator is defined as the transmission time of a single flit to cross from one node to the next. Message destinations are uniformly distributed across the network. Figures 1~3 depict results for the mean message latency predicted by the above model plotted against those provided by the simulator in the 4, 6 and 8-dimensional hypercubes, respectively. Message length is M=32 and 64 flits. Number of virtual channels of per physical channel is V=3, 5 and 7. Hurst parameters are H =0.6, 0.7 and 0.8; Parameter for computing autocorrelation at lag 1 is ρ =0.7, 0.8 and 0.9. We have modelled burstiness over five time scales. The figures reveal that the simulation results closely match those predicted by the analytical model in the steady state region. Its tractability makes it a

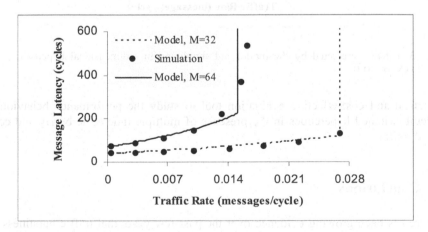

Fig. 1. Latency predicted by the model and simulation in 4-dimensional hypercubes, V=3, $H = 0.6$, $\rho = 0.7$.

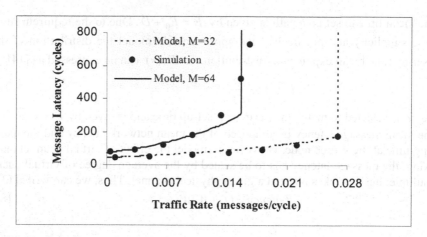

Fig. 2. Latency predicted by the model and simulation in 6-dimensional hypercubes, $V=5$, $H = 0.7, \rho = 0.8$.

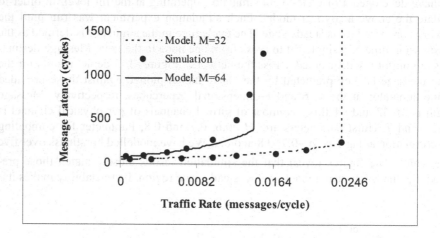

Fig. 3. Latency predicted by the model and simulation in 8-dimensional hypercubes, $V=7$, $H = 0.8, \rho = 0.9$.

practical and cost-effective evaluation tool to study the performance behaviour of circuit-switched hypercubes in the presence of multiple time-scale bursty and corre-lated traffic.

4   Conclusions

There has been growing evidence over the past few years that traffic burstiness and correlation over many time scales appear in a variety of systems including local-area and wide-area networks, digitised multimedia systems, web servers, and parallel computation systems. This fractal-like behaviour of traffic exhibits a totally different behaviour from the conventional Poisson process and has great impact on network performance. In an effort towards providing cost-effective tools for hypercube networks, this paper proposes a analytical model for circuit-switched hypercubes in the presence of multiple time-scale bursty and correlated traffic, which is modeled by the by the superposition of a number of different two-state MMPPs. The validity of the model is demonstrated by comparing analytical results to those obtained through simulation experiments of the actual system.

References

1. Duato, J., Yalamanchili, S., Ni, L.: Interconnection Networks: An Engineering Approach. IEEE Computer Society Press, Los Alamitos (1997).
2. Loucif S., Ould-Khaoua M., Mackenzie L.M.: Modelling Fully-Adaptive Routing in Hypercubes. Telecommun. Syst. 1 (2000) 111-118.
3. Tanenbaum, A.S.: Computer networks (3rd Edition). Prentice-Hall (1996).
4. Chlamtac, I., Ganz, A., Kienzle, M.G.: A Performance Model of a Connection-Oriented Hypercube Interconnection System. Perform. Eval. 2 (1996) 151-167.
5. Colajanni, M., Ciciani, B., Tucci, S.: Performance Analysis of Circuit-Switching Interconnection Networks with Deterministic and Adaptive Routing. Perform. Eval. 1 (1998) 1-26.
6. Min, G., Ould-Khaoua, M.: Message Latency in Hypercubic Computer Networks with Bursty Traffic Pattern. J. Comput. Electrical Engineering. 3 (2004) 207-222.
7. Sharma, V., Varvarigos, E.A.: Circuit Switching with Input Queuing: An Analysis for the D-Dimensional Wraparound Mesh and the Hypercube. IEEE Trans. Parallel Distrib. Syst. 4 (1997) 349-366.
8. Crovella, M.E., Bestavros, A.: Self-Similarity in World Wide Web Traffic: Evidence and Possible Causes. IEEE/ACM Trans. Networking. 6 (1997) 835-846.
9. Leland, W.E., Taqqu, M.S., Willinger, W., Wilson, D.V.: On the Self-Similar Nature of Ethernet Traffic (Ext. Version). IEEE/ACM Trans. Networking. 1 (1994) 1-15.
10. Sahuquillo, J., Nachiondo, T., Cano, J.C., Gil, J.A., Pont, A.: Self-Similarity in SPLASH-2 Workloads on Shared Memory Multiprocessors Systems. Proc. EURO-PDP'2000. IEEE Computer Society Press. (2000) 293-300.
11. Park, K., Willinger, W. (eds.): Self-Similar Network Traffic and Performance Evaluation. John Wiley & Sons, New York (2000).
12. Min, G., Ould-Khaoua, M.: A Performance Model for K-Ary N-Cube Networks with Self-Similar Traffic. Proc. 16th IEEE & ACM PDPS '2002. IEEE Computer Society Press, Florida (2002) CD-ROM.
13. Ould-Khaoua, M.: A Performance Model for Duato's Fully Adaptive Routing Algorithm in K-Ary N-Cubes. IEEE Trans. Comput. 12 (1999) 1-8.
14. Kleinrock, L.: Queueing Systems: Theory, Vol. 1. John Wiley & Sons (1975).
15. Andersen, A.T., Nielsen, B.F.: A Markovian Approach for Modeling Packet Traffic with Long-Range Dependence. IEEE J. Selected Areas Commun. 5 (1998) 719-732.
16. Manjunath, D., Sikdar, B.: Input Queued Switches for Variable Length Packets: Analysis for Poisson and Self-Similar Traffic. Comput. Commun. 6 (2002) 590-610.
17. Neuts, M.F., Li, J.: The Bernoulli Splitting of a Markovian Arrival Process. http://www.maths.adelaide.edu.au/jli/papers/split.pdf. (2002).
18. Fischer, W., Meier-Hellstern, K.: The Markov-modulated Poisson process (MMPP) Cookbook. Perform. Eval. 2 (1993) 149-171.

Leader Election in Hyper-Butterfly Graphs

Wei Shi and Pradip K. Srimani

Department of Computer Science
Clemson University
Clemson, SC 29634 USA

Abstract. Leader election in a network is one of the most important problems in the area of distributed algorithm design. Consider any network of N nodes; a *leader* node is defined to be any node of the network unambiguously identified by some characteristics (unique from all other nodes). A leader election process is defined to be a uniform algorithm (code) executed at each node of the network; at the end of the algorithm execution, exactly one node is elected the *leader* and all other nodes are in the non-leader state [GHS83, LMW86, Tel93, Tel95a, SBTS01] In this paper, our purpose is to propose an election algorithm for the oriented hyper butterfly networks with $\mathcal{O}(N\log N)$ messages.

1 Hyper Butterfly Graphs

1.1 Hypercube

A hypercube H_n, of order n, is defined to be regular symmetric graph $G = (V, E)$ where V is the set of 2^n vertices, each representing a distinct n-bit binary number and E is the set of symmetric edges such that two nodes are connected by an edge iff the Hamming distance between the two nodes is 1 i.e., the number of positions where the bits differ in the binary labels of the two nodes is 1. For example, in H_3, the node 010 is connected to three nodes 110, 000 and 011. It is known that the number of edges in H_n is $n \times 2^{n-1}$ and the diameter of H_n is given by $\mathcal{D}(H_n) = n$.

1.2 Butterfly Graph

A wrapped butterfly network, denoted by B_n, is defined [Lei92] as follows: a vertex is represented as $(z_{n-1} \cdots z_0, \ell)$, where $z_{n-1} \cdots z_0$ is a n-bit binary number and ℓ is an integer, $0 \leq \ell \leq n - 1$.

The edges of B_n are defined by a set of four generators. Consider an arbitrary node $(z_{n-1} \cdots z_0, \ell)$ in B_n. We define $\alpha(\ell) = \ell + 1 \pmod n$ and $\beta(\ell) = \ell - 1 \pmod n$. The four edges node $(z_{n-1} \cdots z_0, \ell)$ has can be derived by the following four generators:

$$g(z_{n-1} \cdots z_0, \ell) = z_{n-1} \cdots z_0, \alpha(\ell)$$
$$g^{-1}(z_{n-1} \cdots z_0, \ell) = z_{n-1} \cdots z_0, \beta(\ell)$$
$$f(z_{n-1} \cdots z_0, \ell) = z_{n-1} \cdots z_{\ell+1}\bar{z}_\ell z_{\ell-1} \cdots z_0, \alpha(\ell)$$
$$f^{-1}(z_{n-1} \cdots z_0, \ell) = z_{n-1} \cdots z_{\beta(\ell)+1}\bar{z}_{\beta(\ell)} z_{\beta(\ell)-1} \cdots z_0, \beta(\ell)$$

Remark 1. We refer to the frist part in the butterfly label, i.e. $z_{m-1} \cdots z_0$ as **complementation index**; and the second part, i.e. ℓ, as **permutation index**.

H. Jin et al. (Eds.): NPC 2004, LNCS 3222, pp. 292–299, 2004.
© IFIP International Federation for Information Processing 2004

1.3 Hyper-Butterfly Graph $HB_{(m,n)}$

Consider two undirected graphs $G = (V_G, E_G)$ and $H = (V_H, E_H)$; the product graph $G \times H$ has node set $V_G \times V_H$. Let u and v be any two nodes in G, and let x and y be any two nodes in H; then, $(\langle u, x \rangle, \langle v, y \rangle)$ is an edge of $G \times H$ iff either (1) (u, v) is an edge of G and $x = y$, or (2) (x, y) is an edge of H and $u = v$.

Definition 1. *A **Hyper-Butterfly** graph $HB_{(m,n)}$, of order (dimension) $(m + n)$ is defined as the product graph of a hypercube H_m of dimension m and a butterfly B_n of dimension n.*

In $HB_{(m,n)}$, each node is assigned a label $(x_{m-1} \cdots x_0, z_{n-1} \cdots z_0, \ell)$ where each x_i and z_j are binary bit, $0 \leq i \leq m-1$ and $0 \leq j < n-1$. ℓ is an integer, $0 \leq \ell \leq n-1$. $x_{m-1} \cdots x_0$ is the *hypercube-part-label* and $(z_{n-1} \cdots z_0, \ell)$ is *butterfly-part-label*. The edges of the $HB_{(m,n)}$ graph are defined by the following $m + 4$ generators:

$$h_i(x_{m-1} \cdots x_0, z_{n-1} \cdots z_0, \ell) =$$
$$(x_{m-1} \cdots x_{i+1} \bar{x}_i x_{i-1} \cdots x_0, z_{n-1} \cdots z_0, \ell) \quad \forall i, \ 0 \leq i \leq m-1$$
$$g(x_{m-1} \cdots x_0, z_{n-1} \cdots z_0, \ell) = (x_{m-1} \cdots x_0, z_{n-1} \cdots z_0, \alpha(\ell)) \quad \alpha(\ell) =$$
$$\ell + 1 (\bmod n)$$
$$g^{-1}(x_{m-1} \cdots x_0, z_{n-1} \cdots z_0, \ell) = (x_{m-1} \cdots x_0, z_{n-1} \cdots z_0, \beta(\ell)) \quad \beta(\ell) =$$
$$\ell - 1 (\bmod n)$$
$$f(x_{m-1} \cdots x_0, z_{n-1} \cdots z_0, \ell) =$$
$$(x_{m-1} \cdots x_0, z_{n-1} \cdots z_{\alpha(\ell)+1} \bar{z}_{\alpha(\ell)} z_{\alpha(\ell)-1} \cdots z_0, \alpha(\ell))$$
$$f^{-1}(x_{m-1} \cdots x_0, z_{n-1} \cdots z_0, \ell) = (x_{m-1} \cdots x_0, z_{n-1} \cdots z_{\ell+1} \bar{z}_\ell z_{\ell-1} \cdots z_0, \beta(\ell))$$

Remark 2.

- The set of $m+4$ generators of the graph $HB_{(m,n)}$, $\Omega = \{h_i, 0 \leq i < m, f, g, f^{-1}, g^{-1}\}$ is closed under inverse; in particular h_i for all i is its own inverse, g is inverse of g^{-1} and f is inverse of f^{-1}; thus the edges in $HB_{(m,n)}$ are bidirectional.
- For an arbitrary n, $n > 2$, for any arbitrary node v of the graph $HB_{(m,n)}$, $\delta(v) \neq v$ where $\delta \in \Omega = \{h_i, 0 \leq i < m, f, g, f^{-1}, g^{-1}\}$; also, for any two $\delta_1, \delta_2 \in \Omega$, $\delta_1(v) \neq \delta_2(v)$.
- Hyper butterfly graph $HB_{(m,n)}$ is a Cayley graph of degree $m + 4$.
- For any m and n, $n \geq 3$, the graph $HB_{(m,n)}$ (1) is a symmetric (undirected) regular graph of degree $m+4$; (2) has $n \times 2^{m+n}$ vertices; and (3) has $(m+4) \times n \times 2^{m+n-1}$ edges.

Definition 2.

- *The m edges generated by the generators h_i are called **hypercube edges** and the 4 edges generated by either of the generators g, f, g^{-1}, f^{-1} are called **butterfly edges**.*
- *Any arbitrary node $v = (h, b) \in HB_{(m,n)}$ has m **hypercube neighbors** $\{(h^{(i)}, b), 1 \leq i \leq m\}$ (reached from v by the m hypercube edges) and has 4 **butterfly neighbors** $\{(h, b^{(j)}), 1 \leq j \leq 4\}$ (reached from v by the 4 butterfly edges).*

Remark 3. Along any hypercube edge, only the hypercube-part-label of a node changes, and along any butterfly edges, only the butterfly-part-label changes.

Remark 4. The labeling of a hyper-butterfly graph is not unique. There exist many possible different label assignments with the same graph using traditional labeling scheme. We arbitrarily choose one such traditional labeling and refer to it as canonical labeling and will refer to the nodes using its canonical label.

Definition 3.

- We use $H_m^{(*,z,\ell)}$ to denote an m-dimensional hypercube subgraph of $HB_{(m,n)}$ where each node has the same butterfly-part-label (z, ℓ).
- We use $B_n^{(h,*,*)}$ to denote an n-dimensional butterfly subgraph of $HB_{(m,n)}$ where each node has the same hypercube-part-label h.
- We use $R_n^{(h,z,*)}$ to denote a ring of n nodes where each node has the same hypercube-part-label h and same complementation index $z = z_0 \cdots z_n$.
- We use $HR_{m,n}^{(*,z,*)}$ to denote the set of nodes that have the same complementation index z. This set of node is actually the product of a $H_m^{(*,z,\ell)}$ and $R_n^{(h,z,*)}$, with the same z value.

2   Leader Election Algorithm in Hyper-Butterfly Graph

Consider a hyper-butterfly graph $HB_{(m,n)}$; a *leader* node is defined to be any node of the graph unambiguously identified by some characteristics (unique from all other nodes). A leader election process is defined to be an uniform algorithm executed at each node of the network; at the end of the algorithm execution, exactly one node is elected the *leader* and all other nodes are in the non-leader state.

Remark 5. If each node knows its canonical label, this election process is trivial. Consider the node having the smallest label, i.e. $(0 \cdots 0, 0 \cdots 0, 0)$ in $HB_{(m,n)}$; we can say that the node with this label will automatically become the leader and all other nodes are non-leaders.

In this paper, as in [Tel95b], we assume that the nodes in the graph do not know their canonical labels. We will still refer to the nodes by some canonical labels for convenience, but these labels or names have no topological significance [Tel95b]. We also assume in this paper that the network is oriented in the sense that each node can differentiate the links incident to it by different generators. (in contrast, a node in an un-oriented star graph distinguishes its adjacent links by different but uninterpreted names). We define the *direction* of a link as the index of the generator that generates the link. So, the link that is associated with generator h_i has direction i, $0 \le i \le n-1$. And the link that is associated with generator g, g^{-1}, f, f^{-1} has direction g, g^{-1}, f, f^{-1} respectively.

The whole elction algorithm in hyper-butterfly graph consists of three major steps. At different step, the graph is divided into different regions, and the leader for each region is elected. At first step, the hyper-butterfly graph $H_{(m,n)}$ is divided into $n \times 2^n$ hypercubes. Within each hypercube, the nodes run a formerly proposed election algorithm for hypercubes. After this step, each hypercube will have a leader node. In the second step, the nodes with the same complementation index are considered in one region. For a certain complementation index z, the region is actually a ring of hypercube, i.e. $HR_{(m,n)}^{(*,z,*)}$. The hypercube leaders elected in the first step will compete with each other and elect one leader in $HR_{(m,n)}^{(*,z,*)}$ for each different z value. The third step is the final step, where the leaders elected in the second step compete with each other and elect one final leader for $HB_{(m,n)}$. In the following sections, we discuss the detail of election algorithm at each step.

Remark 6. It should be noted that in an oriented hyper-butterfly graph, each node can identify the region with the knowledge of direction of edges, i.e. one node can send a message to some other node in the same region by using a sequence of certain directions. the node does not have to know its canonical label in order to identify the region.

2.1 Election Algorithm in $H_m^{(*,z,\ell)}$

In $HB_{(m,n)}$, there are $n \times 2^n$ different butterfly labels, which we denote as (z,ℓ), $0 \le z < 2^n$, $0 \le \ell < n$; and the nodes with the same butterfly part label form a hypercube of dimension m, which we denote as $H_m^{(*,z,\ell)}$.

In this step, each nodes first runs a leader elction algorithm for hypercube []. The algorithm uses only *hypercube edges*, i.e. edges with direction 0 to $n-1$. At the end of this procedure, there will be one leader elected in $H_m^{(*,z,\ell)}$ for each different (z,ℓ) value pair. The details of the algorithm is listed as follows:

After the leader is set at $H_m^{(*,z,\ell)}$. The leader will broadcast its id to all nodes in $H_m^{(*,z,\ell)}$. Each node receives this broadcast message will save the leader's id into a variable HL (abbreviation for hypercube leader).

Lemma 1. *This step requires less than* $7.24 \times n \times 2^{m+n}$ *messages [Tel95b].*

2.2 Election in $HR_{(m,n)}^{(*,z,*)}$

After the first step, there will be a leader in each hypercube $H_m^{(*,z,\ell)}$, $(0 \le z < 2^n, \ 0 \le \ell < n)$. We use $(h(z,\ell), z, \ell)$ to denote the label of the leader in $H_m^{(*,z,\ell)}$, where $h(z,\ell)$ specifies the hypercube part label of the leader.

Remark 7. $h(z,\ell)$ does not denote a particular function to derive the hypercube part label from z and ℓ. $h(z,\ell)$ only indicates that the hypercube part label of the leader varies for different hypercubes. Since the leader in $H_m^{(*,z,\ell)}$ is determinate for any (z,ℓ) value pair, the hypercube part label of leader is also determinative and solely depends on the value of z and ℓ.

In the first step, the leader of each hypercube also broadcasts its id within the hypercube when it becomes the leader. After the broadcast procedure, every node in $H_m^{(*,z,\ell)}$ will be informed with the id of leader, i.e. $(h(z,\ell), z, \ell)$, and has variable HL set to it.

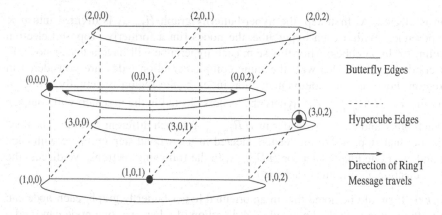

Fig. 1. Example of Leader Election in $HR_{(2,3)}^{(*,0,*)}$ (A subgraph of $HB_{(2,3)}$)

The objective in the second step is to elect leaders in larger regions. In this step, the nodes in hyper-butterfly graph $HB_{(m,n)}$ is considered to be grouped into 2^n new regions: $HR_{(m,n)}^{(*,z,*)}$, $0 \leq z < 2^n$, each consists of n hypercubes with the same complementation index, $H_m^{(*,z,\ell)}$, $0 \leq \ell < n$. Each hypercube has one leader elected from the first step, and there are totally $n \times 2^n$ such hypercube leader, with n in each new region $HR_{(m,n)}^{(*,z,*)}$. In the second step, each hypercube leader $(h(z,\ell), z, \ell)$ invokes procedure $HRElect$ to compete with other $n - 1$ hypercube leaders in the same region $HR_{(m,n)}^{(*,z,*)}$. Only one of them becomes the new leader. After every hypercube leader finishes procedure $HRElect$, there will be only 2^n leaders left, with one in each $HR_{(m,n)}^{(*,z,*)}$, $0 \leq z < 2^n$. The *** code of procedure $HRElect$ is listed below.

Procedure $HRElect(h(z,\ell), z, \ell)$
Initial Conditions:

    1. Node $(h(z,\ell), z, \ell)$ is the leader of $H_m^{(*,z,\ell)}$.
    2. All nodes in $HB_{(m,n)}$ have viarable HL set to the label of the hypercube leader.

Invocation of the Procedure:

    Node $(h(z,\ell), z, \ell)$ sends message $RingTest((h(z,\ell), z, \ell), 0, True)$ along direction g.

Upon receiving message $RingTest(id, i, b)$ from direction g^{-1}:

    //id is the label of the node which invokes procedure $HRElect$.
    //i is an integer from 0 to $n - 1$ and b is a boolean
    //with the value of either $True$ or $False$.
    if $(i < n - 1)$
        {
            if $(b == False || HL > id)$
                send message $RingTest(id, i + 1, False)$ through direction g.

```
        else
                send message RingTest(id, i + 1, True) through direction g.
        }
    else
        {
        // This means the message gets back to the leader node (h(z, ℓ), z, ℓ)
        if (b == True)
                // This node passed all tests in the ring, becomes the new leader.
                Current node (h(z, ℓ), z, ℓ) becomes the leader of HR_{(m,n)}^{(*,z,*)}.
        else
                // Failed the test, becomes non-leader.
                Current node becomes non-leader in HR_{(m,n)}^{(*,z,*)}.
        }
```

As we can see, the procedure can be invoked from any hypercube leader $(h(z, \ell), z, \ell)$. It consists of sending message $RingTest(id, i, b)$ carrying three parameters. The first parameter is the id of the hypercube leader that invokes the procedure. The second parameter i is an integer that counts the number of nodes message $RingTest(id, i, b)$ has passed except the origin node. b is a boolean to indicate if id is large enough to be the leader of the part of $HR_{(m,n)}^{(*,z,*)}$ that the message has passed so far.

Since every node increments i and relays the message through direction g, message $RingTest(id, i, b)$ will go through a ring of n nodes and get back to the origin node $(h(z, \ell), z, \ell)$ after that. At each intermediate node, the variable HL is compared to id that comes from the message. If HL is larger than id, then b is set to $False$ to indicate that the node invoke the procedure is not large enough to be the leader of $HR_{(m,n)}^{(*,z,*)}$. When message $RingTest(id, i, b)$ gets back to the origin node that invokes the procedure, the node checks the value of b and becomes the leader of $HR_{(m,n)}^{(*,z,*)}$ or a non-leader accordingly.

Lemma 2. *For any arbitrary value of z, $0 \le z < 2^n$, after all n hypercube leaders in $HR_{(m,n)}^{(*,z,*)}$ execute procedure $HBElect$ and get back the message $RingTest$, only one of them will become the leader of $HR_{(m,n)}^{(*,z,*)}$ and all others will become non-leader.*

Proof. For any arbitrary value z, there are n hypercube leaders in $HR_{(m,n)}^{(*,z,*)}$. They are $(h(z, \ell), z, \ell)$, $0 \le \ell < n$. Each of them invokes procedure $HRElect$ and will determine to becomes a leader or non-leader depending on the value of b returned from message $RingTest$.

Consider an arbitrary leader $(h(z, \ell), z, \ell)$ among them. This node starts procedure $HRElect$ by sending message $RingTest ((h(z, \ell), z, \ell), 0, True)$ through direction g. Because every node gets the message also relays it through direction g, the message will traversal every node in $R_n^{(h(z, \ell), z, *)}$ which include n nodes: $(h(z, \ell), z, j)$, $0 \le j < n$. And because node $(h(z, \ell), z, j)$ has variable HL set to the id of leader of hypercube

$H_m^{(*,z,j)}$, i.e. $(h(z,j),z,j)$. The id $(h(z,\ell),z,\ell)$ is compared with the id of leaders of other hypercubes $H_m^{(*,z,j)}$, i.e. $(h(z,j),z,j)$, $0 \le j < n$. If some node becomes the leader after executing procedure $HRElect$, it is assured that its id is larger than all other leaders in $H_m^{(*,z,j)}$, $0 \le j < n$. Therefore, from n hypercube leaders $(h(z,\ell),z,\ell)$, $0 \le \ell < n$, only one of them can claim as the leader of $HR_{(m,n)}^{(*,z,*)}$ after executing procedure $HRElect$; all other $n-1$ nodes will become non-leaders.

Remark 8.

- After every hypercube leaders (elected from first step) complete procedure $HRElect$, there will be 2^n nodes remain as leader, with each from $HR_{(m,n)}^{(*,z,*)}$, $0 \le z < 2^n$.
- After a node becomes the leader in $HR_{(m,n)}^{(*,z,*)}$, it broadcast its id to all nodes in $HR_{(m,n)}^{(*,z,*)}$. And the node receives the broadcast message will save the leader's id into variable HRL.

Lemma 3. *There will be* $n \times 2^{m+n} + n^2 \times 2^n$ *number of messages generated in the second step, including procedure* $HRElect$ *and the broadcast process afterwards.*

Proof. There are $n \times 2^n$ hypercube leaders elected from the first step. Each leader executing procedure $HRElect$ generates n messages. And there will be 2^n leaders elected afterwards. Each leader in $HR_{(m,n)}^{(*,z,*)}$, $0 \le z < 2^n$ will broadcast it id, which takes $n \times 2^m$ message. So the total number of message needed in this step is $n \times 2^{m+n} + n^2 \times 2^n$.

2.3   Leader Election in $HB_{(m,n)}$

After the second step, there will be one leader left in each $HR_{(m,n)}^{(*,z,*)}$, $0 \le z < 2^n$. We use $(h(z),z,\ell(z))$ to denote the label of the leader in $HR_{(m,n)}^{(*,z,*)}$.

Remark 9. Similar to the second step, $h(z)$ or $\ell(z)$ does not specify the function to derive the hypercube part label or permutation index of the leader node. They only indicates the dependency relationship with between those labels with z.

In the third step, which is the final step, the objective is to elect one leader for entire hyper-butterfly graph $HB_{(m,n)}$. Since we already have 2^n leaders in each $HR_{(m,n)}^{(*,z,*)}$, we use similar approach as in the second step to elect one node from the those leaders to become the final leader.

In this step, each of the 2^n leaders from the second step sends $TreeTest$ message through a tree structure in butterfly graph. We ensure that the message will get to the nodes with different complementation index, so that the id of each leader will be tested to see if it is larger than the ids of all other leaders. As in procedure $HRElect$, only the node that passes all tests will become the leader which is the leader of entire hyper-butterfly graph $HB_{(m,n)}$. The pseudocode listing of the details of the procedure $HBElect$ to be invoked by every leader of $HR_{(m,n)}^{(*,z,*)}$ is omitted for lack of space.

There are two types of messages used in the procedure. The first type of message is $TreeTest$ which travels down a binary tree because each node distributes the message through direction g and f. The parameter id and b have the same meaning as in the second step, while i indicates the current level of the tree. The other type of message is $TreeReply$ which go through the reversal path of $TreeTest$. Only the leaf nodes will compare the value of HRL with id that comes from the message. The intermediate nodes only act as transmit message $TreeTest$ to both children and collect $TreeReply$ from them. We state the following lemmas (the proofs are omitted for lack of space).

Lemma 4. *Consider the execution of procedure $HBElect$ from any node $(h(z), z, \ell(z))$, there are 2^i nodes that receive both message $TreeTest(id, i, b)$ and $TreeReply(id, i, b)$. These 2^i nodes have the same permutation index and hypercube label, but different complementation index.*

Lemma 5. *After every leader from the second step completely execute procedure $HBElect$, only one node will become leader of $HB_{(m,n)}$. All other leaders will become non-leader.*

Lemma 6. *There are 2^{2n+2} number of messages generated in the third step.*

Theorem 1. *The total number of message needed for a leader election algorithm in $HB_{(m,n)}$ is $8.24 \times n \times 2^{m+n} + (n^2 + 2^{n+2}) \times 2^n$.*

3   Acknowledgement

The work of Pradip Srimani was partially supported by a National Science Foundation award # ANI-0218495.

References

[GHS83]   R. G. Gallagar, P. A. Humblet, and P. M. Spira. A distributed algorithm for minimum weight spanning trees. *ACM Transactions on Programming Languages and Systems*, 5:67–77, 1983.

[Lei92]   F. T. Leighton. *Introductions to Parallel Algorithms and Architectures: Arrays, Trees and Hypercubes*. Morgan Kaufman, 1992.

[LMW86]   M. C. Loui, T. A. Matsuhita, and D. B. West. Election in a complete network with a sense of direction. *Information Processing Letters*, 22:185–187, 1986.

[SBTS01]   W. Shi, A. Bouabdallah, D. Talia, and P. K. Srimani. Leader election in wrapped butterfly networks. In *Proceedings of Parallel Computing 2001*, pages 382–389, Naples, Italy, September 2001.

[Tel93]   G. Tel. Linear election in oriented hypercubes. Technical Report RUU-CS-93-39, Computer Science, Utrecht University, 1993.

[Tel95a]   G. Tel. Linear election in hypercubes. *Parallel Processing Letters*, 5:357–366, 1995.

[Tel95b]   G. Tel. Linear election in hypercubes. *Information Processing Letters*, 5:357–366, 1995.

A New Approach to Local Route Recovery for Multihop TCP in Ad Hoc Wireless Networks

Zhi Li and Yu-Kwong Kwok*

Department of Electrical and Electronic Engineering
The University of Hong Kong, Pokfulam Road, Hong Kong**
ykwok@hku.hk

Abstract. The TCP (Transmission Control Protocol) is a critical component in an ad hoc wireless network because of its pervasive usage in various important applications. However, TCP's congestion control mechanism is notoriously ineffective in dealing with time-varying channel errors even for a single wireless link. Indeed, the adverse effects of the inefficient usage of wireless bandwidth due to the large TCP timers are more profound in a multihop communication session. In this paper, we design and evaluate local recovery (LR) approaches for maintaining smooth operations of a multihop TCP session in an ad hoc network. Based on our NS-2 simulation results, we find that using the proposed LR approaches is better than using various well-known ad hoc routing algorithms which construct completely new routes.

Keywords: wireless TCP, multihop communications, ad hoc networks, routing, local recovery.

1   Introduction

The TCP (Transmission Control Protocol) is the most widely used transport protocol and, more importantly, will continue to be a critical component when the Internet becomes completely pervasive in a wireless manner [6]. Unfortunately, due to the fact that TCP was not designed for a wireless environment, in which link transmission errors are the norm rather than the exception, its performance can be unacceptable under a time-varying communication channel [5]. Specifically, congestion is assumed to be the primary reason for packet losses in TCP. While this is true in wired networks, the throttling actions in a wireless environment can be detrimental. Indeed, unnecessary reduction in network load over a long period of time (TCP's timers are on the order of tens of seconds) leads to very inefficient use of the precious channel bandwidth and high delays.

Recently, many adaptive TCP approaches for various wireless environments have been suggested. The major objective of these schemes is to make TCP respond more intelligently to the lossy wireless links. According to [1,5], there

---

* This research was supported by a grant from the Research Grants Council of the HKSAR Government under project number HKU 7162/03E.
** Corresponding Author: Yu-Kwong Kwok

H. Jin et al. (Eds.): NPC 2004, LNCS 3222, pp. 300–307, 2004.

are three major classes of wireless TCP approaches: end-to-end, link layer, and split-connection approaches. Unfortunately, all these previous approaches are only suitable for use in a single wireless link. For ad hoc networks where devices communicate in a multihop manner, these protocols are inapplicable because we cannot afford to have each pair of intermediate devices on a multihop route to execute these wireless TCP protocols [3,9]. Indeed, if a multihop ad hoc route is broken (e.g., due to deep fading in one of its links), the performance of a TCP session over such a route can be severely affected. The most obvious result is that the TCP sender will eventually discover such breakage after several unsuccessful retransmissions (i.e., after a long delay due to the large TCP timers) and then initiate a new session after setting up a new route. This can lead to unacceptably long delay at the receiver side.

In this paper, we study the performance of two local recovery approaches, which work by swiftly repairing the broken link using a new partial route. In Section 2, we describe our proposed local recovery approaches. Section 3 contains our simulation results generated by the NS-2 [10] platform.

2   The Proposed Approach

When the original route is down, we do not simply inform the source that the route cannot be used. Instead, we suppress the notification which is transmitted to the source by TCP, and then find a new partial route between the separated nodes to replace the broken part of the old route. Our approach, remedial in nature, is a *local recovery* (LR) technique [4]. The essence of LR is to shield the route error from the source in the hope that we can avoid incurring the excessive delay induced by TCP. Indeed, since the problem is found locally, the remedial work should be done locally.

For example, suppose that due to channel fading and nodes' mobility, the link between node N and $N + 1$ is broken. Firstly, we suppress the upstream notification generated by TCP. Afterward, we find if the route table of node N has another route to node $N + 1$. If there is a new route to the $N + 1$ (i.e., the next node of such a route is not $N + 1$), then the broken route is immediately repaired by using this route. If no such route exists, local recovery packets will be sent to repair the route.

A local recovery timer is set to make sure the local recovery process will not consume more time than to re-establish a new route by the source. Thus, if the local recovery timer is expired, we give up local recovery and make use of the full blown ad hoc routing protocol.

In the remedial process, a node N generates the local recovery route request (LRRREQ) packet, which includes the following information: type of the packet, local recovery source address, local recovery destination address, original destination address, local recovery broadcast identifier (ID), and hop count. Whenever node N generates a LRRREQ, the local recovery broadcast ID is increased by one. Thus, the local recovery source and destination addresses, and the local recovery broadcast ID uniquely identify a LRRREQ. Node N broadcasts the

LRRREQ to all nodes within the transmission range. These neighboring nodes then relay the LRRREQ to other neighboring nodes in the same fashion. An intermediate node, upon receiving the LRRREQ, first checks whether it has seen this packet before by searching its LRRREQ cache. If the LRRREQ is in the cache, the newly received copy is discarded; otherwise, the LRRREQ is stored in the cache and is forwarded to the neighbors after the following major modifications are done: incrementing the hop count, updating the previous hop node, and updating the time-to-live (TTL) field.

When node $N + 1$ or some other intermediate node, which has a fresh route to the node $N+1$, receives the LRRREQ, it then generates a local recovery route reply (LRRREP) packet, which includes the following information: type of the packet, local recovery source address, local recovery destination address, original destination address, hop count, and TTL. The LRRREQ is then unicast to the local recovery source along the reverse path until it reaches the local recovery source. During this process, each intermediate node on the reverse path updates its routing table entry to the local recovery destination and original destination.

Although the new partial route is found from node N to node $N+1$, updating is needed for the original route. As described above, there are two cases where updating of the original route must be done. The first case is the event that the local recovery destination receives the LRRREQ. The second case is the event that an intermediate node gets the LRRREQ and it has a fresh route to the local recovery destination in its routing table.

According to the different directions, forward and backward updatings are carried out. The forward updating process is triggered by receiving the update packet, which contains the following information: type of packet, update destination address, original destination address, hop count, and TTL. The backward updating process is triggered by receiving the LRRREP packet. In any updating, the original route should be re-established. In the first case, only backward updating is done, while in the second case, both forward and backward updatings are needed.

In the former case, node $N + 1$ receives the LRRREQ, and thus, backward updating is done through the route of nodes $N + 1$, 3, 2, 1, N. In the latter case, forward updating is done through the route of nodes 2, 3, $N + 1$, while backward updating is done through the route of nodes 2, 1, N. The detailed updating process is as follows: when node 2 receives the LRRREQ and it has a route entry to node $N+1$, node 2 sends the update packet to node 3 according to the route entry to node $N + 1$. Upon receiving the update packet, node 3 should update the route entry to the original destination node D and then check if it is the local recovery destination. The same forward updating process continues until the update packet is received by the local recovery destination. On the other hand, LRRREP is sent to node 1 following the reverse route. Upon receiving the LRRREP, node 1 should update the route entry to the original destination node D and then check if it is the local recovery source. The same backward updating process continues until the LRRREP is received by the local recovery source.

This variant of our approach is similar to the mechanism we described above. The only difference is that the goal of route reconstruction is to find a new partial route from node N directly to the destination.

3   Performance Results

In our study, we use packet level simulations to evaluate the performance of TCP in ad hoc networks. The simulations are implemented in Network Simulator (NS-2) [10] from Lawrence Berkeley National Laboratory (LBNL) with extensions for wireless links from the Monarch project at Carnegie Mellon University [2]. The simulation parameters are as follows:

- number of nodes: 50;
- testing field: $1500m \times 300m$;
- mobile speed: uniformly distributed between 0 and MAXSPEED (we choose MAXSPEED to be 4, 10, 20, 40, 60m/s, respectively);
- mobility model: *modified* random way point model [12];
- traffic load: TCP Reno traffic source;
- radio transmission range: 250m;
- MAC layer: IEEE 802.11b.

Each simulation is run for 200 seconds and repeated for ten times. We compared four protocols in our simulations. They are DSR (Dynamic Source Routing) [7], AODV (Ad Hoc On-Demand Distance Vector) [11], LR1 and LR2. LR1 is the local recovery protocol in finding the new route between node N to the destination. LR2 is the local recovery protocol in finding the new route between node N and node $N + 1$.

To evaluate TCP performance in different routing protocols, we compare them using four metrics:

1. Average End-to-End Delay: the average elapsed time between sending by the source and receiving by the destination, including the processing time and queuing time.
2. Average Throughput: the average effective bit-rate of the received TCP packets at the destination.
3. Delivery Rate: the percentage of packets reaching the destination (note that some packets are lost during the route breakage and the route reconstruction time).
4. Control Overhead: the data rate required by the transportation of the routing packets.

Our first set of simulation results are summarized in Figure 1. We compare the performance of the LR approaches against that of several well-known ad hoc routing protocols: AODV (Ad-Hoc On-Demand Distance Vector) [11], DSR (Dynamic Source Routing) [7], DSDV (Destination Sequenced Distance Vector) [11], and RICA (Receiver-Initiated Channel Adaptive) protocols [8].

Firstly, we find that TCP is idle most of the time when used with the DSDV and DSR routing protocols. On the other hand, other routing protocols can cooperate with TCP quite well. It should be noted that DSDV is table-driven routing algorithm. When the source has no route to the destination, it uses a long time to find a new route. This frequently leads to TCP timeout. Furthermore, the nodes are moving during almost the whole simulation time. Consequently, routes in the table can be stale very quickly and cannot be used. As for DSR, it is an on-demand algorithm, even though it has a route cache containing routes. When using DSR, a mobile device first checks if it has a route to the destination in the cache. Again, similar to the case of DSDV, the routes in the cache become stale very quickly and thus, new routes have to be found. However, as DSR is an on-demand algorithm, it can generally respond much faster than DSDV to find new routes.

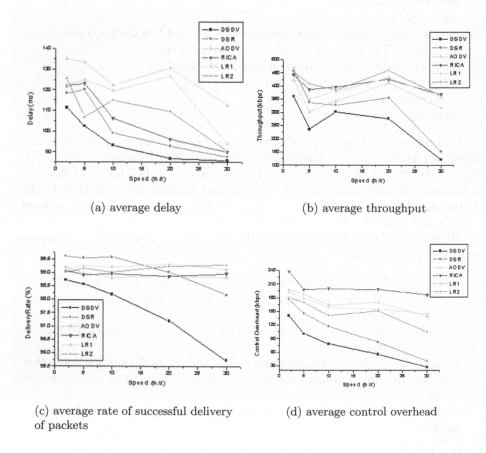

(a) average delay

(b) average throughput

(c) average rate of successful delivery of packets

(d) average control overhead

Fig. 1. Protocol performance.

Figure 1(a) shows the average end-to-end delay of each protocol. It should be noted that the delay is effective delay—the delay of the packets that actually arrive at the destinations. We can see that DSDV has the lowest delay in all protocols. The reason is that each device has a table to contain routes. DSR has higher delay than DSDV because DSR caches only recently used routes. Comparing the other four routing protocols, where TCP almost does not become idle, RICA has the lowest delay and AODV has the highest delay. As RICA always chooses the best route, and the LR approaches can automatically recover the broken route locally, they generate smaller delays compared with AODV.

Figure 1(b) depicts the TCP throughput over the simulation time. Obviously, since DSDV and DSR have much idle time, they have lower throughputs. The LR approaches have higher throughputs than AODV due to the local repairing mechanisms. In particular, LR2 exhibits a better performance than LR1 because the time consumed by node N to find node $N + 1$ is less than that to find the destination on the average. Figure 1(c) shows the delivery rate. DSDV's delivery rate decreases dramatically with increasing device speed. This is because when the speed increases, stale routes are more common. This detrimental effect of mobility also applies to DSR. In the other four routing protocols, the delivery rate has little change with increasing speed. Figure 1(d) shows the control overhead required by the transportation of the routing packets. Again, because of idleness, DSDV and DSR have lower control overheads. RICA has the highest control overhead. The reason is that RICA must transmit CSI (channel state information) [8] packet to assist finding the best path. The LR approaches have less control overheads than AODV because when the route is broken the LR approaches need not inform the source to find a new route. In summary, the LR approaches are the best routing protocols for integrating with TCP in an ad hoc network.

Another set of results is about the evaluation of the TCP performance against different number of nodes (30, 50, 100, and 200 nodes). The mean mobile speed is fixed at 5 m/s and the maximum speed is fixed at 10 m/s. As can be seen in Figure 2, using the Local Recovery algorithms can greatly shorten the end-to-end delay from source to destination and lead to a higher throughput. LR1 and LR2 have higher throughputs than AODV and DSR. Furthermore, LR1 and LR2 have lower delay than AODV. In general, LR2 outperforms LR1. We can draw the following conclusions.

- Local Recovery suppresses the notification to the source so that the saved time can be utilized for local construction of new routes.
- The source does not need to setup a new route so that the buffered packets in the intermediate nodes need not be sent again.
- The unnecessary TCP timeout can be avoided in the source.

However, DSR has the lowest delay in all compared protocols. This is because the delay is calculated by considering the received packets only. In fact, DSR has much longer idle time. For the same reason, DSR has the lowest control overhead. In general, LR has lower control overhead than AODV. Finally, we can see that LR has a higher delivery rate than AODV. Furthermore, in LR and AODV, the delivery rate does not change much with the the number of nodes.

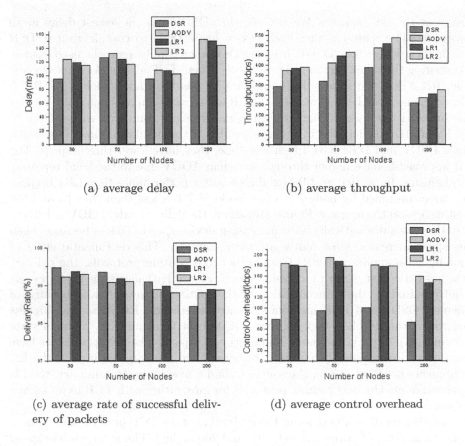

(a) average delay

(b) average throughput

(c) average rate of successful delivery of packets

(d) average control overhead

Fig. 2. Simulation results for various number of nodes.

We also consider the route setup delay of the protocols. The results are shown in Figure 3. In general, DSR has the lowest setup delay in all compared protocols. This is because the DSR source has the route cache to set up connection immediately. However, if a suitable cached route cannot be found, DSR will use a long time to find a new route. Moreover, the setup delay is rather unacceptable, e.g., more than 6 sec. In that case, the route failure causes the TCP sender to become idle until a new trial begins after a long time. AODV and the LR approaches have nearly the same route request and reply mechanisms. They require some time to find the route to set up connection. In particular, LR1 and LR2 have the same setup delay. When the number of node is small, i.e., 30 or 50, AODV and the LR approaches have similar setup delay. However, with a larger number of nodes—100 or 200, the setup delays between AODV and LR become obviously different. The setup delay of the LR approaches are smaller than that of AODV. The reason is that with increased number of nodes, the route re-establishment process is more frequent, especially when TCP synchronization packet has not been received by the destination. Since the LR approaches can suppress the route error notification to the source and locally recover the route, the unnecessary timeout can be avoided or the duration of timeout is much reduced in the TCP source.

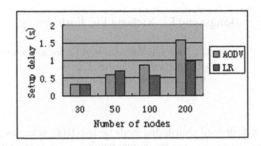

Fig. 3. The proposed local recovery algorithm.

References

1. H. Balakrishnan, V. N. Padmanabhan, S. Seshan, and R. H. Katz, "A Comparison of Mechanisms for Improving TCP Performance over Wireless Links," *IEEE/ACM Transactions on Networking*, vol. 5, no. 6, pp. 756–769, Dec. 1997.
2. J. Broch, D. A. Maltz, D. B. Johnson, Y.-C. Hu, and J. Jetcheva, "A Performance Comparison of Multi-Hop Wireless Ad Hoc Network Routing Protocols," *Proc. MOBICOM*, pp. 85–97, Oct. 1998.
3. K. Chandran, S. Raghunathan, S. Venkatesan, and R. Prakash, "A Feedback-Based Scheme for Improving TCP Performance in Ad Hoc Wireless Networks," *IEEE Personal Communications*, vol. 8, no. 1, pp. 34–39, Feb. 2001.
4. R. Duggirala et al., "Performance Enhancements of Ad Hoc Networks with Localized Route Repair," *IEEE Trans. Computers*, vol. 52, no. 7, pp. 854–861, July 2003.
5. H. Elaarag, "Improving TCP Performance over Mobile Networks," *ACM Computing Surveys*, vol. 34, no. 3, Sept. 2002.
6. S. Floyd, "TCP and Explicit Congestion Notification," *ACM Computer Communications Review*, vol. 24, no. 5, pp. 10–23, 1994.
7. D. B. Johnson and D. Maltz, "Dynamic Source Routing in Ad Hoc Wireless Networks," in *Mobile Computing*, T. Imielinski and H. Korth (eds.), Chapter 5, Kluwer Academic Publishers, 1996.
8. X.-H. Lin, Y.-K. Kwok, and V. K. N. Lau, "A Quantitative Comparison of Ad Hoc Routing Protocols with and without Channel Adaptation," *IEEE Trans. Mobile Computing*, vol. 3, no. 4, Oct.-Dec. 2004.
9. D. A. Maltz, J. Broch, J. Jetcheva, and D. B. Johnson, "The Effects of On-Demand Behavior in Routing Protocols for Multihop Wireless Ad Hoc Networks," *IEEE J. Selected Areas in Comm.*, vol. 17, no. 8, pp. 1439–1453, Aug. 1999.
10. The UCB/LBNL/VINT Network Simulator (NS), URL:http://www.isi.edu/nsnam/ns/, 2003.
11. C. E. Perkins, E. M. Royer, and S. R. Das, "Ad Hoc On-Demand Distance Vector(AODV) Routing," *IETF Internet Draft*, draft-ietf-manet-aodv-10.txt, 2002.
12. J. Yoon, M. Liu, and B. Noble, "Random Waypoint Considered Harmful," *Proc. INFOCOM 2003*.

Graph-Theoretic Analysis of Kautz Topology and DHT Schemes*

Dongsheng Li, Xicheng Lu, Jinshu Su

School of Computer, National University of Defense Technology
Changsha 410073, P.R. China
leedongsh@hotmail.com

Abstract. Many proposed distributed hash table (DHT) schemes for peer-to-peer network are based on some traditional parallel interconnection topologies. In this paper, we show that the Kautz graph is a very good static topology to construct DHT schemes. We demonstrate the optimal diameter and optimal fault tolerance properties of the Kautz graph and prove that the Kautz graph is $(1+o(1))$-congestion-free when using the long path routing algorithm. Then we propose FissionE, a novel DHT scheme based on Kautz graph. FissionE is a constant degree, $O(\log N)$ diameter and $(1+o(1))$-congestion-free. FissionE shows that the DHT scheme with constant degree and constant congestion can achieve $O(\log N)$ diameter, which is better than the lower bound $\Omega(N^{1/d})$ conjectured before.

1 Introduction and Related Work

In recent years, peer-to-peer computing has attracted significant attentions from both industry and academic research. The core component of many proposed peer-to-peer systems is the distributed hash table (DHT) schemes [1] that use a hash table-like interface to publish and lookup data objects. DHT schemes for structured P2P systems have attracted much attention in academic researches for their desirable characteristics, such as scalability, robustness, self-management, and generality.

Many proposed DHT schemes are based on some traditional interconnection topology: Chord [2], Tapestry and Pastry are based on the hypercube topology; CAN [3] is based on the d-torus topology; Koorde [4] and D2B [5] are based on the de Bruijn graph; Viceroy [6], Ulysses [7] are based on the Butterfly topology. Compared with hypercube, de Bruijn or torus topology, Kautz graph has some better properties. In this paper, we demonstrate the optimal diameter and optimal fault tolerance properties of the Kautz graph and prove that the Kautz graph is $(1+o(1))$-congestion-free when using the long path routing algorithm. Then we propose FissionE, a novel DHT scheme based on Kautz graph. FissionE is a $(1+o(1))$-congestion-free DHT scheme with constant degree and $O(\log N)$ diameter.

Two important measures of DHT schemes are degree, the size of routing table to be maintained on each peer, and diameter, the number of hops a query needs to travel

*This paper is supported in part by the National Natural Science Foundation of China under the grant No. 90104001 and 69933030.

H. Jin et al. (Eds.): NPC 2004, LNCS 3222, pp. 308-315, 2004.

in the worst case. In many existing DHT schemes, such as Chord, Tapestry, and Pastry, both the degree and the diameter tend to $O(\log N)$, while in CAN the degree and the diameter are $O(d)$ and $O(dN^{1/d})$ respectively. An open problem posed in [1] is whether there exists DHT scheme with $O(d)$ degree and $O(\log N)$ diameter. Recent work [4,5,6,7,8] has shown that there are DHT algorithms to achieve $O(\log N)$ diameter with $O(1)$ degree, but the algorithms cause severe congestion in P2P networks. Xu et al. [7] systematically studied the degree-diameter tradeoff of DHT schemes and defined the concept of *congestion*, and then clarified the role that *congestion-free* plays in the degree-diameter tradeoff. A conjecture posed in [7] is that "$\Omega(N^{1/d})$ is the asymptotic lower bounds for the diameter when the degree is no more than d and the network is required to be c-congestion-free for some constant c". *FissionE* is a novel constant degree and $(1+o(1))$-congestion-free DHT scheme with $O(\log N)$ diameter. FissionE can achieve better bound than the conjecture above.

FissionE is a constant-degree and $(1+o(1))$-congestion-free DHT scheme with $O(\log_2 N)$ diameter. The average degree of FissionE is 4, and the diameter of FissionE is less than $2*\log_2 N$; the average routing path length of FissionE is about $\log_2 N$. Compared with FissionE, the degree of Ulysses is $O(\log N)$ which is not constant. The expected degree of D2B is constant, but its high probability bound is $O(\log N)$, i.e., a few unlucky peers would be of degree $\Omega(\log N)$. The expected diameter of Viceroy is about $3\log_2 N$, however its $O(\log N)$ diameter is achieved not with certainty but "with high probability". Among the well-known DHT schemes, only CAN and Koorde definitely have constant degree. CAN is of $2d$ degree, but its diameter is $O(dN^{1/d})$, and so it does not scale as well as FissionE. Koorde [4] is constant degree and $O(\log N)$ diameter, but it isn't $(1+o(1))$-congestion-free and it's congestion is severer than that in FissionE.

The remainder of the paper is organized as follows. Section 2 introduces the Kautz graph and its properties. Section 3 proves the low congestion property of the Kautz graph. Section 4 describes the design of FissionE. Conclusions and future work is discussed in Section 5.

2 Static Kautz Graph

Many DHT schemes are based on the traditional interconnection network topologies. Different from dynamic P2P network, the traditional interconnection network poses some limits on the number of nodes it can support and does not support the dynamic joining or departure of nodes. To distinguish them, the traditional interconnection network is called static network in the paper. FissionE exploits Kautz graph as its static topology. This section discusses the Kautz graph and its properties.

Definition 1. The *Kautz string* ξ of length n and base d is defined as a string $a_1 a_2 \ldots a_n$ where $a_j \in \{0,1,2,\ldots,d\}$ $(1 \leq j \leq k)$ and $a_i \neq a_{i+1}$ $(1 \leq i \leq k-1)$.

Definition 2. The *Kautz namespace KautzSpace(d,k)* is defined as the set containing all the Kautz strings of length k and base d, i.e.,
KautzSpace(d,k) = { $a_1 a_2 \ldots a_k$ | $a_i \in \{0,1,2,\ldots,d\}$ $(1 \leq i \leq k)$ and $a_i \neq a_{i+1}$ $(1 \leq i \leq k-1)$}.

Definition 3. The *Kautz graph K(d,k)* [9] is a directed graph whose nodes are labeled with a Kautz string of length k and base d. For simplicity, we name a node with its label. Every node $U=u_1u_2...u_k$ in Kautz graph $K(d,k)$ has d outgoing edges: for each $\alpha \in \{0,1,2,...,d\}$ and $\alpha \neq u_k$, node u has one outgoing edge to node $V=u_2u_3...u_k\alpha$, (denoted by $u \rightarrow v$), i.e., there is an edge from u to v iff v is a left-shifted version of u.

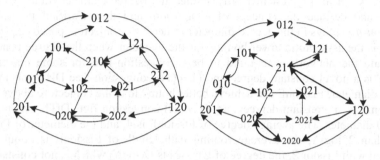

Fig. 1. Kautz graph $K(2,3)$ **Fig. 2.** Neighborhood of FissionE

Obviously there are $N=d^k+d^{k-1}$ nodes in the $K(d,k)$ graph and each node in $K(d,k)$ is of in-degree d and out-degree d. Figure 1 shows Kautz graph $K(2,3)$.

Table 1. The degree-diameter tradeoff of different topologies

Topology	Degree	Diameter	Average path length
de Bruijn	d	$\log_d N$	$\log_d N - 1/(d-1)$ [11]
Hypercube (Chord)	$\log_2 N$	$\log_2 N$	$1/2 \log_2 N$
d-torus (CAN)	$2d$	$1/2 dN^{1/d}$	$1/4 dN^{1/d}$
Butterfly	d	$2 \log_d N(1-o(1))$	about $3/2 \log_d N$ [11]
Kautz (FissionE)	d	$D=\log_d N - \log_d(1+1/d)$	$D-1/(d+1)$

Assuming a graph of fixed degree d and diameter k, the maximum number of nodes N in the graph is the *Moore bound* [10] $1+d+d^2+...+d^k$. The Moore bound is not achievable for any non-trivial graph. The number of nodes in the Kautz graph $K(d,k)$ is $d^{k-1}+d^k$, very close to the Moore bound. In fact, Kautz graph is the densest graph when the diameter is two. From the Moore bound, it is easy to see the low bound of the diameter of a graph with N nodes is $\lceil \log_d(N(d-1)+1) \rceil - 1$ and the diameter k of Kautz graph $K(d,k)$ reaches the lower bound as $\lceil \log_d(N(d-1)+1) \rceil - 1 = \lceil \log_d((d^k+d^{k-1})(d-1)+1) \rceil - 1 = \lceil \log_d(d^{k+1}-d^{k-1}+1) \rceil - 1 = k$. Thus Kautz graph $K(d,k)$ has an optimal diameter.

The Kautz graph also has optimal fault tolerance [13]. That is, Kautz graph $K(d,k)$ of degree d is d-connected (i.e., there are d node disjoint paths between any two nodes). The corresponding de Brujin graph is $(d-1)$-connected. In addition, Kautz graph $K(d,k)$ has a better load balancing feature than the de Bruijn graph as shown in [9]. Table 1 shows the degree-diameter tradeoff of different topologies.

3 Low Congestion Routing in Kautz Graph

There are many routing algorithms for Kautz graph. FissionE uses the *Long Path Routing Algorithm* in Kautz graph [9]. Long path routing in Kautz graph from node U to node V is accomplished by taking the string U and shifting in the symbols of V one at a time until the string U has been replaced by V. For instance, given two nodes $U=u_1u_2...u_k$ and $V=v_1v_2...v_k$, the long routing path from U to V is a path of length k shown as below:

$$U=u_1u_2...u_k{\to}u_2u_3...u_kv_1{\to}u_3u_4...u_kv_1v_2 \to ....{\to}u_kv_1v_2...v_{k-1}{\to}v_1v_2...v_k \quad (\text{if } u_k{\neq}v_1)$$

or a path of length k-1 shown as below:

$$U=u_1u_2...u_k{\to}u_2u_3...u_kv_2 {\to}u_3u_4...u_kv_2v_3 \to....{\to}u_kv_2...v_{k-1}v_k=v_1v_2...v_k \quad (\text{if } u_k{=}v_1)$$

For example, with the long path routing algorithm, the routing path in Kautz graph $K(2,3)$ from node 012 to node 102 is 012$\to$ 121$\to$210$\to$102, and the routing path from 012 to 202 is 012$\to$120$\to$202.

The long path may contain duplicate nodes and the algorithm keeps it for symmetry and simplicity. Obviously, with the long path routing algorithm, the path length between any nodes is k or k-1, and the average path length is $h=d/(d+1)*k+1/(d+1)*(k-1)=k-1/(d+1)$. Compared with the shortest path routing algorithm, the long path routing algorithm has a little longer average routing path length, while it has better load balance characteristics and the average delay is even less than the shortest routing algorithm under heavy load [9] (the severe congestion on some nodes leads to some delay). FissionE adopts the long path routing algorithm.

Now we consider the congestion characteristic of long path routing in Kautz graph. We use the concept "congestion-free" from [7].

Definition 4 [7]. A P2P network is *c-congestion-free* (*c* is constant and $c{\geq}1$) if its static network is both *c-node-congestion-free* and *c-edge-congestion-free* under *uniform all-to-all communication* load. The *c-congestion-free* is also called *constant congestion*. A network is said to be *c-node-congestion-free* if no node is handling more than c times the average traffic per node. A network is said to be *c-edge-congestion-free* if no edge handling more than c times the average traffic per edge. The *uniform all-to-all communication* load is defined as: for each pair of nodes U,V (U$\neq$V), there is a unit of traffic from U to V. The static P2P network is referred to the case that all nodes in the identification space exist and are alive, i.e., nodes in P2P network form the complete static topology.

Now we turn to the congestion property of the Kautz graph and some lemmas referred in the proof are shown after the Theorem 1.

Theorem 1. *When using long path routing algorithm, Kautz graph $K(d,k)$ is $(1+o(1))$-congestion-free.*

Proof. Define S1={$u_1u_2...u_ku_1u_2...u_k \mid u_1u_2...u_ku_1u_2...u_k{\in}KautzSpace(d,2k)$ },
S2={$u_1u_2...u_ku_2...u_k \mid u_1u_2...u_ku_2...u_k \in KautzSpace(d,2k-1)$
   and $u_1u_2...u_k{=}u_ku_2...u_k$ },
S3=$KautzSpace(d,2k)$-S1, S4=$KautzSpace(d,2k-1)$-S2, S=S3$\cup$S4

The uniform all-to-all communication load is represented by the set M:
M={routing paths from U to V $\mid$ U,V are nodes in $K(k,d)$ and U$\neq$V}

Define mapping f: $\forall \delta \in M$, assuming δ is a routing path of length n:

$b_1b_2...b_k \rightarrow b_2b_3...b_{k+1} \rightarrow b_3b_4...b_{k+2} \rightarrow ... \rightarrow b_nb_{n+1}...b_{n+k}$,

then $f(\delta)=b_1b_2...b_k...b_{n+k}$.

From Lemma 1, f is a bijection from M to S. Thus under uniform all-to-all communication load, for any node $R=r_1r_2...r_k$, its load equals the number that the Kautz string $r_1r_2...r_k$ appears as a substring (except for the prefix) of the Kautz strings in S. From Lemma 2, the load L_n of R is:

$$L_n = \begin{cases} k * d^k + (k-1)d^{k-1} - k & (r_1 \neq r_k) \\ k * d^k + (k-1)d^{k-1} - k + 1 & (r_1 = r_k) \end{cases}$$

The average path length in Kautz graph $K(d,k)$ is $h=k-1/(d+1)$, thus the average load of a node is

$Aveg(L_n)=(N-1)*h=(d^k+d^{k-1}-1)*(k-1/(d+1)) = k*d^k+(k-1)*d^{k-1}-k+1/(d+1)$

Because $Max(L_n)- Aveg(L_n)= d/(d+1)<< Aveg(L_n)$, and

$Max(L_n)/Aveg(L_n)<1+1/((k-1)*(d^k+d^{k-1}))=1+1/((k-1)*N)=1+O(1/N\log_d N)=1+o(1)$

Thus the static Kautz graph is $(1+o(1))$-node-congestion-free.

In Kautz graph $K(d,k)$, the edge from $r_1r_2...r_k$ to $r_2...r_kr_{k+1}$ can be uniquely represented by the Kautz sring $r_1r_2...r_kr_{k+1}$, and each Kautz string $b_1b_2...b_kb_{k+1}$ in Kautz namespace $K(d,k+1)$ can be uniquely represented by the edge from node $b_1b_2...b_k$ to node $b_2...b_kb_{k+1}$. Thus under uniform all-to-all communication load, for any edge $e=r_1r_2...r_kr_{k+1}$ in $K(d,k)$, its load equals the number that the Kautz string $r_1r_2...r_kr_{k+1}$ appears as a substring of the Kautz strings in S. From Lemma 3, the load L_n of R is:

$$L_e = \begin{cases} k * d^{k-1} + (k-1)d^{k-2} - k & (r_1 = r_{k+1}) \\ k * d^{k-1} + (k-1)d^{k-2} - k + 1 & (r_1 = r_k \quad and \quad r_2 = r_{k+1}) \\ k * d^{k-1} + (k-1)d^{k-2} & (others) \end{cases}$$

In Kautz graph $K(d,k)$, the average load of edges $Avg(L_e)=N*(N-1)*h/|E|$ ($|E|$ is the number of edges in $K(d,k)$ and $|E|=N*d$), thus

$Avg(L_e)= N*(N-1)*h/(N*d) = (N-1)*h/d = k*d^{k-1}+(k-1)*d^{k-2}-k/d+1/(d*(d+1))$

Because $Max(L_e)- Avg(L_e) = k/d - 1/(d*(d+1)) = h/d << Avg(L_e)$, and

$Max(L_e)/Avg(L_e) =1+(h/d)/((N-1)*h/d)=1+ 1/(N-1)=1+o(1)$

Thus Kautz graph $K(d,k)$ is $(1+o(1))$-edge-congestion-free.

Therefore, Kautz graph $K(d,k)$ is $(1+o(1))$-congestion-free.   □

From Theorem 1, it is easy to get that the Kautz graph is constant congestion.

Now we give the lemmas referred in the proof above.

Lemma 1 *The Mapping f is a bijection from M to S.*

Proof: Obviously, S3∩S4=∅ , S=*KautzSpace*(d,2k) ∪ *KautzSpace*(d,2k-1)-S1-S2.

First we prove that f is an injection.

$\forall \delta \in M$, then δ is a routing path from a certain node $U=u_1u_2...u_k$ to another node $V=v_1v_2...v_k (U \neq V)$:

1) if $u_k \neq v_1$, then the routing path δ would be :

$U=u_1u_2...u_k \rightarrow u_2u_3...u_kv_1 \rightarrow u_3u_4...u_kv_1v_2 \rightarrow ....\rightarrow u_kv_1v_2...v_{k-1} \rightarrow v_1v_2...v_k=V$

Thus $f(\delta)=u_1u_2...u_kv_1v_2...v_k$, thereby $f(\delta) \in KautzSpace(d,2k)$. Since $U \neq V$, thereafter $f(\delta) \notin S1$, thus $f(\delta) \in KautzSpace(d,2k)-S1$, i.e. $f(\delta) \in S3$.

2) if $u_k=v_1$, then the routing path δ would be :

$U= u_1u_2...u_k \rightarrow u_2u_3...u_kv_2 \rightarrow u_3u_4...u_kv_2v_3 \rightarrow ....\rightarrow u_kv_2...v_{k-1}v_k = v_1v_2...v_k =V$

Thus $f(\delta)=u_1u_2...u_kv_2...v_k$, thereby $f(\delta) \in KautzSpace(d,2k-1)$. Since $U \neq V$, i.e. $u_1u_2...u_k \neq u_ku_kv_2...v_k$, thereafter $f(\delta) \notin S2$, and $f(\delta) \in KautzSpace(d,2k-1)$-S2, i.e. $f(\delta) \in S4$.

So $\forall \delta \in M$, $f(\delta) \in S$, that is, the range of mapping f is S, and f is a mapping from M to S. Obviously, the identical routing path can only be mapped to one Kautz string, and different routing paths will be mapped to different Kautz strings, thus f is an injection.

Then we'll prove that f is a surjection.

$\forall \xi \in S$, since $S3 \cap S4 = \Phi$, thus we may find that $\xi \in S3$ or $\xi \in S4$.

If $\xi \in S3$, let $\xi = a_1a_2...a_{2k-1}a_{2k}$. According to the definition of S3, $a_1a_2...a_k$ and $a_{k+1}a_{k+2}...a_{2k}$ are both valid Kautz strings in $KautzSpace(d,k)$, and $a_1a_2...a_k \neq a_{k+1}a_{k+2}...a_{2k}$, $a_{k+1} \neq a_k$. Consider routes δ' in Set M with length k which originate from source node $a_1a_2...a_k$ to destination node: $a_1a_2...a_k \rightarrow a_2a_3...a_ka_{k+1} \rightarrow a_3a_4...a_{k+2} \rightarrow ......\rightarrow a_k...a_{2k-1} \rightarrow a_{k+1}...a_{2k}$, we may find that $\xi=f(\delta')$, i.e. $\exists \delta' \in M$, s.t. $\xi=f(\delta')$.

If $\xi \in S4$, let $\xi = b_1b_2...b_{2k-1}$. According to the definition of S4, we can get that $b_1b_2...b_k$ and $b_kb_{k+1}...b_{2k-1}$ are all valid Kautz strings in $KautzSpace(d,k)$; what's more, $b_1b_2...b_k \neq b_kb_{k+1}...b_{2k-1}$. Consider route δ' with length k-1 in set M which originates from source node $b_1b_2...b_k$ to target node $b_kb_{k+1}...b_{2k-1}$: $b_1b_2...b_k \rightarrow b_2b_3...b_kb_{k+1} \rightarrow b_3b_4...b_{k+2} \rightarrow ...... \rightarrow b_{k-1}b_k...b_{2k-2} \rightarrow b_kb_{k+1}...b_{2k-1}$. Thus we may find $\xi = f(\delta')$, that is, $\exists \delta' \in M$, s.t. $\xi=f(\delta')$.

Thus f is a bijection.   □

Lemma 2 *For any Kautz string $R=r_1r_2...r_k$ in KautzSpace(d,k), the number of R appearing as the substring(except for the prefix) of Kautz strings in set S is:*

$$L_R = \begin{cases} k*d^k + (k-1)d^{k-1} - k & (r_1 \neq r_k) \\ k*d^k + (k-1)d^{k-1} - k + 1 & (r_1 = r_k) \end{cases}$$

Proof. S= $KautzSpace(d,2k) \cup KautzSpace(d,2k-1)$-S1-S2.

Based on theories of combinatorics, the number of times that R appears as a substring (except for the prefix) of Kautz string in $KautzSpace(d,2k)$ are $k*d^k$. (R can be placed in k different places in a Kautz string with length 2k, and the other k places left all have d choices.). Similarly, the number of times that R appears as a substring (except for the prefix) of Kautz string in $KautzSpace(d,2k-1)$ is $(k-1)*d^{k-1}$.

Then we calculate the number of times that R appears in S1 and S2. If R appears as a substring of the Kautz string ξ in S1=$\{u_1u_2...u_ku_1u_2...u_k \mid u_1u_2...u_ku_1u_2...u_k \in KautzSpace(d,2k) \}$ and R appears at No. m place of ξ, assuming $\xi=b_1b_2...b_kb_{k+1}b_{k+2}...b_{2k}=b_1b_2...b_kb_1b_2...b_k$, then $U=b_m...b_kb_1b_2...b_{m-1}$ $(b_m \neq b_{m-1})$, i.e., $r_1 \neq r_k$. Similarly, if R appears in S2, $r_1=r_k$.

Thus if $r_1 \neq r_k$, R would not appear in S2. For each m that satisfies $1<m \leq k$, we could construct a unique Kautz string $\xi'=r_{k-m+2}...r_kr_1r_2...r_kr_1r_2...r_{k-m+1}$ with length 2k: $\xi' \in$ S1, R appears at No. m place of ξ' and R also appears at No. $k+1$ place of $r_1r_2...r_kr_1r_2...r_k$ that is in S1. Therefore, the number of times that R appears in S1 is k and the number of times that R appears in S2 is 0.

If $r_1=r_k$, for each m that satisfies $1<m \leq k$, we could construct a unique Kautz string $\xi' = r_{k-m+1}...r_kr_2...r_kr_2...r_{k-m}r_{k-m+1}$ with length 2k-1: $\xi' \in$ S1 and R appears at No. m place

of ξ'. Therefore, the number of times that R appears in S2 is k-1 and the number of times that R appears in S1 is 0.

Therefore, for any node R=$r_1r_2...r_k$ in Kautz graph $K(k,d)$,

If $r_1 \neq r_k$, $L_R = k*d^k + (k-1)*d^{k-1} - k$.

If $r_1 = r_k$, $L_R = k*d^k + (k-1)*d^{k-1} - (k-1)$.   □

Lemma 3 *For each Kautz string $e=r_1r_2...r_kr_{k+1}$ in KautzSpace(d,k+1), the number of times that e appears as the substring of Kautz strings in set S is:*

$$L_e = \begin{cases} k*d^{k-1} + (k-1)d^{k-2} - k & (r_1 = r_{k+1}) \\ k*d^{k-1} + (k-1)d^{k-2} - k + 1 & (r_1 = r_k, r_2 = r_{k+1}) \\ k*d^{k-1} + (k-1)d^{k-2} & (else) \end{cases}$$

The proof of Lemma3 is similar to Lemma 2 and omitted here.

4 FissionE Sketch

The Kautz graph has optimal diameter and good fault tolerance characteristic. Also it is constant congestion when using long path routing algorithm. Thus the Kautz graph is a good static topology to construct DHT schemes. We propose FissionE, a novel constant degree, $O(\log N)$ diameter and $(1+o(1))$-congestion-free DHT scheme based on the Kautz graph.

FissionE adopts Kautz graph $K(2,k)$ as its static topology. Each peer in FissionE owns a zone in virtual 2-dimensional Cartesian coordinate. The identifiers of zones in FissionE are Kautz strings with base 2, and zones are organized according to their identifiers. The identifier of a peer is the identifier of the zone it owns. When peers join or leave, the "split large and merge small" policy is adopted for maintenance. Then the entire coordinate space is dynamically partitioned among the peers in the system and the identifiers of zones changes dynamically.

FissionE is somewhat similar to Fission scheme [8], and the main differences lie in the neighborhood of peers and the routing algorithm as well as the update algorithms. In FissionE, the neighborhood invariant (i.e., if zone U and V are neighbors, then $||U|-|V||\leq1$) is kept, but there is no brother-edges. An example of FissionE neighborhood is shown in Figure 2. Routing algorithm in FissionE is much like the long path routing algorithm in the Kautz graph, while Fission adopts the short path routing algorithm. The maintenance policy is similar to that in Fission, but the procedure to find fit zone to split or merge is much more complex. Some fault-tolerant mechanisms are also proposed in FissionE. The details of FissinE and Fission are in [8, 14].

Now we show some properties of FissionE. The proof and details are in [14].

Theorem 2 (Congestion Characteristic) *FissionE is $(1+o(1))$-congestion-free.*

Theorem 3 (Performance Characteristic) *In an N-peer FissionE system,*

1. The in-degree of each peer is 2 and the out-degree is between 1 and 4. The average out-degree is 2.

2. The diameter of FissionE systems is less than $2*\log_2 N$.

5 Conclusions and Future Work

The Kautz graph is a good static topology to construct DHT schemes. A novel DHT scheme based on Kautz graph, FissionE, is proposed to achieve constant degree, $O(\log N)$ diameter and $(1+o(1))$-congestion-free. FissionE is a very promising DHT schemes and many topics (such as proximity, heterogeneity, etc.) on FissionE will be investigated thoroughly in our further work.

References

1. Ratnasamy, S., Shenker, S., and Stoica, I.: Routing algorithms for DHTs: some open questions. Proc. of 1st Workshop on peer-to-peer Systems (IPTPs'02), (2002)
2. Stoica, I., Morris, R., Karger. D. *et al.*: Chord: a scalable peer-to-peer lookup service for Internet applications. Proc. of ACM SIGCOMM 2001, ACM Press, New York (2001) 160-177
3. Ratnasamy, S., Francis, P., Handley, M. *et al.*: A scalable content-addressable network. Proc. of ACM SIGCOMM 2001, ACM Press, New York (2001) 149-160
4. Kaashoek, F. and Karger, D. R.. Koorde: A simple degree-optimal hash table. Proc. of 2nd Intl. Workshop on Peer-to-Peer Systems (IPTPS'2003) (2003)
5. Fraigniaud, P., Gauron, P.: The Content-Addressable Network D2B. Tech Rept. 1349, CNRS University paris-Sud, France (2003)
6. Malkhi, D., Naor, M., and Ratajczak, D.: Viceroy: a scalable and dynamic lookup network. Proc. of 21st ACM Symp. on Principles of Distributed Computing (PODC), Monterey, CA (2002)
7. Xu Jun, Kumar Abhishek, Yu Xingxing: On the fundamental tradeoffs between routing table size and network diameter in peer-to-peer networks. IEEE Journal on Selected Areas in Communications (JSAC), No.1 (2004)
8. Li Dongsheng, Fang Xinxin, WANG Yijie *et al.*: A scalable peer-to-peer network with constant degree. Proc. of APPT'2003 (5th International workshop on Advanced Parallel Processing Technologies), LNCS 2834, (2003) 414-425
9. Panchapakesan, G. and Sengupta, A.: On a lightwave network topology using Kautz digraphs. IEEE Transaction on computers, Vol. 48, No. 10, (1999) 1131-1138
10. Bridges, W.G. and Toueg, S.: On the impossibility of directed Moore graphs. Journal of Combinatorial theory, series B, 29 (1980) 330-341
11. Dmitri Loguinov, Anuj Kumar, Vivek Rai, *et al.*: Graph-Theoretic Analysis of Structured Peer-to-Peer Systems: Routing Distances and Fault Resilience. In: Proc. of ACM SIGCOMM' 2003, Karlsruhe, Germany: ACM Press, (2003) 395-406
12. Sivarajan, K. N. and Ramaswami, R.: Lightwave Networks based on de Bruijn Graphs. IEEE/ACM Trans. Networking, Vol.2 (1994) 70-79
13. Chiang Wei-kuo and Chen Rong-Jaye: Distributed Fault-Tolerant Routing in Kautz Networks. Journal of parallel and distributed computing, 20 (1994) 99-106
14. Li Dongsheng, *et al.*: FissionE: A Scalable Constant degree and constant-congestion Peer-to-Peer Network. Tech Rept. PDL-2003-14, National University of Defense technology (2003)

A Parameterized Model of TCP Slow Start

Xiaoheng Deng, Zhigang Chen, Lianming Zhang

School of Info Sci & Tech, Central South University, Changsha, 410083, China
dengxh@hunnu.edu.cn, czg@csu.edu.cn, zlm@hunnu.edu.cn

Abstract. Based on analysis on multiple packet losses of standard slow start caused by exponential growth of congestion window (*cwnd*), this paper proposes a new phase-divided TCP start scheme and designs a parameterized model to reduce packet losses and improve TCP performance. This scheme employs different of *cwnd* growth rules while *cwnd* is under and over the value of half window threshold (*ssthresh*) respectively, namely exponential growth and negatively exponential growth, which greatly decreases probability of multiple packet losses from a window of data and guarantees that a connection smoothly joins the Internet and transforms into congestion avoidance. Parameterized model adjusts the duration of slow start and acceleration of increasing *cwnd* to improve performance of slow start phase through various parameter setting. An adaptive paraeter setting method is designed. And the simulation results show that this new method significantly decreaseds packet losses and improves the stability of TCP and performance of slow start, and also achieves good fairness and friendliness to other TCP connections.

1 Introduction

With expanding of the Internet applications and scale, TCP is widely deployed, providing reliable end-to-end Internet services. Statistic data show that 95 percent of data flows belong to TCP on the Internet [1]. Since TCP was produced, researchers have done many work on it and proposed several enhanced variants [2,3,4]. TCP adopts slide window mechanism to control network congestion and slow start takes effect while a session starts, the sender opens one segment size congestion window and exponentially increases *cwnd* until *cwnd* reaches a threshold, *ssthresh*, therefore, slow start effectively avoids bursty traffic while new connections join network.

Connections are classified into long-lived and short-lived connections according to the duration. Network measurement [1] shows that short-lived flows, such as WEB and TELNET, are the majority, and long-lived flows, like FTP, are the minority but transfer most data packets of TCP flows. Short-lived flows often end before they come to steady state; namely, they often locate at startup phase. Obviously, the performance of slow start directly impacts on the transmission utility of short-lived flows. In practice, short-lived flows convey the data of important Internet services, which require high bandwidth and short delay. In the same way, slow start also takes effect while long-lived flows start and a retransmission timeout takes place, thus impacts on performance of long-lived flows. Although slow start's duration is very short, it is of great significance to improve performance of data transmission. The

H. Jin et al. (Eds.): NPC 2004, LNCS 3222, pp. 316-324, 2004.

congestion window of standard slow start doubles with *RTT*, shown in figure 2 and figure 3, the equation follows as (1),

$$cwnd(t+T) = \begin{cases} 2 \times cwnd(t), \text{ if } cwnd(t) < ssthresh \\ ssthresh, \quad \text{ if } cwnd(t) > ssthresh \end{cases} \tag{1}$$

Researchers have proposed many enhanced schemes to improve slow start, M. Allman [5] has set a larger initial window(LIW) to improve the performance; TCP Fast-start [6] records network parameters of network recently to reduce the start time of a new connection, decrease short abrupt transmission delay, and maintain high utility while network keeps steady. SPAND [7] picks up current network state and gains optimal initial parameters. J. Hoe's method replaces the default setting of *ssthresh* with an estimated value to ensure that *cwnd* reaches an appropriate value [8]. That recent history information is used to initialize parameters of new connections has been presented in [9]. TCP Vegas [10] restricts the exponential window growth, and doubles *cwnd* every other *RTT*. The above approaches partially optimize slow start, but each still has weakness. TCP Fast-start has strict condition of steady network. J. Hoe's method is problematic in practice. Parameter setting based history information violates slow start principle and cannot fit dynamic change of network. TCP Vegas cannot avoid multiple packet losses in one window.

Considering the limitations, we propose a new phase-divided and gradually approaching slow start algorithm, called P-Start. P-Start employs standard slow start mechanism and *cwnd* grows exponentially while congestion window is less than *ssthresh*/2; If *cwnd* is equal or greater than *ssthresh*/2, the congestion window, $cwnd_{i+1}$, is not directly set with *ssthresh* but only increases $(ssthresh-cwnd_i)/2$, and iterates until $(ssthresh-cwnd_i)$ is less than the factor of δ that lies from 2 to *ssthresh*/2. This approach combines exponential and negatively exponential growth, of which congestion window gradually approaches *ssthresh*, to improve stability of TCP and decrease multiple packet losses. The rest of the paper is organized as follows. Section 2 proposes phase-divided and gradually approaching slow start algorithm and the parameterized model; Section 3 validates the algorithm through a series of simulating experiments; Section 4 gives the conclusion and points out further research direction.

2 P-Start

2.1 Motivation of P-Start

TCP slow start probes network bandwidth, and its inherent property of exponential growth of window from one packet results in the following problems: first, congestion window starts with one packet and spends many *RTT*s, which brings low utility of short-lived connections. So researchers propose a larger initial window and adopts fast start [5,6] to reduce the duration of slow start and improve network utility. Second, the source nodes are blind to the available bandwidth and use the default initial *ssthresh*. The exponential growth of congestion window results in severe overflow of the buffer of the bottleneck link and multiple packet losses, which makes self-clock loss and retransmission timeout of TCP. And retransmission timeout causes global synchronization, which greatly degrades network utility and brings oscillation of queuing delay. TCP restarts and regains self-clocking.

Efficient measurement technology, which is used to probe available network bandwidth, adaptively set slow start *ssthresh*, and eliminate the limitation of static parameters setting, is potential method. For dynamics of data flows and delay of system feedback, even though, effective bandwidth measurement cannot gain entire match between *ssthresh* and available bandwidth. In the last *RTT*, the send window increase near *ssthresh/2*, the largest increment, but the sending rate is close to network's capability. The over increment of window causes multiple packet losses.

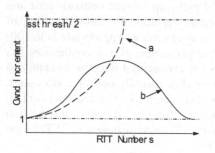

Fig. 1. *Cwnd* acceleration

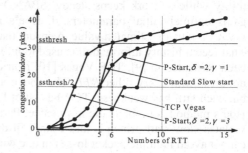

Fig. 2. Comparison of startup mechanisms

The growth of window of standard slow start is shown as curve a in figure 1; the increment of window becomes larger and larger. In fact, while a connection starts, it should gradually increase congestion window from a small one to avoid large initial window, which brings bursty traffic and causes network congestion. When sending rate is near network capacity, the increment should be reduced to smoothly transform into congestion avoidance, which is shown as curve b in figure 1.

2.2 Elements of P-Start

The key idea of P-Start is that congestion window increases exponentially while it is less than *ssthresh/2*, otherwise, increases (*ssthresh-cwnd*)/2 and gradually approaches *ssthresh* until the (*ssthresh-cwnd*) is less than the factor of δ (ssthresh/2$\geqslant \delta \geqslant$2), and then *cwnd* is set with *ssthresh* and transforms into congestion avoidance phase. In contrast to TCP Vegas, P-Start has the same duration when the factor is set with 2, the low bound. It means that the longest process of P-Start is same as long as TCP Vegas's, but P-Start can efficiently decrease probability of multiple packet losses for *cwnd* increment of P-Start becomes smaller and locates middle phase of startup. And *cwnd* can be represented as (2), shown in figure 2 and figure 4.

$$cwnd(t+T) = \begin{cases} 2 \times cwnd(t), & if \; cwnd < ssthresh/2 \\ (cwnd(t)+ssthresh)/2, & if \; ssthresh-cwnd \geq \delta \\ & and \; ssthresh > cwnd \geq ssthresh/2 \\ ssthresh, & else \end{cases} \quad (2)$$

The major feature of P-Start is that *cwnd* increases with a small amplitude at start phase and transition phase to congestion avoidance phase, sending rate changes smoothly with little impact on other shared connections, and maintains network stability, decreases oscillation. Algorithm is shown as following,

```
1. init, cwnd=1, ssthresh=ssth_init, reset δ ;
2. send cwnd packets;
4. if cwnd<ssthresh/2, then cwnd=2*cwnd,   goto 2;
5  if cwnd≥ssthresh/2 and ssthresh-cwnd>δ then
   cwnd=(cwnd+ssthresh)/2, goto 2;
5. else cwnd=ssthresh, goto 5;
6. if received 3 dup-ACKs or retransmision time out,
   then re-enter slow start phase, goto 1;
7. enter congestion avoidance phase;
```

We compare the window change between standard slow start [12] and P-Start. First, we assume that all segments are successfully acked and round trip time is fix. Let $N+1 = \log_2{^{ssthresh}}$, So the duration is equal to $T_{ss} = (N+1) \times RTT$ according to slow start elements. Increment of window are shown in figure 3, in the first N-1 *RTTs*, the total increment is *ssthresh*/4; In the last two *RTTs*, *cwnd* increases *ssthresh*/4 and *ssthresh*/2 respectively, total increment of the last two RTT reaches 3 quarters of *ssthresh*. In high-speed network, congestion window size is very large; The bursty traffic caused by great imcrement of *cwnd* should result in great impact on network stability, packet loss of all connections sharing the bottleneck link, global synchronization and degrading of performance. P-Start is shown in figure 4, while δ =2, the largest increment of *cwnd* is equal to *ssthresh*/4 and occurs twice during slow start, and bursty traffic reduces by 50%. Congestion window changes smoothly, the utility of P-Start is lower than standard slow start's, which is shown in figure 2. But P-Start can maintain network higher utility while network congestion occurs by decreasing packet losses. P-Start is a general slow start, which can be applied in wider areas, through varying δ from 2 to *ssthresh*/2. If δ = *ssthresh*/2, P-Start turns to standard slow start. P-Start reduces its duration and improves utility if δ is set with the value greater than 2.

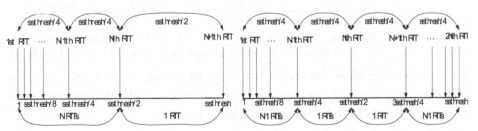

Fig. 3. Window change of slow start of TCP   **Fig. 4.** Window change of P-Start (δ =2)

2.3 Flexible Parameter Setting Model

According to the statement of section 2.2, if δ =2, P-Start has the same duration as TCP Vegas's, however, P-Start diminishes the granularity of increment of *cwnd*, and significantly improves the smoothness of sending rate change, shown in figure 2; and if $\delta = ssthresh/2$, P-Start becomes standard slow start. P-Start can flexibly select the value of δ from $ssthresh/2$ to 2. Compared with standard slow start, the behaviors are same while $cwnd<ssthresh/2$, exponential window growth, but congestion window of P-Start is negatively exponential growth of the difference between $ssthresh$ and $cwnd$, represented as (2). The duration is approximate the double of standard slow start's, which causes low performance at startup phase, shown in figure 2. So it is necessary to improve the performance and synchronously keep smooth transition to congestion avoidance. An increment factor of γ ($\gamma \geq 1$) is introduced, which means that $cwnd$ increases γ packets if one packet is successfully acked. $Cwnd$ becomes ($\gamma +1$) times of the former one during one RTT if all packets are successfully acked, so this factor γ represents the acceleration of $cwnd$ growth. For example, if $\gamma =1$, $\delta =2$, P-Start is the algorithm stated in section 2.2, if $\gamma =3$, $\delta =2$, and $cwnd<ssthresh/2$, $cwnd$ becomes 4 times as the original one, else if $cwnd \geq ssthresh/2$, $cwnd$ increases $\frac{\gamma(ssthresh-cwnd)}{\gamma+1}$ every RTT, namely $3(ssthresh-cwnd)/4$, until $(ssthresh-cwnd)< \delta$, which is shown in figure 2. So $cwnd$ of P-Start can be computed as (4),

$$cwnd(t+T)=\begin{cases}(\gamma+1)\times cwnd(t), & if\ cwnd < ssthresh/2 \\ \dfrac{\gamma\times ssthresh + cwnd(t)}{\gamma+1}, & if\ cwnd \geq ssthresh/2 \\ & and\ ssthresh - cwnd \geq \delta \\ ssthresh, & if\ cwnd > ssthresh\ or\ ssthresh - cwnd < \delta\end{cases} \tag{3}$$

The performance of the above parameterized model is determined by the static parameter setting of γ and δ, P-Start should be more adaptive to the dynamics of Internet. As large initial window has been proposed to improve the performance of slow start with the same effect of the factor δ in P-Start, so the value of δ is decided by large initial window option. For the reason of performance, startup phase cannot last too long, the time taken by various slow start mechanisms are shown in table 1.

Table 1. duration of startup phase (RTT is fix & all packets are successfully acked)

Slow Start	TCP Vegas	P-Start		
		$\gamma =1, \delta =2$	$\gamma =3, \delta =2$	Any given γ, δ
$RTT \times \log_2^{ssthresh}$	$2RTT \times \log_2^{ssthresh}$	$2RTT \times \log_2^{ssthresh/2}$	$2RTT \times \log_4^{ssthresh/2}$	$2RTT \times \log_{\gamma+1}^{(ssthresh/2-\delta)}$

Generally, the duration is no longer than 10 RTTs, P-Start takes time, $T_{ss} = 2RTT \times \log_{\gamma+1}^{(ssthresh/2-\delta)}$, and $ssthresh$ can be gained by the method of J. Hoe [8]. If standard slow start takes time less than 5 RTTs, namely $\log_2^{ssthresh} \leq 5$, P-Start set γ with 1, else if $5 \leq \log_2^{ssthresh} \leq 10$, P-Start sets γ with $\alpha \times \log_2^{ssthresh}/5, \alpha \geq 1$, else γ follows equation (4). And the adaptivity of P-Start needs further research.

$$\log_{\gamma+1}^{(ssthresh/2-\delta)} \leq 5 \tag{4}$$

3 Network Simulations and Validation

To validate P-Start, we implement it in network simulator NS2 [13] in environment of red hat 9.0 linux, network topology is shown in figure 5, and simulation scenarios includes various mechanisms, such as TCP standard slow start, TCP Vegas and P-Start with different parameter setting. We design a series of experiments and compare the simulation results to figure out the advantage of P-Start.

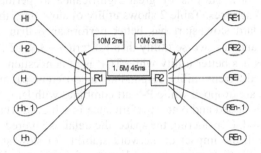

Fig. 5. Topology of network simulation

As shown in figure 5, N connections share a bottleneck link consisted of routers R1, R2, bandwidth of the bottleneck link is 1.5Mbps. Time labeled in figure 5 is one-way delay, packet size is 1024 Bytes, buffer size L is 25 packets size, and type of data transferred in network are FTP.

In experiment one, link is injected 0.5 Mbps background traffic, segment-discarding strategy of bottleneck link is Droptail. The TCP connection we measured has a fixed share of 1Mbps and 8 buffer units. According to network transmission property, product of network bandwidth and delay (BDP) can be computed as follow,

$$BDP = bandwidth \times RTT = 1.0M \times 2(2+45+3) = 12500 Bytes$$

BDP is approximate 12 packets size, and the available buffer size is 8 packets size, so the pipe's capacity is 20 packets. The file size transferred is 60 Kbytes. In TCP protocol, the window of the sender is the smaller one of *cwnd* and the receiver announced window *rwnd*. *Rwnd* is set 18,20,24,36,64 packets size, of which value is set greater, equal and less than actual network bandwidth. Relation between packet losses and window size of various slow start mechanisms is shown in figure 6.

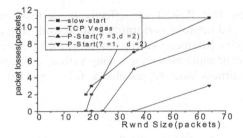

Fig. 6. Packet losses vs. rwnd

Table 2. comparison of utilities

Time	Slow start	TCP Vegas	P-Start	
			$\gamma=1, \delta=2$	$\gamma=3, \delta=2$
2 Sec	48.6%	35.1%	42.7%	69.6%
4 Sec	74.3%	78.2%	68.9%	75.6%
6 Sec	84.1%	91.3%	77.2%	85.2%
8 Sec	87.5%	93.5%	85.4%	88.3%

Throughput of slow start is of great significance to performance of services, especially to WEB services. Table 2 shows utility of slow start, the simulation results indicate that standard slow start has better performance than TCP Vegas and P-Start(γ =1, δ =2), and has worse utility than P-Start(γ =3, δ =2). P-Start gains better utility, TCP Vegas has better utility while TCP is at congestion avoidance phase. P-Start can achieve different utility responding to different parameter configuration. And more packets are dropped while P-Start combines with large initial window of 4, fewer packets are dropped and better performance is achieved while P-Start combines with J. Hoe's method. Considering the space, the detail is ignored.

In order to check the impact on network stability of slow start, we monitor the bursty traffic and instantaneous queue length of bottleneck link if the segment dropping strategy is RED(Random Early Detection). Slow start and P-Start(γ =1, δ =2) start a new FTP connection every 0.5 second and end 0.7 second later. The instantaneous queue length of bottleneck link is shown in figure 8, P-Start can effectively maintain the stability of network for the relatively smoother change of window, which causes smaller oscillation.

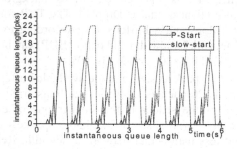

Fig. 7. Comparison of instantaneous queue length

Experiments show that P-Start can effectively decrease packet losses, lighten network oscillation, and improve performance of network with appropriate parameter setting, and the adaptive parameter setting requires further research.

Fairness reflects bandwidth allocation among various connections in the bottleneck link, we use Jain's Fairness Index represented as following [15] :

$$Fairness\ Index = \frac{(\sum_{i=1}^{n} x_i)^2}{n \sum_{i=1}^{n} x_i^2} \qquad (5)$$

Where x_i is the throughput of the *ith* flow and n is the number of total flows. The fairness index is ratio, which lies between 0 and 1. The upper bound value of 1 shows that all flow share the same bandwidth of bottleneck link. Simulations with different number of flows are put up to test fairness of P-Start. We calculate the Fairness Index for TCP Reno and P-Start for each simulation, and the average Fairness Index is 0.9945 and 0.9949 respectively. Simulation results show that P-Start only improves the performance of flows at the start and has no impact on other phases of flow.

4 Conclusion

This paper analyses the impact of TCP slow start on network transmission and difficulties of deployment effective and stable slow start, and proposes a new phase-divided slow start mechanism. This mechanism adjusts the rule of congestion window change, fast and smoothly transforms from slow start to congestion avoidance and decreases the damage caused by multiple packet losses. It has no effect on TCP congestion avoidance but benefits short-lived flows and flows in long fat pipes. The further research is to apply effective and accurate bandwidth measurement technology to dynamically set proper threshold value of slow start, which get over the limitation of static parameter configuration and enhance adaptivity to improve network utility.

Reference

1. K. Thompson, G. J. Miller, and R. Wilder, "Wide-Area Internet Traffic Patterns and Characteristics", IEEE Network, Vol. 11, No. 6, pp. 10-23, November 1997
2. V. Jacobson, "Congestion Avoidance and Control", ACM Computer Communications Review, 18(4) : 314 -329, August 1988
3. V. Jacobson, "Berkeley TCP Evolution from 4.3-Tahoe to 4.3 Reno", Proceedings of the 18th Internet Engineering Task Force, University of British Colombia, Vancouver, BC, Sept. 1990
4. K. Fall, S. Floyd, "Simulation-based Comparisons of Tahoe, Reno, and SACK TCP", Computer Communication Review, V. 26 N. 3, July 1996, pp. 5-21
5. M. Allman, C.Hayes, S.Ostermann, "An Evaluation of TCP with Larger InitialWindows", ACM Computer Communication Review, Vol.28 No. 3, pp 41-52, July, 1998.
6. V. N. Padmanabhan, R. H. Katz, "TCP Fast Start: A Technique for Speeding Up Web Transfers", Proceedings of IEEE GLOBECOM'98, Sydney, Australia, November 1998.
7. S. Seshan, M. Stemm, R. H. Katz, "SPAND: Shared Passive Network Performance Discovery", Proceedings of USITS'97, Monterey, CA, December 1997.
8. J. Hoe, "Improving the Start-up Behavior of a Congestion Control Scheme for TCP", Proceeding of ACM SIGCOMM'96, Stanford, CA, pp. 270-280, August 1996.
9. CHEN Jing, ZHENG Ming Chun, MENG Qiang, "A Network Congestion Control Algorithm Based HistoryConnections and Its Performance Analysis", Journal of Computer Research and Development (in Chinese), Vol 40,No 10, Oct 2003, P1470-1475
10. L.S. Brakmo, L.L. Perterson, "TCP Vegas: End-to-End Congestion Avoidance on a Global Internet", IEEE Journal on Selected Areas in Communication, Vol. 13, Nov. 8, October 1995
11. Claudio Casetti, Mario Gerla, Saverio Mascolo et al, "TCP Westwood: End-to-End Congestion Control for Wired/Wireless Networks", In Wireless Networks Journal 8, 467-479, 2002
12. J. Postel, "Transmission Control Protocol, Request for Comments 793", DDN Network Information Center, SRI International, September 1981.

13.NS project, the network simulator-ns-2 (EB/OL). http://www.isi.edu/nsnam/ns/
14.Haining Wang, Hongjie Xin, Douglas S. Reeves et al, "A Simple Refinement of Slow start of TCP Congestion", ISCC2000, July 04-06,2000 Antibes, France
15.R. Jain, "The art of computer systems performance analysis", John Wiley and sons, AA76.9.E94J32,1991.

SMM: A Truthful Mechanism for Maximum Lifetime Routing in Wireless Ad Hoc Networks

Qing Zhang[1], Huiqiong Chen[2], Weiwei Sun[1], and Bole Shi[1]

[1] Department of Computing and Information Technology, Fudan University
qzhang79@yahoo.com, wwsun@fudan.edu.cn, blshi@fudan.edu.cn
[2] Faculty of Computer Science, Dalhousie University
hchen3@dal.ca

Abstract. As an important metric for wireless ad hoc networks, network lifetime has received great attentions in recent years. Existing lifetime-aware algorithms have an implicit assumption that nodes are cooperative and truthful, and they cannot work properly when the network contains selfish nodes. To make these algorithms achieve their design objectives even in the presence of selfish nodes, in this paper, we propose a truthful mechanism Second-Max-Min (SMM) based on the analysis of current algorithms as well as a DSR-like routing protocol for the mechanism implementation. In SMM mechanism, the source node gives appropriate payments to relay nodes, and the payments are related to the path which has the second maximum lifetime in all possible paths. We show that the payment ratio is relatively small due to the nature of lifetime-aware routing algorithms, which is confirmed by experiments.

1   Introduction

Power-aware routing is a key concern for wireless ad hoc networks due to the limited battery power of nodes. Current research on power-aware routing mainly focuses on two aspects: minimizing the consumed energy of communication (i.e. energy-efficiency) [8] and maximizing the lifetime of whole network (i.e. lifetime-aware) [4–6]. An energy-efficient routing protocol tries to find a path which has the minimal consumed energy. However, the nodes in the minimal energy path will be drain-out of energy quickly if all the packets are routed along this path. Therefore, it would be better to route along nodes which have a higher residual energy, which is discussed by lifetime-aware routing protocols.

Most previous works on power-aware routing have implicitly assumed that nodes are cooperative and truthful. A cooperative node means the node is willing to relay packets for other nodes. A truthful node means the node will reveal its private information, such as its residual energy etc. However, this assumption cannot be taken for granted from the view of an individual node. A node may tend to be selfish, refuse to relay packets for other nodes, or do not tell the truth for its own benefit.

Several protocols have been proposed to stimulate the cooperation of nodes (see [9] for a survey). Further, [2] proposed Ad hoc–VCG, an reactive routing

H. Jin et al. (Eds.): NPC 2004, LNCS 3222, pp. 325–332, 2004.
© IFIP International Federation for Information Processing 2004

protocol coping with the selfish nodes while also achieving the desirable goal of truthfulness and energy-efficiency. However, as we have pointed out, lifetime is also an import metric for network. In the face of selfish nodes, how to make existing lifetime-aware routing algorithms achieve their design objectives is an imperative problem to be solved. But to the best of our knowledge, few works have addressed this problem.

In this paper, we study existing lifetime-aware routing algorithms, and propose a truthful mechanism SMM based on the analysis of current algorithms. Our mechanism deals with selfish node within the framework of algorithmic mechanism design [3]. By giving appropriate payments to relay nodes, the mechanism ensures existing algorithms work properly even the nodes in network are selfish. We also present a DSR-like routing protocol to implement SMM mechanism.

The rest of the paper is organized as follows. Section 2 reviews some related works. Section 3 presents our problem, and analyzes existing solutions. Section 4 proposes the SMM mechanism and presents a DSR-like protocol for the implementation of our mechanism. Section 5 proves the truthfulness of SMM mechanism. Section 6 conducts experiments to examine the performance of payment ratio. We conclude our work in sect. 7.

2   Related Work

Several lifetime-aware routing algorithms which do not consider the effect of selfish nodes have been proposed. MMBCR [4] tries to avoid the path with nodes having the least battery power among all nodes in all possible paths. MRPC [5] identifies the capacity of a node not only by its residual battery power, but also by the expected energy spent in reliably forwarding a packet over a specific link. It selects the path which has the largest packet capacity at the critical node. LPR [6] minimizes the variance in the remaining power of all the nodes and thereby prolong the network lifetime. Other algorithms like CMMBCR [4] and CMRPC [5] can be viewed as a conditional variant of algorithms mentioned above.

To make existing algorithms continue to work when the nodes in network are selfish, we adopt the framework of algorithmic mechanism design. Algorithmic mechanism design considers the problems in a distributed environment where the participants cannot be assumed to follow the algorithm but rather their own self-interest. [3] proposed a formal model for such problems. It can be described as following:

In a distributed environment, there are n agents. Each agent i has some private information t^i, called its *type*. For a mechanism design problem, there is an *output specification* that maps each type vector to a set of allowed outputs $o \in O$. Agent i's preferences are given by a *valuation function* $v(o, t^i)$. A *mechanism* defines a family of *strategies* A^i for each agent i. For each strategy vector $(a^1, \ldots, a^n)$, $a^i \in A^i$, the mechanism computes an *output* $o = o(a^1, \ldots, a^n)$, and a *payment* vector $p = p(p^1, \ldots, p^n)$. Agent i's *utility* is $u^i = p^i - v(o, t^i)$. It is i's goal to maximize its utility. A mechanism is called *truthful* if for every agent i of type t^i and for every strategies a^{-i} of the other agents, i's utility is maximized when it declares its type t^i.

Several standard problems have been studied as the mechanism design problem [3]. In the context of wireless ad hoc network, [2] applies the mechanism design theory to ad hoc energy-efficient routing problem. They proposed a reactive routing protocol Ad hoc–VCG, which achieves the design objectives of truthfulness and energy-efficiency by paying to the intermediate nodes a premium over their actual costs for forwarding packets.

3 Problem Statement and Analysis

In this section, we present the mechanism design problem for lifetime-aware routing in wireless ad hoc networks by considering the selfish nodes.

In a wireless ad hoc network, there are m mobile nodes, each of which has a unique identification and belongs to different users. From the view of a node, it is selfish but economically rational, and its objective is to maximize its own benefit. A rational node means the node is willing to forward packets for others only when it can get payments equal or greater than what it desires. Now, a source node S wants to send a message to a destination node D. There are n possible paths can be found between S and D. Our problem is to select a path from these n possible paths to maximize the lifetime of network and ensure the truthfulness of this selected path.

Section 2 has reviewed some solutions that do not consider the impact of selfish nodes. After pondering existing algorithms, we find these algorithms can be represented by a common form as following:

Let function $g()$ be the common representation of lifetime of all nodes. The factors, such as the residual battery power of node and the transmission power between nodes, can be used as the parameters of $g()$. We treat the minimal lifetime of nodes in a path as the lifetime of the path, and select the path which has the maximal lifetime as the output path, i.e. the output path o can be obtained from the equation:

$$o = \underset{j \in A}{Max}(\underset{i \in j}{Min}(g(R_j^i, \dots))), \tag{1}$$

where R_j^i is the residual battery power of node i in path j, and A is the set of all possible paths.

As we have pointed out, a node may tend to be selfish. To prevent its battery power is consumed for other nodes, a node may refuse to relay packets, or declare a very low lifetime so that it cannot be selected as the relay node. In this case, existing algorithms will fail to work. Our objective is just to design a mechanism which ensures to route along the path selected by (1), and the path is truthful.

4 SMM Mechanism and Protocol

In this section, we propose SMM mechanism to cope with the selfish nodes. We also present a DSR-like protocol to implement our mechanism.

4.1   SMM Mechanism

To design a mechanism, we provide the output function of mechanism, define practical valuation function of nodes, and present appropriate payment function.

The output function $o()$ is given first. According to the lifetime declaration of each node (a node can declare its lifetime at will), the output function $o()$ selects a path from all possible paths by using (1). It can be represented as following:

$$o(a^1, \ldots, a^m) = \underset{j \in A}{Max}(\underset{i \in j}{Min}(a_j^i)), \tag{2}$$

where a^i is the lifetime declaration of node i, a_j^i is the lifetime declaration of node i in path j.

The valuation function of nodes is defined as following:

$$v(o, t^i) = \begin{cases} 0 & : \quad i \notin o \\ \frac{c}{t^i} & : \quad i \in o \end{cases}, \tag{3}$$

where t^i is the lifetime of node i, and o is the output path.

It means that i's evaluation is zero if i does not belong to o, and i's evaluation is inversely proportion to its lifetime if i is one of the node in o. Intuitively, the shorter lifetime i has, the more likely that i is not willing to forward packets for other nodes. Therefore, i would expect more payments.

The goal of a node is to maximize its utility, so it tends to choose favorable strategy and become truthless. If a node declares false lifetime, $o()$ may select an improper path. We have to design an appropriate payment function which can meet the needs of nodes while compatible with the output of algorithm.

We treat the minimal lifetime declaration of nodes in path j as j's lifetime declaration. Assume that the nodes whose lifetime declaration is minimal in all n possible paths are $q_1, \ldots, q_n$, then the lifetime declarations of these n paths are $a_1^{q_1}, \ldots, a_{n-1}^{q_{n-1}}, a_n^{q_n}$. We can simply denote them as $a_1, \ldots, a_{n-1}, a_n$. Without losing generality, we assume $a_1 \leq \ldots \leq a_{n-1} \leq a_n$. The output would be the path n. The payment function $p()$ is defined as following:

$$p(a_j^i) = \begin{cases} 0 & : \quad \forall j \neq n, i \in j \\ \frac{c}{a_{n-1}} & : \quad j = n, i \in n \end{cases}, \tag{4}$$

where c is a constant.

It means that the payments to nodes which do not belong to the output path would be zero, and the payments to nodes in the output path are related to the path which has the second maximum lifetime declaration in all possible paths.

We call our mechanism the Second-Max-Min (SMM) mechanism and will prove the truthfulness of SMM mechanism in the next section.

4.2   Protocol

DSR [7] protocol is an reactive routing protocol which is used to find the shortest hop path between source and destination. To meet the need of the implementation of our SMM mechanism, we make some modifications to DSR protocol.

First, the lifetime declaration of each intermediate node, which is equal to its type through SMM mechanism, is recorded in the request packet. Type is private information for each node. To prevent a node's type information from being known or altered by other nodes, we adopt a PKI-based security model. In this model, the keyed *encryption algorithm* is known to all the nodes in the network, the *encryption* and *decryption keys* are generated by S. When S starts the route discovery phase, it puts the encryption key in the route request packet. Every intermediate node uses the encryption key in the received route request packet and the public encryption algorithm to encrypt its private lifetime declaration. After receiving the route reply packet, S uses the decryption key to decrypt the lifetime declaration of each intermediate node in the packet.

Second, instead of selecting the shortest hop path, we try to choose a path which can maximize the lifetime of network. When S wants to send a packet to D, it starts a timer and launches the route discovery phase. During a period of time T, S may receive several possible paths from the destination. Each path has the information of lifetime declaration of nodes in the path. S can choose a path from these paths by using the output function $o()$ and calculate the payments to each node in the selected path by using the payment function $p()$.

Third, we avoid the route cache optimization techniques used in DSR. The cached routes cannot represent the current state of nodes because every node's type keeps changing. In our implementation, the source node periodically refreshes its cache and triggers a new route discovery process, the intermediate node does not respond to the route requests with cached routes.

Last, unlike DSR, a node processes the route request packet even it has seen the request before. We cannot simply discard the packet because the later arrived packet may have longer minimal lifetime declaration. Therefore, we ignore the judgment whether the node has seen the request before. To prevent heavy traffic, node will discard a packet if it has seen the request more than several times.

5   SMM Mechanism Analysis

In this section, we will show that the design of SMM mechanism can ensure the routing algorithm get its desired output in the presence of selfish nodes.

First, our mechanism guarantees the voluntary participation of all nodes. If a node can get payments equal to or greater than its valuation, it is willing to participate in the protocols. It can be shown that no matter a node belongs to the output path or not, its utility is non-negative in our mechanism.

Second, our mechanism is truthful. It is clear that if all nodes declare their type ($a_j^i = t_j^i$), our mechanism will guarantee the source node chooses algorithm desired path. Here, we prove that SMM mechanism is truthful.

Theorem 1. *SMM mechanism is truthful.*

Proof. To prove our mechanism is truthful, we need to show that every node cannot get more utility than what it gets when declaring its true lifetime, that is cheating cannot increase the utility of a node. We get it in two steps:

First, the lifetime declaration of each path is truthful. We treat the nodes in a path as an entity, and consider the behavior of the path. Assume that there are n possible paths between S and D, and the lifetime of these n paths are $a_1, \ldots, a_{n-1}, a_n$ ($a_1 \leq \ldots \leq a_{n-1} \leq a_n$).

- The path n can be selected as the output path if it declares its true lifetime, its utility u is $\frac{l_n \cdot c}{a_{n-1}} - \sum_{k=1}^{l_n} \frac{c}{a_n^{i_k}} \geq 0$, where l_n is the number of nodes except S and D in path n. Now path n declares a false lifetime $\overline{a_n}$. If $\overline{a_n} \geq a_{n-1}$, n still can be selected as the output path, and its utility does not change. If $\overline{a_n} < a_{n-1}$, n cannot be selected as the output path, and its utility is zero.
- The other paths cannot be selected as the output path if they declare their true lifetime, their utility are zero. Now a path j declares a false lifetime $\overline{a_j}$. If $\overline{a_j} < a_n$, j still cannot be selected as the output path, its utility will not change. If $\overline{a_j} \geq a_n$, j can be selected as the output path, its utility u' is $\frac{l_j \cdot c}{a_n} - \sum_{k=1}^{l_j} \frac{c}{a_j^{i_k}}$, but its expected utility u is larger than u' because $u \geq \frac{l_j \cdot c}{a_j} - \sum_{k=1}^{l_j} \frac{c}{a_j^{i_k}} > u'$. Therefore, there must exist some nodes in path j, such as the node with the minimal lifetime, their utility decrease.

Second, the lifetime declaration of each node in a path is truthful. We consider a node i in path j. No matter i is the node which has the minimal lifetime in path j or not, i cannot get more utility if it declares a false lifetime. The analysis is similar as the first one, we omit it here.

To measure the payment, we define *payment ratio*: Lets path j be the output path, payment ratio is the ratio of payment for path j to valuation of path j. We have following theorem for payment ratio.

Theorem 2. *For SMM mechanism, let path j be the output path, which has the maximum lifetime in all possible paths from S to D; and path s has the second maximum lifetime. Let $Max(a_j^i)$ denote the maximal lifetime declaration of nodes in path j, $Min(a_j^i)$ denote the minimal lifetime declaration of nodes in path j, and $Min(a_s^i)$ denote the minimal lifetime declaration of nodes in path s, then:*

$$\frac{Min(a_j^i)}{Min(a_s^i)} \leq \beta \leq \frac{Max(a_j^i)}{Min(a_s^i)} \tag{5}$$

Proof. We omit the proof due to limitations of space.

The payment ratio β can be used as an important metric to the performance of mechanism. If β is close to 1, the premium that the source node pays to intermediate nodes is low. It means that the mechanism achieves the design objective of algorithm at little additional cost. While β is far more than 1, the premium that the source node pays to intermediate nodes is high. It means that the mechanism achieves the design objective of algorithm at high additional cost. The essence of a lifetime-aware routing algorithm is to distribute the power consumption evenly among nodes, which leads to the result that the lifetime of nodes has the tendency of closing to each other. From Theorem 2, we can conclude that β is close to 1 when the maximal lifetime of nodes in the output path is close to the minimal lifetime of nodes in path which has the second maximum lifetime. Therefore, we can infer that SMM mechanism has excellent payment ratio, which is relatively small and stable.

6   Experiment

We conducted experiments to evaluate the payment ratio of SMM mechanism. The simulation consisted of a network of 50 nodes randomly distributed over a $700 \times 700 m^2$ area. We used the CBR traffic at 4 packets per second, and the packet size was 512 bytes. Random connections were established. The source node refreshed its cache every other 10 sec. Each node was given enough battery power to finish the experiments. The initial values of battery power in all nodes are same. A node could dynamically adjust its transmission power based on the link distance d, and the transmission cost h is $K \cdot d^\alpha$, where α is the signal loss exponent. Two lifetime-aware routing algorithms, MMBCR and MRPC, were implemented. We try to find the influence of different parameters (such as the link distance d, the signal loss exponent α) on payment ratio.

In Fig.1, we present the payment ratio in MMBCR when $\alpha = 2$. It can be observed that the ratio payment is very small and close to 1. We compare the situations when the maximum transmission range R of nodes is $150m$, $200m$ and $250m$ respectively. The effect of transmission range increment lies in two aspects: (1) Each node covers more nodes, so there are more possible paths between the source node and the destination node. It will increase the balance of traffic on nodes and reduce the lifetime variance between nodes; (2) The range of transmission cost will increase due to $h = K \cdot d^\alpha$, which increases the lifetime variance between nodes. In Fig.1, we can find that the payment ratio for $R = 150m$ is higher than the payment ratio for $R = 200m$ and $R = 250m$. This result can be viewed as the effect of the first aspect. The payment ratio for $R = 200m$ is close to the payment ratio for $R = 250m$, which can be viewed as the balance between these two aspects.

In Fig.2, we present the payment ratio in MRPC when $R = 150$. In MRPC, the lifetime of a node is the ratio of its residual battery power to its transmission cost (we does not consider the link's packet error probability). Though the initial battery power of all nodes is same, the transmission cost of nodes is different because the transmission cost relates to the link distance. This experiment can be viewed as a simulation of the initial lifetime of all nodes is different. From Fig.2, we see that the payment ratio increases with the increment of α. It is because that the higher α, the higher the difference between initial lifetime of nodes. As we have pointed out, a lifetime-aware routing algorithm tries to minimize the variance of lifetime between nodes to increase the lifetime of network. It can be observed in Fig.2 that the payment ratio decreases with time.

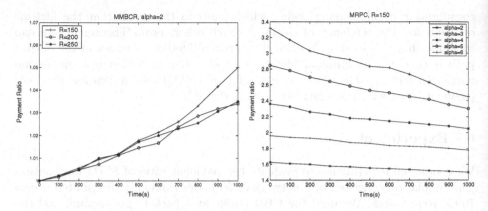

Fig. 1. β vs. R in MMBCR   **Fig. 2.** β vs. α in MRPC

7   Conclusion

In this paper, we dealt with the problem of maximum lifetime routing in ad hoc network with selfish nodes. By applying the framework of algorithm mechanism design, we designed a mechanism SMM. The basic idea of our mechanism is giving appropriate payments to stimulate the cooperation of nodes, and cheating can not increase or even lose the utility. In SMM mechanism, the payments to nodes in the output path are related to the path which has the second maximum lifetime in all possible paths. We proved that SMM mechanism is truthful, and purposed a routing algorithm to implement SMM mechanism. Finally, we conducted experiments to evaluate the performance of our mechanism.

References

1. E. Royer and C-K Toh, A Review of Current Routing Protocols for Ad-Hoc Mobile Wireless Networks, *IEEE Personal Communications Magazine*, April 1999.
2. L. Anderegg and S. Eidenbenz, Ad hoc-VCG: a truthful and cost-efficient routing protocol for mobile ad hoc networks with selfish agents. *Proc. of MobiCom'03*.
3. N. Nisan and A. Ronen, Algorithmic mechanism design, *Proc. of STOC'99*.
4. C.K.Toh, Maximum Battery Life Routing to Support Ubiquitous Mobile Computing in Wireless Ad hoc Networks, *IEEE Communication Magazine*, June 2001.
5. A. Misra and S. Banerjee, MRPC: Maximizing Network Lifetime for reliable routing in Wireless Environments, *IEEE WCNC'02*.
6. M. Maleki, K. Dantu and M. Pedram, Lifetime Prediction Routing in Mobile Ad Hoc Networks, *IEEE WCNC'03*.
7. D. Johnson and D. Maltz. Dynamic source routing in ad hoc wireless networks, *Mobile Computing*, pages 153–181. Kluwer Academic Publishers, 1996.
8. C. E. Jones, K. M. Sivalingam, P. Agrawal, and J. C. Chen, A survey of energy efficient network protocols for wireless networks. *Wireless Networks*, 2001.
9. S. Buchegger and J. Le Boudec, Cooperative Routing in Mobile Ad-hoc Networks: Current Efforts Against Malice and Selfishness, *Proc. of Informatik'02*.

A Dioid Linear Algebra Approach to Study a Class of Continuous Petri Nets

Duan Zhang, Huaping Dai, Youxian Sun

National Laboratory of Industrial Control Technology, Zhejiang University, Hangzhou,
P.R.China, 310027
{dzhang, hpdai, yxsun}@iipc.zju.edu.cn

Abstract. Continuous Event Graphs (CEGs), a subclass of Continuous Petri Nets, are defined as the limiting cases of timed event graphs and Timed Event Multigraphs. A set of dioid algebraic linear equations will be inferred as a novel method of analyzing a special class of CEG, if treated the cumulated token consumed by transitions as state-variables, endowed the monotone nondecreasing functions pointwise minimum as addition, and endowed the lower-semicontinuous mappings, from the collection of monotone nondecreasing functions to itself, the pointwise minimum as addition and composition of mappings as multiplication. As a new modeling approach, it clearly illustrate characteristic of continuous events. Based on the algebraic model, an example of optimal Control is demonstrated.

1 Introduction

It is well know that max-plus algebra is powerful tools for Discrete Event Dynamic Systems (DEDS) [1-3]. Min-plus algebra is the dual of max-plus algebra, and they are both dioid, an idempotent semiring.

Linear model is so popular that it is adopted by most of classic control theory. Many evidences support that max-plus algebra, min-plus algebra, dioid and some other idempotent semirings are appropriate mathematic tools to describe the phenomena of DEDSs, especially synchronization. With the operations of above algebraic systems, some logic nonlinear formulae come to linear formulae. As a by-product of the linearization, the existence of an eventual periodic regime is readily obtained, the performance being characterized in terms of invariants of the original net [3].

An event graph is a Petri net such that each place has only one input arc and one output arc. Timed Event Graphs (TEG) are a subclass of event graphs satisfied that the tokens have to stay a minimum amount of time in the places. The dynamic of TEGs can be represented as a max-plus linear algebraic model [1]. Timed Event Multigraphs (TEMGs), each arc has an integral weight, are extensions of TEGs. The max-plus linear algebraic model of TEMGs was built by G. Cohen [2] and HuaPing Dai [3] in different way respectively. By those linear formulae, the analyses of TEGs and TEMGs are analogous to traditional linear system theory.

H. Jin et al. (Eds.): NPC 2004, LNCS 3222, pp. 333-340, 2004.

Comparing with TEGs or TEMGs, Continuous Event Graphs (CEGs), proposed by R. David and H. Alla [4-6], have continuous places and continuous transitions. As a limiting case of TEMGs, CEGs are applied to describe the continuous events system [7-11], for example the flow control and congest control of TCP [12]. Unfortunately, the building of algebraic model for CEGs is more difficult than TEMGs. G. Cohen [2] induce a min-plus algebraic model considered only the case of continuous places, but no the case of continuous transitions. There is no universal algebraic model is constructed for CEGs so far.

In Section 2, the definition of CEG is reviewed. Some properties of CEGs will be presented in Section 3. A dioid linear algebraic representation of a class of CEGs is given in Section 4 and an example will tackled in Section 5 with the new model.

2   Definition of CEG

Let R is the set of real, $\varpi = +\infty$, $\bar{R} = R \bigcup \{\varpi\}$ and $R^+ = [0, +\infty) \bigcup \{\varpi\}$.

Definition 1. A CEG is a 6-tuplet: $< P, T, R, W, V, M_0 >$; P is a set of continuous places; T is a set of continuous transitions; $R = R_{PT} \bigcup R_{TP}$, where $R_{PT} \subseteq P \times T$ and $R_{TP} \subseteq T \times P$, $< n_1, n_2 > \in R$ represent that n_1 is a input of n_2 and n_2 is a output of n_1; $W : R \to R^+$ is the weight of R; $V : T \to R^+$ is the maximum firing velocities of transitions; $M_0 : P \to R^+$ is the initial markings of places; every place has only one input transition and one output transition; moreover we assume that every transition have at least one input place and one output place.

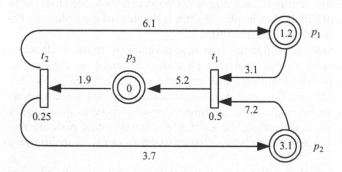

Fig. 1. A CEG

CEGs can be illustrated by directed graphs (Fig. 1) that denote continuous places as double circle, denote continuous transitions as rectangle, and denote the elements of R as arrow.

Definition 2. Let t be a transition, $^\circ t = \{p \in P \,|< p, t > \in R_{PT}\}$ is called the preset of t, $t^\circ = \{p \in P \,|< t, p > \in R_{TP}\}$ is called the postset of t; Let p be a place,

$°p = \{t \in T \mid < t, p > \in R_{TP}\}$ is called the preset of p, $p° = \{t \in T \mid < p, t > \in R_{PT}\}$ is called the postset of p.

Definition 3. Let $Mark(p,\tau)$ denote the token of place p at the epoch τ, $\overline{V}(t,\tau)$ denote the firing velocity of transition t, then:

1) $\overline{V}(t,0) = 0$;

2) if $\forall p \in °t$ $Mark(p,\tau) > 0$, then $\overline{V}(t,\tau) = V(t)$;

3) if $\exists p \in °t$ $Mark(p,\tau) = 0$, denote $T_0 = \{t_0 \in °p \mid p \in °t$ and $Mark(p,\tau) = 0\}$,

then $\overline{V}(t,\tau) = \min\{\min_{p \in T_0}\{\overline{V}(°p,\tau) \times W(°p,p)/W(p,t)\}, V(t)\}$. Note that if there is a

loop satisfied that for any place p in the loop $Mark(p,\tau) - 0$, then for any transition

t in the loop, $\overline{V}(t,\tau) = 0$.

Remark 1. The firing of transition t can lead change of the token of some places:

1) if $p \in t°$, then $\int_{\tau_2}^{\tau_1} W(t,p)\overline{V}(t,\tau) \cdot d\tau$ represents the mark input p from t in

time interval $[\tau_1, \tau_2]$;

2) if $p \in °t$, then $\int_{\tau_2}^{\tau_1} -W(p,t)\overline{V}(t,\tau) \cdot d\tau$ represents the mark input t from p in

time interval $[\tau_1, \tau_2]$.

3   Properties of CEGs

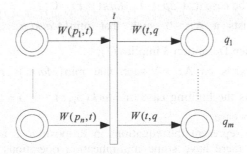

Fig. 2. A continuous transition

Definition 4. $M_{(\cdot)} : [0,+\infty) \to \mathrm{R}^+$ is a monotone nondecreasing function:

1) if $t \in T$, $M_t(\tau)$ is the total mark t consumed from the epoch 0 to τ, namely

$M_t(\tau) = \int_0^\tau \overline{V}(t,u)du$;

2) if $p \in P$, $M_p(\tau)$ is the total mark entered p from the epoch 0 to τ, namely

$$M_p(\tau) = M_0(p) + \int_0^\tau \overline{V}(t,u)du ;$$

Then we consider transition t with $^\circ t = \{p_1, p_2, \dots, p_n\}$ and $t^\circ = \{q_1, q_2, \dots, q_m\}$ as Fig.2.

Proposition 1. For the input places of t,

$$M_{p_i}(\tau) = Mark(p_i, \tau) + M_t(\tau) W(p_i, t) \quad i = 1, 2, \dots, n ; \tag{1}$$

for the output places of t,

$$M_{q_i}(\tau) = M_{q_i}(0) + M_t(\tau) W(t, q_i) \quad i = 1, 2, \dots, m . \tag{2}$$

Proposition 2. Let $t \in T$, there exists $\Delta\tau > 0$ satisfied

$$M_t(\tau + \Delta\tau) = M_t(\tau) + \min\{V(t) \cdot \Delta\tau, M_{p_i}(\tau + \Delta\tau) - M_t(\tau) \cdot W(p_i, t), \quad i = 1, \dots, n\} . \tag{3}$$

Proof. Assume that $Mark(p_i, \tau) > 0 \quad i = 1, 2, \dots, n$. let

$$0 < \Delta\tau < \min_i\{\frac{Mark(p_i, \tau)}{W(p_i, t)V(t)}\} , \tag{4}$$

then $\overline{V}(t, \tau) = V(t)$ holds in time interval $[\tau, \tau + \Delta\tau]$; and

$$M_{p_i}(\tau + \Delta\tau) - M_t(\tau) \cdot W(p_i, t) \geq M_{p_i}(\tau) - M_t(\tau) \cdot W(p_i, t) > V(t) \cdot \Delta\tau , \tag{5}$$

thus (3) satisfied.

Now consider the case that $\exists p \in {}^\circ t \ Mark(p, \tau) = 0$:

1) if there exists a $\Delta\tau > 0$ such that $\min_i\{Mark(p_i, \tau_1)\} = 0$ holds for all $\tau \leq \tau_1 \leq \tau + \Delta\tau$, then Definition 3 implies (3);

2) else there exists no $\Delta\tau > 0$ such that $\min_i\{Mark(p_i, \tau_1)\} = 0$ holds for all $\tau \leq \tau_1 \leq \tau + \Delta\tau$. As the limiting case of $Mark(p_i, \tau) > 0 \quad i = 1, 2, \dots, n$, inequality (3) still holds in this case. □

It is impossible to represent the equations in Proposition 2 as max-plus algebraic linear form, since there have some multiplication operations that are exponential operations under max-plus algebra.

4   Dioid Representation of a Class of CEGs

M is a collection of functions, $\forall \lambda \in M \ \lambda : R \to R^+$, and λ is monotone nondecreasing. A minimization operation $\oplus$ in $\overline{R}$ is defined by

$$\forall r_1, r_2 \in \overline{R} \ r_1 \oplus r_2 = \min(r_1, r_2) . \tag{6}$$

Define the operation $\oplus$ in M as point wise minimization

$$\forall \lambda_1, \lambda_2 \in M \ \lambda_1(\tau) \oplus \lambda_2(\tau) = \min\left(\lambda_1(\tau), \lambda_2(\tau)\right). \tag{7}$$

Obviously, $\forall \lambda \in M \ 0 \oplus \lambda(\tau) = \lambda(\tau)$ and $0 \in M$.

Proposition 3. $\langle M, \oplus \rangle$ is a monoid, the identity element is 0, $\oplus$ is commutative and idempotent.

Proposition 4. $\forall \{\lambda_i\} \subseteq M \ \bigoplus_i \lambda_i(\tau) \in M$, namely M is complete.

A partial-order $\leq$ is induced from $\oplus$ as follow:

$$\forall \lambda_1, \lambda_2 \in M \ \lambda_1(\tau) \leq \lambda_2(\tau) \iff \lambda_1(\tau) \oplus \lambda_2(\tau) = \lambda_2(\tau). \tag{8}$$

Definition 5. Mapping $f : M \to M$ is said to be lower-semicontinuous (l.s.c.) [3] if

$$\forall \{\lambda_i\} \subseteq M \ \bigoplus_i f(\lambda_i(\tau)) = f\left(\bigoplus_i \lambda_i(\tau)\right). \tag{9}$$

Proposition 5. All the l.s.c. mappings on M , denoted F , can be induced a dioid with two operations, $\oplus$ and $\otimes$, defined as follow:

$$\forall f_1, f_2 \in F \ \forall \lambda \in M \quad (f_1 \oplus f_2)(\lambda) = f_1(\lambda) \oplus f_2(\lambda) \tag{10}$$
$$(f_1 \otimes f_2)(\lambda) = f_1(f_2(\lambda)).$$

According to Proposition 4 and Proposition 5, the following holds.

Corollary 1. F is Complete.

For briefness, $\otimes$ may be omitted.

Proposition 6. Let $k \in N$ and $k > 0$, $x \in M^k$ be a variable vector, $v \in M^k$ be constant one, and $A \in F^{k \times k}$, the least solution of equations $x = Ax \oplus v$ is $x = A^* v$, where $A^* = \bigoplus_{i=0}^{\infty} A^i$ [1].

Definition 6. $\forall \lambda \in M$

1) add mapping $[r^+]$, $r \in [0, +\infty)$: $[r^+] \lambda(\tau) = \lambda(\tau) + r$;

2) multiplication mapping $[r^\times]$, $r \in R^+$: $[r^\times] \lambda(\tau) = r \cdot \lambda(\tau)$.

The symbol [ ] may be omitted if no ambiguity. Note that 0^+ and $1^\times$ are both the identity element of $< M, \otimes >$.

Let $F_1 = \{[r^+] \mid r \in [0, +\infty)\}$, $F_2 = \{[r^\times] \mid r \in R^+\}$, and

$$F_0 = \{\bigoplus_{i=1}^{m} \bigotimes_{j=1}^{n} f_{ij} \mid f_{ij} \in F_1 \cup F_2 \ i, j, m, n \in N\}. \tag{11}$$

Theorem 1. $F_0 \in F$.

Proof. Because all the elements of $F_1 \cup F_2$ is l.s.c. . □

Given a class of CEGs satisfied

$$\forall t \in T \quad \max\{V(t_i)\frac{W(t_i, p_i)}{W(p_i, t)} \quad t_i \in {}^{\circ}({}^{\circ}t), p_i = t_i{}^{\circ}\} \leq V(t) . \tag{12}$$

Theorem 2. Performances of the class of CEGs above mentioned could be described as linear algebraic equations.

Proof. Considering a transition $t_k \in T_C$, given that ${}^{\circ}({}^{\circ}t_k) = \{t_{ki} \mid t_{ki} \in {}^{\circ}({}^{\circ}t_k)\} \subseteq T_C$, as above assumed. Let $v_k(\tau) = V(t_k)\tau$, $p_{ki} = t_{ki}{}^{\circ}$, $m_{ki} = \dfrac{M_{p_{ki}}(0)}{W(p_{ki}, t_k)}$, $w_{ki} = \dfrac{W(t_{ki}, p_{ki})}{W(p_{ki}, t_k)}$.

The following equation holds.

$$M_{t_k}(\tau) = \min\{V(t_k)\tau, \frac{M_{p_{ki}}(0) + M_{t_{ki}}(\tau) \cdot W(t_{ki}, p_{ki})}{W(p_{ki}, t_k)}\} . \tag{13}$$

In fact, according to (12), on the one hand once a transition t_{ki} satisfied $Mark(t_{ki}, \tau_0) = 0$, $\forall \tau \geq \tau_0 \ \exists k_{i'} \ s.t. \ Mark(t_{ki'}, \tau) = 0$; On the other hand, let $\tau_0 = \min\{\tau \mid \neg \exists t_{ki} \ Mark(t_{ki}, \tau) = 0\}$, then $\tau_0 = 0$. (13) can be represented as follow:

$$M_{t_k}(\tau) = \bigoplus_{ki}[m_{ki}{}^+][w_{ki}{}^\times]M_{t_{ki}}(\tau) \oplus v_k . \tag{14}$$

Let $x = (t_1, t_2, ..., t_{|T|})^T$ and $v = (v_1, v_2, ..., v_{|T|})^T$. (14) imply

$$x = Ax \oplus v \tag{15}$$

where $A = (a_{ij})$ is a mapping matrix, and $a_{ij} = [m_{ij}{}^+][w_{ij}{}^\times]$.

Corollary 2. The least solution to (15) is $x = A^*v$.

5   Example of Optimal Control

A manufacturing system represented by a CEG is shown in Fig. 5, where $V(t_1) = 1$, $V(t_2) = 1$, $V(t_3) = 1$, $V(t_4) = 1$, $M_{p_1}(0) = 1$, $M_{p_2}(0) = 0$, $M_{p_3}(0) = 1$, $M_{p_4}(0) = 1$, $M_{p_5}(0) = 1$ and $M_{p_6}(0) = m$.

Using Theorem 2, the following equations holds

$$M(\tau) := \begin{bmatrix} M_{t_1}(\tau) \\ M_{t_2}(\tau) \\ M_{t_3}(\tau) \\ M_{t_4}(\tau) \end{bmatrix} = \begin{bmatrix} \varpi & 1^+ & \varpi & \varpi \\ 1^+ & \varpi & m^+ & \varpi \\ \varpi & 1^+ & \varpi & 1^+ \\ \varpi & 1^+ & \varpi & \varpi \end{bmatrix} \begin{bmatrix} M_{t_1}(\tau) \\ M_{t_2}(\tau) \\ M_{t_3}(\tau) \\ M_{t_4}(\tau) \end{bmatrix} \oplus \begin{bmatrix} \tau \\ \tau \\ \tau \\ \tau \end{bmatrix} := AM(\tau) \oplus v . \tag{16}$$

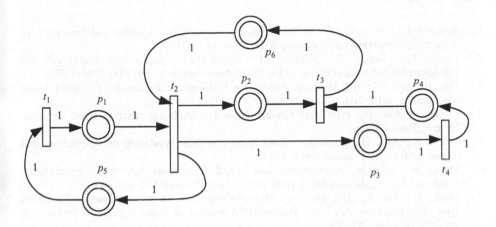

Fig. 3. Example of represented a CEG by dioid Equations

According *Corollary 2*, the least solution to (16) is

$$A^{\bullet}v = \begin{bmatrix} 0^{+} & 1^{+} & (m+1)^{+} & (m+2)^{+} \\ 1^{+} & 0^{+} & m^{+} & (m+1)^{+} \\ 2^{+} & 1^{+} & 0^{+} & 1^{+} \\ 2^{+} & 1^{+} & (m+1)^{+} & 0^{+} \end{bmatrix} \begin{bmatrix} \tau \\ \tau \\ \tau \\ \tau \end{bmatrix}. \tag{17}$$

The solution indicate that m are cannot affect the firing velocity of transition t_3, but that of t_1, t_2 and t_4.

6   Conclusion

In this note, a linear algebraic model $\langle F, \oplus, \otimes \rangle$ for performance evaluation of a class of Continuous event graph has been developed. And an interesting and useful result of the example gives us a novel approach to compute the minimum (optimal) initial tokens of places in a CEG by its algebraic model.

Acknowledgement

This work was supported by National Natural Science Foundation of China (60304018).

References

1. Baccelli, F., Cohen, G., Olsder, G.J., Quadrat, J.P.: Synchronization and Linearity: An Algebra for Discrete Event Systems. Wiley, New York (1992)
2. Cohen, G., Gaubert, S., Quadrat, J.P.: Timed-events graphs with multipliers and homogeneous Min-plus systems. IEEE Trans. Automat.Contr. 43(1998) 1296–1302
3. Dai, H., Sun, Y.: An Algebraic Model for Performance Evaluation of Timed Event Multigraphs. IEEE Trans. Automat. Contr. 48(2003) 1227–1230
4. David, R, Alla, H.: Petri Nets Grafcet Tools for Modeling Discrete Event Systems. Hermes, Paris (1992).
5. David, R., Alla, H.: Continuous Petri Nets. European Workshop on Application and Theory of Petri Nets. Saragosse (1987)
6. David, R., Alla, H.: Autonomous and Timed Continuous Petri Nets. International Conference on Application and Theory of Petri Nets. Paris (1990) 367-386
7. David, R., Xie, X., Alla, H.: Properties of Continuous Models of Transfer Lineswith Unreliable machines and Finite Buffers. IMA Journal of Math. Applied in Business & Industry. 6 (1990) 281-308
8. Alla, H., David, R.: Modeling of Production Systems by Continuous Petri Nets. 3rd International Conference on CAD/CAM, CARS & FOF88. Detroit 3(1988)
9. Le Bail, J., Alla, H., David, R.: Hybrid Petri Net. European Control Conference. Grenoble (1991) 1472-1477
10. Le Bail, J., Alla, H., David, R.: Asymptotic Continuous Petri Nets: An efficient Approximation of Discrete event Systems. IEEE International Conference on Robotics and Automation. Nice (1992)
11. Zerhouni, N., Alla, H.: Asymptotic Continuous Petri Nets: An efficient Approximation of Discrete event Systems. IEEE International Conference on Robotics and Automation. Cincinnati. Cincinnati 2(1990) 1070-1075
12. Baccelli, F., Hong, D.: TCP is Max-Plus Linear and what it tells us on its throughput. INRIA Report. Paris (2000)

A Fully Adaptive Fault-Tolerant Routing Methodology Based on Intermediate Nodes[*]

N.A. Nordbotten[1], M.E. Gómez[2], J. Flich[2], P. López[2], A. Robles[2], T. Skeie[1], O. Lysne[1], and J. Duato[2]

[1] Simula Research Laboratory, P.O. Box 134, N-1325 Lysaker, Norway
nilsno@simula.no
[2] Dept. of Computer Engineering, Universidad Politécnica de Valencia, Camino de Vera, 14, 46071-Valencia, Spain
megomez@gap.upv.es

Abstract. Massively parallel computing systems are being built with thousands of nodes. Because of the high number of components, it is critical to keep these systems running even in the presence of failures. Interconnection networks play a key-role in these systems, and this paper proposes a fault-tolerant routing methodology for use in such networks. The methodology supports any minimal routing function (including fully adaptive routing), does not degrade performance in the absence of faults, does not disable any healthy node, and is easy to implement both in meshes and tori. In order to avoid network failures, the methodology uses a simple mechanism: for some source-destination pairs, packets are forwarded to the destination node through a set of intermediate nodes (without being ejected from the network). The methodology is shown to tolerate a large number of faults (e.g., five/nine faults when using two/three intermediate nodes in a 3D torus). Furthermore, the methodology offers a gracious performance degradation: in an $8 \times 8 \times 8$ torus network with 14 faults the throughput is only decreased by 6.49%.

Keywords: fault-tolerance, direct networks, adaptive routing, virtual channels, bubble flow control.

1 Introduction

There exist many compute-intensive applications that require a huge amount of processing power, and this required computing power can only be provided by massively parallel computers. Examples of these systems are the Earth Simulator [12], the ASCI Red [1], and the BlueGene/L [2].

The huge number of processors and associated devices (memories, switches, links, etc.) significantly increases the probability of failure. It is therefore critical to keep such systems running even in the presence of failures. Much work deal

---

[*] This work was supported by the Spanish MCYT under Grant TIC2003-08154-C06-01.

H. Jin et al. (Eds.): NPC 2004, LNCS 3222, pp. 341–356, 2004.

with failures of processors and memories. In this paper, we consider failures in the interconnection network. These failures may isolate a large fraction of the machine, wasting many healthy processors that otherwise could have been used. Therefore, fault-tolerant mechanisms for interconnection networks are becoming a critical design issue for large massively parallel computers.

There exist several approaches to tolerate failures in the interconnection network. The most prominent technique in commercial systems consists of replicating components. The spare components are switched on in the case of failure while switching off (or bypassing) the faulty components. The main drawback of this approach is the high extra cost of the spare components. Another powerful technique is based on reconfiguring the routing tables in the case of failure, adapting them to the new topology after the failure [5]. This technique is extremely flexible, but this flexibility may also kill performance. However, most of the solutions proposed in the literature are based on designing fault-tolerant routing algorithms able to find an alternative path when a packet meets a fault along the path to its destination. Most of these fault-tolerant routing strategies require a significant amount of extra hardware resources (e.g., virtual channels) to route packets around faulty components depending on either the number of tolerated faults [9] or the number of dimensions in the topology [17]. Alternatively, there exist some fault-tolerant routing strategies that use none or a very small number of extra resources to handle failures at the expense of providing a lower fault-tolerance degree [9,14], disabling a certain number of healthy nodes (either in blocks (fault regions) [6,7] or individually [10,11]), preventing packets from being routed adaptively [15], or drastically increasing the latencies for some packets [19]. Moreover, when faults occur, link utilization may become significantly unbalanced when using those fault-tolerant routing strategies, thus leading to premature network saturation, and consequently, degrading network performance even more.

In [13] we proposed a fault-tolerant routing methodology for n-dimensional meshes and tori, and that only requires one extra virtual channel. In order to avoid network failures, an intermediate node is used for some source-destination pairs.[3] This node is selected in such a way that the faults are avoided when the packets are routed first to the intermediate node and then from this node to the destination node. However, in order to tolerate an acceptable number of faults, an additional mechanism is used, that is, disabling adaptive routing for some paths (i.e., routing packets deterministically).

Disabling adaptivity has two main drawbacks: The first is that it has a negative impact on network performance, because it prevents packets from being adaptively routed. The second is that it needs additional complexity at the routers in order to enable turning off adaptivity on a per packet basis. For these reasons it would be beneficial to use a single mechanism only. In this paper we propose a methodology solely based on intermediate nodes, but instead of using only one intermediate node, we propose to use several ones in order to cir-

---

[3] Intermediate nodes were introduced by Valiant [21] for other purposes, such as traffic balance.

cumvent faulty components. This way, regardless of the number of intermediate nodes being used, the way packets are being routed does not need to be modified, allowing the same router design as in the absence of intermediate nodes to be used. Furthermore, this methodology allows all packets to be adaptively routed, which again contributes to a good network performance.

On the other hand, this approach requires using additional virtual channels as long as more intermediate nodes are used. However, virtual channels are nowadays inexpensive. Current interconnects are able to provide several virtual channels. This is the case for the Cray T3E [20] with five virtual channels, the BlueGene/L [2] with four virtual channels, and InfiniBand switches [16] with 16 virtual channels.

Still, when designing a fault-tolerant routing scheme that requires extra virtual channels, it is desirable to use a bounded number of virtual channels. At the same time one should also tolerate a reasonably large number of faults, avoid disabling any healthy node, maintain a low router complexity, and guarantee routing through adaptive paths in order to provide high network performance both in the absence and in the presence of faults.

The rest of the paper is organized as follows. In Sect. 2, the methodology is presented. The methodology is then illustrated through some example scenarios in Sect. 3. In Sect. 4, the routing algorithm obtained by the methodology is analyzed in terms of performance and fault-tolerance. Finally, in Sect. 5, some conclusions are drawn.

2   The Methodology

The methodology for achieving fault-tolerance through the use of one or more intermediate nodes will now be presented. We will assume a k-ary n-cube (torus) or n-dimensional mesh network. The methodology is valid for any minimal routing function, although it is applied to minimal adaptive routing [18] in this paper. Minimal adaptive routing with v virtual channels allows the use of any minimal path through $v - 1$ virtual (adaptive) channels, whereas the last channel (i.e., the escape channel) uses deterministic routing. Thus, at least two virtual channels per physical channel ($v = 2$) are required. In a torus the escape channel also uses the bubble flow control mechanism [4].

Furthermore, a static fault model is assumed. This means that when a fault is discovered all the processes are stopped, the network is emptied, and a management application is run in order to deal with the fault. Checkpointing techniques must also be used so that applications can be brought back to a consistent state prior to the fault occurred. Detection of faults, checkpointing, and distribution of routing info is assumed to be performed as part of the static fault model, and are therefore not further discussed in this paper.

A fault-free path is computed by the methodology for each source-destination pair. In the presence of faults, those paths that may use some faulty components are not valid. The methodology avoids these faults by using intermediate nodes. Packets are first forwarded to the first intermediate node, then from this node to the second one, and so forth until the packet reaches its final destination. As shown in Fig. 1, the use of intermediate nodes reduces the number of possible paths, and therefore enables avoiding areas containing faults. The original routing algorithm (e.g., minimal adaptive routing) is used in all subpaths. Notice that the packets are not ejected from the network at each intermediate node.

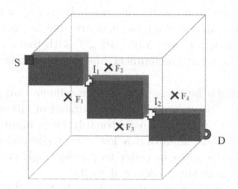

Fig. 1. The use of intermediate nodes (I) limits the number of possible paths, from the source (S) to the destination (D), enabling faults (F) to be avoided

Packets sent through intermediate nodes carry the address of each intermediate node, in addition to the address of the final destination. As the packet reaches each intermediate node, the address of that intermediate node is removed from the packet header, until the packet finally reaches its true destination. In addition, every source node must maintain a table specifying the intermediate node(s) to be used for each destination that requires such measures to be taken. When there are several candidates for the intermediate node(s), one of the alternatives can be selected randomly or more than one alternative could be listed in order to provide additional routing flexibility.

In what follows we will denote the source node as S and the destination node as D. The intermediate nodes are denoted I_x, where I_1 refers to the first intermediate node in a route. Faulty links are denoted as F_i. A node failure can easily be modelled as the failure of all the links of a node.

Deadlock freedom is ensured by having a separate escape channel for each phase. E.g., with two intermediate nodes, one escape channel is used (if required) from S to I_1, another from I_1 to I_2, and a third one from I_2 to D. This way, each phase defines a virtual network, and the packets change virtual network at each intermediate node. Although each virtual network relies on a different escape channel, they all share the same adaptive channel(s). If y is the allowed number of intermediate nodes for each source destination pair, and the minimal adaptive routing algorithm uses one adaptive and one escape channel per physical channel, the methodology requires a total of $y + 2$ virtual channels. Notice that one of them corresponds to the escape channel used in the minimal adaptive routing algorithm. So, for two intermediate nodes, four virtual channels are required.

The escape channels use deterministic Dimension Order Routing (DOR) with the bubble flow control mechanism. With this mechanism, a packet that is injected into the network or cross a network dimension requires two free buffers (i.e., one for the packet itself and one additional free buffer) to guarantee deadlock freedom. Hence, in order to avoid deadlocks, a packet changing virtual network at an intermediate node should be considered as crossing a dimension, and therefore requires two free buffers.

The computational complexity for identifying one intermediate node is $O(1)$ in torus and mesh topologies. For all the paths in the network the computational complexity thus becomes $O(n^2)$. When using two intermediate nodes this increases to $O(n^3)$ in the worst case. However, as we will see in Sect. 4, the number of paths using more than one intermediate node is very low even when there are many faults (e.g., 0.000001% of the paths in a $3 \times 3 \times 3$ torus with six faults). Thus, the methodology has a low computational cost, especially when considering that a static fault model is used.

Next, a methodology for identifying the intermediate nodes is presented. First, the case where only one intermediate node is used is presented. We then show how the method can be extended to the use of multiple intermediate nodes.

2.1   One Intermediate Node

When at most one intermediate node is used for each source-destination pair, the intermediate node I_1 should have the following properties so that the fault(s) F_i are avoided when routing packets from S via I_1 to D:

1. I_1 is reachable from S.
2. D is reachable from I_1.
3. There is no I_1' giving a shorter path than I_1.

The first requirement guarantees that packets can be routed from S to I_1, and the second requirement guarantees that packets can be routed from I_1 to D. The third requirement guarantees that the final path is the shortest possible.

Also notice that, when minimal adaptive routing is used, a node N_2 is reachable from a node N_1 if and only if: For all i, F_i is not on any minimal path from N_1 to N_2.

To identify the possible intermediate nodes, let $\mathcal{T}_{RS}$ be the set of nodes reachable from S and $\mathcal{T}_D$ the set of nodes from which D is reachable. Furthermore, let $l(x, y)$ be the length of the minimal path, in the fault free case, from x to y. We then define $\mathcal{T}_j$ (for $j \geq 0$) in the following way: A node N is in $\mathcal{T}_j$ if, and only if, $l(S, N) + l(N, D) = l(S, D) + j$.

This way, $\mathcal{T}_j$ defines non-overlapping sets of nodes, as shown in figure 2. These sets can easily be identified by starting with the nodes that are reached (i.e., traversed) on any minimal path from S to D (i.e., $j = 0$), and continuing outwards. As can be seen in Figure 2, the sets $\mathcal{T}_j$ are non-empty only for even values of j. This is always the case for meshes, but not always for tori (due to the wraparound links).

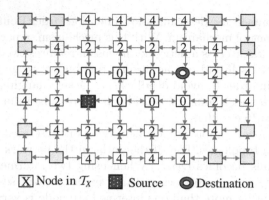

$\boxed{\text{X}}$ Node in T_X ▓ Source   ⬤ Destination

Fig. 2. The nodes in the sets T_j, for $j \le 4$ in a 2D mesh

Theorem 1. *Let j' be the smallest j for which $T_j \cap T_{RS} \cap T_D$ is non-empty. A node N fulfills all three requirements, if and only if, $N \in T_{j'} \cap T_{RS} \cap T_D$.*

Proof. We prove the theorem by induction. The theorem is true for $j = 0$ (i.e., when a minimal route exists):

- Let us assume that there is one node N in the set that does not fulfill the requirements. Then N would either have to be unreachable from S, not have a valid route to D, or not be on a minimal path from S to D. If N is unreachable from S it is by definition not in T_{RS}. If N does not have a valid route to D it is by definition not in T_D. If N is not on a minimal path from S to D it is by definition not in T_0. Because of the properties of set intersection, N must be in all the three sets T_{RS}, T_D, and T_0 to be in the set $T_0 \cap T_{RS} \cap T_D$. Thus, we have a contradiction.
- Let us then assume that there is one node N, outside the set, which fulfills the requirements. N would then have to be outside at least one of the sets T_{RS}, T_D, or T_0. If N is outside T_{RS} it is unreachable from S and therefore does not fulfill requirement one. If N is outside T_D it has no valid route to D and therefore does not fulfill requirement two. If N is outside T_0 it violates our assumption that a minimal route exists (i.e., that $j = 0$). Thus, we have a contradiction in all three cases.

If the theorem is true for $j = m$, then the theorem is also true for $j = m+1$: Concerning requirements one and two, the arguments made for $j = 0$ also hold for $j = m+1$. Furthermore, when $j = m+1$, no route S-I_1-D exists for $j < m+1$. Indeed, as each increase of j adds one additional hop to the path S-I_1-D, all the intermediate nodes found when $j = m+1$ yield paths S-I_1-D of equal lengths. Finally, for the same reason, no shorter path can be found for $j > m+1$. The theorem, therefore, fulfills all three requirements.   □

This way, we start considering the minimal paths ($j = 0$) and then, if necessary, non-minimal paths ($j > 0$) to avoid the fault(s).

2.2   Multiple Intermediate Nodes

In cases where one intermediate node is insufficient, to avoid all the faults when routing from S to D, two or more intermediate nodes can be used. The use of multiple intermediate nodes may also enable shorter paths than those otherwise obtained when using fewer intermediate nodes.

We will now first present a methodology for using two intermediate nodes. We then generalize this methodology so that it can be used, in a recursive way, for any number of intermediate nodes.

Two Intermediate Nodes. When using two intermediate nodes, we are looking for intermediate nodes I_1 and I_2 so that:

- I_1 is reachable from S.
- I_2 is reachable from I_1.
- D is reachable from I_2.
- There are no I_1' and I_2' giving a shorter path than S-I_1-I_2-D.

However, it can be observed that if a suitable I_1 is identified, then the second intermediate node I_2 follows from Theorem 1. Thus, the problem can be reduced to identifying I_1.

In order to solve this problem, let us introduce a variation of $\mathcal{T}_D$, namely $\mathcal{T}_{D1}^k$. We define this new set as the set of nodes that can reach D through one intermediate node (i.e., the 1 in the subscript denotes that one intermediate node is used). This intermediate node is given by Theorem 1, and k here represents the j in the set $\mathcal{T}_j$ used, with Theorem 1, for identifying it. E.g., the set $\mathcal{T}_{D1}^0$ consists of the nodes that have minimal path, via one intermediate node, to D. The set $\mathcal{T}_{D1}^1$, on the other hand, consists of nodes which have a path length equal to the minimal path plus one, via one intermediate node, to D. As before, $\mathcal{T}_{RS}$ denotes the nodes reachable from S.

Theorem 2. *Let j' and k' be the smallest j and k (i.e., so that their sum is minimized) for which $\mathcal{T}_j \cap \mathcal{T}_{RS} \cap \mathcal{T}_{D1}^k$ is non-empty. A node N fulfills all four requirements if, and only if, $N \in \mathcal{T}_{j'} \cap \mathcal{T}_{RS} \cap \mathcal{T}_{D1}^{k'}$.*

Proof. Let us define l as the sum of j and k, i.e., $l = j + k$. We then prove the theorem by induction. The theorem is true for $l = 0$ (i.e., when a minimal path exists):

- Let us assume that there is one node N in the set $\mathcal{T}_0 \cap \mathcal{T}_{RS} \cap \mathcal{T}_{D1}^0$ that gives a path S-N-I_2-D that does not fulfill the requirements. It follows from Theorem 1, and the definition of $\mathcal{T}_{D1}^k$, that I_2 is reachable from N and that D is reachable from I_2. Thus, N must be unreachable from S or the path S-N-I_2-D is not the shortest possible. If N is unreachable from S, N is by definition not in $\mathcal{T}_{RS}$. It also follows from Theorem 1 that the subpath N-I_2-D is the shortest possible. Thus, N can not be on a minimal path from S to D for the path S-N-I_2-D to be a non-minimal path. However, then N is by definition not in $\mathcal{T}_0$. Therefore, we have a contradiction.

– Let us then assume that there is one node N outside the set $T_0 \cap T_{RS} \cap T_{D1}^0$ that fulfills the requirements. N would then have to be outside at least one of the sets T_0, T_{RS}, or T_{D1}^0. If N is outside T_0 it violates our assumption that $l = 0$. If N is outside T_{RS}, it is unreachable from S and therefore violates requirement one. If N is outside of the set T_{D1}^0 it violates requirements two or three, or our assumption that $l = 0$.

If the theorem is true for $l = m$, then it is also true for $l = m + 1$: As for reachability, the same arguments as for $l = 0$ are still valid. Thus, it only remains to be shown that the path $S\text{-}N\text{-}I_2\text{-}D$ is the shortest possible. By definition, when $l = m + 1$, no N exists for $l < m + 1$. Each increase of l adds one hop to the path $S\text{-}N\text{-}I_2\text{-}D$. Thus, all paths where $l = m + 1$ are of equal length, and no shorter path can be found for $l > m + 1$. □

Thus, as before, we start considering the minimal paths (i.e., $j + k = 0$) and then consider non-minimal paths (i.e., $j + k > 0$), if necessary, to avoid all the faults.

Any Number of Intermediate Nodes. Let us now generalize the definition of T_{D1}^k, in order to apply Theorem 2 for any number of intermediate nodes. We therefore define T_{Dz}^k in the following way:

– T_{D0}^0: The set of nodes from which D is reachable without the use of any intermediate node (i.e., the set of nodes defined by the original set T_D).
– T_{Dz}^k, for $z > 0$ and $k \geq 0$: The set of nodes given by $T_{j'} \cap T_{RS} \cap T_{Dz'}^{k'}$, where $z = z' + 1$ and $k = j' + k'$.

Thus, T_{Dz}^k is the set of nodes that reach D through z intermediate nodes, and where k is the number of additional hops, in the path to D, compared to the minimal path. When paths of equal length exist, preference should be given to paths with fewer intermediate nodes.

Notice that the set $T_j \cap T_{RS} \cap T_{D0}^0$ is actually the same as that in Theorem 1, and thus results in paths with one intermediate node. The set $T_j \cap T_{RS} \cap T_{D1}^k$ is that given by Theorem 2, resulting in paths with two intermediate nodes. Similarly, $T_j \cap T_{RS} \cap T_{D2}^k$ gives paths with three intermediate nodes. Continuing this way, an arbitrary number of intermediate nodes can be obtained.

3 Example Scenarios

We will now illustrate the methodology through two example scenarios. A 2D mesh is used for this purpose, although the methodology is also valid for other topologies such as a 3D mesh or torus. For both scenarios we assume that minimal adaptive routing is used, and that at most two intermediate nodes are allowed in each route.

Figure 3a shows a scenario with three faults. Because there are faults present in some of the minimal paths between S and D, an intermediate node is needed.

In order to find a minimal path, we look for an intermediate node within T_0. As shown in Fig. 3a, there are several nodes within T_0 that are either reachable from S, or able to reach D. However, we are only interested in nodes with both of these attributes, i.e., the nodes given by the set $T_0 \cap T_{RS} \cap T_{D0}^0$. In this scenario there is only one such node, i.e., the one identified as a possible intermediate node in the figure. By using this node as the intermediate node, it is guaranteed that the faults are not encountered when packets are routed first from S to I_1 and then from I_1 to D.

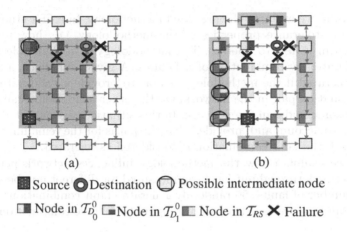

(a)   (b)

▦ Source ◉ Destination ◐ Possible intermediate node

▣ Node in T_{D0}^0 ◪ Node in T_{D1}^0 ◧ Node in T_{RS} ✖ Failure

Fig. 3. (a) The faults are avoided by the use of one intermediate node. The shaded area identifies the nodes in T_0. (b) Two intermediate nodes must be used in order to avoid the faults. The figure shows how the first of these intermediate nodes (i.e., I_1) is identified. The shaded areas identify the nodes in T_2

Figure 3b shows the same fault scenario as in the previous example, except that the source node is different. In this case, all the minimal paths between S and D are blocked by faults. The set $T_0 \cap T_{RS} \cap T_{D0}^0$, giving minimal paths with one intermediate node, is therefore empty. The set $T_0 \cap T_{RS} \cap T_{D1}^0$, giving minimal paths with two intermediate nodes, is also empty. Because preference is given to the paths with the least number of intermediate nodes when the path length is equal, we then try to find an intermediate node within T_2 (because this is a mesh we are only interested in the even values of j) giving a non-minimal path with one intermediate node. However, this set, $T_2 \cap T_{RS} \cap T_{D0}^0$, is also empty.

There are now two more sets giving the same path lengths as the previous one, but using two intermediate nodes instead of one. Which of these two sets are given preference is irrelevant for the correctness of the methodology as they both give the same value for $j + k$ (which should be minimized according to Theorem 2). Increasing j means adding one hop to the path. S-I_1, while increasing k adds one hop to the path I_1-I_2-D.

Anyway, of the two sets, the set $T_0 \cap T_{RS} \cap T_{D1}^2$ is empty, while $T_2 \cap T_{RS} \cap T_{D1}^0$ gives us the possible intermediate nodes shown in Fig. 3b. Thus, the first intermediate node, I_1, can be selected among these three nodes. If I_1' is the first intermediate node, then the second intermediate node, I_2, can be selected among the intermediate nodes that give I_1' a path with one intermediate node to D. In this case, I_2 would be the same as the one identified as I_1 in the first example.

4   Evaluation of the Methodology

In this section, we evaluate the proposed methodology. In a first study, we analyze the fault-tolerance properties of the methodology, i.e., how many faults the mechanism is able to tolerate. The methodology is $n-$fault tolerant if it is able to tolerate any combination of n failures. A given combination of failures, again, is tolerated if the methodology is able to provide a valid path for every source-destination pair in the network. On the other hand, faults can physically disconnect some nodes in the network. In this situation, disconnected nodes are not taken into account and, provided that the paths for the remaining nodes can be computed, the fault combination is considered as tolerated.

Then, we evaluate how the methodology influences network performance. For this, network throughput has been measured for different numbers of faults. For each number of faults, 50 randomly generated fault combinations have been simulated, and the average network throughput for these combinations is provided.

We have applied the methodology to $3 \times 3 \times 3$ (27 nodes) torus and mesh networks, to a 3×3 (9 nodes) torus network, and to an $8 \times 8 \times 8$ (512 nodes) torus network. Although actual systems are built with larger topologies (e.g., a $32 \times 32 \times 64$ torus for the BlueGene/L), smaller networks can be evaluated exhaustively from a fault-tolerant point of view and the results can then easily be extended to larger networks.

4.1   Simulation Model

A detailed event-driven simulator has been used to analyze the performance exhibited by the proposed methodology. The simulator models a direct interconnect network with point-to-point bidirectional serial links. Each router has a non-multiplexed crossbar with queues only at the input ports. Each physical input port uses five virtual channels, each providing buffering resources in order to store up to two packets. A round-robin policy has been chosen to select among packets contending for the same output port.

In order to make a fair evaluation, the same number of virtual channels (i.e., five) is used regardless of the number of intermediate nodes used in the methodology. Virtual channels are used as adaptive or as escape channels, depending on the number of required intermediate nodes. If paths use at most one intermediate node, three virtual channels are used for adaptive routing, whereas the remaining two virtual channels are used for the escape paths. For two inter-mediate nodes, there are two adaptive channels and three are escape channels, and so on. When faults are not present (i.e., when no intermediate nodes are required), four adaptive channels are used. In the escape channel(s), packets are deterministically routed following the DOR routing and the bubble flow con-trol mechanism. Notice that for a given number of intermediate nodes, all the paths in the network will have the same number of adaptive virtual channels, regardless of whether they use intermediate nodes or not.

For each simulation run, we assume that the packet generation rate is con-stant and the same for all of the nodes. The destination of a message is randomly chosen with the same probability for all the nodes. This pattern has been widely used in other evaluation studies [3,8]. In all the simulations, the packet length is set to 128 bytes.

4.2   Fault Analysis Models

For a reduced number of faults in the network, all the possible combinations of faults can be explored. However, as the number of faults increases, the number of possible fault combinations increases exponentially. Therefore, from a particular number of faults, it is impossible to explore all the fault combinations in a reasonable amount of time. We tackle this problem with two approaches. In the first approach, we focus on faults bounded into a limited region of the network. Notice that the worst combinations of faults to be solved by the methodology are those where the faults are closely located. This is because the number of fault-free paths in that region is reduced. Because the number of fault combinations within such a region is much lower than for the entire network, all the fault combinations can be evaluated. Although the results obtained cannot be directly extended to the generic case, where faults may be located over the entire network, it gives us an approximation of the effectiveness of the methodology in the worst case.

For this, we must define the region where the faults are to be located. The region is formed by all the links attached to the nodes that are one hop away from a node (the center node). Therefore we refer to this as a distance 1 region, and it consists of 36 links. However, in a $3 \times 3 \times 3$ torus it only consists of 33 links, as three of the links then are shared by nodes within the region. The center node is randomly selected.[4] Notice that with a high number of faults and for a large number of fault combinations, the center node is hardly accessible, as very few links are non-faulty. So, the distance 1 region actually represents a real worst case to access the center node.

In the second approach, a statistical analysis is performed, analyzing a subset of the fault combinations, where the faults are randomly located over the entire network. From the obtained results, statistical conclusions are extracted about the fault-tolerance degree of the proposed methodology.

---

[4] The selection of the center node does not affect the results in a torus network due to the symmetry of the topology.

Table 1. Fault tolerance achieved by the methodology when using at most one ($I \times 1$), two ($I \times 2$), or three ($I \times 3$) intermediate nodes in a $3 \times 3 \times 3$ torus network. The three rightmost columns show the percentages of the paths that use each number of intermediate nodes when at most three intermediate nodes are used

Link faults	Analysis type	Combinations analyzed	Not tolerated combinations			$I \times 3$ Paths using # I		
			$I \times 1$	$I \times 2$	$I \times 3$	1	2	3
1	Exhau-	81	0%	0%	0%	6.86%	0%	0%
2	stive	3,240	2.50%	0%	0%	12.99%	0.04%	0%
3		85,320	7.44%	0%	0%	18.46%	0.13%	0%
4		1,663,740	14.67%	0%	0%	23.32%	0.31%	0%
5		25,621,596	24.06%	0%	0%	27.62%	0.56%	0%
6		324,540,216	35.49%	0.0002%	0%	31.41%	0.90%	0.000001%
6	Dist.1	1,107,568	54.52%	0.01%	0%	28.09%	1.19%	0.00003%
7		4,272,048	70.31%	0.06%	0%	30.41%	1.78%	0.0004%
8		13,884,156	83.30%	0.31%	0%	32.25%	2.51%	0.002%
9		38,567,100	92.15%	1.06%	0%	33.67%	3.38%	0.008%
10		92,561,040	96.97%	2.99%	0.001%	34.71%	4.36%	0.02%
11		193,536,720	99.01%	6.51%	0.01%	35.42%	5.44%	0.05%
12		354,817,320	99.67%	12.88%	0.62%	35.84%	6.58%	0.11%
6	Stati-	10,000,000	35.46%	0.00%	0%	31.41%	0.90%	0.000001%
7	stical	10,000,000	48.72%	0.00%	0%	34.72%	1.34%	0.00001%
8		10,000,000	62.98%	0.01%	0%	37.61%	1.88%	0.00007%
9		10,000,000	76.51%	0.03%	0%	40.10%	2.53%	0.0002%
10		10,000,000	87.40%	0.09%	0%	42.21%	3.29%	0.0008%
11		10,000,000	94.47%	0.23%	0%	43.98%	4.16%	0.002%
12		10,000,000	98.05%	0.52%	0.00001%	45.44%	5.14%	0.005%
13		10,000,000	99.46%	1.10%	0.0003%	46.60%	6.22%	0.01%
14		10,000,000	99.88%	2.13%	0.0009%	47.50%	7.41%	0.02%

4.3   Evaluation Results

Table 1 shows the fault tolerance achieved by the methodology for a $3 \times 3 \times 3$ torus network. The table shows the results for the three different types of analysis performed (exhaustive, distance 1, and statistical). From the exhaustive analysis results, we can observe that the methodology is only 1-fault tolerant when using only one intermediate node. For two faults present in the network, 2.5% of the fault combinations are not tolerated when using one intermediate node. As the number of faults increases, the percentage of not tolerated combinations grows fast. For six faults, 35.49% of the fault combinations are not supported when using one intermediate node.

By using two intermediate nodes, the methodology greatly increases its fault tolerance degree. In particular, it is 5-fault tolerant as all the fault combinations of up to and including five faults are tolerated. With six faults in the network, two intermediate nodes where sufficient for almost all the fault combinations, except for 0.0002% of the combinations.

With three intermediate nodes, the methodology achieves a very good fault tolerance degree. From the exhaustive analysis results, we observe that using three intermediate nodes allows tolerating all the possible fault combinations up to and including six faults. In the statistical analysis, where 10 million randomly generated fault combinations were analyzed for up to 14 faults[5], the methodology could provide a valid path for every non-disconnected pair of nodes for up to 11 faults. For 12 faults one not tolerated combination was found (in 10,000,000) and this number increased to 89 when 14 faults were present.

However, taking into account the distance 1 analysis (representing the worst case situation) we can observe that with 10 faults in the network there were some not tolerated combinations. Therefore, the methodology is not 10-fault tolerant. Even, from seven up to and including nine faults we can not deduce for sure that the methodology is n-fault tolerant since not all the fault combinations have been tested. However, this strongly indicates that the methodology tolerates nine faults. Anyway, even with a high number of faults, the percentage of not supported fault combinations is very low when using three intermediate nodes. So, the methodology achieves a high fault-tolerance degree.

Table 1 also shows the percentage of paths that use a certain number of intermediate nodes. As can be seen, most of the paths avoid faults by using just one intermediate node, and very few paths need a third intermediate node. Notice that although the third intermediate node is little used, it makes a large difference for the fault-tolerance degree.

Table 2 shows the results achieved for a 3×3 torus network and for a $3 \times 3 \times 3$ mesh network. In the 3×3 torus, all the combinations of up to and including six faults (i.e., 1/3 of the total number of links) have been exhaustively analyzed. The methodology tolerates one fault when using one intermediate node, three faults when using two intermediate nodes, and five faults when using three intermediate nodes. So, the fault-tolerance degree in a 2D torus is lower than in a 3D torus. This is not unexpected considering that a 2D torus provides lower routing flexibility.

For the $3 \times 3 \times 3$ mesh network, the results are not as good as for the torus networks. The methodology requires at least two intermediate nodes in order to be 1-fault tolerant.[6] When using three intermediate nodes, the methodology is 4-fault tolerant, and it is 6-fault tolerant when using four intermediate nodes.

Finally, Fig. 4 shows the performance degradation exhibited by the methodology in an $8 \times 8 \times 8$ torus network when up to two intermediate nodes are used. Notice that in a larger network, like the one used in the performance analysis, the percentage of not tolerated fault combinations, when using two intermediate nodes, is much lower than in a $3 \times 3 \times 3$ torus. Thus, all the randomly generated combinations for the performance evaluation could be solved by the use of at most two intermediate nodes. When only one fault is present in the network,

---

[5] The error due to not analyzing all the combinations is lower than 0.05.

[6] Notice that in a mesh the wraparound links do not exist and it is therefore impossible to communicate to a node on the direct opposite side of the fault without using at least two intermediate nodes (i.e., when S, F, and D are in the same row/column).

Table 2. Fault tolerance degree achieved by the methodology for a 3 × 3 torus network and a 3 × 3 × 3 mesh network. The table shows the percentage of the total number of combinations that are not tolerated. The results have been obtained by exhaustively analyzing all the possible fault combinations

Link faults	3 × 3 torus			3 × 3 × 3 mesh			
	I×1	I×2	I×3	I×1	I×2	I×3	I×4
1	0%	0%	0%	100%	0%	0%	0%
2	11.76%	0%	0%	100%	0%	0%	0%
3	33.82%	0%	0%	100%	0.97%	0%	0%
4	67.06%	1.18%	0%	100%	4.23%	0%	0%
5	91.81%	10.71%	0%	100%	11.65%	0.05%	0%
6	96.49%	40.24%	2.33%	100%	24.89%	0.28%	0%
7	N/A	N/A	N/A	100%	43.67%	1.02%	0.002%
8	N/A	N/A	N/A	100%	64.53%	2.83%	0.02%

only one intermediate node is used. The figure shows for every number of faults, the average throughput achieved. The presented throughput is the average of the individual results obtained when evaluating the 50 randomly generated fault combinations.[7] As can be observed, the throughput decreases as the number of faults in the network increases. However, the decrease in throughput, is very low. In particular, when there are 14 faults, the throughput is on average only decreased by 6.49% compared to the fault-free case (from 474 flits/cycle to 443 flits/cycle). In particular, this degradation is lower than the one obtained with the methodology proposed in [13], where with 5 virtual channels the degradation from the fault-free case to 14 faults was 11.02%.

5   Conclusions

In this paper we have proposed a fault-tolerant routing methodology based on the use of intermediate nodes. The proposed methodology can be applied with any minimal routing function in n-dimensional mesh and torus networks, and it has been applied with minimal adaptive routing in this paper. The main advantage of the proposed mechanism is its simplicity, since the same original routing (e.g., minimal adaptive) continues to be valid. The only requirement on switches is that they should provide the required number of extra virtual channels. However, only a low number of virtual channels is required.

The paper provides the necessary and sufficient conditions, for selecting the intermediate nodes, in order to tolerate as many faults as possible and to provide the shortest paths possible.

The methodology has been shown to be five fault-tolerant when using two intermediate nodes in a 3D torus network. When using three intermediate nodes,

---

[7] The 95% confidence intervals are always smaller than 0.796.

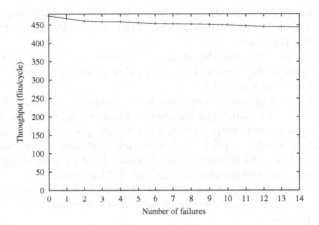

Fig. 4. Overall throughput (flits/cycle) for the proposed methodology in an 8 × 8 × 8 torus network. Five virtual channels are used

the method is nine fault-tolerant for 3D torus networks, five fault-tolerant in 2D torus, and four fault-tolerant in 3D mesh topologies.

Regarding performance, the methodology does not degrade performance in the absence of faults, whereas in the presence of faults it provides a gracious performance degradation. Specifically, it has been shown that the average performance degradation, in an 8 × 8 × 8 torus network with 14 faults, is only 6.49%.

References

1. ASCI Red Web Site. http://www.sandia.gov/ASCI/Red/.
2. IBM BG/L Team. *An Overview of the BlueGene/L Supercomputer.* ACM Supercomputing Conference, 2002.
3. R. Bopana and S. Chalasani. *A Comparison of Adaptive Wormhole Routing Algorithms.* Proc. 20th Annual Int. Symp. Comp. Architecture, 1993.
4. C. Carrion, R. Beivide, J.A. Gregorio, and F. Vallejo. *A Flow Control Mechanism to Avoid Message Deadlock in K-ary N-Cube Networks.* 4th International Conference on High Performance Computing, pp. 332-329, 1997.
5. R.Casado, A. Bermúdez, J. Duato, F.J. Quiles, and J.L. Sánchez. *A protocol for deadlock-free dynamic reconfiguration in high speed local area networks.* IEEE Transactions on Parallel and Distributed Systems, vol. 12, No. 2, pp. 115-132, 2001.
6. A.A. Chien and J.H. Kim. *Planar-adaptive routing: Low-cost adaptive networks for multiprocessors.* Proceedings of the 19th International Symposium on Computer Architecture, pp. 268-277, 1992.
7. S.Chalasani and R.V. Boppana. *Communication in multicomputers with nonconvex faults.* IEEE Transactions on Computers, vol. 46, no. 5, pp. 616-622, 1997.
8. W.J. Dally. *Virtual-channel flow control.* IEEE Transactions on Parallel and Distributed Systems, vol. 3, no. 2, pp. 194-205, 1992.

9. W.J. Dally and H. Aoki. *Deadlock-free adaptive routing in multicomputer networks using virtual channels.* IEEE Transactions on Parallel and Distributed Systems, vol. 4, no. 4, pp 466-475, 1993.

10. W. J. Dally et al., *The Reliable Router: A Reliable and High-Performance Communication Substrate for Parallel Computers.* Proc. Parallel Computer Routing and Communication Workshop, 1994.

11. J. Duato. *A theory of fault-tolerant routing in wormhole networks.* Proc. International Conference on Parallel and Distributed Systems, pp. 600-607, 1994.

12. Earth Simulator Center. http://www.es.jamstec.go.jp/esc/eng/index.html.

13. M.E. Gómez, J. Duato, J. Flich, P. López, and A. Robles / N.A. Nordbotten, O. Lysne, and T. Skeie. *An Efficient Fault-Tolerant Routing Methodology for Meshes and Tori.* Computer Architecture Letters, vol. 3, May 2004.

14. G.J. Glass, and L.M. Ni. *Fault-Tolerant Wormhole Routing in Meshes without Virtual Channels.* IEEE Transactions Parallel and Distributed Systems, vol. 7, no. 6, pp. 620-636, 1996.

15. C.T. Ho and L. Stockmeyer. *A New Approach to Fault-Tolerant Wormhole Routing for Mesh-Connected Parallel Computers.* Proc. 16th International Parallel and Distributed Processing Symposium, 2002.

16. InfiniBand^{TM} Trade Association, *InfiniBand^{TM} architecture. Specification vol. 1. Release 1.0.a.* Available at http://www.infinibandta.com.

17. D.H. Linder and J.C. Harden. *An Adaptive and fault tolerant wormhole routing strategy for k-ary n-cubes.* IEEE Transactions on Computers, vol. C-40, no. 1, pp. 2-12, 1991.

18. V. Puente, J.A. Gregorio, J.M. Prellezo, R. Beivide, J. Duato, and C. Izu. *Adaptive Bubble Router: A Design to Balance Latency and Throughput in Networks for Parallel Computers.* 22nd International Conference on Parallel Processing, 1999.

19. Y.J. Suh, B.V. Dao, J. Duato, and S. Yalamanchili. *Software-based rerouting for fault-tolerant pipelined communication.* IEEE Transactions on Parallel and Distributed Systems, vol. 11, no. 3, pp. 193-211, 2000.

20. S.L. Scott and G.M. Thorson. *The Cray T3E Network: Adaptive Routing in a High Performance 3D Torus.* Symposium on High Performance Interconnects, 1996.

21. L.G. Valiant, *A Scheme for Fast Parallel Communication.* SIAM J. Comput. 11, pp. 350-361, 1982.

Extended DBP for (m,k)-Firm Based QoS

Jiming Chen[1], Zhi Wang[1], Yeqiong Song[2], and Youxian Sun[1]

[1] National Laboratory of Industrial Control Technology,
Zhejiang Univ., Hangzhou 310027, P.R.China
{jmchen, wangzhi, yxsun}@iipc.zju.edu.cn
[2] LORIA - TRIO Campus Scientifique B.P. 239
54506 VANDOEUVRE-les-NANCY, France
{song}@loria.fr

Abstract. In this paper, an extended DBP (E_DBP) scheme is studied for (m,k)-firm constraint. The basic idea of the proposed algorithm takes into account the distance to exit a failure state, which is a symmetrical notion of distance to fall into a failure state in DBP. Quality of Service (QoS) in terms of dynamic failure and delay is evaluated. Simulation results reveal the effectiveness of E_DBP to provide better QoS.

1 Introduction

Real-time media servers for delivering audio/video streams need to service hundreds and, possibly, thousands of applications, each with its own quality of service (QoS) requirements. Many such applications can tolerate the loss of a certain fraction of the information requird from the server, resulting in little or no noticeable degradation in QoS [1] [2]. Consequently, loss-rate is an important performance measure for the QoS to many real-time media applications. We define the term loss-rate as the fraction of packets in a stream either discarded or serviced later than their delay constraints allow (Deadline) [3].

One of the problems with using loss-rate as a performance metric is that it does not describe when losses are allowed to occur. For most loss-tolerant applications, there is usually a restriction on the number of consecutive packet losses that are acceptable. For example, losing a series of consecutive packets from an audio stream might result in the loss of a complete section of audio, rather than merely a reduction in the signal-to-noise ratio.

A suitable performance metric in this case is a window-based loss-rate, i.e. loss-rate constrained over a finite range, or window, of any consecutive packets. More precisely, an application might tolerate at most k-m packet losses for every k arrivals at the various service points across a network. Any service discipline attempting to meet these requirements must ensure that the number of violations to the loss-tolerance specification is minimized (if not zero) across the whole stream. In another way, it is same meaning that at least m packets must be serviced before their deadline in any consecutive k packets. We refer to such QoS requirement as (m,k)-firm constraint. If less than m packets are serviced successfully in any window k, it is said the application experiences a dynamic failure and

H. Jin et al. (Eds.): NPC 2004, LNCS 3222, pp. 357–365, 2004.

the current state is called as failure state. An approach called Distance-based Priority (DBP) based on (m,k)-firm idea has been proposed to schedule multiple packet streams competing for service on a single server each having its own (m,k)-firm constraints [4]. It has been showed in that when streams have same or different (m,k)-firm constraint requirement and are identical (i.e. with same packet transmission time distribution, same packet inter-arrival distribution and same deadline distribution), DBP is especially more beneficial to tightening the probability of dynamic failure than conventional scheduling scheme where all packets are serviced at the same priority level [4]. This idea is then generalized under the name weakly hard real-time to deal with real-time applications that allows some packet losses without violating the desired behaviors of application [5]. In this paper, we proposed an extended DBP (E_DBP) scheme to study (m,k)-firm based QoS, and compared the E_DBP and DBP for streams with (m,k)-firm in terms of probability of dynamic failure and delay.

The rest of paper is structured as follows. Section 2 describes DBP scheme and some relative work. In section 3, E_DBP scheduling is proposed. In section 4, performance metric of QoS about dynamic failure and delay is evaluated through simulation in overloaded scenarios. Finally, we make some concluding remarks.

2   DBP Scheduling on Steams with (m,k)-Firm

We begin this section by defining the problem that we focus on real-time streams with (m,k)-firm . Then, how the DBP scheme works is described. The drawbacks are stated in the last.

2.1   Problem Definition

In order to define the real-time scheduling problem based on (m,k)-firm constraint addressed as part of this paper, we introduce the following definitions:

Application Model. As briefly mentioned in the introduction section, DBP scheduling is designed to study how to efficiently serve multiple streams under (m,k)-firm constraints sharing a single server. This system is called multiple input queues on single server (MIQSS). This model can be used to study a large category of computer and telecommunication systems such as multiple tasks executing in a CPU, transmission of packets issued from multiple packet sources sharing a same transmission medium or network interconnection equipment (switch or router). The proposed model is for n loss-tolerant applications generating n packet streams τ_i $(i = 1, 2, \ldots, n)$ that will be served by a single server. Each stream is formed by a source and a waiting queue, where a packet issued from a source waits until being chosen by the server. The server chooses packets at the head of queues according to its scheduling scheme.

In such a model, scheduling scheme is of prime importance to provide not only (m,k)-firm guarantee for each individual stream (end user's point of view) but also good server utilization (system designer's point of view).

Stream Characterization. A stream τ_i is characterized by a 3-tuple (C_i, D_i, T_i), where C_i is the service time for a packet in stream τ_i. There, it is assumed that all packets in τ_i have the same service time. For the purposes of this paper, where time is divided into fixed-sized slots, each and every packet can be serviced in one such slot. Deadline D_i is the latest time a packet finishes its service. If a packet cannot be finished by D_i, it will be discarded, which is called deadline miss or packet loss. T_i is the inter-arrival time between consecutive packets.

Loss-Tolerance. This is specified by (m,k)-firm constraint, where m is the least number of the packets that should be transmitted successfully by their deadline for any window k of consecutive packet arrivals in the same stream. Otherwise, a stream experiences a dynamic failure. The rate at which a stream experiences dynamic failure is therefore a measure of how often the QoS falls below the acceptable level, which is defined as the *probability of dynamic failure*.

Problem Statement. The problem addressed in this paper is to propose a more effective scheduling scheme than DBP to guarantee better (m,k)-firm based QoS for each stream in terms of dynamic failure and delay at the given resource.

2.2   DBP Outline

DBP was firstly put forward in [4], as a dynamic priority assignment mechanism for streams with (m,k)-firm constraint in a MIQSS model, and targeted primarily at loss tolerant, real-time applications like multimedia.

The basic idea of DBP algorithm is quite simple and straightforward: the closer the stream is to a failure state the higher its priority is. A failure state occurs when the stream's (m,k)-firm requirement is transgressed, i.e., there is more than k - m deadline misses within the last k-length window.

So for each stream τ with (m,k)-firm constraint, the priority is assigned based on the number of consecutive deadline misses that will lead the stream to violate its (m,k)-firm constraint. This number of deadline misses is referred to as *distance to fall into a failure state* from the current state. Examining the recent history of τ, one can do the evaluation of the distance. The key to dealing with it is the k-sequence. If the same distance occurs, Earliest Deadline First (EDF) will be adopted as adjunctive scheme.

The k-sequence is a word of k bits ordered from the most recent to the oldest packet in which each bit keeps memory of whether the deadline is missed (bit= 0) or met (bit=1). In this paper, the leftmost bit represents the oldest. Each new arriving packet causes a shift of all the bits towards left, the leftmost exits from the word and is no longer considered, while the rightmost will be 1 if the packet has met its deadline (i.e. it has been served before its deadline) or 0 otherwise.

The priority is assigned by DBP to a packet at a given instant according to the distance of the current k-sequence to a failure state. By adding consecutive 0s to the right side of k-sequence, we can evaluate the distance easily until a failure state happens. If a stream has already been in a failure state (i.e., less than m 1s in the k-sequence), the highest priority is assigned.

Formally, according to [4], priority is evaluated as follows. Let $s_j = (\delta^j_{i-k_j+1}, \ldots, \delta^j_{i-1}, \delta^j_i)$ denotes the state of the previous k consecutive packets of τ_j, $l_j(n, s)$ denotes the position (from the right) of the nth meet (or 1) in the s_j, then the priority of the $(i+1)^{th}$ packet of τ_j is given by:

$$\Omega^j_{i+1} = k_j - l_j(m_j, s_j) + 1 \qquad (1)$$

We note that if there are less than n 1s in s, $l_j(n, s) = k_j + 1$, the highest priority (Ω=0) will be assigned, this is normal as the stream is in a failure state.

Example1: a stream τ_1 with (3,5)-firm constraint, current k-sequence is 11011, we can get $l_1(3, s_1)$ =4 and Ω^1_{i+1}=5-4+1=2. If the current k-sequence is 10000, then $l_1(3, s_1)$= 5+1, so Ω^1_{i+1}= 0.

2.3 Drawbacks of DBP

Although DBP is more effective to guarantee (m,k)-firm constraint, there are still some drawbacks. The first one is that it only uses the distance to fall into a failure state of k-sequence whereas the whole richer information of "0,1" distribution in k-sequence is neglected. In order to explain this problem, it is enough to consider different k-sequences with (2,5)-firm constraint: 11100 from τ_1 and 11001 from τ_2. They have the same distance (Ω=2). If they arrive at the same time, according to the DBP, EDF algorithm is default adjunctive scheduling scheme. But is EDF optimal to deal with such condition?

It appears that 11100 is less robust than 11001. For example, after a successful service of both, these two k-sequences become 11001($\Omega = 2$)and 10011($\Omega = 4$) respectively.But this is not necessary that we should firstly serve the next packet from τ_1 even if it has earlier deadline. In fact, how to use such information will depend on what we would like to optimize. Maybe it is more complicated to set the priority and get the optimal objection function.

Another shortcoming of DBP is that it assigns priorities considering only one stream source without taking into account the parameters of other streams sharing the same server, which results in local priority that not global one and may lead to "priority inversion" phenomena. Improved algorithms to overcome the problem have been proposed in [6] [7].

3   Extended Distance-Based Priority Scheduling

One of the possible solutions to explore the '0,1' distribution in k-sequence is found when a stream falls in a failure state. Any packet in a failure stream has the same DBP value (Ω=0) but the distance to exit a failure state may be different. Let's take again the (2,5)-firm constraint as an example, DBP assigns the same priority to the following different k-sequences in failure states: 00001 and 10000, but to exit the failure state, 00001 needs only one more 1 whereas

10000 needs two consecutive 1s. Especially in heterogeneous system, the streams have different (m,k)-firm constraints, the above situation will occur frequently, so it is necessary to consider factor of '0,1' distribution.

Based on the information in k-sequence, including the '0,1' distribution, we propose to extend the notion of distance to failure state by introducing the notion of distance to exit failure state.

For each stream with (m,k)-firm in a failure state, the priority is assigned based on the number of consecutive deadlines met that makes the stream back to meet its (m,k)-firm constraint. The number of necessary consecutive deadlines met referred to as *distance to exit a failure state* from the current state.

The distance to exit a failure state is thus the number of consecutive 1s adding to the right side. Formally, given a stream τ_j with constraint parameter m_j and k_j in a failure state, and let $s_j = (\delta^j_{i-k_j+1}, \ldots, \delta^j_{i-1}, \delta^j_i)$ be its current k-sequence. Define $\tilde{l}_j(n,s)$ as the position (from the right side) of the nth miss in the state of s_j, so the distance to exit a failure state of stream is given by equation (2):

$$\Phi^j_{i+1} = k_j - \tilde{l}_j(k_j - m_j + 1, s_j) + 1 \qquad (2)$$

Example2: Φ=2 for 100011 with (4,6)-firm constraint and Φ=1 for 00011 with (3,5)-firm constraint.

In a successful state, priority is assigned according to DBP, while in a failure state priority is assigned by equation (2), in case of priority equality, EDF is adopted, which is referred as E_DBP. As discuss above, the definition of distance to exit a failure state is a symmetrical notion of distance to a failure state, just as if we look at in a mirror, so the negative logic is applied. It is supposed that if the packet in the stream with smaller Φ value gets higher priority, and a successful service for a packet adds 0 to the right of k-sequence, which will make the stream get more chance to be in failure states like DBP to guarantee successful states. But in fact, a packet is serviced by its deadline, 1 will be added to right of k-sequence, which will be more easy to a exit failure state. So it is reasonable to assign higher priority to the packet from the stream having smaller Φ value. The detailed priority assigning process can be described as follows. E_DBP precedence among all being selected packets

- If all streams are in successful states, the smaller DBP value , the higher priority. If DBP value Ω is the same, EDF is adopted.
- If just only stream τ_j is in a failure state, others are in successful states, the packet in the stream τ_j, gets higher priority.
- If many streams are in failure states at the same time, the smaller Φ, the higher priority. If Φ value is the same, EDF is adopted.
- For all cases, if the same deadline, then FIFO.

4   Simulation Result

The new proposed algorithm, E_DBP is compared with DBP through simulation examples given in [4]. QoS in terms of probability of dynamic failure and delay is taken as performance metric. In the results that follow, two packets generation patterns are considered: Poisson and burst. In a Poisson stream, packet inter-arrival times are exponentially distributed. A burst source alternates between ON and OFF states. When in the ON state, packets are generated periodically. No packets are generated when source is in the OFF state. The durations of the ON and the OFF states are exponentially distributed with averages ON_{ave} and OFF_{ave} respectively. Such a stream is often used to model a stream of voice sample in a conversation [8]. We firstly consider the case where all streams in the system have the same timing requirements. We also assume that only the packets that meet their deadline are serviced, which means that drop policy is enabled. Simulation adopts software OPNET8.0.c Modeler. Time duration of all projects is 20000. There we define $\sum_{i=1}^{n} \frac{C_i}{E(T_i)}$ as average system Load and $\sum_{i=1}^{n} \frac{m_i C_i}{k_i E(T_i)}$ as average system (m,k)-Load, where $E(T_i)$ is the mean inter-arrival time. The initial k-sequence is $\underbrace{11 \ldots 1}_{k_i}$ for a stream with windows k_i.

4.1   Evaluation of Dynamic Performances

Poisson Streams The data in the left column in Table.1 shows the probability of dynamic failure in one system with (3,4)-firm constraint. The system consists of five streams. All packets require a constant service time. Service deadlines are set equal to five times the packet service time. The packet inter-arrival time is exponentially distributed and the overall average load is varied from 1.0-2.0 by changing inter-arrival time. As a result, it is shown that new scheme E_DBP can reduce the probability of dynamic failure, especially when it is overloaded. The maximum reduced percent is 9.3% in this case when load equals to 2.0.

The above system considers that all streams have the same deadline requirement with (3,4)-firm. The middle column in the Table.1 shows the results for the heterogeneous system in which steams have different deadline requirement. The system consists of five systems with (9,10)-firm, (3,4)-firm, (1,2)-firm, (1,3)-firm, (1,4)-firm constraint, respectively. The packet service time, arrival pattern, and the deadline in this system are like those for the stream examined in the first example. The arrival rates of the packets are adjusted to get an average system load from 1.3-2.3. Simulation result shows that even at load 1.4-1.6, there is a little abnormal behavior that E_DBP is slightly worse than DBP (1.0% to 2.3% increase). But there is still a strong trend that E_DBP can reduce the probability of dynamic failure, especially about 8.6% at load 2.3.

Burst Streams The data in the right column in Table.1 of probability of dynamic failure in a system with five burst streams. The ON and OFF periods of each stream are exponentially distributed with $ON_{ave}=50$ and $OFF_{ave}=100$. The offered peak load of a stream is therefore three times the average load. When in the ON state, a stream generating one packet is 5 periodically. The deadlines are set to twice the generation period. Overall load varies by changing packet service time. We find that E_DBP is better than DBP to guarantee the

Table 1. Probability of dynamic failure in Poisson streams with same constraint, heterogeneous system and burst streams

Poisson Stream				Heterogeneous system				Burst streams			
Avg Load	DBP	E_DBP	% Rd	Avg Load	DBP	E_DBP	% Rd	Avg Load	DBP	E_DBP	% Rd
1.0	0.055	0.055	-	1.3	0.032	0.032	-	0.5	0.000	0.000	-
1.1	0.096	0.095	0.8	1.4	0.053	0.054	-2.3	0.6	0.006	0.006	3.3
1.2	0.156	0.154	1.3	1.5	0.083	0.084	-1.6	0.7	0.031	0.031	-
1.3	0.229	0.223	2.4	1.6	0.115	0.117	-1.0	0.8	0.078	0.075	4.0
1.4	0.311	0.299	3.9	1.7	0.157	0.157	0.3	0.9	0.150	0.145	3.3
1.5	0.398	0.378	5.0	1.8	0.200	0.198	0.8	1.0	0.227	0.213	6.0
1.6	0.481	0.449	6.5	1.9	0.245	0.240	1.8	1.1	0.296	0.270	8.7
1.7	0.557	0.514	7.8	2.0	0.293	0.284	3.1	1.2	0.371	0.337	9.1
1.8	0.623	0.569	8.7	2.1	0.339	0.323	4.8	1.3	0.449	0.409	8.8
1.9	0.675	0.612	9.2	2.2	0.381	0.362	6.6	1.4	0.509	0.472	7.4
2.0	0.716	0.649	9.3	2.3	0.431	0.394	8.6	1.5	0.556	0.509	8.4

(m,k)-firm constraint and substantially reduce probabilities of dynamic failure obviously with average load varied from 0.5-1.5. At load 1.2, there is maximum reduction percent 9.1%. It is obvious that the probability of dynamic failure is higher in burst case than in Poisson case at the same average load, because the peak load is heavier and the packets are more concentrated in the burst case.

4.2 Delay Analysis

Delay is the time interval between the departures of packet from the source to the arrival at the destination. This is usually referred to as end-to-end delay. In MIQSS model, delay just only means the queue delay. Delay is an important parameter of QoS. Many real-time applications such as voice over IP (VoIP), video-conference, and tele-medicine require guarantees on delay and packet loss. These applications are usually sensitive to delay and loss-tolerance. Smaller delay will make media stream more smoothly. This statistic represents instantaneous measurements of packet waiting times in the queue of server, and delay of all discarded packets is not calculated in this statistic. The simulation results also through the above three examples reveal that E_DBP can reduce the delay than DBP at different degree when (m,k)-load is varied. At some appropriate load duration, queue delay is decreased more effectively, but some light load, it is not so significant. The third example is burst stream, the packets are more concentrated at the ON state, so at a lighter (m,k)-load in burst case, we can still get the similar result with the Poisson stream cases. For the delay in the burst case, it fluctuates acutely because of concentration of packets.

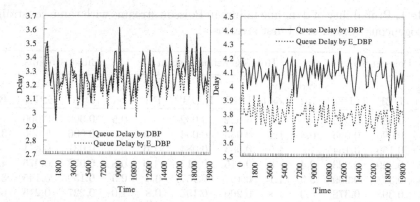

Fig. 1. Queue delay comparison of E_DBP and DBP for Poisson streams with (3,4)-firm at (m,k)-load equals to 1 and 1.5

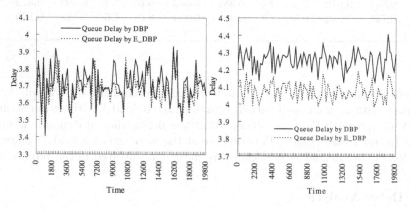

Fig. 2. Queue delay comparison of E_DBP and DBP for heterogeneous system at (m,k)-load equals to 1 and 1.5

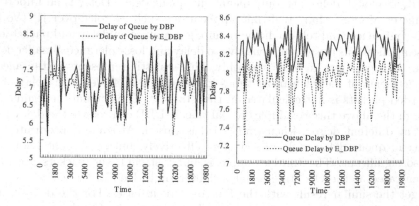

Fig. 3. Queue delay comparison of E_DBP and DBP for burst stream (3,4)-firm at(m,k)-load equals to 0.5 and 1

5   Conclusions

The main original contributions of this paper are:

- Point out the drawbacks of the classic DBP when it is applied to a more general real-time context and corresponding possible solutions.
- Propose E_DBP to correct DBP by taking the distribution of "0,1"in k-sequence into account when stream is in a failure state, and give the equation to calculate the distance to exit failure state.
- Show that E_DBP can get lower probability of dynamic failure and smaller queue delay than classic DBP, which is validated by various cases through simulation based on OPNET 8.0.c.

This improvement is made with a very low computing cost or complexity, only to check minimum 1s, which needs to be added to the right position. Furthermore, this new computing is only needed when the stream is in a failure state. In this sense, our algorithm is interesting in guaranteeing (m,k)-firm QoS in network scheduling. Furthermore, WFQ and RED combined with (m,k)-firm constraint also may be an interesting work.

Acknowledgements

The authors thank the anonymous reviewers for their valuable comments that improve the quality of this paper and financial support of Sino-France Advanced Research Program(No:PRA SI03-02) and NSFC(No:60203030).

References

[1] Mittal, A., Manimaran, G., Siva Ram Murthy, C.: Integrated Dynamic Scheduling of Hard and QoS Degradable Real-Time Tasks in Multiprocessor Systems. Journal of Systems Architecture. **46** (2000) 793–807
[2] El-gendy, M.A., Bose, A., Shin, K.G.: Evolution of the Internet QoS and Support for Soft Real-Time Applications. Proceedings of IEEE. **91** (2003) 1086–1104
[3] Peha, J.M., Tobagi, F.A.: A Cost-Based Scheduling Algorithm to Support Integrated Services. In: Proceedings of IEEE INFOCOM., IEEE (1991) 741–753
[4] Hamdaoui, M., Ramanathan, P.: A Dynamic Priority Assignment Technique for Streams with (m,k)-Firm Deadlines. IEEE Transactions on Computers. **44** (1995) 1443–1451
[5] Bernat, G., Burns, A., Llamosi, A.: A Weakly Hard Real-Time Systems. IEEE Transaction on Computers. **50** (2001) 308–321
[6] Poggi, E.M., Song, Y.Q., Koubaa, A., Wang, Z.: Matrix-DBP for (m,k)-Firm Real-Time Guarantee. In: Proceedings of Real-Time and Embedded System., Paris (2003) 457–482
[7] Chen, J.M., Song, Y.Q., Wang, Z., Sun, Y.X.: Equivalent Matrix-DBP for (m,k)-Firm Deadline. In: Proceedings of IEEE International Symposium on Industrial Electronics. (2004) 675–680
[8] Saleh, M.A., Habib, I.W., Saadawi, T.N.: Simulation Analysis of A Communication Link with Statistically Multiplexed Bursty Voice Sources. IEEE Journal on Selected Areas in Communication. **11** (1993) 432–442

Weighted Fair Scheduling Algorithm for QoS of Input-Queued Switches

Sang-Ho Lee[1], Dong-Ryeol Shin[2], and Hee Yong Youn[2]

[1] Samsung Electronics, System LSI Division, Korea
sangho74.lee@samsung.com
http://nova.skku.ac.kr
[2] Sungkyunkwan University, Information and Communication Engineering, Korea
{drshin, youn}@ece.skku.ac.kr

Abstract. The high speed network usually deals with two main issues. The first is fast switching to get good throughput. At present, the state-of-the-art switches are employing input queued architecture to get high throughput. The second is providing QoS guarantees for a wide range of applications. This is generally considered in output queued switches. For these two requirements, there have been lots of scheduling mechanisms to support both better throughput and QoS guarantees in high speed switching networks. In this paper, we present a scheduling algorithm for providing QoS guarantees and higher throughput in an input queued switch. The proposed algorithm, called Weighted Fair Matching (WFM), which provides QoS guarantees without output queues, i.e., WFM is a flow based algorithm that achieves asymptotically 100% throughput with no speed up while providing QoS.

Keywords: scheduling algorithm, input queued switch, QoS

1 Introduction

The input queued switch overcomes the scalability problem occurring in the output queued switches. However, it is well known that the input-queued switch with a FIFO queue in each input port suffers the Head-of-Line (HOL) blocking problem which limits the throughput to 58% [1].

Lots of algorithms have been suggested to improve the throughput. In order to overcome the performance reduction due to HOL blocking, most of proposed input queued switches have separate queues called Virtual Output Queue(VOQ) for different output ports at each input port. With VOQs, Input queued switches need matching algorithm to make input-output port pairs.

Parallel Iterative Matching (PIM), which is one of Maximum Size Matching schemes, is a three-phase scheduling algorithm which uses parallelism, randomness and iteration to achieve higher throughput[2]. Some variations of PIM such as iSLIP[3] appeared. iSLIP is very efficient and its throughput can reach 100% but does not address QoS problems.

H. Jin et al. (Eds.): NPC 2004, LNCS 3222, pp. 366–373, 2004.
© IFIP International Federation for Information Processing 2004

Another proposed algorithm is RPA which realizes Maximum Weighted Matching (MWM) scheme [4], which is based on reservation rounds where the switching input ports indicate their most urgent data transfer needs. RPA took a similar approach with different scheduling algorithm as a proposed method presented in this paper.

There has been a large amount of works on providing service guarantees in the integrated service networks. Various scheduling algorithms are proposed to provide QoS guarantees. Generalized Processor Sharing (GPS) is considered an ideal scheduling discipline[5]. The GPS is based on a fluid model where the packets are assumed to be infinitely divisible and multiple sessions may transmit traffic through the outgoing link simultaneously. Weighted Fair Queuing (WFQ) is a packetized generalized process sharing[6]. Some variations of WFQ, Self-Clocked Fair Queuing(SCFQ), Virtual-Clock(VC), Deficit Round Robin (DRR) etc. appeared in the literature to address the computational problem of WFQ.

Most of algorithms for QoS provisioning have been done in the context of output queued switch where the speed of the switching fabric and output buffer memory is required to N times the input line speed. As line speeds increase and as routers have more input ports, the required fabric speed becomes infeasible and non-scalable. For these reasons, in addition to the demand for high throughput on routers or switches with input queued architecture, there is an increasing need for supporting applications with diverse performance requirements where QoS is guaranteed.

However there has been a restriction to provide QoS guarantees in an input queued switch: input queued switch is scalable but lead to some packets not being promptly transmitted across switch fabric because enqueued packets can not be isolated, which may lead to violating QoS. Therefore the goal of providing QoS guarantees in the input queued switch is to design a scheduling algorithm which can provide QoS requirements so that queued packets are transmitted across the switch fabric promptly (i.e., throughput maximization).

In this paper, we propose a scheduling algorithm for providing QoS guarantees and high throughput in an input queued switch. The proposed algorithm, called Weighted Fair Matching (WFM), which is a flow based algorithm that provides bandwidth allocation. Like other matching algorithms, it can achieve asymptotically 100% throughput under uniform traffic.

The WFM in input queued switches is unique in a sense that the selection right and corresponding matching mechanism based on virtual finishing time of WFQ is done at the output port where the number of connections to the output ports and the virtual finishing time stamps already computed and transferred by input ports are involved.

This paper is organized as follows. Section 2 gives a basic principle of the proposed scheduling method. Section 3 shows the performance based on simulation. The conclusion is drawn in section 4.

2   Weighted Fair Matching Algorithm

We now propose an algorithm, WFM, which applies Weighted Fair Queueing (WFQ) [6] at the input port switch. This algorithm operates as a scheduler to avoid HOL-blocking and to provide QoS guarantees simultaneously. Like other scheduling algorithms in input queued switch, WFM uses multiple virtual queues at the input port for each output port. In this section, we first describe how to derive a WFQ in the input queued switch and then present a WFM.

2.1   Applying Weighted Fair Queueing

The GPS is an ideal scheme for fluid traffics which are assumed to be infinitely divisible and multiple connections may transmit traffic through the output port simultaneously at different rates. Its packetized version, WFQ scheduling algorithm can be thought of as a way to emulate the hypothetical GPS discipline by a practical packet-by-packet transmission scheme.

For an $N \times N$ output queued switch, the bandwidth of each output port is shared by N flows. In this case, each output port has a WFQ system which is composed of a WFQ server and N queues for N flows. In every slot, each output port's WFQ server selects one among its own queues.

Figure 1 depicts the overall block diagram of WFM in a 2×2 input queued switch. We shall denote the kth input and output ports by I_k and O_k, respectively. Let $F(i,j)$ is the flow which is switched from I_i to O_j.

Applying WFQ to the input queued switch is not much different from the case of the output queued switch. In the input queued switch, the flow, $F(i,j)$, is a backlogged Q_i^j which denotes a virtual output queue for O_j in I_i. Like output queued switches, there are N WFQ systems. Let S_j be a WFQ server in O_j. This server includes a virtual-time for tracking normalized fair service amount. As shown in Fig.1, a WFQ system for O_j is composed of S_j and N VOQs located in the input ports and destined for O_j.

In input ports, all arriving packets are tagged with virtual finishing times computed according to WFQ based on allocated bandwidth. The time-stamp,i $TS_{i,j}^k$, associated with k'th packet of the $F(i,k)$ is calculated as follows:

$$TS_{i,k}^k = max\{v_j(t), TS_{i,j}^{k-1}\} + \frac{L_{i,j}^k}{\omega_{i,j}} \tag{1}$$

where $L_{i,j}^k$ denotes a packet length and $v_j(t)$ the virtual-time of S_j.

2.2   Description of WFM

In the previous subsection, we described WFQ to share each output port in input queued switch. For input queued switches, the main problem is how to match input-output ports to get high throughput. In [14], WFQ is used to make input-output port matching with simple sequential scheduling. But this approach did not show to provide QoS in an input queued switch.

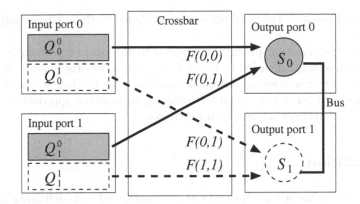

Fig. 1. Weighted fair queueing in an 2×2 input queued switch

We propose a scheduling scheme which operates as not only matching input-output ports but also providing QoS. As shown in figure 1, the switch model for WFM has non-buffered crossbar and its all output ports are connected to a shared medium, called a bus whose main role broadcasts information on input-output port matching to all output ports concerned. Three steps are used to resolve the conflict among input ports using. It is described as follows:

Step 1: Request. Each input port sends a request to every output port for which it has a queued cell. Each request corresponds to nonempty VOQ and includes the time-stamp (i.e., virtual finishing time), $TS_{i,j}^k$, of the cell at the head of the VOQ. All received requests along time-stamps are stored at a request array of each output. The request array of O_j is denoted by R_j and It consists of N elements, denoted by $R_j[i]$ with $1 \leq i \leq N$, which contains corresponding virtual finishing time. In addition, if an output port receives one or more requests, it counts the number of connections destined for itself which is denoted by C_j.

Step 2: Sort and Output Port Selection. Every output ports are sorted based on the number of received requests (i.e., C_j) in an increasing order. It determines turns of which output port is granted the right to select an input port ahead of other output ports. The reason why a sorting operation is performed with an ascending order is that an output port with the smallest number of backlogged flow has less input ports to match so that it is granted to make its selection earlier than the others, which brings a higher probability of matching pairs. For example, if two output ports have a relation with $v'_m(t) > v'_n(t)$, The input-output pair for O_m should be determined earlier than O_n.

Step 3: Input Port Selection and Matching. Once granted to choose input ports, the output port picks up an input port with smallest virtual finishing time expressed by via time-stamps. Furthermore, at most one input port among unmatched input ports is chosen. On selecting an input port, the information about "matched ports" is transferred (or broadcasted) by a common bus to all output ports so that the same input is not permitted to be selected by another output. This process is repeated until all matchings are done sequentially at the output port.

In short, the selection priority is granted to the output port with smallest number of connections denoted by C_j (via step 2), on the other hand, the matching mechanism by the selected output is done based on the time-stamps of input ports connected (via step 3), which is different from other approaches taken in RPA where a matching is done by input ports.

3   Simulation

We perform simulations to illustrate the capability of fast switching and QoS provisioning of the proposed method. With simulation experiments, we show about switching performance, delay control capability, bandwidth allocation capability, and fairness. Each subsection describes those results.

3.1   Switching Performance

Simulation is performed on a 16×16 switch, where each input has 16 flows for each output port, totally 256 flows. Each flow reserves same bandwidth as each weight. To evaluate switching capability, we measured average delay time and compared it with iSLIP and RPA algorithms. In this simulation iSLIP operate as 4-iteration, because the minimum required number of iteration iSLIP is $log_2 N$ [3]. Concerning the input traffic, we consider two types of models.

1. Uniform traffic : cells arrive with Bernoulli arrival process, the cell output ports are selected with random independently
2. Bursty traffic : cells arrive with on-off arrival process modulated by a two-state Markov chain with destinations uniformly distributed over all output ports

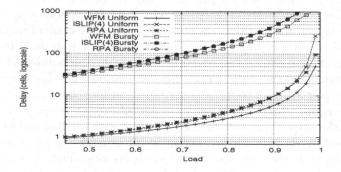

Fig. 2. Average delay under uniform traffic

Fig. 2 shows the curves of the average cell delay normalized with respect to slot time. For the uniform traffic, WFM provides improvement over iSLIP in average delay. At light loads below 60%, All have similar delay time, while for high load above 60%, delay time with WFM are less than half of iSLIP and RPA. For the loads less than 90%, RPA have longest delay time. As the result WFM provide improved delay performance over iSLIP and RPA, which is due to transient delay at a start and priority assignment. Hence, iSLIP is capable of achieving 100% denotes that WFM achieve 100% throughput for uniform traffic.

For the bursty traffic, WFM has also best performance. In this work, the bursty on length is 32.

3.2 Delay Control Capability

Fig. 3 shows the capability of delay control. The simulation is performed under the same situation as in section 3.1, but all flows to each output port have different weights. Each output port has 16 flows, the flows' weights are configured as 1 to 16. We took samples for $F(1,1)$, $F(4,1)$, $F(8,1)$, $F(12,1)$ and $F(16,1)$ at O_1.

The delay control ability of WFM is compared with output queued switches. The result of the output queued switch is shown in Fig. 4. At light loads below 60%, each flow's delay is almost identical that of output queued switch, while for high load above 60%, delay time of all flows are more than those of output queued switch. However, WFM can control each flow's delay.

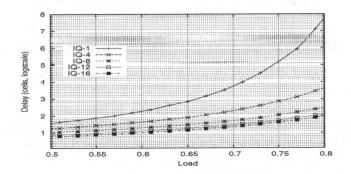

Fig. 3. Delay per flow using WFM

3.3 Throughput with Weighted Fair Bandwidth Allocation

In this subsection, we demonstrate WFM's ability of allocating bandwidth among input ports in proportion to their reservations. The simulation is performed on a 8×8 switch where each input port has one flow, totally 8 flows, destined to O_1. Each flow is assigned the weight as 1 to 8. As shown Fig. 5, the bandwidth

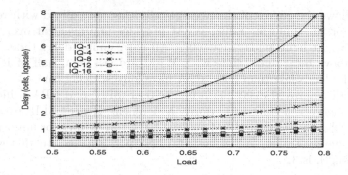

Fig. 4. Delay per flow using WFQ in output queued switch

is distributed in proportion to each flow's weight under uniform traffic. WFM
can allocate the switch bandwidth.

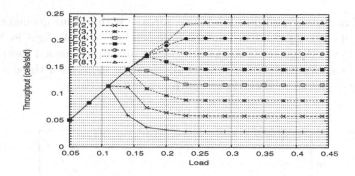

Fig. 5. Throughput per flow under uniform traffic

Fig. 6 presents the result under bursty traffic with busrty length 32. The
bandwidth of each flow is also allocated in proportion to it's weight.

4   Conclusion

In this paper we proposed a scheme, called weighted fair matching (WFM) for
providing QoS in an input queued switch. We described how to apply a weighted
fair queueing of the output queued switch to the input queued switch and proposed a simple matching method. The WFM is a flow based fair scheduling
algorithm and operate sequentially. Its main feature is to provide good throughput and to allocate the output bandwidth in a simple manner. We showed that
the proposed scheme achieved 100% throughput with low latency and provided
QoS guarantees.

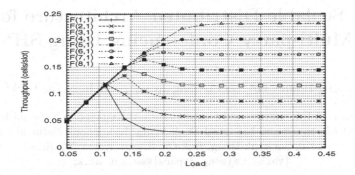

Fig. 6. Throughput per flow under bursty traffic

References

1. M. Karol, M. Hluchyj, S. Morgan : Input versus output queueing on a space division switch, IEEE Transactions on Commumnication, vol.35 (1987) 1347–1356
2. T. Anderson, S. Owicki, I. Saxe, C. Thacker : High speed switch scheduling for local area networks, ACM Transactions on Computer Systems, vol.11 (1993) 1871–1894
3. Mckeon N., Mekkittikul A.: A practcal scheduling algorithm to achieve 100% throughput in input-queued switches, Proceedings of IEEE INFOCOM'98, vol. 2 (1998) 792-799
4. Ajmone Marsan M., Bianco A., Leonardi E. : RPA: a simple efficient and flexible policy for input buffered ATM switches, IEEE Communication Letters, vol.1 (1997) 83-86
5. Parekh A.K. Gallager R.G: A generalized processor sharing approach to flow control in integrated services network, ACM Transactions on Computer Systems, Vol. 11 (1993), 319-352
6. A.Demers, S. Keshav, S. Shenker: Analysis and Simulation of a Fair Queuing Algorithm, Proceedings of SIGCOMM89, (1989) 3-12
7. S. Golestani: A self-clocked fair queueing scheme for broadband applications, Proceedings of IEEE INFOCOM'94, (1994) 636-645.
8. L. Zhang: VirtualClock: a new traffic control algorithm for packet switching networks, ACM Transactions on Computer Systems, Vol. 9, (MAY 1991) 101-124
9. M. Shreedhar, G. Varghese: Efficient fair queueing using deficit round robin, Proceedings of SIGCOMM, (1995).
10. Ge Nong, Mounir Hamdi: On the provision of Quality-of-Service Guarantees for Input Queued Switches, IEEE Communications Magazine, (December 2000) 62-69
11. D. Stiliadis, A.Varma: Providing bandwidth guarantees in an input-buffered crossbar switch, Proceedings of IEEE INFOCOM'95, (1995) 960-968
12. N. Ni, L. N. Bhuyan: Fair scheduling and buffer management in internet routers, Proceedings of IEEE INFOCOM'02, (2002) 1141-1150
13. Xiao Zhang, L. N. Bhuyan: Deficit Round-Robin Scheduling for Input-Queued Switches, IEEE Journal on selected areas in communications, Vol. 21, (MAY 2003) 584-594
14. Sang Ho Lee and Dong Ryeol Shin: "A simple pipelined scheduling for input queued switch", ISCIS 2003 , November 2003, 844-851.

A Scalable Distributed Architecture for Multi-party Conferencing Using SIP

Young-Hoon Cho[1], Moon-Sang Jeong[2], and Jong-Tae Park[2]

[1] Department of Information and Communication, Kyungpook National University
[2] School of Electronic and Electrical Engineering, Kyungpook National University
1370, Sankyuk-Dong, Buk-Gu, Taegu, Korea 702-701
{yhcho,msjeong,jtpark}@ee.knu.ac.kr

Abstract. As various multimedia communication services are increasingly required by Internet users, several signaling protocols have been proposed for the efficient control of complex multimedia communication services. However, the model and architecture of multi-party conferencing which is currently being standardized by IETF has some limitation in scalability to meet the requirement for the management of large-scale multimedia conferencing service. In this article, we have presented a new scalable distributed architecture for the efficient management of large-scale multimedia conferencing service which is based on SIP. The high scalability is achieved by adding, deleting and modifying the multiple mixers and composing conference server network in a distributed way, in a real-time, and without disruption of services. The SIP-based control mechanism for achieving the scalability has been designed in detail. Finally, the performance of the proposed architecture has been evaluated by simulation.

1 Introduction

Internet telephony services provide not only traditional voice services, but also application services based on packet, so these are applied in various multimedia communication services such as video, and multi-party conferencing. Demands for Internet telephony services are steadily increasing. Additionally, signaling protocols, applications, and models have been developed for efficient control of complex multimedia communication services.

Internet telephony services use IETF standard protocols such as H.323, SIP, and MGCP for call control and signaling. An ITU-T's H.323 defines the terminal and other components to provide multimedia communication on a packet network [1]. An SIP (Session Initiation Protocol) is an application layer signaling protocol standardized by IETF which defines initiation, modification, and termination of multimedia communication session between users [2]. Because SIP supports flexibility, user mobility, and various merits, its application area is wide.

Currently, a great deal of research about conferencing models and controlling mechanisms using SIP are being conducted to provide complex multi-party

H. Jin et al. (Eds.): NPC 2004, LNCS 3222, pp. 374–381, 2004.

conferencing. IETF MMUSIC working group studies the general requirements of Internet multimedia conference structure for supporting multi-party conferencing [3]. IETF SIPPING working group proposes several drafts for multi-party conferencing based on SIP [4]. Stream processing like mixing and encoding about various types of media, and performance evaluation are studied in a conference based on centralized server model [8]. Based on the handling method for signaling and redistribution of stream, a conferencing model can be generally divided into end system mixing, multicast, centralized server, and full mesh and the characteristics of each models are described as shown in Table 1.

Table 1. Characteristics of conferencing models

Model	Signaling	Media	Inviting	Joining	Scalability
End System Mixing	Tree	Tree	INVITE	INVITE	Small
Multicast	Pairs	Multicast	INVITE	Multicast Join	Large
Centralized Server	Star	Star	REFER	INVITE	Medium
Full Mesh	Star	Full Mesh	REFER+ Server msg.	INVITE+ Server msg.	Medium

Even though multicast model has huge scalability, but it is hard to apply because multicast is not deployed widely. Currently, the centralized server model is adopted as basic multi-party conferencing model. However, this model has limitations of scalability such as triangular transmission by using single conference server, bottleneck by traffic concentration, and processing overload. Thus, a new scalable conferencing model supporting large scale multi-party conference is needed. More specifically, a new model needs to be designed which can facilitate the transition to the new model and the integration with the existing conferencing model, using standard signaling method. In this paper, we suggest a new scalable distributed architecture for multi-party conferencing using SIP that can reduce traffic and processing load, and that can support scalability by constructing a special network for conferencing servers.

In this architecture, a participant host acquires information of the adjacent conferencing server, and several conferencing servers can join a conference using this information. Stream can be delivered efficiently in this architecture. A distributed conference can be constructed from the existing conferencing model by using the standard signaling procedure, and can distribute load by constructing a conference server network without changing the end host. Using adjacent conference server information and data distribution mechanism, it can provide a virtual multicast conference.

In this paper, we analyze the features of the existing multi-party conferencing models using SIP, and propose a new distributed architecture for multi-party conferencing which can support scalability, load distribution, and traffic distribution. Specifically, we describe a signaling procedure and conferencing mechanism that can make this architecture more scalable.

2   Distributed Conferencing Architecture

In the case of a centralized conferencing model, there are some problems due to the conference control mechanism using single server. First, according to server location, although the conference server is far away from the participants, data transmission between participants is always performed through the conference server. Bottleneck may occur because the traffic of all participants may be concentrated to the server, and the processing load of the server can increase rapidly because the server must mix and encode all the streams. A centralized conferencing model has limitation of scalability in a large scale conference environment. Therefore, a new multi-party conferencing model that can deliver stream effectively and can provide scalability is needed. A new distributed conferencing model which can provide scalability is thus proposed.

We propose distributed conferencing architecture for the large-scale multimedia conferencing service. In Fig. 1, we describe the distributed conferencing architecture which vertically consists of three tiers: a conference management tier, a mixer tier for multimedia stream processing, and the participants. The salient feature of the architecture is that the conference management tier is configured in a distributed way.

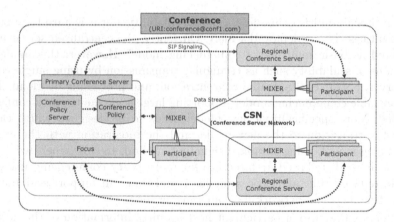

Fig. 1. Distributed Conferencing Architecture

In the distributed conferencing architecture, a conference consists of several local conference servers (CS). Each local conference server contains a focus which is responsible for the management of the corresponding local conferencing service. The focus also manages the corresponding mixers in the region for load sharing and media streaming. In the architecture, one of the conference servers is designated as a primary conference server (PCS). The conference is horizontally comprised of PCS, several regional CSs for signaling and streaming of the conference. Both the PCS and the regional CS control the conferencing operations using the SIP signaling with some extension in accordance with the conference policy. The CS also handles mixing and redistribution of multimedia streams such as conference video and audio streams. The set of CSs involved in the conference constitute a network called as a conference server network (CSN).

The PCS is responsible for the control of the whole conference in an integrated way. It sets up the CSN and modifies the CSN. It also controls the access to the conference server so that the participants should first get the permission from the PCS to participate in a specific conference session. The PCS announces the conference session information using session announcement protocol (SAP) [12], and handles participation requests. The PCS can add and delete mixers according to the scale of conference, so that it can compose the CSN properly. Thus, the control and mixing operations are distributed in the proposed distributed conferencing architecture, so that the processing overload and traffic concentration can be reduced. These features can greatly enhance the scalability of the conferencing system.

Basically, one of the CSs in a conference is selected automatically to play the role of PCS. If the PCS leaves the CSN, a PCS transition procedure occurs so that another CS in the CSN can be the PCS. Through this, conferencing can be maintained without unnecessary CS. Since the CSN can be configured independently of participants, participants don't have to take care of the composition of the CSN. This makes the signaling and stream procedure of the centralized conferencing model to be used without modification. Additionally, the triangular transmission which is caused by accessing the remote server can be eliminated, and delay and traffic in the core network can be reduced accordingly.

In order to efficiently support the conferencing operation of the proposed distributed architecture, we have extended the SIP signaling method for the exchange of ACS information between the primary focus and the participants. This can be achieved by using ACSInfo header. ACSInfo header is newly defined extended SIP signaling information for the proposed distributed conferencing architecture. The primary focus uses the ACSInfo header information to configure a conference mixer network. The format of the ACSInfo header which is defined in the distributed conferencing model is show below.

```
ACSInfo: SIP-URI or hostport
```

However, even if an end host does not send ACS information, a CS can handle conference composition and signaling process. That is, if the end host is a 'Conference Unaware UA', it can participate in a conference.

A NOTIFY message is used to exchange the information of the participants when the conference status is changed. When participants join a conference, participants subscribe by using the conference notification message, and receive a notification message which contains the current conference status such as participant status, conference server status, PCS transition notification and CS table exchange. Using the participant status notification message, the PCS broadcasts the status change information to all the participants when a participant joins and leaves. The CS status message includes the information on the configuration of CSN and stream transmission mechanism. The CS table exchange message includes the participant list and the stream type of the mixer.

3   Signaling of Distributed Conferencing Architecture

A distributed conferencing uses SIP signaling to construct a conference and CSN. A conference server operates like a general SIP UA, and a user can join a conference by submitting a connection request to the CS. Figure 2 shows a test network that is designed to examine conference composition procedures of the distributed conferencing. Procedures of invitation, joining, and leaving a test network, changing conference session, and making a PCS transition are examined.

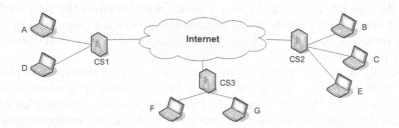

Fig. 2. Test Network for Distributed Conferencing

- **Conference Initiation**

  Because a distributed conferencing is based on the dial-in conferencing model, the signaling procedure for invitation is to the same as the dial-in model. When host A invites host B, a CS1 that is the ACS of A takes charge of the current conference signaling. Host A requests the creation of a session to the CS1 and then CS1 becomes the PCS for additional signaling and conference control. Finally, host A and B are connected with the CS1 according to the test network.

- **Inviting and Joining**

  After a conference is created, if a participant wishes to invite a new user, the participant sends a REFER message to the relevant host. Then, the end host can join a conference by sending an INVITE message to the CS. If a end host wishes to join a conference, the host can acquire the session information about the conference by SAP and access the CS using the INVITE message. At this time, access point is always the PCS. The PCS connects with the current CS using the INVTE message of the participant, or if necessary, handles all signaling procedures after the CSN is composed by adding CS.

  If the ACS information of a new participant is equal to the ACS information of existent participants in a single CS conference, it is better to change for efficient stream flowing. For example, when host A invites host C and where host B and C have the same ACS information, the CS transition is occurred. The CS transition procedure is identical to PCS transition procedure.

  When a new participant joins a conference, the new CS can participate in the conference according to the CS policy. At this time, a new conference session is formed between the conference servers. If the PCS decides to participate in a new CS, the PCS sends an INVTE message to the new CS. The CSN initiates a conference session, and the conferencing model of the CSN can be a full mesh, centralized, end system mixing, or hybrid type according to the conference's policy, If the CSN is established and a new CS is added, participants who have the new CS as ACS reestablish their session. For this, a PCS requires relevant participants to reconnect with the new CS sending a REFER message. Accordingly, relevant participants send an INVITE message to the new CS and terminate the session with the old CS.

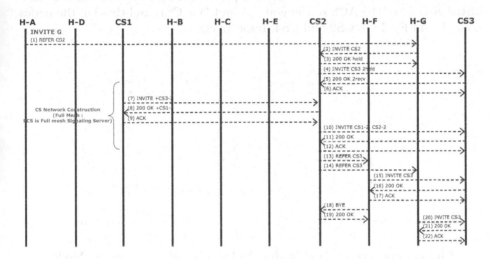

Fig. 3. Signaling Procedures for Joining and CSN Composition

Fig. 3 shows the signaling procedure for inviting a host G where hosts A and D are connected with a CS1, and host B, C, E, and F are connected with CS2. Because hosts F and G have CS3 as their ACS, a CS transition and a CSN re-composition will take place.

• **Leaving**

When a participant wishes to leave a conference session while conference progresses, the participant sends a BYE message to the connected CS. The participant's leaving can leads to CS's leaving in CSN. When a participant leaves, if the number of participants belonging to a CS is lower than the value of minimum CS participants decided by policy, the CS leaves the CSN. Therefore, CS send REFER message to participants belonging to itself that participants will reestablish connection with another CS. When all of remaining participants leave CS, the CS sends a BYE message to the PCS and leaves the CSN. If the CS is a PCS, a PCS transition occurs. The PCS passes the role of PCS to one of the remaining CS, and notifies all participant of the PCS change by sending a NOTIFY message to everyone.

4   Performance Analysis

In this section, we evaluated the performance of the distributed multi-party conferencing model. In particular, we compare the performance of the existing centralized conferencing model with the distributed model that we have proposed. We have measured a signaling delay, a stream transmission delay and a processing load of a conference server for the test network which is shown in Fig. 2. In the centralized mode of conferencing management, the CS1 play the role of the centralized server, whereas in a distributed model, the management operations and the stream distribution is performed by CS1, CS2 and CS3 in a distributed way. The ACS of the nodes A and D is CS1, and those of the nodes B, C, E and F, G are CS2 and CS3, respectively.

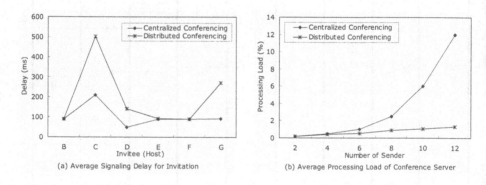

(a) Average Signaling Delay for Invitation   (b) Average Processing Load of Conference Server

Fig. 4. Performance Analysis for the Distributed Conferencing Model

Fig. 4 (a) shows the delay characteristics when the participant A invites other participants B, C, D, E, F and G. The delay is measured in the average signaling completion time. Initially, the participant A invites the participant B, and in this case, the average signaling delay is identical in both distributed and centralized models. This is indicated by the delay due to inviting the participant B. However, when the participant C is invited, the CSN is re-configured. A new conference server CS2 is joined to handle the media requests from the new participant C, and the existing participant B should be assigned to the CS2. This re-adjustment generates some delay so that the invitation completion time for the participant C is large as shown in Fig. 4 (a). This pattern of re-configuration continues to invite other participants D, E, F, and G, and the related signaling delay times are shown. As shown in Figure 4, the distributed conferencing model creates larger delay time than that of the centralized conferencing model. However, when the number of participants is large, and they are grouped and located in different regions, the signaling delay can be reduced since the regional CS can perform the conference management functions which are related to the corresponding region.

Fig. 4 (b) shows the result of measuring the processing load for encoding/decoding and mixing at the conference server for the transmission of stream.

Both the processing load of the centralized conferencing model and that of the distributed conferencing model are shown in comparison. As shown in Fig. 4 (b), the processing load of the centralized model drastically increases as the number of participants increase, while in the distributed model, the processing load is almost constant. This illustrates the fact that the distributed model performs n better than the centralized model with regard to the scalability.

In the case of a large conference, because a number of hosts connected to each CS are smaller than the centralized conferencing, a processing load of each CS is lower than the centralize server. Especially, if a CSN may be constructed a tree topology instead of a full mesh topology in a test network, a load of CSs may be more decreased.

5   Conclusion

In this paper, we suggest a new distributed conferencing architecture which can provide better scalability that appears to be very important feature in a wide-scale Internet community. We specifically design signaling procedures and conferencing mechanisms for this architecture. The proposed architecture facilitates both the integration with the existing models and transition from the existing models, providing efficient load and traffic distribution, thereby achieving great scalability. For further study, we are planning to apply the architecture in a real environment and to evaluate the performance enhancement by comparison with other works.

References

1. ITU-T "Recommendation H.323: Packet-based Multimedia Communications Systems", ITU, Geneva, November 2000
2. J. Rosenberg, H. Schulzrinne, Camarillo, G., Johnston, A., Peterson, J., Sparks, R., Handley, M. and E. Schooler, "SIP: Session Initiation Protocol", RFC 3261, June 2002.
3. M. Handley, J. Crowcroft, C. Bormann and J. Ott, "The Internet Multimedia Conferencing Architecture", Internet-Draft, MMUSIC WG, July 2000
4. J. Rosenberg and H. Schulzrinne, "Models for Multi Party Conferencing in SIP", Internet-Draft, SIPPING WG, July 2003
5. O. Levin and R.Even, "High Level Requirements for Tightly Coupled SIP Conferencing", Internet-Draft, SIPPING WG, April 2003
6. J. Rosenberg, "A Framework for Conferencing with the Session Initiation Protocol", Internet-Draft, SIPPING WG, May 2003
7. A. Johnston and O. Levin, "Session Initiation Protocol Call Control - Conferencing for User Agents", Internet-Draft, SIPPING WG, June 2003
8. Kundan Singh, Gautam Nair and Henning Schulzrinne, "Centralized Conferencing using SIP", Proceedings of the 2nd IP-Telephony Workshop, April 2001
9. J. Veizades, E. Guttman, C. Perkins and S. Kaplan, "Service Location Protocol", RFC 2165, June 1997
10. M. Handley, C. Perkins and E. Whelan, "Service Announcement Protocol", RFX 2974, October 2000

DC-mesh: A Contracted High-Dimensional Mesh for Dynamic Clustering

Masaru Takesue

Dept. Electronics and Information Engr., Hosei University, Tokyo 184-8584 Japan
takesue@ami.ei.hosei.ac.jp

Abstract. This paper proposes a *DC-mesh* network that allows requesting nodes to be put into clusters while the requests are sent to a target node, as well as is easy to layout on an LSI chip. To organize the DC-mesh, we use the partitioning in the word space based on the Hamming code [1]. We introduce an index scheme, (parity-value,information-value), in the word space, and map it onto a 4-D (dimensional) mesh so that the Hamming distance between the words in each partition is preserved in the Manhattan distance between the corresponding nodes on the mesh; two of the dimensions are contracted for easy wiring. The resultant DC-mesh consists of a number of local 2-D meshes and a single global 2-D mesh; all processing nodes linked to one local mesh are connected to one node of the global mesh via a bus to compensate for the contraction. A subset of the nodes in a partition organizes a dynamic cluster. The diameter equals the greater of the diameters of local and global meshes.

1 Introduction

To reduce communication latency in multiprocessors, a cache hierarchy in a *static cluster*, of which member nodes are fixed in hardware, is a popular technique. However, the static cluster cannot adapt efficiently to the change of communication patterns, due to the contention on per-cluster resources such as the directory for cache coherence, and because of the complexity of cache protocols.

For hypercube-connected systems, a *dynamic cluster* can be organized of which member nodes are determined during the requests are sent to the target node [2], exploiting the partitioning of the n-bit word space based on the n-bit Hamming code [1]; one cluster consists of a subset of nodes in a partition. No per-cluster resource is required for the clustering. The distance between the representative and another nodes in each cluster is less than three.

The hypercube, however, needs long wires to layout, that will lead to an unacceptably long signal-delay in a future LSI chip [3]. This paper addresses such networks that need no long wires, but also can produce dynamic clusters. As a network with such properties, we propose a *DC-mesh* (*Dynamically Clustering mesh*). To organize the mesh, we map the partitions in the word space [1] onto a high-dimensional mesh so that the Hamming distance in the word space is preserved in the Manhattan distance on the mesh as completely as possible.

H. Jin et al. (Eds.): NPC 2004, LNCS 3222, pp. 382–389, 2004.

We start with a 2-D (dimensional) array of the words indexed by their parity and information values. With a reflected Gray code sequence, we map the array onto a 4-D mesh, but contract two of the dimensions for easy layout. This leads to multiple local 2-D meshes and a single global 2-D mesh that are disconnected with each other. To obtain the DC-mesh, we connect all processing nodes linked to a local mesh together with one node of the global mesh via a bus.

Related work: Commercial and research systems adopt static clusters: STiNG [4] and SGI Origin [5] use the ring and an extended hypercube, respectively. The Stanford Dash is configured into the mesh [6]. A research chip, Hydra [7], has 4 processors and exploits two buses between their caches. A chip reconfigurable for several types of applications includes 64 processing nodes, that are connected with each other by the mesh [8].

The Ψ-cube [1] can produce dynamic clusters since it is organized through recursive partitioning based on the Hamming code. But this network will be unacceptable in an LSI chip due to its long buses, though it is much easier to wire than the hypercube. It is possible to organize dynamic clusters in multistage networks if each network switch has a directory [9]. Dynamic clusters are also organized by freezing the memory blocks in a specified cache and allowing the other caches to access the frozen blocks with no cache coherence [10].

A few methods based on the Hamming code and/or other linear codes have been reported to map the resources such as I/O processors onto the hypercube so that each node is adjacent to at least one resource [11] or a specified number of resources [12,13]. However, those methods exploit none of the properties of Hamming codes exploited in our partitioning.

In the rest of the paper, Section 2 describes the properties of partitions [1]. Section 3 organizes the DC-mesh, and describes the routing method for clustering. Section 4 summarizes the paper and discusses future research

2 Properties of the Partitions

This section describes the properties of Hamming code-based partitions that are used to organize the DC-mesh and dynamic clusters; for the detail, see [1].

A *codeword* c of the n-bit Hamming code $\psi(n,k)$ has p-bit parity for k-bit information, where the p is the smallest integer that satisfies $(2^p - 1) \geq n$, and $k + p = n$. Assuming no or a single-bit error in a received word w, the *syndrome* $\varepsilon = w \cdot H_n^t$ indicates the erroneous bit position if $\varepsilon \neq 0$, or no error otherwise, where H_n^t is the transpose of the parity-check matrix H_n for $\psi(n,k)$.

For partitioning, we exploit not only single-bit errors, but also *detectable* double-bit errors for which $\varepsilon > n$. Then, of a pair of erroneous bit positions (d, f) $(d + f = \varepsilon,\ d < f)$, we fix position f equal to 2^{p-1}; so $d = \varepsilon \oplus f$. The number N_d of detectable double-bit errors is equal to $(2^p - 1 - n)$.

The *error vector* e_ε for syndrome ε has bit(s) of 1 at position(s) $s\ (= \varepsilon)$ or (d, f) $(d + f = \varepsilon)$, and bits of 0 in the other positions. Let T_c denote the partition represented by word c, and put a word w with syndrome ε into partition T_c, where $c = w \oplus e_\varepsilon$ and $\oplus$ is the exOR operation. Then the n-bit word space is partitioned into 2^k *partitions each of* 2^p *words*. The Hamming distance between the *leader* (i.e., the representative) word c and word w is less than 3.

We produce *multiple suits* of codewords from the *original suit* S_0 of codewords for the parity-check matrix H_n. Then the suits organize another set of partitions for the word space, i.e., 2^p *suits each of* 2^k *(code) words*. Partitioned with any suit, the 2^p words in each obtained partition are those in different (2^p) suits. Thus every word belongs to one of the 2^p partitions each obtained with a separate suit, and is the leader when partitioned with the suit including the word.

To avoid traffic congestion on a single leader when clustering the requests for a target node t (see Section 3), we send the request from a requesting node s to one (ℓ) of its 2^p *leaders* (each in a separate suit). This routing is based on the following property: Let $S_{\ni t}$ be the suit including a word t, and assume that a word ℓ is included in both suit $S_{\ni t}$ and partition T_s. Then word ℓ is unique and is obtained by $\ell = s \oplus e_\varepsilon$, where ε is the syndrome for $s \oplus t$ with suit S_0.

3   DC-meshes

This section presents an indexed word space, the mapping from the space to the node-address space of the DC-mesh, and its structure and routing method.

3.1   Indexed Word Space

We assign the index (i, j) to the word, denoted by $w_{i,j}$, of which parity and information parts have values i and j, respectively; then an array of 2^p rows and 2^k columns is organized. We denote the ith row and j^{th} column by P_i and I_j. Let ψ-*neighbors* of a word $w_{i,j}$ be the non-leaders in the partition $T_{w_{i,j}}$. Recall that N_d number of double-bit error words have incorrect bits in positions (d, f). Let d' denote the position d in the parity part, and $N_{d'}$ refer to the number of double-bit error words with erroneous positions (d', f). Then,

Theorem 1. *Of the* ψ-*neighbors of word* $w_{i,j}$, k *words are in row* P_i, $(p + N_{d'})$ *words are in column* I_j, *and* $(N_d - N_{d'})$ *words are at the cross-points of row* $P_{i \oplus e_f}$ *and columns* $I_{j \oplus e_d}$ $(d \in$ *information-part), i.e., words* $w_{i \oplus e_f, j \oplus e_d}$.

Proof. Of the single-bit error words of word $w_{i,j}$, k words have each an error in an information bit, so those words are in row P_i. Likewise, p words each with an error at a parity position are located in column I_j. Moreover, of the double-bit error words, $N_{d'}$ words each with errors at positions (d', f) are in column I_j, so a total of $(p + N_{d'})$ words are in the I_j. Since $(N_d - N_{d'})$ number of double-bit error words each have a pair (d, f) $(d \in$ information-part) of error positions, those words are located in the cross-points of row $P_{i \oplus e_f}$ and columns $I_{j \oplus e_d}$.

3.2   Structure of the DC-meshes

The parity size p does not vary so much (equals 3 or 4) for up to the n of 15, so we map each column I_j onto one *local 2-D mesh*, i.e., a *basic block* of the

DC-mesh. Let node (i, j) be the node on which word $w_{i,j}$ is mapped. In parallel with this mapping, we map each row P_i $(0 \le i < 2^p)$ onto a 2-D mesh, so that it consists of the nodes (i, j) $(j = 0, \ldots, 2^k - 1)$ each of different local meshes for columns I_j. Then a 4-D mesh is obtained.

Since a 4-D mesh is generally difficult to layout, we contract the 2^p number of 2-D meshes for rows into a separate 2-D mesh, called *global mesh*, that is produced by contracting all 2^p nodes (i, j) $(i = 0, \ldots, 2^p - 1)$ in the local mesh for each column I_j into a single node, denoted by $*j$, of the global mesh. Then we obtain 2^k local meshes for the columns and one global mesh for the rows; note that these meshes have no connection with each other.

The DC-mesh is organized as follows: We connect one *processing node* to a node of a local mesh by a direct link, and all processing nodes connected with the local mesh for I_j together to node $*j$ of the global mesh by a bus. Moreover, to preserve the ψ-neighbor relation of the word space on the DC-mesh as completely as possible, we exploit the Gray code as the mapping function (see Definition 1) in the word-to-node mapping described above, since this code allows the adjacency relation in the word space to be preserved on the mesh [14].

Let $i(r_1)$ and $i(c_1)$ be the upper r_1 bits and the lower c_1 $(r_1 + c_1 = p)$ bits of index i. Likewise, the upper r_2, middle c_2, and lower d_2 $(r_2 + c_2 + d_2 = k)$ bits of index j are denoted by $j(r_2)$, $j(c_2)$, and $j(d_2)$, where d_2 equals $(n - 8)$ if $n > 8$ or 0 otherwise, and keeps the size of global mesh small, i.e., less than or equal to 4×4. Let $*(j/2^{d_2})$ denote the set of (words in the) 2^{d_2} columns of which indices j are the same in the r_2-bit and c_2-bit portions, but are different from each other in the d_2-bit portion. Indices (x_g, y_g) and (x_ℓ, y_ℓ) are used for the nodes in the global mesh M^g and the local mesh $M^\ell_{x_g, y_g, z_g}$, respectively. We denote the mth code in the sequence of len-bit Gray codes by $G(m, len)$.

Definition 1. *(Mapping Method) We map word $w_{i,j}$ in column I_j on the node (x_ℓ, y_ℓ) of the local $2^{r_1} \times 2^{c_1}$ mesh $M^\ell_{x_g, y_g, z_g}$, and map the set $*(j/2^{d_2})$ of 2^{d_2} columns on the node (x_g, y_g) of the global $2^{r_2} \times 2^{c_2}$ mesh M^g, where $x_\ell = G^{-1}(i(r_1), r_1)$, $y_\ell = G^{-1}(i(c_1), c_1)$, $x_g = G^{-1}(j(r_2), r_2)$, $y_g = G^{-1}(j(c_2), c_2)$, $z_g = j(d_2)$, and G^{-1} is the inverse of G.*

The mapping when $n = 6$ (and hence, $k = p = 3$) is shown in Fig. 1. A mesh node is shown by the rectangle, outside of which the node index is shown (only for $M^\ell_{0,0}$ and M^g, for space). The two-digit integer ij for M^ℓ or $*j$ for M^g inside the node represents the index, (i, j) or $*(j/2^{d_2})$ $(2^{d_2} = 1$, in this case), of the word or column-set mapped on the node. Each column I_j is mapped onto a 2×4 M^ℓ $(r_1 = 1$ and $c_1 = 2)$. Word $w_{5,0}$ $(i = 5)$ in column I_0, for instance, is mapped on node $(G^{-1}(5(r_1), r_1), G^{-1}(5(c_1), c_1)) = (1, 1)$ of $M^\ell_{0,0}$. The 2×4 M^g $(r_2 = 1$ and $c_2 = 2)$ for rows is obtained by mapping the set $*j$ of a single column (since $d_2 = 0$) onto node $(G^{-1}(j(r_2), r_2), G^{-1}(j(c_2), c_2))$. For example, column $*3$ is mapped on node $(0, 2)$ of M^g.

The mapping when $n = 10$ (so $p = 4$ and $k = 6$) is shown in Fig. 2. In this case, $r_1 = c_1 = 2$ and $r_2 = c_2 = d_2 = 2$, so both M^ℓ and M^g are of 4×4; one M^ℓ is shown by the rectangle. Indices x_g and y_g for M^ℓ meshes (and hence, of the M^g

nodes) are shown in the left-most and upper-most parts. Since $2^{d_2} = 4$, the set
$*(j/4)$ of four columns, denoted by $*(j/4)z_g$ $(z_g = 0, \ldots, 3)$ in the M^ℓ box ($j/4$ is
expressed by a hexadecimal number), are mapped on the node $*(j/4)$ with index
$(G^{-1}(j(r_2), r_2), G^{-1}(j(c_2), c_2))$ of the M^g; this leads to the quintuplet of four
M^ℓs with indices $(G^{-1}(j(r_2), r_2), G^{-1}(j(c_2), c_2), z_g)$ $(z_g = 0, \ldots, 3)$ and the M^g
node. Index z_g (shown in the parentheses near the two M^ℓs in two quintuplets,
for space) of M^ℓ equals 0, 1, 2, and 3 respectively for the upper-left, upper-right,
lower-left, and lower-right meshes in each quintuplet. To increase the bandwidth
in M^g, adjacent nodes of the M^g are connected by four $(= 2^{d_2})$ links.

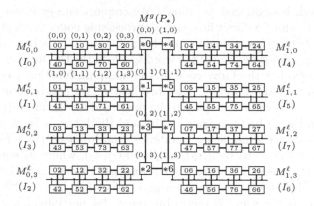

Fig. 1. The 64-node DC-mesh.

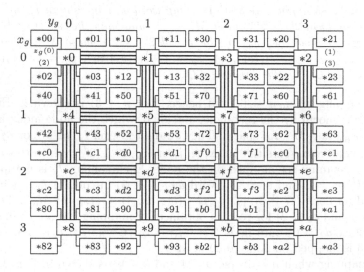

Fig. 2. The 1k-node DC-mesh.

3.3   Routing and Clustering in the DC-mesh

Assume a source and a target addresses, $((x_{g(s)}, y_{g(s)}, z_{g(s)}), (x_{\ell(s)}, y_{\ell(s)}))$ and $((x_{g(t)}, y_{g(t)}, z_{g(t)}), (x_{\ell(t)}, y_{\ell(t)}))$, of a massage in the DC-mesh. Then the message is sent according to the following XY-routing:

Definition 2. *(Routing Method) The message is sent to the target in the local mesh* $M^{\ell}_{x_{g(s)}, y_{g(s)}, z_{g(s)}}$ *if the global indices of the source and target are the same;* $(x_{g(s)}, y_{g(s)}, z_{g(s)}) = (x_{g(t)}, y_{g(t)}, z_{g(t)})$. *Otherwise, it is first sent to node* $(x_{g(s)}, y_{g(s)})$ *of the global mesh* M^g *via the local bus* $z_{g(s)}$ *of the source, next to node* $(x_{g(t)}, y_{g(t)})$ *on the* M^g *if* $x_{g(s)} \neq x_{g(t)}$ *or* $y_{g(s)} \neq y_{g(t)}$ *(this step is not required if* $x_{g(s)} = x_{g(t)}$ *and* $y_{g(s)} = y_{g(t)}$), *last to the target* $(x_{\ell(t)}, y_{\ell(t)})$ *in the local mesh* $M^{\ell}_{x_{g(t)}, y_{g(t)}, z_{g(t)}}$ *via the target's local bus* $z_{g(t)}$.

Theorem 2. *The Manhattan distance required for a message transfer equals* $|x_{\ell(s)} - x_{\ell(t)}| + |y_{\ell(s)} - y_{\ell(t)}|$ *if* $(x_{g(s)}, y_{g(s)}, z_{g(s)}) = (x_{g(t)}, y_{g(t)}, z_{g(t)})$, $|x_{g(s)} - x_{g(t)}| + |y_{g(s)} - y_{g(t)}|$ *if* $x_{g(s)} \neq x_{g(t)}$ *or* $y_{g(s)} \neq y_{g(t)}$, *or 0 otherwise.*

Proof. This is clear since the message is sent via the local mesh in the first case, through the global network in the second case, and via the local buses otherwise, assuming that the connection, such as a point-to-point link and a bus, between a network node and a processing node is not counted in the distance.

Thus the diameter of DC-mesh is equal to the greater of the diameters of local and global meshes. For the clustering, we use the value of word $w_{i,j}$ mapped on node (i, j) as its address. The word value is easy to obtain by $i = G(x_{\ell}, r_1) \circ G(y_{\ell}, c_1)$, and $j = G(x_g, r_2) \circ G(y_g, c_2) \circ z_g$, where $\circ$ is concatenation. A dynamic cluster is produced of a subset of the nodes in a partition. Let C_x be a dynamic cluster produced from the partition T_x represented by node x; note that node x may not be in the C_x, but we say that it is represented by node x. Recall that $S_{\ni t}$ denotes the suit of words that includes word t. Then,

Theorem 3. *(Dynamic Clustering) If a node s requesting for a service from a target node t sends the request to node $\ell = s \oplus e_{\varepsilon}$ included in both partition T_s and suit $S_{\ni t}$, then node s is put into the cluster C_{ℓ}, where ε is the syndrome for $s \oplus t$ with suit S_0. Moreover, node s is put into different clusters, C_{ℓ_1} and C_{ℓ_2}, for separate targets, t_1 and t_2, if they are in different suits, $S_{\ni t_1}$ and $S_{\ni t_2}$.*

Proof. There is a unique node ℓ included in both partition T_s and suit $S_{\ni t}$ (see Section 2). Since *all* requesting nodes send their requests to one of the nodes in suit $S_{\ni t}$, those nodes are partitioned into *clusters* . Particularly, node s is put into cluster C_{ℓ}. For different target nodes, t_1 and t_2, such that $S_{\ni t_1} \neq S_{\ni t_2}$, node s belongs to separate clusters, C_{ℓ_1} and C_{ℓ_2}, because leader nodes, $\ell_1 (= s \oplus e_{\varepsilon 1})$ and $\ell_2 (= s \oplus e_{\varepsilon 2})$, are in different suits, $S_{\ni t_1}$ and $S_{\ni t_2}$, where $\varepsilon 1$ and $\varepsilon 2$ are the syndromes for $s \oplus t_1$ and $s \oplus t_2$ both with suit S_0.

The Hamming distance between node s and leader ℓ is less than 3 since $s \in C_{\ell} \subseteq T_{\ell}$ (or $\ell \in T_s$). The type of a request sent from leader ℓ to target t and its issue timing depend on the applications. For instance, leader ℓ relays the first received request to the target for cache coherence, or produces a request after receiving all requests and sends it to the target for barrier synchronization.

Last we describes how the ψ-neighbor relation is preserved in the partitions (and clusters) produced on the DC-mesh. We denote the Hamming and Manhattan distances between indexes i and i' by $HD(i, i')$ and $MD(i, i')$.

Theorem 4. *(Preservation of the ψ-Neighbor Relation) The ψ-neighbor relation in the partitions of the word space is almost preserved in the partitions on the DC-mesh. Strictly, the Hamming distance of 1 in the word space is preserved in the Manhattan distance on the mesh, while the Hamming distance of 2 is mapped to the Manhattan distance greater than 0.*

Proof. Let's consider the ψ-neighbors of node (i, j). Then the $(p + N_{d'})$ number of ψ-neighbors are in the M^ℓ for column I_j (Theorem 1). Each of the p nodes has an index (i', j) (for a single-bit error in the parity part), and hence, $HD(i, i')$ between the nodes (i, j) and (i', j) equals one. So $MD(i, i') = 1$ for those node, owing to the mapping function G. Likewise, each of the $N_{d'}$ number of ψ-neighbors has an index (i'', j) (for an error in double bits both on parity positions), so that $HD(i, i'') = 2$. Generally, $MD(i, i'') \geq 2$ even with the mapping function G (though $MD(i, i'') = 2$ for the mesh of which size is less than or equal to 4×4 such as shown in Figs. 1 and 2). Since each of the k number of ψ-neighbors has an index (i, j') (for a single-bit error in the information part), it is in the M^ℓ for column $I_{j'}$. So the distance $HD(j, j')$ of 1 is preserved in the distance $MD(j, j')$ because the message is then sent from node $*j$ to node $*j'$ on the M^g. Each of the $(N_d - N_{d'})$ number of nodes has an index (i', j') (for an error in double bits, one of which is in the information part). Then the HD between nodes (i, j) and (i', j') equals $HD(i, i') + HD(j, j') = 2$, but $MD(i, i') + MD(j, j') = 1$ since $MD(j, j') = 1$ and $MD(i, i') = 0$; the latter is the distance from node $*j'$ of the M^g to node (i', j') via the bus.

4   Conclusions

We have proposed the DC-mesh for the dynamic clustering of nodes, as well as for easy layout on an LSI chip, exploiting the properties of partitioning based on the Hamming code. We first arranged the word space into an array so that the word with the parity value i and the information value j has index (i, j). Next, we mapped the indexed word space onto the node space of a 4-D (dimensional) mesh, according to the inverse of Gray code. Last, we contracted two dimensions of the obtained mesh for an easy layout.

The resultant DC-mesh consists of multiple local 2-D meshes and a single global 2-D mesh; each local mesh is connected to a node of the global mesh by a bus to compensate for the contracted dimentions. The diameter of the DC-mesh is equal to the maximum of the diameters of local and global meshes.

A dynamic cluster for a service in a target node is organized in a partition if its member node sends a request to its leader node, that is determined by the addresses of the member and target nodes. Since the effective number of dimensions of the DC-mesh is greater than 2, the Hamming distance, that is less than 3, between the leader and non-leader words in each partition of the word space is almost preserved in the Manhattan distance between the corrsponding nodes on the DC-mesh.

To increase the bandwidth between the local and global meshes, we can exploit multiple buses and hence, multiple global meshes, leading to a fat DC-mesh. Another approach to DC networks is to connect the nodes in each partition with each other by a single bus, leading to a bused fat-hypercube (fat due to the connections corresponding to double-bit errors). In any case, we need to evaluate the performance of these DC networks by simulation with real applications.

References

1. M. Takesue: Ψ-Cubes: Recursive Bused Fat-Hypercubes for Multilevel Snoopy Caches. Proc. Int. Symp. on Parallel Architectures, Algorithms, and Networks. IEEE CS Press (1999) 62-67
2. M. Takesue: An Adaptive Local Protocol for Reducing Coherence Latency in Clustered Computations. Proc. ISCA 12th Int. Conf. on Parallel and Distributed Computing Systems (1999) 21–26
3. D. Matzke: Will Physical Scalability Sabotage Performance Gains? IEEE Computer **30** (1997) 37-39
4. T. Lovett and R. Clapp: STiNG: A ccNUMA Computer System for the Commercial Marketplace. Proc. 23th Int. Symp. on Computer Architectures (1996) 308-317
5. J. Laudon and D. Lenoski: The SGI Origin: A ccNUMA Highly Scalable Server. Proc. 24th Int. Symp. on Computer Architectures (1997) 241-251
6. D. Lenoski, J. Laudon, K. Gharachorloo, W.-D. Weber, A. Gupta, J. Hennessy, M. Horowitz, and M. S. Lam: The Stanford Dash Multiprocessor. IEEE Computer **25** (1992) 63–79
7. K. Olukotun et al.: The Case for a Single Chip Multiprocessor. Proc. 7th Int. Conf. on Architectural Support for Programming Languages and Operating Systems (1996) 2-11
8. K. Sankaralingam et al.: Exploiting ILP, TLP, and DLP with the Polymorphous Architecture. Proc. 30th Int. Symp. on Computer Architectures (2003) 422-433
9. R. R. Iyer and L. N. Bhuyan: Design and Evaluation of a Switch Cache Architecture for CC-NUMA Multiprocessors. IEEE Trans. on Computers **49** (2000) 779-797.
10. M. Takesue: Schemes for Reducing Communication Latency in Regular Computations on DSM Multiprocessors. Proc. Int. Conf. on Parallel Processing (1998) 164-171
11. A. L. N. Reddy: Parallel Input/Output Architectures for Multiprocessors. Ph.D. dissertation, Dept. of Electrical and Computer Engr., Univ. of Illinois, Urbana (1990)
12. H.-L. Chen and N.-F. Tzeng: Efficient Resource Placement in Hypercubes Using Multiple-Adjacency Codes. IEEE Trans. on Computers **43** (1994) 23-33.
13. N.-F. Tzeng, and G.-L. Feng: Resource Allocation in Cube Network Systems Based on the Covering Radius. IEEE Trans. on Parallel and Distributed Systems **7** (1996) 328-342
14. Y. Saad and M. H. Schltz: Topological Properties of Hypercubes. IEEE Trans. on Computers **37** (1988) 867-872

The Effect of Adaptivity on the Performance of the OTIS-Hypercube Under Different Traffic Patterns

H.H. Najaf-abadi [1], H. Sarbazi-Azad [2,1]

[1] School of Computer Science, IPM, Tehran, Iran.
{h_hashemi, azad}@ipm.ir
[2] Computer Engineering Dept., Sharif Univ. of Technology, Tehran, Iran
azad@sharif.edu

Abstract. The OTIS-hypercube is an optoelectronic architecture for interconnecting the processing nodes of a multiprocessor system. In this paper, an empirical performance evaluation of the OTIS-hypercube is conducted for different traffic patterns and routing algorithms. It is shown that, depending on the traffic pattern, minimal path routing may not have the best performance and that adaptivity may be of no improvement. All judgments made are based on observations from the results of extensive simulation experiments of the interconnection network. In addition, logical explanations are suggested for the cause of certain noticeable performance characteristics.

1. Introduction

In order to exploit the speed and power advantages of optical interconnect (in communication distances exceeding a few millimeters [1, 2]), the OTIS architecture for interconnection networks has been suggested by Marsden et al. [3], Hendrick et al. [4] and Zane et al. [5]. Algorithmic properties of specific, cases such as the OTIS-hypercube and OTIS-mesh, have also been developed in the literature [7-13]. However, previous studies have, to our best knowledge, only considered topological and algorithmic issues in OTIS computers, and no study has evaluated the performance of these systems in sight of parameters such as bandwidth and message latency, in view of realistic implementation assumptions.

The main purpose of this work is to take a step in this direction by initially developing a deadlock-free routing scheme for the OTIS-hypercube, and evaluating the performance of the network under realistic conditions and structural constraints. To this end, extensive simulation experiments have been conducted on the network, with different routing algorithms, traffic patterns, traffic loads, network sizes, message lengths and number of virtual channels.

2. The OTIS-Hypercube and Its Router Structure

In the OTIS-hypercube parallel computer, there are 2^{2N} processors organized as 2^N groups of 2^N nodes each. The processors in each group form an N dimensional

H. Jin et al. (Eds.): NPC 2004, LNCS 3222, pp. 390-398, 2004.

hypercube that employs electrical interconnect. The inter-group interconnections are realized by optics. In the OTIS interconnect system, processor (i, j), i.e. processor j of group i, is connected via optics to processor (j, i).

A node, in the n-dimensional OTIS-hypercube, or OTIS-H_n for short, consists of a processing element (PE) and a switching element (SE). The PE contains a processor and some local memory. A node is connected, through its SE, to its intra-group neighboring nodes using n input and n output electronic channels. Two electronic channels are used by the PE to inject/eject messages to/from the network. Messages generated by the PE are transferred to the router through the injection channel. At the destination node, messages are transferred to the local PE through the ejection channel. The optical channel is used to connect a node to its transpose node in some other group for inter-group communication. The router contains flit buffers for each incoming channel. A number of flit buffers are associated with each physical input channel. The flit buffers associated with each channel may be organized into several lanes (or virtual channels), and the buffers in each virtual channel can be allocated independently of the buffers in any other virtual channel [6]. The concept of virtual channels has been first introduced in the context of the design of deadlock free routing algorithms, where the physical bandwidth of each channel is multiplexed between a number of messages [6]. However, virtual channels can also reduce network contention. The input and output virtual channels are connected by a crossbar switch that can simultaneously connect multiple input channels to multiple output channels given that there is no contention over the output channels.

3. Message Routing in the OTIS-Hypercube

The routing scheme used for inter-group routing and the routing algorithm used for intra-group routing collectively determine the exact routing algorithm in an OTIS-hypercube network. In what follows, we refer to different *routing schemes* in order to identify only the manner in which a message travels between different sub-graphs (groups) of the network to reach its destination. Two basic routing schemes can be suggested for any source-destination pair of nodes in an OTIS-network. In the first scheme, a message is routed in the local sub-graph in which it starts until it reaches the node that has the same node address as the destination node. From that node, the optical channel is taken into another sub-graph. In this sub-graph, the message is routed until it reaches a node that has the same node address as the sub-graph address of the destination node. Once there, the message takes its final optical hop to the destination node. In the second basic scheme, a message is first routed to a node that has a node address equal to the sub-graph address of the destination. Once there, the optical channel takes the message to the sub-graph of the destination node. The message is then routed to the destination node within this sub-graph.

Of the two former routing schemes, the one that takes a shorter path depends on the full address of the source and destination nodes. When considering the OTIS-hypercube, this can be determined easily. If the number of differing bits of the full address of the source and destination nodes is less than that of the source node and the transpose of address of the destination node, the first routing scheme will result in a shorter path. Otherwise, the second scheme will. However, it should be obvious that in the first routing scheme, once the first optical channel has been taken, the remainder of routing can be conducted by the second scheme. Therefore, if in each intermediate node, a message is routed according to the basic scheme that takes a shorter path to the destination of the message (without considering the source node), a minimal-path routing scheme, the third scheme, is obtained.

Routing within a hypercube may be deterministic, partially adaptive or fully adaptive. Any of these routing techniques may be used for intra-group routing in the OTIS-hypercube network. In order for a routing algorithm to be deadlock-free, cyclic buffer dependencies between messages and the virtual channels they allocate, must not occur. In the hypercube network, dimension order routing, a well-known deterministic routing algorithm, is inherently deadlock-free. Partially adaptive routing algorithms based on the turn model [14], such as p-cube routing, are also deadlock free. For fully adaptive routing to be deadlock free, virtual channel utilization must be restricted in a way, such as that suggested in [15]. But in an OTIS-hypercube, cyclic buffer dependencies between channels may also occur through the optical connections between groups.

To prevent the occurrence of such cyclic buffer dependencies, messages that enter a group through an optical channel must traverse that group through a separate set of virtual channels from those of messages originating in that group. Therefore, we suggest that the virtual channels of each electronic channel be split into two equal sets, i.e. each group be split into two virtual groups, v_1 and v_2. After being injected into the network, a message traverses the source group through v_1. But once an optical channel has been taken and the message has entered another group, that group is traversed through v_2.

When messages traverse only one optical channel in their path (the second routing scheme), no restriction is necessary on the utilization of the virtual channels of optical channels. But when messages traverse two optical channels (the first routing scheme), cyclic dependencies may still occur if all the virtual channels of optical channels are allowed to be utilized by messages taking their first optical hop. Thus, for the first routing scheme (and consequently the minimal scheme), one of the virtual channels of all optical channels must be reserved for messages that are traversing a second optical channel (entering their destination node). All the other virtual channels of optical channels can be allowed to be traversed with no restriction.

Since a message that has traversed its second optical channel has definitely entered its destination node, it can not be part of a cyclic buffer dependency. It is for this reason that reserving one of the virtual channels of each optical channel, specifically for such messages, eliminates the possibility of the occurrence of cyclic buffer dependencies through the optical channels. In this manner, the deadlock-free nature of the specific hypercube routing algorithm, used for inter-group routing, will be is preserved in the OTIS-hypercube.

4. Empirical Performance Evaluation

The traffic patterns considered in our evaluation are
Uniform: destination node can be any network node with an equal probability,
Complement: node $(a_{n-1}...a_1a_0)$ sends message to node $(\bar{a}_{n-1}...\bar{a}_1\bar{a}_0)$,

Bit-reverse: node $(a_{n-1} \ldots a_1 a_0)$ sends message to node $(a_0 a_1 \ldots a_{n-1})$,

Bit-flip: node $(a_{n-1} \ldots a_1 a_0)$ sends message to node $(\bar{a}_0 \bar{a}_1 \ldots \bar{a}_{n-1})$,

Butterfly: node $(a_{n-1} \ldots a_1 a_0)$ sends message to node $(a_0 a_{n-2} \ldots a_1 a_{n-1})$,

Perfect-shuffle: node $(a_{n-1} \ldots a_1 a_0)$ sends message to node $(a_{n-2} a_{n-3} \ldots a_0 a_{n-1})$.

To evaluate the functionality of the OTIS-hypercube network under different conditions, a discrete-event simulator has been developed that mimics the behavior of the described routing algorithms at the flit level. In each simulation experiment, a minimum of 120,000 messages were delivered and the average message latency calculated. Statistics gathering was inhibited for the first 10,000 messages to avoid distortions due to startup transience. The average message latency is defined as the average amount of time from the generation of a message until the last data flit of that message is consumed at the local PE at the destination node. The network cycle time is defined as the transmission time of a single flit from one router to the next, through an electric channel. The transmission time of a flit, through an optical channel is however a fraction of the network cycle time. Messages are generated at each node according to a Poisson process with a mean inter-arrival rate of λ_g messages per cycle. All messages have a fixed length of M flits. The destination node of each message has been determined through a uniform random number generator to simulate a uniform traffic pattern.

Numerous simulation experiments have been performed for different scenarios of the traffic load, traffic pattern and routing algorithm for various message lengths and network configurations. However, message length and network configuration have been observed to be of no effect on the proportional performance of different scenarios. Hence for brevity, we report the results for only a typical setting. This setting consists of a six dimensional OTIS-hypercube with four virtual channels per physical channel. The ratio of optical channel transmission time to electronic channel transmission time is equal to 1/10 and messages have a fixed length of 32 flits.

In the following subsections, we measure the performance of different traffic patterns by means of the *saturation point*. The saturation point is the maximum injection rate at which the average delay is still bounded. It is assumed that when the average message latency is higher than 200000 unit cycles, the network enters saturation region.

4.1. Uniform, Bit-Flip, Bit-Reverse, and Butterfly Traffic Patterns

In an OTIS-hypercube with uniform traffic, regardless of the routing scheme, the performance of adaptive routing is superior to that of deterministic and p-cube routing, as can be seen in Figure 1. Furthermore, the minimal routing scheme performs better than the first and second routing schemes. But the interesting point is that deterministic routing saturates at a higher generation rate than that of p-cube routing. The OTIS-hypercube inherits this performance characteristic for uniform traffic from the hypercube network (Glass and Ni have reported such a characteristic for the performance of the hypercube network [14]). Due to the fact that, when used individually, the first and second schemes do not always rout messages through an optimal path, one would expect the minimal routing scheme to saturate at much higher generation rates. But for adaptive routing, the difference between the performance of minimal routing and that of the first or second routing scheme is less than what may have been predicted. Thus, considering the extra complexity of implementing the minimal routing scheme, this scheme may not be an efficient option for such a system in which traffic is uniform. But, as will be shown in the following sections, for other traffic patterns, minimal routing may even result in performance poorer than that of the first or second schemes.

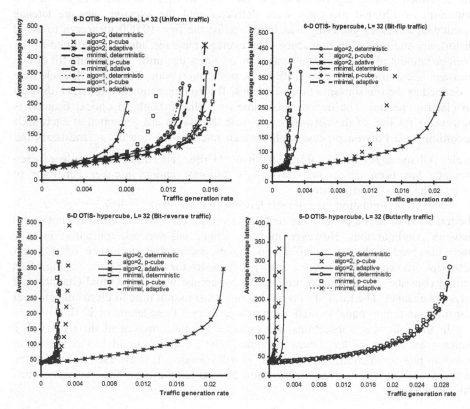

Fig. 1: Average message latency of uniform, bit flip, bit reverse, and butterfly traffic patterns

As shown in Figure 1 for bit-flip traffic, compared to the minimal routing scheme, the network saturates at a much higher generation rate when the second scheme is used, with bit-flip traffic for all three inter-group routing algorithms. This is while messages travel a longer average distance with the second scheme. An explanation for this is that, with the first routing scheme, all messages generated by bit-flip traffic in a specific group, exit that group through the same optical channel (the optical channel exiting a node whose address is the bit-flip of the group address), creating a bottleneck in the network. It is also apparent from the results that, with the second routing scheme, the generation rate for which the network saturates is greater for P-cube routing than that for deterministic routing. The reason for this is that with bit-flip traffic in an OTIS-hypercube, when the second routing scheme is used, the traffic within each sub-graph is also bit-flip traffic. As shown in [14], a hypercube network with P-cube routing saturates at a higher generation rate than that of deterministic routing for bit-flip traffic. This is while P-cube routing saturates at a lower rate than deterministic routing for uniform traffic.

In the results obtained for bit-reverse traffic, also shown in Figure 1, it is observed that the generation rate for which the second routing scheme saturates is greater than that for minimal routing. However, the difference between p-cube and deterministic routing is less than that for bit-flip traffic. The reason why the performance of the minimal routing scheme is so poor with bit-reverse traffic stems from the inefficiency of the first routing scheme. Similar to bit-flip traffic, the first routing scheme (not shown in this figure) causes all messages that are injected into a group to exit that group through a single optical channel (the optical channel exiting a node whose address is the bit-reverse of the group address). But this is not the case for the second routing scheme where messages use the optical channels to exit their source group evenly. With the second routing scheme used for bit-reverse traffic in an OTIS-hypercube, the traffic within each group is also bit-reverse traffic. This explains the superior performance of p-cube routing over deterministic routing, when the second scheme is used.

With Butterfly traffic, results of which are depicted in Figure 1, the performance of minimal routing is unquestionably better than that of the second routing scheme. Left out from this figure to preserve clarity, are the results of the first routing scheme. These results have, however, shown the performance of the first routing scheme to be very close to that of the minimal routing scheme. But the interesting point is that, with the minimal scheme, there seems to be hardly any difference between the different routing algorithms. This is due to the fact that with butterfly traffic, the Hamming distance between the source and destination nodes of any message is equal to 2. It is thus, unsurprising that the degree of adaptivity with which those two hops are traversed is almost of no effect on the performance of the network. Another point is that, since the Hamming distance between the source and destination nodes is so small, the first routing scheme will almost always be selected by the minimal routing scheme. This explains why, for butterfly traffic, the performance of minimal routing is so close to that of the first routing scheme and why these two schemes are superior to the second scheme.

4.2. Complement and Perfect-Shuffle Traffic Patterns

With complement traffic, hardly any difference can be observed between the performance of minimal routing and that of the second routing scheme. This can be observed in the results of Figure 2-a. But the first routing scheme saturates at a much higher generation rate than the other two schemes. The first routing scheme results in the path from source to destination of a message to be equal to the diameter of the network. Therefore, the second routing scheme will never rout messages through a longer path than that of the first scheme. Thus with minimal routing, the second scheme will always be selected. This explains why the minimal scheme and second scheme perform equally. With a complement traffic pattern, all messages injected into a specific group are destined to the same destination group (the address of which is complement to that of the source group address). Thus, with the second routing scheme, all messages are routed to the same node in the source group, i.e. they all exit the source group through the same optical channel. As a result, excessive traffic load is imposed on some optical channels while others are left absolutely unused. Even the traffic load on the electronic channels becomes unequally distributed. But this is not the case for the first routing scheme, by which complement traffic is distributed evenly over the optical channels. This explains why, as depicted in Figure 2-b, the first routing scheme saturates at a much higher generation rate than that of the second scheme, even though messages traverse a longer average distance with the first scheme. In an OTIS-hypercube with complement traffic, there is also complement traffic within each group when the first routing scheme is used.

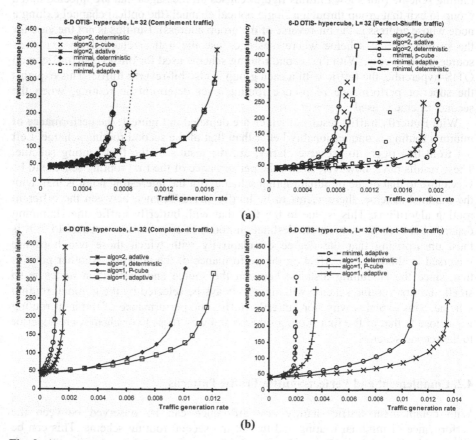

Fig. 2: Average message latency of complement and perfect-shuffle traffic patterns for (a) low and (b) high generation rates.

When the second routing scheme is used for perfect-shuffle traffic, all messages injected into a sub-graph exit that sub-graph, the traffic pattern within each group becomes somewhat similar to the perfect-shuffle pattern. The only difference corresponds to the LSB of the destination address. Therefore, considering that results presented in [14] show that with perfect-shuffle traffic in the hypercube, p-cube routing saturates at a lower generation rate than that of deterministic routing, it is acceptable that through one of two optical channels and the other optical channels exiting that sub-graph are left unused. This, as in the case of complement traffic, results in the uneven distribution of traffic on optical channels, and consequently the second routing scheme suffers from early saturation. But unlike complement traffic, the minimal routing of perfect-shuffle traffic does not always utilize the second scheme. Nevertheless, the poor performance of the second routing scheme does affect the performance of the minimal routing scheme. As a result, minimal routing saturates at a generation rate only slightly higher than that of the second scheme, as revealed in Figure 2-a.

In contrast to complement traffic, even the first routing scheme does not distribute perfect-shuffle traffic equally over the optical channels. Since the MSB (most significant bit) of the group address is rotated into the LSB (least significant bit) of the node address, the first routing scheme causes all messages of the same source group to exit that group through the optical channels of nodes with either even or odd addresses, depending on the MSB of the group address. Nonetheless, the first scheme does maintain superior performance over the second scheme. This can be observed in the results of Figure 2-b. The results obtained for adaptive intra-group routing based on the second routing scheme, shown in Figure 2-a, have been included in Figure 2-b once again to facilitate the comparison of the performance of the different routing schemes in this traffic pattern.

5. Conclusions and Future Work

A simulation-based evaluation of the performance of the OTIS-hypercube network has been conducted for three different inter-group routing schemes that we have defined (*first*, *second* and *minimal* routing schemes), three different intra-group routing algorithms (deterministic, fully adaptive and partially adaptive routing) and five different traffic patterns (uniform, complement, bit-reverse, bit-flip, butterfly, perfect-shuffle). We have shown that the method of routing messages between different groups of the network (the inter-group routing scheme) and the intra-group routing algorithm are of considerable influence on the performance of the OTIS-hypercube. However, we observe that (with the exception of uniform traffic) the inter-group routing scheme is generally of greater effect on performance than intra-group routing. Traffic patterns have also been found to be deeply influential on performance. It is found that with bit-flip, and bit-reverse traffic, the network saturates at higher generation rates when the second inter-group routing scheme is used, whereas poor performance is attained with the first routing scheme. The converse holds for butterfly, complement and perfect-shuffle traffic. This is while minimal routing is of superior performance only with uniform traffic.

Consideration of these characteristics can serve as a guideline to the optimal mapping of tasks to nodes by the operating system of such multiprocessor systems. Our next objective is to derive a mathematical performance model of wormhole routing in the OTIS-hypercube, and to validate its prediction accuracy using simulation experiments.

References

1. M. Feldman, S. Esener, C. Guest and S. Lee, "Comparison between electrical and free space optical interconnects based on power and speed considerations", *applied optics*, 27(9): 1742-1751, May 1988.
2. F. Kiamilev, P. Marchand, A. Krishnamoorthy, S. Esener, and S. Lee, "Performance comparison between optoelectronic and VLSI multistage interconnection networks", *journal of lightwave technology*, 9(12): 1674-1692, Dec. 1991.
3. G. C. Marsden, P. J. Marchand, P. Harvey, and S. C. Esener, "Optical transpose interconnect system architectures", *Optical Letters*, 18(13): 1083-1085, July 1993.
4. W. Hendrick, O. Kibar, P. Marchand, C. Fan, D. V. Blerkom, F. McCormick, I. Cokgor, M. Hansen, and Esener, "Modeling and optimization of the optical transpose interconnection system", *Optoelectronic technology Center*, Sept. 1995.
5. F. Zane, P. Marchand, R. Paturi, and S. Esener, "Scalable network architectures using the optical transpose interconnection system (OTIS)", In proceedings of the second International Conference on Massively Parallel Processing using Optical Interconnections (MPPOI'96), pages 114-121, San Antonio, Texas, 1996.
6. W.J. Dally, "Virtual channel flow control", IEEE TPDS, 3 (2) (1992), 194-205.
7. S. Sahni, C.-F. Wang, "BPC permutations on the OTIS-hypercube optoelectronic computer", Informatica, 22: 263-269, 1998.
8. S. Sahni and C.-F. Wang, "BPC permutations on the OTIS-mesh optoelectronic computer", In proceedings of the fourth international conference on massively parallel processing using optical interconnections (MPPOI'97), pages 130-135, 1997.
9. C.-F. Wang and S. Sahni, "Matrix multiplication on the OTIS-mesh optoelectronic computer", In Proceedings of the sixth international conference on Massively Parallel Processing using Optical Interconnections (MPPOI'99), pages 131-138, 1999.
10. C. -F. Wang and S. Sahni, "Image processing on the OTIS-mesh optoelectronic computer", IEEE TPDS, 11(2): 97-107, 2000.
11. C. -F. Wang and S. Sahni "Basic operations on the OTIS-mesh optoelectronic computer", IEEE TPDS, 9(12): 1226-1236, 1998.
12. S. Rajasekeran and S. Sahni "Randomized routing, selection and sorting on the OTIS-mesh", IEEE TPDS, 9(9): 833-840, 1998.
13. A. Osterloh, "Sorting on the OTIS-mesh", In Proceedings of the 14th International Parallel and Distributed Processing Symposium (IPDPS'2000), pp. 269-274, 2000.
14. C. J. Glass and L. M. NI, "The Turn model for adaptive routing", *J. ACM*, vol. 5, pp. 874–902, 1994.
15. J. Duato, T. Pinkston, "A general theory for deadlock-free adaptive routing using a mixed set of resources", IEEE Transaction on Parallel and Distributed Systems, Vol. 12, 2001, pp. 1219-1235.

An Empirical Autocorrelation Form for Modeling LRD Traffic Series

Ming Li[1], Jingao Liu[1], and Dongyang Long[2]

[1] School of Information Science & Technology, East China Normal University
Shanghai 200026, PR China
{mli, jgliu}@ee.ecnu.edu.cn
[2] Department of Computer Science, Zhongshan University, Guangzhou 510275, PR China
{issldy}@zsu.edu.cn

Abstract. Paxson and Floyd (*IEEE/ACM T. Netw.* 1995) remarked the limitation of fractional Gaussian noise (FGN)) in accurately modeling LRD network traffic series. Beran (1994) suggested developing a sufficient class of parametric correlation form for modeling whole correlation structure of LRD series. M. Li (*Electr. Letts.*, 2000) gave an empirical correlation form. This paper[1] extends Li's previous letter by analyzing it in Hilbert space and showing its flexibility in data modeling by comparing it with FGN (a commonly used traffic model). The verifications with real traffic suggest that the discussed correlation structure can be used to flexibly model LRD traffic series.

1 Introduction

Modeling long-range dependent (LRD) series has been widely studied, see e.g., [1] ~ [6], where exactly self-similar (ess) process (i.e., fractional Gaussian noise (FGN)) is a commonly used tool, e.g., [1] [2] [5] [7]. However, in communication networks, autocorrelation function (ACF) form of ess processes is too narrow for accurately modeling actual series [8]. On the other hand, accurate models of actual series are at the heart of some applications. For instance, accurate models of actual traffic series are crucial to performance evaluation of communication networks [9]. In addition, ACF has impact on queuing systems [10]. Motivated by those, we extend Li's early work [6] for an empirically derived 3-parameter ACF form in Section 2. Verifications of this ACF form are given in Section 3 and conclusions in Section 4.

1 This paper is in part sponsored by the Scientific Research Foundation for the Returned Overseas Chinese Scholars, State Education Ministry, PRC.

2 Empirical 3-Parameter Correlation Form

Let x be an LRD time series and r be its ACF. Then, $r(\tau) \sim c\tau^{-\beta}$ $(\tau \to \infty)$, where $c > 0$ is a constant, $0 < \beta < 1$. Then, we aims at finding a function $R(\tau)$ to best fit $r(\tau)$.

Generally, an ACF is nonlinear. Thus, modeling a measured ACF can be regarded as an issue of nonlinear least squares fitting. If a model is characterized by several parameters, nonlinear least squares in multi-dimensions may result in a set of nonlinear equations. Since a set of nonlinear equations may have no (real) solutions [11], it is needed to prove the existence of solutions. As numerical solutions for the root finding of a set of nonlinear equations are in the sense of approximation, a criterion is needed to evaluate the quality of curve fitting.

Denote a measured traffic trace as $x(t_i)$, indicating the number of bytes in a packet at t_i, $i \in I_0$ $(= 0, 1, 2, \cdots)$. Let r be the measured ACF of x, R be the modeling of r and $M^2(R) = E[(R - r)^2]$ be the mean square error. Then, $M^2(R)$ is used to evaluate the quality of curve fitting. In our scheme, $M^2(R) < 10^{-4}$ was required. Hence, our method to model r is to find R that fits r with the constrain of $M^2(R) < 10^{-4}$.

Let the error $e = R - r$. Construct the functional below

$$f(e) = \sqrt{\sum_k [R(k) - r(k)]^2}. \tag{1}$$

Based on the experiments, we present the following normalized correlation form

$$R(k) = (|k| + 1)^{-a} + Lu(|k| - m), a \geq 0, 1 \geq L \geq 0, m = 1, 2, \cdots, k \in I, \tag{2}$$

where u is the unit step function. Consequently, $f(e)$ stands for a 3-D cost function

$$J(a, L, m) \triangleq f(e). \tag{3}$$

Due to the evenness of ACF, we only consider $k \geq 0$ in what follows. An approximated root (a_0, L_0, m_0) of $J = 0$ can be determined by iteration based on nonlinear least squares fitting for a given r. The existence of solutions is explained below.

In fact, a measured traffic trace is of finite length. Without losing the generality, the maximum possible length of x is assumed as $p \in I_0$. Let $N \in I_0$ and $N \gg p$. Then, N may be regarded as an "infinite" in the engineering sense. Denote

$$\|r\| = \sqrt{<r, r>} = \sqrt{\sum_0^{N-1} |r|^2}. \text{ Then, } l_N^2 = \{r; \|r\| < \infty\} \text{ is a Hilbert space [5]. Denote}$$

$$\mathcal{A}_1 = \{R; R(k) = c[(k+1)^{-a} + Lu(k - m)]\}. \text{ Then, } \mathcal{A}_1 \subset l_N^2.$$

Statement. Let $r \in l_N^2$ be a measured autocorrelation sequence. There exists a unique element $R \in \mathcal{A}_1$ such that $\|r - R\| = \inf_{s \in \mathcal{A}_1} \|r - s\|$, where $\|r - R\| = f(e)$.

Proof: l_N^2 is an obvious convex set and $f(e)$ is a convex functional defined on l_N^2. Therefore, the extremum of $f(e)$ exists. Thus, Statement follows.

According to Statement, for a given $r \in l_N^2$, if $R = R(k; a_0, L_0, m_0)$ is such that $\|r - R\| = \inf_{s \in \mathcal{A}_1} \|r - s\|$, (a_0, L_0, m_0) is called approximated root of $J = 0$ and $(a_0, L_0, m_0) =$ arg min $J(a, L, m)$. Thus, if $M^2(R) < 10^{-4}$, $R(k; a_0, L_0, m_0)$ is acceptable in our scheme. In the paper, (a_0, L_0, m_0) is obtained by Levenberg-Marquardt method [11].

3 Verifications

Four well known real-traffic traces (dec-pkt-1, dec-pkt-2, dec-pkt-3 and dec-pkt-4) are analyzed. Denote $R(k)$ as $R(k; a, L, m)$. Then, the cost function for dec-pkt-1 is given by $J(a, L, m) = \|R(k; a, L, m) - r_{pkt1}(k)\|$, where $r_{pkt1}(k)$ is the measured ACF of dec-pkt-1. By Levenberg-Marquardt method, one obtains $(a_0, L_0, m_0) = (2.091, 0.377, 1)$. At this point, $M^2(R) = 1.952 \times 10^{-5}$. Therefore, $r_{pkt1}(k)$ is modeled by

$$R(k) = (k + 1)^{-2.091} + 0.377u(k - 1). \tag{4}$$

Fig. 1 indicates dec-pkt-1 and Fig.2 the fitting the data for modeling $r_{pkt1}(k)$.

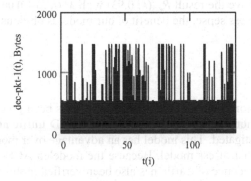

Fig. 1. TCP trace of dec-pkt-1

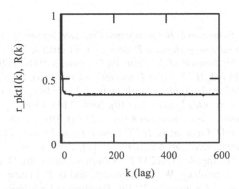

Fig. 2. The result of fitting the data: ...... measured ACF; — modeled ACF

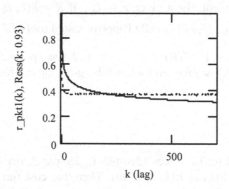

Fig. 3. Fitting $r_{pkt1}(k)$ with ess model: ...... measured ACF; — modeled ACF with FGN

Similarly, we have (2.088, 0.402, 1), (3.14, 0.341, 1), and (3.14, 0.341, 1) for $r_{pkt2}(k)$, $r_{pkt3}(k)$ and $r_{pkt4}(k)$, respectively.

To evaluate the benefit of model (2), we use FGN to fit $r_{pkt1}(k)$. The normalized ACF of FGN is given by $R_{ess}(k, H) = 0.5[(k + 1)^{2H} - 2k^{2H} + (k - 1)^{2H}]$. By using least squares fitting, we have the result $R_{ess}(k; 0.93)$ with $\hat{M}^2(R_{ess}) = 0.003$. As $R_{ess}(k; 0.93)$ is the best result in the ess sense, the benefit of our model is obvious, see Fig. 3.

4 Conclusions

A correlation form for modeling LRD traffic series has been given. The verifications show that it has a noteworthy flexibility to model LRD traffic and satisfactorily fits the real traffic investigated. This model has an advantage over models based on single parameter such as that of ess model. Because the modeled ACFs are non-summable, the long-range dependence of traffic has also been verified in this way.

References

1. B. B. Mandelbrot, *Gaussian Self-Affinity and Fractals*, Springer, 2001.
2. J. Beran, *Statistics for Long-Memory Processes*. Chapman & Hall, 1994.
3. M. Li and C.-H. Chi, *Journal of the Franklin Institute*, 340 (6/7), 2003, 503-514.
4. V. Paxson and S. Floyd, *IEEE/ACM T. on Networking*, 3 (3), June 1995, 226-244.
5. M. Li, W. Zhao, and et al., *Applied Mathematical Modelling*, 27 (3), 2003, 155-168.
6. M. Li, and et al, *Electronics Letters*, 36 (19), 2000, 1168-1169.
7. V. Paxson, *Computer Communication Review*, 27 (5), 1997, 5-18.
8. B. Tsybakov and N. D. Georganas, *IEEE T. on Inform. Theory*, 44 (5), 1998, 1713-1725.
9. A. Adas, *IEEE Communications Magazine*, 35 (7), 1997, 82-89.
10. S. Q. Li and C. L. Hwang, *IEEE/ACM T. on Networking*, 1 (6), Dec. 1993, 678-692.
11. W. H. Press, S. A. Teukolsky, W. T. Vetterling, and B. P. Flannery, *Numerical Recipes in C: The Art of Scientific Computing*, 2nd Ed., Cambridge University Press, 1992.

Statistical Error Analysis on Recording LRD Traffic Time Series

Ming Li

School of Information Science & Technology, East China Normal University
Shanghai 200026, PR China
ming_lihk@yahoo.com

Abstract. Measurement of LRD traffic time series is the first stage to experimental research of traffic patterns. From a view of measurement, if the length of a measured series is too short, an estimate of a specific objective (e.g., autocorrelation function) may not achieve a given accuracy. On the other hand, if a measured series is over-long, it will be too much for storage space and cost too much computation time. Thus, a meaningful issue in measurement is how to determine the record length of an LRD traffic series with a given degree of accuracy of the estimate of interest. In this paper, we present a formula for requiring the record length of LRD traffic series according to a given bound of accuracy of autocorrelation function estimation of fractional Gaussian noise and a given value of H. Further, we apply our approach to assessing some widely used traces in the traffic research, giving a theoretical evaluation of those traces from a view of statistical error analysis.

1 Introduction

The Internet is a complex system such that conventionally scientific computations are quite limited in the performance research of the global Internet. Therefore, measurement plays a key role in the performance research because measured data of real traffic reflect the information about real-life situations of the global Internet under current protocols and infrastructure.

By analyzing measured data, findings regarding traffic were achieved in the last decade. In summary, 1) traffic is of long-range dependence (LRD), and 2) traffic is asymptotically self-similar [1]. The research of this paper will show that the particularity of LRD is also reflected in measurement.

Recording traffic is the first stage for the experimental research of traffic patterns. Here, we ask for a question how to validate the reasonableness of measured traffic data. To explain this question, we ask for another question whether there was another global Internet that was superior to the current one we are using so that it could be used for measurement validation, e.g., data validation/assessment, in the standardization sense. Unfortunately, the answer is NO. The global Internet has the property of *uniqueness*. In addition, simulating the Internet encounters painful difficulties [2]. For those reasons, conventional approaches for validation/assessment of measurement

H. Jin et al. (Eds.): NPC 2004, LNCS 3222, pp. 403-406, 2004.

data in the field of measurement (e.g., [3]) fail for the Internet traffic measurement. Hence, the theoretical research in measurement of LRD traffic is expected.

For measuring a random sequence, an important thing is that a measured sequence should have enough length so as to provide an enough accurate estimate of an objective (e.g., autocorrelation function (ACF)). In the field of measurement, however, length requirements of a measured random sequence are traditionally for those with short-range dependence (SRD), e.g., [4]. Intuitively, length requirements of LRD sequences should be distinctly different from those of SRD sequences because LRD processes evidently differ from SRD ones. However, we have not seen any reports about record length requirements for traffic measurement, to our best knowledge (except Li's early note [5]). This paper will show that the length requirement of a measured LRD sequence does drastically differ from that of SRD one. Note that the result in this paper is based on ACF estimation of fractional Gaussian noise (FGN). However, parameters to be considered in practice may not be ACF of FGN in mono-fractal but others, e.g., the Hurst function [6]. Therefore, the result in this paper may be conservative but it may yet be a reference guideline for record length of traffic in academic research and practice.

The rest of paper is organized as follows. In Section 2, we present the formula for requiring record length of measured LRD traffic with a given accuracy and a given value of H based on ACF estimation of FGN. Discussions are given in Section 3 and conclusions in Section 4.

2 Upper Bound of Standard Deviation

Denote $x(i) = x(t_i)$ ($i = 0$, 1, 2, ...) as a traffic trace, representing the number of bytes in a packet on a packet-by-packet basis at the time t_i. Mathematically, $x(i)$ is LRD if its ACF $r(k)$ is non-summable while $x(i)$ is called asymptotically self-similar if $x(ai)$ ($a > 0$) asymptotically has the same statistics as $x(i)$.

In mathematics, the true ACF of $x(i)$ is computed over infinite interval. However, any physically measured data sequences are finite in record length. Let a positive integer L be the data block size of $x(i)$. Then, $r(k)$ is estimated over finite interval. As known, a useful (actually widely used) model of traffic is FGN [7] [8]. Its normalized ACF is given by $0.5[(k+1)^{2H} - 2k^{2H} + (k-1)^{2H}]$, where H is the Hurst parameter. We take it as a representative of LRD traffic for our research about record length.

Suppose $r(\tau)$ is the true ACF of FGN and $R(\tau)$ is its estimate with L length. Then, R is a random variable. Let $M^2(R)$ be the mean square error in terms of $R(\tau)$. Then, $M^2(R) = \text{Var}(R)$ [4]. We aim at finding a relationship that represents $M^2(R)$ as a two-dimension function of L and H so as to establish a reference guideline for requiring record length for a given degree of accuracy. We represent this relationship by the following theorem.

Theorem. Let $x(t)$ be a FGN function with $H \in (0.5, 1)$. Let $r(\tau)$ be the true ACF of $x(t)$. Let L be the block size of data. Let $R(\tau)$ be an estimate of $r(\tau)$ with L length. Let $\text{Var}[R(\tau)]$ be the variance of $R(\tau)$. Then,

$$\text{Var}[R(\tau)] \le \frac{\sigma^4}{L(2H+1)}[(L+1)^{2H+1} - 2L^{2H+1} + (L-1)^{2H+1}], \tag{1}$$

where σ^2 is the variance of FGN.

The proof of Theorem is omitted due to the limit space. Without losing the generality, we consider $\sigma = 1$. Denote $s(L, H)$ as the bound of standard deviation in the normalized case. Then, one has

$$s(L, H) = \sqrt{\frac{1}{L(2H+1)}[(L+1)^{2H+1} - 2L^{2H+1} + (L-1)^{2H+1}]}. \tag{2}$$

Following (2), we see that $s(L, H)$ is an increasing function of H.

3 Discussions

From (2), it is seen that a large L is required for a large value of H (strong LRD) for a given s. In engineering, accuracy is usually considered from the perspective of order of magnitude. When $H = 0.55$, 0.75 and 0.95, one has $s(L,H)\big|_{L=2^7, H=0.55} = 0.118$, $s(L,H)\big|_{L=2^8, H=0.75} = 0.306$, and $s(L,H)\big|_{L=2^{23}, H=0.95} = 0.621$. These show that Ls vary in orders of magnitude when $H = 0.55$, 0.75 and 0.95 for a given s, implying a series with larger value of H requires larger L for a given s.

An exact value of $s(L, H)$ usually does not equal to the real accuracy of the correlation estimation of a measured LRD-traffic sequence because FGN is only an asymptotical expression for real traffic [9] and traffic is multi-fractal in nature. On the other hand, there are errors in data transmission, data storage, measurement, numerical computations, and data processing. In addition, there are many factors causing errors and uncertainties due to the natural shifts, e.g., various shifts occurring in devices, or some purposeful changes in communication systems. Therefore, the concrete accuracy value is not as pressing as accuracy-order for the considerations in measurement design. For that reason, we emphasize that the contribution of $s(L, H)$ lies in that it provides a relationship between s, L and H for a reference guideline in the design stage of measurement.

Table 1 lists some well known traces on WAN. Now, we evaluate 1Lbl-pkt-4.TCP of 1.3×10^6 length, which is the shortest one in Table 1. For $H = 0.90$ (strong LRD) and s being in the order of 0.1, we can select $L = 2^9$. Because Theorem provides a conservative guideline due to inequality used in the derivations and the assumption of mono-fractal model of FGN, we verify that those traces are quite lengthy for ACF estimation as well as general patterns/structures of traffic.

Table 1. Six TCP packet traces

Dataset	Date	Duration	Packets
dec-pkt-1.TCP	08Mar95	10PM-11PM	3.3 million
dec-pkt-2.TCP	09Mar95	2AM-3AM	3.9 million
dec-pkt-3.TCP	09Mar95	10AM-11AM	4.3 million
dec-pkt-4.TCP	09Mar95	2PM-3PM	5.7 million
Lbl-pkt-4.TCP	21Jan94	2AM-3AM	1.3 million
Lbl-pkt-5.TCP	28Jan94	2AM-3AM	1.3 million

4 Conclusions

We have derived a formula representing the accuracy of the correlation estimation of FGN as a 2-D function of the record length and the Hurst parameter. It may be conservative for real traffic but it may yet serve as a reference guideline in measurement. Based on the present formula, the noteworthy difference between measuring LRD and SRD sequences has been pointed out.

Acknowledgments

Special thanks go to Vern Paxson for his experienced help. This research is in part sponsored by the Scientific Research Foundation for the Returned Overseas Chinese Scholars, Sate Education Ministry, PRC.

References

1. E. Leland, M. S. Taqqu, W. Willinger, and D. V. Wilson, *IEEE/ACM Trans. on Networking*, 2 (1), Feb. 1994, 1-15.
2. S. Floyd and V. Paxson, *IEEE/ACM Trans. on Networking*, 9 (4), Aug. 2001, 392-403.
3. M. Li, translated, *Measurement uncertainty: ANSI/ASME PTC 19.1-1985 (Instruments and Apparatus)*, Chinese version, Ship Mechanics Information Editorial Board, 1993.
4. J. S. Bendat and A. G. Piersol, *Random Data: Analysis and Measurement Procedure*, 3rd Edition, John Wiley & Sons, 2000.
5. M. Li, and et al., *IEEE ICII2001*, vol. 2, 2001, 45-49.
6. S. C. Lim and S. V. Muniandy, *Physics Letters* A, 206 (5-6), 1995, 311-317.
7. J. Beran, *Statistics for Long-Memory Processes*, Chapman & Hall, 1994.
8. M. Li, W. Zhao, and et al., *Applied Mathematical Modelling*, 27 (3), 2003, 155-168.
9. M. Li, and et al., *Electronics Letters*, 36 (19), 2000, 1168-1169.

Load Balancing Routing in Low-Cost Parallel QoS Sensitive Network Architecture

Furong Wang , Ye Wu

Huazhong University of Science and Technology,
Wuhan, Hubei, China
Wangfurong@hust.edu.cn
Minibeepcn@yahoo.com.cn

Abstract. A low-cost parallel QoS Sensitive domain, which supports load balancing network architecture, is developed in the paper. To deal with the scaling problem, a large network, thus, is structured by grouping nodes into parallel domains. Different from traditional approaches, especially hierarchical structure, parallel structure aggregates the topologies of domains in a new way. The corresponding routing algorithm, which adopts two skills for low-cost routing, QoS line segment and swapping matrix, is to emphasize particularly on load balancing within networks. Finally, Simulation results show appealing performances in terms of different metrics.

1 Introduction

QoS Routing is a process for the purpose of finding a path from the source node to the destination node and satisfying end-system performance requirements. Routing messages of a multi-metric QoS routing algorithm, consume enormous amount of network resources. For instance, an algorithm in [6] for finding a route with additive QoS constraints is proposed, but its price for broadcasting routing messages is scarcely taken into account. Meanwhile, the seriousness of load balancing is intended to cause a prodigious waste and congestion partially or full-scaly. QoS routing based on parallel-domain network, better than traditional aggregation suggested in PNNI[1], effactually reduce the outburst of unbalanced traffic load by ameliorating route computation versus QoS provisioning and route computation versus load balancing.

2 Network Architecture and Domain Models

A domain is modeled as a tuple (N, M, E), where N is the set of nodes, $M \subset N$ is the set of border nodes, and E is the set of physical links. The QoS parameter of a physical link is denoted as a QoS pair (D, B), in which D is the best delay of the link and B is the residual bandwidth. If a path is made up of $n-1$ physical links, each of which is characterized with a QoS pair (D_k, B_k), the QoS pair of a physical path is denoted as:

H. Jin et al. (Eds.): NPC 2004, LNCS 3222, pp. 407-410, 2004.

$$\left(D',B'\right)=\left(\sum_{k=0}^{n-1}D_k,\min_k B_k\right)$$

When there exist m ($m>1$) paths between two nodes, a QoS pair set like $\{(D'_0, B'_0), (D'_1, B'_1)... (D'_m, B'_m)\}$ must be used to denote QoS information between two nodes. A network, denoted as (G, L) consists of a set of domains and joint links, where $G = \{g_i = (N_i, M_i, E_i), 1 \leq i \leq |G|\}$. L is the set of inter-domain links, each of which is denoted in the same way as the intra-domain links in a domain.

3 QoS Sensitive Aggregations

Fig. 1 shows two line segments of a physical path between two nodes denoted by [*low_left, high_right*] at time T_1 and T_2. Different line segments would have different **crankback** and **err-denial**. Similarly, the QoS approximation of a logical inter-domain path can also be denoted by a line segment such as l_{path}, which must include three essential parts, the originating node and domain, the outgoing/incoming border node and domain, and the current incoming/outgoing border node and domain.

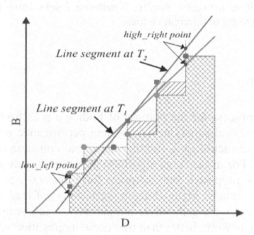

Fig. 1. A line Segment are generated by the least square method applied on its QoS pair set. The shift of line segments may occur with the process of time. Route requests in the unshaded area between the line segment and the staircase can not be served at all, which is called *crankback* that is caused by the distortion of line segment. Meanwhile, it would reject feasible requests as it doesn't cover some areas that belong to staircase, which is called *err-denial*

A line segment can be evaluated for its approximate residual traffic load on the path. For a line segment $[(D_0, B_0), (D_1, B_1)]$, its residual traffic load is defined as:

$$B_{path} = \left\{\int_{D_0}^{D_1}\left[\frac{(B_1-B_0)D}{(D_1-D_0)}+\frac{(B_0D_1-B_1D_0)}{(D_1-D_0)}\right]\right\}\Big/(D_1-D_0)=\frac{B_0+B_1}{2}$$

There are totally λ outgoing border nodes w, x... z within domain Y adjacent to domain Z and node i is the current incoming border node within domain Z, or there are totally λ incoming border nodes w, x... z within domain Y and node i is the current outgoing border node within domain Y. When a route request originates from node o within domain X, the swapping matrix for node i is defined as follows:

$$
\begin{bmatrix} l_{owi} \\ l_{oxi} \\ \vdots \\ l_{ozi} \end{bmatrix}_{\lambda \times 1} = \begin{bmatrix} \left(D_{low\_left}, B_{low\_left}\right)_{owi} & \left(D_{high\_right}, B_{high\_right}\right)_{owi} \\ \left(D_{low\_left}, B_{low\_left}\right)_{oxi} & \left(D_{high\_right}, B_{high\_right}\right)_{oxi} \\ \vdots & \vdots \\ \left(D_{low\_left}, B_{low\_left}\right)_{ozi} & \left(D_{high\_right}, B_{high\_right}\right)_{ozi} \end{bmatrix}_{\lambda \times 4}
$$

4   Line-Segment and Balance-Swapping Routing Algorithm

A problem with two constraints called "*shortest weight-constrained path*" was listed in [4]. Furthermore, as a four-metric routing algorithm, *LBRA*'s nature is close to the centralized bandwidth-delay routing algorithm (*CBDRA*) as in [3]. Like [5], *LBRA* prefers source routing mechanism to Hop-by-Hop routing mechanism because it needs the topological border information to analyze resource allocations. There are totally two conjoint levels in *LBRA*, inter-domain routing level and intra-domain routing level. Intra-domain routing level is analogous to *CBDRA* if residual traffic load is not taken into account. Suppose that there is a route request from node o with the QoS pair (d_{req}, b_{req}). Let D_i, $D_{i+1}...D_{i+n}$ be the estimated sum of delay from the source node to outgoing border node i, $i+1...i+n$ within the same domain, which incoming node k doesn't lie in. The link between node i and node k is an inter-domain link$_{ik}$ (D_{ik}, B_{ik}). So is the link between node $i+1...$ and node k.

```
j = 0; B'path = 0;
do{
    if (Bik < breq) break;
    else{
        use (Dik, Bik) and loi to form swapping matrix Mi;
        B'path = B'path + Boik;    j ++;
}
    i ++;
}while(n+1 times)
B'path = B'path / j;
if(B'path > Bpath){
        D'k = Dmin(Mi);
            if((D'k < Dk)) && (Dk <= dreq)){
                Dk = D'k;         }  Bpath = B'path;
}
```

An outgoing node runs LBRA similar to an incoming node, except that the out going node use [(D$_{ik}$, B$_{ik}$), (D'$_{ik}$, B'$_{ik}$)] and l$_{oi}$ to form a swapping matrix M$_i$.

5   Simulation Results

The simulated network consists of 9 domains with a total of 253 nodes. The number of borders varies from 4 to 6. All nodes are connected by directed links and each node is connected to at least 2 other nodes in the same domain. The delay of each link

410   F. Wang and Y. Wu

is between 2 *ms* to 15 *ms* and the bandwidth ranges from 640K to 6.4M *Bytes/s*. Fig.2 reflects routing success ratio w.r.t. bandwidth and link utilization.

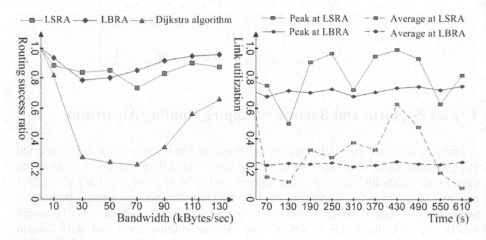

Fig. 2. In the left sub-figure, LBRA outperforms Dijkstra algorithm and LSRA as in [2] in routing success ratio evaluation w.r.t bandwidth. In the right sub-figure, LBRA doesn't cause any congestion and keep the smooth trend of link utilization on the random link, while LSRA fails to obviate the outburst of unbalanced traffic load

6   Conclusions

In the paper, I use line segments and swapping matrix to achieve a load-balancing QoS sensitive network and develop *LBRA* which can find the most appropriate QoS route. Simulations show a stable and high performance of different metrics.

References

1. The ATMForum: Private Network-to-network Interface Specification Version 1.0 (pnni 1.0). fpnni-0055.000 (1996)
2. King-Shan Lui, Klara Nahrstedt: Topology Aggregation and Routing in Bandwidth-delay Sensitive Networks. In Proceedings of GLOBECOM '00. IEEE (2000)
3. Z. Wang, J. Crowcroft: Quality-of-service Routing for Supporting Multimedia Applications. In IEEE Journal on Selected Areas in Communications. Vol.14. (1996)
4. M. R. Garey, D. S. Johnson: Computers and Intractability - A Guide to the Theory of NPCompleteness. Freeman, California, USA (1979)
5. D. Estrin, Y. Rekhter, and S. Hotz: Scalable Inter-Domain Routing Architecture. In Proceedings of ACM SIGCOMM'92, Maryland (1992)
6. Turgay Korkmaz, Marwan Krunz, and Spyros Tragoudas: An Efficient Algorithm for Finding a Path Subject to Two Additive Constraints. In Computer Communications Journal, Vol. 25. (2002) 225-238

Reversible Cellular Automata Based Encryption

Marcin Seredynski[1,3], Krzysztof Pienkosz[1] and Pascal Bouvry[2]

[1] Warsaw University of Technology
Nowowiejska 15/19, 00-665 Warsaw, Poland
seredynski@acn.waw.pl, K.Pienkosz@ia.pw.edu.pl
[2] Luxembourg University of Applied Sciences
6, rue Coudenhove Kalergi, L-1359, Luxembourg-Kirchberg, Luxembourg
pascal.bouvry@univ.lu
[3] Polish-Japanese Institute of Information Technology, Research Center
Koszykowa 86, 02-008 Warsaw, Poland

Abstract. In this paper cellular automata (CA) are applied to construct a symmetric-key encryption algorithm. A new block cipher based on one dimensional, uniform and reversible CA is proposed. A class of CA with rules specifically constructed to be reversible is used. The algorithm uses 224 bit key. It is shown that the algorithm satisfies safety criterion called Strict Avalanche Criterion. Due to a huge key space a brut-force attack appears practically impossible.

1 Introduction

The increased use of computers resulted in a strong demand for means to protect information and to provide various security services. Encryption is a primary method of protecting valuable electronic information. It transforms the message (plaintext) into the cipher text. The opposite operation is called decryption. Two forms of encryption are in common use. They are called symmetric-key and public-key encryption [3]. If both sender and receiver use the same key, or it is easy to obtain one from another then the system is referred to as symmetric key. If the sender and receiver each uses different key, and it is computationally infeasible to determine one from another without knowing some additional secret information then the system is referred to as a public-key. There are two classes of symmetric-key encryption algorithms. They are called block and stream ciphers. A block cipher breaks up the message into blocks of fixed length and encrypts one block at a time. A stream cipher encrypts a data stream one bit or one byte at a time. This paper deals with symmetric-key block ciphers.

In this paper we apply CAs to construct a new symmetric-key algorithm. CAs are highly parallel and distributed systems, which are able to perform complex computations. They have been used so far in both symmetric-key and public-key cryptography. CA-based public cipher was proposed by Guan [1]. Stream CA-based encryption algorithm was first proposed by Wolfram [9] and later some other algorithms were

H. Jin et al. (Eds.): NPC 2004, LNCS 3222, pp. 411–418, 2004.
© IFIP International Federation for Information Processing 2004

developed by Tomassini et al. [6], and recently by Seredynski et al. [4]. Block cipher using both reversible and irreversible rules was proposed by Gutowitz [2].

This paper presents a new encryption algorithm based on a class of reversible CA with rules specially designed to be reversible. It is organized as follows. The coming section defines elementary and reversible CA. Section 3 presents the idea on how particular reversible CA class can be used for encryption. Detailed description of the encryption algorithm based on reversible CAs and its analysis can be found in section 4. Section 5 concludes the paper.

2 Cellular Automata

2.1 Elementary Cellular Automata

One-dimensional CA is an array of cells. Each cell is assigned a value over some state alphabet. CA is defined by four parameters: *size, initial state, neighborhood, rule* and *boundary conditions*. Size defines number of cells. Each cell updates its value synchronously in discrete time steps accordingly to some rule. Such rule is defined over the *neighborhood* which is typically composed of the cell itself and its *r* left and right neighbors:

$$s_i^{t+1} = R(s_{i-r}^t, ..., s_{i-1}^t, s_i^t, s_{i+1}^t, ..., s_{i+r}^t), \tag{1}$$

where s_i^t is a value (state) of *i-th* cell in step *t* and *r* is radius of the neighborhood. Example of rule definition for radius 1 neighborhood is shown on Fig.1.

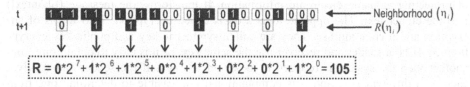

Fig. 1. Elementary rule 105 definition

There are 8 possible neighborhood configurations for radius 1 neighborhood. As shown on Fig. 1 state transition must be defined for each possible case.

When dealing with finite CA, *cyclic boundary conditions* are usually applied which means that CA can be treated as a ring. Changing values of all cells in step *t* is called CA *iteration*. Before the first iteration can take place some initial values must be assigned to all cells. This is called the *initial state* of CA. By updating values in all cells the initial state is transformed into a new configuration. When each cell updates its state according to the same rule, CA is said to be *uniform*. Otherwise such CA is called *non-uniform*. In this paper one-dimensional, uniform CA defined over binary state alphabet with neighborhood size two and three is used.

2.2 Reversible Cellular Automata

When analyzing elementary CA it turns out that only a small number of rules have the property of being reversible. For example, among all 256 radius 1 CA only six are reversible. This is why class of CA with rules specially created to be reversible is considered. Different reversible CA classes are presented in [5]. In this paper we are using reversible CA class presented by Wolfram [8]. In this class rule depends not on one but on two steps back:

$$s_i^{t+1} = R(s_{i-r}^t, \dots, s_{i-1}^t, s_i^t, s_i^{t+1}, s_{i+1}^t, \dots, s_{i+r}^t). \qquad (2)$$

In the elementary CA value s_i^{t+1} of i-th cell in configuration $t+1$ depends on the value of the state of itself and r of its neighbors in configuration t. In this reversible class additional dependency is added. Now, the value of the central cell s_i^{t-1} in step $t-1$ is also considered. Such a rule can be simply constructed by taking elementary CA rule and adding dependency on two steps back ($t-1$). Example of such rule definition is shown on the Fig.2.

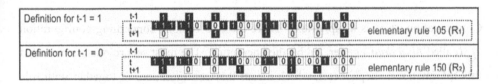

Fig. 2. Reversible rule 105/150 definition

Definition of the rule is now composed of two elementary rules. The first one is defining state transition in case when in step $t-1$ central cell was in a state 1, and the second one, when that cell was in the state 0. Fig. 2 gives an example of reversible rule based on two elementary rules: 105 and 150. These two rules are complementary to each other. Knowing one value it is possible to calculate the second one using the following formula:

$$R_2 = 2^d - R_1 - 1, \qquad (3)$$

where $d = 2^{2*r+1}$. The same rule is used in forward and backward iteration. The total number of radius r rules is 2^d. Since a reversible rule depends now on two steps back, CA initial state must be composed of two successive configurations labeled q_0 and q_1.

3   The Idea of Using Reversible CA Class in a Block Cipher

When using reversible CA described in the previous section, plaintext is encoded as a part of CA initial state - configuration q_1. Configuration q_0 is set up with random data. Encryption is done by forward iteration of the CA by fixed number of steps according to some reversible rule. This rule forms a secret *key*. Encryption algorithm is shown on Fig. 3.

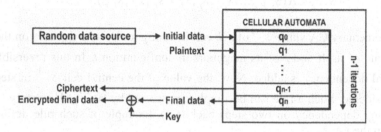

Fig. 3. Encryption using reversible cellular automata

Configuration q_{n-1} is a ciphertext. There are two options concerning configuration q_n (called *final data*) generated by the encryption. The most secure one assumes that this information is kept secret, which means that configuration q_n together with rule forms the *key*. The disadvantage of this option is that the *key* changes with each encryption. This is because the *key* is now a function of the rule, plaintext and random initial data. In the second option, the final configuration q_n is encrypted using *Vernam* cipher [3]. It is done by applying exclusive-OR operation (XOR, $\oplus$) on the final configuration q_n and the *key*. Now encrypted final configuration no longer has to be kept secret, and can be added to the ciphertext. To obtain final data for decryption, XOR operation must be applied to encrypted final configuration and the *key*.

For the decryption, the same operations are applied in reverse order. CA initial state is composed of the *final data* and the ciphertext. CA is then iterated for the same number of steps as used for encryption. The same secret rule taken from the *key* is used.

Good encryption algorithm should satisfy the *Strict Avalanche Criterion* (SAC) [7]. This means that each output bit should change with a probability of one half whenever a single input bit is complemented. In this paper, we are using 32 cells radius 2 CAs and 64 cells radius 3 CAs. In order to satisfy SAC, 32 cells radius 2 CAs should be iterated for at least 22 iterations, while 64 cells radius 3 CAs should be iterated for at least 19 iterations. These results are based on 10000 experiments for each parameters set (CA size/rule size/iteration number). For each experiment randomly generated rule and initial configuration were used.

4 Cipher Based on Reversible Cellular Automata

Our cipher is composed of four one-dimensional CA labeled CA32L, CA32R, CA64, and CAS. Both CA32L and CA32R are composed of 32 cells. CA64 is composed of 64 cells and CAS is composed of 16 cells. There are two inputs to the encryption function: plaintext and the key. The plaintext is divided into 64 bit blocks. The key is 224 bits in length (see Sec. 4.2). Automata CA32L, CA32R, CAS use radius 2 reversible rules and CA64 uses radius 3 reversible rule. Encryption process of a single plaintext block consists of 16 rounds (typical number for block ciphers). Each round is composed of 4 operations: iterations in CA64, CA32L, CA32R and *Shift* transformation.

4.1 Details of a Single Round

Fig. 4 presents details of a single round of encryption.

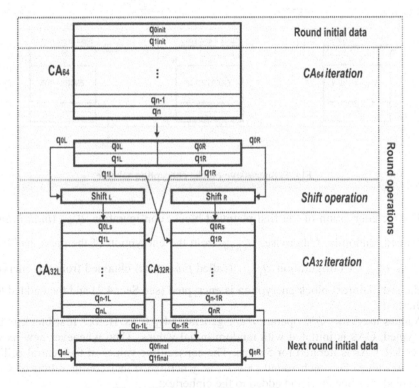

Fig. 4. Single round of the algorithm

Each round starts with two 64-bit values labeled q_{0init} and q_{1init} that form initial state of CA64. In the first round of encryption, q_{1init} is a plaintext to be encrypted.

Configuration q_{0init} called *initial data* is described latter. In case of rounds 2-16, both configurations get their values from the result of the preceding round. After being initiated, CA64 is iterated for 19 steps. The result is divided into four 32 bit values labeled q_{0L}, q_{0R}, q_{1L} and q_{1R}. Then configurations q_{0L} and q_{0R} are shifted respectively left and right by *ns* cell positions (described latter). Shifted values together with q_{1L} and q_{1R} form initial state of CA32L, CA32R. Next, both CA are iterated for 22 steps. The result forms two 64 bit values labeled $q_{0\,final}$ and $q_{1\,final}$. This values become initial data for the next round: $q_{0\,final}$ becomes q_{0init} and $q_{1\,final}$ becomes q_{1init}. After the last round $q_{0\,final}$ is a 64 bit ciphertext block.

Successive blocks encryption is shown on the Fig.5.

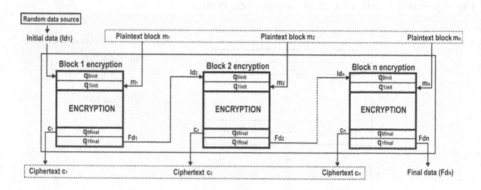

Fig. 5. Successive blocks encryption scheme

For the encryption of the first plaintext block, configuration q_{0init} (*initial data*) is generated randomly. Otherwise, $q_{1\,final}$ from the encryption of the previous block is used as q_{0init}. Configuration $q_{1\,final}$ (called *final data*) obtained from the encryption of the last plaintext block encryption is encrypted (see Sec. 4.2) and then added to the ciphertext.

Values used for *Shift* operation are generated by CAS. Before first block is being encrypted, CAS is initiated with random initial values. Then whenever new *ns* value is needed, CAS is iterated for 5 steps. The consecutive values of the central cell form 5-bit *ns* value. For each round new *ns* is generated. Final configuration of CAS is encrypted (see Sec. 4.2) and added to the ciphertext.

Decryption is using the same operations in reverse order. The only difference is that the selected output from CA32L is shifted right and output from CA32R is shifted left.

4.2 Key Structure

Each automata runs with its own reversible rule. The key is composed of 4 rules corresponding to each automaton in the following order: CA32L, CA32R, CA64, CAS. There are three radius 2 rules (CA32L, CA32R, CAS) and one radius 3 rule (CA64). Each radius 2 rule is 32 bits in length while radius 3 rule is 128 bits in length. This makes the key size of 224 bits. *Final data* configuration ($q_{1 final}$) is encrypted using XOR operation and bits 0-63 of the key and final configuration of CAS is encrypted using the same operation and bits 192-223. The key should be generated using some high quality random number generator.

4.3 Cryptanalysis

There are 2^{224} possible keys, which means that a brute-force attack appears practically impossible.

Another attack consists in assuming to find final states of CA32L, CA32R, CAS. Indeed the knowledge of the two successive configurations of the CA makes finding a rule much easier. For CA32L and CA32R the final state is composed of the last ciphertext block and *final data* configuration. Last ciphertext block is known so we only need to find out two 32 bits *final data* configurations. For CAS final state is composed of two last 16 bit configurations. Knowledge of the final state of CAS enables finding values used in *Shift* transformation. Since final states of CA32L, CA32R and CAS were encrypted using XOR operation and some random data (key) it can only be found by enumeration. There are 2^{32} possible values of *final data* configurations of CA32L, CA32R and final state of CAS. We also need to know the rule used for CA64. There no information on any configuration used in CAS, which means that there is no way of telling which rule was used. Described attack assumes verifying 2^{224} possible combinations of "final states of CA32L/CA32R/CAS / CA64 rule" ($2^{32} * 2^{32} * 2^{32} * 2^{128}$). Complexity of this task is just the same as the one for brute-force attack.

Greater security can be achieved by using larger block size but it reduces encryption/decryption speed.

4.4 Cipher Properties

Our reversible CA-based cipher works in a mode that is similar to CBC mode [3] in terms of achieved result. The same plaintext block that appears in the whole plaintext more than once produces different blocks of ciphertext. This is because encryption of each plaintext block starts with some initial data taken from the encryption of the previous block (each time a different value). In DES like ciphers there is still problem with encryption of the same plaintext more than once, or when two encrypted plaintext begin with the same information (in both cases the same key is used). In the first case the same ciphertext will be produced, while in the second case both plaintexts will be encrypted the same way until the first difference is reached. It is possible to overcome this problem by encrypting some random data block first. In the proposed cipher encrypting the same plaintext with the same key will always result in a different ciphertext. This is achieved by using randomly generated data and new initial configuration of automaton CAs for encryption of each plaintext.

5 Conclusions

In this paper we have presented an idea on how a particular class of reversible CAs can be used in cryptography. We have given an example of a new block encryption algorithm based on that idea. One dimensional, radius 2 and radius 3 CAs are used. The algorithm uses 64-bit blocks as an input. The same operations are used for both encryption and decryption. Strict Avalanche Criterion is satisfied. Due to a huge key space a brute-force attack appears practically impossible.

References

1. Guan, P.: Cellular Automaton Public-Key Cryptosystem. Complex Systems 1 (1987) 51-56
2. Gutowitz, H.: Cryptography with Dynamical Systems, manuscript
3. Menezes, A., van Oorschot, P., Vanstone, S.: Handbook of Applied Cryptography, CRC Press (1996)
4. Seredynski, F., Bouvry, P., Zomaya, A.Y.: Cellular Programming and Symmetric Key Cryptography Systems. In: E.Cantú-Paz et al. (eds.): Genetic and Evolutionary Computation – GECCO 2003. LNCS 2724. Part II. Springer (2003) 1369-1381
5. Toffoli, T., Margolus, N.: Invertible cellular automata: a review. Physica D 666. North-Holland, Amsterdam (1997)
6. Tomassini, M., Perrenoud, M.: Stream Ciphers with One and Two-Dimensional Cellular Automata. In: M. Schoenauer et al. (eds.): Parallel Problem Solving from Nature – PPSN VI. LNCS 1917. Springer (2000) 722-731
7. Webster, A.F., Tavares, S.E.: On the Design of S-Boxes, Advances in Cryptology : Crypto '85 Proceedings. Springer. LNCS 218. Springer (1985) 523-534
8. Wolfram, S.: A New Kind of Science, Wolfram Media (2002) 435-441
9. Wolfram, S.: Cryptography with Cellular Automata in Advances in Cryptology : Crypto '85Proceedings. LNCS 218. Springer (1985) 429-432

Ontology Based Cooperative Intrusion Detection System*

Yanxiang He, Wei Chen, Min Yang, and Wenling Peng

Computer School, State Key Lab of Software Engineering
Wuhan University, Wuhan 430072, China
{yxhe,chenwei,myang,wlpeng}@whu.edu.cn

Abstract. As malicious intrusions span sites more frequently, network security plays the vital role in internet. Intrusion detection system(IDS) is expected to provide powerful protection against malicious behaviors. However, high false negative and false positive prevent intrusion detection system from practically using. After survey of present intrusion detection systems, we believe more accurate and efficient detection result can be obtained by using multi-sensor cooperative detection. To aiding cooperative detection, an ontology consisting of attribute nodes and value nodes is presented after analysis of IDSs rules and various classes of computer intrusions. On the basis of ontology, a matchmaking method is given to improve flexibility of detection. Cooperative detection framework based on the ontology is also discussed. The ontology proposed in paper has two advantages. First, it makes the detection more flexible and second it provides global locality information to support cooperation.

1 Introduction

Since intrusion detection was introduced in the mid-1980s [1], intrusion detection system(IDS) has developed for almost thirty years to enhance computer security. However high false negative and false positive prevent ID system from practically using. After analyzing the reason of high false alarms rate, we think the inefficient detection is partly caused by insufficient audit data sources and lack of cooperating multi-sensors data. Many of IDSs depend on only one kind of sources: network data or host based data. However many intrusions can shows character in both of these two data sources. If more sensors data can be utilized to perform intrusion detection, the alert will be more accurate.

The key problem is how to correlate multi-sensor information to evaluating the security state of monitored system. In this paper, we argue a cooperating detection framework based on ontology. Ontology can provide detection system with the ability to share a common conceptual understanding and provide relationships among heterogeneous audit data. Based on ontology we present our cooperative framework to correlate the information from multi-sensor. A flexible and efficient matching algorithm is also given to perform detection.

---

* Supported by the National Natural Science Foundation of China under Grant No. 90104005

H. Jin et al. (Eds.): NPC 2004, LNCS 3222, pp. 419–426, 2004.

The remainder of the paper is organized as follows: Section 2 presents related work in cooperative detection by using multi-sensor. In Section 3 we present the ontology established from host and network data feature, give the matchmaking algorithm and the ontology based cooperating function. Some experiment results will be present in Section 4. In Section 5, we conclude our work and discuss future research.

2   Relate Work

Some of IDSs have used both of host and network data to perform detection. DIDS[3] accepts the notable event records from each of the host and LAN monitors and sends them to the expert system. The expert system is responsible for evaluating and reporting on the security state of the monitored system. The detection model is the basis of the rule base and consists of 6 layers, each layer representing the result of a transformation performed on the data. EMERALD[4] is a scalable distributed intrusion detection system that operates on three different levels in a large enterprise network. EMERALD introduces a recursive framework for coordinate analyses from distributed monitors to provide a global detection. However neither of these two systems addresses data sharing between host and network data.

In [5] Peng addresses that most intrusions are not isolated but related as different stages of attack sequence, with the early stages preparing for the later ones. Proposed approach correlated alerts using prerequisites of intrusions. It can discover high-level intrusion scenario and reduce the impact of false alert. But the detection rate is constrained by the low-level IDSs. Frincke in[6] proposes principles for a framework to support cooperative intrusion detection across multiple domains and describes a prototype cooperative data sharing system illustrating many of those principles.

An ontology is an explicit specification of the concepts and relationships and is widely used in many research areas, such as semantic web, knowledge management, AI etc. There are not much literature reports about applying ontology to IDS. In [7] Pinkston gives a target-centric ontology to descript the concepts within ID domain and relations between them. They implement their ontology model by DAML+OIL language. But they do not seem to make full use of correlating and inheritance relationship to perform detection.

3   The Ontology Based Cooperative Detection

3.1   Ontology

The term ontology means a specification of a conceptualization. An ontology is a description (like a formal specification of a program) of the concepts and relationships in a specific domain. Using ontology in intrusion detection system is to provide powerful constructs that can guide cooperating detector to exchange machine interpretable message. Understanding other cooperating detectors' message and description of current status is vital in cooperating work. We design an ontology after analysis some IDSs rules and the security vulnerabilities published by Common Vulnerabilities and Exposures (CVE)[8]. Compare to the ontology provided by [7], our ontology focuses on the features that can be observed by each sensor. We not intend to estimate the motivation of the intruder as [7] have done.

The complete ontology includes two kinds of nodes: value nodes and attribute nodes. Attribute nodes describe all the features that can be observed by multi-sensor and value nodes are the children of some attribute nodes which represent the possible value of their parent attribute node. Fig. 1 illustrates a part of our ontology which only has attribute nodes. The complete ontology not is given because it would make the illustration clumsy. At the root of the ontology is attack signature. The subclass of root is attribute nodes that represent different features from heterogeneous sensors including host sensors, network sensors, router logs etc. The higher level node of ontology means more abstract feature and is the locality of the lower level nodes. By the ontology, we can know on which sensor we can find concerned information. For example, if we require the memory total usage information. We can learn from the ontology that, this value can be obtained from the system status sensor on the host. This is useful in cooperative detection process because it help us to locate the required information.

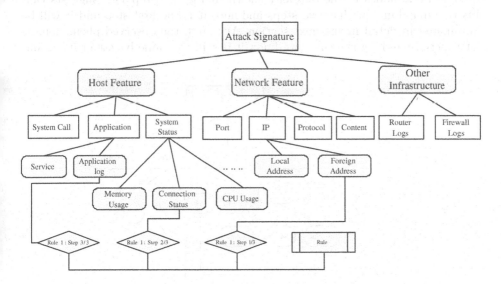

Fig. 1. The Overview of Ontology

3.2 Ontology Based Matching

Signature intrusion detection system often uses string matching or more powerful expert system to perform matchmaking. String matching system, such as snort [9,10], is a simple substring matching of the characters in the text. Such a mechanism of course is not of considerable flexibility. If attack signature changes a little, the system will neglect it. For example, a backdoor server uses port '666' to connect with client. If the server changes communication port to '555', the string matching system will not detect it until another rule added to rules base. The expert system are more powerful and flexible, however execution efficiency is influenced by more complex mechanism. In our approach we give matchmaking method based on above ontology that is a little similar to the powerful expert system but has high execution efficiency.

Each node in the above ontology (in Fig. 1) is feature nodes that show the attributes of collection information. In the complete ontology will also include the value nodes which show the value distribution. The parent of value nodes is the attribute that has these values. If the attribute has a continuous value, some discrete preprocessing should be taken.In the above given example, the intruder changes backdoor program communication port form suspicious '666' to a seldom used port '555' and establishes the connection from an unknown foreign address other than the known suspicious one. To illustrate this scenario, a rule node 'Rule1: Step 1/2' and the observed suspicious data node 'intrusion' are attached to some value nodes in the ontology shown in Fig. 2. 'Step 1/2' suggests that this rule matchmaking has two steps and here it is the first step and it will be illuminated in detail in the next section. Although the observed phenomena is not exactly matching the rule , we know it is still the same backdoor intrusion.

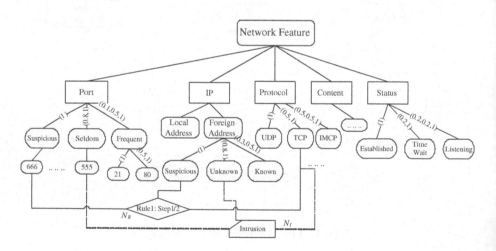

Fig. 2. Ontology based Matchmaking

To evaluate the relationship and similarities among the rules and data, each edge between value node and its parent node is assigned a weight. The weigh from 0 to 1 shows the relationship among the different values that has the same parent node. The 1 means the two values nodes has the maximum similarity while 0 means the minimum. For example, the 'Port' node has the values of 'Suspicious', 'Seldom used', 'Frequent used' and we store the weight of node N by vector $V_N(w_1, w_2, ..w_n)$. w_i means the weight between N and its brother node i. In above example, the three vectors are $V_{\text{suspicious}}(1)$, $V_{\text{seldom}}(0.8, 1)$, $V_{\text{frequent}}(0.1, 0.5, 1)$ and 0.8 in $V_{\text{seldom}}(0.8, 1)$ means the weight between 'Suspicious' and 'Seldom used' is 0.8.The weight is empirically assigned by expert and will be adjusted according to feedback of result. The autonomous adaptive weight assigning method has more advantage [11], which will be our future work. The weight between 'Suspicious' and 'Seldom Used' is 0.8 because a seldom used port is always utilized by intruder to perform malicious communication. However, the weight between 'Suspicious' and 'Frequent used' is only 0.1 as the frequent used port does not seem used by intruder.

There exists a set of paths, marked as $path\_set(N_R, N_I)$, that from node 'Rule'(N_R)to 'Intrusion'(N_I) which will be utilized to evaluate the similarity between two nodes. It is not necessary to traverse all paths that between N_R and N_I and only path between two attached nodes that have the same attribute parent node are considered. In the above example, only three paths, path from '666' to '555', path from 'Suspicious' to 'Unknown' and path from 'TCP' to 'TCP', are considered. If N_R and N_I are attached to the same node in one path, the detector will give the maximum score 1. If not, the similarity score depends on the path weight between the two nodes N_i, N_j which they are attached to separately. Then the total score is calculated by sum up all the path similarity score.

$$path\_simi\_score_{path(i,j)} = V_i(w_1, w_2, ..w_n) * (0_1, 0_2, ..e_j.., 0_n)' \quad (e_j = 1) \quad (1)$$

$$total\_score(N_R, N_I) = \frac{\sum\limits_{path(i,j)\in path\_set(N_R,N_I)} path\_simi\_score_{path(i,j)}}{\text{Count}(pathset(N_R, N_I))} \quad (2)$$

The total score in the above example is:

$$total\_score = \frac{((0.8, 1) * (1, 0)' + (0.8, 1) * (1, 0)' + 1)}{3} = 0.8667$$

If the total_score exceeds the threshold, it means the observed data matches the rule and is suspicious intrusion. During the intrusion detection process, lots of rules will be loaded and attached to ontology. The similarity score of each audit data toward the relevant rules is evaluated by total_score function. To make the matchmaking more efficient, we do not need to calculate all total_score between audit data node N_{data} and each rules. One prior fact is that if the total_score can exceed the threshold, at least one path_simi_score belong to the same path set exceeds the threshold. By utilizing this priori fact we filter the rules before calculating the total_score function which influence the execution speed mostly. The matchmaking algorithm is given as below.

```
Boolean:IntrusionMatchMaking(Var RuleSet:Rst; AuditData Node:Ndata)
 {
   Queue: Q;
// AttachedNodeSet function gives all the nodes that Ndata is attached to
   For each node N in AttachedNodeSet(Ndata)
     FOR each rule R in Rst
       IF path_simi_score path(N,Rj) > Threshold THEN
       insert(Q, R) ;  // If the path_simi_score exceed the threshold,
       The rule R will be insert to queue
         continue ;     // Quit inner loop
     END FOR
   END FOR
//Calculate the total score of the Ndata and rule in Q
   FOR each R in Q
     IF total_score(Ndata,R) > Threshold THEN RETURN TRUE;
   END FOR
   RETURN FALSE;
 }
```

3.3 Apply Ontology to Cooperating Detection

The relationship between value nodes and attribute node can be applied to more accurate and efficient matchmaking method for signature detection. At the same time, the relationship between the attribute nodes provides fundamental information to perform cooperating detection. The parent node indicates the locality of the children nodes. For example, if the memory total usage information is wanted during cooperating detection process, the ontology tells the detector to obtain this information from the system status sensor on the host. Ontology provides the machine interpretable knowledge in cooperating detection process.

To give more accurate alert, detectors try to collect as more information as possible before drawing the conclusion. Rules become more complicate when signatures information in rule may distribute on different sensors. For example, a complete rule in Fig. 1 is composed by three sub-rules. When detector finishes first detection on network sensors, it will examine connection status on host. The ontology indicates the detector where to get the desired information, and then the detector will send a query request to system status monitor on host. Before beginning the third step, the detector again learns from the ontology about the locality of application logs. This scenario is common in cooperating detection. If the backdoor intruder communicates with the backdoor server in encrypted commands, the network sensor can only detect some connection using strange port and unable to decrypt the content of connection. So the decrypted commands can only be obtained from application logs on host.

Facing the multi-step rule, the detectors perform sub-rule detections individually and the detection result is stored in local database temporarily. Each sub-alert has a TTL (Time to Live) tag. When the sub-alert expires, it will be deleted from database. When the last step sub-rule detection is finished, the detector cooperates and queries each sub-rule detection result on relevant local database.

4   Experiment

An experiment is designed to test our approach. The edges and nodes of the ontology are stored in relational database. Because of the infrastructure limitation, we only implement cooperating detection among the host and network. A WinPcap based tool was used to collect network packets and Strace for NT[12] to trace NT system call on Windows 2000 Server operation system. Some host logs, such as memory usage and network connecting status are also utilized in detection. According to the rules of the snort and CVE, we design 21 rules which are mostly R2L(Remote to Local) and U2R(User to Root) detection rules because R2L and U2R intrusion is not easy to detect while our cooperating approach is suitable to detection these intrusion by using both host and network audit data. Most of these rules are two-step rule including sub-rule on network and host.Then we ran intrusion tool Netbus to evaluate our intrusion detection prototype. During the simulation we change the communication port of Netbus to test our ontology-based matchmaking algorithm. The default port for Netbus is 20034 and we change the default port to 20038 and 80 separately. We also ran snort 2.1.1 to detect simulated intrusion and compared the detection rate with our prototype

Table 1. Detection Results Comparison between Snort and Our Prototype

Netbus	Detected by Snort	Detected by Prototype	False Alerts by Snort	False Alerts by Prototype
Default Port	Y	Y		
Port:20038	N	Y	38	12
Port:80	N	N		

Table 1 compares the detection result and false alerts between snort and our prototype. The experiment result shows the superiority of our prototype over snort. From the result in the second line, we can find our approach is more flexible than Snort because ontology-based matchmaking algorithm is employed in our approach. However, if the attack has been changed too much, our method shows its limitation. Because of the co-operation of network and host detector, the false alarm rate decreases in our method. More complicated experiments are on designing, such as intruder's communication in encrypted commands and new intrusion evolved from old one. We expect more conspicuous improvement shown by our prototype.

5   Conclusion and Ongoing Efforts

In this paper, we present an ontology to describe relationship among features observed by multi-senor. There exist two kinds of nodes in ontology: value nodes and attribute nodes. By assigning the weight to the edge between values nodes and their parent attributed node, we provide a more flexible matchmaking method for intrusion detection. At the same time, the relationship between attribute nodes and their parent can indicate the locality of desired information. An ontology based cooperative detection function is also given in the paper.

We will employ more sensors to perform multi-sensor cooperating detection in our prototype and more complicated experiment will be designed to evaluate our approach. Our future work will focus on the improvement of ontology in intrusion detection domain and the ontology based matchmaking and cooperation method. In our future work, we also intend to design autonomous adaptive method to adjust the weights by feedback from detect result.

References

1. D.E. Denning, An Intrusion Detection Model, IEEE Transactions on Software Engineering, vol. SE-13, pp. 222-232, February 1987.
2. Stefan Axelsson. Intrusion Detection Systems: A survey and Taxonomy. Technical Report 99-15, Dept. of Computer Engineering, Chalmers University of Technology, Sweden, March2000
3. Steven R Snapp, Stephen E. Smaha, Daniel M Teal, and Tim Grance. The DIDS (distributed intrusion detection system) prototype. In Proceedings of the Summer USENIX Conference, pages 227-233, San Antonio, Texas, 8-12 June 1992.
4. Philip A Porras and Peter G Neumann. EMERALD: Event monitoring enabling responses to anomalous live disturbances. In Proceedings of the 20th National Information Systems Security Conference, pages 353-365, Baltimore, Maryland, USA, 7-10 October 1997.
5. Peng Ning, Correlating Alerts Using Prerequisites of Intrusions. Department of Computer Science, NC State University.
   http://www.mts.jhu.edu/ marchette/ID04/ Papers/CorrelationModel.pdf
6. Deborah Frincke, Don Tobin etc. A Framework for Cooperative Intrusion Detection. Proceedings of the 21 st National Information Systems Security Conference, pp. 361-373, October 1998
7. John Pinkston, Jeffrey Undercoffer etc. A Target-Centric Ontology for Intrusion Detection . University of Maryland, Baltimore County Department of Computer Science and Electrical Engineering
8. CVE, Common Vulnerabilities and Exposures ,http://www.cve.mitre.org/
9. Snort. Open Source Network Intrusion Detection System. http://www.snort.org
10. M. Roesch, Snort - lightweight intrusion detection for networks, 13th Administration Conference, LISA'99, Seattle, WA, Nov 1999
11. W. Lee, S.J. Stolfo, and K. Mok. A data mining framework for adaptive intrusion detection. the Proceedings of the 1999 IEEE Symposium on Security and Privacy, IEEE Computer Society Press.
12. Strace for NT.http://razor.bindview.com/tools/desc/strace

Adding Security to Network Via Network Processors

Hao Yin[1], Zhangxi Tan[1], Chuang Lin[1], Guangxi Zhu[2]

[1] Department of Computer Science and Technology, Tsinghua University, China
{hyin, xtan, clin}@csnet1.cs.tsinghua.edu.cn
[2] Department of Electronic & Information Engineering, Huazhong University of Sci.&Tech,
China
{gxzhu}@mail.hust.edu.cn

Abstract. With the increasing need of security, cryptographic processing becomes a crucial issue for network devices. Traditionally security functions are implemented with Application Specific Integrated Circuit (ASIC) or General-Purposed Processors (GPPs). Network processors (NPs) are emerging as a programmable alternative to the conventional solutions to deliver high performance and flexibility at moderate cost. This work compares and analyzes architectural characteristics of many widespread cryptographic algorithms on Intel IXP2800 network processor. In addition, we investigate several implementation and optimization principles that can improve the cryptographic performance on NPs. Most of the results reported here should be applicable to other network processors since they have similar components and architectures.

1 Introduction

Information security is an indispensable concern owing to the growing demands for trusted communication and electronic commerce. For example, a collection of applications such as secure IP (IPSEC) and virtual private networks (VPNs) has been widely deployed in nodal processing. However, cryptographic algorithms are all computational intensive [1]. To address this problem and add security functions to network equipment, such as secure gateway, a straightforward approach to achieve comparable performance is to implement them in hardware. Unfortunately, many security chips or coprocessors are only designed for a few algorithms, while most Internet security standards are written to allow flexible in algorithm selection. In addition, cryptographic hardware is not cheap or readily exportable.

On the other hand, Network processors (NPs) are an emerging class of programmable processors used as a building block for implementing packet processing applications such as switches and routers [2]. They are highly optimized for packet processing and I/O operations. As demands for communication security grow, cryptographic processing becomes another type of application domain. Currently, there are two approaches to add security into NPs: 1) Security functionality is directly built into the same silicon as the Network Process. Nevertheless, this method is still inflexible in implementation of multiple algorithms. 2) Implement cryptographic applications on NPs using software, which provides a good trade-off between performance

H. Jin et al. (Eds.): NPC 2004, LNCS 3222, pp. 427–434, 2004.

and flexibility. Compared to other similar approaches, such as software implementation over general-purposed processors (GPPs), this approach has the following advantages: a) NPs utilize system-on-chip (SoC) technology and have better performance-price ratio than GPPs. b) NPs often involve multi-thread and multi-core architecture, thus various parallelism can be exploited to boost performance. So, in this paper, we focus on software implementation over NPs.

Clearly, the most challenging work for software implementations is to provide some performance guarantees. Most of recent studies [2][3] related with cryptographic issues on NPs assume a symmetric multiprocessor (SMP) or super scalar architecture with multi-level caches, which are more similar with GPPs and ignore many characteristics like hardware multi-thread, asynchronous I/O in real-life NPs. This work aims to conduct studies of architectural properties of several widespread cryptographic algorithms on an actual platform - Intel IXP2800 network processor. Their implementation and optimization principles have been proposed. The rest of this article is organized as follows. In section 2 we briefly review the architecture of IXP2800. Then, we detail the selection of cryptographic algorithms and their characteristics in section 3. Next, we propose several optimization principles and illustrate the results through benchmarks in section 4. Finally, we summarize this work and offer some suggestions for network processor designs.

2   Architecture of Intel IXP2800

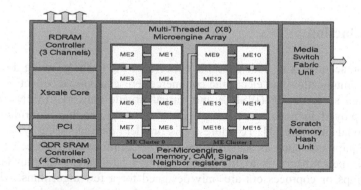

Fig. 1. The hardware architecture of Intel IXP2800

Closely examining the hardware architecture of IXP2800 shown in Fig. 1 helps to elucidate our implementation and optimization. IXP2800 is a 32-bit RISC based multi-core system that exploits system-on-chip (SOC) technique for deep packet inspection, traffic management and forwarding at high speed. The 700 Mhz XScale core is a general purpose processor used for control plane tasks (slow-path processing). The sixteen 1.4 Ghz microengines (MEs) are data plane PEs, which are connected in two clusters. IXP2800 has distributed, shared memory hierarchy which supports two types of external memory: RDRAM and QDR SRAM. In addition, the processor includes a 16KB on-chip Scratch SRAM shared among all MEs and plenty of registers in conjunction with a small amount of local memory per ME. Memory access latencies have not kept pace with ME processing speed. For instance, the minimum read latency for fastest shared SRAM (Scratch) is 100 ME cycles. To solve this problem, IXP architecture uses 8 "zero thread switching overhead" hardware threads for interleave operation - one thread does computation while others block waiting for memory operations to complete.

3 Selection of Cryptographic Algorithms

There are three such application domains for cryptographic processing: Public-key ciphers, Private-key ciphers and Hash functions. In this article, public-key ciphers are not studied, since many of them are not practically applicable to be implemented on fast-path of NP. First, large code storage is required. Besides, public-key ciphers are usually used for short sessions and private key managements, while private-key ciphers are critical for long session performance. Therefore, we will only focus our effort on private-key ciphers and hash functions. The former can be further classified into block ciphers and stream ciphers. Of the many algorithms, we select a subset of 10 algorithms based on their representativeness, popularity and availability. The summaries and characteristics of these algorithms are presented in Table 1.

Type	Name	Block Size (bits)	Round	Table Size (bytes)	Special Requirements	Description or Applications
Block Cipher	DES [4]	64	16	256		The first commercial -grade modern cipher
	AES [5]	128	10	5120		802.11i
	IDEA [6]	64	9	0	Multiply Unit	PGP, SSH/SSL
	RC5 [7]	64	16	136	32-bit variable rotation engine	Wireless Transport Layer Security in WAP
	RC6 [8]	128	20	176	Multiply Unit, 32-bit variable rotation engine	AES candidate, improved version of RC5
	Blowfish [9]	64	16	4168		Norton Utilities
Stream Cipher	RC4 [10]	-	-	256		SSL/TSL, 802.1x
	SEAL [11]	-	64+2	<4096ᵃ		Disk encryption
Hash Function	MD5 [12]	512	64	0		Digital Signature
	SHA-1 [13]	512	80	0		

ᵃ The table size of SEAL is variable concerning the output length. Here lists the upper bound.

Table 1. Selection and characteristics of cryptographic algorithms

4 Optimization and Benchmark

4.1 Methodology

To observe architectural characteristics of cryptographic algorithms and utilization of internal re-sources, as well as the performance bottlenecks, we conduct our experiments under Workbench 3.1, which is a cycle-accurate simulator of IXP2800. We configure MEs working at 1.4 Ghz, SRAM at 200 Mhz and RDRAM at 400 Mhz. All the source codes are compiled using Intel Microengine C compiler 3.1 with optimization level -O2 enabled. When encounter operations such as rotation that can not be directly expressed using C operators but supported by instructions of IXP, we implement them with inline assembly codes. Hence, our optimization principles do not focus on specific instructions unique to one target but general features applicable to a wide range of NPs. In addition, to test the scalability of parallel optimization we exploit up to 8 MEs (64 threads in total) in one ME cluster as described earlier.

4.2 Instruction Characteristics

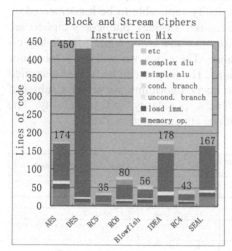 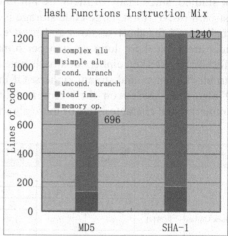

Fig. 2. Raw code sides and instruction mix

In this section we present the experimental statistics on instruction distribution of these algorithms. These metrics are essential information for understanding their dynamic properties and developing implementation and optimization principles. Figure 2 illustrates the instruction mix profile and code size of all selected algorithms. The following gives indications on their instruction patterns and great differences:

◆ Most block ciphers and stream ciphers need small code storages (less then 200 lines of code). The only exception is DES because it has several complex bit operations. Hash functions usually need more code storage.

◆ The most frequently used instructions are ALU instructions, especially simple ALU instructions like add, shift and logic. As a whole, ALU instructions occupy a significant share of the total instruction mix, which is 79.9% on average

◆ Branch instructions are less used in every algorithm. The average percent is 1.5% (0.8% for unconditional branch and 0.7% for conditional branch).

◆ For memory and load immediate instructions, there are significant differences among all selected algorithms. Stream ciphers and some block ciphers (AES and Blowfish) tend to have a relative high percentage of memory instructions (exceeding 15%) than Hash functions. The average percent of memory instructions of the 10 algorithms is only 4%.

4.3 Optimization Principles and Benchmarks

We describe our optimization and benchmarks in two subsections. The first one focuses on general implementation and optimization principles for single thread within one ME. The second one considers multi-thread and performs scalability tests with multiple MEs.

Optimizations for single thread
Generic implementation and optimization rules
    These rules are NP-independent and most of them are suitable for optimizations on GPPs. Their goal is to minimize the overall computation complexity and downcast expensive operations.
◆   Take full advantage of rich register resource and distributed memory hierarchy: To minimize access latencies, some frequently used tables should be placed into registers and per-ME local memories as much as possible.
◆   Avoid using complex instructions: Instructions like multiplication which consume more than one cycle of time should be avoided.
◆   Pre-calculate part of algorithms: Aside from table initialization and key scheduling mentioned earlier, immediate data used in inner loops can also be pre-loaded.
◆   Unroll loops: This can prevent the flush of pipeline and save extra clock cycles. Besides, unrolling loops can reduce calculations concerning iteration variables and make addressing in arrays more efficiently.
NP-dependent memory optimizations
    These principles make use of special optimized memory and I/O units on NPs to increase ME utilization rate and stretch the computation capacity to the outmost.
◆   Align memory operations: Access to data size smaller than those supported by the hardware incurs overhead (i.e. table access in RC4 and DES). Thus, to achieve optimal performance tables should be aligned at hardware boundaries.
◆   Memory burst read and write: On most NPs, memory burst operations can be directly issued at instruction level. IXP2800 allows 32 bytes Scratch/SRAM or 64 bytes RDRAM burst reference within one instruction. Employing this, memory instructions will be further reduced. In our benchmark, reading plaintext and writing back ciphertext are all burst at their block size.
◆   Latency hiding and I/O parallelization: This makes use of asynchronous memory operations to 'hide' long memory access latencies and improve the ME utilization rate. The core idea is to continue calculations while 'waiting' for references to be completed. Further, with the mechanism of complete signals and command queues, multiple memory references can be issued simultaneously.

Fig. 3 presents single thread throughputs of selected algorithms applying different optimization principles. Related internal statistics of ME are given in Fig. 4. As is evident from the plot, Hash functions have the best performance (MD5 1219 Mb/s) followed by stream ciphers and block ciphers. DES achieves the lowest throughput

(32.2 Mb/s after optimization) because it works at bit level while 32-bit IXP2800 has a weak support on bit instructions.

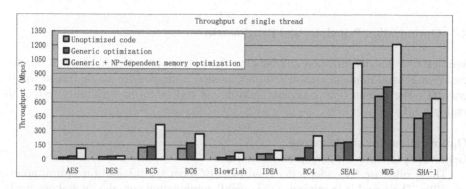

Fig. 3. Single thread performance with different optimization principles

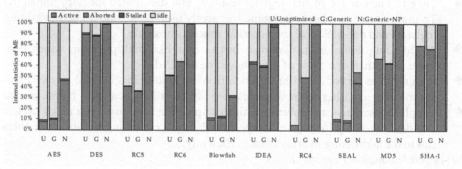

Fig. 4. Internal Statistics of ME

The effect of pipeline optimizations seems quite limited. This is because of the short pipeline architecture of NPs and low percentage of branch instructions (<2%) in cryptographic algorithms. The execution statistics also prove this. Most stream and block ciphers suffer from low ME utilization rate ('active' in Fig. 4), but generic optimizations do not take long memory reference latencies into account. On the other hand, NP-dependent memory optimizations effectively 'hide' them and increase ME utilization rate significantly, especially for algorithms which have a relative high percentage of memory operations. For instance, SEAL receives 438% performance The effect of pipeline optimizations seems quite limited. This is because of the short pipeline architecture of NPs and low percentage of branch instructions (<2%) in cryptographic algorithms. The execution statistics also prove this. Most stream and block ciphers suffer from low ME utilization rate ('active' in Fig. 4), but generic optimizations do not take long memory reference latencies into account. On the other hand, NP-dependent memory optimizations effectively 'hide' them and increase ME utilization rate significantly, especially for algorithms which have a relative high percentage of memory operations. For instance, SEAL receives 438% performance boost after applying memory optimizations. Even though Hash functions have less than 1% memory instructions, memory optimizations still yield more speedup than generic optimizations. From Fig. 4, we also observe that all algorithms except AES, Blowfish and SEAL get a near 100% ME utilization rate after memory optimizations. Hence, ME computing power is still their bottleneck. On the contrary, not the memory bandwidth but long access latency limits the throughput of AES, Blowfish and SEAL. Because, none of tested algorithms has its ME 'stalled' owing to fullness of target memory queues or ME command queues.

Scalability test

An obvious way to improve the cryptographic applications on NPs is to use parallelism. Three types of parallelism can be used: flow-level, block-level and intra-block parallelism. We select flow-level and block-level parallelism to see how well the overall throughput scale using multiple threads and MEs of IXP2800. All block ciphers are implemented in Cipher Block Chaining (CBC) mode. When encrypted with CBC mode, block read/write operations can be paralleled, which are handled by single thread using I/O parallelization. Thus, we assign one hardware thread to one flow and no thread communication is required. Fig. 5 presents the overall throughputs of the selected algorithms with our multi-ME and multi-thread implementation.

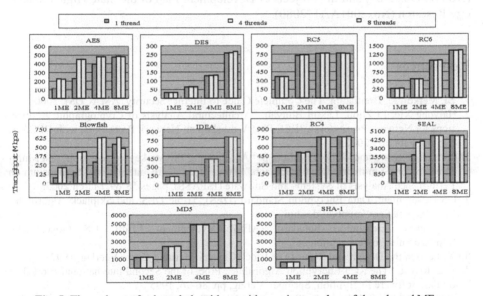

Fig. 5. Throughput of selected algorithms with varying number of threads and MEs

5   Summary

This study selects ten widely used cryptographic algorithms and analyze their instruction architectures on Intel IXP2800 network processor. We suggest several hardware improvements can be made on current NPs to help 'software' implementations on data path PEs:

◆ Increase cache size on PEs to hold large tables and lessen the pressure on shared memory and bus.
◆ Enlarge the size of memory queue and command queue to reduce the 'stalled' possibility of PE.
◆ Improve communications among different PEs to help intra-block parallelism.
◆ Adopt a new memory system to shorten the access latency.

We believe that in combination of these improvements the proposed implementation and optimization principles could go a long way to improving cryptographic processing performance on network processors.

Acknowledgment

This research was supported by Intel IXA University Research Plan (No. 9077), the Natural Science Foundation of China (No.90104002, 60173012 and 60372019), the Projects of Development Plan of the State Key Fundamental Research (No.G1999032707) and the Projects of Development Plan of the State High Technology Research (No. 2001AA112080).

References

1. M. Merkow, J. Breithaupt, The Complete Guide to Internet Security, AMACOM, 2000
2. Haiyong Xie, Li Zhou, Laxmi Bhuyan, "Architectural Analysis of Cryptographic Applications for Network Processors", IEEE First Workshop on Network Processors, with HPCA-8, Boston, February 2002.
3. Praveen Dongara and T. N. Vijaykumar, "Accelerating Private-key cryptography via Multithreading on Sym-metric Multiprocessors", Proc. of the IEEE International Symposium on Performance Analysis of Systems and Software (ISPASS), pages 58-69, March 2003.
4. US Government. Data Encryption Standard (DES), Triple DES, and Skipjack Algorithms. http://csrc.nist.gov/cryptval/des.htm.
5. Advanced Encryption Standard (AES) Development Effort, US Government, http://csrc.nist.gov/encryption/aes/
6. X. Lai, On the Design and Security of Block Ciphers, Hartung-Gorre Veerlag, 1992
7. R.L. Rivest, "The RC5 Encryption Algorithm", Proc. of the Second International Workshop on Fast Software Encryption, Springer-Verlag, pp. 86-96, 1995
8. R. Rivest, M. Robshaw, R. Sidney, Y. Yin, The RC6 block cipher, RSA Security, http://csrc.nist.gov/encryption/aes/round2/AESAlgs/RC6.
9. B. Schneier, "Description of a New Variable-Length Key, 64-Bit Block Cipher", Proc. of the Cambridge Security Workshop, Springer-Verlag, pp. 191-204, 1994.
10. B. Schneier, Applied Crytography, 2nd Edition, John Wiley & Sons, 1996.
11. P. Rogaway and D. Coppersmith, "A Software-Optimized Encryption Algorithm", Proc. of the Cambridge Security Workshop, Springer-Verlag, pp. 56-63, 1994
12. R. Rivest,The MD5 Message-Digest Algorithm, RFC 1321, April 1992
13. Alfred J. Menezes, Paul C. van Oorschot and Scott A. Vanstone. Handbook of Applied Cryptography, CRC Press 1996

A Method to Obtain Signatures from Honeypots Data

Chi-Hung Chi[1], Ming Li[2] (corresponding author), and Dongxi Liu[1]

[1] School of Computing, National University of Singapore, Singapore 117543
{Chich, liudx}@comp.nus.edu.sg

[2] School of Information Science & Technology, East China Normal University
Shanghai 200062, PR. China
ming_lihk@yahoo.com

Abstract. Building intrusion detection model in an automatic and online way is worth discussing for timely detecting new attacks. This paper gives a scheme to automatically construct snort rules based on data captured by honeypots on line. Since traffic data to honeypots represent abnormal activities, activity patterns extracted from those data can be used as attack signatures. Packets captured by honeypots are unwelcome, but it appears unnecessary to translate each of them into a signature to use entire payload as activity pattern. In this paper, we present a way based on system specifications of honeypots. It can reflect seriousness level of captured packets. Relying on discussed system specifications, only critical packets are chosen to generate signatures and discriminating values are extracted from packet payload as activity patterns. After formalizing packet structure and syntax of snort rule, we design an algorithm to generate snort rules immediately once it meets critical packets.

1 Introduction

Techniques in an intrusion detection system (IDS) can usually be classified into two. One is anomaly detection and the other misuse detection. Anomaly detection views behaviors deviated significantly from normal profile as attacks, e.g., [6] [7]. Misuse detection systems detect attacks by finding the activities matched with attack signatures, which are drawn from known attacks [3] [4] [5]. This approach is effective to detect known attacks but hard to identify new attacks due to the lack of corresponding signatures.

In order to enable misuse detection systems to identify new attacks adaptively, we explore a method to construct attack signatures from data gathered by honeypots in an automatic and online way. A honeypot is security resource whose value lies in being probed, attacked, or compromised [1]. Generally, honeypots play no role in production systems. Hence, traffic to and from honeypots are suspicious, providing us with opportunities to get pure intrusive packets. Inspired by this feature of honeypots, we can extract patterns of these packets and use them as signatures for misuse detection systems. Here, we choose snort [3] as our target system. Since signatures between different signature-based IDSs can be mutually translated [8], the present approach can be extended to other misuse detection systems.

H. Jin et al. (Eds.): NPC 2004, LNCS 3222, pp. 435-442, 2004.
© IFIP International Federation for Information Processing 2004

It is usually unnecessary to map each packet to a snort rule. E.G., if a scanning packet or ICMP echo request (ping) is captured, it may not provide distinct information to identify abnormal activities as an intruder may fake its source IP address. Generally, choosing which part of the packet payload as signatures is difficult since a successful attack usually involves a sequence of packets. Therefore, instead of constructing a snort rule for each of them, we only maps chosen packets for system specifications of honeypots. Moreover, our method can extract discriminating values from packet payload as activity pattern rather than use the entire payloads as signatures. In the course of building signatures, system specifications are important. They are specified by honeypots administrator and made up of system commanders, system calls, system configuration files and even some machine instructions.

In summary, the contributions in this paper are 1) a new usage of honeypots, which differs from traditional usage; 2) system specifications based way to recognize critical packets and extract discriminating values as activity pattern; and 3) an automatic and online method to generate attack signatures. In the rest of paper, § 2 describes our requirements to the new usage of honeypots, § 3 discusses our method and § 4 concludes the paper.

2 Requirements to Honeypots

There are many types of honeypots. According to interaction level, they are classified into three [1]: low-interaction, medium-interaction and high-interaction honeypots. Low-interaction honeypots emulate some services, medium-interaction ones also emulate services (but they can response attackers' request to some extent) while high-interaction ones are real operating systems and services. This paper concerns with high-interaction, as we need to collect real data coming from intruders instead of simply detecting unauthorized scans or connection attempts.

In a honeynet, production traffic only goes to production network while intrusion traffic goes to all hosts since intruders try to attack as many systems as possible. When intruders use new attack methods, conventional misuse detection systems in production network may be difficult to sense them. However, when they are equipped with honeypots that can update signature bases of misuse detection systems, it will enable misuse detection systems to adapt new attacks quickly. This paper focuses on how honeypots generate snort rules. The issue of how they exchange between honeypots and snorts is not contained in this paper.

Main requirements to honeypots are data control, data capture and data collection [1]. To the honeypots in our scheme, we have two requirements for our purpose:
1) Correspondence between honeypots and servers in production network. This means each honeypot corresponds to a server or several same servers, and vice versa.
2) Security levels between corresponding honeypots and servers. The security level of honeypots should be as secure as the corresponding servers.

3 Generating Signatures Online

By generating signatures online, we mean generating snort rules on line once honeypots capture suspicious packets without the intervention of administrators. To this end, we consider two issues. One is the specific procedure to map a given packet to a snort rule (§ 3.1). The other is the way to choose the packets among those captured by honeypots to map and extract the activity patterns from the payload (§ 3.2).

3.1 Mapping a Packet to a Snort Rule

To map a given packet to a snort rule, it needs to describe packet structure and the syntax of snort rules formally. We introduce the mapping procedure from a given IP packet to a snort rule in this subsection.

Consider formalizing packet structure. A packet is a stream of raw bits in essence. How to interpret this stream is determined by its structure, which is usually specified as standards. Snort currently can analyze four types of protocols (IP, TCP, UDP and ICMP). Below, we take IP as an example to show how to formalize IP packet structure.

For our purpose, an IP packet structure is described as: $<srcIP, dstIP, ttl, tos, fragbits, ipoption, protocol, payload>$, where

--$srcIP$ is the source IP address, and $dstIP$ the destination IP address;

--ttl is the time to live(ttl) filed, and tos is the type of service field;

--$fragbits$ is the fragment flag filed, including three bits that can be checked, namely, the

reserved (R) bit, more fragments (M) bit and the don't fragment (D) bit;

--$ipoption$ is the options field. There eight option types, including strict source routing (ssr),

loose source routing (lsr), IP security option (seq), time stamp (ts), record route (rr), end of list

(eol), no option (nop), and stream identifier (satid).

--$protocol$ is the type of transport packet being carried;

--$payload$ is the data encapsulated in IP packet.

In the above structure, we omit some fields of less interesting for our research, e.g., check sum field. In addition, suppose $count(ipoption)$ indicate the count of $ipoption$. Then, $ipoption[i]$ $(0 \leq i < count(ipoption))$ denotes each option's type. If p is an IP packet, we use $p.srcIP$ to denote p's source address, $p.dstIP$ to denote p's destination address, and so on.

The previous syntax of snort rules is the target of signature constructing. If a non-terminal symbol is defined only with a terminal symbol, the non-terminal symbol will be replaced by the corresponding terminal symbol when generating a rule. Otherwise, we have to determine which terminal symbol should be chosen according to packet content.

Let us discuss mapping procedure. The major work of mapping is to determine values of BNF non-terminal symbols in snort rule syntax. Suppose p is an IP packet. Algorithm 1 produces a snort rule from p. In addition, option "msg" ":" "Signature from honeypots" ";" is desirable to be included in each generated snort rule so as to facilitate management of rule bases, but we omit this option in *algorithm 1* for simplicity.

Algorithm 1. *Mapping procedure between a given packet and a snort rule*
INPUT: *an IP packet pt*
OUTPUT: *a snort rule*
1.   let ip_patterns = "ttl" ":" "*p.ttl*" ";" "tos" ":" "*p.tos*" ";";
2.   let ip_patterns += "fragbits" ":"+*substring*("RDM", *p.fragbits*)+";" ;
3.   for *i*=0 to *count*(*p.ipoption*)-1, do
     let ip_patterns += "ipopts" ":" "*p.ipoption*[i]" ";";
4.   if *p.protocol*∉ {TCP, UDP, ICMP}, then
         \<protocol> ::= "ip";
     \<rport> ::= "any";
     \<options> ::= ip_patterns+"content" ":" "*p. payload*" ";";
5.   if *p.protocol*=UDP, then
     \<protocol> ::= "udp";
     \<rport> ::= "*p.payload.destPort*";
     \<options> ::= ip_patterns+"content" ":" "*p. payload.payload*" ";" ;
6.   if *p.protocol*=TCP, then
     \<protocol> ::= "tcp";
     \<rport> ::= "*p.payload.destPort*";
     let tcp_flags= *substring*("12UAPRSF", *p.flags*);
     if tcp_flags= "", then tcp_flags= "0";
     let tcp_patterns = "flags" ":"+ tcp_flags + ";";
     \<options> ::= ip_patterns+tcp_patterns+"content" ":"
         "*p. payload.payload*" ";" ;
7.   if *p.protocol*=ICMP, then
     \<protocol> ::= "icmp";
     \<rport> ::= "any";
     let icmp_patterns = "itype" ":" "*p.payload.type*" ";";
     let icmp_patterns += "icode" ":" "*p.payload.code*" ";";
     let icmp_patterns += "icmp_id" ":" "*p.echo_id*" ";";
     let icmp_patterns += "icmp_seq" ":" "*p.echo_seq*" ";";
     \<options>::=ip_patterns+icmp_patterns+"content"
         ":" "*p.payload.payload*" ";" ;
8.   return;

In the above algorithm, "+" is used to concatenate two terminal symbols in BNF; "" represents an empty string; *substring*(*str, indicator*) extracts a substring from *str* according to the indicator. For example, for *substring*("12UAPRSF", *p.flags*), if *p.flags*= 0x55, then substring "2ARF" is generated. It should be noted that *algorithm 1* simply map the *p*'s payload, which will be improved in the following section.

3.2 System Specifications, Critical Packets, Discriminating Values, and Building Signature

Using *algorithm* 1, one can map fields of a given packet to the corresponding constructs of a snort rule. Nevertheless, it is still not enough to build accurate and efficient attack signatures. As stated previously, it may be unnecessary to map every captured packet to a snort rule and extracting activity pattern from packet payload is also a difficult task. In this subsection, we address both problems by turning to the knowledge in system specifications of honeypots.

Different definitions of system specifications can be used for different purposes. For example, to describe hardware system for a computer, one can use CPU frequency, memory and hard disk size, network speed as system specifications. Here, we concern with the system specifications of honeypots to characterize the seriousness level of captured packets regarding network security.

Generally, intruders exploit vulnerabilities of programs to obtain necessary privilege to implement attacks. In the course of attacks, in particular for attacks on hosts like R2L attacks in [9], an intruder uses system calls (even some specific machine instructions) to change the execution path and uses system commands to change the system state, or modify system configuration files to leave back doors. For examples, using *WinExec* executes the shell code in buffer overflow attack; copying worm or Trojan programs in malicious code attack. It can be concluded that, among packets captured by honeypots, those containing system calls, commands or configuration files will represent more serious intrusive activities than those without such information.

Therefore, system specifications of a honeypot are defined as a set of system calls, system commands, system configuration files, or even machine instructions. C is used to denote system specifications. For example, smd.exe, win.ini, WinExec, dir, cp are all elements of C in Microsoft Windows; fork, passwd, ln belong to C on unix or linux platform; machine instruction "Jump" is also an element of C.

For each honeypot, its administrator should specify its system specifications explicitly. That C is empty means that nothing is considered to be serious. In this case, no rules will be generated. On the other hand, if C contains all possible objects on honeypots, then almost every captured packet will result in a snort rule. For example, if file index.htm of web server on honeypots is included in C, then an unwelcome browser to this file will generate a snort rule, and obviously this rule will cause false positives in production network. Fortunately, an administrator often knows his system very well. In other words, he knows what system specifications are, and which specifications are more important. Therefore, he can give a reasonable system specifications C for a honeypot.

A list of probes captured by a honeypot in a 30-day period is given in [12], where some "ordinary" packets (such as the ICMP echo request packets and DNS version query packets) are included. Suppose p is a normal packet and r is the snort rule by using *algorithm* 1. r will match packets in normal production traffic, which will cause false alarms. Therefore, we do not map "ordinary" packet captured by honeypots to a snort rule, and instead, only critical packets are chosen to do so. Below we describe the definition of critical packets.

Definition 1. Suppose $p_1 \to p_2 \to p_3 \ldots \to p_n$ is a series of packets captured by honeypots for an attack. $p_i(1 \leq i \leq n)$ is a critical packet for the attack, if the following conditions hold:

a) The payload of p_i contains c, $c \in C$;

b) For $\forall p_j(1 \leq j \leq i)$, p_j is not critical, which are ordinary packets.

In order to implement attacks, ordinary packets are usually used by an intruder to gather information about target hosts. Critical packets help an intruder to get necessary privileges or install backdoor programs. The packets following critical packets represent intruder's activities on honeypots after getting some privileges, such as create directory, modify files, etc. These packets also contain system calls. However, we don't translate them into snort rules because they rely on the critical packets. Since snort rule is per-packet based signature, we only define one critical packet in a successful attack. In fact, if misuse detection system uses state-transition signatures as stated in [4], in which every state represents an occurrence of events, we can choose many critical packets to build such kind of signatures.

For attacks on network, packets may contain no system calls or system commands, such as tear drops attacks and syn flood attack. The goals of these attacks are usually to crash the target systems or make them deny services. Constructing signature based on critical packets may not cover this kind of attacks. However, attacks on network only involve packet headers that have more strict structure. Thus, they have much less variations and new attacks than those on hosts.

In *algorithm* 1, the entire packet payload is used as the argument value of *content* option. Hence, *content* option in the resulting rule contains more than enough bits to characterize activity pattern. It will result in two drawbacks: 1) matching snort rules to network traffic will be low efficient because there are more bits to deal with; and 2) it is possible to make false negatives because finding longer bit sequence exactly in network traffic is more difficult and the change of some redundant bits will cause variants of attacks and lead to miss matching. To avoid these drawbacks, we should identify the representative subsequence of bits in packet payload as activity patterns, called discriminating value of the packet. For a critical packet, only its discriminating value is used as the argument value of *content* options. A formal definition of discriminating value is given below.

Definition 2. Suppose p is a critical packet captured by honeypots. The discriminating value of p is a triple (*serv, op, c*) or a pair (*serv, c*), where

a) *serv* is the service type;

b) *op* is the type of service operation;

c) $c \in C$ is contained by p's payload.

If the service is based on TCP or UDP, then discriminating values will take the triple form, otherwise the pair form. For example, discriminating value for an HTTP packet can be (HTTP, GET, cmd.exe); discriminating value for the attack based on buffer overflow on IP protocol software can be (IP, *WinExec*). In the first case, field *serv* can be characterized by the destination port uniquely, such as 80 for HTTP and 23 for TELNET; field *op* can be determined by interpreting packet payload according to the packet format of service *serv*. In the second case, field *serv* can be determined by using protocol name, i.e. IP or ICMP. In the both cases, field c can be gotten by looking up each element of C and one of the found elements can be used as c. Because $p.payload$ maybe contains several elements of C, we use a heuristic method to choose the most distinct one. Suppose n elements c_i ($1 \leq i \leq n$) have been found and $pos(c_i)$ is the position of c_i in $p.payload$. Then c_i with minimum $pos(c_i)$ is chosen as c.

Combining critical packets with discriminating values, *algorithm* 1 can be improved to be *algorithm* 2. For simplicity, only the modifications are listed.

Algorithm 2. *Building snort rules with critical packets and discriminating values*
  INPUT: *critical packet p from a honeypot, System Specifications C*
  OUTPUT: *a snort rule or null*

1. $Sp = \Phi$;
2. for $\forall c \in C$, if *found*(c, $p.payload.payload$), then
     $Sp = Sp \cup \{(\, c, pos(c))\}$;
3. if $Sp = \Phi$, then
     return *null*;
4. Let $c = c'$, where $(c', pos(c')) \in Sp$ and $pos(c') = min(\{pos(c'') \mid (c'', pos(c'')) \in Sp\})$;
   ......
5. if $p.protocol \notin \{TCP, UDP, ICMP\}$, then
   ......
   <options> ::= ip_patterns+"content" ":" "c" ";";
6. if $p.protocol = UDP$, then
   ......
   Let op be operation type of service in $p.payload.payload$;
   <options> ::= ip_patterns+"content" ":" "op" ";" + "content" ":" "c" ";" ;
7. if $p.protocol = TCP$, then
   ......
   Let op be operation type of service in $p.payload.payload$;
   <options> ::= ip_patterns+"content" ":" "op" ";" + "content" ":" "c" ";" ;
8. if $p.protocol = ICMP$, then
   ......
   <options>::=ip_patterns+icmp_patterns+"content" ":" "c" ";" ;
9. return;

Compared with *algorithm* 1, *algorithm* 2 has two differences. The first one is to check whether p is a critical packet, and if not, it will not generate snort rules for p, and if yes, c in discriminating values will be calculated. The second is to use c and op as the argument value of *content* option. As a result, *algorithm* 2 can produce more compact and flexible snort rules to identify the variants of attacks. In addition, we ignore the details to interpret the operation type op.

The above explanations imply that the present method is not simply to translate each captured packet to a snort rule. Owing to the limit space, cases to show the application of the present method is not given.

4 Conclusions and Acknowledgements

A usage of honeypots for on-line building snort rules from the data captured by honeypots has been discussed. We have analyzed the requirements to honeypots with respect to assuring honeypots to generate useful signatures for detecting attacks in production network. System specifications used to recognize critical packets and extract discriminating values as activity pattern have been explained. Algorithms for automatic and online generation of attack signatures have been derived. This research is under a grant for the project Pervasive Virtual Community in Cyberspace (R-252-000-079-112), Singapore. The paper is in part sponsored by SRF for ROCS, State Education Ministry, PRC.

References

1. L. Spitzner, Honeypots: *Tracking Hackers*, Addison-Wesley, 2002.
2. Honeynet Project, Know Your Enemy, Honeynets, http://project.honeynet.org/papers/honeynet/.
3. M. Roesch, Snort-lightweight intrusion detection for networks, *1999 USENIX*, 1999.
4. K. Ilgun and et al, *IEEE T. on Software Eng.*, 21 (3), 1995, 181-199.
5. V. Paxson, *Computer Networks*, 31 (23/24), 1999, 2435-2463.
6. M. Li, An approach to reliably identifying signs of DDOS flood attacks based on LRD traffic pattern recognition, to appear on *Computer & Security*, 2004.
7. R. A. Kemmerer and G. Vigna, *Supplement to Computer*, 35 (4), 2002, 27-30.
8. S. T. Eckmann, *Proc., RAID 2001, LNCS 2212*, 2001, 69-84.
9. K. Kendall, *A Database of Computer Attacks for the Evaluation of Intrusion Detection Systems*, Master Thesis, MIT, 1999.
10. M. Roesch and C. Green, Snort users manual, http://www.snort.org/docs/ SnortUsers-Manual.pdf
11. http://project.honeynet.org/papers/enemy/probed.txt.

A Framework for Adaptive Anomaly Detection Based on Support Vector Data Description*

Min Yang, HuanGuo Zhang, JianMing Fu, and Fei Yan

School of Computer, State Key Laboratory of Software Engineering,
Wuhan University, Wuhan 430072, Hubei, China
yangm75@hotmail.com

Abstract. To improve the efficiency and usability of adaptive anomaly detection system, we propose a new framework based on Support Vector Data Description (SVDD) method. This framework includes two main techniques: online change detection and unsupervised anomaly detection. The first one enables automatically obtain model training data by measuring and distinguishing change caused by intensive attacks from normal behavior change and then filtering most intensive attacks. The second retrains model periodically and detects the forthcoming data. Results of experiments with the KDD'99 network data show that these techniques can handle intensive attacks effectively and adapt to the concept drift while still detecting attacks. As a result, false positive rate is reduced from 13.43% to 4.45%.

1 Introduction

Intrusion detection is a necessary complement to traditional intrusion prevention techniques to guarantee network security. There are two general approaches for intrusion detection: misuse detection and anomaly detection [1]. Compared with misuse detection, anomaly detection has the advantage that it can detect new types of attacks. However, at the same time, it suffers from high false alarm especially when normal behavior changes over time. In practice, users, networks or system activities cannot be invariant when environment changes over time. This phenomenon is called concept drift [2]. To guarantee the accuracy of adapting to concept drift while still recognizing anomalous activities, adaptive anomaly detection systems have to retrain and update their models with online or newly collected data frequently [3].

Unsupervised learning algorithms, which train models with unlabelled data, are promising for adaptive anomaly detection and have been studied by researchers in recent years [3,4,5,6]. In [3], a general adaptive model generation system to anomaly detection is presented, which uses a probability-based algorithm for building models over noisy data periodically. SmartSifer, an online

---

* Supported by the National Natural Science Foundations of China under Grant No.90104005 and No.66973034, supported by the National 863 Project under Grant No.2002aa141051, supported by the Doctoral Science Foundation of Ministry of Education under Grant No.20020486046

H. Jin et al. (Eds.): NPC 2004, LNCS 3222, pp. 443–450, 2004.

unsupervised learning algorithm for anomaly detection based on a probabilistic model, adjusts the model after each input datum [4]. More recently, several different unsupervised learning algorithms are applied to anomaly detection, including cluster-based algorithm, k-nearest neighbor based algorithm, LOF approach, and one-class SVM algorithm [7]. The work most similar to our SVDD-based unsupervised anomaly detection is one-class SVM based anomaly detection. Those algorithms as well as previous probabilistic based algorithms [3,4] make an important assumption of attack ratio that attacks can be taken as outliers because they are rare and qualitatively different from normal data. Therefore, these algorithms can use real time data to constantly update or periodically retrain their models directly. However,the assumption of attack ratio, i.e. normal data greatly outnumber the attacks, limits the application of these algorithms in practice because the number of large-scale DoS attacks and probing attacks has been increasing alarmingly over the past few years. As a result,the assumption does not hold when a burst of intensive attacks causes a large number of anomaly instances in a short time.

In this paper, we present a new framework for adaptive anomaly detection, which extends traditional unsupervised method and overcomes the limitations of the assumption of attack ratio. In the framework, we introduce the SVDD algorithm to anomaly detection. Also, an SVDD-based online change detection algorithm is presented to distinguish changes caused by intensive attacks from concept drift. With the aid of change detection algorithm, intensive attacks is filtered first, and then model retraining is realized safely.

The rest of this paper is organized as follows. In section 2, we describe the SVDD algorithm and introduce the change point detect algorithm; based on these algorithms, we then present the SVDD-based adaptive anomaly detection framework. In section 3, we discusses our experiments with KDD'99 data. We summarize our conclusions in section 4.

2   SVDD-based Anomaly Detection

SVDD [8] is an unsupervised support vector machine algorithm for outlier detection. The goal of SVDD is to distinguish one class of data, called target data, from the rest of the feature space. To do this, SVDD learns an optimal hypersphere around target data after mapping the whole dataset to high dimensional feature space. The hypersphere as descriptive model for target data is used to classify data into target data or non-target data (also be called outliers). For SVDD-based anomaly detection we take normal data as target class and all kind of known and unknown attacks as outliers.

2.1   SVDD

Let $\{x_i\} \subseteq \chi$ be a training dataset of N data points, with $\chi \subseteq R^d$ Using a nonlinear transformation Φ from χ to some high dimensional feature space, we search for the optimal enclosing hypersphere that is as small as possible while at the same time, including most of the training data. This can be formulated as the following optimization problem:

$$\min_{R,\xi,a} \ R^2 + \frac{1}{vN} \sum_i \xi_i \qquad (1)$$

subject to $\ \| \Phi(x_i) - a \|^2 \le R^2 + \xi_i, \ \ \xi_i \ge 0, \ \ i = 1, \ldots, N \ ,$

where a is the center of the hypersphere and R is its radius. Parameter v controls the tradeoff between the radius of hypershpere and the number of points that it contains. It is expected that if R and a solve this problem, the decision function $f(x) = sgn(R^2 - \| \Phi(x) - a \|^2)$ is determined by location of x in the feature space. To solve this problem we introduce the Lagrangian:

$$L = R^2 - \sum_i (R^2 + \xi_i - \| \Phi(x_i) - a \|^2) \alpha_i - \sum_i \xi_i \beta_i + \frac{1}{vN} \sum_i \xi_i \ . \qquad (2)$$

Setting to zeros the derivative of L with respect to R, a and ξ_i, leads to

$$a = \sum_i \alpha_i \Phi(x_i), \quad \alpha = \frac{1}{vN} - \beta_i \le \frac{1}{vN}, \quad \sum_i \alpha_i = 1 \ . \qquad (3)$$

We then turn the Lagrangian into the Wolfe dual form with kernel function:

$$\min_{\alpha} \ \sum_{i,j} \alpha_i \alpha_j K(x_i, x_j) - \sum_i \alpha_i K(x_i, x_i) \qquad (4)$$

subject to $\ \sum_i \alpha_i = 1, \ \ 0 < \alpha_i < \frac{1}{vN}, \ \ i = 1, \ldots, N \ .$

Throughout this paper we use the Gaussian kernel: $K(x_i, x_j) = exp(-q \| x_i - x_j \|^2)$, with width parameter q. The optimal α 's can be obtained after the dual problem is solved. Few special points with $0 < \alpha_i < 1/vN$ just lie on the surface of hypershere and are called *support vectors* . The first equation of (3) means that a can be expressed as the linear combination of $\Phi(x)$, and then R can be computed from any *support vector* x_k:

$$R^2 = \| \Phi(x_k) - a \|^2 = K(x_k, x_k) - 2 \sum_i \alpha_i K(x_i, x_k) + \sum_{i,j} (i,j) \alpha_i \alpha_j K(x_i, x_j). \qquad (5)$$

2.2 Change Detection Algorithm

The main idea of our change detection algorithm comes from the change point detection theory. The objective of change point detection is to determine if the observed time series is statistically homogeneous, and if not, to find the point in time when the change happens [9]. In our application, real time data from sensors are processed into multi-dimensional time series. Compared with traditional change detection algorithm Cumulative Sum (CUSUM), our SVDD-based algorithm could be easily applied to multi-dimensional series.

The idea of SVDD-based change detection is simple. SVDD always try to find an optimal hypersphere for the target class, which is the great majority in the training data. Thus the region of the hypersphere is a representative of the probability density function that generates the target class. Hence, comparing the geometries and location of hyperspheres has the equal effect with comparing training data that the hypersheres build on.

Fig.1 demonstrates the change detection algorithm. Two adjoining sliding windows with same size m are placed on the series to produce adjoining subset of data flow. The two windows are moving forward with fixed increment step simultaneously. At time t, subset $W_1 = \{x_{t-m}, \ldots, x_{t-1}\}$ and $W_2 = \{x_t, \ldots, x_{t+m-1}\}$ are obtained by the two windows. If we use them as training data to build SVDD models independently, we get hypersphere S_1 defined by center a_1 and radius R_1 for W_1 and hypersphere S_2 defined by center a_2 and radius R_2 for W_2. A unexpected change at time t, which means a different distribution of data after t, may result in different location and geometries of S_1 and S_2. We use a change detection index $I(t)$ to reflect the dissimilarity between S_1 and S_2:

$$I(t) = \| a_1 - a_2 \| / (R_1 + R_2) \ . \tag{6}$$

According to 3.1, a_1, a_2, and $\| a_1 - a_2 \|$ can be computed:

$$a_1 = \sum_i \alpha_{1i} \cdot \Phi(x_{1i}), \qquad a_2 = \sum_j \alpha_{2j} \cdot \Phi(x_{2j}) \ ,$$

$$\| a_1 - a_2 \|^2 = \sum_{i,j} \alpha_{1i}\alpha_{1j} K(x_{1i}, x_{1j}) + \sum_{i,j} \alpha_{1i}\alpha_{1j} K(x_{1i}, x_{1j}) - 2\sum_{i,j} \alpha_{1i}\alpha_{2j} K(x_{1i}, x_{2j}).$$

Radii of the hyperspheres can also be computed from their *support vectors* according to (5). It can be found that, although $I(t)$ is defined in the feature space, it can be computed in the input space using the kernel function.

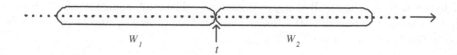

$$W_1 \qquad\qquad t \qquad\qquad W_2$$

Fig. 1. Data series and sliding windows at time t. The right arrow indicates the direction of data generation.

With the continual generation of input data, the two windows are moving simultaneously with a fixed increment w that is predefined and $I(t)$ is computed every time. We then get a index curve of $I(t)$, and abrupt changes are easily detected whenever the index $I(t)$ peaks or is over a threshold λ.

There are two parameters, w and m, and a threshold λ which need to be considered. Window size m is selected based on several factors. It should not be too small. Otherwise, it can't reflect the data distribution, and will get $I(t)$ unsteady even for purely normal data flow. Nonetheless a too large m is also infeasible and unnecessary because it will increase the computing complexity. We are not able to find a universal value of m for any application, but we can find a proper value for our application by testing different m in normal data flow until getting steady change index values with a little variance. The moving increment, w, could range from 1 to m. This depends on the acceptable degree of detection delay. The index $I(t)$ measures the extent of change. In our application, we assume sudden a burst of large-scale intensive attacks will cause abrupt changes in data flow while concept drift raises mild and gradual changes in data flow. The threshold λ is used to detect abrupt change. If one $I(t)$ in index curve goes above λ, it indicates an ongoing intensive attack.

2.3 Adaptive Anomaly Detection Framework

Based on SVDD algorithm and change detection algorithm, we design an adaptive anomaly detection framework, which consists of four main components: preprocessor, change detector, model generator, and anomaly detector. The preprocessor transforms the raw network packets from sensors into formatted data, and then sends these data to the anomaly detector and the change detector. The anomaly detector uses a SVDD model to classify normal and intrusive data and raises alarm for ongoing intrusion. The change detector uses change detect algorithm to detect the intensive attacks and prepares training data for the model generator. The training data are stored in database and they are sent to the model generator when model update condition is triggered. The model generator learns a new model with new training data, and feeds model to anomaly detector periodically.

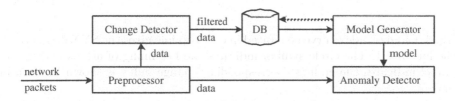

Fig. 2. Adaptive Anomaly Detection Framework

3   Experiment

We conducted experiments on KDD'99 dataset [10] , which is prepared for network intrusion detection. In the dataset, the network traffic data are connection-based. Each connection instance, described by 7 symbolic attributes and 34 continuous attributes, corresponds to a TCP/IP connection. The symbolic attributes must be transformed into numeric attribute to adapt to the SVDD algorithm. And attributes scaling is needed in order to ensure that the effect of some attributes is not dwarfed by others that have larger scales. The detail of these data preprocessing methods is described in our previous paper [11].

Experiment 1 (Exp1) is designed to evaluate the change detection algorithm for detecting intensive attacks. We take SYN flood DoS attack as an example. KDD'99 provides a typical 10 percent subset consisting of 494,020 instances, in which most instances are attacks. We reserve all of its 97,277 normal instances and filter most attacks to get a new set $C1$. In $C1$, 5 SYN flood attacks are reserved, which include more than 100,000 instances. Besides SYN flood attacks, all other kinds of at-tacks are less than 900 in $C1$.

We first illustrate how the change index can reflect the influence of SYN flood attacks. Fig. 3 displays the change index values obtained on $C1$ data flow, where the sliding windows size m is 3,000 and the increment w for windows is 3,000. SVDD parameter v is 0.001 and Gaussian kernel parameter q is 0.02.

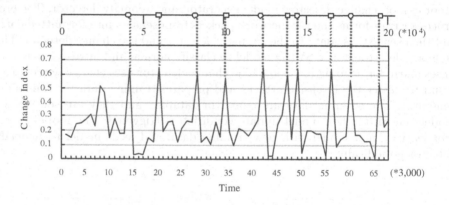

Fig. 3. Change index curve generated in $C1$. Top line gives the SYN flood attack schedule in $C1$. The circle symbol indicates the beginning of attack and square symbol indicates the ending. Corresponding change index is shown by bottom curve

In Fig. 3, when the threshold λ is 0.53, all changes caused by SYN flood attacks are correctly detected, with no false positive. It is natural that not only the starting of a SYN flood but also the withdrawing of the attack produce peaks in change index curve. These data falling in the two peaks should be rejected by the training dataset. In fact, the change detection algorithm not only can be used to prepare training dataset, but also can act as an intensive DoS attacks detector if we set a proper parameter, such as w. When detecting these kinds of DoS attacks, we are most concern with how to detect them as soon as possible so that we can take some response actions early to reduce the damage. With a 3,000 increment for windows, the average alarm delay for five SYN flood attacks is 342 connections. This means that we become aware of an attack in its first 342 connections. We can use less increment step for window to get early change alarm. In the set $C1$, when w is 500, the average alarm delay is 105. Theoretically, a smaller w is good for less delay time, but in fact a very smaller w is unpractical because SVDD's efficiency problem though online version of SVDD [12] is employed.

Experiment 2 is designed to test our adaptive anomaly detection system. The experiment compares the performance of static method with adaptive learning strategy. On the basis of the Exp1, $C1$ is filtered and generate a new dataset $C2$ in which attack instances are about 1%.

In order to compare the adaptive manner with the static manner, first 20,000 normal records of $C2$ are extracted to get an initial training dataset. An initial model is build based on this initial training dataset. Exp2-1 is an experiment for adaptive manner which updates the model periodically. In this mode, a retrain period for model training and update is set. First the initial model is used, then at the end of every period, a new model is trained using data collected in this period and the old model is replaced with the new generated one. In Exp2-1, retrain period is set 20,000. Exp2-2 is a static manner experiment without updating the model. It just uses the initial model to detect the rest of $C2$ set, and the model remains unchanged during the detecting process.

Table 1. Results of Exp2-1 and Exp2-2

Experiment	Elapsed time (thousand of instances)			
	20	40	60	80 (all)
	False positive rate(%)			
Exp2-1	4.87	4.33	5.39	4.45
Exp2-2	4.87	6.43	9.52	13.43
	Detection rate(%)			
Exp2-1	96.33	92.66	88.76	89.27
Exp2-2	96.33	95.17	92.80	92.35

In initial dataset, the parameter v and q are selected through cross validation to obtain the minimum false positive rate. We set v 0.01 and q 0.5 when false positive rate is 1.06%. In Exp2-1, the two parameters are unchanged. Table 1 shows the detection rates and false positive rates for Exp2-1 and Exp2-2 over elapsed time, i.e. more instances are seen. The static model in Exp2-1 is able to detect 92.35% of the attacks in the dataset $C2$ at the end of all data. However, the false positive rate is increasing with time, and reaches 13.43% at the end, which indicates the influence of concept drift in $C2$. At the time, the adaptive manner (Exp2-2) continuously adapts to the concept drift and thus improves the false positive. Consequently, it generates significantly less false positive rate($< 5\%$) as well as a comparable detection rate with static model.

4 Conclusion

Because of the limitation of application and the difficult of deployment of the previous adaptive system, in this paper, we present a new framework for adaptive anomaly detection based on SVDD. In order to implement the automatic collection of training data for model update, we design a change detection algorithm to find intensive attacks and to filter them from real time data. Then detection models are periodically regenerated with online collected training data. Our system significantly reduces human intervention as well as deployment costs. Results of experiments with the KDD'99 network data and preliminary analysis show that it can adapt to the network behavior changes while still detect attacks.

References

1. J.Mchugh. Intrusion and intrusion detection. International Journal of Information Security, 1(1): 14-35, 2001.
2. T.Lane, C.E.Brodley. Approaches to Online Learning and Concept Drift for User Identification in Computer Security. In Fourth International Conference on Knowledge Discovery and Data Mining, New York, NY, USA, Aug. 1998, 259-263.
3. E. Eskin, M. Miller, Z.-D. Zhong, G. Yi, W.-A. Lee, and S. Stolfo. Adaptive model generation for intrusion detection systems. In Proceedings of the ACMCCS Workshop on Intrusion Detection and Prevention, Athens, Greece, 2000.
4. K. Yamanishi, J. Takeuchi, and G. Williams. On-line unsupervised outlier detection using finite mixtures with discounting learning algorithms. In Proceedings of the Sixth ACM SIGKDD International Conference on Knowledge Discovery and Data Mining, Boston, MA, Aug. 2000, 320-324.
5. M. Hossain and S. M. Bridges. A framework for an adaptive intrusion detection system with data mining.In Proceedings of the 13th Annual Canadian Information Technology Security Symposium, Ottawa, Canada, June 2001.
6. W. Fan. Cost-sensitive, scalable and adaptive learning using ensemble-based methods. Ph.D. dissertation, Columbia University, Feb. 2001.
7. E. Eskin, A. Arnold, M, Prerau, L. Portnoy and S. Stolfo. A Geometric Framework for Unsupervised Anomaly DetectionDetecting Intrusions in Unlabeled Data. In D. Barbara and S. Jajodia (editors), Applications of Data Mining in Computer Security, Kluwer, 2002.
8. D.M.J. Tax, R.P.W. Duin. Support vector domain description. Pattern Recognition Letters, 20(11-13): 1191-1199, 1999.
9. M. Basseville, I. V. Nikiforov. Detection of Abrupt Changes : Theory and Application. Prentice Hall, 1993.
10. http://kdd.ics.uci.edu/databases/kddcup99/task.html.
11. M.Luo, H.G Zhang , L.N.Wang, and J. Chen. A Research on Intrusion Detection Based on Unsupervised Clustering and Support Vector Machine. In Proceedings of Fifth International Conference on Information and Communications Security, Huhhot, China, Oct. 2003, 325-336.
12. D.M.J. Tax, P.Laskov. Online SVM Learning: From Classification to Data Description and Back. In Proceedings of IEEE International Workshop on Neural Networks for Signal Processing, Toulouse, France, September 17-19, 2003, 499-508.

Design and Analysis of Improved GSM Authentication Protocol for Roaming Users

GeneBeck Hahn[1], Taekyoung Kwon[2], Sinkyu Kim[3], and JooSeok Song[1]

[1] Department of Computer Science, Yonsei University, Seoul, Korea
{gbhahn, jssong}@emerald.yonsei.ac.kr
[2] School of Computer Engineering, Sejong University, Seoul, Korea
{tkwon}@sejong.ac.kr
[3] National Security Research Institute, Daejeon, Korea
{skkim}@etri.re.kr

Abstract. In this paper, we improve the GSM (Global System for Mobile Communications) authentication protocol to reduce the signaling loads on the network. The proposed protocol introduces a notion of the enhanced user profile containing a few of VLR IDs for the location areas where a mobile user is most likely to visit. We decrease the authentication costs for roaming users by exploiting the enhanced user profile. Our protocol is analyzed with regard to efficiency and is compared with the original protocol.

1 Introduction

GSM, an european standard for the second generation mobile networks, intrinsically provides three security functions[1][2].

- Authentication for subscriber's identity
- Anonymity for subscriber's identity
- Confidentiality for data on the radio path

While providing the security functions listed above, the GSM networks suffers from excessive signaling loads for the transmission of authentication parameters. This indicates that the GSM authentication protocol requires significantly high costs while a number of communicating mobile users frequently move through the location areas. Considering the tremendously growing mobile users, this problem must become critical[2]. In this paper, we improve the GSM authentication protocol to reduce the costs of roaming user authentication. The basic concept of our protocol is to utilize the enhanced user profile containing a group of VLR (Visitor Location Register) IDs. Among the VLRs, the master VLR is defined as a VLR to which a mobile user performs location registration, while slave VLR is a VLR to which a mobile user performs location update. It means that a mobile user moves from the location area covered by master VLR to the other areas covered by slave VLRs. In our protocol, the master VLR manages several slave VLRs to reduce the signaling traffics for authenticating roaming

H. Jin et al. (Eds.): NPC 2004, LNCS 3222, pp. 451–458, 2004.
© IFIP International Federation for Information Processing 2004

users. This paper is organized as follows. Section 2 summarizes the operations
of GSM authentication protocol and describes its drawbacks. Section 3 proposes
an improved GSM authentication protocol without modifying the fundamentals
of GSM systems. In Section 4, we show that our protocol improves the original
protocol with regard to efficiency. Finally, Section 5 concludes this paper.

2   GSM Authentication Protocol

GSM authentication protocol utilizes the challenge-response mechanism with
secret key protocol which is used for either the mobile user authentication or
the session key generation. In GSM systems, the communicating users store the
session key in the SIM (Subscriber Identity Module) card and the network stores
the key in the secure database called AuC (Authentication Center)[4]. SIM is
unique to each mobile user and can be inserted to the mobile terminal. Also,
SIM contains the service related information for each mobile user and a unique
128 bit key Ki that is used to identify and authenticate itself to the network[5].

2.1   Original Protocol

The detailed operations of original protocol are summarized as follows[7][8].

1. While entering a new location area, a mobile user sends an authentication
   request which involves the TMSI (Temporary Mobile Subscriber Identity)
   and LAI (Location Area Identity) to the VLR.
2. The VLR checks the TMSI and derives an IMSI (International Mobile Subscriber Identity) from the TMSI. Then, the VLR forwards it to the HLR.
3. The HLR/AuC generates a 128 bit RAND corresponding to the received
   IMSI. Then, the HLR derives a 32 bit SRES (Signed RESult), 64 bit Kc
   through A3, A8 algorithm. This is done by using the RAND and the private
   key of the mobile user, results of which are returned to the VLR with RAND.
4. The VLR chooses a RAND from one of the triplet and forwards it to the
   mobile terminal.
5. The mobile terminal generates SRES, Kc through A3, A8 algorithm. This
   is also done by using the RAND and Ki stored in the SIM. The session key
   Kc is kept for the secure communication and the SRES is sent to the VLR.
6. Finally, the VLR compares it with the SRES sent from the HLR. If the two
   are equal, the mobile user is regarded as legal and the user authentication is
   completed.

2.2   Drawbacks of the GSM Authentication Protocol

In order to perform the user authentication, the VLR must contact to the HLR
since the private key of a mobile user is stored in the HLR. The problem is that
the triplets provided by the HLR are sent to the VLR via various intermediate
links and this incurs dramatic signaling traffics to GSM networks. Besides, the

excessive stream of signaling traffics may increase the authentication delay. As we will see, large portions of the GSM network traffics are generated from the consistent signaling between mobile users and network[5][9]. Fig. 1 depicts the flow of signaling messages generated while a mobile user performs either the location registration or update.

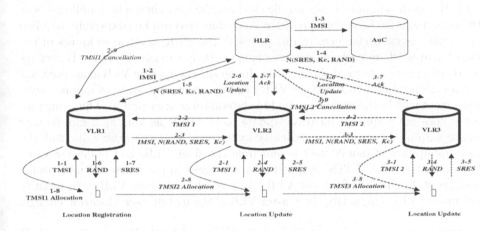

Fig. 1. GSM authentication protocol for roaming users

Since we explained the authentication procedure during location registration in Section 2.1, we skip this in this section. Instead, we illustrate the authentication procedure during location update. A mobile user first performs location registration to VLR1. As a result of successful authentication, VLR1 allocates a TMSI1 to the mobile user. In this point, we assume that the mobile user subsequently moves to the area covered by VLR2. Then, following steps of user authentication are performed.

2-1 The mobile user sends a TMSI1 to VLR2.

2-2 VLR2 forwards the TMSI1 to the location area managed by VLR1.

2-3 VLR2 receives an IMSI, together with a few of authentication triplets from VLR1.

2-4 VLR2 chooses a RAND from one of the authentication triplets and sends it to the mobile terminal.

2-5 The mobile terminal calculates a SRES and send it back to VLR2. VLR2 then performs the user authentication.

2-6 After the user authentication is completed successfully, VLR2 sends a location update message to HLR and updates the location of the mobile user.

2-7 HLR returns an acknowledgement for the user's location update to VLR2.

2-8 VLR2 assigns a TMSI2 to the mobile terminal.

2-9 HLR finally transmits a TMSI1 cancellation message to VLR1.

In case that the mobile user moves to the location area managed by VLR3, the similar steps of authentication procedure are performed.

3   Proposed Protocol for GSM Roaming Users

3.1   Basic Idea

In order to reduce the signaling traffics for roaming user authentication, our protocol exploits the enhanced user profile. The enhanced user profile is maintained in the HLR and the mobile terminal. The location areas corresponding to the VLR IDs in the enhanced user profile can be selectively chosen by mobile users at the enrollment to the service provider. Also, the areas can be adaptively modified by mobile users' preference. In our protocol, the HLR in advance knows of the location ares where each mobile user is most likely to visit. Besides, the master VLR manages a group of slave VLRs. In detail, the master VLR transmits authentication triplets to the slave VLRs and maintains the state of mobile users' movement within the areas specified in the enhanced user profile. Thus, our protocol does not require a location update to the HLR as long as a mobile user roams within a group of areas indicated by the enhanced user profile. Instead, the location update of mobile user is sent from the slave VLRs to the master VLR. For doing this, the TMSIs assigned from the areas in the enhanced user profile must contain the ID of master VLR. As a result, the slave VLRs can identify the master VLR and notify the master VLR of the mobile user's location change.

Our protocol must be installed on the HLR and VLR. As a result, the HLR knows of the master VLR by checking the VLR ID in the enhanced user profile when a mobile user performs location registration. The HLR regard the other VLRs in the enhanced user profile as slave VLRs and delegate its role to the master VLR. In addition to the fields for the VLR IDs in the enhanced user profile, we consider another field for the case where a mobile user moves to the area that is not indicated by the enhanced user profile. In this case, the VLR ID for the corresponding area is inserted into this field and the original protocol is performed. Specifically, the current VLR receives the authentication triplets from the master VLR and performs the authentication procedure. When the user authentication is completed successfully, the VLR transmits a location update directly to the HLR for the consistency between itself and HLR.

3.2   Protocol Description

Fig. 2 illustrates the functional steps of our protocol and describes the flow of signaling messages while a mobile user crosses several areas specified in the enhanced user profile. The main steps that must be focused on are the authentication procedure during location update. As presented in Fig. 2, our protocol utilizes the enhanced user profile containing three VLR IDs, i.e., VLR1, VLR2 and VLR3. The noticeable difference between the original protocol and our protocol is that the VLR1 acts as master VLR and VLR2/VLR3 act as slave VLRs. In case that a mobile user performs location registration to VLR1, the original protocol is performed and this is depicted in the step 1-1 through 1-8. If the mobile user moves to the area covered by VLR2, following steps of authentication procedure are performed.

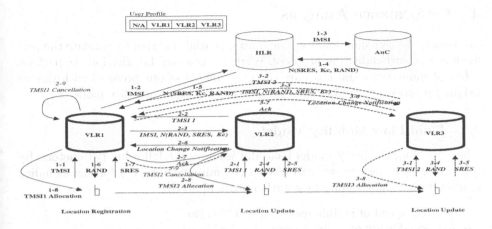

Fig. 2. Proposed GSM authentication protocol for roaming users

2-1 The mobile user sends a TMSI1 to VLR2.

2-2 VLR2 forwards the TMSI1 to the area where a mobile user performs location registration, i.e., the area managed by VLR1.

2-3 VLR2 receives an IMSI along with the authentication triplets from VLR1.

2-4 VLR2 chooses a RAND from one of the triplets and sends it to the mobile terminal.

2-5 The mobile terminal calculates a SRES and returns it to VLR2. The SRES is used to check the validity of the mobile user.

2-6 After the user authentication is completed successfully, VLR2 sends a location change notification to VLR1.

2-7 VLR1 forwards an Ack to VLR2.

2-8 VLR2 allocates a new TMSI, i.e., TMSI2 to the mobile terminal.

2-9 VLR1 sends a TMSI1 cancellation message to itself, i.e., the area that previously allocated a TMSI to the mobile terminal.

When the mobile user moves to the area managed by VLR3, similar steps of authentication procedure are performed and this is presented in the step 3-1 through 3-9. In summary, the proposed protocol can trace the location areas where a mobile user is most likely to visit. Basically, our protocol exploits the concept of mobile users' local movement, i.e., the local mobility. Specifically, large number of mobile users can be regarded as commuters roaming within a few of limited areas including home, office, school, etc. This stems from the fact that the mobility pattern of most roaming users could be quite routine and their roaming coverage might be confined to a few areas. By using the localized feature of user roaming, our protocol does not entirely rely on the HLR for whole steps of user authentication. Thus, the proposed protocol can perform an efficient roaming user authentication.

4   Performance Analysis

We regard the signaling loads as the most essential criterion to evaluate the performance of authentication protocol. While focusing on the criterion, we perform a few of simulations and compare the performance of our protocol with that of original protocol. For doing this, we use the Fluid flow mobility model[2].

4.1   Fluid Flow Mobility Model

The Fluid Flow mobility model basically assumes the following parameters. By using these parameters, we can obtain the numerical results for the signaling traffics during the roaming user authentication[2][11].

- Average speed of mobile users : $v = 6.3km/hr$
- Average density of mobile users : $\rho = 267/km^2$
- Moving direction of mobile users : $[\,0, 2\pi\,]$
- Border length of a location area : $l = 8.65$km
- Total border length of a location area : $L = 34.6$km
- One HLR for 64 location areas, each controlled by one VLR

At first, we can compute the number of location registrations to VLR.

$$R_{Reg,VLR} = \rho * v * L = \frac{267 * 6.3 * 34.6}{3600\pi} = 5.14/s \qquad (1)$$

We can also derive the number of location registrations generated at HLR.

$$R_{Reg,HLR} = R_{Reg,VLR} * Number of Areas = 5.14/s * 64 = 328.96/s \qquad (2)$$

4.2   Numerical Results for the Authentication Signaling Loads

We define the parameters to calculate the costs of roaming user authentication:

- TC_{HV} : Transmission Cost between HLR and VLR
- TC_{VV} : Transmission Cost between VLR and VLR
- TC_{HM} : Transmission Cost between HLR and Master VLR
- TC_{MS} : Transmission Cost between Master VLR and Slave VLR
- TC_{VM} : Transmission Cost between VLR and Mobile Terminal
- PC_H, PC_V : Processing Cost at HLR, VLR
- PC_M, PC_S : Processing Cost at Master VLR, Slave VLR

According to the signaling flows described in Fig. 1 and 2, the authentication costs for the original protocol and our protocol can be derived as:

$$AC_{original\_reg} = 4TC_{VM} + 2TC_{HV} + 3PC_V + 2PC_H \qquad (3)$$

$$AC_{proposed\_reg} = 4TC_{VM} + 2TC_{HM} + 3PC_V + 2PC_H \qquad (4)$$

$$AC_{original\_up} = 4TC_{VM} + 3TC_{HV} + 2TC_{VV} + 6PC_V + PC_H \quad (5)$$

$$AC_{proposed\_up} = 4TC_{VM} + 4TC_{MS} + TC_{VV} + 4PC_S + 2PC_M \quad (6)$$

We assume that the transmission cost is proportional to the distance between the network entities. We also assume that the transmission cost through wireless link is much higher than the transmission cost through wired link. Additional parameters are depicted as follows.

- p : Residential probability to the areas indicated by the enhanced user profile
- r : Registration ratio to the location areas

By using the aforementioned parameters, we present a few of simulation results. Fig. 3 shows the authentication signaling loads with the varying residential probabilities. We obtain the simulation results for the time interval 100(sec). As presented in Fig. 3, our protocol ensures better performance than the original protocol as p increases. When p is 0, the performance of both protocol is equal since in this case, the mobile users move through the areas that are not specified in the enhanced user profile. The gap of performance between the two protocol gets into maximum when p is 1. This stems from the fact the the mobile users roam only within the areas indicated by the enhanced user profile.

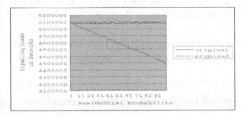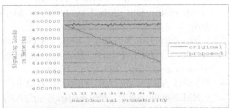

Fig. 3. Results with varying p where Registration Ratio = 10%, 30%

Fig. 4 shows the results with the varying registration ratio. Similarly, our protocol ensures better performance than the original protocol as r decreases. As r decreases, the authentication cost during the location update is incrementally added to the total signaling loads. By examining all the simulation results, we can conclude that our protocol generates less signaling traffics than the original protocol while authenticating the roaming users.

5   Conclusion and Future Work

In this paper, we design and analyze the improved authentication protocol for GSM roaming users. Our protocol aims at reducing the excessive signaling traffics for roaming user authentication. For doing this, we exploit the enhanced user profile and utilize the localized features of users' mobility. As a result of performance evaluations, we present that our protocol avoids the inefficiency of original

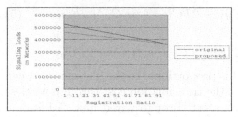 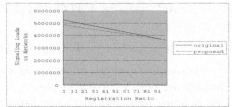

Fig. 4. Results with varying Registration Ratio where p = 100%, 60%

protocol where whole steps of roaming user authentication procedure must rely on the HLR. Our protocol does not make much modifications to the fundamentals of GSM systems. Thus, our protocol can satisfy the security requirements of GSM authentication protocol. Specifically, our protocol can maintain the similar level of security implications as original protocol.

References

1. Sanjoy Paul, "Privacy and Authentication Needs of PCS", *IEEE Personal Communications* , pp. 11-15, Aug. 1995.
2. Cjii Hwa Lee, Min Shiang Hwang, Wei Pang Yang, "Enhanced Privacy and Authentication for the global system for Mobile Communications ,", *Wireless Networks* , Vol. 5, pp. 231-243, 1999.
3. Chi-Chun Lo, Yu-Jen Chen, "A Secure Communication Architecture for GSM Networks ,", *IEEE Pacific Rim Conference on Communications , Computers and Signal Processing* , pp. 221-224, 1999.
4. Khalid Al-Twail, Ali Akrami, Habib Youssef, "A New Authentication Protocol for GSM Networks ,", *Proceedings of IEEE Annual Conference on Local Computer Networks* , pp. 21-30, 1998.
5. Dan Brown, "Techniques for Privacy and Authentication in Personal Communication System ,", *IEEE Personal Communications* , pp. 6-10, August, 1995.
6. Samarakoon, M.I., Honary, B, "Novel authentication and key agreement protocol for low processing power and systems resource requirements in portable communications systems ,", *Novel DSP Algorithms and Architectures for Radio Systems (1999/184), IEE Colloquium on* , pp. 9/1 -9/5, 1999.
7. Khalid Al-Tawil, Ali Akrami, "A New Authentication Protocol for Roaming Users in GSM Networks ,", *Proceedings. IEEE Int'l Symposium on Computer and Communications* , pp. 93-99, 1999.
8. Sesharri Mohan, "Privacy and Authentication Protocols for PCS ,", *IEEE Personal Communications* , pp. 34-38, 1996.
9. 3GPP TS 03.20 V8.1.0(2000-10) 3rd Generation Partnership Project; Digital Cellular Telecommunications System (Phase 2+); Security related Network Functions(Release 1999)
10. ETSI TS 100 614 V8.0.0(2000-04) Digital Cellular Telecommunications System (Phase 2+); Security Management (GSM 12.03 Version 8.0.0 Release 1999)
11. S.Mohan, R.Jain, "Two User Location Strategies for Personal Communications Service ,", *IEEE Personal Communications* , First Quarter, pp. 42-50, 1994.
12. L.Kleinrock, Queueing Systems, Vol.1, Wiley-Interscience, 1975

A Novel Intrusion Detection Method

ShengYi Jiang [1], QingHua Li [2], Hui Wang [3]

Computer School, Huazhong University of Science & Technology,
430074, Hubei, wuhan, China
[1]Jiangshengyi@163.com, [2]Liqh@263.net, [3]Wh621004@yahoo.com

Abstract. It is an important issue for the security of network that how to detect new intrusions attack. This paper investigates unsupervised intrusion detection method. A distance definition for mixed attributes, a simple method calculating cluster radius threshold, a outlier factor measured deviating degree of a cluster, and a novel intrusion detection method are proposed in this paper. The experimental results show that the method has promising performance with high detection rate and low false alarm rate, also can detect new intrusion.

1. Introduction

The signature-based detection methods and supervised anomaly detection methods can only detect previously known intrusion, at same time signature database and labeled data has to be manually processed. To upper flaws, unsupervised anomaly detection methods have been addressed recently [1-4]. However, existing unsupervised methods have some problems: (1)They cannot deal with categorical attributes or deal with categorical attributes too complicatedly. (2)The results of detection are sensitive to the parameter, and it is difficult to select the parameter. (3) It isn't reasonable that the objects in the small clusters are labeled anomalous. This paper is mainly concerned with these problems.

2. Notation and Definition

Suppose dataset D is featured by m attributes(m_C categorical and m_N continuous), categorical attributes before continuous attribute, D_i is the set of i-th attribute value.

Definition 1: Given a cluster C and $a_i \in D_i$, then the support of a_i in C with respect to D_i is defined as $Sup_{C|D_i}(a_i) = |\{object|object \in C, object.D_i = a_i\}|$.

Definition 2: Given a cluster C, the cluster summary information (*CSI*) for C is defined as: $CSI = \{kind, n, Summary\}$, *kind* for the type of the cluster C with 'normal' or 'attack', n for the size of the cluster C, *Summary* describes the frequency information for categorical attribute value and the centroid of numerical attributes.

$Summary = \{< Stat_i, Cen > | Stat_i = \{(a_j, Sup_{C|D_i}(a_i)) | a_j \in D_i\}, 1 \le i, j \le m_C, Cen = (p_{m_C+1}, p_{m_C+2}, \cdots p_{m_C+m_N})\}$

H. Jin et al. (Eds.): NPC 2004, LNCS 3222, pp. 459-462, 2004.
© IFIP International Federation for Information Processing 2004

Definition 3: Given clusters C, C_1, C_2 and objects $p = \{p_i | i \in [1, m]\}$, $q = \{q_i | i \in [1, m]\}$

(1) The distance between objects p and cluster C is defined as $d(p, C) = (d_C + d_N)/m$,

where $d_C = m_C - \sum_{i=1}^{m_C} Sup_{C|D_i}(p_i)/|C|$, $d_N = \sqrt{\sum_{i=m_C+1}^{m_C+m_M} |p_i - c_i|^2}$.

(2) The distance between clusters C_1 and C_2 is defined as $d(C_1, C_2) = (d_C + d_N)/m$,

$$d_C = m_C - \frac{1}{|C_1| \cdot |C_2|} \sum_{i=1}^{m_C} \sum_{p \in C_1} Sup_{C_1|D_i}(p_i) \cdot Sup_{C_2|D_i}(p_i) = m_C - \frac{1}{|C_1| \cdot |C_2|} \sum_{i=1}^{m_C} \sum_{q \in C_2} Sup_{C_1|D_i}(q_i) \cdot Sup_{C_2|D_i}(q_i),$$

$$d_N = \sqrt{\sum_{i=m_C+1}^{m_C+m_M} |c_i^{(1)} - c_i^{(2)}|^2}.$$

Definition 4: Let $C = \{C_1, C_2, \cdots, C_k\}$ is the result of clustering on training data D, The outlier factor of cluster C_i is defined as harmonic means of distances between cluster C_i and other clusters: $OF(C_i) = (k-1)/\sum_{j \neq i} \frac{1}{d(C_i, C_j)}$.

3. The Clustering-Based Intrusion Detecting Method

3.1 Clustering

We use the least distance principle to cluster dataset into hyper spheres with almost the same radius [3]. The details about the clustering are described as follows.

    Step 1: Initialize the set of clusters, S, to the empty set, read a new object p.

    Step 2: Create a cluster with the object p.

    Step 3: If no objects are left in the database then turn to step 6, else read a new object p, find the cluster C in S that is closest to the object p. In other words, find a cluster C in S, such that for all C' in S, $d(p, C) \leq d(p, C')$.

    Step 4: If $d(p, C) > r$ turn to step 2, where r is threshold.

    Step 5: else merge object p into cluster C and, modify the *CSI* of cluster C.

    Step 6: Stop.

3.2 The Intrusion Detection Method

Our intrusion detection method is composed of modeling and detecting module.

  (1) Setting up model

    Step 1,**Clustering**:Cluster training set T_1 and produce clusters $C = \{C_1, C_2, \cdots, C_k\}$.

    Step 2, **Labeling clusters**: Sort clusters $C = \{C_1, C_2, \cdots, C_k\}$ and make them meet $OF(C_1) \leq OF(C_2) \leq \cdots \leq OF(C_k)$. Search the smallest b_1, which satisfies

$\sum_{i=1}^{b_1}|C_i|/|T_1| \geq \varepsilon$, and then label clusters $C_1, C_2, \cdots, C_{b_1}$ with 'normal' while

$C_{b_1+1}, C_{b_1+2}, \cdots, C_k$ with 'attack'.

Step 3, **Producing model**: The model is made up of the cluster summary information and the radius threshold r.

(2) Detecting attack

For any object p in testing set T_2, find a cluster C_{i_0} which is closest to p, if $d(p, C_{i_0}) \leq r$ then classify p by the label of C_{i_0}, else regard p as new attack.

3.3 Tuning Parameters

(1) Selecting threshold r

According to the process of clustering, threshold r should greater than inter-cluster distance and less than intra-cluster. So we guess logically that r should be close to average distance of any pair's objects. The details are described as follows:

①Choosing randomly N0 pairs of objects in the dataset D.

②Computing the distances between each pair objects.

③ Computing the average EX and standard deviation DX of distances from ②.

④ Selecting r in the range of [EX -0.25DX,EX].

(2) Selecting parameter ε

$1-\varepsilon$ is the approximation ratio of outlier to whole dataset. A rule of thumb in statistics is that the proportion of contaminated data in a dataset is usually less than 5% and almost always less than 15%, so we general let ε be about 0.95. If we have prior knowledge on the ratio, we may select ε more accurate.

4. Experimental Results

The 10% subset of KDDCUP99[6] is used to evaluate our algorithm. We divide the subset into two subset P1, P2. P1 contains 40459 records (96% normal). P2 contains some unknown attacks type in the P1. We set up model on training set P1, and test model on testing set P2. By computing, EX=0.063, DX=0.043, let ε=0.95, the table 1 show detection result with distinct r. The table 2 shows contrast of results on dataset KDDCUP99 among methods.

Table 1 Detection result with distinct r

	r=0.031	r=0.042	r=0.052	r=0.063	r=0.073	r=0.084
Total detection rate	98.79%	98.53%	98.47%	93.33%	93.18%	27.69%
False alarm rate	1.24%	0.12%	0.40%	1.37%	1.36%	0.43%
Detection rate for unknown attack	37.40%	33.60%	33.56%	58.92%	57.81%	21.24%

Table 2 The contrast of results with different methods on dataset KDDCUP99

Ref.	Detection rate	False alarm rate	Detection rate for unknown attack
[1]	55%-82%	0.8%-4.9%	/
[2]	43.1%-75.2%	/	/
[3]	35.7%-88%	1.44%-8.14%	/
[4]	28%-93%	0.5%-10%	/
[5]	91.8%	0.5%	/
Our method	27.69%-98.79%	0.4%-1.37%	21.24%-58.92%

5. Conclusion

In practice, unsupervised detection methods are important, because these methods can be applied to raw collected system data and do not need to be manually labeled which can be an expensive process. In this paper, we presented a new unsupervised intrusion detection method,the method needn't any prior classification about training data and the knowledge about new attacks. The experimental results show that our method outperforms the existing methods on accuracy.

Acknowledgments

This work is supported by NSFC of P.R.China(No.60273075).

Reference

1. Yamanishi,K.,Takeuchi. J. and Williams, G. On-line unsupervised outlier detection using finite mixtures with discounting learning algorithms. In: Proceedings of the Sixth ACM SIGKDD00, Boston, MA, USA, pp 320-324
2. Yamanishi, K.,Takeuchi, J. Discovering outlier filtering rules from unlabeled data: combining a supervised learner with an unsupervised learner.In:Proceedings of the seventh ACM SIGKDD international conference on Knowledge discovery and data mining , 2001
3. Portnoy, L.,Eskin,E. and Stolfo,S. J.Intrusion Detection with Unlabeled Data using Clustering.In: Proceedings of ACM CSS Workshop on Data Mining Applied to Security (DMSA-2001). Philadelphia, PA: November 5-8, 2001
4. Eskin,E.,Arnold,A.,Prerau,M.,Portnoy, L. and Stolfo, S. A geometric framework for unsupervised anomaly detection: Detecting intrusions in unlabeled data. In Data Mining for Security Applications, 2002
5. Charles Elkan .Results of the KDD'99 Classifier Learning Contest. URL: http://www.cs.ucsd.edu/users/elkan/clresults.html
6. Merz, C. J.,Merphy,P. UCI repository of machine learning databases. URL: http://www.ics.uci.edu/ mlearn/ MLRRepository.html

An Implementation of Storage-Based Synchronous Remote Mirroring for SANs

Ji-wu Shu, Rui Yan, Dongchan Wen, and Weimin Zheng

Department of Computer Science and Technology, Tsinghua University,
Beijing 100084, China

Abstract. Remote mirroring ensures that all data written to a primary storage device are also written to a remote secondary storage device to support disaster recoverability. In this study, we designed and implemented a storage-based synchronous remote mirroring for SAN-attached storage nodes. Taking advantage of the high bandwidth and long-distance linking ability of dedicated fiber connections, this approach provides a consistent and up-to-date copy in a remote location to meet the demand for disaster recovery. This system has no host or application overhead, and it is also independent of the actual storage unit. In addition, we present a disk failover solution. The performance results indicate that the bandwidth of the storage node with mirroring under a heavy load was 98.67% of the bandwidth without mirroring, which was only a slight performance loss. This means that our synchronous remote mirroring has little impact on the host's average response time and the actual bandwidth of the storage node.

1 Introduction

Remote mirroring ensures that all data written to a primary storage are also written to a remote secondary storage to support disaster recoverability. It can be implemented at various levels, including the file system, the volume manager, the driver, the host bus adapter (HBA) and the storage control unit[1] [14]. In general, there are two locations at which mirroring are implemented: the storage control unit and the host. Each location has its own advantages and disadvantages.

IBM's Peer-to-Peer Remote Copy (PPRC)[1] and EMC's Symmetrix Remote Data FacilitySRDF[2] use a synchronous protocol at the level of the storage control unit. Today's storage control units contain general-purpose processors, in addition to special-purpose elements for moving and computing blocks of data. Therefore, remote mirroring is provided by storage subsystems as advanced copy functions. But it costs a lot and depends on the actual disk's storage subsystem. Veritas's Volume Replicator [3] is a remote mirroring solution at the level of the host's device driver. It intercepts write operations at the host device driver level and sends the changes to a remote device. So it is kept independent of the actual storage unit. However, it takes a toll on the host CPU cycles and communication bandwidth, and it is difficult to manage because it needs to interact with all the

H. Jin et al. (Eds.): NPC 2004, LNCS 3222, pp. 463–472, 2004.

hosts where replication software is installed. NetApp's SnapMirror[4] is a remote mirroring solution using an asynchronous protocol at the level of the host's file system, but it is not suitable for block-level I/O access in the SAN environment.

In this study, we designed and implemented synchronous remote mirroring at the level of the storage control unit for Tsinghua Mass Storage Network System (TH-MSNS) [5][6], an implementation of the FC-SAN. Based on the high bandwidth and long-distance linking ability of dedicated fiber connections, this approach provides a consistent and up-to-date data copy in a remote location to meet the demand for disaster recovery. This implementation of remote mirroring has no host or application overhead, and it is also independent of the actual storage unit. In addition, we present a failover solution for disk failure. The performance results indicate that our synchronous remote mirroring does not have a significant effect on the average command response time or on the actual bandwidth of the storage node.

2   Introduction of the TH-MSNS

The TH-MSNS[5][6] is an implementation of an FC-SAN. In the TH-MSNS, the storage nodes provide storage services. A storage node is composed of a general-purpose server, SCSI disk arrays, and fibre channel adapters, and it has a software module named the SCSI target simulator [7][8] running on it. By using the SCSI target simulator to control the I/O process to access disk arrays, the TH-MSNS can implement basic functions of FC disk arrays while only using general SCSI disk arrays. Because of this, it is low cost, highly flexible and can achieve considerable performance [5]. Figure 1 shows the I/O path of the TH-MSNS. The file system and SCSI driver in the host converts the application's I/O requests to SCSI commands and data, and then the FC HBA driver encapsulates

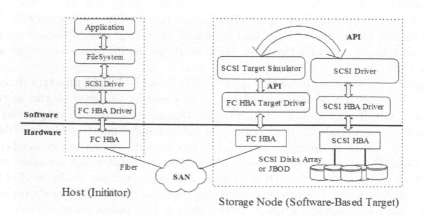

Fig. 1. The I/O path of the TH-MSNS

them into FC frames using Fibre Channel Protocol (FCP)[9] and sends them to the SAN. When the FC HBA on the storage node receives the frames, the FC target driver transforms them back into SCSI commands and data. Then the SCSI target simulator, a kernel module running on the storage node, queues and fills up the SCSI requests' structures, and finally prompts the API of the SCSI driver layer to commit the SCSI requests to the SCSI subsystem. After the SCSI subsystem has completed the SCSI commands, the SCSI target simulator returns the command status or data to the host. Therefore, by the coordination of the SCSI target simulator and the FC target driver, the SCSI disk arrays of the storage node can be directly mapped to the host as its own local disks. So the storage node is equal to the storage control unit in the SAN environment at the basic function of storage service.

3   Design and Implementation of Remote Mirroring for the TH-MSNS

3.1   The Architecture of Remote Mirroring

Figure 2 shows the architecture of remote mirroring for the TH-MSNS. We added a remote storage node with the same structure and configuration as the

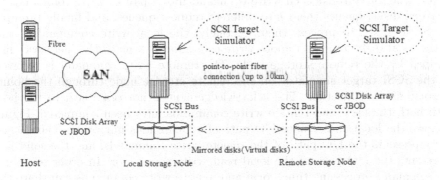

Fig. 2. The architecture of remote mirroring for TH-MSNS

local storage node. By adding an FC HBA in the local storage node to connect point-to-point with the remote storage node, the remote storage node's disks are regarded as the local storage node's own disks. Therefore, the storage node and remote storage node can constitute a mirrored pair. The write commands from the host can be mirrored to the remote storage node by the SCSI target simulator on the local storage node. So the data on the storage node can be mirrored to the remote storage node. The remote storage node can be located up to 10km away from the local storage node using fibre channel technology, and this distance can also been extended by using extenders.

The advantages of this approach of remote mirroring are as follows.

- It has low cost and high flexibility because the remote mirroring is implemented by software modules, not by special hardware.
- The actual storage unit is independent because the host's SCSI commands are redirected to the storage node's SCSI driver layer, which provides a common API for I/O access and hides the detail of the low-level storage subsystem.
- The mirroring process is transparent to the host, and does not consume any of the host's resource. Moreover, the remote storage node is also transparent to the host, because the SCSI target simulator can prevent the remote disks being mapped by the host.

3.2 Synchronous Mirroring

Synchronous remote mirroring writes data not only to a local disk but also to a remote mirror disk at the same time. The acknowledgement is not be sent back until all the data is written to both disks. In many cases, both copies of the data are also locally protected by RAID[10]. This approach provides a consistent and up-to-date copy in a remote location to meet the demand for disaster recovery.

In the mirroring architecture we presented, the SCSI target simulator on the local storage node receives SCSI commands and data from the FC target driver. Then it converts each write command into a pair of write commands to mirrored disks, queues them into different request queues, and finally prompts the SCSI driver to process them. Actually, the local write command is sent to the local disk, and the remote write command is sent to the 'network' disk mapped by the remote storage node. The remote write command is received by the SCSI target simulator on the remote storage node through the point-to-point fiber connection. The acknowledgement is not sent back to the host until both the local and remote write commands have been completed. Figure 3 shows the local and remote I/O path of synchronous mirroring. The dashed line represents the I/O path of the remote write commands, and the solid line represents the I/O path of the local read/write commands. In order to reduce the command processing time, local and remote write commands can share the same data buffer. It is not necessary to apply the data buffer for the remote write command; the data pointer only has to be pointed to the data buffer of the local write command. Local write and remote commands can be committed to the SCSI driver at almost the same time, and can be executed by different HBAs concurrently. In this way, commands can be executed more efficiently.

There are two device chain structures in the SCSI target simulator: the local disk chain and the remote disk chain. Figure 4 shows the local and remote disk chains. The structure of the local disk in the local disk chain contains a pointer which points to the structure of its mirrored disk. The relationship of mirrored disks can also be created between two local disks, just like the software RAID 1. When a SCSI command arrives, the SCSI target simulator analyzes the SCSI command's target disk and finds the remote mirrored disk through the pointer

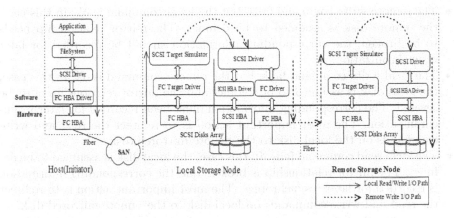

Fig. 3. The I/O path of remote mirroring for the TH-MSNS

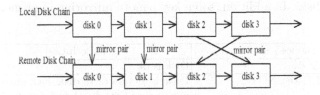

Fig. 4. The local and remote disk chains

mentioned above. Then the SCSI target simulator fills the mirrored write request using the information of the mirrored disk such as the number of the SCSI host bus, target, or LUN and so on. Furthermore, the SCSI target simulator only maps the local disk to the host, so the remote disk is invisible to host.

3.3 Disk Fail Over

Although both the local and remote disks are also locally protected by RAID, many circumstances could cause a SCSI command's failure. Some examples include the power failure of the disk array, an unplugged SCSI cable, a break in the fiber connection or the failure of the RAID. Because of this, it is necessary to monitor all write commands locally and remotely. When a command is returned with an abnormal status, some actions must be taken immediately to ensure the services' continuity.

For the accidents mentioned above, SCSI commands will timeout. The SCSI driver layer will try to recover it or retry command. If these actions fail, the SCSI driver will return the SCSI command with the timeout status to the SCSI target simulator. The SCSI target simulator analyzes the status of the local and remote command, and adopts different measures to meet different instances.

- The remote write command fails, but the local command is ok. In this case, the remote disk is assumed to be defunct. The mirror relationship needs to be broken; the corresponding information should be recorded for later resynchronization.
- The local write command fails, but the remote command is ok. In this case, the local disk is assumed to be defunct and the mirror relationship must be severed. The corresponding information must been recorded for later resynchronization. The most important action is to redirect the read and write commands on the local disk to the remote mirrored disk.
- The local read command fails. In this case, the local disk is assumed to be defunct. The mirror relationship is broken, and the corresponding information is recorded for later resynchronize. The most important action is to redirect the read and write commands on local disk to the remote mirrored disk.

In order to perform the disk failover, the local disk's structure contains a status identifier to record the status of the local disk. Table 1 shows the possible status of the local disks. In addition, some key remote mirroring implementation tech-

Device's state	Description
DEVICE_OK	Disk is ok.
DEVICE_DEFUNCT	Disk is defunct. If disk has mirrored, it means that both local and remote disks are defunct.
DEVICE_MIRRORED	Disk has mirrored, both local and remote disks are ok.
DEVICE_LOCAL_DEFUNCT	Disk has mirrored. Remote disk is ok, but local disk is defunct.
DEVICE_MIRROR_DEFUNCT	Disk has mirrored. Local disk is ok, but remote disk is defunct.
DEVICE_SYNCING	Disk is synchronizing.

Table 1. The status of the local disk

niques, such as software LUN masking, online resynchronization and disaster tolerance, have been introduced in another paper [11].

4 Performance Evaluation

The synchronous remote mirroring system was tested, and its performance was evaluated and analyzed. Because the read command is executed locally in the process of mirroring, our testing only used the write command. Table 2 shows the test configuration of the host and storage nodes.

Host A

CPU	Intel Xeon 700MHz × 4
Memory	1G
OS	Linux (kernel: 2.4.18)
FC HBA	Emulex LP9822Gb/s

Host B

CPU	Intel Itanium 2 1GHz × 2
Memory	2G
OS	Linux (kernel:2.4.18-e12)
FC HBA	Emulex LP982(2Gb/s)

Storage node and its storage subsystem

CPU	Intel Xeon 2.4GHz × 1
Memory	1G
OS	Linux (kernel: 2.4.18)
FC HBA	Emulex LP982 (Initiator mode2Gb/s) Qlogic ISP 2300 (Target mode2Gb/s)
RAID Controller	Adaptec Ultra160 RAID Controller 2110S
SCSI Disks	Seagate Cheetah (73GB 10KRPM) × 7 configured as JBOD

Table 2. Test configuration of hosts and storage node

4.1 Comparison of Average Command Response Times

The average response time of the command is a very important factor to evaluate the performance and quality of services. In this test, a host issues commands with different data block sizes to its one 'network' disk, which is provided by the local storage node. The goal is to compare the average response time of each command both with mirroring and without. The Iometer[12] benchmarking kit was used. The host issues sequential write commands with different block size ranging from 64KB to 2048 KB. This test adopts a host configured as host A (given above) and two storage nodes: a local storage node and a remote storage node. Table 3 shows the test results. The results show that synchronous mirroring has little impact on the average command response time for different block sizes.

Block Size	Command Average Response Time	
	No mirror(ms)	Mirror(ms)
64KB	1.718	1.795
128KB	3.482	3.573
192KB	5.335	5.357
256KB	7.083	7.202
512KB	13.573	14.469
768KB	21.214	21.561
1024KB	24.797	28.610
1536KB	42.245	44.048
2048KB	58.141	58.323

Table 3. Comparison of average command response time on different block sizes

4.2   The Total Execution Time for Replication in a Large Amount of Data

In this test, we used command dd on the host to replicate a large amount of data (10GB-50GB) to the network disk. By comparing the total execution time with and without mirroring, we evaluated the performance of synchronous mirroring. Command dd is able to directly generate read/write block-level requests. This test adopts a host configured as host A and two storage nodes. Figure 5 shows the test results. The results show that synchronous mirroring has little impact on the total execution time for replicating a large amount of data.

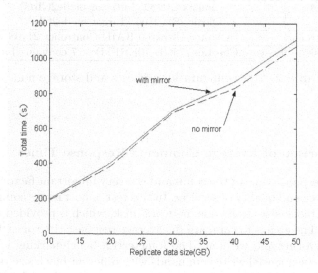

Fig. 5. The total execution time for replication of a large amount of data

4.3   The Storage Node Bandwidth with Heavy Loads

In this test, we adopted seven hosts, local and remote storage nodes which both have 7 SCSI disks and are mapped to the hosts. Each host accesses its one network disk respectively. We ran IOzone [13]benchmarking kit on each host to offer the local storage node a heavy load. The test used sequential 100% write requests with different record sizes ranging from 4 KB to 4096 KB. The hosts file system were ext2, and the test files size was 15 GB. We compared the bandwidth of local storage node with mirroring and without mirroring. The seven hosts were configured as host B. Figure 6 shows the results. The results show the bandwidth of storage node with different record sizes. With the host cache, the results appear higher than actual bandwidth of the storage node. In the figure, the black bars represent the results without mirroring, with an average bandwidth

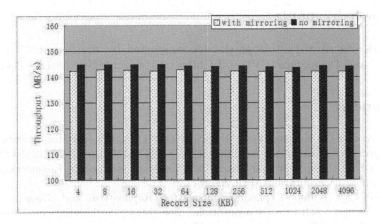

Fig. 6. A comparison of storage node bandwidth with heavy loads

of 144.314MB/s, while the white bars represent the results with mirroring, with
an average bandwidth of 142.399MB/s. The bandwidth of storage node with
mirroring is 98.67% of that without mirroring. The performance loss is very
little.

In addition, the SCSI HBA we adopted in the test was an Ultra 160 card, so
the max throughput in theory was only 160Mbyte/s. Furthermore, the storage
node is a server which is only responsible for I/O operations without caring other
services, so its CPU has not heavily load. Actually, its CPU utilization is less
than 20% at most time.

5   Conclusion

In this study, we designed and implemented a storage-based synchronous remote
mirroring system for the TH-MSNS. Based on the high bandwidth and long-
distance linking ability of dedicated fiber connections, this approach provides a
consistent and up-to-date data copy in a remote location to meet the demands
of disaster recovery. This system is independent of the actual storage unit, and
the process of mirroring is transparent to the hosts. In addition, we present a
disk failover solution. In the performance evaluation, we compared the average
command response time with different block sizes, the total execute time in
replicating a large amount of data, and the bandwidth of storage node under
heavy loads, both with and without synchronous mirroring. The performance
results indicate that the bandwidth of storage node with mirroring under heavy
loads is 98.67% of the bandwidth of storage node without performing mirroring,
a result showing only slight performance loss. This means that our synchronous
remote mirroring has little impact on the host's average response time and the
actual bandwidth of the storage node.

Acknowledgements

The work described in this paper was supported by the National High-Tech Research and Development Plan of China under Grant No. 2001AA111110.

References

1. A.C.Azagury,M.E.Factor,W.F.Micka. Advanced Functions for Storage Subsystems: Supporting Continuous Availability, IBM SYSTEM Journal VOL 42 ,NO 2,2003.
2. Using EMC SnapView and MirrorView for Remote Backup, Engineering White Paper,EMC Corporation(April 2002).
3. VERITAS Volume Replicator Successful Replication and Disaster Recovery, Veritas Software. Corporation. See http://eval.vertias.com/downloads/pro/volume_replicator_whitepaper.pdf
4. Patterson, R.H., et al. SnapMirror: File-System-Based Asynchronous Mirroring for Disaster Recovery. In First USENIX conference on File and Storage Technologies. 2002. Monterey, CA, USA
5. Shu Ji-wu, et al. A Highly Efficient FC-SAN Based On Load Stream. Xingming Zhou, Stefan Jahnichen, Ming Xu, and Jiannong Cao eds., The Fifth International Workshop on Advanced Parallel Processing Technologies, LECTURE NOTES IN COMPUTER SCIENCE 2834, pp.31-40,2003,
6. Technical Report: Design and Implementation of the TH-MSNS (In Chinese), Computer Science Department, Tsinghua University, P.R. China, 2003, http://storage.cs.tsinghua.edu.cn/
7. Ashish Palekar, Narendran Ganapathy. Design and Implement of A LINUX SCSI Target for Storage Area Networks. Proceedings of the 5th Annual Linux Showcase & Conference, 2001.Oakland ,USA.
8. Jae-Chang Namgoong ,Chan-Ik Park . Design and Implement of a Fibre Channel Network Driver for SAN-Attached RAID Controllers. IEEE Parallel and Distributed Systems, 2001.
9. Fibre Channel Protocol for SCSI (FCP) , ANSI X.272, rev4.5, 1995
10. D.Patterson, G.Gibson, and R.Katz, "A Case for Redundant Arrays of Inexpensive Disks (RAID)", ACM SIGMOD, June 1998.
11. YAO Jun, SHU Ji-wu, ZHENG Wei-minA Distributed Storage Cluster Design for Remote Mirroring based on Storage Area NetworkIEEE Transactions on computers(Submitted), also in http://storage.cs.tsinghua.edu.cn
12. Jerry Sievert. Iometer: The I/O Performance Analysis Tool for Servers. http://www.intel.com/design/servers/devtools/iometer/index.htm
13. IOzone Filesystem Benchmark. http://www.iozone.org/
14. Richard Barker, Paul Massiglia ,Storage Area Network Essentials: a complete guide to understanding and implementing SANS. Publish by John Wiley&Sons, Inc.,New York, 2001.
15. Draft, T10 Project 1561-D, SCSI Architecture Model - 3 (SAM-3), Revision 3 16 September 2002, http://www.t10.org/scsi-3.html

A Network Bandwidth Computation Technique for IP Storage with QoS Guarantees

Young Jin Nam[1], Junkil Ryu[1], Chanik Park[1], and Jong Suk Ahn[2]

[1] Department of Computer Science and Engineering
Pohang University of Science and Technology/PIRL
Kyungbuk, Republic of Korea
{yjnam,lancer,cipark}@postech.ac.kr
[2] Department of Computer Engineering
Dongguk University, Seoul, Republic of Korea
jahn@dgu.ac.kr

Abstract. IP storage becomes more commonplace with the prevalence of the iSCSI (Internet SCSI) protocol that enables the SCSI protocol to run over the existing IP network. Meanwhile, storage QoS that assures a required storage service for each storage client has gained in importance with increased opportunities for multiple storage clients to share the same IP storage. Considering the existence of other competing network traffic in IP network, we have to provide storage I/O traffic with guaranteed network bandwidth. Most importantly, we need to calculate the required network bandwidth to assure a given storage QoS requirement between a storage client and IP storage. This paper proposes a network bandwidth computation technique that not only accounts for the overhead caused by the underlying network protocols, but also guarantees the minimum data transfer delay over the IP network. Performance evaluations with various I/O workload patterns on our IP storage testbed verify the correctness of the proposed technique; that is, allocating a part (0.6–20%) of the entire network bandwidth can assure the given storage QoS requirements.

1 Introduction

Storage Area Networks (SAN), such as Fiber Channel and Gigabit Ethernet, have enabled a plethora of storage systems to be maintained as a storage pool, resulting in reduced total cost of ownership, effective storage resource management, etc. Such SAN-based storage systems are advantageous in terms of scalability and configurability, compared with SCSI bus-based storage systems. Accordingly, a few data transmission protocols have newly emerged to support the SAN environment. Fiber Channel protocol (FCP) is developed for FC-based SAN, and iSCSI recently ratified by Internet Engineering Task Force is made for IP SAN. A main advantage of iSCSI is that the iSCSI can operate on standard network components, such as Ethernet [1]; that is, it exploits existing features and tools that have been developed for the IP network. Thus, this paper focuses

H. Jin et al. (Eds.): NPC 2004, LNCS 3222, pp. 473–480, 2004.

on the storage environment using IP-based SAN (IP storage), where storage devices are attached to IP networks, and storage clients communicate with the storage devices via the iSCSI protocol [1]. An initiator-mode iSCSI protocol runs on the storage client, whereas a target-mode iSCSI protocol operates on the IP storage. Note that the traditional SCSI protocol operates on top of the iSCSI protocol layer that transmits a given SCSI command to its associated IP storage over the IP network.

With the advance in storage technologies in terms of storage space and I/O performance, the chances increase that multiple storage clients share the same storage. A different storage client may require a different storage service, called storage Quality of Service (QoS); that is, each storage client requires receiving a guaranteed storage service, independently of the status of the I/O services in other storage clients. Unfortunately, the storage itself does not contain any feature of assuring storage QoS. As a result, recent research efforts [2,3] try to add the QoS feature to various types of storage systems. However, notice that the previous research emphasizes the QoS issue only within the storage system, whereas it is assumed that the SAN itself has no QoS issues. Note that, FC-based SAN is used only for storage I/O traffic. IP storage, however, transmits its data over the IP network, where storage I/O traffic is likely to coexist with the other network traffic. Considering this situation leads us to preserve an amount of network bandwidth for the storage I/O traffic between a storage client and its associated IP storage to avoid any probable interference with the other network traffic. A naive approach is to allocate the full network bandwidth (or separate dedicated IP network) that is large enough to serve the storage I/O traffic with QoS guarantee for a pair of a storage client and its associated IP storage. However, it can be easily inferred that this approach ends up being with under-utilization of IP network resources, even though it can certainly guarantee a given storage QoS requirement. By contrast, unless enough network bandwidth resides between the storage client and the IP storage, the storage QoS requirement is no longer guaranteed with lower I/O throughput (I/O requests per seconds) and higher response time due to increased data transfer delays.

This paper emphasizes the problem of computing the required network bandwidth to meet a given storage QoS requirement. It proposes a network bandwidth computation technique that not only accounts for overhead caused by the underlying network protocols, but also guarantees the minimum data transfer delay over the IP network. In the case of FC-based SAN environments, Ward *et. al.* in [4] proposed a scheme to automatically design an FC-based SAN that not only serves a given set of storage I/O traffic between storage clients and storage systems, but also minimizes the system cost.

2   Problem Description

We begin by defining a few notations to be used throughout the paper. C_i and Q_i represent the storage client i and its storage QoS requirement, respectively. Generally, the storage QoS requirement is defined as $Q_i = \{f_i, iops_i, sz_i, s_i, rt_i\}$.

The notation of f_i represents the ratio of read I/O requests. In addition, $iops_i$, sz_i, and rt_i represent the number of I/O requests per second (briefly IOPS), an average I/O request size, and an average response time requested from C_i, respectively. I/O access pattern is random with $s_i = 0$ and purely sequential with $s_i = 1$. Note that our network bandwidth computation does not depend on the value of s_i. We denote with $b_i^{c \to s}$ and $b_i^{s \to c}$ the network bandwidth allocated for the direction from C_i and its associated IP storage and for its opposite direction, respectively. Then, the problem that this paper will solve can be described as follows: *Compute $b_i^{c \to s}$ and $b_i^{s \to c}$ that satisfy the given Q_i for the storage client C_i and its associated IP storage.* Note that we assume that the storage resources except for network resources (bandwidth) have been appropriately reserved to satisfy the storage QoS requirement Q_i.

3   The Proposed Technique

To begin, we will explain the protocol layering for iSCSI protocol and the specific behavior of the iSCSI protocol for read and write I/O requests. The iSCSI protocol data unit (PDU) consists of a 48-byte iSCSI header and iSCSI data of a variable length. The maximum iSCSI data length relies on the types of underlying Ethernet cards. Typically, it ranges from 1,394 through 8,894 bytes. The TCP/IP headers and Ethernet header respectively occupy 40 bytes and 18 bytes.

Figure 1 presents the protocol behaviors for read and write I/O requests. In the case of the read I/O request, as shown in Figure 1(a), the storage client sends the READ SCSI command to the IP storage. Next, after reading the requested data from its internal disk drives, the IP storage transmits the data to the storage client in the DATA_IN phase. Note that the data are to be fragmented into smaller pieces according to the maximum iSCSI data length. Finally, the IP storage sends the response message to the storage client. The iSCSI

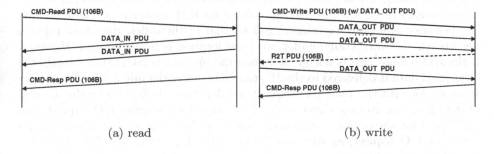

(a) read   (b) write

Fig. 1. iSCSI protocol behaviors for read and write I/O requests: (a) read and (b) write

protocol behavior for the write I/O request is more complicated than that of the read I/O request because of free buffer management and performance optimization techniques like immediate/unsolicited data transmission. The storage client sends the WRITE SCSI command to the IP storage. Unless the data size is greater than the maximum iSCSI data length, it is transmitted along with the write SCSI command. This results in collapsing the COMMAND phase and the DATA_OUT phase [1]. It is called immediate data transmission [1]. If the data size is greater than FirstBurstLength, the storage client transfers the data of the first FirstBurstLength bytes to the IP storage without receiving the Ready to Transfer (R2T) message from the IP storage that is used to secure free buffer space to store the write data. This process is called unsolicited data transmission [1]. Note that the immediate data transmission is combined with the unsolicited data transmission. Afterwards, the storage client transfers data only when it receives the R2T message from the IP storage. It is called solicit data transmission [1].

In what follows, we derive a set of equations to compute the required network bandwidth to meet a given storage QoS requirement. We start by computing the amount of data transfer, including the underlying protocol overhead for given read and write I/O requests of size s_i. We denote with $D_r^{c \to s}(sz_i)$ the amount of data transfer from the storage client to the IP storage for the read I/O request of size sz_i, and $D_r^{s \to c}(sz_i)$ for the opposite direction. From the protocol behavior for the read I/O request, as shown in Figure 1(a), we can easily obtain $D_r^{c \to s}(sz_i)$ and $D_r^{s \to c}(sz_i)$ as follows:

$$D_r^{c \to s}(sz_i) = ov_{prot}, \tag{1}$$

$$D_r^{s \to c}(sz_i) = 2ov_{prot} + \lfloor \frac{sz_i}{\hat{S}_f} \rfloor S_f + sz_i \bmod \hat{S}_f, \tag{2}$$

where $\hat{S}_f = S_f - ov_{prot}$. The notation of ov_{prot} represents the 106-byte protocol overhead caused by the Ethernet header, the TCP/IP header, and the iSCSI header. The notation of S_f represents the underlying Ethernet frame size.

Next, we calculate the amount of data transfer for the write I/O request. To begin, the storage client sends the agreed-upon amount of data (unsolicited data transmission) to IP storage without having an R2T message. We assume that the behavior of each data transfer follows that of the solicit data transmission because the network traffic under our consideration is heavy enough. However, if the I/O request size is not greater than the maximum iSCSI data length, the associated data is delivered to the IP storage by using the immediate data transmission. As with the read I/O request, we denote with $D_w^{c \to s}(sz_i)$ the amount of data from the storage client to the IP storage for the write I/O request, and $D_w^{s \to c}(sz_i)$ for the opposite direction. Based on the iSCSI protocol behavior for the write I/O request, as shown in Figure 1(b), $D_w^{c \to s}(sz_i)$ and $D_w^{s \to c}(sz_i)$ can be obtained as follows:

$$D_w^{c \to s}(sz_i) = \begin{cases} ov_{prot} + sz_i & \text{if } sz_i \leq \hat{S}_f \\ ov_{prot} + \lfloor \frac{sz_i}{\hat{S}_f} \rfloor S_f + sz_i \bmod \hat{S}_f & \text{otherwise} \end{cases}, \tag{3}$$

$$D_w^{s \to c}(sz_i) = \begin{cases} ov_{prot} & \text{if } sz_i \leq \texttt{FirstBurstLength} \\ 2ov_{prot} & \text{otherwise} \end{cases}. \tag{4}$$

If the data size is not greater than the maximum iSCSI data length of $\hat{S}_f$, $D_w^{c \to z}(sz_i)$ is $ov_{prot} + sz_i$. Otherwise, it includes $\lfloor \frac{sz_i}{\hat{S}_f} \rfloor$ times of the maximum Ethernet frame size of S_f and the remaining data with the protocol overhead of ov_{prot}. As for $D_w^{s \to c}(sz_i)$, if the data size is not greater than $\texttt{FirstBurstLength}$, $D_w^{s \to c}(sz_i)$ is equal to the size of the iSCSI response message. Otherwise, it becomes two times of ov_{prot}, because the R2T message is also delivered to the storage client as well as the iSCSI response message.

Next, we define with $\hat{b}_i^{c \to s}$ the average amount of data transfer including the underlying protocol overhead from the storage client to the IP storage for the sz_i sized I/O request. In addition, we define with $\hat{b}_i^{s \to c}$ for the opposite direction. From Equation (1)–(4), we can obtain $\hat{b}_i^{c \to s}$ and $\hat{b}_i^{s \to c}$ as follows:

$$\hat{b}_i^{c \to s} = \{f_i D_r^{c \to s}(sz_i) + (1 - f_i) D_w^{c \to s}(sz_i)\} iops_i, \tag{5}$$

$$\hat{b}_i^{s \to c} = \{f_i D_r^{s \to c}(sz_i) + (1 - f_i) D_w^{s \to c}(sz_i)\} iops_i. \tag{6}$$

The network bandwidth allocation with $\hat{b}_i^{c \to s}$ and $\hat{b}_i^{s \to c}$ is expected to assure the requested maximum storage bandwidth derived by multiplying sz_i and $iops_i$. However, they may not guarantee the demanded response time of rt_i. For example, notice that Equation (5) and (6) result in a lower network bandwidth with a smaller $sz_i \cdot iops_i$. This implies that the chances increase that each I/O request of size sz_i experiences a longer transmission delay on IP network that is most likely to entail a violation of the demanded response time.

Thus, we introduce the minimum network bandwidth to assure the demanded response time of rt_i. We denote with $m_i^{c \to s}$ and $m_i^{s \to c}$ the minimum network bandwidth for each direction. The values of $m_i^{c \to s}$ and $m_i^{s \to c}$ are determined such that the transmission delay of each I/O request are not greater than $\alpha_i \cdot rt_i$, where $0 < \alpha_i < 1$. Usually, α_i is determined according to the marginal response time to meet rt_i in the phase of designing the associated IP storage [2,5,3]. For example, if the IP storage is designed to assure 15msec for given $rt_i = 20$msec, the values of α_i can range from 0 through 0.25. We compute $m_i^{c \to s}$ and $m_i^{s \to c}$ from a simple relationship that the expected transmission delay is inversely proportional to the allocated network bandwidth without accounting for the effects of traffic congestion control, IP routing, the transmission buffer size, TCP retransmission, etc. The $m_i^{c \to s}$ and $m_i^{s \to c}$ are written as follows:

$$m_i^{c \to s} = \frac{max\{\lfloor f_i \rfloor D_r^{c \to s}(sz_i), \lfloor 1 - f_i \rfloor D_w^{c \to s}(sz_i)\}}{\alpha_i rt_i}, \tag{7}$$

$$m_i^{s \to c} = \frac{max\{\lfloor f_i \rfloor D_r^{s \to c}(sz_i), \lfloor 1 - f_i \rfloor D_w^{s \to c}(sz_i)\}}{\alpha_i rt_i}. \tag{8}$$

By denoting with $b_i^{c \to s}$ and $b_i^{s \to c}$ the network bandwidth for each direction required to guarantee a given Q_i, we finally have $b_i^{c \to s}$ and $b_i^{s \to c}$ as follows:

$$b_i^{c \to s} = max\{\hat{b}_i^{c \to s}, m_i^{c \to s}\}, \tag{9}$$

$$b_i^{s \to c} = max\{\hat{b}_i^{s \to c}, m_i^{s \to c}\}. \tag{10}$$

4   Performance Evaluations

We set up an experimental testbed for IP storage to evaluate the performance of the proposed technique. We use two Intel Pentium III based desktops for the storage client and the IP storage. Both systems are attached to a Gigabit IP network via Gigabit Ethernet cards and a switch. Assume that no other traffic exists between the two systems. The maximum size of the Ethernet frame is 1500 bytes. The Linux kernel 2.4.18 works on top of the storage client and IP storage. The storage client includes the initiator-mode iSCSI driver developed by the University of New Hampshire [6], and the IP storage contains the target-mode iSCSI driver for operating the iSCSI protocol. The network bandwidth is controlled by Token Bucket Filtering (TBF) [7]. We believe that this type of end-to-end traffic control works because no other traffic exists between the storage client and the IP storage.

Table 1 shows the measured $iops_i$ and rt_i for various QoS requirements of Q_1–Q_4 when the amount of network bandwidth is computed by the proposed technique. In addition, they are compared with the results with the full network bandwidth for the same QoS requirements. We denote with `prot-rt` and `full` for the proposed technique and the full network bandwidth, respectively. Each

Table 1. Results of $iops_i$ and rt_i for the various QoS requirements of Q_1–Q_8 by the proposed technique (`prot-rt`) and the full network bandwidth allocation (`full`)

QoS	Technique	Toward IP storage	Toward client	$iops_i$	rt_i
Q_1	prot-rt	0.05MB/s	0.60MB/s	84(100%)	9.74ms
	full	100.00MB/s	100MB/s	82(100%)	9.70ms
Q_2	prot-rt	1.84MB/s	0.17MB/s	265(99%)	2.59ms
	full	100.00MB/s	100MB/s	266(100%)	2.58ms
Q_3	prot-rt	0.03MB/s	19.19MB/s	77(100%)	15.66ms
	full	100.00MB/s	100MB/s	76(100%)	15.34ms
Q_4	prot-rt	15.67MB/s	0.02MB/s	211(100%)	20.28ms
	full	100.00MB/s	100MB/s	208(100%)	21.54ms

of the storage QoS requirements is represented as follows: $Q_1 = \{f_1 = 1, iops_1 = 82, sz_1 = 1KB, s_1 = 0, rt_1 = 10ms\}$, $Q_2 = \{f_2 = 0, iops_2 = 266, sz_2 = 1KB, s_2 = 0, rt_2 = 3ms\}$, $Q_3 = \{f_3 = 1, iops_3 = 76, sz_3 = 64KB, s_3 = 0, rt_3 = 18ms\}$, and $Q_4 = \{f_4 = 0, iops_4 = 208, sz_4 = 64KB, s_4 = 0, rt_4 = 22ms\}$. The first two requirements are for the small read and write I/O requests as in OLTP applications, and the others are for the large read and write I/O requests in scientific applications [5]. Since the network bandwidth allocation is independent of storage access patterns, we assume that all the storage access patterns are purely random. In addition, the demanded IOPS of $iops_i$ and its associated response time of rt_i are configured by injecting a set of I/O workload patterns and measuring each performance. Note that the $iops_i$ and rt_i of the QoS requirements fall into neither too light traffic that makes the IP storage mostly idle nor too heavy traffic that overloads the system. The results reveal that the allocation of only 0.6–20% of the full network bandwidth computed by the proposed technique can meet the given storage QoS requirements. Observe that the proposed technique can compute an appropriate amount of network bandwidth to provide the same quality of storage service as the case when the full network bandwidth is allocated. The percentage values in the $iops_i$ column represent the percentage of the measured IOPS with respect to the demanded IOPS.

Table 2 shows the measured $iops_i$ and rt_i for the QoS requirements of Q_1–Q_4 for the prot and naive techniques. The prot technique computes the required network bandwidth only by considering the underlying protocol overhead, as shown in Equation (5)–(6); that is, $\hat{b}_i^{c\rightarrow s}$ and $\hat{b}_i^{s\rightarrow c}$. The naive technique simply calculates the network bandwidth by multiplying $iops_i$ and sz_i. It assigns the same bandwidth for each direction. As expected, the naive technique cannot guarantee even demanded $iops_i$, because it does not account for the underlying protocol overhead in Ethernet, TCP/IP, and iSCSI layers at all. Notice that

Table 2. Results of $iops_i$ and rt_i for the various QoS requirements of Q_1–Q_8 by the technique using Equation (5)–(6) (prot) and the technique using $iops_i{\cdot}sz_i$ (naive)

QoS	Technique	Toward IP storage	Toward client	$iops_i$	rt_i
Q_1	naive	0.06MB/s	0.06MB/s	64(77%)	28.82ms
	prot	0.01MB/s	0.12MB/s	80(96%)	12.99ms
Q_2	naive	0.26MB/s	0.26MB/s	238(89%)	9.25ms
	prot	0.29MB/s	0.03MB/s	262(98%)	3.54ms
Q_3	naive	4.78MB/s	4.78MB/s	69(91%)	22.31ms
	prot	0.01MB/s	5.19MB/s	74(96%)	19.33ms
Q_4	naive	13.06MB/s	13.06MB/s	194(93%)	25.13ms
	prot	14.08MB/s	0.02MB/s	208(99%)	22.05ms

the smaller sized I/O request causes higher protocol overhead, as expected from Equation (1)–(4). In addition, the results show that read I/O requests creates more protocol overhead than write I/O requests. It can be expected mainly from Equation (2)–(3). By contrast, the prot technique guarantees more than 96% of the required $iops_i$. However, it does not satisfy the demanded response time of rt_i because of the transmission delay on IP network. Recall that, as shown in Table 1, the proposed prot-rt technique can meet both the $iops_i$ and the rt_i by effectively allotting the network bandwidth for each direction between the storage client and the IP storage.

5 Conclusion and Future Work

This paper addressed the problem of effectively allocating network bandwidth to assure a given QoS requirement for IP storage. It defined a specification of the storage QoS requirement, and it proposed a technique to compute the demanded network bandwidth to meet the storage QoS requirement that not only accounts for the overhead caused by the underlying network protocols, but also guarantees the minimum data transfer delay over the IP network. Performance evaluations with various I/O workload patterns on our IP storage testbed verified the correctness of the proposed technique; that is, allocating a part (0.6–20%) of the entire network bandwidth can assure the given storage QoS requirements. Currently, we have been revising Equation (9)–(10) to additionally account for real-world I/O workload patterns featured by self-similarity and the condition of traffic congestion.

Acknowledgments

The authors would like to thank the Ministry of Education of Korea for its financial support toward the Electrical and Computer Engineering Division at POSTECH through its BK21 program. This research was also supported in part by the Korea Science and Engineering Foundation (KOSEF) under grant number R01-2003-000-10739-0 and by HY-SDR IT Research Center.

References

1. Meth, K., Satran, J.: Design of the iscsi protocol. In: Proceedings of the Mass Storage Systems and Technologies/20th IEEE/11th NASA Goddard Conference. (2003)
2. Nam, Y.J.: Dynamic Storage QoS Control for Storage Cluster and RAID Performance Enhancement Techniques. Ph.D Dissertation, POSTECH (2004)
3. Anderson, E., Hobbs, M., Keeton, K., Spence, S., Uysal, M., Veitch, A.: Hippodrome: Running rings around storage administration. In: Proceedings of Conference on File and Storage Technologies. (2002)
4. Ward, J., O'Sullivan, M., Shahoumian, T., Wilkes, J.: Appia: Automatic storage area network design. In: Proceedings of Conference on File and Storage Technologies. (2002)
5. Alvarez, G., Borowsky, E., Go, S., Romer, T., Becker-Szendy, R., Golding, R., Merchant, A., Spasojevic, M., Veitch, A., Wikes, J.: Minerva: An automated resource provisioning tool for large-scale storage systems. ACM Transactions on Computer Systems 19 (2001) 483–518
6. UNH: iscsi reference implementation. http://www.iol.unh.edu/consortiums/iscsi/ (2004)
7. Hurbert, B.: Linux advanced routing & traffic control. http://lartc.org/howto (2003)

Paramecium: Assembling Raw Nodes into Composite Cells*

Ming Chen, Guangwen Yang, Yongwei Wu, and Xuezheng Liu

Dept. of Computer Science and Technology, Tsinghua University
cm01@mails.tsinghua.edu.cn, ygw@mail.tsinghua.edu.cn, wuyw@tsinghua.edu.cn,
xuezhengliu00@mails.tsinghua.edu.cn

Abstract. In conventional DHTs, each node is assigned an exclusive slice of identifier space. Simple it is, such arrangement may be rough. In this paper we propose a generic component structure: several independent nodes constitute a cell; a slice of identifier space is under nodes' condominium; part of nodes in the same cell cooperatively and transparently shield the internal dynamism and structure of the cell from outsiders; this type of structure can be recursively repeated. Cells act like raw nodes in conventional DHTs and cell components can be used as bricks to construct any DHT-like systems. This approach provides encapsulation, scalable hierarchy, and enhanced security with bare incurred complexity.

1 Introduction

Many Distributed Hash Tables (DHTs) ([1], [2], [3], [4], [5], [6]) have been proposed in recent years. A distinguishing feature provided by these systems is scalable routing performance while keeping a scalable routing table size in each node. Of those algorithms, every node has a unique numerical identifier and the identifier space is allocated among participant living nodes, which is solely responsible for its assigned exclusive slice, or zone, of identifier space. There is no central node and every node is identical and *visible* to all other nodes. The methodology discarding role difference is simple but may be rigid in practice.

In previous decade, success in object-oriented programming revealed the power of encapsulation: objects encapsulate internal implementations and states; they supersede discrete functions and variables, and communicate through exported public properties and methods. We are enlightened to present Paramecium architecture: raw nodes aggregate into composite cells, which communicate with each other through exported constituent nodes. The extension is simple but promising in two traits: encapsulation and shared zone.

---

* This project is supported by the National Natural Science Foundation of China under Grant No. 60373004, No. 60373005, and No. 60273007, and by the National High Technology Development Program of China under Grant No. 2002AA104580

H. Jin et al. (Eds.): NPC 2004, LNCS 3222, pp. 481–484, 2004.

2 Design of Paramecium

Paramecium's goal is to shield highly dynamic behaviors of *unstable* nodes in system and improve security in P2P's open environment. To achieve this goal, Paramecium brings in encapsulation and condominium through cell structure. In this section, we describe Paramecium's cell structure, necessary exported properties and functions. To be generic, we only depict abstract implementation of Paramecium, and leave specific-related issues to concrete implementation. For conciseness, the difference and comparison between Paramecium and other conventional DHTs are here emphasis.

2.1 Cell Structure

Atom Cell Adjacent independent nodes in identifier space constitute an atom cell, which could be identified by an exclusive slice, named *cell zone*, of identifier space. The set of all cell zones covers the whole identifier space. A node resides and only resides in one atom cell. And a cell can be made up of only one node. There is no existent dissociative node. Nodes in the same atom cell are called *sibling nodes*.

Sibling nodes can be organized into flat structure (eg: full connection or DHTs), or hierarchic structure (eg: spanning tree). Paramecium does not specify any material internal structure, including cell zone's division among sibling nodes, and maintenance mechanism in a cell.

Nodes in a cell are categorized into two role types: *boundary nodes* and *hidden nodes*. As representatives of their resident cells, boundary nodes are responsible for requests from nodes in different cells. Hidden nodes facilitate sibling boundary nodes to perform exported functions of resident cell, but they don't serve as representatives. Besides a certain type of request, hidden nodes will reject any request from outsiders. Hidden nodes can directly request non-sibling boundary nodes for services, or sibling boundary nodes for relaying requests. Every node, whether boundary node or hidden node, provides a type of service called *giveMeRepresentatives*. The semantic of *giveMeRepresentatives* is self-explaining and straightforward: when a node X receives a request of this type, X corresponds with the representatives of its resident cell. Role's selection depends on node's discretion and *giveMeRepresentatives*'s implementation. The latter is specific-related and out of the concern of Paramecium. Drawing an analogy between Paramecium and class, we can image that similar to a class, boundary nodes are cell's public methods while hidden nodes are its protected or private methods. Boundary nodes encapsulate implementation of resident cells and export corresponding properties and functions. Hidden nodes' rejection to outer requests enforces the rule of encapsulation. We suggest that representatives free hidden nodes from inter-cell level business, allowing them to concentrate on internal affair. To be concise, we use cell and cell's boundary nodes exchangeably in the rest of this paper if no confusion exists.

Evolve to Organism As a natural extension, the cell structure can be recursively repeated: cells conglomerate into a larger and higher level cell (organism). The grammar expressed in BNF (Backus-Naur Form) is: *cell ::= cell|{cell}*. All cells immediately forming a new cell X are called $X's$ *child cell*. This is a hierarchic architecture abiding with the principle of encapsulation. Child cells can serve in two ways: as boundary cells or as hidden cells. Only boundary cells are exported to the outside world of their resident cell. The implementation, maintenance, and internal dynamics of a cell are shielded by its boundary cells, similar to an atom cell. A higher level cell has no knowledge and interest of low level businesses. Considering the consequential benefit, the incurred complexity should be justifiable.

2.2   Modification to Conventional DHTs

Routing Table In addition to its own zone and traditional routing table called inter-cell routing table here in Paramecium, a node must maintain the state composed of its resident cell zone and its *intra-cell routing table*. Each entry in the intra-cell routing table contains NodeID, zone, and other implementation-related information of a sibling, node or subcell. A node's intra-cell routing table can include partial or entire siblings. The connection topology in a cell and the maintenance of intra-cell routing table depend on concrete implementation.

The inter-cell table can be constructed and maintained by Chord[2], Pastry[3], or other DHT protocols. Although an entry in an inter-cell routing table points to an appropriate top-layer cell, the content is cell's boundary node, as well as cell's zone. The selection of boundary nodes through service *giveMeRepresentatives* is also implementation-related. But we must remember that all sibling boundary nodes are eligible candidates. Sibling nodes/subcells can *share* a completely same inter-routing table. Thus, only part of nodes have to actively maintain inter-routing tables and disseminate results to their siblings. This difference tells Paramecium from other DHTs.

Routing The amendment to conventional routing schemas is trivial. A node first checks whether the routing target falls into its resident cell's zone. If yes, the node employs implementation-related approach with the help of intra-cell routing table to route the request (the simplest scenario is that when sibling nodes are full-connected, the final target can be reached in one-hop by local lookup). Otherwise, the request is routed by inter-cell routing table and specific inter-cell routing algorithm.

Node join The join operation is intuitive. Assumed a node X wants to join an existing Paramecium system, X first finds an atom cell C whose zone covers X through routing algorithm described in above paragraph. X then informs other sibling nodes residing in C of joining message. Meanwhile, X learns intra-cell and inter-cell routing tables from them. If X only acts as hidden node, there is no perceivable changes to other cells. Otherwise, other cells will eventually detect the X's arrival in process of periodical update of inter-cell routing table by the service *giveMeRepresentatives*.

Node departure Ordinarily, a node can crash or leave system unpredictably to relevant nodes. Similar to node's join, the departure of a hidden node does not affect other cells' routing table except the node's sibling nodes' intra-cell routing table. The effectiveness of encapsulation apply here again.

3   Related Work

There are many existing or under development DHTs. To the best as we know, Paramecium is the first general architecture that introduces the concepts of encapsulation and jointly governed zone by a group of nodes.

There are some similarities between Paramecium and CAN[1], Chord[2], Pastry[3], Tapestry[4], SkipNet[5], and Koorde[6]. In these conventional DHTs, however, each node exclusively takes portion of identifier space and exposes itself to others in a system level. Nodes can share partial routing table, but they don't support encapsulation, too.

4   Conclusion

Recognizing that raw nodes acting as bricks to build DHTs may not be flexible, Paramecium extends the construction unit from primitive node to composite cell which is made of nodes/subcells in a intuitive and efficient way. The cell structure shields its internal dynamism and structure through the distinguished characteristics of encapsulation: cells interact with each other only through boundary nodes/subcells. Recursive cell composition provides analogy to hierarchal structure in a scalable way. With the help of the trait of jointly shared zone among sibling nodes/subcells, Paramecium can also enhance security to some degree through Practical Byzantine-like algorithms.

References

1. S. Ratnasamy, P. Francis, M. Handley, R. Karp, and S. Shenker. *A Scalable Content-Addressable Network*. In ICSI Technical Report, Jan. 2001.
2. I. Stoica, R. Morris, D. Karger, F. Kaashoek, H. Balakrishnan. *Chord: A Scalable Peer-to-Peer Lookup Service for Internet Applications*. In Proceedings ACM Sigcomm 2001, San Diego, CA, Aug. 2001.
3. A. Druschel and P. Rowstron. *Pastry: Scalable, Distributed Object Location and Routing for Large-scale Peer-to-peer System*. In proceedings of the 18th IFIP/ACM International Conference on Distributed Systems Platforms (Middleware 2001).
4. B. Y. Zhao, J. Kubiatowicz, A. D. Joseph. *Tapestry: An Infrastructure for Fault-toleratnt Wide-area Location and Routing*. Technical Report UCB/CSD-01-1141.
5. Nicholas J. A. Harvey, Michael B. Jones, S. Saroiu, M. Theimer and A. Wolman. *SkipNet: A Scalable Overlay Network with Practical Locality Properties*. Proceedings of the USENIX Symposium on Internet Technologies and Systems USITS 2003.
6. Frans Kaashoek and David R. Karger. *Koorde: A Simple Degree-optimal Hash Table*. In Proceedings of the 2nd International Workshop on Peer-to-Peer Systems (IPTPS'03).

The Flexible Replication Method in an Object-Oriented Data Storage System[1]

Youhui Zhang, Jinfeng Hu, Weimin Zheng

Institute of High Performance Computing Technology
Dept. of Computer Science, Tsinghua Univ.
100084, Beijing, P.R.C
zyh02@tsinghua.edu.cn

Abstract. This paper introduces a replication method for object-oriented data storage that is highly flexible to fit different applications to improve availability. In view of semantics of different applications, this method defines three data-consistency criteria and then developers are able to select the most appropriate criteria for their programs through storage APIs. One criterion realizes a quasi-linearizability consistency, which will cause non-linearizability in a low probability but may not impair the semantic of applications. Another is a weaker one that can be used by many Internet services to provide more read throughput, and the third implements a stronger consistency to fulfill strict linearizability. In addition, they all accord with one single algorithm frame and are different from each other in a few details. Compared with conventional application-specific replication methods, this method has higher flexibility.

1 Introduction

We implement an object-oriented data management layer as a cluster infrastructure software, specifically for the construction of Internet services. The impedance mismatch problem [1] is avoided because its interface is compatible with Java Data Objects API [2], an emerging standard for transparent data access in Java.

However, existing replication methods [3][4][5] cannot be adopted by OStorage. Therefore, we design one replication method that can be embedded in storage APIs. Users can employ it to set parameters on replication consistency and ease the development.

In the replication method, the principles, including high flexibility, low latency and adjustability are emphasized. The flexible replication method defines and implements three consistency criteria, soft consistency, general consistency and rough consistency. General consistency realizes a quasi-linearizability consistency, which will cause non-linearizability in a low possibility but do not impair the semantic of applications. Moreover, it does not introduce any total order multicast to solve consensus problem so that the latency is very low. Soft consistency is a weaker one that does not

---

[1] Supported by High Technology and Development Program of China (No. 2002AA1Z2103).

H. Jin et al. (Eds.): NPC 2004, LNCS 3222, pp. 485-488, 2004.

support linearizability at all to support more read throughput. And the third implements a stronger consistency to fulfill strict linearizability. They accord with one single algorithm frame and are different from each other in some details.

The rest of this paper is organized as follows. Section 2 presents three consistency criteria and emphasizes solutions of key issues. Section 3 summarizes this paper.

2   Replication Algorithms

To simplify the presentation of the method, the system model is described abstractly as follows.

- Reliable point-to-point communication is supported by the low-level network protocol with FIFO property. Reliability means the network layer guarantees a receiver will get the message in latency μ after sending, or the receiver can be assumed wrong.
- A system-global loosely synchronized clock is implemented using Network Time Protocol, whose max time error, τ, is less than 1ms.
- Nodes and network links may crash, but we assume Byzantine failures and network partition will not occur.
- The atomic data cell is called object, which is a data block with variable size.
- Three kinds of permitted commands upon an object are read, overwrite and recover-read, while creating and deleting are two forms of overwrite operation. When a crashed storage node, named Brick, recovers, the objects it holds is outdated and it will send a recover-read command to other Bricks to update data.
  In addition, some terminologies are introduced.
- A command C is described as <type, O, D, timestamp> where type is one of overwrite, read and recover-read, O is the object to operate, D is null if type is not overwrite and timestamp denotes the time when this command is invoked.
- An object O is described as <OID, D, ctype, ctimestamp> where OID is its identification, ctype is the type of the latest command on it and ctimestamp is timestamp of that command.

Several copies of an object O are distributed to a set of Bricks that is noted as view(O). Each copy is called a replica. Before an objected O is created, some Bricks should be selected to form view(O).

2.1   General Consistency Algorithm

General consistency is almost equal to linearizability and can be used in most applications. A global loosely synchronized clock algorithm is applied to keep the order of commands in general consistency criteria. And there may be a tiny clock error between every two nodes, which makes causality unsatisfied in a low probability. Its principles of different operations are described as follows.

Read: One read command is sent to any Brick in view(O). While no successful response returns, it will be redirected to another Brick until the data is obtained.

Write: A overwrite command is sent to every Brick in view(O) and waits for a response. Once the first successful response returns, the overwrite command is assumed accomplished. In addition, Thomas write rule [6] is employed here. That is, it attaches timestamps to commands and objects, and only the latest update is accepted. Then, the timestamp of an object is the one from its latest command.

2.2 Soft Consistency Algorithm

Linearizability is too strict for some applications that need faster response (especially for read). Soft consistency algorithm is therefore designed. Compared with linearizability, soft consistency is defined as follows.

CS is the set of all actual commands. The execution is said to be soft consistent if there exists a sequence S on CS satisfies these two conditions.

- Ca is before Cb in S if Ca<<Cb; But if Cb is a read command, it is not necessary to satisfy this condition.
- This condition is as same as that of linearizability.

It allows read commands to obtain stale data in fact. Compared with general consistency, it is only different in the implementation of read. That is, read command is executed as soon as received without concerning any other conditions. For many Internet services it is valuable. For example, a cluster-based email server maintains two mailboxes for every user, and it will save any email to both boxes. On reception of an email for user U, the server updates box u1 firstly. At that time, the user visits his/her box u2 that has not been refreshed, so he/she will get the stale data. But it does not impair the usage of mailboxes because users can imagine the email is still in transmission, which still observes email protocols.

2.3 Rough Consistency Algorithm

Rough consistency offers strict linearizability, but it introduces more latency. This algorithm employs a global token system [7] to replace the loosely synchronized clock.

Before a command is sent, a global token is applied to attach it whose number is increased seriatim. Bricks operate commands in accordance with the sequence of tokens, and it is prohibitive to operate a command which token number is not larger one than the prior. In this case, the Brick has to wait for commands between the twos.

In addition, only if all successful responses of every Brick in view(O) have returned, the overwrite command is assumed accomplished. So total order is maintained strictly and the adverse circumstance in general consistency will never happen.

2.4 How to Recover

When a crashed Brick recovers, the data it holds is outdated and should be refreshed. So it sends a recover-read command to other Bricks and buffers commands received until all data are updated. Because general consistency algorithm does not solve

488   Y. Zhang, J. Hu, and W. Zheng

consensus problem, after carrying out a recover-read command on object o, one Brick may receive a overwrite command on O accomplished in another Brick before the recover-read command. Therefore linearizability cannot be maintained. The solution is a the command will be put off for a period of time, T_{lim} (equal to T) to execute.

3 Conclusion

General consistency realizes a quasi-linearizability consistency, which will cause non- linearizability in a low possibility but developers can adopt rough consistency or improve the applications to avoid this case. Soft consistency is a weaker one that permits applications to obtain stale data and is fit for some Internet services. Moreover, rough consistency realizes strict linearizability but introduces longer latency.

References

1. Steven D. Gribble and Eric A. Brewer and Joseph M. Hellerstein and David Culler. Scalable, Distributed Data Structures for Internet Service Construction, 4th Symposium on Operating System Design & Implementation, San Diego (2000).
2. C. Russell, Java Data Objects 1.0 Proposed Final Draft, JSR12, Sun Microsystems Inc., available from http://access1.sun.com/jdo (2001).
3. Idit Keidar. Totally Ordered Broadcast In The Face Of Network Partitions. Chapter 3 Exploiting Group Communication for Replication in Partitionable Networks, Laboratory for Computer Science Massachusetts Institute of Technology (1999).
4. R. Guerraoui and A. Schiper. Fault-Tolerance by Replication in Distributed Systems. In Proc Conference on Reliable Software Technologies (invited paper). Springer Verlag, LNCS 1088 (1996) 38-57.
5. David L. Mills. Improved algorithms for synchronizing computer network clocks. In the Proceedings of ACM SIGCOMM, London, UK (1994). 317–327.
6. Robert Thomas. A majority consensus approach to con-currency control for multiple copy databases. ACM Trans. on Database Systems (1979). 180-209.
7. Y. Amir, L. Moser, P. Melliar Smith, D. Agarwal, and P. Ciarfella. Fast message ordering and membership using a logical token-passing ring. In Proceedings of the 13th International Conference on Distributed Computing Systems, Pittsburgh, Pennsylvania, USA (1993). 551-560.

Enlarge Bandwidth of Multimedia Server with Network Attached Storage System

Dan Feng, Yuhui Deng, Ke Zhou, Fang Wang

Key Laboratory of Data Storage System, Ministry of Education
College of Computer, Huazhong University of Science and Technology
Wuhan 430074, China
dfeng@hust.edu.cn

Abstract. Network attached storage system is proposed to solve the bottleneck problem of the multimedia server. It adds a network channel to the RAID and data can be transferred between the Net-RAID and clients directly. The architecture avoids expensive store-and-forward data copying between the multimedia server and storage devices when clients download/upload data from/to the server. The system performance of the proposed architecture is evaluated through a prototype implementation with multiple network disk arrays. In multi-user environment, data transfer rate is measured 2~3 times higher than that with a traditional disk array, and service time is about 3 times shorter. Experimental results show that the architecture removes the server bottleneck and dynamically increases system bandwidth with the expansion of storage system capacity.

1 Introduction

Multimedia service is pervasive on the Internet now and continues to grow rapidly. Most multimedia service provider systems have adopted a typical system architecture in which the storage devices are attached privately to the server. [1],[2] When a client browses some multimedia data from the server, data should be fetched from the storage devices and then forwarded to the client by the server. Unfortunately, with the steady growth of Internet subscribers, the multimedia server quickly becomes a system bottleneck.

More recently, there have been some research efforts invested in solving the bottleneck problem of the multimedia servers. A distributed server architecture that places the streaming servers close to the user clusters has been proposed, [3] where the system is able to achieve scalable storage and streaming capacities by introducing more repository servers and local servers as the traffic increases. A scalable multimedia server based on a clustered architecture is discussed, [4] where a group of nodes are connected by a switch (interconnection network). These related works have made it progressive to enhance the aggregate bandwidth of the multimedia system.

In this paper, Network attached Redundant Arrays of Independent Disks(Net-RAID) is proposed to solve the server bottleneck. There are two different channels in the disk array. One is SCSI (Small Computer System Interface) bus to make the disk

H. Jin et al. (Eds.): NPC 2004, LNCS 3222, pp. 489–492, 2004.

array work as a normal storage system. And the other is network interface to transfer data between clients and the disk array directly. A multimedia server with Net-RAIDs is implemented and the experimental results show that the bandwidth of the server is enlarged by the Net-RAIDs.

2 Architecture of Multimedia Server System with Net-RAIDs

A multimedia server is designed with the network attached RAID. It is shown in Fig.1. All Net-RAIDs are centrally controlled by the server through the SCSI channel for the convenience of management just like a normal storage system, while all network interfaces of Net-RAIDs are allowed parallel data transmission. By keeping the SCSI channel of Net-RAID connected to the multimedia file server to exert central control, it strikes a good balance between a centralized file management and a distributed data storage.

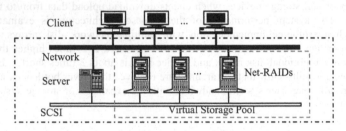

Fig. 1. Multimedia Server with Net-RAIDs

Storage system capacity must keep pace with the continuous growth of multimedia data. The system in Fig.1 achieves this capacity scalability by expanding the system storage capacity incrementally with additional Net-RAIDs along with associated network interfaces that expand data transmission rate proportionally.

3 The Redirection of Data Transfer

All Net-RAIDs in the system are collected as a virtual storage pool. The virtual storage protocol consists of virtual layer, logic map layer and data redirection layer. The virtual layer is used to simulate a standard block device driver and register the virtual storage pool. The logic map layer provides standard interface with block buffer cache and realizes the address map of the virtual storage pool. Different logic map layer leads to different virtual storage pool functions. The data redirection layer provides an interface for physical device drivers, and redirects the data requests from the host to the physical devices.

For example, a File Transfer Protocol(FTP) session consists of two connections. One is control connection for a client to connect with the server and it is kept in the whole session. Another is data connection for the server to transfer data with a client and it is established when data should be downloaded/uploaded to the server. Because

FTP uses different logical channels to transport control and data packet, we move the logical channel of data connection from the server to the physical network channel of Net-RAID.

When the client downloads a file, the server parses the data information (start address and data length) of the requested file over SCSI channel. Afterwards, the server sends the data information and client information to Net-RAID over the network. A data connection is established between the Net-RAID and the client. Net-RAID gets the requested data from SCSI disks in terms of the data information, and transfers the data to the client directly according to the client information.

4 Performance Measurement

In order to get a performance comparison between the prototype and the traditional system where the disk array is only attached to the server, we configure a HUST-RAID[6] that has the same hardware platform as Net-RAID, except for NIC. The HUST-RAID is directly attached to the multimedia server through the SCSI channel. Peak read and write performances of HUST-RAID are 46MB/s and 33MB/s, respectively. The multimedia server is configured as a FTP server and it is connected to the 100Mbps Ethernet.

The performance of the system is measured by the aggregate bandwidth when a number of clients download/upload files from/to the server simultaneously. Table 1 shows the performance comparison between the prototype and the traditional system. The aggregate bandwidth of the prototype is larger than that of the traditional one and it approaches the network bandwidth. In multi-user environment, the data transfer rate is 2~3 times higher than that with a traditional disk array.

Table 1 Performance comparison between the prototype and the traditional system

operation	Number of clients	Traditional System			Prototype system with Net-RAID		
		Data transfer rate(MB/s)	Average rate (MB/s)	Aggregate bandwidth (MB/s)	Data transfer rate(MB/s)	Average rate (MB/s)	Aggregate bandwidth (MB/s)
Download File	1	6.75	6.75	6.75	7.36	7.36	7.36
	2	2.83	2.62	5	4.82	4.67	9.33
		2.41			4.51		
	3	1.28	1.25	3.76	3.28	3.34	10.01
		1.12			4.01		
		1.36			2.72		
	4	0.88	0.82	3.29	2.62	2.48	9.93
		0.93			2.35		
		0.76			3.11		
		0.72			1.85		

When we add another Net-RAID to the prototype system, the aggregate bandwidth is nearly 20MB/s(see Table 2). It shows that the performance of the system increases almost linearly with the increase of the number of Net-RAIDs, and the system bottleneck has been removed from the server to network.

Table 2 Performance comparison when two Net-RAIDs are in the system

Operation	Number of clients	Traditional Architecture		Prototype system with Net-RAID	
		Data transfer rate(MB/s)	Aggregate bandwidth (MB/s)	Data transfer rate(MB/s)	Aggregate bandwidth (MB/s)
Download File	3	3.23	9.94	6.67	19.03
		3.32		6.85	
		3.57		5.51	
Upload File	3	4.50	10.10	6.37	18.40
		2.96		5.35	
		2.64		6.68	

5   Conclusions

An innovative network attached Disk array architecture, called Net-RAID, is proposed and implemented. It adds a network channel to the RAID and data can be transferred between the Net-RAID and clients directly. The architecture removes the server bottleneck and dynamically increases system bandwidth with the expansion of storage system capacity. Experimental results provide useful insights into the performance behavior of the system. The architecture can also be adopted to transfer massive data in other different servers, such as database server, HTTP server and so on.

6   Acknowledgements

This research is supported by National Nature Science Foundation of China (No. 60273074), and the Special Foundation of Excellent Ph.D. Thesis of China.

References

1. H. Radha, Y. Chen, K. Parthasarathy, R. Cohen: Scalable Internet Video Using MPEG-4, Image Communications, 15, 1999.
2. J. Pieper, S .Srinivasan, B. Dom: Streaming-Media Knowledge Discovery, IEEE Computer, Vol. 34, No. 9, (2001) 68-74
3. SA Barnett and GJ Anido: A cost comparison of distributed and centralized approaches to video-on-demand, IEEE J. Select. Areas Commun., vol. 14. (1996) 1173-1183
4. R. Tewari, D. Dias, R. Mukherjee, H. Vin: High Availability for Clustered Multimedia Servers, Proc. Int. Conf. Multimedia Computing and Systems, Tokyo, (1996) 144
5. Milind Buddhikot, Gurudatta, Parulkar, and Jerome, Cox, Jr.: Design of a Large Scale Multimedia Storage Server. Journal of Computer Networks and ISDN Systems. Elsevier, North Holland (1994) 504-524
6. Cheng peng, Jiangling Zhang, Hai Jin "Design of High Performance RAID in Real-Time system". ACM, Computer Architecture News, Vol. 27. (1999)

The NDMP-Plus Prototype Design and Implementation for Network Based Data Management

Kai Ouyang, Jingli Zhou, Tao Xia, Shengsheng Yu

Key Laboratory of Data Storage System, Ministry of Education,
Huazhong University of Science and Technology, Wuhan 430074, China
{oykai, ljzhou, xiatao, ssyu}@mail.hust.edu.cn

Abstract: Network based data management/backup/restore is the key component in the data storage centre. This paper proposes a new network based data
management --- NDMP-Plus. We firstly discuss the components of the NDMP-
Plus architecture. Then, we detail two new techniques in NDMP-Plus --- VSL
(Virtual Storage Layer) and the negotiation mechanism. VSL is the core component to implement the flexibility, which could avoid the network communication with the storage media directly. And the negotiation mechanism is the
key mechanism to improve the performance. Furthermore, we carry out an experiment to evaluate the performance of NDMP-Plus. The result of it suggests
that NDMP-Plus has stronger flexibility and higher performance than the original NDMP.

1. Introduction

In modern data storage centre, it is too difficult for the administrator to man-
age/backup/restore over thousands of millions of data using the distributed file systems (e.g. NFS, CIFS and DAFS [1]). To implement data backup/restore management,
NDMP (Network Data Management Protocol) is then introduced [2]. However, because of the lack of flexibility of the NDMP framework, we introduce new techniques
for NDMP in this paper to enhance the flexibility and performance. In particular, we
propose the NDMP-Plus prototype originating from NDMP but differing in the interior design of the architecture. Compared with NDMP, the NDMP-Plus prototype has
two new features as follows:

(1) NDMP-Plus introduces VSL (Virtual Storage Layer), by which it can erase
the difference between the data service and the tape service of NDMP and provide a
new uniform service --- the data+ service used as either the data provider or backup
server dynamically. VSL could also avoid the network communication with the storage media directly.

(2) NDMP-Plus provides one negotiation mechanism, by which it can decide the
data transmission format dynamically and enhance performance (e.g. the data can be
transmitted in the form of the tape device or the file-system to the data backup server).
While NDMP merely uses tape device format to transmit data, which will bring some
unnecessary processes in some cases (e.g. backup data from one NAS to another) and
decline performance.

H. Jin et al. (Eds.): NPC 2004, LNCS 3222, pp. 493–497, 2004.

2. The Architecture of NDMP-Plus

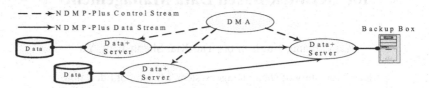

Fig. 1. The basic architecture of NDMP-Plus

The NDMP-Plus basic architecture, as shown in Fig. 1, provides DMA (Data Management Application) and the data+ service. The administrator uses DMA to manage, backup and restore data. The data+ service is a uniform service for all the NDMP-Plus compliant hosts. Compared with the data service and the tape service of NDMP, the data+ service of NDMP-Plus provides the uniform interface to all storage devices. In the glossary of NDMP-Plus, there is no primary or secondary storage device; all storage devices are the same to the data+ service and classified by the working method of the storage media.

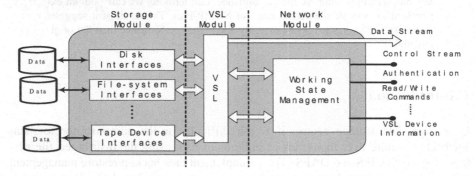

Fig. 2. The Components of The Data+ Service

A data+ service is composed of the VSL module, the network module and the storage modules, as shown in Fig. 2. A fundamental issue in the data+ service is how the backup/restore manipulation and the storage media are associated. To address it, this paper provides a media-independent module --- the VSL module. VSL instances one storage media to a VSL device entity and provides the information of that storage media to the network modules. The storage module involves one or more sub-storage media module. Each kind of sub-storage media modules is classified by the read/write method and the storage format of data.

3. The Implementation of VSL

VSL is a key component to realize the flexibility of the NDMP-Plus prototype, manage the storage modules and provide a series of uniform VSL interfaces. The internal frame of VSL is shown in Fig. 3.

VSL employs the pair --- {MediaID, DeviceID} to identify every logic storage partition the administrator can access. Both MediaID and DeviceID are globally exclusive numbers in the scope of VSL, hence DMA can use DeviceID to access the right logic storage partition and VSL can use MediaID to redirect the access to the real storage media. In practice, VSL provides a structure (VSLStorage) to describe an abstract storage module and a structure (VSLPartition) to describe a logic storage partition. And then the two structures cooperate with each other to implement the management of VSL.

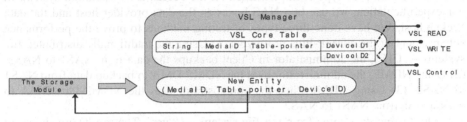

Fig. 3. The Internal Frame of VSL

4. The Negotiation Mechanism

In the glossary of NDMP-Plus, one session means that one connection between the data provider server and the data backup server can be used to do only one type of the procedure (either backup or restore) more than one time. Compared with NMDP, at the outset of one session, NDMP-Plus need do the negotiation mechanism for this session, as shown in Fig. 4.

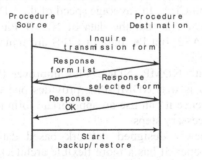

Fig. 4. The Negotiation Procedure

We take the backup procedure for example to illustrate the negotiation mechanism. After one connection is established, firstly, the procedure source inquires the procedure destination to provide the transmission form, and then the procedure destination provides the form list to the source. Secondly, the source selects the appropriate form as the transmission form of this session and notifies the destination. Finally, this backup or restore procedure can start up. The restore procedure is almost the same as the backup procedure, in which the backup server is the procedure source.

Based on the above discussion, the backup procedure is the same as the restore procedure from the network communication viewpoint. Through the negotiation mechanism, the procedure destination provides the transmission form to negotiate.

5. Evaluation and Conclusion

The NDMP-Plus prototype is implemented on the FreeBSD4.7 operation system. In our experimentation, we use two NAS boxes as the data provider host and the data backup host. We have done three types of testing methods to prove the performance enhancement of the NDMP-Plus prototype: (1) Using the traditionally distributed file systems --- CIFS, the administrator in Client backups the data from NAS1 to NAS2; (2) Using NDMP, the administrator uses the NDMP DMA to backup data from NAS1 to NAS2; (3) Using NDMP-Plus, the administrator uses the NDMP-Plus DMA to backup data from NAS1 to NAS2.

Our testing data come from the file-system --- "/usr". The results are shown in Table 1.

Table 1. The "/usr" Performance of Client Benchmarks

Method	Time-consumer (s)	Transmission Speed (KB/s)	Network traffic (KB/s)	CPU Utilization (%)
CIFS	1813	399.36	794.7	30 - 50
NDMP	832	870.4	About zero	About 2
NDMP-Plus	759	952.32	About zero	About 2

Based on the data of Table 1, we can reach the conclusion as follows:

(1) Compared with CIFS, the average speed of the NDMP-Plus backup methods speedup 90%. The reason is that the data of NDMP-Plus are transmitted directly between NAS1 and NAS2, but the data of CIFS are transmitted from NAS1 to the client, and then to NAS2.

(2) Compared with NDMP, NDMP-Plus improves the transmission speed by about 9%. The reason is that NDMP-Plus provides one negotiation mechanism to select the data form; hence it can use an appropriate form to transmit data more efficiently, avoiding unnecessary steps.

We present a newly designed network based data management prototype (NDMP-Plus) in this paper. It has a more flexible architecture and a higher performance than NDMP. The future work may focus on further enhancing the performance of NDMP-Plus and implementing the snapshot technology [3].

References

1. Kostas Magoutis.: Design and Implementation of a Direct Access File System (DAFS) Kernel Server for FreeBSD. Proceeding of the BSDCon 2002 Conference, February 11-14, 2002
2. R.Stager, H.Skardal.: Network Data Management Protocol Version 5 (Internet Draft). http://www.ndmp.org/download/sdk_v5/index.shtml (February 2000)
3. Y.H.Kim, D.J.Kang, and Y.H.Bak, M.J.Kim.: Snapshot Technique for Shared Large Storage in SAN Environments. CCN2002, Boston (2002) 520-525

Further Optimized Parallel Algorithm of Watershed Segmentation Based on Boundary Components Graph[1]

Haifang Zhou[1], Xuejun Yang[1], Yu Tang[2], Nong Xiao[1]

[1] Institute of Computer, National University of Defense Technology, Changsha, China
[2] Institute of Electronic Technology, National University of Defense Technology
{haifang_zhou, yutang18}@sina.com

Abstract. *Watershed segmentation/transform* is a classical method for image segmentation in gray scale mathematical morphology. Nevertheless watershed algorithm has strong recursive nature, so straightforward parallel one has a very low efficiency. Firstly, the advantages and disadvantages of some existing parallel algorithms are analyzed. Then, a *Further Optimized Parallel Watershed Algorithm* (FOPWA) is presented based on boundary components graph. As the experiments show, FOPWA optimizes both running time and relative speedup, and has more flexibility.

1 Introduction

Watershed segmentation/transform is a classical and effective method for image segmentation in gray scale mathematical morphology. This method, with a wide perspective, has been applied successfully into some fields like remote sensing images processing of satellite and radar, biomedical applications and computer vision. However, watershed transform is a relatively time consuming task for its low efficiency, and in above fields, such as in remote sensing applications large size images, e.g. 1024×1024, 3000×3000 or larger, are not uncommon and must be processed in real time usually. Therefore, to study watershed algorithm easy to be paralleled is meaningful in real applications.

2 Related Work

Meijster and Roerdink had proposed a three-stage parallel watershed algorithm (M-R algorithm for short) in [1] based on components graph, which was designed for a ring-architecture with shared memory. But there are some potential logic errors/limits in M-R algorithm, as shown in [2]. Therefore, [2] pointed out an improved parallel

---

[1] This work is partially supported by the National 863 High Technology Plan of China under the grant No. 2002AA1Z201, 2002AA104510 and 2002AA714021, and the Grid Project sponsored by China ministry of education under the grant No. CG2003-GA00103.

H. Jin et al. (Eds.): NPC 2004, LNCS 3222, pp. 498–501, 2004.

watershed algorithm (IPWA for short) for distributed memory system, which got better performance. With the further study, we find that the adaptability of these two algorithms is limited: 1) The parallel efficiency of two algorithms is very low when they meet images with content of large size objects. 2) They are only designed for the segmentation of the images containing many plateaus with large area. 3) Because of simplified computation of plateaus, algorithms probably end up with images that contain thick watersheds, which need post-processing.

Moga and Cramariuc etc. had given some parallel methods of watershed transform based on definition by topographical distance [3]. We have learned from [4] that the proposed method based on Ordered Queue (OQ for short) is derived from optimal sequential watershed algorithm, but its scalability is quite limited. While an alternative solution, namely image integration by sequential scanning, introduced by [5], provides an equitable work load on multiprocessors, and hence a better relative speedup, but the absolute running time of this algorithm is very long. And then literature [6] proposed a method named rain-falling or hill-climbing simulation, which reduced re-scanning overhead through computing lower-complete image, but introduced undesirable overhead caused by the lower distance computation and preserved data dependent character of the algorithm. In addition, these algorithms do not construct watershed lines, but only labeled regions [3], needing post-processing.

3 An Optimized Parallel Method: FOPWA

Considering positive and negative contributions of above algorithms we proposed a *Further Optimized Parallel Watershed Algorithm* (FOPWA) based on definition of watershed transform by topographical distance. Topographical distance based watershed transform is started by detecting minima of the input data (called *seed pixels*); ordered region growing is then performed according to *lower distance*. Lower distance is formally defined as following:

Definition 1. Let $D \subseteq Z^2$, f be a digital gray value image in domain D, and G be underlying grid of f. $f(p)$ denotes the gray value of pixel p. *Lower distance d* is defined as: $d(p) = 0$ if p is a minimum; otherwise, $d(p)$ equals the length of the shortest path $\{p = p_0, p_1, ..., p_s = q\}$ from p to a pixel q such that $\forall i \in \{1, 2, ..., s\}$, $(p_{i-1}, p_i) \in G$, $f(q) < f(p)$, and, if $s > 1$, $\forall i \in \{1, 2, ..., s-1\}$, $f(p_i) = f(p_{i-1})$.

Each non-seed pixel is put into different catchments (regions) in an increasing order of gray levels. This recursive label propagation is called *flooding*. We define a 2D ordering relation to satisfy parallel requirement for flooding.

Definition 2. *2D ordering relation* can be formulated by two conditions: Condition 1. If $f(q) = \min_{r \in N_G(p)} \{f(r) | f(r) < f(p)\}$, then q is the preceding-pixel of p (also called p is flooded by q), and $L(p) = L(q)$. $L(.)$ denotes the output label image. Condition 2. If $f(p) = f(q)$ and $d(p) = d(q) + 1$, then $L(p) = L(q)$. Where $d(p)$ stands for lower distance of p with initial value ∞ ($d(p) = \infty$), which denotes a maximum value, and $N_G(p)$ for the set of neighboring pixels of p with respect to surrounding pattern.

We also assigned a unique label to each of boundary pixels with preceding-pixels, which are looked as seed-pixel like minima. Consequently, based on this 2D ordering relation, each processor can correctly and exhaustively delimit the extent of regions crossing the local sub-domains, regardless of what is happening in other processors; hence parallel computing could be realized. We name these additional seed-pixels as *pseudo seed-pixels*. Then, we define a *Boundary Components Graph* (BCG) to record the ordering relation between pseudo seed-pixel and its preceding for flooding and merging in later steps. Note that BCG is only related to boundary pixels of each sub-domain, not all pixels in the input image, so the size of components graph is reduced.

Definition 3. Considering the input image f as a direct valued graph $G = (V, E, f)$, in which V is the set of pixels in the graph, and E is the set of edges of the graph defining the connectivity. BCG $G^* = (V^*, E^*, f^*)$ ($f^* = f$) can be defined as following:

1) If $v \in V \wedge L(v) = H$ or $L(v) \neq H \wedge (\exists p, p \in V \wedge p \in N_G(v) \wedge L(p) = H)$, then $v \in V^*$. 2) $\forall u, v \in V^*$, if $L(u) \neq H \wedge L(v) = H$, and u and v satisfies Condition 1 or Condition 2 described above, then $(u, v) \in E^*$. 3) $\forall u, v \in V^*$, if $L(u) \neq H \wedge L(v) = H \wedge f^*(u) = f^*(v) \wedge d(u) = d(v) = \infty$, then $(u, v) \in E^*$.

For the implementation, the global domain D of size $X \times Y$ is split among N processors in sub-domains D_i; FOPWA has four stages: 1) Detecting real and pseudo seed-pixels and building local BCGs. 2) Local flooding. We use Ordered Queue (OQ) to realize the local watershed transform, for OQ is derived from optimal serial watershed algorithm that can obtain relatively shorter running time of local tasks. 3) Global merging. We use similar process to merging components graphs as IPWA [2]. 4) Broadcasting the merging result to each processor to updating the local results.

4   Experiments and Conclusion

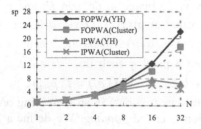 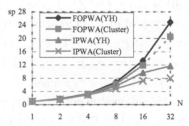

Fig. 1. The comparison of FOPWA and IPWA in speedups. The left is the speedup curves of two algorithms for the test image *Lena* with size of 512×512. The right is for the test image *Airport* with size of 1024×1024

Firstly, we realized FOPWA and IPWA [2] on two parallel platforms, and tested for various images with different size (256/512/1024/2048). Moreover, performance of FOPWA is also compared with existing algorithms in running time and speedup. One of the two parallel platforms is a Cluster system with 16 nodes. Another parallel platform is YinHe supercomputer (YH for short), which includes 32 processors.

Fig.1 compares FOPWA with IPWA in speedup on two different platforms (dashed curves represent speedup trend for Cluster system when number of processors is over 16). From this figure, we can draw some conclusions: 1) FOPWA outperforms IPWA, and has better scalability. 2) FOPWA is less data dependent. 3) The result got from YH is better than that from Cluster for YH has better network.

FOPWA outperforms other existing parallel algorithms by combining the advantages of components-graph based method and distance based method but not introducing additional overhead. Table 1 compares performance of FOPWA with some existing parallel algorithms. As the experiments show, FOPWA optimizes both running time and relative speedup, and has more flexibility and adaptability, compared against old methods.

Table 1. The comparison of FOPWA and other parallel algorithms in serial time and speedups on YH. Test image is *Airport* with size of 1024×1024, N is the number of nodes in system.

Algorithms	Serial time (s)	Speedup(N=16)	Speedup(N=32)
Rigid OQ-based	11.402	5.548	7.358
Sequential scanning	52.882	14.964	26.296
Rain-falling	5.958	2.877	4.532
Connected component	11.883	11.777	21.527
IPWA	1.445	9.658	11.709
FOPWA	1.312	13.299	24.876

References

1. Meijster, A., Roerdink, J. B. T. M.: A proposal for the implementation of a parallel watershed algorithm. In Hlavac, V., Sara, R. (eds.): Computer Analysis of Images and Patterns. New York. (1995) 790-795.
2. Zhou, H. F., Jiang, Y. H., X.J. Yang, X. J.: An Improved Parallel Watershed Algorithm for Distributed Memory System. In Zhou, W. L. (ed.): Proceedings of the 5th International Conference on Algorithms and Architecture for Parallel Processing. IEEE Computer Society. Los Alamitos (2002) 310-314.
3. Zhou, H. F., Jiang Y. H., Yang, X. J.: Researches on serial and parallel strategies of watershed transform. Journal of national university of defense technology. Vol. 24(6). (2002)71-76. (in Chinese, cited by EI)
4. Moga, A. N., Viero, T., Dobrin, B. P.: Implementation of a distributed watershed algorithm. In Serra, J., Soille, P. (eds.): Computational Imaging and Vision Mathematical Morphology and Its Applications to Image Processing. Dordrecht, the Netherlands. (1994) 281-288
5. Moga, A. N., Viero, T., Gabbouj, M., et al.: Parallel watershed algorithm based on sequential scannings. In Pitas, I. (ed.): Proceedings 1995 IEEE Workshop on Nonlinear Signal and Image Processing, Vol. II. Neos Marmaras, Greece. (1995) 991-994
6. Cramariuc, B., Gabbouj, M.: A parallel watershed algorithm based on rain falling simulation. In Proceedings 12th European Conference on Circuit Theory and Design, Vol. 1. Istanbul, Turkey. (1995) 339-342.

The Transmitted Strategy of Proxy Cache Based on Segmented Video

Zhiwen Xu, Xiaoxin Guo, Yunjie Pang, and Zhengxuan Wang

Faculty of Computer Science and Technology, Jilin University,
Changchun City, 130012, Jilin Province, China
xuzhiwen@public.cc.jl.cn

Abstract. Using proxy cache is a key technique that may help to reduce
the loads of the server, network bandwidth and startup delays. Basing on
the popularity of clients' request to segment video,we extend the length
for batch and patch by using dynamic cache of proxy cache for streaming media. Present transmission schemes using dynamic cache such that
unicast suffix batch, unicast patch, multicast patch, multicast merge and
optimal batch patch by proxy cache based on segmented video. And then
quantitatively explore the impact of the choice of transmission scheme,
cache allocation policy, proxy cache size, and availability of unicast versus multicast capability, on the resultant transmission cost.

1 Introduction

We consider that video stream from a server travels through Internet to the end
clients. We assume that clients always request playback from the beginning of a
video. The proxy receives the client request and, if the prefix video is available in
the proxy, streams the prefix directly to the client. If the video is not present in
the proxy, the latter will contact the server and streams the received data from
the server to the client. We, according to the popularity of video application
from the clients, store the segmented videos in proxy cache, therefore enhance
the byte hit ratio of proxy cache.

In order to raising the efficiency of proxy cache for streaming videos, we
present the video segmented cache scheme based on the popularity of video requests from the clients. We segment the video into small parts, for being cached
and substituted. Suppose the minimal cache allocation unit length is b, we segment video into the multiple of b. The value of b is determined according to
the startup delays in the Internet environments. In later discussion, we simply
assume that the video length unit is b, therefore video unit can be independently
cached and substituted. The length of the prefix cache unit is also b. According
to the popularity of video requests, we cache the video segmentation of different
size and insure that segmented cache can obtain maximal percentage of byte
hits radio. We extend the length for batch and patch by using dynamic cache of
proxy cache for streaming media. Present transmission schemes using dynamic
cache such that unicast suffix batch, unicast patch, multicast patch, multicast
merge and optimal batch patch by proxy cache based on segmented video.

H. Jin et al. (Eds.): NPC 2004, LNCS 3222, pp. 502–507, 2004.

2   Proxy Cache Based on Segmented Video

The f_i measures the relative popularity of a video: every access to the video repository has a probability of f_i requesting video i. Let λ_i be the access rate of video i and λ be the aggregate access rate to the video repository. The storage vector $V = (V_1, V_2, \ldots, V_N)$ specifies that a prefix of length V_i seconds for each video i is cached at the proxy, i=1,2,...,N. The storage vector $U = (U_1, U_2, \ldots, U_N)$ specifies that a segmented cache of length U_i seconds for each video i is cached at the proxy, i=1,2,...,N. The length of video i cached at the proxy is $V_i + U_i$. Let C_s and C_p represent respectively the costs associated with transmitting one byte of video data on the server-proxy path and proxy-client path. $C_i(V_i, U_i)$ is the transmission cost per unit time for video i when the length of proxy cache is $V_i + U_i$. The r_i represent the stream rate of video i resource.

2.1   Unicast Suffix Batch Based on Segmented Video

Unicast suffix batch using dynamic cache based on segmented video is a simple batch scheme, which makes use of proxy cache to provide immediate playback. It is designed for the unicast transmission of video from the proxy to the clients. Suppose the first video request i arrives at time 0. The proxy will immediately transmit the video prefix to the client. Unicast batch processing makes the transmission time from server to proxy be as late as possible, and ensures it the playback on the client side is continuous. That is to say, the first frame of suffix is scheduled to reach the client at time V_i. The length of prefix cache which depends on the network environment, but the other length U_i of cache in proxy cache is relative to the speed of customer's request for this video, that is to say, we determine the length of cache U_i according to the popularization of video. For any request arriving in time $(0, V_i + U_i)$, the proxy just forwards the incoming suffix (of length $L_i - V_i - U_i$) to the client, and new transmitted suffix should come from server. Actually, several video suffix requests are transmitted in batch using dynamic cache. Segment-based unicast transmission and prefix cache can solve the problem of startup delays. But batch transmission using dynamic cache can increase transmission efficiency because its maximum unit is realized by dynamic cache windows and different from the others. Suppose there is a Poisson distribution process, and the average request number is $1 + (V_i + U_i)\lambda_i$ in time $[0, V_i + U_i]$, these requests cause the transmission of suffix $[V_i + U_i, L_i]$ from the server, and the average transmission cost of video i is :

$$c_i(V_i, U_i) = (c_s \frac{L_i - V_i - U_i}{1 + (V_i + U_i)\lambda_i} + c_p L_i)\lambda_i r_i \qquad (1)$$

2.2   Unicast Patch Based on Segmented Video

Unicast patch for proxy cache based on segmented video using dynamic cache can save network resource. The first request of video i arrives at time 0, and the video non-stored in proxy cache arrives at time $V_i + U_i$ from server (Fig.1).

Suppose another customer's request arrives at time t_2, $V_i + U_i < t_2 < L_i$. One method is to read the video non-cached in proxy from server directly. The other is to use patch processing technique. We suppose to handle $[V_i + U_i, t_2]$ from the patch of server, since segment $[t_2, L_i]$ have been scheduled to transmit, the patch is set at time $t_2 + V_i + U_i$, then the client must receive at the same time from two channels and deliver the content of the suffix and patch. So a patch depends on a suffix threshold G_i. Measured from the beginning of the suffix, if we begin delivering from the nearest suffix, and request the arrival within G_i, the proxy will schedules a patch from the server for it. Otherwise, it starts a new complete transmission of the suffix. Suppose a Poisson arrival process, between the initiations of the two consecutive transmission of the suffix, the average number is $1 + \lambda_i(V_i + U_i + G_i)$. These requests are only in one transmission of the suffix $[V_i + U_i, L_i]$ from the server, the total length of patches from the server for these requests is:

$$\lambda_i G_i \int_0^{G_i} x/G_i dx = \lambda G_i^2/2 \tag{2}$$

This is because, the distribution of arrivals in time interval $[V_i + U_i, V_i + U_i + G_i]$ follows a uniform distribution in a Poission arrival process. The average transmission cost of the video i is:

$$c_i(V_i, U_i) = c_s \lambda_i r_i \frac{\lambda_i G_i^2/2 + L_i - V_i - U_i}{1 + \lambda(V_i + U_i + G_i)} + c_p \lambda_i r_i L_i \tag{3}$$

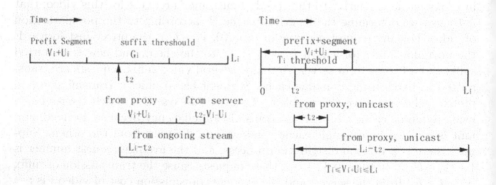

Fig. 1. Unicast patch   **Fig. 2.** Case 1

2.3   Multicast Patch Based on Segmented Video

If the path from the proxy to the client is multicast transmission, proxy can use the scheme of segmented multicast patch using dynamic cache. Suppose the request of video i arrives at time 0 (fig.2), proxy begins to transmit video $V_i + U_i$ by multicast at time 0, the server begins to transmit suffix of video to the client at time $V_i + U_i$, and the proxy transmits received data to client by multicast patch using dynamic cache. If that T_i is the domain value that control the transmission frequency of whole stream. Suppose a request shortly after the stream transmitting arrives at $t_2(0 < t_2 \leq T_i)$, the video transmission to the clients can be classified into two cases according to the relationship between $V_i + U_i$ and T_i:

Case 1: $T_i \leq V_i + U_i \leq L_i$ (Fig.2), the client receives $[0, t_2]$ segment by using unicast from proxy through a single channel, and receives $[t_2, L_i]$ segment by using a processing multicast. Suppose this is the Poisson distribution, in this circumstance, the value transmission function $g_1(V_i, U_i, T_i)$ is:

$$\frac{\lambda_i r_i}{1 + \lambda_i T_i}[(L_i - V_i - U_i)c_s + L_i c_p + \frac{\lambda_i T_i^2}{2}c_p] \tag{4}$$

Case 2: $0 \leq V_i + U_i < T_i$ (Fig.3), if $0 < t_2 \leq V_i + U_i$, transmission construction is the same as case 1. If $V_i + U_i < t_2 \leq T_i$, the client receives $[0, V_i + U_i]$ segment by using unicast from proxy through a single channel, and receives $[t_2, L_i]$ by using the processing multicast. The server transmits $[V_i + U_i, t_2]$ through proxy to client by using unicast. Suppose its process is the Poisson distribution, then the transmission cost function $g_2(V_i, U_i, T_i)$ is:

$$\frac{\lambda_i r_i}{1 + \lambda_i T_i}[(L_i - V_i - U_i)c_s + L_i c_p + \frac{\lambda_i(V_i + U_i)^2}{2}c_p + \frac{\lambda_i(T_i - V_i - U_i)^2}{2}(c_s + c_p)] \tag{5}$$

We denote the cost of transmission with k(k=1,2), $h_k(V_i, U_i)$ is the minimum transmission cost of the transmission value function: $h_k(V_i, U_i) = \min\{g_k(V_i, U_i, T_i), 0 \leq T_i \leq L_i\}$. For a given $V_i + U_i$ cache proxy, the average transmission value is: $c_i(V_i, U_i) = \min\{h_1(V_i, U_i), h_2(V_i, U_i)\}$.

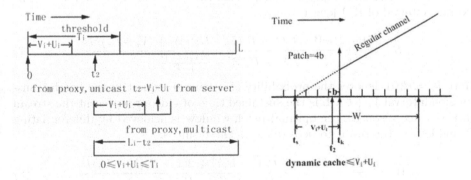

Fig. 3. Case 2   **Fig. 4.** optimal multicast patch

2.4 Multicast Stream Merging Based on Segmented Video

The key issue of stream merging is deciding how to merge a later stream into an earlier stream. Closest Target policy [5] is one online heuristic policy whose performance is close to optimal offline stream merging. Our scheme for multicast Merge integrates dynamic cache and stream merging. It uses Closest Target policy to decide how to merge a later stream into an earlier stream. For a video segmentation required by the client, if a prefix of the segmentation is at the proxy, it is transmitted directly from the proxy to the client. The suffix not stored at proxy cache is transmitted from the server as late as possible while still ensuring continuous playback at the client. Let P_j be the probability of requiring a j-second , $0 \leq j \leq L_i$. This can be obtained by monitoring a running system. The average transmission cost of video is:

$$c_i(V_i, U_i) = \sum_{j=b}^{V_i+U_i} jP_jb_ic_p + \sum_{j=V_i-U_i+b}^{L_i} (j(c_p + c_s) - (V_i + U_i)c_s))P_jr_i \quad (6)$$

2.5 Batch Patch Based on Segmented Dynamic Cache

Recently White and Crowecroft [8] have introduced the concept of optimal batch patch for prefix cache in order to minimize the average stream rate of the server. We present optimal batch patch using dynamic cache based on segmented video. The common clients, before applying to the server for conventional channel RM, are transmitted in batches as one interval. This interval is fixed, symbolized as V_i+U_i, with an optimal patch window W. RM denotes regular channel. It exceeds this window, initiating a new conventional regular channel RM is more efficient than sending the patch within $V_i + U_i$(Fig.4). A length of RM is transmitted as a startup interval of RM, while a non-RM length is transmitted as a non-startup interval. The RM length and the average interval of startup patch, it is that in the interval of two adjacent RM periods random chosen by computer. The average interval of RM length is:

$$R = \frac{(1 - P)rW^2 + (1 - P)(V_i + U_i)rW + (V_i + U_i)rL}{2(V_i + U_i)W + \frac{2(V_i+U_i)^2}{1-P}} \quad (7)$$

Here $P = P(0)$ denotes the probability of getting 0 request in the batch transmission interval $V_i + U_i$. L is the sustained time of video, r represent the stream rate of video resource, the optimal patch window is achieved by differentiating R and letting the result to be 0 request. The result is:

$$W = \frac{-(V_i + U_i) + \sqrt{P(V_i + U_i)^2 + 2(1 - P)(V_i + U_i)L}}{(V_i + U_i)(1 - P)} \quad (8)$$

The optimal batch patch uses dynamic cache to transmit the request of batch and patch in interval V_i+U_i. The value of b for prefix cache can not be too large, generally in seconds. If the value is too large, that will extend the clients' waiting time. In proxy cache based on segmented video, by utilizing dynamic cache technique, the total length of prefix and segmented cache in the proxy cache is considered as the unit of batch transmission and patch. If $t_2 < V_i + U_i \leq W$, there exists multiple patch streams with batch of $V_i + U_i$, and the dynamic cache, which is in proxy cache, completes processing the patch within the exact time of the patch streams, then the value from the server to the proxy becomes $1/(1+((V_i+U_i)\lambda_i)$. If $t_2 < W < V_i+U_i$, there exists multiple patch streams with W, and use of length W for dynamic cache in proxy cache, completes processing the patch within the exact time of the multiple patch streams, then the value from the sever to the proxy becomes$1/(1+W\lambda)$. These two cases can both reduce the output from the server and enhance the efficiency of proxy cache.

3   Conclusions

We present the segmented proxy cache technique based on the popularity of video, and extend the length of batch transmission by using dynamic cache. Further more, we put forward several schemes which are based on video segment such as unicast batch transmission, unicast patch, multicast patch, multicast stream merging and optimal batch patch schemes, and study the impact on the transmission cost caused by the choice of transmission schemes. The evaluation exposits that even to relative small proxy cache, elaborately designed transmission scheme, with dynamic cache based segmented video, can produce significant cost saving. Its performance is prior to the optimal prefix cache, proportional priority cache and 0-1 cache schemes.

References

1. C. Aggarwal, J. Wolf, and P. Yu : On optimal batching policies for video-on-demand storage servers. In Proc. of IEEE International Conference on Multimedia Computing and Systems, June 1996.
2. K.L.Wu, P.S.Yu: Segment-Based Proxy Caching of Multimedia Streams. In: Proc. of IEEE INFOCOM, May, 2001.
3. S.Sen, J.Reforrd, D.Towsley: Proxy Prefix Caching for Multimedia Streaming. In: Proc. Of IEEE INFOCOM, Mar.1999.
4. K. Hua, Y. Cai and S. Sheu: Patching: A multicast techniquefor true video-on-demand services. In: Proc. ACM Multimedia, September 1998.
5. D.Eager, M.Vernon and J.Zahorjan: Optimal and efficient merging schedules for video-on-demand servers. In Proc.ACM Multimedia, November 1999.
6. B. Wang, S. Sen, M. Adler and D. Towsley: Proxy-based distribution of streaming video over unicast/multicast connections. In: Tech. Rep. 01-05, Department of Computer Science, University of Massachusetts, Amherst,2001.
7. O.Verscheure, C.Venketramani, P.Frossard, L.Amini: Joint server scheduling and proxy caching for video delivery. In: IBM Technical Report Number RC21981, 2001.
8. Paul P.White,Jon Crowcroft:Optimised Batch Patching with Classes of Service. In: ACM Cpmputer Communication Review (2000), Vol 30.

The Strategy of Batch Using Dynamic Cache for Streaming Media

Zhiwen Xu, Xiaoxin Guo, Yunjie Pang, and Zhengxuan Wang

Faculty of Computer Science and Technology, Jilin University,
Changchun City, 130012, Jilin Province, China
xuzhiwen@public.cc.jl.cn

Abstract. The batch is an important technique for delivering video over
Internet or VoD. It is a key method to improve effect for video multicast.
In this paper, we research the batch strategy of proxy cache for streaming
media using dynamic cache, proposed the three kind of cache algorithm
for proxy cache: window batch, size batch, efficient batch. These methods increased the length of batch, solved the problem for latency time
of batch in video muticast, improved the byte-hit ratio of proxy cache
for streaming media, and economized the resources of network backbone.
Event-driven simulations are conducted to evaluate these kinds of strategy are better than prefix cache and segment cache.

1 Introduction

The batch is one important technique for transmitting video multicast and VoD.
It makes it possible to transmit video and the media required by all the clients
within b of the duration time. Therefore through only one transmission, multi-
application within duration time b can be satisfied. Although this method saves
the transmission resource, users need to wait during the time interval b. What's
more, in the process to transmit video, the length of b is not allowed to be too
long, which limits the use of batch technique. In the paper, we make use of the
technique based on the proxy cache for streaming media and dynamic cache to
solve the following problems: to lengthen time of batch, enhance the byte-hit
ratio of proxy cache, ensure that we can transmit the video to the users without
waiting time.

2 The Batch Using Dynamic Cache for Streaming Media

In the proxy cache based on segmented streaming media[2], we cache the prefix
first to ensure there's no startup delay. The segmented cache, employing prefetch technique caches only a part of video, according to the popularity for the
users' requests. When two or more users apply for the same video, we can save
network resource as long as we can transmit the entire requirement at a time.
In proxy cache, we employ dynamic movable time windows to cache video, and
make replacement by using an algorithm called FIFO in order to make sure that

H. Jin et al. (Eds.): NPC 2004, LNCS 3222, pp. 508–512, 2004.
© IFIP International Federation for Information Processing 2004

applicants can directly receive video from the proxy cache, needless to wait. In this paper, we put forward three batch strategies: window batch, size patch, efficient batch.

2.1 Window Batch

If the time length of the video is L_h minutes, then the simplest strategy of batch is used to transmit the video in batch with a set length in the window. We set W to be the width of batch for each video clip, and L_h/W will determine the times of multicast required. When two users (or more) apply to video, than that video required by the very first applicant is transmitted through the server by the proxy. The latter users required the video that is transmitted by the proxy cache. If the average request ratio reaches λ, then the average of the users who require video service can be simply believed to be λW. If two or less applicants apply for a certain video when we are window batch of the video, then the data stream in batch can be omitted. There exists one problem about how to select. The number of applications from the users is uncertain, which is determined by the random changes in the requesting process. When there are no more than two applicants within the window batch time, we don't employ the batch technique. In the proxy cache of segmented streaming video, the length of the video cached in the proxy is $2^i b$. Set the length of the window based on window batch to be W, and $W=2^i b$. when batch takes place in time W, then we should make a judgment whether the batch saves the value. Let us suppose the requests used of batch are respectively $A_1, A_2, ..., A_j$, then the value of j/W should be smaller than the threshold value of proxy cache, otherwise we can not transmit the video used of batch. In this way, we can surely enhance the efficiency of proxy cache and simplify the replacement algorithm of cache.

2.2 Size Batch

Generally, for the service providers, to cover as many users as possible in the batch is their great concern, because the income of the system is directly related to the average length of batch. Set C_s represents the value of the video stream of batch when seeing video and N' is the average of the users within batch. If P is the worth for each delivering video in the batch, then the worth of transmitted video in the batch is N'P. In order to maintain the income for network resource, N'P $\geq C_s$ is necessary. Let us define K $\doteq C_s/P$, and N'$\geq$K, then the longer the length of batch, the larger income of the system. In size batch, there involves one question, automatic selection. Higher number of the users in batch results from higher arrival ratio. Low byte-hit ratio results in low yield of the system. Before multicast, the yield is ensured by the requests from M$\geq$K users in batch. The time length needed by dynamic cache in the proxy cache is the time brought by collecting M users. When M=2, the practicability is useful.

2.3   Efficient Batch

In the batch process, the smaller capacity the proxy cache is taken up, the larger the quantity within batch. The higher the byte-hit radio of proxy cache, the higher the efficiency. The length of video with popularity λ is L_i, and that length in the proxy cache is V_i. The users make applications at time $A_0, A_1, ..., A_n$ in turn and $A_0=0$. When k=1,2,...,n, $(A_k - A_{k-1}) \leq L_i/\lambda V_i$, we can ensure it is beneficial for every video request within batch. That is to say, we transmitted those requested video in batch which help to save network resources.

3   Analysis for Batch Strategy

We analyze the performance of the batch schemes mentioned above. We focus on a particular video in the system, with the request's arrival process being Poisson with rate λ. In the various schemes for evaluation, we are interested in the following closely related performance measure: (a) Its distribution is represented by $f_s(s)$, and the mean value is S'. The average of the concurrent stream indicates the average required in the system. Probably it is also related to the saved bandwidth, compared with pure VoD, because in the pure VoD, the average number of concurrent stream's requested is λL_h, the saved bandwidth can be defined as $\eta = 1 - S'/(\lambda L_h)$. (b) The batch size N, both its distribution $f_N(n)$ and its mean N'. Note that N' is related to S' by the $\lambda T_h = $ S' N'. Indeed, by the above formula, within the display time of a certain video, the arrival average of the users' requests can be simply represented by λL_h, which is equal S'N'. (c) For a random user, the delay is represented by D, whose distribution $f_D(t)$ is expressed by D'. The proxy cache requires the smallest dynamically cache batch size for D.

3.1   Analysis for Window Batch

In the fixed window batch strategy, the distribution of the batch size is a Poisson process, expressed by N'= λ W. The video is accurate batch once in every W second, therefore S'=L_h/W and $\eta = 1 - 1/(\lambda W)$. D is a $\sim$ U(0,W) uniformly distribution and D'=W/2. in fixed gating, the possibility of the request i(i $\geq$ 1)in batch is given by $\lambda W^i e^{-\lambda W}/(i!(1 - e^{-\lambda W}))$, therefore N'=$\lambda W/(1 - e^{-\lambda w})$ and

$$S' = \frac{L_h}{W}(1 - e^{-\lambda w}) \tag{1}$$

As expect ,when $\lambda \longrightarrow 0, S' \longrightarrow \lambda L_h$, and when $lim_{\lambda \longrightarrow \infty} S' = L_h/W$, then S'$\leq L_h$/W. The bandwidth saved is $\eta = 1 - (1 - (1 - e^{-\lambda w})(\lambda W))$. Given one arrival in the batch window, and this arrival time in the window is distributed evenly, therefore the distribution function related to the users' delay for a certain video is $f_D(t)=1/W$, for $0 \leq t \leq W$ and D'=W/2. T=0, when the proxy cache can't transmit the video in the batch. In automatic selection, the distribution of the batch size is $P(N = i) = (\lambda W)^{i-1} e^{-\lambda w}/(i-1)!$, for $i \geq 1$, therefore N'=1+λW and

$$S' = \frac{\lambda T_h}{1 + \lambda w} \tag{2}$$

and $\eta = \lambda W/(1+\lambda W)$, the request distribution is given by the following formula:

$$f_D(t) = \frac{1}{1 + \lambda W}\delta(t - W) + \frac{\lambda W}{1 + \lambda W}\frac{1}{W} \tag{3}$$

for $0 \leq t \leq W$, where $\delta(t)$ is the usual impulse function with $\delta(t) = 0$ for $t \neq 0$ and $\int_{-\infty}^{\infty} \delta(t)dt = 1$. It accounts for the first user in each batch having a delay of W while the remaining users in the batch having a delay uniformly distributed between o and W, then the function works out that for the first user of each batch, there is a time interval W. Therefore D' can be given:

$$D' = \frac{\lambda W + 2}{2(1 + \lambda W)}W \tag{4}$$

The cache size of batch for proxy cache is D', and the request number in batch is N'.

3.2   Analysis for Size Batch

The video films collect M requests at a time in batch, therefore N is decided, which is equal to M. As a result N'=M, $S'=\lambda L_h/M$,$\eta = 1-1/M$. Let W represent the batch period, which is variable at random and equal (M-1), the summation of exponential variables. Its distribution can be given:

$$g_w(W) = \frac{\lambda(\lambda W)^{M-2}}{M - 2}e^{-\lambda W} \tag{5}$$

The users' request duration can be given according to the movement status on W:

$$f_D(x) = \frac{1}{M}g_w(x) + \frac{M+2}{M}\int_x^{\infty} \frac{g_w(W)}{W}dW + \frac{\delta(W)}{M} \tag{6}$$

D'=(M-1)/(2λ), which is equal to half of average batch period. The cache size in batch is T=(M-1)/λ.

3.3   Analysis for Efficient Batch

In the efficient batch scheme, N=j, its distribution can be given:

$$P(N = j) = \frac{(\lambda A_j)^{j-1}}{(j - 1)!} \tag{7}$$

The users' request distribution is

$$f_D(x) = \frac{L_i}{\lambda V_i}e^{-\lambda x} \tag{8}$$

All the requests is transmitted in this batch scheme. The time of duration is smaller than $L_i/\lambda V_i$, when M=2. The proxy cache size T= A_n, and the request number of batch is S(t)=n.

512   Z. Xu et al.

4 Performance and Conclusion

We compared these three batch policies with the full video approach, the variable-sized segment approach, and the prefix schemes in terms of the impact they imposed on byte hit ratio and startup delay, in the following aspects: the cache size, the popularity of the video.

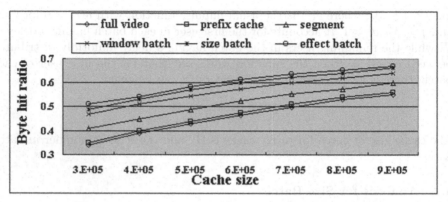

Fig.1. The relation of byte hit radio and cache size

The window batch of the proxy cache is the simplest and most practical strategy. Efficient batch of the proxy cache has the highest byte hit ratio(Fig.1).Within the whole range of cache size, the effect of the dynamic cache approach, variable-size segment-based strategy and the prefix strategy all effectively solve the problem of startup delay.

Efficient batch, size batch, window batch further improve the byte hit ratio of the proxy cache and solve the wait delay existed in batch for VoD. Efficient batch has the highest byte hit ratio. Window batch has the following characteristics: convenient usage, simply and practical replacement algorithm of cache, high byte hit ratio. These three kinds of batch strategies can enhance the efficiency of the proxy cache together with the segment strategy.

References

1. Z.Miao, A.Ortega: Proxy caching for efficient video services over the Internet.In Proc. Of Int, Web Caching Workshop, Apr. 1999.
2. K.L.Wu, P.S.Yu: Segment-Based Proxy Caching of Multimedia Streams. In: Proc. of IEEE INFOCOM, May, 2001.
3. S.Sen, J.Reforrd, D.Towsley: Proxy Prefix Caching for Multimedia Streaming. In: Proc. Of IEEE INFOCOM, Mar.1999.
4. S. Ramesh, I. Rhee, and K. Guo: Multicast with Cache (MCache): Anadaptive Zero-Delay Video-on-Demand Service. in: Proc. IEEE INFOCOM, April 2001.

New Regions of Interest Image Coding Using Up-Down Bitplanes Shift for Network Applications

Li-bao Zhang, Ke Wang

¹ College of Communication Engineering, Jilin University,
Changchun 130025, China
{ZHANG Li-bao, WANG Ke, libaozhang}@163.com

Abstract. Regions Of Interest (ROI) image coding is one of the most significant features in JPEG2000 for network applications. In this paper, a new approach for ROI coding so-call Up-Down Bitplanes Shift (UDBShift) is presented. This new method separates all bitplanes into three parts: Important Significant Bitplanes (ISB), General Significant Bitplanes (GSB) and Least Significant Bitplanes (LSB). The certain number bitplanes of ROIs are up-shifted to ISB based on different degrees of interest of every ROI. Then, partial BG bitplanes are downshifted to LSB according to encoding requirement. Finally, The residual significant bitplanes of ROIs and BG that are saved in GSB are not shifted. Simulation results show significant improvement in reduction of reduction of transmission time and enhanced flexibility at the expense of a small complexity. Additionally, it can support arbitrarily shaped multiple ROI coding with different degrees of interest without coding the ROI shapes.

1 Introduction

The functionality of ROI is important in applications where certain parts of the image are of higher importance than others. In such a case, these ROIs need to be encoded at higher quality than the background (BG). During the transmission of the image, these regions need to be transmitted first or at a higher priority, as for example in the case of progressive transmission. JPEG 2000 standard in [1] and [2] not only supports ROI coding firstly, but defines two coding algorithms that are called Maxshift (maximum shift) method [3] in part 1 and the general scaling-based method in part 2 along with the syntax of a compressed codestream. In these methods, a region of interest of the image can have a better quality than the rest at any decoding bit-rate.

Although the Maxshift method is efficient, three disadvantages are inevitable [4]. First, this method requires decoding of all ROI coefficients before accessing bitplanes of the BG and uses large shifting values that significantly increase the number of total bit-planes to encode. Second, it is inflexible in interactive net browser. Third, It is difficult that this method handles multiple ROIs of any shapes. The general scaling-based method can support multiple ROI coding. But it needs to code every ROI shape, which not only improves coding complexity, but also restricts every ROI shape.

H. Jin et al. (Eds.): NPC 2004, LNCS 3222, pp. 513-516, 2004.
© IFIP International Federation for Information Processing 2004

In this paper, a new method so-call up-down bitplanes Shift (UDBShift) is presented. This new method separates all bitplanes into three parts: Important Significant Bitplanes (ISB), General Significant Bitplanes (GSB) and Least Significant Bitplanes (LSB). The experiment results show that the UDBShift method has three primary advantages: (1) it can support arbitrarily shaped multiple ROI coding with different degrees of interest without coding the ROI shapes; (2) it enables the flexible adjustment of compression quality in every ROI and BG by using appropriate scaling values based on bit rate; (3) it can ensure that all ROIs can be encoded at higher quality than the BG based on requirement. So the UDBShift method is more efficient and flexible than the two standard methods in JPEG2000 for network transmission.

2 Description of UDBShift Method

2.1 UDBShift Method for Single ROI

The UDBShift method is based on the ROI coding theory that at low bit rates, ROI in an image is desired to sustain higher quality than BG, while at the high bit rates, both ROI and BG can be coded with high quality and the difference between them is not very noticeable. First, the wavelet transform is performed, and the transformed coefficients are eventually quantized. Then, all bitplanes are divided into three parts: Important Significant Bitplanes (ISB), General Significant Bitplanes (GSB) and Least Significant Bitplanes (LSB). The certain number bitplanes of ROI called ISBs are upshifted. And some BG bitplanes so-called LSBs are downshifted based on encoding requirement. Finally, The residual significant bitplanes of ROI and BG that are called GSBs are not shifted. Fig.1 shows the ROI coding comparison of the UDBShift method and the PSBShift method [4] for single ROI of an image.

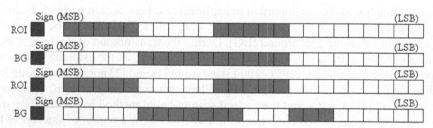

Fig. 1. Comparison of PSBShift method (top) and UDBShift method (bottom) for single ROI

Bitplanes that have not been sent in their entirety, in each subband, are arithmetically encoded again skipping all coefficients that do not belong to the ROI. We can encode every bitplane using arithmetic coding based on context modeling. At the decoder, all bits higher than original MSB will be downshifted until them come back to real value and all bits lower than the original LSB will be up-shifted to real value. If ROI need to have higher quality than BG, the larger scaling value can be used and the results would be closer to the general scaling-based method.

2.2 Multiple ROI Coding Using UDBShift Method

In an image, multiple ROI coding requires multiple ROIs to be coded with different quality according to different degrees of interest. Maxshift method may support multiple ROI coding, but when the number of ROIs increases rapidly, large shifting values that significantly increase the number of total bit-planes to encode is used. Largely increasing the scaling value of wavelet coefficients significantly reduces the compression efficiency. In the worst case, the scaling value of bitplanes may result in bit overflow. In addition, Maxshift only scales all ROI's bitplane using same scaling value. The general scaling-based method can ensure multiple ROI coding in different scaling values, while this method needs to code ROI shape and is only supported by rectangle or ellipse ROI shape in current JPEG 2000 standard. The UDBShift method can support efficient multiple ROI coding by modulate the shifting value of ISBs and LSBs. Fig. 2 shows the method with scaling different bitplanes of three ROIs. First, this method ensures that all ROIs have the same scaling value S_V. And the certain number bitplanes of ROIs are upshifted to ISB based on different degrees of interest of every ROI (Fig. 2 shows that the important significant bitplanes are chosen as $S_1=6, S_2=5, S_3=4$). Second, certain parts of BG bitplanes are downshifted to LSB based on encoding requirement. Finally, The residual significant bitplanes of ROIs and BG that are saved in GSB are not shifted.

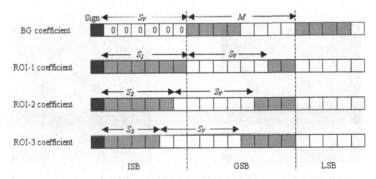

Fig. 2. UDBShift method for three multiple ROI coding ($S_1=6, S_2=5, S_3=4$)

3 Experimental Results and Conclusions

In Fig. 3, one figure gives multiple ROI coding results for Lena from low bit rates to mediate bit rates. Three ROIs are defined in image. The priority order of these ROIs is ROI-1>ROI-2>ROI-3. The up-shifted numbers of ISBs should be chosen as $s_{ROI-1}>s_{ROI-2}>s_{ROI-3}$, e.g., $s_{ROI-1}=6$, $s_{ROI-2}=5$, $s_{ROI-3}=4$. At low bit rates (e.g., bpp<1.0), all ROIs have the higher quality than BG. ROI-1 has the highest quality among three ROIs. When bit rates increases, BG quality increases quickly. This is because the up-shifted numbers of the ISBs of ROI-2, ROI-3 are not large enough. Three ROIs can reach the lossless quality firstly because some least significant BG bitplanes down-shift. The reconstructed quality (PSNR) of three ROIs is given in Fig. 4.

The proposed method can support arbitrarily shaped multiple ROI coding with different degrees of interest without coding the ROI shapes, which is very important to interactive network transmission and the distance servers based on large images. We expect this idea is valuable for future research in ROI coding and its applications.

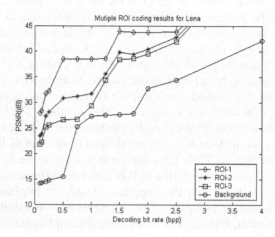

Fig. 3. Multiple ROI coding results for Lena from low bit rates to mediate bit rates

Fig. 4. The reconstructed Lena image with three ROIs. ROI-1 is face region, the ROI-2 is feather region and ROI-3 is hat region using UDBShift method: 0.25 bpp (left), 1.0 bpp (right)

References

1. ISO/IEC, ISO/IEC 15444-1, Information technology JPEG 2000 image coding system-Part 1: Core coding system. http://www.jpeg.org (2003)
2. ISO/IEC JTC 1/SC 29/WC 1 (ITU-Y SC8) JPEG 2000 Part II Final Committee Draft Version 1.0 (2000) December
3. C. Christopoulos, J. Askelf and M. Larsson, Efficient methods for encoding regions of interest in the upcoming JPEG 2000 still image coding standard, IEEE Signal Processing Letters, Vol. 7, no.9 (2000) 247-249
4. L. Liu and G. Fan, A new JPEG 2000 Region of interest image coding method: Partial Significant bitpanes shift, IEEE Signal Processing Letters, Vol. 10, no.4 (2003) 35-38

Bridging the Gap Between Micro and Nanotechnology: Using Lab-on-a-Chip to Enable Nanosensors for Genomics, Proteomics, and Diagnostic Screening

Jonathan M. Cooper, Erik A. Johannessen, and David R.S. Cumming

Department of Electronics and Electrical Engineering, University of Glasgow,
Glasgow, G12 8LT, UK
jmcooper@elec.gla.ac.uk

Abstract. The growing need for accurate and fast methods of DNA and protein determination in the post human genome era has generated considerable interest in the development of new microfluidic analytical platforms, fabricated using methods adapted from the semi-conductor industry. These methods have resulted in the development of the Lab-on-a-Chip concept, a technology which often involves having a miniaturised biochip (as an analytical device), with rather larger instrumentation associated with the control of the associated sensors and of fluidics. This talk will explore the development of new Lab-on-a-Chip platforms for DNA, protein and cell screening, using microfluidics as a packaging technology in order to enable advances in nanoscale science to be implemented in a Lab-on-a-Chip format. The talk will also show how system on a chip methods can be integrated with Lab-on-a-Chip devices to create remote and distributed intelligent sensors, which can be used in a variety of diagnostic applications, including for example chemical sensing within the GI tract.

1. International Context of the Work

The invention of the transistor enabled the first radiotelemetry capsules, which utilised simple circuits for in vivo telemetric studies of the gastro-intestinal (GI) tract [1]. These units could only transmit from a single sensor channel, and were difficult to assemble due to the use of discrete components [2]. The measurement parameters consisted of either temperature, pH or pressure, and the first attempts of conducting real time non-invasive physiological measurements suffered from poor reliability, low sensitivity and short lifetimes of the devices. The first successful pH gut profiles were achieved in 1972 [3], with subsequent improvements in sensitivity and lifetime [4, 5]. Single channel radiotelemetry capsules have since been applied for the detection of disease and abnormalities in the GI tract [6-8] where restricted access prevents the use of traditional endoscopy [9].

Most radiotelemetry capsules utilise laboratory type sensors such as glass pH electrodes, resistance thermometers [10] or moving inductive coils as pressure transducers [11]. The relatively large size of these sensors limits the functional

H. Jin et al. (Eds.): NPC 2004, LNCS 3222, pp. 517-521, 2004.
© IFIP International Federation for Information Processing 2004

complexity of the pill for a given size of capsule. Adapting existing semiconductor fabrication technologies to sensor development [12-17] has enabled the development of highly functional units for data collection, whilst the exploitation of integrated circuitry for sensor control, signal conditioning and wireless transmission [18] has extended the concept of single channel radiotelemetry to remote distributed sensing from microelectronic pills.

2. Current Activity at the University of Glasgow

Our current research on sensor integration and onboard data processing has therefore focused on the development of microsystems capable of performing simultaneous multiparameter physiological analysis [19,20]. The technology has a range of applications in the detection of disease and abnormalities in medical research. The overall aim has been to deliver enhanced functionality, reduced size and power consumption, through system level integration on a common integrated circuit platform comprising sensors, analogue and digital signal processing, and signal transmission. We have already created a platform which comprises a novel analytical microsystem incorporating a four channel microsensor array for real time determination of temperature, pH, conductivity and oxygen (work pioneered by professor Cooper). The sensors were fabricated using electron beam and photolithographic pattern integration, and were controlled by an application specific integrated circuit (ASIC), which sampled the data with 10 bit resolution prior to communication off chip as a single interleaved data stream. An integrated radio transmitter sends the signal to a local receiver (base station), prior to data acquisition on a computer (work pioneered by Dr Cumming). We have now presented real time wireless data transmission from a model *in vitro* experimental set-up, for the first time.

The sensors comprised a silicon diode to measure the body core temperature, whilst also compensating for temperature induced signal changes in the other sensors; an ion selective field effect transistor, ISFET to measure pH; a pair of direct contact gold electrodes to measure conductivity; and a three-electrode electrochemical cell, to detect the level of dissolved oxygen in solution. All of these measurements will, in the future, be used to perform *in vivo* physiological analysis of the GI-tract. For example, temperature sensors will not only be used to measure changes in the body core temperature, but may also be identify local changes associated with tissue inflammation and ulcers. Likewise, the pH sensor may be used for the determination of the presence of pathological conditions associated with abnormal pH levels, particularly those associated with pancreatic disease and hypertension, inflammatory bowel disease, the activity of fermenting bacteria, the level of acid excretion, reflux to the oesophagus, and the effect of GI specific drugs on target organs. The conductivity sensor will be used to monitor the contents of the GI tract by measuring water and salt absorption, bile secretion and the breakdown of organic components into charged colloids. Finally, the oxygen sensor will measure the oxygen gradient from the proximal to the distal GI tract. This will, in future enable a variety of syndromes to be investigated including the growth of aerobic bacteria or bacterial infection concomitant with low oxygen tension, as well as the role of oxygen in the formation of radicals causing cellular injury and pathophysiological conditions (inflammation and gastric ulceration). The implementation of a generic oxygen sensor will also enable the development of first generation enzyme linked amperometric biosensors, thus greatly extending the range of future applications to include e.g. glucose and lactate sensing, as well as immunosensing protocols.

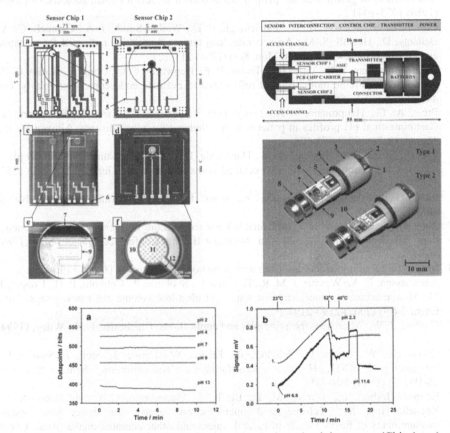

Figure 1: (Top left) showing the ISFET, temperature and conductivity sensor (Chip 1, a,c) and the electrochemical oxygen sensor (Chip 2, b, d). Figures e and f show detail of the pH and oxygen sensor, respectively; (Middle) Schematic (top right) and photo (below) of the Glasgow IDEAS capsule. Although the capsule is currently too large to swallow, the hybrid approach towards its construction provides considerable experimental flexibility. It is estimated that the volume of the pill could be readily reduced by ca. 40% through careful layout of the packaging and surface mount; (Bottom) a recording of pH and temperature using wireless transmission of data from a model gut system, showing the importance of temperature sensing. As expected the response of the pH sensor has a Nernstian dependence on temperature (although the reverse is not true, and the temperature sensor does not have a pH dependence). The Figure also shows that there is no signal cross-talk across the capsule, between sensors, despite the fact that they are located proximal to each other on the chip (and share the same microsystem for signal collection and transmission).

520   J.M. Cooper, E.A. Johannessen, and D.R.S. Cumming

References

1. Mackay, S., Jacobson, B.: Endoradiosonde. Nature 179 (1957) 1239-1240
2. Wolff, H.S.: The radio pill. New Scientist 12 (1961) 419-421
3. Meldrum, S.J., Watson, B. W., Riddle, H. C., Bown, R. L., Sladen, G.E.: pH Profile of gut as measured by radiotelemetry capsule. Brit. Med. Journal 2 (1972) 104-106
4. Evans, D. F., Pye, G., Bramley, R., Clark, A. G., Dyson, T. J., Hardcastle, J. D.: Measurement of gastrointestinal pH profiles in normal ambulant human subjects. Gut 29(8) (1988) 1035-1041
5. Colson, R. H., Watson, B. W., Fairclough, P. D., Walker-Smith, J. A., Campell, C. A., Bellamy, D., Hinsull, S. M.: An accurate, long-term, pH sensitive radio pill for ingestion and implantation. Biotelem. Pat. Mon. 8(4) (1981) 213-227
6. Kadirkamanathan, S. S., Yazaki, E., Evans, D. F., Hepworth, C. C., Gong, F., Swain, C. P.: An ambulant porcine model of acid reflux used to evaluate endoscopic gastroplasty. Gut 44(6) (1999) 782-788
7. Press, A. G., Hauptmann, I. A., Hauptmann, L., Fuchs, B., Ewe, K., Ramadori, G.: Gastrointestinal pH profiles in patients with inflammatory bowel disease. Aliment Pharm. Therap. 12(7) (1998) 673-678
8. Pye, G., Evans, D. F., Ledingham, S., Hardcastle, J. D.: Gastrointestinal intraluminal pH in normal subjects and those with colorectal adenoma or carcinoma. Gut 31(12) (1990) 1355-1357
9. Iddan, G., Meron, G., Glukhovsky, A., Swain, P.: Wireless capsule endoscopy. Nature 405(6785) (2000) 417
10. Zhou, G. X.: Swallowable or implantable body temperature telemeter - Body temperature radio pill. Proc. IEEE Fifteenth Ann. Northeast Bioeng. Conference, Boston, MA, (1989) 165-166
11. Mackay, S.: Radio telemetering from within the body. Science 134 (1961) 1196-1202
12. Johannessen, E. A., Weaver, J. M. R., Bourova, L., Svoboda, P., Cobbold, P. H., Cooper, J. M.: Micromachined nanocalorimetric sensor for ultra-low-volume cell-based assays. Anal. Chem. 74(9) (2002) 2190-2197
13. Gardner, J. W.: Microsensors: principles and applications. Chichester, U.K.: Wiley, (1994) 1-331
14. Gumbrecht, W., Peters, D., Schelter, W., Erhard, W., Henke, J., Steil, J., Sykora, U.: Integrated pO2, pCO2, pH sensor system for online blood monitoring. Sens. Actuators B, 18-19(1-3) (1994) 704-708
15. Belmont-Herbert, C., Tercier, M. L., Buffle, J., Fiaccabrino, G. C., de Rooij, N. F., Koudelka-Hep, M.: Gel-integrated microelectrode arrays for direct voltammetric measurements of heavy metals in natural waters and other complex media. Anal. Chem. 70(14) (1998) 2949-2956
16. Jobst, G., Urban, G., Jachimowicz, A., Kohl, F., Tilado, O.: Thin film Clark-type oxygen sensor based on novel polymer membrane systems for in vivo and biosensor applications. Biosens. Bioelectron. 8(3-4) (1993) 123-128
17. Bergveld, P.: Development, operation, and application of the ion-sensitive field effect transistor as a tool for electrophysiology. IEEE Trans. Biomed. Eng. 19 (1972) 342-351
18. Asada, G., Burstein, A., Chong, D., Dong, M., Fielding, M., Kruglick, E., Ho, J., Lin, F. , Lin, T. H., Marcy, H., Mukai, R., Nelson, P., Newbery, F., Pister, K. S. J., Pottie, G., Sarcelize, H., Stafsudd, O. M., Valoff, S., Young, G., Kaiser, W. J.: Low power wireless communication and signal processing circuits for distributed microsystems. IEEE Int. Symp. Circuits and Systems 4 (1997) 2817-2820

19. Tang, T.B., Johannessen, E.A., Wang, L., Astaras, A., Beaumont, S., Murray, A.F, Cooper, J.M., Cumming, D.R.S.: Miniature Wireless Integrated Multisensor Microsystem for Industrial and Biomedical Applications. IEEE Transactions in Sensors **2** (2003) 628-635
20. Johannessen, E.A., Tang, T.B., Wang, L., Astaras, A., Beaumont, S., Murray, A.F, Cumming, D.R.S., Cooper, J.M.: Remote Distributed Sensors for Biological Measurement in a Microsystems Format. Accepted in IEEE Transactions in Biology and Medicine, 2003

The Development of Biosensors and Biochips in IECAS*

Xinxia Cai, Dafu Cui

State Key Lab of Transducer Technology
Institute of Electronics, Chinese Academy of Sciences (IECAS)
P.O. Box 2652, Beijing 100080, China
xxcai@mail.ie.ac.cn

Abstract In this paper, the thin film electrode disposable biosensors capable with low cost, high reliability, robustness, low volume sample and hand-held multichannel meter were developed. Various biomolecules, such as glucose, lactate, b-hydroxybutyrate, cholesterol, hemoglobin and creatine kinase in low volume (less than 3 µL) have been detected. It is significant for the applications in home health care, clinical diagnostics and physiological identification and physical performance of athlete. Biochips based on micro-electro-mechanical-systems (MEMS) technology supply novel biochemical analytical technologies, which offer many advantages including high sample throughput, high integration, and reduced cost. Biochips are rapidly developed in recent years. This paper also will show the research results of biochips based on MEMS technology, including DNA purification chips, DNA-PCR chips, capillary electrophoresis chips, PCR-CE chips, LAPS (light addressable potential sensor) for DNA detection, DNA SPR (surface plasmon resonance) and DNA FET (field effect transistor) sensors. These biochips have potential applications in health care diagnosis, environment monitoring, gene sequencing and high through drug screening.

1. The Research and Development of Biosensors in IECAS

It is known that biosensors will be integrated and miniaturized, and be used to replace existing, more time consuming analytical methods for monitoring and detecting [1, 2]. In this work, the thin film electrode biosensors with 2-electrode construction and hand-held meter were developed. The surface of the working electrode of the biosensor, modified with nanoscale materials of electrodeposited platinum or carboxymethylcellulose (CMC), has the porous performance and has excellent hydrophilicity, thus the electrode possesses huge surface and high catalytic activities for electrolytic processes.

---

* This work is supported by the Hi-Tech R. & D. Program of China (2002AA404510, 2002AA302106), the NSFC (60276039, 20299030, and 60341005), the Chinese Academy of Sciences (KGCX2-SW-602-2), the SRF for ROCS of SEM and the Ministry of Personnel of China.

H. Jin et al. (Eds.): NPC 2004, LNCS 3222, pp. 522–525, 2004.
© IFIP International Federation for Information Processing 2004

Various biomolecules, such as glucose [3], lactate [3], b-hydroxybutyrate [4], cholesterol [4], hemoglobin [7] and creatine kinase [8] in low volume were detected as shown in Table 1[5]. Compared with the strips in market and the existing analytical instruments, the produced disposable biosensors (Figure 1a) are capable with low cost, high reliability, robustness, low volume sample and the created portable multichannel meters (Figure 1b) can be used for test human metabolites without reagents. It is significant for the applications in home health care, clinical diagnostics and physiological identification and physical performance of athlete. Also it has the potential applications in food, beverage, environmental, pharmaceutical, bioprocess and antiterrorism.

Table 1. The biosensors characteristics achieved [5]

Test Molecules	Sample Solution	Nanoscale Materials	Test Time	Measurement Range	Correlation Coefficient
Glucose	Buffer	Pt nanoparticals	12 s	0.5~12 mM	0.998
	Serum	Pt nanoparticals	27 s	1~30 mM	0.965
Lactate	Buffer	Pt nanoparticals	15 s	0.5~15 mM	0.998
	Serum	Pt nanoparticals	25 s	0.5~10 mM	0.988
β-hydroxybutyrate	Buffer	Pt nanoparticals	20 s	0.01~4 mM	0.999
	Serum	Pt nanoparticals	20 s	0.01~6 mM	0.946
Cholesterol	Buffer	Pt nanoparticals	30 s	0.1~5 mM	0.995
Hemoglobin	Buffer	Nanoporous CMC	90 s	10μM~3 mM	0.995
Creatine kinase	Buffer	Nanoporous CMC	140 s	8~800 U/mL	0.980
			280 s	8~800 U/L	0.960

(a)   (b)

Figure 1. The photos of the thin film electrode biosensors fabricated in laboratory throughput and the meter: (a) the disposable biosensors packed in vacuum; (b) the portable multichannel meter.

2. Current Research on Biochips in IECAS

Biochips based on micro-electro-mechanical-systems (MEMS) technology supply novel biochemical analytical technologies, which offer many advantages including high sample throughput, high integration, and reduced cost. Biochips are rapidly developed in recent years [9]. The research results of biochips based on MEMS technology are described as below:

(1)   Two types of DNA purification chips based on solid phase extraction (SPE) technology have been fabricated and studied. Both two chips were used to purify the DNA from PCR products. The silicon chip was also used to purify DNA from yeast bacteria.

(2)   DNA-PCR chip were fabricated on glass and silicon substrates using MEMS technology (Figure 2a), and a portable temperature controller (Figure 2b) for PCR chip has been developed [10]. PCR reaction has been realized successfully in this system.

(3)   PDMS electrophoresis microchip was constructed by molding method. A novel method to fabricate PDMS sandwiched microfluidic chip was presented and the microchip has been demonstrated as a capillary electrophoresis device for double-stranded DNA (dsDNA) and amino acid separation (Figure 3) [11].

(4)   Fundamental research of integrated chip, including materials compatibility and microfabricated process possibility has been done. PDMS sandwiched PCR-CE chip and PCR-CE electrochemical detection chip have been designed and microfabricated.

(5)   Novel technologies for DNA detection, including light addressable potential sensor (LAPS), SPR sensors and DNA FET, have been developed and good results have been obtained.

The above research on biochips based on MEMS, has laid a foundation for potential applications in health care diagnosis, environment monitoring, gene sequencing and high through drug screening.

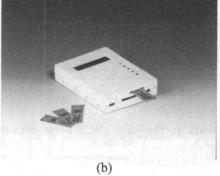

(a)   (b)

Figure 2. (a) The mounted chip of DNA-PCR; (b) a photo of the thermal circler. [10]

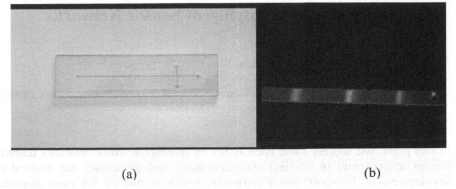

(a)   (b)

Figure 3. (a) The photo of PDMS microchip for DNA separation; (b) the separation image of DNA fragments labeled by SYBR Green I. [11]

References

1. Cooper, J.M.: Towards Electronic Petri-dishes and Picolitre-scale Single-cell Technologies. Trends in Biotechnology, 17(6), (1999) 226-230.
2. Wang, E.K.: Biosensors. Analytical Chemistry in the 21st Century, Science Press, Beijing (2001) 216-227
3. Nenggao Rao, Rihui Xi, Huaqing Li, Li Wang, Xinxia Cai, Thin-film biosensor array for the determination of glucose and L-lactate, The 6th East Asian Conference on Chemical Sensors, Guilin, China. (2005). Accepted.
4. Li, H., Wang, L., Rao, N., Cui, D., Cai, X.: Thin-film Biosensor Array for Simultaneous Amperometric Measurement of β-hydroxybutyrate and Cholesterol. The 6th East Asian Conference on Chemical Sensors, Guilin, China. (2005). Accepted.
5. Cui, X.: Thin Film Electrode Biosensors with Nanoscale Materials. The Second International Forum on Post-Genome Technologies (2'IFPT)—Genomic Analysis and Bio-Nanoscience, Nanjing, China, (2004) 231-232.
6. Li, H., Yang, Q., Luo, X., Liu, C., Jiang, L., Cui, D., Cai, X.: Multi-channel Electrochemical Detection System Based on LabView. Proceedings of 2004 International Conference on Information Acquisition. Hefei, China, (2004) 224-227.
7. Jiang, L., Liu, C., Li, H., Luo, X., Wu, Y., Cai, X.: Performance of Amperometric Biosensors for Determination of Hemoglobin, The Second International Forum on Post-Genome Technologies (2'IFPT)—Genomic Analysis and Bio-Nanoscience, Nanjing, China, (2004) 287-289.
8. Liu, C., Jiang, L., Li, H., Luo, X., Cai, X.: Measurement of Creatine Kinase Using Disposable Electrochemical Biosensor. The Second International Forum on Post-Genome Technologies (2'IFPT)—Genomic Analysis and Bio-Nanoscience, Nanjing, China, (2004) 277-279.
9. Gregory, T.A. Kovacs: Chemical and Biosensors and Actuators. Micromachined Transducers Sourcebook. McGraw-Hill Companies Inc., (1998)
10. Zhao, Z., Cui, Z., Cui, D., Xia, S.: Monolithically Integrated PCR Biochip for DNA Amplification. Sensors and Actuators A **108** (2003) 162-167.
11. Liu, C., Cui, D.: Separation Imaging of DNA Fragments in Poly (Dimethylsiloxane) Microchip. Proceedings of 2004 International Conference on Information Acquisition, Hefei, China, (2004) 205-207.

Open Issues on Intelligent Sensor Networks

Yiqiang Chen, Wen Gao, Junfa Liu

Institute of Computing Technology, Chinese Academy of Sciences, Beijing, China, 100080
{yqchen, wgao, jfliu}@ict.ac.cn

In this paper, we address some open issues on intelligent sensor networks research. Recent advancement in wireless communications and electronics has enabled the development of low-cost sensor networks, which is one of the most important technologies for 21st century. The sensor networks can be used in various application areas, such as security and surveillance applications, smart classroom, monitoring of natural habitats and ecosystems, medical monitoring etc. Although there have been great improvements in research on sensor networks, there still lie some open issues need to be solved to make the whole system works well. First is sensor node platform. The key issue is about how to design and implement a kind of cheaper node than the Berkeley Motes and iPaq-based Sensor Node that are two famous platforms. Second is energy awareness. Energy efficiency is the crucial problem in sensor networks. There are various sources of energy consumption in sensor networks, such as Processing Unit, Radio, Sensors, Actuators. Some results show that the actuation energy is the highest and the communication energy is the next. Node-level techniques and Network-level techniques are employed for various efficient energy management methods. Third are the time and space issues. Time synchronization is a critical piece of infrastructure of sensor network. Almost all forms of sensor data fusion and coordinated actuation require synchronized physical time for reasoning about events in the physical world. The clock accuracy and precision requirements are often more crucial in sensor networks than in traditional distributed systems. The space issues comprise the node localization and sensor coverage problems. They are both essential to support services and applications in sensor networks. Fourth are the protocols of sensor networks. The protocol stack consists of the physical layer, data link layer, network layer, transport layer and application layer. The physical layer addresses the needs of simple but robust modulation, transmission, and receiving techniques. Since the environment is noisy and sensor nodes can be mobile, the medium access control (MAC) protocol must be power-aware and able to minimize collision with neighbors' broadcasts. The network layer takes care of routing the data supplied by the transport layer. The transport layer helps to maintain the flow of data if a sensor networks application requires it. Depending on different sensing tasks, different types of application software can be built and used on the application layer. The last issue is the collaborative signal processing. The nodes in sensor network must collaborate to collect and process data to generate useful information. Important technical issues include the degree of information sharing between nodes and how nodes fuse the information from other nodes. Also one needs to consider the tradeoffs between the better system performance and the resource limitation in collaborative signal and information processing. The above all will make the system more intelligent.

H. Jin et al. (Eds.): NPC 2004, LNCS 3222, pp. 526-526, 2004.

Enabling Anytime Anywhere Wireless Sensor Networks

John Crawford

Crossbow Technology, Inc., 41 Daggett Drive, San Jose, CA 95134 USA
www.xbow.com

Abstract. A self-configuring wireless sensor network (WSN) system will be presented. This "smart-dust" system, deployed in more than 500 installations, and based on the UC Berkeley, open-source TinyOS embedded operating system, is the most widely used WSN worldwide. Applications and their requirements and characteristics will be presented, along with markets and the latest technology. Key technical issues with real-world deployments will be explored.

H. Jin et al. (Eds.): NPC 2004, LNCS 3222, pp. 527-527, 2004.

A Query-Aware Routing Algorithm in Sensor Networks

Jinbao Li [1,2], Jianzhong Li [1,2], Shengfei Shi [1]

[1] Harbin Institute of Technology, 150001, Harbin, China
[2] Heilongjiang University, 150080, Harbin, China
lijb6912@vip.sina.com, lijzh@hit.edu.cn

Abstract. Wireless sensor networks have become increasingly popular due to the variety applications in both military and civilian fields. Routing algorithms are critical for enabling the successful operations of sensor networks. A number of routing algorithms have been proposed. However, all the routing algorithms are considered in isolation from the particular communication needs of the data management. This paper focuses on the design of the routing algorithms considering the needs of processing data query in sensor networks. A query-aware routing algorithm is proposed. The algorithm has the following advantages comparing with other routing algorithms. First, it processes as many queries as possible while routing. Second, the broadcast is executed locally so that the energy required by globe broadcasts is saved. Third, routing is executed by searching and generating a binary-tree and only two boundary nodes selected to broadcast message when broadcast is needed so that the number of broadcast is reduced dramatically and the cover range of local broadcast is increased. Finally, multiple routing paths for many routing requirements are found by merging routing requirements and through only one random walk in the sensor network. Experimental results show that the proposed algorithm has better performance and scalibility than other routing algorithms.

1 Introduction

Recent advances in micro-electronics and wireless technologies enable the creation of small, cheap, and smart sensors. In the past few years, smart sensor devices have matured to the point that it is now possible to deploy large, distributed sensor networks in an ad-hoc fashion. These sensors monitor various measurements such as temperature, pressure, humidity, movement, noise level, chemical and etc. Such networks pose new challenges in data processing and dissemination because of their limited resources such as processing ability, bandwidth and energy. Even though each single sensor has limited capabilities, the network consisting of a large number of such sensors are powerful enough to deal with complex monitoring missions. Wireless sensor networks have become increasingly popular due to their variety applications in both military and civilian fields ranging from battlefield surveillance to natural habitat monitoring. Sensor networks are attracting more and more attentions.

Routing is critical for enabling successful operations of sensor networks. Traditional routing schemes are not suitable for sensor networks, so many new routing algorithms have been developed [1, 2, 3, 4, 5].

H. Jin et al. (Eds.): NPC 2004, LNCS 3222, pp. 528-535, 2004.

The directed diffusion routing algorithm is proposed in [1], which provides a mechanism for doing a limited flood of a query toward the event and then setting up reverse gradients to send data back along the best route. This algorithm employs the techniques of the initial low-rate data flooding and gradual reinforcement of better paths to accommodate certain levels of network and sink dynamics. In order to find the best path, this routing algorithm resorts to flooding the query throughout the entire network. Directed diffusion results in high quality paths, but requires an initial flood of the query for exploration.

The Geo-Routing algorithms were considered in [9] and [10]. Geo-Routing algorithms rely on localized nodes, and provide savings over a complete network flood by limiting the flooding to a geographical region, but they do not work without the geography information of sensor nodes.

[2] proposed a random routing algorithm, Rumor Routing. Rumor routing intends to work in conjunction with diffusion, bringing innovations from GRAB[11] and GOSSIP[12] routing to this context. In Rumor Routing, each node maintains a neighbor table and an event table. The event table is generated by an agent. The agent broadcasts an event to the farther nodes and builds up an event table. A query can use the information in its neighbor's table and the event table to form a route path. If the querying node has a path to the sink, then the sink is looked up in this path directly. Otherwise, a neighbor node of it is selected to continue querying. Rumor Routing requires to maintain a neighbor table and an event neighbor table, which consumes too much energy.

[3] described TTDD, a Two-Tier Data Dissemination approach that provides data delivery to multiple mobile sinks. Each data source in TTDD proactively builds a grid structure which enables the mobile sinks to continuously receive data on the move by flooding queries within a local cell only. TTDD handles multiple mobile sinks efficiently, but it is only suitable for sensor networks without mobile sensor nodes.

[5] implemented a cluster based routing algorithm. The basic idea is to divide sensor nodes in a network into some clusters. Each cluster is managed by a head. Routing is executed by the head. In this routing method, not only does the maintenance of clusters require much cost, but also the head may become a bottleneck of the processing information and communication.

[4] provided a routing mechanism to obtain the information in sensor networks, ACQUIRE, which considers each query as an active entity. This entity searches result by transmitting query (in random or other way) in the network. In ACQUIRE, a neighbor table is maintained dynamically at each intermediate node. This table contains the neighbors within d hops away from this node. Each active entity can use its neighbors to generate part of query result. When the query result is completely generated, it is returned to the querying node along the reversed path. ACQUIRE generates efficient routes by selecting a proper d and refresh the frequency c, but it is not suitable for the case with high refresh frequency ($0.08 < c < 1$).

In summary, all the current routing algorithms, except the one in [4], considered the energy efficiency and extending the network lifetime in isolation from the particular communication needs of the data management and loss the opportunity for cross-layer optimization to design and adapt routing algorithms to the particular routing needs of the data management layer. Although [4] considered the query processing while routing, it is not suitable for the case with high refresh frequency ($0.08 < c < 1$).

This paper focuses on the design of the routing algorithms taking account of the needs of processing data query in sensor networks. A query-aware routing algorithm is proposed. The algorithm has the following advantages comparing with other routing algorithms. First, it processes as many queries as possible while routing. Second, the broadcast is executed locally so that the energy required by globe broadcasts is saved. Third, routing is executed by searching and generating a binary-tree and only two boundary nodes selected to broadcast message when broadcast is needed so that the number of broadcast is reduced dramatically and the cover range of local broadcast is increased. Finally, multiple routing paths for many routing requirements are found by merging routing requirements and through only one random walk in the sensor network. Experimental results show that the proposed algorithm has high performance and scalibility than other routing algorithms.

2   Query-Aware Routing Algorithm

All nodes in sensor networks are assumed to be homogeneous and uniformly distributed. S is the sink and D is the source. Routing from S to D is to find a multi-hop path from S to D. In this paper, routing not only is considered as a simple path seeking, but also executes queries with routing. We call this kind of routing as query-aware routing. Query-aware routing is considered as searching on a dynamic generated binary tree whose nodes are sensor nodes in the sensor network with S as the root and search target as leaves. Since D is the search target, D must be on a leaf. Routing from S to D is a procesure of depth first (or width first) search. With an increase in the depth, the binary tree will increase. Once D is found, the routing is successful, D becomes a leaf node and the multi-hop path is generated. If predefined search depth is reached without finding D, the search fails and a failure message is sent to S. We first discuss some basic concepts and then give the query-aware routing algorithm DFRS in details.

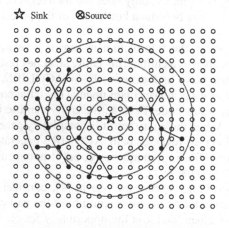

Fig. 1 DFRS

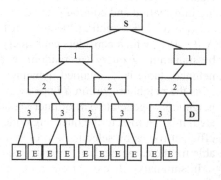

Fig. 2 Routing-Tree

A **Routing Tree** is a binary tree randomly generated for routing. The height of the tree is denoted as *Hop_End* in the rest of the paper. The generation procedure of a routing tree in a sensor network is shown in fig.1. An example routing tree is shown in fig.2.

Sink node *S* is the node which sends routing request to the source node, which is the root of the routing tree. *S* is the start node of a route.

Target node *D* is the destination node of a routing, which is on the leaf of the routing tree.

The minimum routing search depth, *Hop_End*, is determined by the diameter *R* of the sensor network and the effective transmission radius *r*, i.e. *Hop_End* = *R/r*. In actual applications, the search depth is often more than *R/r*, that is *Hop_End* = $(1+\varepsilon)R/r$, where $0<\varepsilon<1$ is a constant.

A **boundary node of a node *n*** is a node in the node set *B*, where *B=C-c*, *C* is the node set in the circle with radius *r*, *c* is the node set in the circle with radius *r-a*, *r* is the communication radius of *n*, and *a<r* is a parameter.

In sensor networks, nodes exchange and transmit messages with their neighbors. A message has *message type* and *message content*. Message type includes *RRQ, RRRQ, FR* and *NT*. The message content of a message of type *RRQ* is composed by *sink node id (SID), target node id (DID), query id (QID), query (Query)*, and *current search depth H*. The message content of a message of type *RRRQ* is composed by *sink node id (SID), query node id (QID)*, and *returned result (Result)*. The message content of a message of type *FR* is composed by *target node id (DID)* and *Query or Result*. A message of type *NT* is composed by *node id (NID)* and *node type (NodeType)*. If *NodeType=boundary*, the corresponding node is a boundary node.

After the sink sends *RRQ* request to its neighbors, the nodes that accept the *RRQ* message process the message content with the following algorithm DFRS. *H* in the *RRQ* is computed by $(1+\varepsilon)R/r$.

```
Algorithm DFRS
Input: RRQ message, RRRQ message, FR message or NT message.
Output: Send the processed RRQ, RRRQ, FR or NT message out.
1 MessageProcessing(Message) {//function invoked after current node
    m receive message from i
2   if (haveMultiMessage())
3     Merge the message to sigle message;
4   while (Message){
5     if (Message.Type == RRRQ) { // Message is a message of RRRQ
6       if (Message.Message.SID==m.ID)//m is the node which sends
      the message
7         ProcessResult(Message) //process query result.
8       else
9         Send(Message,i);  //transmit message RRRQ to parent node
10    }
11    else if (Message.Type == RRQ) {  // Message is RRQ message
12      if(m.ID == Message.DID) {  // m is target node
13        Result=Process(Message.Query); //process query
14        CreateMessage(RMessage);   //construct RRRQ message
15        Send(RMessage,i);}   //return query result to parent i
16      if(Message.H>0 && HaveBoundaryNode(Message.QID)){
17        Message.H--;
18        CreateMessage(RMessage); //construct FR message, trans-
    mit RRQ
19        if (m.B(l))
20          Send(RMessage,m.B(l));  //search sub-trees in left
    first order
21        else if (m.B(r))
```

```
22              Send(RMessage,m.B(r));  //search sub-trees in right
        first order
23            else{//select two boundary points of m, m.B(l) and
        m.B(r)
24              SelectBoundaryNode(BoundaryNodeBuffer);
25              Send(RMessage,m.B(l));}  // search sub-trees in left
        first order
26            }
27          else if (IsBoundary(m)) {  //m is boundary node of i
28            CreateMessage(RMessage);  //construct RM message:m is
        boundary node
29            Send(RMessage,i);}//inform parent,m is boundary node
30         if(Mesage.H==0){//reach max search depth, search right sub-
        tree
31            Mesage.H++;          //refresh H of RRQ
32            UpdateMessage(RMessage);
33            Send(Message,i);}
34          }
35          else if(Message.Type == FR){
36            Send(Message.Message,0) //transmit PRQ to neighbors of m
37            Timer(T0);} //waiting for result from boundary node
38          else if(Message.Type == RM && Message.NodeType == boundary)
39            Store(Message.NID) //store boundary node of m to Bound-
        aryNodeBuffer
40          Message = Message->next;
41        }
42  }
```

Fig.1 and Fig. 2 illustrate the routing procedure of DFRS. From the sink *S*, the routing tree is depth first traversed. The traversal of the routing tree is also a procedure of the generation of this tree. When traversing the routing tree, once the target node is found, the traversal is finished when the tree is generated.

During the traversal of the routing tree, if multiple queries can be executed concurrently, the efficiency will be improved. Based on the above idea, the routing requests from other nodes are merged dynamically when executing the routing. That is, once the routing requests are satisfied, these routing requests are merged to the executing routing request. In the following routing process, once the target node of some routing is reached, then the query result is returned while the other routing requests continue being executed until all the target nodes are found or the specified search depth is reached.

In DFRS, the following strategies are used to reduce the number of broadcasts to save energy.

(1). Process as many queries as possible while routing so that the routes are sufficiently used and the required energy is reduced.

(2). Broadcast is executed locally so that the energy required by globe broadcasts is saved.

(3). Transmit message by boundary nodes so that the cover range of local broadcast is increased and the number of repeatedly received messages is decreased.

(4). Routing is executed by searching and generating a binary-tree. Only two boundary nodes selected to broadcast message when broadcast is needed, and thus the number of broadcast is reduced dramatically.

(5). Multiple routing paths for multiple routing requirements are found by merging routing requirements and through one random walk in the sensor network.

3   Experiments and Analysis

In order to test the proposed algorithm DFRS, a simulation environment for sensor networks is built. The number of the nodes in the sensor networks is varied from 1850 to 7400, and all nodes are distributed within an area of $x \times 750$, where x is from 1000 to 4000. For simplicity, the nodes in the network are uniformly deployed in a grid with size 20×20.

The following assumptions are used for the experiments: (1) each transmitted message during routing is in one package; (2) it consumes one unit of energy to transmit one package; (2) no energy is consumed when a node receives a package; (4) effective communication radius of all the nodes are 100 units of length; (5) initial energy of each node is 150 units of energy; (6) the target node and sink node of a routing are generated randomly.

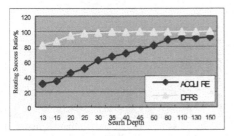

Fig. 3 Routing Success Ratio,N=1850

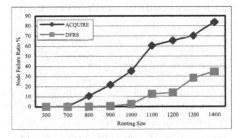

Fig. 4 Node Failure Ratio, N=1850

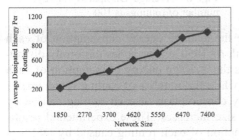

Fig. 5 Routing Success Ratio , the number of routings is 1000

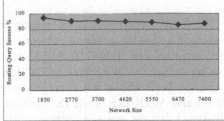

Fig. 6 Average Dissipated Energy, the number of routings is 1000

The first experiment is to investigate the success ratios of DFRS and ACQUIRE in a simulation sensor network with $N=1850$ sensor nodes uniformly distributed in an area of 1000×750. DFRS and ACQUIRE are executed in the simulation sensor network. Fig. 3 shows the success ratios of DFRS and ACQUIRE while search depth varied from 13 to 150 without any failure node. From fig.3, it can be seen that DFRS has higher success ratio than ACQUIRE. The success ratio of DFRS is much higher than ACQUIRE in case of the search depth being smaller.

The second experiment is to investigate the ratio of the disabled nodes during routing in a simulation sensor network with N=1850 sensor nodes uniformly distributed in an area of 1000×750. Fig 4 shows the ratios of the disabled nodes by running DFRS and ACQUIRE while increasing the number of routings with same success ratio. Fig. 4 illustrated that the ratio of disabled nodes caused by ACQUIRE higher than that caused by DFRS, and thus DFRS keeps the sensor network having longer lifetime.

The third experiment is to investigate the scalibility of DFRS in a simulation sensor network with the number of sensor nodes varying from 1850 to 7400 and the size of deployment area of the sensor nodes varying from 1000×750 to 4000×750 correspondingly in terms of the success ratio and energy consumption. Fig.5 shows the success ratio of DFRS while the number of sensor nodes varies from 1850 to 7400. The experimental results show that the success ratio of DFRS keeps about 90% while the network size varies. Fig 6 shows that the average energy consumption of DFRS increases linearly when the size of the network varies. The experimental results tell that the scalibility of DFRS is very high.

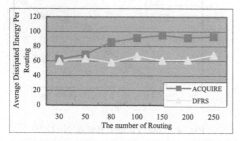

Fig. 7 Average Dissipated Energy, N=1000   **Fig. 8** Average Dissipated Energy, the number of routings is 100

The fourth experiment is to investigate the average energy consumption of each routing in a simulation sensor network with N=1850 sensor nodes uniformly distributed in an area of 1000×750. Fig.7 shows the average energy consumption of each routing caused by DFRS and ACQUIRE while the number of routing requirements increases. Fig.8 shows the average energy consumption of each routing caused by DFRS and ACQUIRE while the network size increases. These experimental results illustrated that the average energy consumption of each routing caused by DFRS is much lower than that caused by ACQUIRE.

4   Conclusion

A query aware routing algorithm, DFRS, is presented in this paper. DFRS not only considers the energy efficiency and extending the network lifetime but also considers the particular communication needs of the query processing in sensor networks. The experimental results show that DFRS has better performance and scalibility.

References

1. Chalermek Intanagonwiwat, Ramesh Govindan, Deborah Estrin, John Heidemann, and Fabio Silva, Directed Diffusion for Wireless Sensor networks, *ACM/IEEE Transactions on Networking, 11* (1), pp. 2-16, February, 2002.
2. David Braginsky and Deborah Estrin, Rumor Routing Algorithm For Sensor networks, *In Proceedings of the First Workshop on Sensor networkss and Applications (WSNA), September 28 2002*
3. HaiYun Luo, A Two-Tier Data Dissemination Model for Large-scale Wireless Sensor networkss, *ACM MOBICOM (International Conference on Mobile Computing and Networking) 2002*, Atlanta, Georgia, Sep. 2002
4. N. Sadagopan, B. Krishnamachari, A. Helmy, The ACQUIRE Mechanism for Efficient Querying in Sensor networkss, *First IEEE International Workshop on Sensor networks Protocols and Applications (SNPA), in conjunction with IEEE ICC 2003*, May 2003, Anchorage, AK, USA.
5. M. Younis, M. Youssef, K. Arisha, Energy-Aware Routing in Cluster-Based Sensor networks, *Proceedings of the 10th IEEE/ACM International Symposium on Modeling, Analysis and Simulation of Computer and Telecommunication Systems (MASCOTS2002)*, Fort Worth, Texas, October 2002.
6. A. Helmy, S. Garg, P. Pamu, N. Nahata, "Contact Based Architecture for Resource Discovery (CARD) in Large Scale MANets", Third IEEE/ACM International Workshop on Wireless, Mobile and Ad Hoc Networks (WMAN), part of IEEE/ACM IPDPS 2003, April 2003, Nice, France.
7. Lan F. Akyildiz, Weilian Su, Yogesh Sankarasubramaniam, Erdal Cayirci, A Survey on Sensor networks. IEEE Communications Magazine, August 2002.
8. Rajgopal Kannan, Ramaraju Kalidindi, S. S. Iyengar and V. Kumar, Energy and Rate based MAC Protocol for Wireless Sensor Networks, *ACM SIGMOD Record* Vol. 32 No. 4, pp. 60-65 (2003).
9. Yan Yu, Ramesh Govindan and Deborah Estrin.Geographical and Energy Aware Routing: A Recursive Data Dissemination Protocol for Wireless Sensor Networks. UCLA Computer Science Department Technical Report UCLA/CSD-TR-01-0023, May 2001.
10. Brad Karp and II. T. Kung. GPSR: Greedy perimeter stateless routing for wireless networks. In *Proceedings of the ACM/IEEE International Conference on Mobile Computing and Network ing*, pages 243–254, Boston, Mass., USA, August 2000
11. "GRAdient Broadcast: A Robust, Long-lived Large Sensor Network", http://irl.cs.ucla.edu/papers/grab-tech-report.ps
12. M. Lin, K. Marzullo, S. Masini. Gossip versus deterministic flooding: Low message overhead and high reliability for broadcasting on small networks. UCSD Technical Report TR CS99- 0637. http://citeseer.nj.nec.com/278404.html

Sensors Network Optimization by a Novel Genetic Algorithm

Hui Wang[a], Anna L. Buczak[b1], Hong Jin[a], Hongan Wang[a], Baosen Li[c]

[a] Institute of Software, Chinese Academy of Sciences
wanghui@ios.cn
[b] Lockheed Martin Advanced Technology Laboratories, Cherry Hill, NJ 08002
[c] Zibo Electric Power Compnay, 61 Xin Cun Xi Lu, Zibo.Shandong, 255032

Abstract. This paper describes the optimization of a sensor network by a novel Genetic Algorithm (GA) that we call King Mutation C2. For a given distribution of sensors, the goal of the system is to determine the optimal combination of sensors that can detect and/or locate the objects. An optimal combination is the one that minimizes the power consumption of the entire sensor network and gives the best accuracy of location of desired objects. The system constructs a GA with the appropriate internal structure for the optimization problem at hand, and King Mutation C2 finds the quasi-optimal combination of sensors that can detect and/or locate the objects. The study is performed for the sensor network optimization problem with five objects to detect/track and the results obtained by a canonical GA and King Mutation C2 are compared.

1 Introduction

During the last four decades there has been a growing interest in algorithms that rely on analogies to natural phenomena. One type of such algorithms is the Genetic Algorithms (GAs) that imitate the principles of natural evolution [9, 7]. GA has been widely used for combinatorial optimization, structural design, scheduling and other engineering problems [8, 13].

In this paper we are approaching the problem of optimization of a sensor network by Genetic Algorithms from a practical standpoint: we are interested in obtaining the quasi-optimal solutions fast. The sensor network is comprised of randomly distributed unattended ground sensors that are remotely deployed and after deployment their location is known. Objects in a space are monitored by limited numbers of those low cost - low power sensors. The advantages of using several of those sensors outweigh the expected performance degradation since a system of several inexpensive sensors in the same area offers a redundancy that provides acceptable performance. The complete system consists of modules that perform self-organization, object tracking, track fusion, ID fusion, communication, etc. [4]. This paper focuses on the optimization of sensor selection performed by genetic algorithms in the Self-Organization module.

---

[1] This work was performed by Anna L. Buczak when she was with Honeywell Laboratories.

H. Jin et al. (Eds.): NPC 2004, LNCS 3222, pp. 536–543, 2004.

2 Optimization of a Sensor Network

We are performing optimization of a sensor network. The network is comprised of remotely deployed unattended ground sensors that can be used for object detection, tracking and identification. A sensor can be used for tracking an object, if this object resides in the sensor's field-of-view (FOV) and if the sensor is turned on. The sensor network adapts its structure in order to achieve the goals specified by a human. Sensor selection is often performed in order to minimize the power consumption of the sensor network, by choosing the sensors that need to be turned on or off at a given moment in time.

The goal of optimization is to find sensors for tracking all the objects identified in network objective (that can be seen as the optimization goal) in a way that optimizes certain metrics. In case of object tracking two metrics should be optimized: the accuracy of object tracking and the power utilization of the sensor network. This multi-objective optimization is performed by Genetic Algorithms. For each object identified in network objective, optimization has to find m sensors needed for accurate tracking of objects. The value of m depends on the physical characteristics of the sensors used.

Our problem falls in the category of combinatorial optimization problems: the system has to choose tuples of sensors that need to be on. There is a need of one tuple per object and the same sensor can be used for multiple objects as long as these objects are within its FOV. If we have k objects and we need m sensors per object, 1 to k m-tuples are needed. The size of the search space is described by:

$$SearchSpace = \prod_{i=1}^{k} (NumberOfMTuplesForIthObject) = \prod_{i=1}^{k} \binom{n}{m} = \prod_{i=1}^{k} \left(\frac{n_i!}{(n_i - m)! \cdot m!} \right) \quad (1)$$

where ni is number of sensors that can detect object i. The search space is exponentially increasing with the number of sensors and objects, discontinuous, with non-ordered (feature type) parameters.

3 Internal GA Structure for Sensor Network Optimization

In our design each individual of the Genetic Algorithm population is comprised of several genes. Each of the genes contains on sensor's identification. All the sensors, which are chosen by GA to be active at a given moment, have their identification coded in the genes. There is a unique identification associated with each sensor and the genes use a binary encoding for identification.

The GA's internal structure (i.e. number of genes) depends on Network Objective. Whenever this objective changes, the number of genes of the GA also changes. Network Objective includes a list of suspected objects and required operations associated with them. If the operation is to locate the object, there are as many genes as necessary for location, for example in case of acoustic bearing sensors this number is three (Fig1).

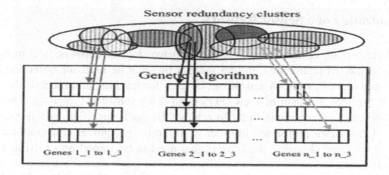

Fig. 1. Internal structure of GA for location

When performing object tracking we encounter a multi-objective optimization problem. The fitness function of GA takes into account both objectives: maximization of the location accuracy (i.e. minimization of the position tracking error) and minimization of the network power consumption. The fitness function has the following form:

$$Fitness = -(w_1 \cdot \sum_{i=1}^{k} E_i + w_2 \cdot \sum_{j=1}^{l} P_j + \sum_{i=1}^{k} PenaltyForEachE_i ExceedingThreshold) \quad (2)$$

where E_i (i=1,2,…, n) are the estimated position errors for i-th object and P_j (j=1,2,…, m) are the power consumption of j-th sensor, k is the number of objects, l is the total number of selected sensors and w_1 and w_2 are weights. The last term is a penalty added for each of position errors exceeding a predefined threshold. This penalty increases significantly the range of population fitness and thus improves GA convergence but solutions that exceed the penalty are still valid. For estimating the position errors (E_i), we are using the GDOP error [6]. The smaller the GDOP error of a sensor triplet, the better the position accuracy of the object will be achieved.

4 Genetic Algorithm with Special Reproduction Operators

The difficulties inherent in GA design are to determine the stopping criterion, the proper GA population size, probabilities of crossover and mutation. The difficulty in determining the stopping criterion comes from the fact, that GA convergence is problem dependent [6,8,15,17]. Wolpert et al. [15] presented a number of "no free lunch" (NFL) theorems and established that for any algorithm, any elevated performance over one class of problems is exactly paid for in performance over another class. Our goal is to obtain a quasi-optimal solution in the shortest possible time for the sensor network optimization problem. We make no claims in this paper to the generality of the GA developed and its speed of convergence for other problems.

4.1 Genetic Algorithm with King Strategy

The King Genetic Algorithm that we developed has been inspired by the reproduction process of the bees. There are three kinds of bees: the queen, worker bees, and drones. If mated with drones, the queen's eggs will become worker bees, otherwise they will become drones. In bees' colonies the queen plays the most important role in generating the offspring: only she can lay eggs. Inspired by this phenomenon, a novel GA that we call King GA, was proposed [14]. In King GA, a special individual, the best individual in the population, is always selected in the reproduction process to be one of the parents. This reproduction process is shown in Fig. 2a.

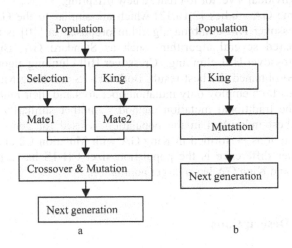

Fig. 2. : The reproduction in a) King GA; b) King Mutation.

4.2 Special Mutation Operator

In Genetic Algorithms, mutation was first introduced as an auxiliary operator to ensure population diversity. Many papers [1,6] pointed out the importance of mutation, but the mutation methods proposed were very similar, the difference merely being the value of the mutation rate, or whether the rate was constant or adaptive. Our previous experiments with GAs [5] showed that when mutation performs a strong enough search, crossover is not necessary for finding the optimum of multi-modal functions with non-ordered parameters. Therefore we proposed King Mutation, a version of King GA in which only mutation takes place. The reproduction process of King Mutation is shown in Figure 2b.

Mutation in GAs is the process by which one or more genes in an individual are modified. Generally, each gene is chosen for mutation with a probability of mutation P_m that is determined in the initialization step of the genetic algorithm. In the new mutation operator that we are proposing, called Mutation C2, exactly two chromosomes of an individual are randomly selected to be mutated. Any number of genes in a chromosome may undergo mutation. Each gene in a chromosome to be mutated is mutated with probability P_m. King Mutation algorithm with only the mutation of type Mutation C2 is called King MutationC2.

King GA with Mutation C2 is similar to Evolutionary Strategies [16], ES($1+\lambda$). In ES($1+\lambda$) algorithm, there is only one parent which is the best individual in the population; the parent generates λ children; in the next reproduction process, the best individual from the parent and its λ children is selected as the new parent to generate children. So King GA with Mutation C2 is very similar to ES($1+\lambda$), but the mutation method is quite different. In ES($1+\lambda$), the main reproduction operator is Gaussian mutation, in which a random value from a Gaussian distribution is added to each element of an individual's vector to create a new offspring.

There are some GA studies [2,10,12] which are similar to the GA we proposed here. Jones' Crossover Hill-climbing algorithm proposed in [10] is similar to King GA. He compared several algorithms such as Standard GA, Bit-flipping Hill-climbing, and Crossover Hill-climbing. Crossover Hill-climbing algorithm with only one step (CH-1S) obtained the best result. Both CH-1S and King Mutation C2 have no crossover; they both employ only mutation operators and their mutations are quite different from the traditional mutation method. Another similarity is that in both algorithms, the best individual in the population is used for generating offspring. However the mutations performed in King GA with Mutation C2 and in CH-1S are dissimilar; another difference is the population size: CH-1S has a population of 2 individuals only and King GA has a larger population.

5 Experiment Descriptions

In an attempt to examine the quality of the GA proposed, we performed a set of experiments that compared the performance of King Mutation C2 and canonical GA on optimization of a sensor network for five objects. In the experiments performed we used an area of 25 by 25 kilometers with 81 sensors uniformly distributed. Each sensor's FOV is a circle with a radius of 5 kilometers and there are about 20 sensors that can detect each object. For each of the experiments performed the Percentage of Total Search Space (PTSS) covered by GA was computed using the following equation:

$$\text{Percentage Total Search Space} = 100 * FFE / SS_n \% \tag{3}$$

where SS_n is the whole search space for n objects and the number of sensors identified above. FFE is the actual number of fitness function evaluations performed by GA.

Effectiveness is used to compare the performance of different GAs. For each set of the experiments performed with the same values of n and P the Effectiveness was computed as:

$$\text{Effectiveness} = \text{Number of Optimal Runs} / \text{Total Number of Runs} \tag{4}$$

The experiments with different population size are listed on Table 1. For canonical GA, the crossover rate is set to 0.9 and the mutation rate is set to 1/IndividualLength;

for King Mutation C2, the crossover rate is 0 and the mutation rate is set to 1/ChromosomeLength. We performed experiments with population sizes: 5, 10, 20, 50, and 100. For each population size a canonical GA and King Mutation C2 was run 30 times and the results in Table 1 are the average of those runs. Both methods have the same stopping criterion, the algorithms stop iteration if there is no improvement in the fitness function after a certain number of consecutive generations (This number is 5000 in our experiment).

Table 1: Experiment results for 5 objects

	GA Method	Generation#	Fitness	PTSS	Effectiveness
P=5	King Mutation C2	5505	-551.35	5.76E-12	0.80
	GA	8565	-889.86	8.95E-12	0.00
P=10	King Mutation C2	6147	-530.54	1.29E-11	0.95
	GA	10151	-672.98	2.12E-11	0.00
P=20	King Mutation C2	5857	-529.34	2.45E-11	1.00
	GA	11453	-642.60	4.79E-11	0.15
P=50	King Mutation C2	5345	-529.34	5.59E-11	1.00
	GA	11228	-562.07	1.17E-10	0.20
P=100	King Mutation C2	5281	-529.34	1.10E-10	1.00
	GA	10142	-548.54	2.12E-10	0.20

P: Population size;
Generation#: Number of generations.

Canonical GA results are pretty poor for small population sizes. With increasing population size, the fitness achieved by canonical GA becomes closer to the optimum. The best effectiveness achieved by canonical GA is for the largest population (100 individuals) and is only 0.2 meaning that it is very difficult for the canonical GA to perform optimization for a sensor network with five objects.

Results of King Mutation C2 are much superior to those of a canonical GA: it can obtain quasi-optimal solutions with high probability, the effectiveness being 0.8 and 0.95 for populations of size 5 and 10 respectively. Its effectiveness becomes 1 for population sizes of 20 or larger.

Consistently for each population size, King Mutation C2 gave a better result than the canonical GA: a much higher effectiveness and a higher fitness value. King Mutation C2 also covered roughly two times smaller search space (PTSS) than the canonical GA in each case. Small PTSS is very important in real-world applications since it leads to the reduction of the computation time, allowing for a real time application of the algorithm.

6 Conclusion

This paper describes a system performing self-organization of a sensor network. The goal of the system is to choose sensors necessary to perform object detection or tracking while minimizing the power consumption of the entire network. In this paper, special emphasis is placed on the optimization performed by genetic algorithms.

The exponential grow of the search space (with the increasing number of sensors and objects) makes the problem intractable for most optimization techniques in a reasonable time frame. Genetic Algorithms are chosen for the task, given their high robustness in complex search spaces. In case of multi-objective optimization problems, such as object tracking, convergence is much more difficult to achieve. With the increasing number of objects, Effectiveness of canonical GAs is rapidly decreasing. The increase of GA search space makes the genetic search of the standard genetic algorithm inefficient and consequently the computation time needed for convergence becomes very large. This makes it necessary to improve the canonical genetic algorithm to speed up the convergence of the algorithm when the number of objects increases.

We proposed a novel Genetic Algorithm with King selection strategy that somewhat imitates the reproduction process of bees. The new King selection strategy, especially when coupled with a new mutation operator (Mutation C2) significantly improves the performance of GA for the optimization of sensor network. The new algorithm is very robust, giving good results for a wide range of population sizes. This is in contrast with traditional GAs where it is very difficult to set the value of population size, crossover and mutation rates.

References

1. H. Aguirre, K. Tanaka, "Parallel Varying Mutation Genetic Algorithms", Proceedings of the Congress on Evolutionary Computation, Hawaii, USA, May 2002.
2. S. Areibi, "An Integrated Genetic Algorithm With Dynamic Hill Climbing for VLSI Circuit Partitioning", Genetic and Evolutionary Computation Conference (GECCO-2000), Las Vegas, Nevada, July 2000, IEEE
3. T. Blickle, L. Thiele, "A Comparison of Selection Schemes used in Genetic Algorithms", Swiss Federal Institute of Technology. TIK-Report 1995.
4. L. Buczak, H. Wang, H. Darabi, M.A. Jafari, "Genetic Algorithm Convergence Study for Sensor Network Optimization", Information Sciences. Pages 267-282. Volume 133, Issues 3-4. 2001.4.
5. L. Buczak, H. Wang, "Optimization of Fitness Functions with Non-Ordered Parameters by Genetic Algorithms", Congress on Evolutionary Computation '2001, Korea.2001.5
6. K. Deb, S. Agrawal, "Understanding Interactions Among Genetic Algorithm Parameters", Foundations of Genetic Algorithms5, W. Banzhaf, C. Reeves (eds.), Morgan Kaufmann Publishers, Inc., San Francisco, CA, 1999.
7. K. De Jong. "Genetic algorithms are not function optimizers". Foundations of Genetic Algorithms 2, pages 5--17, San Mateo, CA, 1993. Morgan Kaufmann.
8. D.B. Fogel, Evolutionary Computation – Toward a New Philosophy of Machine Intelligence, IEEE Press, 1995.

9. J. Holland, Adaptation in Natural and Artificial Systems, University of Michigan Press, 1975
10. Terry Jones, "Crossover, Macromutation, and Population-based Search", Proceedings of the Sixth International Conference on Genetic Algorithms. July 15-19, 1995
11. Kadar, "Optimum Geometry Selection For Sensor Fusion", Signal Processing, Sensor Fusion and Target Recognition VII, I. Kadar (ed.), SPIE Vol. 3374, pp.13-15, The International Society for Optical Engineering, Bellingham, 1998.
12. Bing Li, Weisun Jiang, "A Novel Stochastic Optimization Algorithm", IEEE Transactions on System, Man, and Cybernetics, ---Part B: Cybernetics, Vol. 30. No.1, February 2000.
13. Z. Michalewicz, Genetic Algorithms + Data Structures = Evolution Programs, Springer-Verlag, 1996.
14. H. Wang, A. Buczak, H. Wang, "A Novel Genetic Algorithm with King Strategy", ANNIE 2003, St. Louis, USA. 2003.11
15. D. H. Wolpert and W. G. MacReady. "No free lunch theorems for optimization". IEEE Transactions on Evolutionary Computation, April 1996.
16. Hans-Paul Schwefel, Evolution and Optimum Seeking. A Wiley-Interscience Publication. John Wiley & Sons, Inc. 1994.
17. M. Srinivas, L.M. Patnaik, "Adaptive Probabilities of Crossover and Mutation in Genetic Algorithms", IEEE Transactions on Systems, Man and Cybernetics. Vol. 24, No.4, pp. 656-667, April 1994.

Online Mining in Sensor Networks[*]

Xiuli Ma[1], Dongqing Yang[1], Shiwei Tang[1], Qiong Luo[2], Dehui Zhang[1],
Shuangfeng Li[1]

[1]School of Electronics Engineering and Computer Science, National Laboratory on Machine
Perception, Peking University, Beijing, China, 100871
{xlma, dqyang, dhzhang, sfli}@db.pku.edu.cn, tsw@pku.edu.cn
[2]Department of Computer Science, The Hong Kong University of Science and Technology,
Clear Water Bay, Kowloon, Hong Kong
luo@cs.ust.hk

Abstract. Online mining in large sensor networks just starts to attract interest.
Finding patterns in such an environment is both compelling and challenging.
The goal of this position paper is to understand the challenges and to identify
the research problems in online mining for sensor networks. As an initial step,
we identify the following three problems to work on: (1) sensor data irregularities detection; (2) sensor data clustering; and (3) sensory attribute correlations
discovery. We also outline our preliminary proposal of solutions to these problems.

1 Introduction

Recent technology advances have enabled the development of small, battery-powered,
wireless sensor nodes [2][6][20]. These tiny sensor nodes, equipped with sensing,
computation, and communication capabilities, can be deployed in large numbers in
wide geographical areas to monitor, detect and report time-critical events. Consequently, wireless networks consisting of such sensors create exciting opportunities for
large-scale, data-intensive measurement and surveillance applications. In many of
these applications, it is essential to mine the sensor readings for patterns in real time
in order to make intelligent decisions promptly. In this paper, we study the challenges,
problems, and possible solutions of online mining for sensor networks.

Research on data mining has been fruitful; however, online mining for sensor networks faces several new challenges. First, sensors have serious resource constraints
including battery lifetime, communication bandwidth, CPU capacity and storage [15].
Second, sensor node mobility increases the complexity of sensor data because a sensor may be in a different neighborhood at any point of time [7][19]. Third, sensor data
come in time-ordered streams over networks. These challenges make traditional mining techniques inapplicable, because traditionally mining is centralized, computationally expensive, and focused on disk-resident transactional data.

---

[*] This work is supported by the National Grand Fundamental Research 973 Program of China
under Grant No.G1999032705

H. Jin et al. (Eds.): NPC 2004, LNCS 3222, pp. 544-550, 2004.

In response to these challenges, we propose to develop mining techniques that are specifically geared for sensor network environments. Our goal is to process as much data as possible in a decentralized fashion while keeping the communication, storage and computation cost low.

As a start point, we propose three operations of online mining in sensor networks: (1) detection of sensor data irregularities, (2) clustering of sensor data, and (3) discovery of sensory attribute correlations. These mining operations are useful for practical applications as well as for network management, because the patterns found can be used for both decision making in applications and system performance tuning. For example, irregularities in sensory data are of interest of monitoring applications. In addition, for this kind of applications, the communication cost can be reduced if only abnormal sensory values, as opposed to all values, need to be transmitted.

The rest of the paper is organized as follows. In Section 2, we illustrate the need for online mining in sensor networks using an example. Our design of online mining in sensor networks is presented in Section 3. We present related work in Section 4 and conclude in Section 5.

2 A Motivating Example

There have been initial applications of sensor networks on wild life habitat surveillance [15], battlefield troop coordination, and traffic monitoring. As a motivating example for online mining in sensor networks, we describe a possible application on wild giant panda monitoring and protection in China. Suppose weather sensors are deployed throughout a panda habitat and wearable sensors attached to the pandas in the habitat. The sensors acquire sensor data on attributes such as temperature, light, sound, humidity, and acceleration. In addition, there is a panda of interest named Huanhuan. The following is a few questions that scientists on site may ask:

1) Is Huanhuan having any abnormal symptoms compared with its past data? What other pandas are having abnormal symptoms and what are these abnormal symptoms?

2) What pandas have a similar physical status to Huanhuan's? What pandas are similar to one other and on what sensory attributes are they similar?

3) What attributes of Huanhuan's are correlated and how are they correlated? What attributes of pandas are correlated with the humidity of their habitat? What symptoms of pandas are correlated to what attributes of the habitat?

Answers to these questions are important for habitat maintenance and panda protection, and these questions all require online mining of sensor data.

3 Design of Online Mining

In this section, we identify the following three problems of online mining in sensor networks and outline our preliminary solutions.

3.1 Detection of Sensor Data Irregularities

The problem of irregularities detection is to find those sensory values that deviate significantly from the norm. This problem is especially important in the sensor network setting because it can be used to identify abnormal or interesting events or faulty sensors.

We break this problem into two smaller problems. One is to detect irregular patterns of multiple sensory attributes and the other to detect irregular sensory data of a single attribute with respect to time or space. The irregular multi-attribute pattern detection problem has the assumption that there are some normal patterns among multiple sensory attributes, which is true in some natural phenomena. Once these normal patterns are broken somewhere, the irregularity is detected and reported. In contrast, the irregular single-attribute sensor data detection problem examines the temporal and spatial characteristics of a sensor node and detects any irregularity in comparison with the node's previous data or the data of the neighbor nodes.

3.1.1 Detection of Irregular Patterns

We propose a new approach named *pattern variation discovery* to solve this problem. Our approach works in the following four steps: i) Selection of a reference frame. This frame consists of the directions along which we want to look for irregularities among multiple sensory attributes. An analyst can explicitly specify the reference frame. It is also possible to discover the reference frame that results in a lot of irregularities. ii) Definition of normal patterns. This definition can be models of multiple sensory attributes or constraints among multiple attributes. iii) Incremental maintenance of the normal patterns. Whenever a sensor gets a new round of readings, the normal patterns are adjusted incrementally. iv) Discovery of irregularity. Whenever a normal pattern is broken at some point along the reference frame, an irregularity appears. That is, the pattern variation happens.

For example, we want to discover the irregular distribution pattern among multiple sensory attributes along time. Then, for each time point, we can put the values of a group of sensory attributes at a series of sensor nodes into a matrix, which represents a distribution status. The problem then becomes to discover the irregular matrix among a set of matrices. An irregular matrix represents that, at the corresponding time point, the distribution pattern of all the sensory attributes on all the nodes are irregular. Because our approach involves a lot of comparisons between matrices, we propose to use the technique of Singular Value Decomposition (SVD) [4]. SVD is a powerful data reduction and approximation technique, which extracts the useful features of a matrix. Using SVD, we can get a vector of singular values out of a matrix. Consequently, matrix comparison becomes vector comparison, which is less computationally expensive and reduces communication cost. Additionally, integrating SVD with the sliding window mechanism, we can handle streaming sensory data.

3.1.2 Detection of Irregular Sensor Data

Detection of irregularities is tightly interrelated to modeling of sensor data. Therefore, we propose to detect irregular single-attribute sensor data with respect to time or space by building models.

For temporal irregularities in sensor data, we build a model of the sensory data as the readings of a node come in. When some reading substantially affects the coefficients of the model, it is identified as an irregularity. With resource constraints of sensor nodes, we may need to approximate the distribution of data instead of maintaining all historical data. In many applications, it suffices to consider the most recent N values in a sliding time window.

For spatial irregularities in sensor data, we build a statistical model of readings of neighboring nodes. If some readings of a node differ from what the model anticipates based on the readings of the neighboring nodes, an irregularity is detected. In order to reduce resource consumption, we may define the neighboring nodes to be those only a single hop away on the network. As a node moves geographically, the parameters of its model is incrementally adjusted. Distributed modeling is also possible.

Finally, there is a tradeoff between model accuracy and resource consumption. On one hand, modeling can reduce resource consumption because only model parameters are stored and transmitted instead of a large amount of sensor data. On the other hand, highly accurate models may result in a large size and frequent updates of data, which increases resource consumption.

3.2 Clustering of Sensor Data

We propose a new approach named *multi-dimensional clustering* of sensor data. This approach works as follows. First, cluster the sensor data along each sensor attribute separately. All resulted clusters form a set of clusters, which we call the Cluster Set. Second, construct a bipartite graph G with the Sensor Set (the set of sensor nodes) and the Cluster Set being the two vertex sets. If some sensory attribute value of a sensor v belongs to cluster u, there is an edge pointing from v to u. Last, find all of the maximal complete bipartite sub-graphs, i.e., the maximal bipartite cliques of G. These cliques identify "which sensor nodes have similar sensory readings on which attributes".

Figure 1 illustrates an example of multi-dimensional clustering. In the bipartite graph, the set of vertices on the top is clusters of sensor data by single-attribute of sensors, e.g., T1, T2, and T3 are clusters by the temperature attribute, L1, L2, L3 by light, and H1, H2, H3 by humidity correspondingly. The set of vertices in the bottom of the figure is the sensor nodes, with the dark ones being representative nodes of a clique. There are three cliques of the sensor nodes in the figure.

The cliques resulted from multi-dimensional clustering are useful not only for data analysis applications but also for network management and query optimization. Since all sensor nodes in one clique are similar, we can select a representative node for each clique to work on behalf of its clique in order to save power consumption with a reduced accuracy of data. This selection can be based on the residual energy of a node or the distance between the node and the base station. We can also select representative nodes based on a cost function of assigned tasks. In addition, the role of a representative node can be rotated among the nodes in one clique for load balancing.

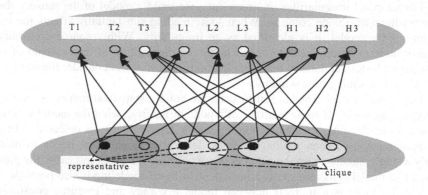

Fig. 1. Multi-dimension clustering

3.3 Discovery of Sensory Attributes Correlations

Sensory attributes are rarely independent and correlations are common. For example, empirical evidence has shown that temperature and humidity are closely correlated in some natural environment. Therefore, efficiently identifying correlations among multiple sensory attributes is important for data analysis applications. For instance, we can estimate the changes of some attributes from the changes of the correlated attributes.

We treat readings of each sensory attribute as a data stream, i.e., a sequence of data items x_i at the sequence number i. As we are interested in correlation between data changes of various sensory attributes, e.g., correlation between the change of temperature values and that of light values, we replace each sensory data value x_i with its difference from its previous data item, $\Delta_i = x_i - x_{i-1}$. Thus, a time series of sensor data is represented as a sequence of Δ_i.

Let $S_1, \ldots, S_{m-1}, S_m$ be a collection of m sensor data streams, each for one attribute. One way of representing these data streams is to use a matrix A with time points and attributes being row and column indexes. We can then group data by correlated attributes or correlated time points [4][10] in this matrix. Recall that we propose to use the SVD technique (Singular Value Decomposition) for matrix reduction in pattern variation discovery. Here, this technique can also be used to find the best subspace that identifies the strongest linear correlations in the underlying data set [10]. Additionally, SVD tries to identify similarity patterns (rectangular regions) of related values in the A matrix, and the similarity of each row with the patterns [4]. It will naturally group similar "attribute-name" into attribute groups with similar behavior. In pattern variation discovery, we use SVD to speed up the comparison among multiple matrices. Here, in correlation discovery, we use SVD to consider the correlation among the rows within one matrix.

Alternatively, we can consider sensory attributes correlations as inter-transaction association rules [13]. For example, a rule or correlation says that "if node A's attribute x goes up at time point 1, B's attribute y will (with an 80% possibility) go up at time point 2 and C's attribute x will go down at time point 3". However, in the context of a large-scale mobile sensor network, the problem is more complex and challenging than traditional market basket analysis.

4 Related Work

There has been much work in the areas of sensor networks, data mining, and data streams, but little work has been done at the intersection of these areas.

Sensor networking protocols have attracted a tremendous amount of research effort [6]. Sensor databases and query processing techniques have been proposed for acquiring and managing sensor data [14][15]. However, existing sensor databases lack support for complex, online mining operations.

There is extensive literature regarding outlier (irregularity) detection [12][21]. However, none of these approaches is directly applicable to a sensor network environment. There is also initial work on modeling sensor data, including a distributed model based on kernel density estimators [16], and a distributed regression framework [9].

Although the clustering problem has been widely studied [5], we have not seen any previous work on multi-dimensional clustering. Existing sensor network clustering methods [3][8][22] mainly concern about the distance among nodes and the network topology, not sensory data. Recently, the clustering problem has also been studied in data streams [1][18].

There is some work on correlated data items [11] with respect to their accesses in order to improve data accessibility in sensor networks. In comparison, we focus on finding out correlations among sensory values. A related problem is identifying correlations among streams [10]. There has also been initial work on online analytical processing and mining for data streams [1][17][18]. However, they seldom consider the unique challenge in sensor networks.

5 Conclusions

We have identified the challenges for online mining in large-scale, mobile sensor network environments. The main concern is to satisfy the mining accuracy requirements while maintaining the resource consumption to a minimum. We identify three research problems to work on: (1) sensor data irregularities detection; (2) sensor data clustering; and (3) sensory attributes correlations discovery. We provide preliminary considerations towards solving these problems. We believe that the patterns discovered can not only enable the applications to gain insight into the sensor data, but also be used to tune the system performance. As future work, we will consider more about energy-awareness, adaptivity, and fault-tolerance of online mining for sensor networks in addition to a further study of our proposed approaches.

References

1. C.C.Aggarwal, J.Han, J.Wang, P.S.Yu. A Framework for Clustering Evolving Data Streams. VLDB2003.
2. I.F.Akyildiz, W.Su, Y.Sankarasubramaniam, and E.Cayirci. Wireless Sensor Networks: A Survey. Computer Networks, Vol.38, No.4, pp.393-422, 2002.
3. S.Bandyopadhyay and E.J.Coyle. An Energy Efficient Hierarchical Clustering Algorithm for Wireless Sensor Networks. IEEE INFOCOM 2003.
4. D.Barbara, W.Dumouchel, C.Faoutsos and P.Haas. The New Jersey Data Reduction Report. IEEE Data Engineering Bulletin, Vol.20, No.4, pp.3-45, 1997.
5. V.Estivill-Castro. Why So Many Clustering Algorithms----A Position Paper. SIGKDD Explorations. Vol.4, Iss.1, 2002.
6. D.Estrin, R.Govindan, J.Heidemann, and S.Kumar. Next Century Challenges: Scalable Coordination in Sensor Networks. MobiCOM 1999
7. M.J.Franklin. Challenges in Ubiquitous Data Management. Informatics 2001.
8. S.Ghiasi, A.Srivastava, X.Yang, and M.Sarrafzadeh. Optimal Energy Aware Clustering in Sensor Networks. Sensors 2002, 2, pp.258-269.
9. C.Guestrin, P.Bodik, R.Thibaux, M.Paskin and S.Madden. Distributed Regression: an Efficient Framework for Modeling Sensor Network Data. IPSN 2004.
10. S.Guha, D.Gunopulos, and N.Koudas. Correlating Synchronous and Asynchronous Data Streams. KDD 2003, pp. 529-534.
11. T.Hara, N.Murakami, and S.Nishio. Replica Allocation for Correlated Data Items in Ad Hoc Sensor Networks. SIGMOD Record, Vol.33, No.1, pp.38-43, March 2004.
12. E.M.Knorr and R.T.Ng. Algorithms for Mining Distance-based Outliers in Large Datasets. VLDB 1998.
13. H.Lu, L.Feng, J.Han. Beyond Intra-transaction Association Analysis: Mining Multi-dimensional Inter-transaction Association Rules. ACM Transaction on Information system, Vol.18, No.4, pp.423-454, 2000.
14. S.Madden, M.J.Franklin, J.M.Hellerstein, and W.Hong. TAG: A Tiny Aggregation Service for Ad-hoc Sensor Networks. In Symposium on OSDI, 2002.
15. S. Madden, M.J.Franklin, J.M.Hellerstein, and W.Hong. The Design of an Acquisitional Query Processor for Sensor Networks. SIGMOD 2003.
16. T.Palpanas, D.Papadopoulos, V.Kalogeraki, and D.Gunopulos. Distributed Deviation Detection in Sensor Networks. SIGMOD Record, Vol.32, No.4, Dec.2003
17. T.Palpanas, M.Vlachos, E.Keogh, D. Gunopulos, and W.Truppel. Online Amnesic Approximation of Streaming Time Series. ICDE 2004.
18. N.H.Park and W.S.Lee. Statistical Grid-based Clustering over Data Streams. SIGMOD Record, Vol.33, No.1, March 2004.
19. F.Perich, A.Joshi, T.Finin, and Y.Yesha. On Data Management in Pervasive Computing Environments. IEEE Transactions on Knowledge and Data Engineering. Vol. 16, No. 5, May 2004.
20. G.J.Pottie and W.J.Kaiser. Wireless Integrated Network Sensors. Communications of the ACM. Vol.43, No.5, pp.51-58, May 2000.
21. S.Sarawagi, R.Agrawal, and N.Megiddo. Discovery-driven Exploration of OLAP Data Cubes. EDBT 1998.
22. O.Younis and S.Fahmy. Distributed Clustering in Ad-hoc Sensor Networks: A Hybrid, Energy-efficient Approach. IEEE INFOCOM 2004.

The HKUST Frog Pond - A Case Study of Sensory Data Analysis

Wenwei Xue, Bingsheng He, Hejun Wu, and Qiong Luo

Department of Computer Science
The Hong Kong University of Science and Technology
Clear Water Bay, Kowloon
Hong Kong, China
{wwxue, saven, whjnn, luo}@cs.ust.hk

Abstract. Many sensor network applications are data-centric, and data analysis plays an important role in these applications. However, it is a challenging task to find out what specific problems and requirements sensory data analysis will face, because these applications are tightly embedded in the physical world and the sensory data reflect the physical phenomena being monitored. In this paper, we propose to use field studies as an alternative for identifying these problems and requirements. Specifically, we deployed an experimental sensor network for monitoring the frog pond in our university and analyzed the collected sensory data. We present our methodology of sensory data collection and analysis. We also discuss preliminary analytical results from the collected sensory data, together with our generalization for similar sensor network applications. We find that this case study helped us identify and understand several problems, either general or specific, in real-world sensor network application deployment and sensory data analysis.

1 Introduction

Sensor network applications pose a number of novel problems for networking ([4][9][10]) and data management ([7][15]). Nevertheless, many more problems and requirements in real-world sensor network applications are to be identified and understood, especially for sensory data analysis. Due to the tight integration of these applications with the physical world, field studies are effective, sometimes necessary, for identifying problems and requirements. In this paper, we present a case study of sensory data analysis for a small-scale real-world sensor network application. Our goal is to identify and understand problems and requirements specifically for sensory data analysis.

From our case study, we observe that most of the problems in our sensory data analysis rose because the sensor network application was deeply embedded in the physical environment and the sensory data reflected the physical phenomena under study. For instance, we find that even though there were inherent trends in the readings of individual sensors as well as strong correlations between readings of multiple sensors, outliers were common and the causes of some outliers were hard to determine.

H. Jin et al. (Eds.): NPC 2004, LNCS 3222, pp. 551-558, 2004.

The remainder of the paper is organized as follows. Section 2 introduces the deployment of the case study. Section 3 presents our preliminary analytical results of the collected sensory data and discusses the generalization of our experience. Section 4 compares related work and Section 5 concludes the paper.

2   Deployment of the Case Study

We started the case study around a frog pond on the HKUST campus in April 2004. The frog pond is located at the northeastern corner of the campus and is surrounded by two pagodas and various plants. Throughout the late spring, the frogs in the pond croak loudly all day long.

The smart sensor nodes we used in the case study were the Crossbow MICA2 motes [3]. Each mote consists of an Atmel Atmega128L low-power micro-controller running TinyOS [13] with a 900MHz radio channel. Mote 0 connects with a PC-grade base station through a PC interface card, and other motes each consists of a MICA2-compatible sensor board. The scale of the case study was small due to our resource limit.

We deployed a total of nine MICA2 motes in two groups, with each group in a pagoda around the frog pond. Fig. 1 shows the deployment of the two groups. The base station (Mote 0) of each group was connected to the serial port of a notebook through a MIB510CA interface board and a serial cable.

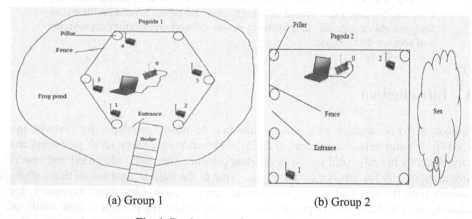

(a) Group 1   (b) Group 2

Fig. 1. Deployment of two groups of Motes

Group 1 was deployed in the pagoda that is surrounded by the frog pond. Each of Motes 1-5 was attached with a MTS310CA sensor board, which includes a temperature sensor, a light sensor, a microphone, a 2-axis accelerometer and a 2-axis magnetometer. We installed TinyDB [12] on the motes and used the TinyDB GUI to collect sensor readings and to log the readings to a text file.

Group 2 was deployed in the pagoda that is near the frog pond and overlooks the sea. Its Motes 1-2 used the MTS420CA weather sensor boards. This type of sensor board consists of a humidity and temperature sensor, a barometric pressure and temperature sensor, an ambient light sensor, a 2-axis accelerometer and a GPS module. We configured the Xlisten program and the corresponding on-mote module XSensorMTS400 downloaded from the TinyOS SourceForge CVS [14] for logging the sensory data from this type of sensors.

It was cloudy with intermittent rain on the day of our data collection. We collected one-day data in four two-hour periods of the day: 6:30 – 8:30 (morning), 12:30 – 14:30 (noon), 17:30 – 19:30 (dusk), and 22:00 – 24:00 (night). We set the sample period to be 30 seconds. At the end of the eight-hour data collection, we logged thousands of sensor readings per group.

We used homegrown programs to pre-process the collected sensory data before conducting further analysis. First, we converted the sensor readings from raw ADC counts generated by the sensor boards to more human-friendly engineering units (e.g., Celsius degrees for temperature) using conversion formulas provided by Crossbow. Next, we parsed and imported the sensor readings (both ADC counts and engineering units) into a Microsoft Access database. Finally, we used SQL queries and Microsoft Excel Charts to perform preliminary data analysis.

3   Sensory Data Analysis

In this section, we analyze the sensory data we collected in the experiment. From a database perspective, our focus of the analysis is on identifying and understanding the problems and requirements that are specific for sensory data. Apparently, the analytical results we present here are preliminary. However, the methodology and insights gained from these initial analytical results are valuable for more advanced analysis and are otherwise unavailable or less convincing without the case study.

3.1   Trends in Readings of Individual Sensors

We first give an analysis of individual sensor readings using some typical examples. **Light**. Fig.2 shows the light readings of Mote 1 and Mote 5 in Group 1. We pick these two motes because in our deployment they were the nearest (Mote 1) and farthest (Mote 5) motes from the Group 1 base station. Each point in the figure corresponds to one light reading. In the morning, the light readings kept on increasing due to the sunrise. At noon, the light readings were at the highest for the day and slightly decreased past noon. At dusk, the light readings decreased sharply due to the sunset and then jumped up to a certain level because the lamps around the pagoda were lit. The light readings at night remained almost constant with the lamplight.

The two motes in Fig. 2 had similar readings. The other three motes of Group 1 also had similar readings to these two. This similarity was because the area of a pagoda is small and thus the motes in this group were located near to one another. The proximity of motes also made readings of other sensors (e.g., humidity, temperature) of a group similar.

However, for Group 2, the readings of the ambient light sensors remained a constant value of 131.448624 Lux due to a bug in the XSensorMTS400 program that we used. As a result, a comparison of light readings between the two groups is not done. We are developing our own data logging programs for future usage.

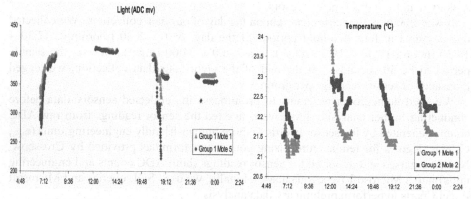

Fig. 2. Light readings of Group 1   **Fig. 3.** Temperature readings of two groups

Temperature. Fig. 3 shows the temperature readings of Group 1 Mote 1 and Group 2 Mote 2. We put the readings from different groups in one figure for comparison purpose. Again, temperature readings from motes of the same group were similar due to their proximity.

The temperature readings of Group 1 motes varied from 21 to 24°C, whereas those of Group 2 motes varied from 21 to 23°C. The temperature measured by Group 2 was often slightly higher than that measured by Group 1 (except around noontime), even though the two pagodas were within a distance of 20 meters from each other. We think there are two possible reasons: (1) the temperature sensors of the two groups are made by different companies and therefore differ in hardware characteristics, (2) the microclimates in the two pagodas differ due to their different geographical locations.

Humidity. Humidity sensors were available only in Group 2. The humidity readings of the two motes in Group 2 are illustrated in Fig. 4. Most of the time, the readings remained at the level of around 90%.

Note there were some abnormally high humidity readings (larger than 130%) of Mote 1 at the beginning of the morning period. These abnormal readings were because some rain drops splashed onto the Mote by accident. The water made the humidity sensor malfunction and return abnormally high readings. This kind of physical failure is not uncommon and is recoverable [11]. After being dried, the sensor returned to normal operation.

Noise. Microphone sensors were available only in Group 1. Fig. 5 shows the noise readings of Mote 1 and Mote 5 in Group 1. Unlike temperature, light, and humidity readings, which are more continuous, the noise readings are more discrete. The scattered data points in the noise readings in Fig. 5 usually suggest the actual, sudden changes (events) in the sound level in the environment. In comparison, those outlier points in temperature, light, and humidity readings in the previous figures were often due to errors.

From Fig. 5 we see that the frogs croaked most actively in the early morning and were most quiet around noontime. Also, some of the high data points in the figure were because people passing by were talking.

Correlation. Our analysis on correlation of sensor readings is limited and will be an important part of our future work. So far we have found that the temperature and humidity readings were inversely correlated and that the temperature and light readings were not correlated as found in other environments [5].

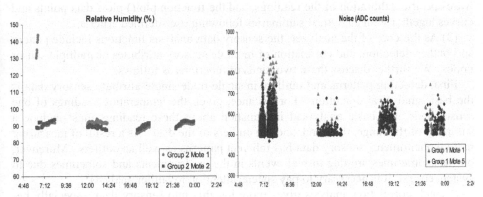

Fig. 4. Humidity readings of Group 2   **Fig. 5.** Noise readings of Group 1

3.2 Discussion

Having presented our initial results with a specific sensor network application, we discuss how to generalize our findings to similar sensor network applications.

We start by summarizing the problems that we have encountered in the application deployment and data analysis. First, both hardware problems and software bugs are common in sensor network applications. The reasons include sensor networks being an emerging technology and the typical application environment being the physical world full of unpredictable events and changes. Second, data pre-processing and post-processing constitutes a large amount of work in order to facilitate sensory data analysis. This work mainly includes data cleaning and format conversion prior to analysis and visualization after analysis. Third, sensory data exhibits regularities as well as abnormalities, and the causes of outliers are hard to determine.

Based on this summary of experienced problems, we propose the following three requirements for a sensory data analyzer.

(1) The analyzer should have data acquisition functions that are fault-tolerant and adaptive, since the sensory data collection process determines the quality of sensory data. The fault-tolerance requirement is because hardware malfunctioning is common in field studies, as we have already experienced. It is thus desirable that a data collector is able to recover, to migrate the work from a failed node to a normal node, and to resume the work. The adaptivity requirement is to take advantage of the patterns and regularities captured in sensor readings. For instance, continuous quantities such as

temperature can be measured with a sampling frequency adapted to the changes in the temperature readings in order to improve power efficiency while keeping the quality of sensory data unaffected.

(2) The analyzer should have a set of basic functions for data pre-processing and post-processing operations. Data pre-processing is to further ensure the quality of data for analysis. Data post-processing is mainly for the presentation of analytical results. For example, the function convert() converts sensor readings from raw ADC counts to human-friendly engineering units, the function calibrate() performs hardware-specific calibration of the readings, and the function plot() plots data points and curves together with analytical summaries following user-defined criteria.

(3) As the core of the analyzer, the sensory data analysis functions include pattern and outlier detection, and correlation of multiple sensory attributes or multiple sensor nodes. We further discuss these two kinds of functions as follows.

First, detecting patterns and outliers in single-node single-attribute sensory data is the basic analytical operation. For instance, given the temperature readings of one sensor node, the basic analytical information about these readings must include a summary of the range, the trend, and the outliers of the data. As a result of measuring natural phenomena, sensory data has inherent patterns as well as outliers. Moreover, outliers sometimes are due to real events in the environments and sometimes due to system errors. It is necessary to pay special attention to outlier analysis.

Second, correlation analysis gives more insights into sensory data, especially because each sensor node has multiple sensory attributes and multiple sensor nodes work concurrently in a geographical region. The inherent correlations between natural phenomena as well as the temporal and spatial correlations of sensor nodes will be useful for both sensor network applications and system deployment. For example, when an application is detecting transient changes such as a sudden increase in the noise level, it can utilize the spatial correlation of a cluster of adjacent nodes to detect the noise with a high fidelity. In other words, if one sensor node detects a sudden increase of noise level, it might be a real event as well as a system error. But if multiple nearby nodes report the same event, the probability of a system error is much lower and that of a real event is much higher than reported by a single node.

In summary, we find several problems in sensory data analysis, ranging from hardware or software problems in the deployed applications to difficulties in producing meaningful analytical results out of sensory data. Correspondingly, we propose several requirements for sensory data analysis systems, including fault-tolerance and adaptivity of data collection, a set of data pre-processing and post-processing functions, and basic data analysis functions such as pattern, outlier, and correlation detection. Our ultimate goal is to build a general sensory data analysis system for various data-centric sensor network monitoring applications.

4   Related Work

A number of sensor network projects have real-world deployment, including ALERT [1], GDI ([8][11]), PODS [2], Surveillance and NIMS [6].

ALERT (Automated Local Evaluation in Real Time) is a well-known, practical sensor network application [1]. It provides real time rainfall and water level information for forecast of flooding. ALERT mainly focuses on special-purpose sensory data statistics and uses them for prediction.

Both GDI ([8][11]) and PODS [2] deployed sensor networks in outdoor environments mainly for the purpose of system performance study. Specifically, GDI deployed a multi-tier sensor network for habit monitoring whereas PODS was deployed in Hawaii Volcanoes National Park.

Surveillance and NIMS [6] are two demonstrations. Surveillance built an energy-efficient surveillance system using a wireless sensor network, and NIMS focused on new, mobile sensing devices on a suspended infrastructure.

In comparison, our case study is at a smaller scale and a finer level, with a focus on identifying general problems and requirements for advanced sensory data analysis in real-world applications.

5   Conclusions

In this paper, we describe our case study of deploying a small-scale monitoring application at the frog pond in our university and analyzing the collected sensory data. Our goal is to identify the problems and requirements for sensory data analysis in real-world sensor network applications. We find that (1) data collection and logging functions need to be failure-aware and easy to resume, (2) data pre-processing such as format conversion and post-preprocessing such as visualization is necessary for sensory data analysis, and (3) essential sensory data analysis functions include pattern and outlier detection for readings of individual sensors and correlation detection for readings of multiple sensors.

Our future work includes designing and implementing advanced sensory data analysis tools and conducting larger-scale studies using these tools.

Acknowledgement

Funding for this work is provided by the Hong Kong Research Grant Council through Grant HKUST6158/03E.

References

1. ALERT Systems Organization Homepage. http://www.alertsystems.org.
2. Edoardo Biagioni and Kent Bridges. The Application of Remote Sensor Technology to Assist the Recovery of Rare and Endangered Species. In Special issue on Distributed Sensor Networks for the International Journal of High Performance Computing Applications, Vol. 16, No. 3, August 2002.
3. Crossbow, Inc. Wireless Sensor Network Products. http://www.xbow.com.

4. Deborah Estrin, Ramesh Govindan, John Heidemann, and Satish Kumar. Next Century Challenges: Scalable Coordination in Sensor Networks. MobiCOM 1999.
5. Wei Hong and Samuel Madden. Implementation and Research Issues in Query Processing for Wireless Sensor Networks. MDM 2004 Tutorial.
6. Intel Research – Exploratory Research – Sensor Networks. http://intel.com/research/exploratory/wireless_sensors.htm.
7. Samuel Madden, Michael J. Franklin, Joseph M. Hellerstein, and Wei Hong. The Design of an Acquisitional Query Processor for Sensor Networks. SIGMOD Conference 2003.
8. Alan Mainwaring, Joseph Polastre, Robert Szewczyk, David Culler, and John Anderson. Wireless Sensor Networks for Habit Monitoring. WSNA 2002.
9. Loren Schwiebert, Sandeep K. S. Gupta, and Jennifer Weinmann. Research Challenges in Wireless Networks of Biomedical Sensors. MobiCOM 2001.
10. David C. Steere, Antonio Baptista, Dylan McNamee, Calton Pu, and Jonathan Walpole. Research Challenges in Environmental Observation and Forecasting Systems. MobiCOM 2000.
11. Robert Szewczyk, Joseph Polastre, Alan Mainwaring, and David Culler. Lessons from a Sensor Network Expedition. EWSN 2004.
12. TinyDB: A Declarative Database for Sensor Networks. http://telegraph.cs.berkeley.edu/tinydb/.
13. TinyOS. http://www.tinyos.net.
14. SourceForge.net. CVS Repository: TinyOS. http://sourceforge.net/cvs/?group_id=28656.
15. Yong Yao and Johannes Gehrke. Query Processing for Sensor Networks. CIDR 2003.

BLOSSOMS: A CAS/HKUST Joint Project to Build Lightweight Optimized Sensor Systems on a Massive Scale*

Wen Gao[1], Lionel M. Ni[2], and Zhiwei Xu[1]

[1]Institute of Computing Technology
Chinese Academy of Sciences
Beijing, China 100080
{wgao,zxu}@ict.ac.cn
[2]Department of Computer Science
The Hong Kong University of Science and Technology
Clear Water Bay, Kowloon, Hong Kong, China SAR
ni@cs.ust.hk

Abstract. A joint effort between the Chinese Academy of Sciences and the Hong Kong University of Science and Technology, the BLOSSOMS sensor network project aims to identify research issues at all levels from practical applications down to the design of sensor nodes. In this project, a heterogeneous sensor array including different types of application-dependent sensors as well as monitoring sensors and intruding sensors are being developed. Application-dependent power-aware communication protocols are also being studied for communications among sensor nodes. An ontology-based middleware is built to relieve the burden of application developers from collecting, classifying and processing messy sensing contexts. This project will also develop a set of tools allowing researchers to model, simulate/emulate, analyze, and monitor various functions of sensor networks.

1 Introduction

Recent advances in wireless communication and hardware have enabled the dense deployment of distributed sensor networks and opened a wide range of application domains, such as environmental monitoring for endangered species or ecosystems of changes in light, temperature, pressure, acoustics; security surveillance preventing attacks in the forms of chemical, biological, or radiological weapons; target tracking of moving objects; and battlefield awareness [1]. All these applications may have information collected from sensor nodes to be sent to the gateway (sink) from time to time. By exploiting the sensor network's spatial coverage and multiplicity of sensing modalities, the network can achieve a good global measurement. Research in sensor networks has received a great deal of attention worldwide, where the most notable

---

* This research is supported in part by Hong Kong RGC Grant HKUST6161/03E.

H. Jin et al. (Eds.): NPC 2004, LNCS 3222, pp. 559–564, 2004.

one is Berkeley's MOTE [2], due to its potential impact on so many application domains.

In March 2004, recognizing the importance of sensor networks, the Chinese Academy of Sciences and the Hong Kong University of Science and Technology have jointly launched an effort to investigate both fundamental and practical research issues in sensor networks. The goal of this research is to build lightweight optimized sensor systems on a massive scale, namely the BLOSSOMS project. The objective of this research project is to identify research issues at all levels from practical applications down to the design of sensor nodes. As a multidiscipline research, this project involves researchers from different disciplines including hardware design, embedded systems, wired and wireless communications, software engineering, distributed query processing, machine learning, and performance evaluation. In a short period of time, the project has made a very good progress. This paper will give an overview of the BLOSSOMS project and introduce some research directions being investigated.

2   Project Overview

Figure 1 shows the system architecture of the BLOSSOMS project. There are four layers. The bottom two layers are implemented in individual sensor nodes, while the top two layers are executed at gateway nodes or some application nodes. Typically, a gateway node will broadcast a command to all active sensor nodes and selected active sensor nodes will report the result back to the gateway node. The communication among the sensor nodes and gateway nodes is wireless and usually short ranged to reduce power consumption, such as ZigBee. The communication among gateway nodes and application nodes can be either wired or wireless and typically adopts the standard protocols, such as 802.11x and TCP/UDP/IP. In addition, the MEADOWS module (on the left side of the figure) provides a set of tools for sensor network studies. The following sub-sections describe each BLOSSOMS component in more detail.

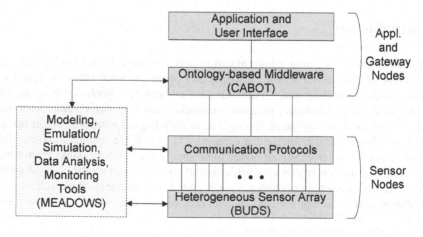

Figure 1: The BLOSSOMS system architecture.

2.1 BUDS: Heterogeneous Sensor Nodes

A sensor node is an embedded system consisting of four basic components, namely a sensing unit, a processing unit, a communication unit, and a power unit. Additionally, there may be application-dependent, optional units such as a mobilizer, a location finding system, and a power generator [1]. Our research on sensor node architecture is currently undertaking at ICT/CAS. The goal is to build multifunctional sensing nodes, called BUDS, targeting on applications such as intelligent transportation systems, precision agriculture, remote medical care, and public safety monitoring system. Efforts are made to tackle the following technical issues:

- the development of an embedded operating system for ultra low power sensor nodes;
- the design of general sensor nodes and system integration method;
- the design of special-purpose sensor nodes, such as video sensors, monitoring sensors, and intruding sensors; and
- the low power management and high reliability design at the system level.

While the general sensors require ultra low power consumption, the special sensors may have different requirements, such as a powerful CPU.

The monitoring sensor is a special sensor needed to help debug and monitor the behavior of other sensors. The monitoring sensor will operate on two frequencies. One is the same as other sensors, which only operates in the listening mode to observe the behavior of other sensors. Another frequency is used to report the collected information to the MEADOWS for further analysis. Power consumption is not a critical issue for such sensors. The intruding sensor is used to simulate malicious sensors trying to attack a working sensor array. We will use the standard low power ZigBee as the wireless communication mechanism.

2.2 Communication Protocols

The communication protocol plays a major role to allow commands to be propagated from gateway nodes to active sensor nodes and to collect replies from some sensor nodes to the gateway nodes. The communication pattern is application dependent and many protocols for different applications have been proposed (e.g., [3]). Furthermore, sensor nodes are unlikely to have a global unique ID, which is too expensive. This creates a new challenge to develop content-based routing among sensor nodes.

If the location of each sensor node can be identified, more useful information can then be collected. Determining the location of sensor nodes is another challenge to be addressed in this research. We are investigating both anchor-free [4] and anchor-based location sensing techniques [5].

2.3 CABOT: Ontology-Based Middleware

Applications of sensor networks often need to be aware of their contexts, which could be related to sensors, time, location, and security. These applications typically have to carry out tedious tasks of gathering, classifying and processing messy context information due to lack of middleware support. The middleware support for these applications is a major topic in pervasive computing. CABOT is a user-centric middleware being developed to provide infrastructural support of sensor network applications. The main responsibilities of CABOT are to provide (a) the resource management of sensor networks, (b) the analysis of dynamic environments, and (c) the development support of context-aware pervasive computing. Current features of Cabot include:

- The support of extensible context gathering (decoupling applications and sensor networks), application-customized context classifying (subscribing interested context information in application-specific ways) and intelligent context processing (reasoning on application requirements).

- The provision of development support for context-aware pervasive applications. This relieves application developers from the tedious programming of gathering, classifying and processing messy context information in sensor networks.

- The provision of naming services to facilitate effective collaboration amongst applications and sensor networks.

CABOT also takes into account the privacy issue. The privacy services in CABOT are able to modify or even hide some certain kinds of sensor contexts based on user identities and relevant privacy policies. For further details about CABOT, please refer to another paper in this workshop [6].

2.4 Application and User Interface

On top of CABOT, many applications may be developed. One application being developed is a location-estimation system. Such systems can be used to support many location based services, such as location based content delivery and object and people tracking. It is still a challenging problem how to predict accurately the location of a wireless device in an indoor environment, especially when one holds a small device with limited computational and power resources. On receiving signals from various access points distributed in an indoor wireless environment, it is natural to ask: where is the user now in the building? And, how may we best help the user [7]?

The above questions present a challenge for computer science in general and artificial intelligence in particular. We have developed an integrated framework called LEAPS (location estimation and action prediction system), which provides solutions for a number of location-related applications, including location queries and location-based user behavior recognition [8]. Such a system can be useful for a variety of applications. In education, the system can provide a student walking in the faculty office area after a class with information about professors, their office hours and class information. The system can offer help by giving directions to the right office. For people suffering from various cognitive limitations in hospitals and care facilities, the technique can discover when a person's behavior is out of the norm and provide help in a timely manner. For students in a university campus, the plan recognizer can enable intelligent pre-fetching of class-content-related information. For shoppers in a busy business environment such as a shopping mall, services and products can be offered not only according to people's current location, but also according to their intended goals and actions. Plan recognition using a relational model also allows prediction of new locations that a user might be visiting even if the location is new to a user.

Some applications require integrated data access, communication, and actions on heterogeneous devices. For instance, a lab monitoring application may need to acquire sensor readings from the environment and to operate network cameras to capture the scene upon the detection of a suspicious event. For these applications, a declarative, SQL (Structured Query Language) interface is useful in order to specify the data interested and actions intended. The interface provides a relational view of the data flowing from sensors as well as an abstraction of device-oriented operations (actions). Systems support and optimization mechanisms are implemented behind the interface for ease of application development and performance [9].

2.5 MEADOWS: A Suite of Evaluation Tools

We are developing a collection of tools for large-scale, in-depth studies on sensor networks. Specifically, these tools are on modeling, emulation, and data analysis for wireless sensor networks (MEADOWS) [11] in addition to monitoring. We have designed a hierarchical power consumption model for sensor databases, a distributed emulator called VMNet (Virtual Mote Network) of sensor networks [10], and a few data analysis functions for sensory data. These tools will interact with all layers of BLOSSOMS closely. On one hand, information about real systems (e.g., sensor node statistics from the BUDS layer) provides system parameters for MEADOWS; on the other hand, MEADOWS enables analysis and validation of real systems.

3 Conclusions

We have presented an overview of the BLOSSOMS project being investigated at CAS and HKUST. Building a working sensor (BUDS) is a major challenge to the project. The MEADOWS tools are also essential because they allow us to simulate the behavior of large-scale sensor applications. The CABOT middleware provides infrastructural support for applications and the LEAPS system allows location-based applications to be easily built. This project involves close collaboration of researchers from different disciplines because of the broad project scope. At the time of writing, the project is still in its beginning stage. As the project moves forward, we expect to identify more research issues and produce more research results.

References

1. I. Akyildiz, W. Su, Y. Sankarasubramaniam and E. Cayirci, "A Survey on Sensor Networks," *IEEE Communications*, August 2002, pp. 102-114.
2. J. Hill, R. Szewczyk, A. Woo, S. Hollar, D. Culler and K. Pister, "System Architecture Directions for Network Sensors," *ASPLOS* 2000.
3. C. Intanagonwiwat, R. Govindan and D. Estrin, "Directed Diffusion," *MobiCom 2000*, pp. 56-67, 2000.
4. J. Ma, M. Gao, Y.M. Zhu and L.M. Ni, "Anchor-free Localization with Refinement in Sensor Networks," submitted for publication, July 2004.

5. L.M. Ni, Y.H. Liu, Y.C. Lau and A.P. Patil, "LANDMARC: Indoor Location Sensing Using Active RFID," *First IEEE International Conference on Pervasive Computing and Communications (PerCom'03),* March 2003.
6. Chang Xu, S.C. Cheung, Cindy Lo, K.C. Leung, and Jun Wei, "Cabot: On the Ontology for the Middleware Support of Context-Aware Pervasive Applications," *Proc. of the IFIP NPC'04 Workshop on Building Intelligent Sensor Networks (BISON '04),* October 2004.
7. J. Yin, X.Y. Chai and Q. Yang, "High-level Goal Recognition in a Wireless LAN," in *Proc. of the Nineteenth National Conference on Artificial Intelligence (AAAI-04),* San Jose, CA USA, July 2004.
8. Q. Yang, Y.Q. Chen, J. Yin and X.Y. Chai, "LEAPS: A Location Estimation and Action Prediction System in a Wireless LAN Environment," *Proc. of the IFIP NPC'04 Workshop on Building Intelligent Sensor Networks (BISON '04),* October 2004.
9. W. Xue and Q. Luo, "AORTA: Action-Oriented Query Processing in Pervasive Computing". Under submission, July 2004.
10. H. Wu, Q. Luo, P. Zheng, B. He, and L. M. Ni. "Accurate Emulation of Wireless Sensor Networks", *Proc. of the IFIP NPC'04 Workshop on Building Intelligent Sensor Networks (BISON '04),* October 2004.
11. Q. Luo, L. M. Ni, B. He, H. Wu, and W. Xue, "MEADOWS: Modeling, Emulation, Analysis of Data of Wireless Sensors," *Proc. of the VLDB Workshop on Data Management for Sensor Networks (DMSN'04),* August 2004.

A Pervasive Sensor Node Architecture

Li Cui, Fei Wang, Haiyong Luo, Hailing Ju, and Tianpu Li

Institute of Computing Technology
Chinese Academy of Sciences
Beijing, P.R.China 100080
lcui@ict.ac.cn

Abstract. A set of sensor nodes is the basic component of a sensor network. Many researchers are currently engaged in developing pervasive sensor nodes due to the great promise and potential with applications shown by various wireless remote sensor networks. This short paper describes the concept of sensor node architecture and current research activities on sensor node development at ICTCAS.

1 The Concept of Sensor Node Architecture

A sensor network is made up of the following parts, namely a set of *sensor nodes* which are distributed in a sensor field, a *sink* which communicates with the *task manager* via *Internet* interfacing with users. A set of sensor nodes is the basic component of a sensor network. Many researchers are currently engaged in developing pervasive sensor nodes [1-3] due to the great promise and potential with applications shown by various wireless remote sensor networks [4 10]. A sensor node is composed of four basic components as shown in Fig. 1. They are *a sensing unit, a processing unit, a communication unit and a power unit.*

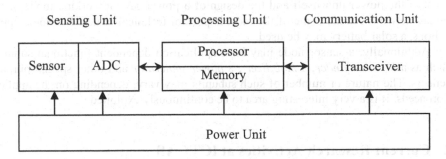

Fig. 1. The components of a sensor node

Sensing units are usually made up of application specific sensors and ADCs (analog to digital converters), which digitalize the analog signals produced by the sensors when they sensed particular phenomenon. In some cases, an actuator is also needed.

H. Jin et al. (Eds.): NPC 2004, LNCS 3222, pp. 565-567, 2004.

Obviously sensors play a key role in a sensor network which are the very front end connecting our physical world to the computational world and the Internet. Although MEMS technology has been making steady progress in the past decades, there is still large space for the further development of smart front end sensors. Among them, various chemical and biochemical sensors remain one of the most challenging sensor groups to be explored and developed, e.g. sensors to detect toxic or explosive trace in public areas, sensors for diagnostic analysis and sensors used under extreme conditions. New sensing principle, new sensing material and new sensor design need to be invented and adopted.

The processing unit is usually associated with an embedded operating system, a microcontroller and a storage part. It manages data acquisition, analyzes the raw sensing data and formulates answers to specific user requests. It also controls the communication and performs a wide variety of application specified tasks. Energy and cost are two key constraints for processing components. Nodes may have different types of processors for certain specific tasks. For example, a video sensor node may need a more powerful processor to run than a common temperature sensor. A small embedded operation system such as Berkeley's TinyOS [2] is another key issue for an embedded system. Besides the basic ability for process management and resource management, it may also possess the capability for software tailor and real time management, the ability to provide support for embedded middleware, network protocols and embedded database.

The transceiver connects the sensor node to the network. Usually each of the sensor nodes has the capability to transmit data to and receive data from another node and the sink. The latter may further communicate with the task manager via Internet (or Satellite) and information reaches the end user. A transceiver is the most power-consuming component of the node. Thus the study of multi-hop communications and complex power saving modes of operation, e.g. having multiple different sleep states, is crucial in this content.

The power unit delivers power to all the working parts of the node. Because of the limited capacity of the power unit, e.g. the limited lifetime of a battery, the development of the power unit itself and the design of a power saving working mode of the sensor network remain some of the most important technical issues. For some applications, a solar battery may be used.

Additionally, a sensor node may have application dependent functional subunits such as a *location finder*, a *mobilizer* , a *power generator* and other special-purpose sensors. The nature or number of such subunits may vary, depending on the application needs. It is a very interesting area to be continuously exploited.

2 Current Research Activities at ICTCAS

Research on sensor node architecture is currently undertaking at ICTCAS. Our goal is to build multifunctional sensing nodes targeting on applications such as intelligent transportation system, precision agriculture, remote medical care and public safety monitoring and notification and so on.

Efforts are made to tackle the following technical issues:

1) The development of new type of chemical sensors for the detection or monitoring of explosives using new sensing principle and materials, e.g. function polymer and nano materials; the design of special-purpose sensor nodes, such as video sensors, monitoring sensors, and intruding sensors;

2) The development of an embedded operating system for an ultra low power sensor node. Besides the basic ability for process control and resource management, it will also possess the capability for software tailing and real time management, the ability to provide support for embedded middleware, network protocols and embedded database;

3) The design of sensor node hardware and system integration. Here low power consumption and high reliability design are our main concern;

4) Hardware and software co-design systematically to manage low power consumption and high reliability.

Besides the research projects on the basic level for sensor node architecture development as mentioned above, other projects on the network communication level is also undertaking at ICTCAS, including the study on multi-hop self-contained sensor network architecture, the development of related communication protocols, middleware and algorithm, complex power saving modes of operations and so on.

References

1. Crossbow, Inc. Wireless Sensor Network Products. http://www.xbow.com
2. TinyOS. http://www.tinyos.net
3. http://robotics.eecs.berkeley.edu/~pister/SmartDust/
4. Akyildiz, I.F.; Weilian Su; Sankarasubramaniam, Y.; Cayirci, E.: A survey on sensor networks. Communications Magazine, IEEE , V 40 (2002) 102–114
5. Arici, T. and Altunbasak, Y.: Adaptive Sensing for Environment Monitoring using Wireless Sensor Networks. Proc. IEEE Wireless Communications and Networking Conference (WCNC), Atlanta, GA, (2004)
6. Mainwaring, A., Culler, D., Polastre, J., Szewczyk, R., Anderson, J.: Wireless Sensor Networks for Habitat Monitoring. Proceedings of the 1st ACM international workshop on Wireless sensor networks and applications (2002)
7. http://www.alertsystems.org
8. Delin, K.A., and Jackson, S.P.: The sensor web: A new instrument comcept. SPIE's Symposium on Integrated Optics, 20-26, Jan. (2001)
9. Schwiebert, L., Gupta, S.K.S., and Weinmann. J.: Research challenges in wireless networks of biomedical sensors. In Mobile Computing and Networking, (2001) 151-165
10. Korhonen, J.Parkka and M.Van GILS: Health monitoring in the home of the future. IEEE Engineering in Medicine and Biology Magazine May (2003) 66-73

Cabot: On the Ontology for the Middleware Support of Context-Aware Pervasive Applications

Chang Xu[1], S.C. Cheung[1], Cindy Lo[1], K.C. Leung[1] and Jun Wei[2]

[1]Department of Computer Science, Hong Kong University of Science and Technology
Clear Water Bay, Kowloon, Hong Kong
{changxu, scc, cindylo, lkchiu}@cs.ust.hk
[2]Technology Center of Software Engineering, Institute of Software,
Chinese Academy of Science
wj@otcaix.iscas.ac.cn

Abstract. Middleware support is a major topic in pervasive computing. Existing studies mainly address the issues in the organization of and the collaboration amongst devices and services, but pay little attention to the design support of context-aware pervasive applications. Most of these applications are required to be adaptable to dynamic environments and self-managed. However, most context-aware pervasive applications nowadays have to carry out tedious tasks of gathering, classifying and processing messy context information due to lack of the necessary middleware support. To address this problem, we propose a novel approach based on ontology technology, and apply it in our *Cabot* project. Our approach defines a context ontology catered for the pervasive computing environment. The ontology acts as the context information agreement amongst all computing components to support applications with flexible context gathering and classifying capabilities. This allows a domain ontology database to be constructed for storing the semantics relationship of concepts used in the pervasive computing environment. The ontology database supports applications with rich context processing capabilities. With the aid of ontology technology, *Cabot* further helps alleviate the impact of the naming problem, and support advanced user space switching. A case study is given to show how *Cabot* assists developers in designing context-aware pervasive applications.

1 Introduction

A pervasive computing environment encompasses a spectrum of computation and communication devices that seamlessly augment human thoughts and activities [1]. Due to the non-trivial context management inherent in pervasive computing, a suitable software infrastructure is needed to assist the development of context-aware pervasive applications. We refer the **context** of a computation task to as the circumstances or situations in which the task takes place. Most context-aware pervasive applications are required to be adaptable to highly dynamic environments and self-managed. Therefore, the design of such applications is a challenging research issue.

At present, developers of context-aware pervasive applications need to write tedious and repetitive codes to handle context management, which concerns the following three functions:

H. Jin et al. (Eds.): NPC 2004, LNCS 3222, pp. 568–575, 2004.

- **Context gathering:** Gather proper context information from relevant context sources in a flexible way rather than specifying them explicitly. When an application is interested in object movement, the middleware should be able to select proper sensors to collect context information about object movement.
- **Context classifying:** Classify context information into different categories in an application-specific way. An application may hope to analyze a certain scenario where the subject is "human being", the action is "enter" and the area is "office 4208". The common context classification is only based on context type (e.g. sound, location, temperature, etc.), which cannot meet such requirements.
- **Context processing:** Support applications with stronger context processing capabilities, e.g. context reasoning (knowing "car" is a subclass of "vehicle" helps an application interested in vehicle movement collect context information about cars) and context filtering (filtering certain context information for privacy purpose).

Existing studies on the middleware support mainly address the issues in the organization of and the collaboration amongst devices and services in the pervasive computing environment, but pay little attention to the design support of context-aware pervasive applications. None of proposed middleware infrastructures like *Gaia* [1], *Easy-Living* [2], *i-Land* [3], *Aura* [4] and *Interactive Workspaces* [5] can effectively assist application developers to handle all the above tasks.

Other studies focusing on context-awareness in [7][8][9] mainly analyze some useful features of context information and propose some helpful frameworks, yet still leaving the context processing duties to clients.

In this paper, we propose a novel approach based on ontology technology, and apply it in our *Cabot* project. Three important concepts, namely, context ontology, context pattern and context matching will be defined. Users use context patterns to subscribe their interested context information, while the middleware uses these context patterns to execute context matching for users. Context pattern helps implement flexible context gathering and classifying, and also contributes to enhancing applications with stronger context processing capabilities.

The remainder of this paper is organized as follows: Sec. 2 introduces related work in recent years; Sec. 3 presents the *Cabot* project – a software infrastructure supporting context-aware pervasive applications built on ontology technology; Sec. 4 further talks about some relevant issues about *Cabot*; Sec. 5 is a case study; and the last section concludes our contributions and explores future work.

2 Related Work

Existing studies on context-awareness are mostly concerned with either the frameworks that support the abstraction of context information or the context models that support data queries. Some typical works includes Cooltown project [7], Sentient Computing project [8] and Owl context service [9]. Their proposed context models generally lack formal bases; some of them even ignore the temporal aspects of context information.

Published research projects in the middleware support for pervasive computing include *Gaia, EasyLiving, i-Land, Aura* and *Interactive Workspaces*.

Gaia is a middleware project focusing on general-purpose pervasive environment. It makes use of active spaces [1] to encapsulate all low-level devices and services to provide a uniform interface such that developers can utilize and control the pervasive computing environment more easily. *Aura* is similar to *Gaia*, but uses a different approach. *Aura* has a context observer to monitor environmental changes that would trigger *Aura* to perform pre-defined actions. Each environment is managed by a distinct *Aura* system, and multiple *Aura* systems can cooperate to perform tasks.

i-Land works in a special environment that consists of a *DynaWall*, an *InteracTable* and a *CommChair* [3]. *DynaWall* is a wall-size touch screen, while *InteracTable* is a display on table. *CommChair* is a chair with computer network support. All devices can interact with each other and serve for presentations and discussions. *Interactive Workspaces* is another project sharing the same objectives with *i-Land*. It mainly focuses on the collaboration between a PDA and large screen projectors.

EasyLiving is a computer-centric system focusing on the living environment. A typical living environment has projectors, wireless keyboards, mice, finger-print recognizers, cameras, etc. Cameras can capture events in the house, and the images will be used for recognizing people and tracing their locations.

These projects work on the management of computing resources, while *Cabot* focuses on how to flexibly gather and classify context information and make further processing including context reasoning and context filtering.

3 Cabot System Architecture

In *Cabot*'s point of view, a complete pervasive computing environment is composed of Application Layer, Middleware Layer and Sensor Layer (Fig. 1).

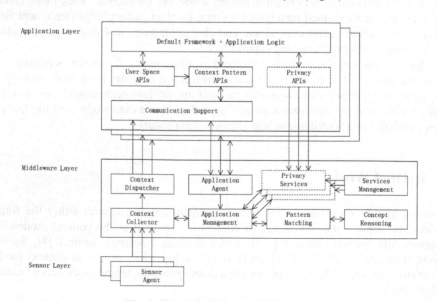

Fig. 1. The *Cabot* system architecture

Context-aware pervasive applications run at the Application Layer. This layer has complete client support in terms of *APIs*. Applications can use context pattern *APIs* to manage (subscribe, update or remove) their own context patterns. Other *APIs* include user space *APIs* and privacy *APIs*. They are related to user space management and privacy services respectively. An application framework is provided for application development. Usually, users do not have to pay attention to the details of communication with the middleware. They only need to focus on application logics, that is, make clear what their interested context information is and how to handle it.

The Middleware Layer is the kernel part. This layer implements five fundamental functionalities: (a) **application management** to be in charge of all registered applications, (b) **context pattern management** to be responsible for context pattern manipulations, (c) **context pattern matching** to be invoked automatically when the middleware receives any incoming context information, (d) **context semantics reasoning** to infer the semantic relations between concepts for reasoning, and (e) **third-party service management** to allow the middleware to integrate external context filtering services (e.g. privacy services) such that further context processing can be facilitated. The privacy services currently provided allows to modify or to hide some certain kinds of context information based on user identities and relevant privacy policies.

A concept related to the Sensor Layer is active entity. Active entities can be physical devices, software components or human beings. They periodically or non-periodically send context information to the middleware. Physical devices collect sensed context information (e.g., Tom enters into office 4208); software components generate derived context information (e.g., Cindy is busy); and human beings supply profiled context information (e.g., Cedric is supervised by Prof. Cheung). We regard each "qualified" active entity as a sensor agent. By "qualified", we mean that each active entity can exchange context information with the middleware based on a predefined context ontology.

4 Main Cabot Features

4.1 Context Ontology and Context Pattern

Most middleware infrastructures have limitations in supporting applications to flexibly subscribe context information. Usually, context subscription is based on context type. It may be inconvenient when users want to gather the context information mentioned in Sec. 1. Due to lack of the necessary support, users have to gather all relevant context information, and do analysis by themselves. This increases the network traffic in context transmission and the analysis workload in context processing.

Our approach is based on ontology technology. We propose context ontology, an ontology document catered for the pervasive computing environment. The context ontology acts as the context information agreement to which all applications, sensor agents and the middleware should conform in pervasive computing. Fig. 2 illustrates some major concepts (classes) and relations (properties) in the context ontology.

An **environment context** is defined by instantiating each ontology concept. When only part of ontology concepts is instantiated, it is called a **context pattern**. Applications subscribe their interested environment contexts to the middleware by means of context patterns.

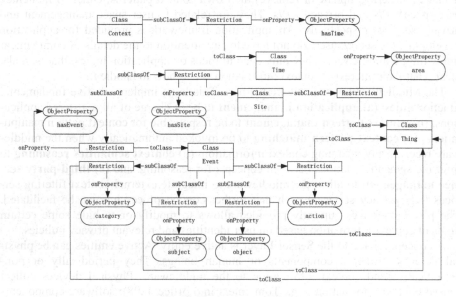

Fig. 2. The context ontology

4.2 Context Matching and Concept Semantics Reasoning

Cabot performs context matching between received environment contexts and subscribed context patterns. Both of them are transmitted, stored and processed in *XML* documents in practice. So an efficient tool for managing *XML* documents and an expressive language for describing matching rules are imminent. We utilize *xlinkit* to perform context matching. It is a software framework for checking the consistency of distributed *XML* documents. It comprises a rule language based on First Order Logic (*FOL*) and *XPath* notation [6]. For each incoming environment context, *xlinkit* checks whether it can be matched for any context pattern stored in the pattern repository according to pre-defined matching rules. The matching rules are written like this:

```
<forall var="context" in="/Context">
  <not><exists var="pattern" in="/Repository/hasPattern/Pattern">
  ......
  </exists></not>
</forall>
```

The omitted part is the kernel matching criteria that can be classified into three modes: exact matching mode, equivalent matching mode and plug-in matching mode.

If we require that a matching is recognized when a concept has exactly the same value in both the environment context and the context pattern, it is called **exact matching mode**. In the **equivalent matching mode**, the semantics relation between two concepts is identified to check equivalence. For example, when "weather" and "climate" or "enter" and "come into" appear in pairs, a matching is recognized. The

plug-in matching mode further allows a context pattern to concern richer context information. When a more specific concept (say "car") encounters a more general concept (say "vehicle"), this mode accepts it. The context matching example in Fig. 3 adopts all the three matching modes.

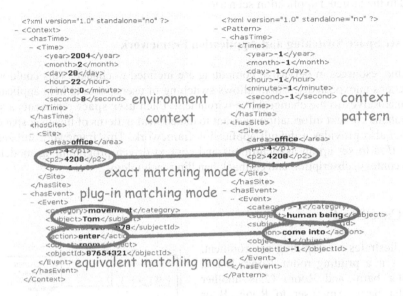

Fig. 3. A context matching example

When all concepts between an environment context and a context pattern are matched, *Cabot* asserts this environment context to be "qualified" for this context pattern.

The use of *xlinkit*'s built-in comparison operators is not enough for supporting context matching. So an operator special for concept semantics reasoning is required in *Cabot* implementation. This operator acts as the interface of a concept semantics reasoning subsystem built on a pervasive computing domain ontology database.

The domain ontology database stores much knowledge on semantics relations between concepts used in the pervasive computing environment. For example, "weather" is similar to "climate", and "car" is a subclass of "vehicle". Based on the domain ontology, the reasoning subsystem infers the semantics relation between two concepts as **equivalent, subsumed, including, intersecting** or **disjoint**.

The inferred semantics relation is the foundation of context matching. Let a concept in the environment context be c_1, and the counterpart in the context pattern be c_2:

- **Exact matching:** c_1 and c_2 are said to be matched when they are exactly the same;
- **Equivalent matching:** c_1 and c_2 are said to be matched when they are exactly the same, or have an equivalent relation;
- **Plug-in matching:** c_1 and c_2 are said to be matched when they are exactly the same, or have an equivalent or subsumed relation.

Some knowledge on concept semantics relations (e.g., "desk" is similar to "table") helps implement some special tasks (e.g., monitoring the abnormal movement of table-like things). Another usage of the ontology reasoning is to alleviate the naming problem across different sensor agents. For example, having known that "light" is similar to "lighting/ray/beam", a light-detecting application can behave better when facing different naming standards. In order to have applications enhanced with some certain reasoning capability, *Cabot* needs to incorporate the corresponding ontology related to the targeted application scenario.

4.3   User Space Switching and Application Framework

Available resources in pervasive computing are inclined to change. This could affect applications unexpectedly. *Cabot* allows switching of user spaces to help applications adapt themselves to the changeable environment. Each **user space** represents a space that contains context information relevant to the context patterns of this user space.

Cabot also provides a default application framework. This framework utilizes the *Cabot APIs* to set up an asynchronous and context-driven programming model that adopts context subscription and callback handling technology.

5   A Case Study

Fig. 4 illustrates a computing environment. Room A is a printing room, Room B is a computer barn, and Room C is another computer barn. Any user to Room B or Room C will pass the Gate first.

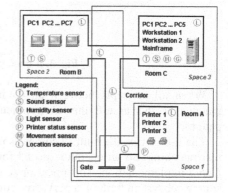

An administrator, Peter, responsible for equipment maintenance usually stays in Room A, supplying printer paper when necessary and monitoring the coming users. Sometime, he goes to Room A and Room B to check whether everything is going well.

Suppose that temperature and sound context information is required to evaluate the PC status in Room B. But for Room C, ad-

Fig. 4. A practical case

ditional humidity and light context information is also needed. Peter hopes to know the current equipment status once entering Room B or Room C, and no matter in which room he is resident, continuous monitoring of printers and coming users is expected.

We assume that all required sensors have been installed properly (Fig. 4). The following is the application design solution that comprises three user spaces (Fig. 4):

- **Space 1:** (Gate + Room A) Activating condition: Peter leaves Room B or Room C. Context patterns: (1) printer (area: Room A, subject: printer), and (2) people (area: Gate, category: movement, subject: people, action: enter).
- **Space 2:** (Gate + Room A + Room B) Activating condition: Peter enters Room B. Extra context patterns (to Space 1): (1) temperature (area: Room B, category: temperature, subject: PC), and (2) sound (area: Room B, category: sound, subject: PC).
- **Space 3:** (Gate + Room A + Room C) Activating condition: Peter enters Room C. Extra context patterns (to Space 1): (1) temperature (area: Room C, category: tem-

perature, subject: computer), (2) sound (area: Room C, category: sound, subject: computer), (3) humidity (area: Room C, category: humidity, subject: air), and (4) brightness (area: Room C, category: light, subject: fluorescent lamp).

Cabot supports this application with two distinct capabilities: (1) context reasoning (e.g. "someone comes into ..." = "somebody enters ..."); (2) context subscription with plug-in matching (e.g. "computer" = "PC" + "workstation" + "mainframe" in Space 3).

6 Conclusions and Future Work

In this paper, we have overviewed several existing middleware infrastructures for pervasive computing. Their supports of context management are inadequate. To address this problem, we develop *Cabot* with the use of ontology technology.

A useful concept, context pattern, is introduced into *Cabot* to facilitate the context gathering, classifying and processing. In order to alleviate the naming problem and to enhance the expressiveness of context patterns, *Cabot* supports three flexible context matching modes. *Cabot* also allows the automatic and manual switching between user spaces to help realize adaptable context-aware pervasive applications.

At present, Cabot is still at a prototype stage. New functionalities and features (e.g. context trigger and context deriving) will be incorporated into the future releases of *Cabot*.

Reference

[1]   M. Román, C. K. Hess, R. Cerqueira, A. Ranganathan, R. H. Campbell, K. Nahrstedt, Gaia: A Middleware Infrastructure to Enable Active Spaces, in *IEEE Pervasive Computing*, pp. 74-83, Oct-Dec 2002.

[2]   B. Brumitt, B. Meyers, J. Krumm, A. Kern, and S. Shafer, EasyLiving: Technologies for Intelligent Environments, presented at Handheld and Ubiquitous Computing (HUC), Bristol, England, 2000.

[3]   P. Tandler, Software Infrastructure for Ubiquitous Computing Environments: Supporting Synchronous Collaboration with Heterogeneous Devices, at Ubicomp 2001: Ubiquitous Computing, Atlanta, Georgia, 2001.

[4]   J. P. Sousa and D. Garlan, Aura: An Architectural Framework for User Mobility in Ubiquitous Computing Environments, presented at IEEE Conference on Software Architecture, Montreal, 2002.

[5]   A. Fox, B. Johanson, P. Hanrahan, and T. Winograd, Integrating Information Appliances into an Interactive Workspace, *IEEE Computer Graphics & Applications*, vol. 20, 2000.

[6]   C. Nentwich, W. Emmerich, A. Finkelstein, Consistency Management with Repair Actions, in the *Proc. of the 25th International Conference on Software Engineering (ICSE'03)*, Portland, Oregon, USA, May 2003.

[7]   T. Kindberg, et al, People, Places, Things: Web Presence for the Real World, *Technical Report HPL-2000-16*, Hewlett-Packard Labs, 2000.

[8]   A. Harter, et al, The Anatomy of a Context-Aware Application, in *Mobile Computing and Networking*, pages 59-68, 1999.

[9]   M. Ebling, G.D.H. Hunt, H. Lei, Issues for Context Services for Pervasive Computing, in *Middleware 2001 Workshop on Middleware for Mobile Computing*, Heidelberg, 2001.

Accurate Emulation of Wireless Sensor Networks

Hejun Wu[+], Qiong Luo[+], Pei Zheng[*], Bingsheng He[+], and Lionel M. Ni[+]

[+] Department of Computer Science
The Hong Kong University of Science and Technology
Clear Water Bay, Kowloon
Hong Kong, China
{whjnn, luo, saven, ni}@cs.ust.hk
[*] Department of Computer Science
Arcadia University
450 South Easton Road
Glenside, PA 19038, USA
zheng@arcadia.edu

Abstract. Wireless sensor networks (WSNs) have a wide range of useful, data-centric applications, and major techniques involved in these applications include in-network query processing and query-informed routing. Both techniques require realistic environments and detailed system feedback for development and evaluation. Unfortunately, neither real sensor networks nor existing simulators/emulators are suitable for this requirement. In this design paper, we propose a distributed sensor network emulator, a Virtual Mote Network (VMNet), to meet this requirement. We describe the system architecture, the synchronization of the nodes and the virtual time emulation with a focus on mechanisms that are effective for accurate emulation.

1. Introduction

Wireless sensor networks (WSNs) enable applications to obtain up-to-date information about the physical world. This information is especially valuable for environments in which it is inefficient, difficult or dangerous for people to collect data on site by themselves. However, such environments also make it hard to study techniques for data-centric WSN applications in real sensor networks. Furthermore, major techniques in data-centric WSNs, such as in-network query processing [8][11] and query-informed routing [3], need a realistic development and evaluation environment with system feedback at a suitable level of detail. In this design paper, we propose to develop an accurate sensor network emulator in order to facilitate studies of techniques for data-centric WSN applications.

Traditionally, simulators and emulators are useful tools for networking research in that they simulate or emulate real networking protocols and provide a controllable environment for studies. This usefulness is even greater for WSN applications, because real WSNs are in frequent upgrades and their deployment is tightly embedded in the physical environment. As evidence, several sensor network simulators and emulators [9] have been developed for large-scale WSN studies.

H. Jin et al. (Eds.): NPC 2004, LNCS 3222, pp. 576-583, 2004.

If we focus on developing and debugging WSN applictions in a realistic environment, existing tools such as TOSSIM [7] and EmStar [4] are excellent choices. However, with the advance of data-centric WSN applications, such as environmental monitoring and assisted living, more requirements for simulation and emulation are posed for developing and evaluating techniques in these applications. For instance, in-network query processing and query-informed routing, two major cross-layer techniques for data-centric WSN applications, require the WSN to return information about sensor node power consumption and response time in order to make decisions for network routing and query processing. Evaluation of alternatives of each technique also requires this information for performance comparison. Unfortunately, current WSN simulators/emulators are insufficient to address this need. Specifically, an accurate emulation of timing and power consumption for node execution and communication is missing in current WSN simulators and emulators.

Aiming at accurate emulation of a WSN for data-centric applications, we propose a WSN emulator called a Virtual Mote Network (VMNet). A VMNet consists of virtual sensor nodes connected through a virtual channel. Each virtual sensor node in turn consists of an emulated CPU as well as emulated hardware peripherals (e.g., sensing units and radio frequency units). The emulated CPU executes software that can run on real sensor nodes and reports execution time at the granularity of the emulated CPU cycle. The emulated hardware peripherals generate interrupts with realistic delays. The virtual channel is emulated through UDP (User Datagram Protocol) on networked PCs with emulated bit errors, delays, and packet collision. Putting all these units together, the timing information of the software under study (e.g., an in-network query processor or a query-informed router) can be accurately emulated and be fed back for the execution and evaluation of the software.

The remainder of this paper is structured as follows. Section 2 introduces the background of our work. Section 3 presents the design of VMNet, including the architecture and components. Section 4 discusses related work briefly and Section 5 concludes.

2. Background

2.1. Terminology

The following terms are used throughout the paper:

Node and **Mote**: both refer to a sensor node consisting of computation, sensing, and communication units. The two terms are used interchangeably.

Real (Target) vs. **Virtual (Emulated)**: A real or target component is one in a real WSN and its counterpart in VMNet is virtual or emulated. For instance, a real CPU is in a real sensor node and a virtual CPU in a virtual mote. Similarly, we refer to the execution time of real software being emulated as the virtual time (not the time of executing the emulation itself).

2.2. Overview of a Target WSN

Fig. 1 shows a typical WSN. The sensor mote in the WSN is MICA2 by crossbow
[2]. We choose MICA2 as the target because it is most commonly used.

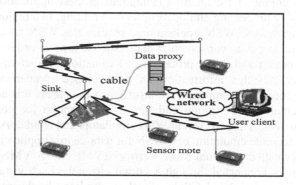

Fig. 1. A Typical WSN

The WSN in Fig. 1 consists of several components, each of which performs different functions. Table 1 lists these components and their composition. Each sensor
node in the WSN runs application software (e.g., a query processor) developed using
TinyOS [3]. The sink node acts as the root of the WSN and communicates with the
data proxy. The data proxy in turn communicates with the user client. Note that the
data proxy and the user client can be on the same PC.

Table 1. Components of a WSN

Components	Composition
Sensor mote (MICA2)	A main board (MPR410) with the Atmega 128, 8 bit, 7.3827MHz CPU and the Chipcon CC1000, 38kb/s, CSMA radio circuit, and a sensor board (MTS300)
Sink node	A main board (MPR410) and a PC interface card with a serial port
Data proxy	A PC that communicates with the sink node via a serial port
User client	A PC that runs the user interface program

The operation of the WSN is as follows: Use the user client to post commands and
queries. These queries are parsed by the data proxy and are disseminated via the sink
node to the network. If a mote acquires data that satisfy a query, it sends the sensory
data tuples to the data proxy through the sink node. The data proxy forwards the
result to the user client.

3. VMNet Design

Our VMNet is designed via a divide-and-conquer approach. First, we analyze the
target WSN, and divide the WSN into components. Second, we design the architecture of the emulator based on the architecture of the real WSN. Third, we design each
emulated component based on its counterpart in the real WSN.

3.1. VMNet Architecture

The architecture of VMNet (Fig. 2) resembles that of a real WSN. It consists of the virtual sink node (VM 0) and other virtual motes connected through virtual channels. Real application software runs on the virtual motes for sensing, processing, and routing. Emulated radio signals travel on the virtual channels. Additionally, the Application User Interface (AUI) and the Network Manager (NM) reside on VM0 for application management (corresponds to the data proxy and the user client in the real WSN) and network emulation management respectively.

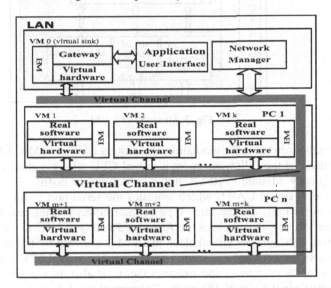

Fig. 2. VMNet architecture

VMNet is designed to be a distributed system in order to achieve fast emulation, high accuracy and scalability. It employs a wired Local Area Network (LAN) to emulate the wireless network. Each real mote in the target WSN is emulated by a program running on the LAN. From our past experience [13], this parallel architecture that VMNet adopts has shown high fidelity and scalability in emulating general wireless networks.

In brief, the architecture of VMNet abstracts the common features of WSNs. Although VMNet can only emulate one type of WSNs at one time, the generality of its architecture makes it easy to switch to other WSNs.

3.2. Virtual Mote

A virtual mote (VM) has three components: the virtual hardware, the real software and the Emulation Manager (EM). Fig. 3 shows the structure of a VM.

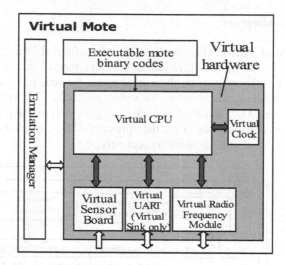

Fig. 3. Structure of a VM

The virtual hardware is the emulation of a mote's hardware (MICA2 in this paper). It is composed of the following units: a virtual CPU with a virtual clock, a Virtual Radio Frequency Module (VRFM) and a virtual sensor board. In the virtual sink node, there is a virtual UART, which emulates the serial port of the sink node. The virtual hardware units are the same type as their corresponding real hardware. For instance, the virtual CPU emulates the Atmega 128 CPU of MICA2 mote.

The virtual CPU and the virtual clock in a VM are critical for the accuracy of emulation, because they control execution and timing. The virtual CPU parses the executable binary codes of a mote and executes them. It also interacts with other virtual hardware units via the virtual I/O ports. The virtual clock is incremented by the virtual CPU per mote CPU clock cycle and records the virtual time in a VM.

The emulation manager manages mote emulation and logs the emulated actions, the execution time of various modes and runtime status of these units.

VM 0 (the virtual sink) is different from other VMs in that it has the virtual UART but no virtual sensor board. The difference is emulated by the gateway software, which operates on the virtual UART and disregards the virtual sensor board.

All three components – the virtual hardware, the real application software and the emulation manager, are separate from one another in a VM. There is a clear interface between the three components. This design ensures the reusability of our emulator when the target application or hardware changes. It also provides a reasonable solution to the conflict between the generality and the accuracy (specificity) of emulation.

3.3. Virtual Channel

The virtual channel generates network effects using three software modules: the bit error module, the delay module and the collision module (shown in Fig. 4). Let us first describe the transmission process of data on a virtual channel connected with a VM. When outgoing bits are sent from the Virtual Radio Frequency Module (VRFM) of the VM to the virtual channel, they pass through the three modules and stay in a buffer (in the lower right corner of Fig. 4) for wrapping. When all bits of a packet arrive in the buffer, the virtual channel wraps them into a packet and sends out the packet via UDP. When an incoming UDP packet arrives at the virtual channel, it is put into a queue (lower left of Fig. 4) and is decomposed into bits to be sent to the VRFM of the VM via another buffer (on the left of Fig. 4).

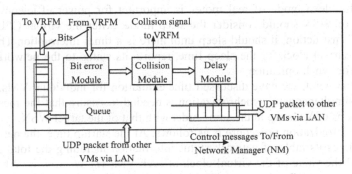

Fig. 4. Virtual Channel

The bit error module uses an experiential radio signal error data model to generate the error rate. The bit error rate model is a table with two attributes: distance and bit error rate, which is defined as: (number of error bits received by the receiver) / (number of total bits sent by the sender). The module randomly generates the bit error at a rate that the table specifies.

The transmission delay module adds a delay to the virtual time of the outgoing packet. The collision module emulates radio signal collision by performing two operations: *carrier sense* and *collision*. Both operations need information about the virtual time and the data transmission status of all VMs. This information is kept in the Network Manager.

In the *carrier sense* operation, the collision module asks the network manager whether if a sending VM can hear any VMs that are transmitting data. If so, the sending VM will wait a random time defined by the network protocols. In the *collision* operation, the collision module destroys the current bit to be sent on one of the two conditions: (1) another VM is transmitting and the sender of the bit can hear that transmitting VM, or (2) another VM is sending to the same destination as this sender.

3.4. Virtual Time

The major criterion for the accuracy of our emulation is the emulated time, or the virtual time. Mathematic models are one way to estimate time, but it is hard to achieve a high accuracy with simple models. In VMNet, we follow the approach of real execution. That is, the emulator executes the real software and measures the virtual time of the execution.

We have described the timing mechanism in the virtual CPU with a virtual clock in Section 3.2. Moreover, the working time of hardware peripherals such as sensing time and transmitting time are also emulated. Let us take the virtual sensor board as an example. When the virtual sensor board receives a command from the virtual CPU, it checks the virtual clock and after a delay (the length of delay is based on measurements in real systems) sends an interruption signal to the interruption port connected to the virtual CPU. When the virtual CPU receives the interruption signal, it executes the sensor data interruption service program. Therefore, the virtual time together with the interruption is accurately emulated. The timing and the interruption of RFM and other hardware peripherals are emulated similarly.

Since the sleep mode of real motes is important for power efficiency, accurate emulation of WSN should consider the sleep mode. After the virtual CPU executes the "sleep" instruction, it should sleep until there is a timer interruption The VM advances its virtual clock by the sleep time, reports its status to the network manager and waits for synchronization.

Up to this point, we have discussed time emulation for individual VMs. Because VMs run simultaneously, synchronization is needed to ensure that the messages and the operations of VMs are in the same order with that of the target WSN.

The synchronization procedure is as follows: At the startup time, the network manager initializes its table of network status information including the total number of VMs n and the value of the virtual clock of each VM: vt_0, vt_1... vt_{n-1}. Whenever the VMs run for a predefined interval T which is called the synchronization interval, they pause and report to the network manager. After every VM has reported to the network manager that its virtual clock has advanced by T, the network manager sends out a broadcast message to inform the VMs to resume running.

It is possible that when the fastest VMs (with a virtual time vt) are waiting, other VMs may exceed the fastest VMs. This does not matter as the message order is not affected and the exceeded time will be synchronized in next interval. In order to ensure correct ordering of messages, the virtual channel queues received UDP packets. The packets are sorted by their virtual time in the ascending order. This queue method avoids the semantic error: When a message is processed, it finds there is another message in the buffer that should be processed earlier.

In summary, the virtual time is carefully emulated in VMNet for accuracy. VMNet adopts a virtual CPU with a virtual clock for each VM to manage the timing. The virtual hardware peripherals of a VM generate interruptions with realistic delays. The sleep mode of a VM is considered and is gracefully handled. Synchronization of multiple VMs is performed periodically to ensure the correctness of emulation.

4. Related Work

Previous work, including Glomosim [12], Maisie[10] and SWiMNET [1], has shown that parallel and distributed architectures can speed up simulations. In this direction, our effort on VMNet is an outgrowth of our previous work on a distributed wire-line and wireless network emulation framework EMPOWER [13]. Our previous work EMWIN [14] gives the experiences in emulating wireless networks.

In the area of sensor network simulation and emulation, UC Berkeley's TOSSIM [7] simulates the network at the bit level. It is useful for debugging applications but it has not provided detailed timing information of the target. UCLA's EmStar [4][6] is another simulator of WSNs. It has not focused on detailed performance evaluation of the target WSN yet.

5.   Conclusions and Future Work

We have presented our design of VMNet, a distributed emulator for WSNs with accurate system feedback. We are currently implementing VMNet, with a focus on the accurate estimation of application execution time. We plan to add power consumption emulation as well as mobility emulation to VMNet in the near future.

Acknowledgement

This work is part of the BLOSSOMS project [5]. Funding for this work is provided by the Hong Kong Research Grant Council through Grants IIKUST6158/03E and HKUST6161/03E.

Reference

[1] Azzedine Boukerche, Alessandro Fabbri. Partitioning Parallel Simulation of Wireless Networks. The 2000 Winter Simulation Conference (WSC), 2000.
[2] Crossbow Technology, Inc. http://www.xbow.com/.
[3] Robert Castañeda, Samir R. Das. Query Localization Techniques for On-Demand Routing Protocols in Ad Hoc Networks. Proceedings of the 5th annual ACM/IEEE international conference on Mobile computing and networking, 1999.
[4] EmStar. http://cvs.cens.ucla.edu/emstar/.
[5] Wen Gao, Lionel M. Ni, Zhiwei Xu. BLOSSOMS: A CAS/HKUST Joint Project to Build Lightweight Optimized Sensor Systems on a Massive Scale. The IFIP NPC'04 Workshop on Building Intelligent Sensor Networks (BISON'04), 2004.
[6] Lewis Girod, Jeremy Elson, Alberto Cerpa, Thanos Stathopoulos, Nithya Ramanathan, Deborah Estrin. EmStar: a Software Environment for Developing and Deploying Wireless Sensor Networks. USENIX, 2004.
[7] Philip Levis, Nelson Lee, Matt Welsh, David Culler. TOSSIM: accurate and scalable simulation of entire TinyOS applications. The first international conference on Embedded networked sensor systems, 2003.
[8] Samuel Madden, Michael J. Franklin, Joseph M. Hellerstein, Wei Hong. The design of an acquisitional query processor for sensor networks. SIGMOD, 2003.
[9] NS-2: The Network Simulator: http://www.isi.edu/nsnam/ns/.
[10] Joel Short, Rajive Bagrodia, Leonard Kleinrock. Mobile wireless network system simulation, Wireless Networks 1, 1995.
[11] Yong Yao, Johannes Gehrke. Query Processing in Sensor Networks. CIDR 2003.
[12] Xiang Zeng, Rajive Bagrodia, and Mario Gerla. Glomosim: a library for parallel simulation of large-scale wireless networks. The 12th Workshop on Parallel and Distributed Simulations (PADS), 1998.
[13] Pei Zheng, Lionel M. Ni. EMPOWER: A Network Emulator for Wireless and Wired Networks. INFOCOM, 2003.
[14] Pei Zheng and Lionel M. Ni. EMWIN: Emulating a Mobile Wireles Network using a Wired Network. The International Workshop on Wireless Mobile Multimedia, 2002.

LEAPS: A Location Estimation and Action Prediction System in a Wireless LAN Environment

Qiang Yang[1], Yiqiang Chen[2], Jie Yin[1], and Xiaoyong Chai[1]

[1] Department of Computer Science
Hong Kong University of Science and Technology
Clearwater Bay, Kowloon Hong Kong, China
{qyang,yinjie,carnamel}@cs.ust.hk
[2] Shanghai Division, Institute of Computing technology
Chinese Academy of Sciences
Building 13 Block 116, Lane 572, Bi Bo Road, Pu Dong District
Shanghai, China, 201203
yqchen@ict.ac.cn

Abstract. Location estimation and user behavior recognition are research issues that go hand in hand. In the past, these two issues have been investigated separately. In this paper, we present an integrated framework called LEAPS (location estimation and action prediction), jointly developed by Hong Kong University of Science and Technology, and the Institute of Computing, Shanghai, of the Chinese Academy of Sciences that combines two areas of interest, namely, location estimation and plan recognition, in a coherent whole. Under this framework, we have been carrying out several investigations, including action and plan recognition from low-level signals and location estimation by intelligently selecting access points (AP). Our two-layered model, including a sensor-level model and an action and goal prediction model, allows for future extensions in more advanced features and services.

1 Introduction

In recent years, the research area of indoor location estimation and user behavior prediction have attracted intense attention. Much work has been done in the computer network and pervasive computing areas on using the signal strength values from the access points (AP) to determine locations using various geometric and probabilistic knowledge. Similarly, different statistical models have been proposed in artificial intelligence and data mining area for recognizing and predicting a user's behavior and plans. However, no work has attempted to combine location estimation with high-level behavior recognition, and to use machine learning and probabilistic reasoning to help with low-level location estimation. In this paper, we survey the work in location estimation and high-level plan recognition, and present our own integrated framework for accomplishing both tasks. Through our integrated system known as LEAPS (Location Estimation and Action Prediction System), we present our research results in three different tasks, including using machine learning methods for access point selection and using location estimation for high-level goal recognition.

H. Jin et al. (Eds.): NPC 2004, LNCS 3222, pp. 584–591, 2004.

Our two-layered model for LEAPS is shown in Figure 1, which includes a sensor model, and an action and goal recognition model. This framework allows several different tasks to be accomplished, ranging from low level to high level. It also allows for more advanced extensions in the future. Below, we discuss the different layers in turn.

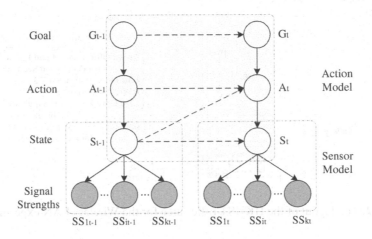

Fig. 1. Two level model for the LEAPS framework

2 Wireless Environment for LEAPS

Our experimental test bed is set up in the faculty office area of Computer Science Department in the Academic Building of Hong Kong University of Science and Technology. The building is equipped with IEEE 802.11b wireless Ethernet network in the 2.4 GHz frequency bandwidth. The layout of the floor is shown in Figure 2. Experiments were carried out in the five hallways (HW1~HW5) and two printing rooms as labeled in the figure. The five hallways are labeled as HW1 to HW5. There are also two rooms in the area.

There are a total of 25 base stations that are detectable in the environment, of which three base stations that are distributed within the area are marked with concrete circles in the figure. Among the other 22 bases stations, some are located on the same floor outside of the area while the others are located on the different floors. The IEEE 802.11b standard works over the radio frequencies in the 2.4 GHz band. However, accurate location estimation using measurements of signal strength is a longstanding complex and difficult task due to the *noisy characteristics* of signal propagation. Subject to reflection, refraction, diffraction and absorption by structures and even human bodies, signal propagation suffers from severe multi-path fading effects in an indoor environment. As a result, a transmitted signal can reach the receiver through different paths, each having its own amplitude and phase. Figure 3 gives a typical example of the normalized histogram of the signal strength received from a base station at a fixed location.

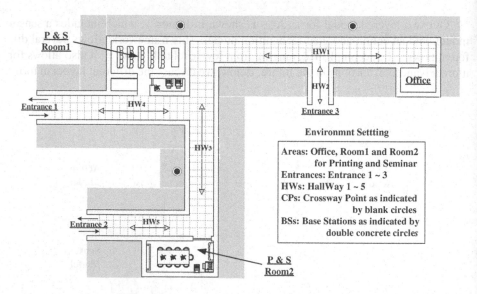

Fig. 2. The layout of the HKUST office area for the Wireless LAN experiments

3   Indoor Location Estimation at the Sensor Level

Deterministic Techniques In general, the location estimation research can be classified into two categories: deterministic techniques and probabilistic techniques. Deterministic techniques [2, 8] use deterministic inference methods to estimate a user's location. The RADAR system by Microsoft Research [2] proposes nearest neighbor heuristics and triangulation methods to infer a user's location. It maintains a radio map which tabulates the signal strength received from different access points at selected locations. Each signal-strength measurement is then compared against the radio map and the coordinates of the best matches are averaged to give the location estimate. The accuracy of RADAR is about three meters with fifty percent probability. The LANDMARC system [8] exploits the idea of reference points to alleviate the effects caused by the fluctuation of RFID signal strength. The accuracy is roughly one to three meters. However, the placement of reference tags should be carefully designed since it has a significant effect on the performance of the system. Moveover, the RFID readers are so expensive that it is infeasible for localization in a large area.

Probabilistic Framework Another branch of research is the probabilistic techniques [14, 13, 11, 6] construct a conditional probability distribution over locations in the environment of interest. In [6], Ladd et al. uses probabilistic inference methods for localization. They first use Bayesian inference to compute the conditional probability over locations, based on received signal-strength measurements from nine access points in the environment. Then a postprocessing step, which utilizes the spatial constraints of a user's movement trajectories, is used to refine the location estimate and reject the results with significant change in the location space. Depending on the postprocessing step is used or not, the accuracy of this method is 83% and 77% within 1.5 meter.

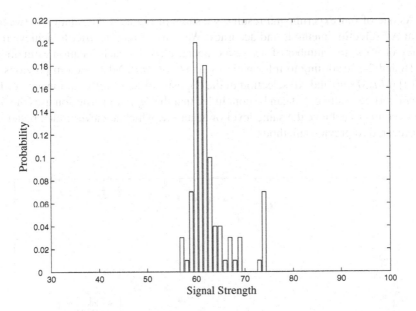

Fig. 3. An example of signal strength distribution

The LEAPS *Framework to Location Estimation* Our LEAPS framework for location estimation is divided into two phases. The first phase is done offline, where the main purpose is to perform intelligent AP selection. We divide this phase into the following steps:

1. First, a feature selection algorithm is applied to find a subset S of AP's that can give the best performance. This subset will then be used as the basis for subsequent computation.
2. A subsequent clustering analysis is then applied to the set S and data collected in the offline phase, in order to partition the grid space into clusters. Each cluster will then provide a subsequent location model.
3. Finally, a decision tree model is constructed for each cluster, based on the AP's given in S. For each cluster only a subset of AP's from S is selected, which further reduces the number of AP's needed for location estimation within each cluster.

The second phase is an online phase, in which a new trace of signal strengths is taken as input and the current location is estimated. This phase is done in two steps:

1. First, the signal strength values from the selected AP's from the set S is used to determine the cluster the current client is most likely located within.
2. Then, the decision tree from the identified cluster is used to determine, at a finer level, which grid the client belongs to. This step will use a subset of the AP's given in S, which further reduces the number of AP's used in a computation. In addition, the AP's that are used only involve arithmetic comparison, which is one of the cheapest computations as computational energy is concerned.

As one of our experimental results, we show in Figure 4 the relation between different AP selection methods and accuracy. We can see that in order to achieve the accuracy of 90%, the number of access points required by each location estimation are 12, 18 and 24, according to information gain (*InfoGain*), MLE used in previous work of [14] (*MaxMean*) and AP selection in the opposite order of information gain ordering (*MinMean*), respectively. It can be concluded that the *InfoGain* criterion uses the fewest access points to achieve the same level of accuracy, which achieves much better result as compared to previous methods.

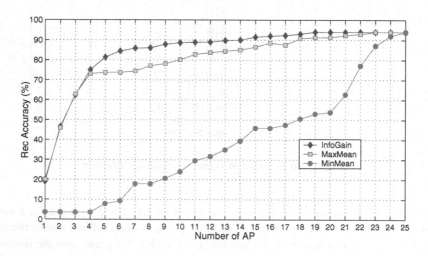

Fig. 4. AP selection and its impact on accuracy

4   User Behavior Recognition in LEAPS

Being able to predict a user's location is one thing, but the eventual purpose of location estimation is to infer users' high-level behavior patterns from low-level sensory data, and provide useful services. Such a task is what we call *location-based plan recognition*. Being able to accomplish this task is critical to many applications. For people suffering from various cognitive limitations in hospitals and care facilities, the technique can discover when a person's behavior is out of the norm and provide help in a timely manner [9]. For shoppers in a busy business environment such as a shopping mall, services and products can be offered not only according to people's current location, but also according to their intended goals and actions.

In our current work, we have taken a first step in inferring high-level user goals from low-level mobile data in an indoor environment, where a wireless LAN is available. In this section, we summarize our statistical model for goal recognition, where a full report can be found in [12], where a two-level dynamic Bayesian network model (DBN) is applied. This model integrates DBN with and a fast-inferencing model based on n-grams for goal inference. We show that this architecture allows us to incorporate domain knowledge, whereby we achieve a nice tradeoff between model accuracy and inferencing efficiency.

Previous Work on Plan Recognition In the artificial intelligence area, recognizing complex high-level behaviors has traditionally been the focus of plan recognition [5, 7]. A Bayesian network was used for plan recognition in story understanding [4] . In [3], a corpus-based N-gram model was introduced to predict the goal from a given sequence of command actions in the UNIX domain. In addition, other advanced stochastic models for recognizing high-level behaviors were proposed such as Dynamic Bayesian Networks (DBN) [1] and Probabilistic State Dependent Grammars [10]. However, most of the work in plan recognition has been restricted to the high level for inference, and the challenge of dealing with low-level sensor models has not been addressed. Only in recent years, attempts have been made to integrate high-level behavior models with low-level sensor models. The work of [9] presents an approach by applying a Bayesian model to predict a user's transportation mode based on location readings from GPS devices in an urban environment.

The Dynamic Bayesian Network Model To represent different degrees of uncertainty in a time series, researchers have proposed various probabilistic models. Among them, the dynamic Bayesian network model has been shown to be well suited for goal recognition tasks. It includes two time slices numbered t and $t-1$ respectively. The shaded nodes SSi_t represent the strength variables of signals received from multiple base stations, which are directly observable. All the other variables - the physical location S_t of the user, the action A_t the user is taking and the goal G_t the user is pursuing - are hidden, with the values to be inferred from the raw signals.

To balance between recognition accuracy and computational complexity, we propose a novel two-level model. The complete DBN model is separated into two different models. The lower part of the DBN starting from the observation layer to the action layer corresponds to the lower level of the architecture. An N-gram model is applied above the action model to infer goals.

In this framework, a low-level DBN model is responsible for computing the most plausible sequence of actions $A_1, A_2, \ldots, A_t$ from the observations $o_1, o_2, \ldots, o_t$ obtained up to time t. The task is carried out by the method of smoothing, which estimates the hidden states of the past given all the evidence up to the current time point t, $P(A_\tau|o_1, o_2, \ldots, o_t)$, where $\tau \leq t$. To test the validity of the model, we have collected 570 traces for 19 goals of a professor to be modeled in the office area. Figure 5 shows the recognition process of one trace belonging to the goal "Seminar-in-Room1", with respect to three other goals among the 19 goals.

5   Conclusions and Future Work

In this paper, we presented an integrated approach towards addressing the problem of inferring high-level goals from low-level noisy signals, as well as estimating a users' current locations, in a complex indoor environment using an RF-based wireless LAN.

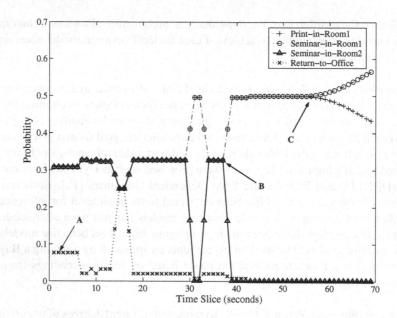

Fig. 5. Behavior recognition for four goals in our experiment

For location estimation, we applied machine learning techniques to select an optimal subset of access points that allow the best balance in accuracy and power saving. For the task of action prediction and plan recognition, we model the problem based on the framework of dynamic Bayesian network, using a two-level n-gram based model. The experiments demonstrate that the two-level approach is more efficient than the whole DBN solution while the accuracy is comparable. The three-layered model, including the sensor model, the action model and the goal model, provides an integrated framework for location estimation and high-level goal recognition.

Acknowledgement

The authors are supported by a grant from Hong Kong RGC and the Hong Kong University of Science and Technology. This research is conducted at the Hong Kong University of Science and Technology.

References

[1] D. Albrecht, I. Zukerman, and A. Nicholson. Bayesian models for keyhole plan recognition in an adventure game. *User Modelling and User-adapted Interaction*, 8(1–2):5–47, 1998.
[2] P. Bahl and V. N. Padmanabhan. RADAR: An in-building RF-based user location and tracking system. In *Proceedings of IEEE INFOCOM2000*, pages 775–784, 2000.
[3] N. Blaylock and J. Allen. Corpus-based statitical goal recognition. In *Proceedings of the Eighteenth International Joint Conference on Artificial Intelligence*, pages 1303–1308, Mexico, August 2003.

[4] E. Charniak and R. Goldman. A bayesian model of plan recognition. *Artificial Intelligence Journal*, 64:53–79, 1993.

[5] H. Kautz and J. F. Allen. Generalized plan recognition. In *Proceedings of AAAI1986*, pages 32–38, 1986.

[6] A. Ladd, K. Bekris, G. Marceau, A. Rudys, L. Kavraki, and D. Wallach. Robotics-based location sensing using wireless ethernet. In *Proceedings of MOBICOM2002*, Atlanta, Georgia, USA, September 2002.

[7] N. Lesh and O. Etzioni. A sound and fast goal recognizer. In *Proceedings of IJCAI95*, pages 1704–1710, Montreal, Canada, 1995.

[8] L. M. Ni, Y. Liu, Y. C. Lau, and A. P. Patil. Landmarc: Indoor location sensing using active rfid. In *IEEE International Conference in Pervasive Computing and Communications 2003 (PerCom 2003)*, Dallas, TX, USA, March 2003.

[9] D. J. Patterson, L. Liao, L. Fox, and H. Kautz. Inferring high-level behavior from low-level sensors. In *Proceedings of UBICOMP2003*, Seattle, WA, 2003.

[10] D. V. Pynadath and M. P. Wellman. Probabilistic state-dependent grammars for plan recognition. In *Proceedings of the Sixteenth Conference on UAI*, pages 507–514, San Francisco, CA, 2000.

[11] T. Roos, P. Myllymaki, H. Tirri, P. Misikangas, and J. Sievanen. A probabilistic approach to WLAN user location estimation. *International Journal of Wireless Information Networks*, 9(3):155–164, July 2002.

[12] Jie Yin, Xiaoyong Chai, and Qiang Yang. High-level goal recognition in a wireless lan. In *Proceedings of the Nineteenth National Conference on Artificial Intelligence (AAAI-04)*, San Jose, CA USA.

[13] M. Youssef and A. Agrawala. Handling samples correlation in the horus system. In *IEEE InfoCom 2003*, Hong Kong, March 2004.

[14] M. Youssef, A. Agrawala, and U. Shankar. WLAN location determination via clustering and probability distributions. In *Proceedings of IEEE PerCom2003*, March 2003.

Reliable Splitted Multipath Routing for Wireless Sensor Networks

Jian Wu, Stefan Dulman, and Paul Havinga

EEMCS Faculty, University of Twente, the Netherlands
{jian,dulman,havinga}@cs.utwente.nl

Abstract. In wireless sensor networks (WSN) the reliability of the system can be increased by providing several paths from the source node to the destination node and by sending the same packet through each of them (the algorithm is known as *multipath routing*). Using this technique, the traffic increases significantly. In this paper, we analyze the combination between a new multipath routing mechanism and a data-splitting scheme that results in an efficient solution for achieving high delivery ratios while keeping the traffic at a low value. Simulation results are presented in order to characterize the performances of the algorithm.

1 Introduction

Sensor nodes have many failure modes [4], each one of them decreasing the performance of the network. The algorithms presented in this paper will assure that the gathered data will reach its destination in the network by assuming as a regular fact that nodes may be not available during the routing procedure. Additional energy will be required only for a small amount of computations; this is almost negligible compared with the energy used for communications [5].

The algorithm starts by discovering n multiple paths from the source to the destination. Sending the same data over all discovered paths is a solution in case of node failures but it requires large quantities of network resources (such as bandwidth and energy). Our contribution is to develop a new multipath routing algorithm that will discover several disjoint paths between a source an a destination nodes. Then, we will make use of the *Turbo Erasure Correction codes* to split the original data packet into k parts (further referred to as *subpackets*) and then compute n-k redundant packets. Finally send these n subpackets instead of the whole packet, across n multipath. The basic principle is to transmit a sequence of n subpackets, out of which only k subpackets are necessary to reconstruct the original packet. The receiver's robustness to missing packets is increased, which also implies that a return feedback channel is not needed anymore.

This work is performed as a part of the European EYES project (IST-2001-34734) on self-organizing and collaborative energy-efficient sensor networks [2]. It addresses the convergence of distributed information processing, wireless communication and mobile computing.

H. Jin et al. (Eds.): NPC 2004, LNCS 3222, pp. 592–600, 2004.

2   Multipath On-Demand Routing

Multipath Routing allows the establishment of multiple disjoint paths between source and destination, which provides an easy mechanism to increase the likelihood of reliable data delivery by sending multiple copies of data along different paths. Based on Dynamic Source Routing (DSR) [3], we designed a new multipath routing algorithm Multipath On-Demand Algorithm (further referred to as MDR). The algorithm provides several paths from sources to destinations. A data splitting algorithm as presented in Section 3 will be used to safely route data while keeping the amount of traffic low. The two phases of the algorithm are described below.

2.1   Route Request Phase

The source initiates the Route Request phase by sending a request message to notify the destination that it has a packet for it. The route request message contains the following fields:

- *snodeID* the source node ID
- *dnodeID* the destination node ID
- *floodID* the route request message ID
- *lasthop* the ID of the node forwarding this message
- *ack* the ID of the last hop

Each node in the network has an unique ID and each message source maintains a counter of the requests sent, such that each route request message in the network is uniquely identified by the first three fields. The *ack* field is needed to distinguish between the messages received by a node. In this way, a route request message can be immediately classified as being received for the first time, or being just a passive acknowledgement of a previously sent message.

When a source node has to transmit a message to a destination, it first checks its cache to see if there are any routes to that destination that did not expire. If the number of routes found is big enough for the maximum given failing probability of the nodes in the network, it uses them. If not, it generates a new route request message filling the ack field with its own ID. When receiving such a message, a node checks its local data structure to see if it has received another route request message having the same three fields identical. If not, it creates a new entry in the data structure and stores this information plus the ID of the node from which it received it. From additional messages received the node has to store only the name of the neighbor. It can easily check and mark if the source of the message is a first order neighbor by looking at the lasthop or ack fields.

The node will forward only the first route request message it gets. It has to change only the ack field with the lasthop value and the lasthop with its own ID. After receiving several such messages each node knows who are its neighbors and more than that, which ones are closer to the source (further referred as the *n-1* neighbor list) and which one closer to the destination (further referred as the *n+1* neighbor list). In fact, each data structure stores them in two separate lists according to the previous rule. If the node identifies itself as being the destination of the message it initiates the second phase of the algorithm.

2.2   Route Reply Phase

The Route Reply phase is the part of the algorithm in which several paths between the destination and the source are reported to the source (if they exist). Because each intermediate node keeps information about the neighbors, the complete path between the source and the destination has not to be stored inside the route reply message, which contains the following fields:

- *snodeID* the source node ID
- *dnodeID* the destination node ID
- *floodID* the flood message ID
- *lasthop* the ID of the node forwarding this message
- *nexthop* the ID of the node to which the message is forwarded
- *ack* the ID of the last hop
- *hops* the number of the hops the message traveled through
- *detours* the number of detours a message can take

The *nexthop* field contains the ID of the node that has to receive this message. This information is provided by each node from their local data structure. The *hops* field is incremented with each hop the message travel and represents the current path length. The *detours* field specifies how many times the reply message is allowed to travel in an opposite direction (from source to destination). When the first route reply message arrives at the source, this node stores the ID of the node that forwarded the message and the path length. It also sets up a timer to measure the interval that it will wait for other reply messages to come. When this timer expires it splits the original data message according to the number of paths, the maximum probability of failure and the length of the paths and forwards it. A node that receives a route reply addressed to it, will modify the last four fields of the message according to the new parameters. Afterwards, it will forward it to the first neighbor in the *n-1* neighbor list. If this list is empty and the detours field is not empty, it chooses the first neighbor in the *n+1* neighbor list and also decreases the *detour* variable by 1. A node that receives a route reply not addressed to it, searches its own data structure to find the entry corresponding to the first three fields. If such an entry is found, it removes the forwarding node from both *n-1* and *n+1* neighbor lists.

A node that forwarded a message has to take care of two more things: first it sets a flag in his data structure saying that it will not forward any other message and second, it waits for the passive acknowledgement. If this does not arrive it assumes that the node to which it send the message is no longer there, is broken or it forwarded a message previously and it deletes it from his lists. It will try re-sending the message to the next neighbor in the lists, until the lists become empty or the *detour* field becomes 0.

The previous step of removing nodes from the list is needed to ensure that the source will receive only disjoint paths. If for various reasons, the paths from the destination to the source have to be known, each node that forwards a route reply message can append its ID to it. This way, the messages will grow in length, but this growth is controlled and involves only a subset of the nodes.

3 Data Splitting Across Multiple Paths

The route discovery process of MDR provides multiple disjoint paths between source and destination. In this section we try to predict the number of paths that will succeed in delivery subpackets. Furthermore, we will give an approximation that allows for a term that can be used to increase the chance of successful delivery of the entire message at the trade-off of added redundancy.

Of course, one can send the whole message along each of the available paths, but the overhead induced by this will be too high. The entire data package to be sent from the source to the destination over the available n disjoint paths will be split up into smaller subpackets of equal size with added redundancy. The number of created subpackets corresponds to the number of available paths. Only a smaller number of these subpackets will then be needed at the destination to reconstruct the original message. In the following, we will focus on approximating a value k that gives, with high probability, the number of successful paths. This value will then be used to determine the amount of redundancy to be added for the split message transmission in Section 4. The total number of subpackets as well as the added redundancy is a function dependent on the multipath degree and on the failing probabilities of the available paths. As these values change according to the positions of the source and the destination in the network, each source must be able to decide on the parameters for the error correcting codes before the transmission of the actual data subpackets.

Suppose we want to send a data package from a source to a destination and the process of MDR is finished with k different paths whose reputation coefficient is sufficient. Each path has some rate $p_i (i = 1, \ldots, n)$ that corresponds to the probability of successfully delivering a message to the destination. This setting corresponds to a repeated Bernoulli experiment. So the estimated number k of successful path is given by

$$k = \sum_{i=1}^{n} p_i$$

When to estimate the number of successful path k, we consider the possibility of a packet failure independent of the packet size. The effect of packet size on the failure possibility depends on many different factors in the system. One large packet is better for MAC layer and OS scheduling, however has higher chance of failure during physical transmission. Many small packets put more burdens on MAC layer and OS scheduling, while each of them has better chance of success in physical layer. So in this paper, we do not consider the influence of packet size on the failing possibility. According to the previous work in [1], we gave an estimate for the number of successful paths with a given value α that serves as a desired bound on the delivery. Given the probabilities of failure for n disjoint paths in the multipath routing, the (maximum) number k of paths that are successful in 1-α of all deliveries can be expressed as

$$k = x_\alpha \cdot \sqrt{\sum_{i=1}^{n} p_i(1-p_i)} + \sum_{i=1}^{n} p_i$$

x_α is the corresponding bound from the standard normal distribution for different level of α (see Table 1 for some values). Obviously, the estimated value for k corresponds to a bound of α=50%. In this case, the coefficient x_α is 0, and we obtain the same estimation as in the previous expression.

α	5%	10%	15%	20%	50%
x_α	-1.65	-1.28	-1.03	-0.85	0

Table 1. Some values for the bound α

4   Turbo Erasure Correction

The design of error correction meets the requirements of our split-multipath scheme. The Turbo Erasure correction code (TEC) described in this section is based on the well know Reed-Solomon error correction code (RSC).

RSC codes are linear block codes, which are often denoted $RS(n,k)$ with s-bit symbols. The encoder takes k data symbols and adds check symbols to make an n symbol codeword. RSC codes correct up to t errors in a codeword where $2t = n - k$. For a symbol size s, the maximum codeword length (n) is $n = 2s - 1$. Because a RSC codes correct symbol errors, they can potentially correct many bit errors. This makes RSC code very good at correcting large clusters of errors. Moreover if the position of the error is known (error which is called erasure), then the decoding procedures can correct up to $2t$ erasures. It means that RSC could correct the same number of errors as the redundancy added. In TEC, when a data packet arrives, it is divided into k subpackets each with L bits. Then these subpackets were put into a two-dimensional array with $k \times L$ bit as shown in Figure 1. Further let $L = L' \times s$ and every s bits form a symbol in finite field $GF(2^s)$. The encoding could be carried out in two stages. The outer-codes are Reed-Solomon codes over $GF(2^s)$ which protect against subpacket loses. Each column of information symbols in $GF(2^s)$ is encoded into a code word of $C_0(n,k)$, where the number of redundant symbols $R = n - k$. In total there are L' outer code words in this array. Then a header h is added to each row, which keep the index of each subpacket and the number of padding added. The inter encoding is optional which gives extra reliability over link errors. A binary BCH code could be used for each row as an inner correction code. After the TEC encoding, each row of subpacket is sent on n different path established by the multipath routing algorithm. As along as more than k of them are received in the destination node the TEC is able to reconstruct the original packet.

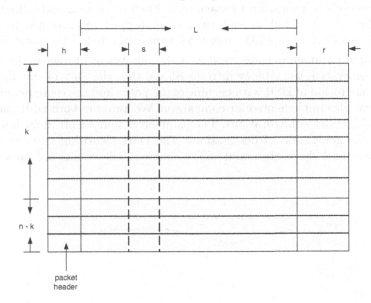

Fig. 1. Turbo Erasure Correction Code

The desired characteristics of the TEC are summarized below:

- BURST CORRECTION: Errors occurs because of link failure. Normally the whole subpacket is lost instead of bit errors.
- ERASURE CORRECTION: The index in the subpacket header help to location the error in the decoding, which resulting in erasures,
- ADAPTABILITY: The number of multipath degree and link quality channel varies over a wide range in a short period of time. TEC can adapt to the changes quickly.

5 Simulation and Results

We have implemented the simulation of MDR algorithm and try to quantify the amount of overhead it introduces versus the improvements obtained. The simulations were performed using our own mobility framework designed for the OMNeT++ simulator.

We have considered 50 nodes randomly distributed inside a rectangle surface (500 by 800 units). For the movement of nodes we used the Random Way Point algorithm. The average sleep time of a node was chosen 5.5 seconds. We are assuming that all the links in the network are bidirectional. Sets of up to 10 simulations were performed for different combinations of the average speed of nodes and transmission ranges. Usually, the speeds were considered in the interval 2 - 20 units/second and the transmission range in the interval 100 - 325 units. One of the nodes defined as being the source node, and randomly chose a destination each 0.5 seconds to forward a message to it. Each simulation had a limit of 200 seconds (in fact after 200 seconds the source stopped generating requests and the simulations ran until all the messages were exhausted in the network).

The main parameters considered were the number of messages, the amount of traffic generated, the latency introduced and the reliability of the algorithm. An implementation of DSR with caching of the paths and the route maintenance enabled was also implemented for comparison. We have run both DSR and MDR for several network configurations. The parameters were identical for both cases and also the generation of destinations. The DSR algorithm had the caching of the paths and the route maintenance enabled. The results are presented in Figure 2.

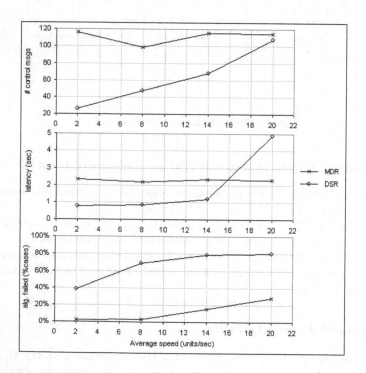

Fig. 2. Comparison MDR/DSR

The figure shows that the number of overhead messages is higher for the MDR algorithm. A closer look at the message sizes shows that the MDR traffic compared to the DSR traffic varies from a 4.04:1 to a 1.02:1 ratio (from the lower average speed to the higher one).

After the paths are created, the source will deliver one data packet that takes one round to travel through one hop. In this case, the latency of DSR is smaller with low mobility. With the increase of speed, the situation changes. In practice we assume data packets far larger than control messages. As future work we are going to investigate the latency from this point of view as well. The last graph in Figure 2 shows the average number of failed cases for the two algorithms. The MDR algorithm performs way better than DSR. The figure shows clearly the two objectives of our algorithm: it improves the reliability a lot and it makes the network almost immune to higher average speed of the nodes.

A failed case is the situation in which the source had a data message to deliver to the destination but failed reaching it. There are two reasons for it:

- the route discovery mechanism did not return any valid paths between the source and the destination;
- although there were several paths available, the data packets got lost on the way (due to mobility issues).

The MDR algorithm performs way better than DSR, so this is the advantage for which we pay with higher number of control messages and higher latency.

6   Conclusions

This paper introduced a splitted multipath scheme to improve the reliability of data routing in wireless sensor networks by keeping the traffic at a low level. An on-demand multipah routing algorithm offers the data source with several paths to any destination (if available). It is used in combination with a data splitting method based on Turbo Erasure Coding.

We have implemented this scheme and estimated the main characteristics. It greatly increases the reliability of packet delivery in wireless sensor network, while keep the total network traffic much lower than the traditional multipath routing. At the same time the latency of splitted mulitpath routing is shorter than any retransmission scheme

The future work will focus on integrating path estimation in the MDR, so that the failing probabilities of each node could be obtained in the routing process. Also we have in mind modifying the Route Reply phase to better deal with failures. This will allow also caching of routes also. The effect of caching the routes and maintaining them has still to be determined.Our scheme, although focused on WSNs, can be incorporated into any routing scheme to improve reliable packet delivery in the face of a dynamic (wireless) environment where nodes move and connections break.

References

[1] S. Dulman, T. Nieberg, J. Wu, and P. Havinga. Trade-off between traffic overhead and reliability in multipath routing for wireless sensor networks. In *Proceedings of the Wireless Communications and Networking Conference*, 2003.

600   J. Wu, S. Dulman, and P. Havinga

[2] EYES project. website. http://eyes.eu.org.
[3] David B Johnson and David A Maltz. Dynamic source routing in ad hoc wireless networks. In Imielinski and Korth, editors, *Mobile Computing*, volume 353. Kluwer Academic Publishers, 1996.
[4] S. Marti, T.J. Giuli, K. Lai, and M. Baker. Mitigating routing misbehaviour in mobile ad hoc networks. In *Proceedings of the Sixth Annual International Conference on Mobile Computing and Networking*, pages 255–265, 2000.
[5] G.J. Pottie and R. Molva. Embedding the internet: wireless integrated network sensors. In *Communications of ACM, 43(5), 51–58*, 2000.

Reliable Data Aggregation for
Real-Time Queries in Wireless Sensor Systems

Kam-Yiu Lam[1], Henry C.W. Pang[1], Sang H. Son[2] and BiYu Liang[1]

[1] Department of Computer Science, City University of Hong Kong
83 Tat Chee Avenue, Kowloon, HONG KONG
cskylam@cityu.edu.hk, henry@cs.cityu.edu.hk
[2] Department of Computer Science, University of Virginia
Charlotte, Virginia, USA
son@cs.virginia.edu

Abstract. In this paper, we study the reliability issue in aggregating data versions for execution of real-time queries in a wireless sensor network in which sensor nodes are distributed to monitor the events occurred in the environment. We extend the *Parallel Data Shipping with Priority Transmission (PAST)* scheme to be workload sensitive (the new algorithm is called *PAST with Workload Sensitivity (PAST-WS)*) in selecting the coordinator node and the paths for transmitting the data from the participating nodes to the coordinator node. PAST-WS considers the workload at each relay node to minimize the total cost and delay in data transmission. PAST-WS not only reduces the data aggregation cost significantly, but also distributes the aggregation workload more evenly among the nodes in the system. Both properties are very important for extending the lifetime of sensor networks since the energy consumption rate of the nodes highly depends on the data transmission workloads.

1 Introduction

In this paper, we study the use of in-networking processing approach [MFH03] for processing of *real-time queries* which access to sensor databases maintained by sensor nodes distributed in the system to generate timely responses if certain events are detected or emergency situations occur [SKH03, YG03]. If the communication workload is concentrated on some nodes, not only the energy consumption rate of the nodes will be heavy, the message loss problem will also be very serious due to high collision probability in data transmission. It is quite common that the sampled value for a data item may contain errors due to noises. Thus, the result generated from a query may contain error too if the data items accessed by the query contain error. In [LPSL04], a *parallel data shipping* scheme, called PAST, is proposed to gather the right versions of data items using the time-stamping method for a real-time query at a coordinator node so that they are relatively consistent with reduced data transmission cost. In this paper, we extend PAST by considering the data communication workload among the relay nodes in choosing the path for collecting sensor data for execution of a query. Our objective is to satisfy the constraints of the queries and at the same time

H. Jin et al. (Eds.): NPC 2004, LNCS 3222, pp. 601–610, 2004.

to minimize the communication overhead and improve the reliability in data communication by evenly distribute the communication workload in the system.

2   System Model

A wireless sensor system consists of a *base station* (BS) and a collection of *sensor nodes* distributed in the system environment which is divided into a number of square grids with length of r as shown in Figure 1. It is assumed that the nodes within the same grid capture the same signals of their surrounding environment. The length r of a grid is defined such that a node can directly communicate with all the nodes in its neighboring grids. Each sensor node generates sensor data values following a pre-defined sampling period which is defined based on the dynamic property of the sampled entities. A real-time query T_i can formally be defined as a tuple: $\{D_i, Op_i, <_i, O_i, \Delta_i, R_i\}$. Op_i is the set of read operations with each operation access to a sensor data item (O_i). To simplify the discussion, it is assumed that the required data items of a query are defined at the *grid* level. The set of operations Op_i in a real-time query is associated with precedence constraints $(<_i)$ on their execution orders. Due to the responsive nature of a real-time query and the dynamic nature of the system environment, it is important that the values of the data items accessed by a real-time query are representing the *current* information ("real-time status of the entities") in the environment. Each real-time query has a *currency* requirement (Δ_i) on its set of data items. Failing to meet the requirement implies that they are too "*old*" and not correctly describing the current situation. Since a timely response is critical to important events occurring in the environments, each real-time query is given a *deadline* on its completion time. In addition to meeting the deadline and currency requirement, another important issue is the reliability of the results generated from a query. As the query result generated from a set of data items may contain errors, it is important to provide multiple results by accessing multiple data versions of data items in processing a real-time query to improve the reliability and accuracy of the results. Therefore, a real-time query is associated with a result interval (R_i), which specifies the time interval of data items for generating the results.

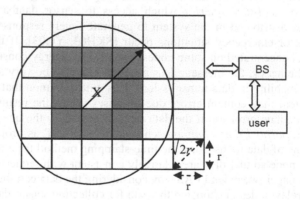

Figure 1: System Model.

In this paper, we adopt relative consistency as the correct notion for ensuring the correctness of the results and meeting the currency requirement of a real-time query [LP04, SBLC03]. Each data version of x is assigned a time-stamp at its generation time to indicate the start time of the validity of the data version. It will become invalid when the next version is generated. We use a time bound, *upper valid time (UVT)* and *lower valid time (LVT)* to label the validity interval of a data version. The set of data items for execution of a real-time query are *relatively consistent* if they are temporally correlated to each other, i.e., representing the status of entities in the environment at the *same time point*.

Relative consistency: Given a set of data versions V from different data items, the versions in V are relatively consistent if $\bigcap\{VI(x_i) \mid x_i \in V\} \neq \Phi$, where $VI(x_i) = [LVT(x_i), UVT(x_i)]$.

To meeting relative consistency requirement, the deadline constraints and currency requirement, for query T_i, the validity of all its accessed data versions should not be earlier than $(D_i - \Delta_i)$, where D_i and Δ_i are the deadline and the currency requirement of T_i, respectively, i.e. $(\bigcap\{VI(x_i) \mid x_i \in V\}) \bigcap [D_i - \Delta_i, D_i] \neq \Phi$. The time window ($D_i$ to $(D_i - \Delta_i)$) is called the *valid time window* for the set of valid results of the query.

3   A Parallel Data Shipping Scheme - PAST

In *Parallel Data Shipping with Priority Transmission (*PAST) [LPSL04], the participating nodes of a query submit data versions to a carefully selected coordinator node in a *parallel* and *synchronized* fashion. The submission of data versions from the participating nodes is synchronized depending on the farthest participating nodes from the coordinator node.

Once the base station receives a real-time query, it will determine: (1) which node (grid) should be assigned as the coordinator node such that the total transmission cost of the data versions from the participating nodes to the coordinator node is minimized, and (2) which data versions from each participating node should be sent to the coordinator node. The data transmission delay from a participating node to the coordinator node is measured in terms of the number of hops in communication between them as we assume that the data transmission delay for sending a data version through one hop is a constant t_d. Let $G_{all} = \{g_1, g_2, g_3, \ldots, g_n\}$ be the set of grids in the system and F_{ij} is defined as the distance (in number of hops) between grid i and grid j where $i, j = 1, \ldots, n$. Suppose T_i wants to access to u grids/nodes and its required nodes are in the grids set $G_i = \{g_{i1}, g_{i2}, g_{i3}, \ldots, g_{i,u}\}$ and $u = |G_i|$. Let F_{totalX} be the total transmission length defined in terms of hops for choosing grid X as the grid where the coordinator node is residing. Then, $F_{totalX} = \sum_{j \in G_i} F_{X,j}$. Let D_{max} be the

maximum data transmission delay of all the participating nodes of a query measured in grid using the shortest distance. The set of data versions to be submitted from each participating node is those data versions which are valid within the interval from $(D_i - C_i - D_{max} - R_i)$ to $(D_i - C_i - D_{max})$. The maximum number of hops H_i of the participating nodes from the coordinator node is then: $H_i = D_{max} / t_d$. Let the coordinates of a grid k be (X_k, Y_k) and $S_{g_{ik}}(H_i)$ be the set of grids which can be reached by the data versions originated from g_{ik} with a distance of no more than H_i:

$$S_{g_{ik}}(H_i) = \left\{ g_{ij} \middle| F_{g_{ik}, j} \leq H_i, j \in G_{all} \right\} \qquad \text{eqn. (1)}.$$

Eqn. (1) defines a square region with a participating node as the central point of the square and the boundary is H_i hop counts from the grid where the participating node is residing. Then, we calculate the coordinates of the coordinator node which is within the intersect regions of all the participating nodes to minimize the total hop counts is getting all the data items from the participating nodes.

Once the coordinator node and the set of data versions for transmission have been determined, the information together with result interval requirement R_i will be sent to the participating nodes. The transmission of data versions from the participating nodes to the coordinator node through the relay nodes are prioritized so that the arrival time of the data is close to the expected time. The priority of a data message M_i for query T_i at node N_j is calculated as: (D_i – Current time) / number of hops from N_j to the coordinator. A higher priority is assigned to a data message for transmission if the calculated value is smaller. The query will be processed at the coordinator node according to the order of the operations defined in the query and following the relative consistency requirement.

4   Workload Sensitive Data Aggregation – PAST-WS

In this section, we introduce the extension of PAST, *PAST with Workload Sensitivity (PAST-WS)*, with purpose to improve the reliability and to reduce the cost and delay in data transmission from the participating nodes to the coordinator node [IEGH02]. Although the total aggregation distance defined in hop counts from the participating nodes to the coordinator node is minimize in PAST, it has ignored the data loss problem in choosing the coordinator node and the aggregation paths. PAST-WS resolves this problem by calculating the mean number of data re-transmissions in choosing the coordinator node and the aggregation paths instead of using the physical hop counts. Another important benefit of the proposed scheme is that the data transmission workload will be more evenly distributed among the nodes in the system. Thus, the energy consumption rate of each node will remain similar over the network, enabling a longer system lifetime.

4.1 Error Modeling for Data Aggregation in Sensor Networks

After determining the coordinator node using PAST, the base station will determine the paths and the start times for the participating nodes to submit their data versions. Since the grids are in a square shape, the shortest path defined in terms of hop counts to the coordinator node can easily be calculated, i.e., it is the shortest line connecting the participating node and the coordinator node using a shortest path searching algorithm. However, this may not be the best one in terms of number of communication messages and total transmission time due to retransmissions. In particular, if multiple sensor nodes want to send messages to the same node N at the same time (or within its transmission time), the receiver N may not be able to receive all of them due to collisions. For the calculation of the error probability of message loss, the base station maintains an array indicating the current relay workload of each node in processing real-time queries in the system. The begin time and the end time of the activated queries are also recorded. When the end time of a query is expired, the array will be updated accordingly.

We model the probability of message loss at a node P_n as a function of the number of nodes (n) concurrently sending data to it. We assume that the transmission delay (S) and transmission period (P) are the same for all senders. For the case $n = 2$, i.e. there are two senders to the same receiver, the probability of having a conflict in transmission is $p2 = S/P$. This can be observed in Figure 2. If node 2 sends a message during the first conflict time interval (marked grey in Figure 2), the message from node 2 may be lost since the receiver is receiving a message from node 1. Within a period, if a message from node 1 is sent after the first conflict time interval, there will be no loss of node 2 message. So the message loss probability for the case of having two senders is S/P.

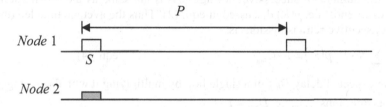

Figure 2: Data Collisions Probability for two senders.

In an interval of time P, at most $m = \lfloor P/S \rfloor$ messages can be sent, i.e. a period can be divided into m small time intervals in which only one message can be sent. Since there are n (suppose $n < m$) senders, there are m^n number of combinations for choosing message transmission intervals for these nodes. Among these m^n possibilities, there are $C_m^1 \cdot C_{m-1}^1 \cdots C_{m-(n-1)}^1 = m(m-1)\cdots(m-n+1) = \dfrac{m!}{(m-n)!}$ combinations that will not cause any message loss .Thus the probability of message loss from any node is:

$$1-(1-P_n)^n = 1 - \frac{m!/(m-n)!}{m^n}$$

That is:

$$P_n = 1 - \left(\frac{m!}{m^n \cdot (m-n)!} \right)^{1/n} \qquad \text{eqn. (2).}$$

We can solve equation (2) to get p_n for different values of n. After we do this for $n = 1, 2, \ldots, m$, we get the distribution of loss probability.

To calculate the average transmission cost for a single hop (measured in hop counts), we assume that the receiving node is the relay node of k nodes. Then, the loss probability of message sending to the receiving node is p_k. So the probability of successfully sending data to the receiving node by sending once is $1 - p_k$. The probability that the sender needs to send twice (i.e. the first message sent is lost, and the second one is received) is $p_k(1-p_k)$. Similarly, the probability that the sender need to send K times is (i.e. the first $(K-1)$ transmissions are all lost, and the final one is received) is $p(K) = p_k^{K-1}(1-p_k)$. So the expected message cost of sending one message through a single hop to the receiving node is:

$$C_{hop} = \sum_{K=1}^{N} K \cdot p(K) = \sum_{K=1}^{N} K \cdot p_k^{K-1}(1-p_k) \qquad \text{eqn. (3).}$$

The cost of a path C_{path} is the sum of the costs of all the hops in the path. When the probability of message loss is considered in calculating the propagation cost, the message transmission delay of a path is no longer a constant proportional to number of hop counts. It is a random variable and larger than that of no message loss case. We can estimate the average number of times a message that has to be sent in one single hop. In order to calculate the mean delay of a path, we need to estimate the mean time length of intervals between consecutive message resend events. The probability distribution of the number of successive message loss is the same as the distribution of the number of resends, i.e. $p(K)$ discussed in eqn. (2). Thus the average time length between two consecutive retransmissions is:

$$\sum_{K=1}^{N} K \cdot P \cdot p(K) = P \cdot C_{hop} \qquad \text{eqn. (4)}$$

We get the expected delay D_{hop} of a single hop by multiplying it with the average number of retransmissions C_{hop}, i.e. $D_{hop} = P \cdot C_{hop}^2$.

4.2 Calculating the Aggregation Path and Coordinator Node

In choosing the path for data propagation, we need to ensure that the expected delay satisfies the currency requirement such that $(D_i - C_i - D_{hop}) > 0$. Algorithm 1 shows the steps of finding the coordinator node and the best path to forward the data versions to the coordinator node. If message loss is considered, the delay is larger than that of no message loss. The set of possible coordinators under the case of message loss is a subset of that of the case with no message loss. In this way, we exclude most of the impossible candidates for the coordinator node. Assuming a straight path (the shortest connection path between a participating node and the possible coordinator node), we find a coordinator node satisfying the currency requirement with the minimum cost. Finally, we find a feasible replacement of the maximum for each path; and for each replacement, we calculate the reduction in cost. We choose the replacement with the maximum cost reduction. The final step is repeated until there is no feasible replacement.

Objective: To find the coordinator node and the paths from the participating nodes of T_i with total minimum communication cost.
Inputs: The node status of all the participating nodes: n (number of receivers), S (mean message delay to send a data version) and P (mean data transmission period); $G_i = \{G_{i1}, G_{i2}, G_{i3},....., G_{iu}\}$, R_i
Outputs: The coordinator node and the set of paths from the participating nodes with minimum communication cost.

Call Algorithm 1 (PAST) to find the set of possible coordinator S;
    for each coordinator node c_node in S

{ /* exclude non-candidate coordinators from S */
      for each participating node p_node in G_i {
          $path$ = the straight path from c_node to p_node;

$$D = \sum_{H \in path} D_{hop}(H);$$

          if $(D > \Delta_i - C_i - R_i)$ **then**   {
             $S = S - \{c\_node\}$; /* cannot be a coordinator */
    break; /* break and continue to check the next c_node */}
          }
}
if($S == \Phi$) **then abort**; /* no feasible solution */
C_{min} = **infinity**;
for each node c_node **in** S **do**
{ /* assuming a straight path (the shortest path), find the coordinator node with
minimum cost */
        C_{total} = 0;
      for each participating node p_node in G_i
        { $path$ = the straight path from c_node to p_node;
            C_{path} = Sum of C_{hop} of each hop of the $path$;
            $C_{total} = C_{total} + C_{path}$;}
            if $(C_{total} < C_{min})$ {
                        $coordinator\_node = c\_node$;
                        $C_{min} = C_{total}$;}

}
S_{path} = the set of straight path (the shortest path) from participating nodes to
$coordinator\_node$;
   do
{ /* adjust the paths */
        C_{max} = 0;
        R_{path} = **NULL**; /* path to be replaced */
           R_{max} = **NULL**; /* path which will replace R_{path} */
        F = **false**;
      for each $path$ in S_{path}
      { C_R = 0;
            for each replacement r of $path$ {
                if(r satisfies delay constraint **AND** $C_{path} - C_r + \Delta C_{decrease} -$
       $\Delta C_{increase} > C_R$){
                   $C_R = C_{path} - C_r + \Delta C_{decrease} - \Delta C_{increase}$; /* cost reduction */
                   $R = r$;}
           }
        if($C_R > 0$) {
                     F = **true**;
           if($C_R > C_{max}$)
           { $R_{max} = R$;
               $C_{max} = C_R$;
               $R_{path} = path$;}
        }
    }
    $S_{path} = S_{path} + \{R_{max}\} - \{R_{path}\}$; /* replace the path R_{path} with R_{max} */
} **while**(F == **true**);
return S_{path}, $coordinator\_node$;

Algorithm 1: Finding the coordinator node and the path loss.

5   Performance Results

Figures 3 through 6 show the results when we vary the size of a real-time query. As shown in Figure 3, increasing the query size (number of grids), the data transmission workload will be increased. Comparing with PAST, the data transmission workload of PAST-WS is consistently lower as shown in Figures 3 and 4. Figure 5 and Figure 6 show the distribution of data transmission workload of the nodes in the system. It can be seen that the workload is more evenly distributed in PAST-WS than in PAST. The numbers of heavy and medium loaded grids in PAST-WS are smaller than in PAST. In addition, we have measured the mean value and variance in workload of the nodes. Consistent with the results in Figures 5 and 6, both the mean and variance of PAST-WS are smaller than that of PAST.

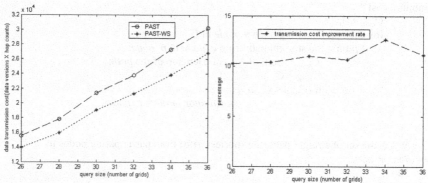

Figure 3: Query Size Vs. Data transmission cost

Figure 4: Percentage improvement of PAST-WS

Figures 7 and 8 show the results of PAST-WS and PAST respectively when we vary the currency requirement of a query. We can see that PAST-WS only not gives a smaller transmission cost, it can complete more queries successfully, i.e., meeting the deadline, currency and result requirements. In PAST, due to long aggregation time and heavy workload as a result of re-transmissions, a large number of queries can only be partially completed and some of them are even failed, i.e., no results are generated, especially when the currency requirement is tight. The situation is less serious in PAST-WS as shown in Figure 7 as its data transmission workload is lower after considering the workloads of the relay nodes in choosing the coordinator node and the relay nodes. We also have investigated the impact of varying the locality factor of a query to their performance. (Due to space limitation, we do not show the result figures.) Similar to the results discussed before, PAST-WS shows a better performance.

6   Conclusions

In this paper, we have studied how to improve the reliability in data aggregation for execution of real-time queries in a wireless sensor system. The real-time queries are

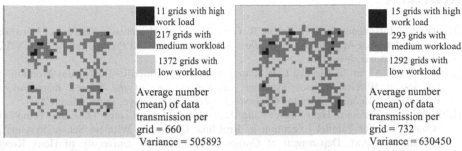

Figure 5 legend:
11 grids with high work load
217 grids with medium workload
1372 grids with low workload
Average number (mean) of data transmission per grid = 660
Variance = 505893

Figure 6 legend:
15 grids with high work load
293 grids with medium workload
1292 grids with low workload
Average number (mean) of data transmission per grid = 732
Variance = 630450

Figure 5: Distribution of transmission workload (PAST-WS)

Figure 6: Distribution of transmission workload (PAST)

associated with a deadline on their completion times and it is important to generate the results before the deadlines since it is mainly for generating responses to the events occurred in the system. To meet the query processing requirements with minimum data transmission cost, a parallel execution scheme, called PAST was proposed. However, the workload at the relay nodes was not taken into consideration in selecting the coordinator node and the aggregation paths. If the workload at the relay nodes is heavy, the data loss probability will be high and the consequence is either some data are lost or a lot of re-transmissions are required. A lot of re-transmission not only increases the energy consumption rate at the relay nodes, but also increases the data transmission workload in the system and the delay in gathering the data versions for processing of the queries. In this paper, we extend the PAST to include a workload sensitive scheme in selecting the coordinator node and the paths for data aggregation. The new algorithm is called PAST-WS. Simulation results have shown that PAST-WS can significantly reduce the aggregation workload and delay and at the same time can distribute the aggregation workload evenly in the system.

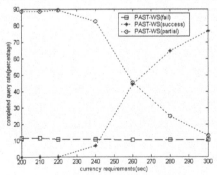

Figure 7: Currency Vs. Completed query percentage(PAST-WS)

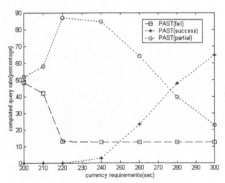

Figure 8: Currency Vs. Completed query percentage (PAST)

References

[IEGH02] C. Intanagonwiwat, D. Estrin, R. Govindan and J. Heidemann, "Impact of Network Density on Data Aggregation in Wireless Sensor Networks", in *Proceedings of ICDCS'02*, Vienna, Austria, July 2002.

[LP04] Kam-Yiu Lam and Henry C.W. Pang, "Correct Execution of Continuous Monitoring Queries in Wireless Sensor Systems", in *Proceedings of the Second International Workshop on Mobile Distributed Computing (MDC'2004)*, Tokyo, Japan, March 2004.

[LPSL04] Kam-Yiu Lam, Henry C.W. Pang, Sang H. Son, BiYu Liang, "On Using Temporal Consistency for Parallel Execution of Real-time Queries in Wireless Sensor Systems", Technical Report, Department of Computer Science, City University of Hong Kong (www.cs.cityu.edu.hk/~henry).

[MFH03] S. Madden, M. J. Franklin and J.M. Hellerstein, "The Design of an Acquisitional Query Processor For Sensor Networks", in *Proceedings of SIGMOD 2003*, June 9-12, San Diego, CA.

[SBLC03] Mohamed A. Sharaf, Jonathan Beaver, Alexandros Labrinidis, Panos Chrysanthis, "TiNA: A Scheme for Temporal Coherency-Aware in-Network Aggregation", in *Proceedings of 2003 International Workshop in Mobile Data Engineering*.

[SKH03] Narayanan Sadagopan, Bhaskar Krishnamachari and Ahmed Helmy, "Active Query Forwarding in Sensor Networks (ACQUIRE)", to appear in *Ad Hoc Networks*.

[YG03] Y. Yao and J. E. Gehrke, "Query Processing in Sensor Networks", in *Proceedings of the First Biennial Conference on Innovative Data Systems Research (CIDR 2003)*, Asilomar, California, January 2003.

The Design of a DRM System Using PKI and a Licensing Agent

KeunWang Lee[1], JaePyo Park[2], KwangHyoung Lee[2], JongHee Lee[2], and
HeeSook Kim[3]

[1] Dept.of Science Chungwoon University, Korea
kwlee@cwunet.ac.kr
[2] School of Computing, Soong-sil University, Korea
[3] Asan Information Polytechnic College, Korea

Abstract. As the logistic environment of digital contents is rapidly
changing, the protection of digital rights for digital content has been
recognized as a very critical issue that needs to be dealt with effectively.
Digital Rights Management (DRM) has taken much interest in Internet Service Providers (ISPs), authors and publishers of digital content
in order to create a trusted environment for access and use of digital
resources. In this paper, PKI (Public Key Infrastructure) and a licensing agent are used in order to prevent illegal use of digital contents by
unauthorized users. In addition, a DRM system is proposed and designed
which performs proprietary encryption and real-time decoding using the
I-frame-under-container method to protect copyright of video data.

1 Introduction

As the distribution environment for digital resources undergoes rapid changes
resulting from the proliferation of the Internet and increased interconnection
among computers, the demand for multimedia content such as music, images,
movies, publications etc. in digital form is rapidly increasing. Since such digital content can be duplicated without deterioration in quality, the protection
of digital copyrights for preventing such unauthorized duplication is emerging
as an important issue. For content protection and management, information
protection, technology for providing stability and security and digital copyright
management DRM (Digital Rights Management) technology for management
of copyrights and the monitoring/tracing of overall distribution of contents is
necessary [1,2]. DRM can be defined as a management technology which continuously protects and manages the rights and interests of copyright holders [3,4].
A comprehensive measure for protecting copyrights from attempted copyright
infringement against digital contents is being pursued by utilizing DRM technology, and various researches are being carried out to create a trusted environment within which creation, distribution and use of copyrighted media are being
performed [5,6]. Several companies such as InterTrust, ContentGuard etc. are
offering various types of DRM solutions. However, in existing DRM technology,
static copyright management is performed by inserting protection conditions,

H. Jin et al. (Eds.): NPC 2004, LNCS 3222, pp. 611–617, 2004.

authoring management, etc., into the contents; therefore, due to limitations in monitoring and tracing functionality, not only is dynamic control of copyright difficult to achieve, but there is also difficulty in obtaining proof of illegal conduct should copyright infringement (such as illegal copying) occur. As such, a digital copyright management technology which is applicable in all types of online and offline content and enables dynamic copyright management, as well as real-time monitoring and tracing, must be developed [7].

In this paper, an integrated DRM system is proposed and designed which provides user certification for multimedia contents in online and offline conditions by using PKI and a licensing agent, and prevents illegal use by unauthorized users through encryption of the data itself.

2   Related Works

Existing DRM technology does not take privacy protection into consideration since the protection of user's privacy is not directly necessary for copyright protection. Due to this, user information leaked during the process of user certification for issuing licenses reported usage details for monitoring illegal usage of contents; therefore, problems related to user privacy infringements occurred [8]. Microsoft's WMRM (Windows Media Rights Manager) is an end-to-end DRM system which distributes digital media files to content providers and consumers in a secure manner [9,10]. WMRM distributes media, such as music or video, to content providers through the Internet in a protected form through the encryption of files. In WMRM, each server or client instance receives a key pair through the individualization process; instances which are considered cracked or unsafe are excluded from service through the certificate cancellation list. WMRM is widely used in incorporated form with the Windows Media Player; however, it only supports a limited number of file formats since its flexibility in dynamic environments is limited–it only supports Windows Media Player. In addition, one disadvantage of the WMRM is since its user certification process for issuing licenses does not use any specific protection mechanism, user information such as user IDs or e-mail addresses are leaked.

3   System Architecture

Data protection of original content and authentication should not be implemented by simple access right control on existing content or password-based authentication but by user authentication using PKI and through inserting related information into original content using data encryption. The proposed system has a client/server architecture and its overall layout is illustrated in Fig. 1.

When a content is registered on the server using an external interface, processing for content monitoring is performed by an agent module and encryption is performed on the content. In order to use the content, user authentication is performed by the licensing agent sent from the server: for authorized users, the content is executed by the application program, and for unauthorized users,

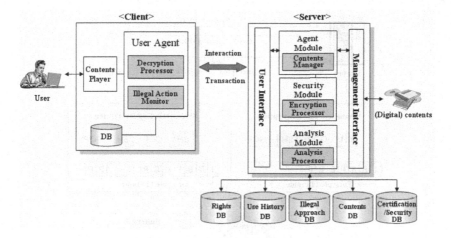

Fig. 1. System Architecture

a warning message is output. Real-time monitoring against illegal activities is performed on the content by the licensing agent, and all illegal activities of all users are stored on the server's database through a monitoring interface.

4   Authentication and Encipherment Mechanism

4.1   Encryption and Decryption of Video Data

When the server which receives a request for use of content performs user authentication, the symmetric key needed for decoding is encrypted using the user's public key then sent to the client so that the video data's I frame which is encrypted can be decrypted for the client for playback. Figure 2 illustrates the encryption and decryption process of the video data which is the content used in this system.

The video data stored on the server is generated by extracting the I frame of each video content then applying encryption using a symmetric key. Any user can download the server's video data; however, the data cannot be used without proper authorization since the I frame is encrypted. The symmetric key algorithm is used since it can minimize the time required for encryption and decryption. If the downloaded video data is to be played back to the client, the user issues a use request to the server, which then performs authentication depending on whether the user is an authorized one. In this authentication process, a PKI algorithm is used. The symmetric key of the video data requested is encrypted using the user's public key and then sent to the client.

The client's agent decrypts the symmetric keys using the user's private keys, then extracts the I frame of the video data to be played back by using these symmetric keys, then stores it on the buffer together with the B and P frames

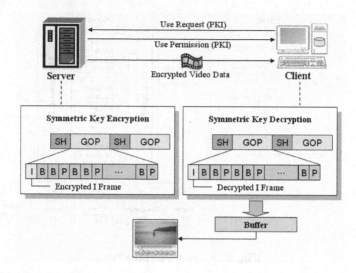

Fig. 2. Encryption & Decryption Processing

to perform playback. While all the video data is being played back, the delayed frames should be calculated to determine the initial buffer size.

4.2 License Certification Method

The author of the content sends the created content to a content publisher. Then, the content publisher encrypts (E) the content using an arbitrary symmetrical key Ks to generate the encrypted content C, which is then sent to the content provider to be stored on the content provider's server.

$$C = EKs[data]$$

The user can download a desired content from the content provider's server. However, the user cannot execute the downloaded content arbitrarily because it is encrypted.

Step 1. User Registration Protocol

The user has to register first in order to use the content. The user registration process is shown in Fig. 3.

The user connects to a system server which functions as a license server and sends the user's certificate cert_u. The system server verifies the user's certificate cert_u through its specified certification path; if the certificate is correct, it sends the user's agent.

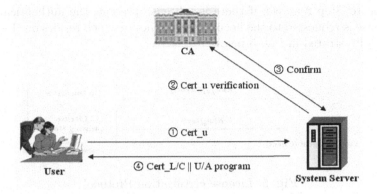

Fig. 3. User Registration Protocol

Step 2. License Issuing Protocol

The user installs a license agent (LA) program which is then executed. When the user executes an encrypted content, the license agent installed on the user's PC connects to the system server and obtains a license, as shown in Fig. 4.

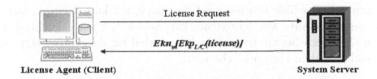

Fig. 4. License Issuance Protocol

The license agent connects to the system server and requests a license for the desired content. The system server issues a license including the license ID, user ID, content ID and privileges. Here, the license is encrypted using the user's public key for security reasons (as shown below), and signed using the user's private key and then transmitted.

$$EKuu[EkpL/C(license)]$$

Here, ku is the public key while kp is the private key. Therefore, kuu is the user's public key and kpL/C is the private key of the license clearing house (L/C).

Step 3. License Certification Protocol

When the user executes an encrypted content, the license agent checks whether there is a license present. If there is no license present, a license is requested according to Step 2 above; if there is a license present, the authentication for that license is requested to the license clearing house which resides on the system server, as illustrated in Fig. 5 below.

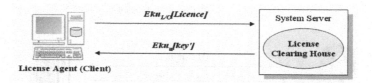

License Agent (Client)

Fig. 5. License certification Protocol

When the license clearing house receives an authentication request for the license from the license agent, it checks the privileges from the license information list and then performs authentication. If the user's license is valid for the time up to a specific date, it checks whether that time has expired; if it is a license for the allowed number of usage, the number is decremented by 1. Then, after performing operations on the key value using the user's ID (as shown below), encryption is done using the user's public key then the key is sent to the user.

$$Ekuu[key'] \qquad (where\ \ key' = ks \oplus user\_ID)$$

The user agent, which has received the encrypted key, decrypts that key by using the user's private key to extract key, which is then calculated with the user_ID in the user's license to get the key needed for decrypting the encrypted content, which is then shown to the user.

5   Performance Evaluation

To evaluate the performance of the system proposed in this paper, we implemented a prototype version of the system using Visual C++ 6.0 and MS-SQL 2000. The encryption time for the video data and the initial playback delay time due to decoding time were both measured at a PC that have Intel(R) P-IV, CPU 2.4GHz and 512M RAM. The result of comparison between the conventional method of playing back an already encrypted video data file after decoding (non-realtime decoding method), and the method of playing back while decoding in real time, which is proposed in this paper, is shown in Fig. 6. To measure time accurately, a total of 30 video data files were segmented in minute units for the comparison. As the test result shows, in the conventional method of playback after decoding the entire video data file, the larger the file size, the longer the initial delay time for playback; whereas in the proposed method, it has been shown that the initial delay time has been reduced significantly.

The result shows that, in the proposed method, the delay time until the start time of video data playback (including decoding time) is much shorter than that of the conventional method. In addition, even with real-time decoding, stable playback was demonstrated without interruption of playback or noise.

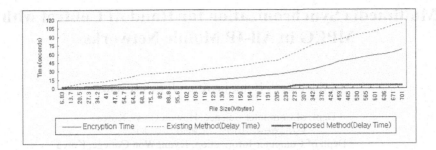

Fig. 6. Encryption Time and Delay Time Comparison

6   Conclusion

In this paper, a DRM system for digital copyright protection using a licensing agent which is based on PKI has been proposed and designed. The licensing agent performs user authentication using PKI methodology, performs encryption of the data itself at the system server using container methodology, and decoding is performed in real time for the client under copyright protection of multimedia data. As a follow-up, complete implementation of the proposed system and a safety evaluation of the user authentication process are necessary.

References

1. James Cannady, Jay Harrell, "A Comparative Analysis of Current Intrusion Detection Technologies," http://iw.gtri.gatech.edu/Papers/ids_rev.html, Feb., 1998.
2. Jai Sundar B., Spafford E., "Software Agents for Intrusion Detection," Technical Report, Department of Computer Science, Purdue University, 1997.
3. J.Dubl,"Digital Rights Management: A Defination", IDC 2001.
4. J.Dubl, S.Kevorkian, "Understanding DRM system: An IDC White paper", IDC, 2001.
5. Kentaro Endo, The Building up of national Regional and International Registers for works and objects of related rights," Proc. of International Conference on WIPO, Seoul, Korea October 25-27, 2000.
6. V. K Gupta, "Technological measures of protection," Proc. of International Conference on WIPO, Seoul, Korea October 28-29, 2000.
7. P. Vora, D, Reynolds, L. Dickinson, J. Erickson, D. Banks, "Privacy and Digital Rights Managements", A Position paper for the W3C Workshop on Digital Rights Management, January 2001.
8. D. K. Mulligan and A. Burstein, Implementing Copyright Limitations in Rights Expression Languages, in 2002 ACM Workshop on Digital Rights Management, Washington DC, November 18 2002.
9. J. S. Erickson, Fair use, DRM, and trusted computing, Communications of the ACM, vol. 46, no. 4, pp. 34-39, April 2003.
10. Microsoft's press releases of the PocketPC 2002 launch, Oct 8, 2001. Available at ww.microsoft.com/presspass/events/pocketpc2002/default.asp.

Multimedia Synchronization for Handoff Control with MPEG in All-IP Mobile Networks

Gi-Sung Lee[1], Hong-jin Kim[2], Il-Sun Hwang[3]

[1] Dept. of Computer Science Howon Univ., Korea
ygslee@sunny.howon.ac.kr
[2] Dept. of Computer Information, KyungWon College, Korea
[3] R&D Network Management, KISTI, Korea

Abstract. This paper proposes a handoff management scheme for the synchronization algorithm of an all-IP based multimedia system. The synchronization algorithm and handoff management method are proposed to realize smooth play-out of a multimedia stream with minimum loss under handoff conditions which normally occur due to the movement of mobile hosts. Handoffs, which frequently occur under mobile environments, result in loss of multimedia streams stored in base stations due to the change of base station. As a result, the multimedia stream shows a low QoS due to disruption of the stream at play-out. The proposed scheme shows that it not only provides a stream of continuous play-out but also shows a higher packet play-out rate and lower loss rate than previous methods.

1. Introduction

The recent explosive increase in Internet utilization has accelerated the emergence of new services based on the mobile computing environment. As a result, the existing service architecture, which is based on simple communication between the client and the server, is no longer capable of satisfying the needs of users who want to utilize various types of high-speed multimedia services [1,2]. This limitation of existing communication service architecture can be overcome by expanding the concept of service provision from one that is single system based to a mobile system connected by a wireless network: the mobile environment provides key functionalities which enable such performance expansion. In a mobile environment, play-out of multimedia data on a mobile host is difficult due to inherent characteristics in wireless networks such as the high data loss rate, long delays and low network bandwidth. The distributed multimedia systems which are connected to the wireless network in large numbers use buffers to overcome network delays and unpredictable losses.

A Base Station (BS) transmits Group of Picture (GoPs) of MPEG from multiple multimedia servers. However, if the expected play-out time is faster than the arrival time, unpredicted delays and increase in traffic can cause failures in play-out of subframes. To solve this problem, buffering is needed at BS in order to reduce interpacket jitter delay between the multimedia server and BS in a mobile environment. A mobile network offers the advantage that Mobile Hosts (MH) can move within the network

H. Jin et al. (Eds.): NPC 2004, LNCS 3222, pp. 618-625, 2004.

[3,4,6]. However, the disadvantage is that multimedia streams transmitted to a BS must be retransmitted. The disadvantage of handoff is that the MPEG video data stored in a BS buffer can be lost. In this paper, the BS and the MH were configured with a 2-jitter buffer and 1-jitter buffer, respectively. In addition, for the GOP (I, P, B) of the MPEG video generated and lost during handoff, the I-picture of the MPEG video of the old BS is transmitted to the new BS. The proposed method aims to enable play-out of the substream stored in the buffer of new BS without retransmission so that adverse effects on play-out that result from loss of media are prevented.

2. Related Work

Current research has reached a level, in which synchronization schemes based on wireless communications are incorporated into conventional ones. D. K. Y. Yau and S.S. Lam adopted a frame rate adjustment scheme in which the CPU processing time of a video server is adjusted according to the frame transmission rate, and traffic load on network links is monitored using kernel-level threads. This leads to a reduction in network traffic by increasing or decreasing frame transmission rates. However, one drawback of this approach is that control is performed only on the server side [4].

M. Woo, N. U. Qazi, and A. Ghafoor defined a BS as an interface between wired/wireless networks. For wired networks, the interface defines buffering in the BS to reduce jitter delay between packets. One possible shortcoming of this approach is an attempt to apply buffering to synchronization by assigning existing wireless communication channels [5].

Azzedine Boukerche proposed an efficient distributed synchronization problem in wireless and mobile multimedia systems to ensure and facilitate mobile client access to multimedia objects [1] He also proposed synchronization and handoff management schemes that allow mobile hosts to receive time-dependant multimedia streams without delivery interruption while moving from one cell to another [2]. But in this method, delay and overhead due to forwarding of MMU data from the buffer of an old BS to a new BS adversely affects the play-out of MMU in MH.

3. Multimedia Synchronization for Handoff in MPEG GOP

3.1 System Architecture

This system supports k multimedia server nodes, m BS, and n MHs. The BS communicates with ith MH in the mth cell. These MHs access the server via the BS. This system monitors variations in the start time for transmission as well as buffers at the BS, using variables such as arrival time of subframes transmitted from multimedia servers and delay jitter. Some advantages of this system include its capability to overcome the limitations of mobile communications like small memory size and low bandwidths. The MPEG video data stored in the multimedia server are composed of data streams split into GOP_k^i units in the sequence, based on a synchronization group, not on the same byte. Figure 1 shows the configuration for the proposed system. Handoff refers to a state in which a MH moves out of range of a BS and comes into range of another. If handoff takes place during MPEG video transmission, data being transmitted from the BS buffer are lost. This system has architecture which passes only I-frames specific to MPEG videos into buffer of new BS for the transmission and the play-out. Figure 1 shows an overview of system modules for synchronization of MPEG videos in mobile environments. MPEG video streams are retrieved from a frame of a certain type stored within the database in the multimedia server, and the sender transmits them to the MH via the BS. The MH receives bit streams in a frame of a certain type from the multimedia server. The frames stored in the buffer are converted by the MPEG decoder, and are then played out.

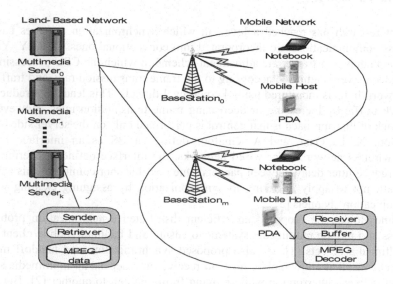

Fig. 1. Synchronization System for MPEG Video

3.2 Control of Multimedia Server's Transfer Rate

There are MPEG frame in 3 types: I, P and B frames. During the decoding process, I and P frames are considered more important than B frames. If the GoP loss rate increases due to overload, the server's transfer rate can be reduced by selectively discarding B frames to reduce the loss rate of I, P frames so that the reception rate of I, P frames increases. Therefore, the picture quality is better than if no transmission rate control is applied on the server. If, at time t, time is insufficient when t_d is imminent, GoP is discarded. That is, if the number of possible transmissions r_t is 0, GoP is discarded. Here, the server's transmission rate is controlled by selective discarding of GoP according to the loss rate of transmitted GoP. Taking this into consideration, a method for controlling the server's transfer rate according to the GOP loss rate within the network has been proposed in figure 2.

Procedure Control of Server's Transmission Rate

If($\rho >= B_{ltt}$){

 While (wait until message of B_{nomal} is received from BS)

  Wait //decrement

else if ($T_{1L} < \rho < T_{1H}$)

 Transmit/maintain $GoP(I, P, B)_k^i$

else

 While (wait until message of B_{nomal} is received from BS)

  transmit $GoP(I)_k^i$ // increment

Fig. 2. Control of server's transmission rate according to GoP loss rate

3.3 Controlling the Play-Out Time of the MH

In the method proposed by Chen [4], the server's transmission time is reconfigured using feedback information from MH; here, a new transmission time is set. However, this involves a complicated method of setting the new transmission time, and is not suitable for an Mobile environment where there is no guaranteed limit for loss and delay. In selecting a control for delay variation under such a network environment, resetting the estimated play-out time of MH is more desirable than controlling the server's transmission time. The proposed algorithm for controlling the estimated play-out time according to the delay variation of the synchronization method within the media is illustrated in figure 3. After receiving RTT GoP, packets are separated and a two-stage synchronization process within the media is applied. In the first stage,

Procedure Controlling the estimated play-out time

While (not EOF) {

Get a new GoP;

D=SCR-STR;

if ($D > \tau_p$){ Insert into decoding buffer;}

 If($D > 0$){ Insert into Delay buffer; }

 Else{ Discard;} }

If ($B_{dL} < \overline{D} < B_{dL}$) // $\overline{D}$ is average delay time

 continue;

else if ($\overline{D} <= B_{dL}$){

 $P_\tau = P_\tau - \delta$; // P_τ is interval time, δ is max jitter time

 continue; }

Else{ $P_\tau = P_\tau + \delta$

continue; }

Fig. 3. Controlling the estimated play-out time

the amount of GoP delay occurring within the mobile network is calculated. Since the server transmits packets based on SCR, the received SCR is the time of the server's packet transmission, and the STC of MH at reception point is the packet's arrival time. Therefore, the delay can be calculated in the difference between the received packet's SCR value and the STC value of MH at arrival time. The second stage is the process of reconfiguring the estimated play-out time of MH according to network delay: it consists of estimated play-out time delay action and estimated play-out time progression action. The average delay $\overline{D}$ is calculated by passing the delay D experienced by each packet through a low-pass filter

3.4 Handoff Control

This paper is intended to enable a MH to implement the play-out of media streams within QoS limits, without any loss of multimedia data or additional delays accompanying message transmission during a handoff. In this paper, the HM_i provides multimedia service via the BS_m. The BS is classified into a primary BS and non-primary BS. The former is a BS responsible for sending MPEG video data in GOP units to the MS, while the latter is a BS adjoining the primary BS.

The buffer size within BS has the two-jitter size, while the one within MH has the one-jitter size. Such buffer configurations offer the advantage of disallowing loss of MPEG video during a handoff, unlike the configuration scheme where the buffer works only within BS. This configuration strategy also offers complementary configurations for MH's small memory size. Handoff occurs when MH_i travels out of range of $BS_{current}$ into the range of BS_{new} . $BS_{current}$ reports a handoff message to the multimedia server and starts handoff processing. The algorithm is described as follows.

Algorithm Handoff Control

1. MH_i performs playout for a time equal to (GoP x γ) x λ regardless of handoff. Here, γ is the play-out speed time required by the substream and λ is the maximum jitter time within the media.
2. MH_i notifies the $Handoff_{on}$ message indicating handoff has occurred to the multimedia server and $BS_{current}$.
3. Setting performed: $BS_{old} = BS_{current}$ and $BS_{current} = BS_{new}$.
4. BS_{new} sends message $Handoff_{on}$ to multimedia server and notifies that the multimedia server to stops transmission of GOP.
5. Each multimedia server transmits $GOP(I)_k^i$ to BS_{new} as soon as it receives $Handoff_{on}$.
6. Only the $GOP(I)_k^i$ of the MPEG video which exists in the buffer of BS_{old} is forwarded to the buffer of BS_{new} .

7. After it has received $GOP_k^i(I)$ from the buffer of BS_{old} through the server, it sends $Handoff_{off}$ message to the multimedia server and mobile host to notify that handoff has been completed successfully.

8. MH_i sends request messages to each server to perform a normal transfer.

4. Performance Evaluation

Presented are the simulation experiments we carried out to evaluate the performance of our synchronization scheme. We developed a distributed discrete-event model to simulate a cellar wireless multimedia system. Simulation is performed using IBM compatible PCs with Pentium or an equivalent processor. Interfaces and algorithms were written using the JAVA development kit JDK 1.3, which were stored in Microsoft MDB as simulation.mdb files. For the purpose of this paper, we have assumed that all simulations are performed in mobile environments. In order to ensure proper packet processing, we applied the information used for actual simulations, computed using the Poisson distribution, equally to mobile networks which have 300 channel for 60 cells. One thousand GOP frames were used in performance evaluation experiments to which a maximum delay jitter time of 600ms was applied. Table 1 displays the simulation parameters we used in our experiments.

Table 1. Simulation parameters

Number of cells	60	Forward time to BS	100ms
Number of servers	4	Rate of handoff	5% of MMUs
Buffer size of a MH	1 Jitter	RTT to request/deliver a GOP	100ms
Buffer size of a BS	2 Jitter	Average Jitter	200ms
Play-out times/GOP	250ms	Maximum Jitter	600ms

Figure 5 shows the GoP loss rate of MH. Here we can see that, if control is performed, the number of transmitted GoPs is reduced if the loss rate is increased so that the loss rate is reduced.

Figure 5 shows the loss rate of GOP at MH. Here, the GoP from 15 to 20 seconds is subject to handoff, therefore the buffer data of BS_{old} is sent to the buffer of BS_{new} in order to prevent the loss of MPEG video's I-frame as a result of handoff. In addition, for handoff, by delaying 10 ms of maximum delay jitter λ at the I-picture interval time τ of GOP_k^i at MH_i, a method for obtaining more time for moving data at BS_{old} to the buffer of BS_{new} has been proposed.

As shown in Figure 5, previous research results failed to deal with handoff and as such suffer from loss of substream data in the buffer of BS_{old}.

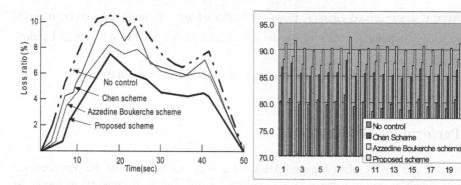

Fig. 5. Comparisons of GoP loss rate in MH   **Fig. 6.** Comparisons of play-out rate

Figure 6 shows the results of 31 tests in which the arrival time was changed for each experiment. In Test 2 and 8, minimum delay and maximum delay were adjusted to 50ms and 600ms each; compared with the no control case, the play-out rate was improved by 6% for the Chen scheme, by 8% for the Azzedin-Boukerche scheme and by about 10% for the scheme proposed in this thesis.

In Test 4, 9 and 26, minimum delay and maximum delay were adjusted to 20ms and 800ms, respectively, to induce overflow and starvation. In these cases, while network traffic conditions worsened, the play-out rate was improved by 5% for the first variance and by 8-9% for the second variance. In average, the play-out rate was about 79% for the conventional method, 85% for the first variance and 91% for the second variance.

5. Conclusions

We proposed a scheme that uses MPEG-frame within GOP in mobile networks. In addition, delay and overhead due to forwarding of MMU data from the buffer of an old BS to a new BS adversely effects play-out of MMU in MH. Therefore, to solve this problem, we propose an algorithm which forwards only the I-frame of MPEG-frame to the new BS. The MPEG-frames within the buffer of MH are presented as adding maximum delay jitter to the interval time of GOP because the play-out policy is related to the occupancy rate of the buffer during handoff. Therefore, we propose an algorithm that performs each overflow policy and underflow policy based on buffer watermarking. Moreover, we propose a scheme that not only deals with hand-off quickly by controlling the buffer and play-out policy, but also properly handles limiting factors for mobile communications such as small memory size and low bandwidths. The proposed scheme allows the BSs to control handoff and the play-out policy, and further provides a solution to the problems of handoff in mobile networks. After evaluation, it has been shown that the proposed scheme offers continuous MPEG data play-out, higher packet play-out rates, and lower packet loss rates, relative to the conventional scheme.

Reference

1. Azzedine Boukerche, Sungbum Hong and Tom Jacob, "MoSync : A Synchronization Scheme for Cellular Wireless and Mobile Multimedia System", Proc. Ninth International Symposium on Modeling, Analysis and Simulation of Computer and Telecommunication Systems IEEE 2001.
2. Ernst Biersack, Werner Geyer, "Synchronization Delivery and Play-out of Distributed Stored Multimedia Streams", Multimedia Systems , Vol. 7 N.1 , 70-90, 1999.
3. D. K. K. Y. Yau, S. S. Lam, "Adaptive Rate-Controlled Scheduling for Multimedia Applications", Multimedia 96 Processing, 4th ACM, Boston. Ma. pp. 129-140. 1996.
4. T. D. C. Little, and Arif Ghafoor, "Multimedia Synchronization Protocols for Broadband Integrated Services," IEEE Journal on selected Areas in Comm., Vol. 9, No.9, Dec. 1991.
5. Z. Chen, S. Than, R. Campbell, and Y.Li, "Real time video and audio in the world wide web", Proc. Fourth International World Wide Web Conference, 1995.
6. W. Geyer, "Stream Synchronization in a Scalable Video Server Array," Master's thesis, Institute Eurecom, Sophia Antipolis, France, Sept., 1995.
7. Dae-Jea Cho, Kee-Young Yoo, "The Study on Development of a Multimedia Synchronization Algorithm for Internet Based VOD Services", KIPS, Vol. 8-B, No 1, pp 74-80, Feb., 2001.
8. Gi-Sung Lee, Jeung-gyu Jee, Sok-Pal Cho, "Buffering Management Scheme for Multimedia Synchronization in Mobile Information System," Lecture Notes in Computer Science Vol. 2660, pp 545-554, June, 2003.

Fuzzy Logic Adaptive Mobile Location Estimation

Jongchan Lee[1], Seung-Jae Yoo[2], Dong Chun Lee[3]

[1]Radio Access Research Team ETRI, Korea
chan2000@etri.re.kr
[2]Dept. of Information Security Joongbu Univ., Korea
[3]Dept. of Computer Science, Howon Univ., Korea

Abstract. In this study, we propose a novel mobile tracking scheme which utilizes the fuzzy-based decision making with the consideration of the information such as previous location, moving direction and distance to the base station as well as received signal strength, thereby resulting to the estimation performance even much better than the previous schemes. Our scheme divides a cell into many blocks based on the signal strength and then estimate in stepwise the optimal block where a mobile locates using Multi-Criteria Decision Making (MCDM). Through numerical results, we show that our proposed mobile tracking method provides a better performance than the conventional method using the received signal strength.

1 Introduction

In the microcell-based or picocell-based mobile communication network frequent movements of a mobile terminal or host bring about excessive traffics into the network and may degrade the quality of services (QoS) severely. If its location can be estimated, network resources may be more effectively allocated and better QoS can be provisioned with the combination of handoff optimization. Moreover the location estimation technology may be used in other new applications such as the emergency call for disaster recovery. It will have viable roles in the communication networks of next generation. Global Positioning System (GPS) was initially developed for military purposes but it is also utilized for civil applications such as local traffic information services and geo-location based applications. However incorporating GPS receivers into handsets raises questions of cost, size and power consumption [1].

Other methods for location estimation are based on radio signal propagation such as signposts, dead reckoning, circular or hyperbolic trilateration systems, etc. Many methods and systems have been proposed based on radio signal strength measurement of a mobile object's transmitter by a set of base stations [2, 3, 4]. Recently, adaptive schemes based on the use of cellular systems and on fuzzy logic [5], hidden Markov models [6, 7] and pattern recognition methods [8] have been used to estimate the position of mobiles. The system studied in [2] estimates mobile location using information on contours but it does not provide a realistic search procedure. In [3] the estimation is based on the signal strength received at a multi-beam antenna of a base station in the multi-path environment, and the angle of its arrival (AOA). AOA is measured under the assumption that the signal is in line of sight (LOS), but LOS

H. Jin et al. (Eds.): NPC 2004, LNCS 3222, pp. 626-634, 2004.

signal may not be received in the microcell where reflections and diffractions occur due to dense building environment. In this situation AOA of the strongest reflected signal is utilized for estimation, and therefore the location estimated differs greatly from real one. Time of arrival (TOA) of a signal from a mobile to neighboring base stations are used in [9], but this scheme has two problems. First, an accurate synchronization is essential between all sending endpoints and all receiving ones in the system. An error of 1 μs in synchronization results to 300 m error in location. Secondly this scheme is not suitable for the microcellular environment because it also assumes LOS environment. Time difference of arrival (TDOA) of signals from two base stations is considered in [10]. TOA scheme and TDOA scheme have been studied for IS-95B where PN code of CDMA system can be used for the location estimation. Enhanced Observed Time Difference (E-OTD) is a TDOA positioning method based on OTD feature already existing in GSM. The mobile measures arrival time of signals from three or more cell sites in a network. In this method the position of mobile is determined by trilateration [11]. E-OTD, which relies upon the visibility of at least three cell sites to calculate it, is not a good solution for rural areas where cell-site separation is large. However, it promises to work well in areas of high cell-site density and indoors.

The above-mentioned schemes such as AOA, TOA and TDOA have problems as follows.

- These schemes assume that the cellular system consists of LOS areas. They get good results only under this assumption.
- The microcellular system such as IMT-2000 has NLOS areas which are affected by specific reflections and diffractions. In this situation these schemes have great errors in estimation.
- In the microcellular environment the points of the same average signal strength form not a circular contour but a distorted one. These schemes ignore the fact that the propagation rule is affected by many parameters.
- They rely only on the information related to radio signal such as signal strength. Their accuracies are affected by short-term fading, shadowing or diffraction.

In this study, to enhance estimation accuracy, we propose a scheme based on Multi-Criteria Decision Making (MCDM) which considers multiple parameters: the signal strength, the distance between the base station and mobile, the moving direction, and the previous location. This process is based on three step location estimations which can determine the mobile position by gradually reducing the area of the mobile position [12]. Using MCDM, the estimator first estimates the locating sector in the sector estimation step, then estimates the locating zone in the zone estimation step, and then finally estimates the locating block in the block estimate step.

2 Estimation Procedure

Figure 1 shows how our scheme divides a cell into many blocks based on the signal strength and then estimates the optimal block stepwise where the mobile is located using MCDM.

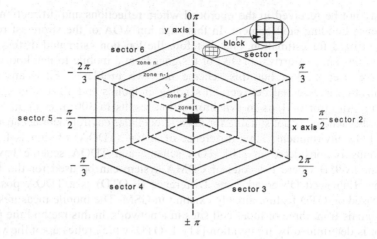

Fig. 1. Sector, Zone and Block

The location of a mobile within a cell can be defined by dividing each cell into sectors, zones and blocks and relating these to the signal level received by it at that point. It is done automatically in three phases of sector definition, zone definition and block definition. Then the location definition block is constructed with these results. They are performed at the system initialization before executing the location estimation. The sector definition phase divides a cell into sectors, and assigns a sector number to blocks belonging to each sector. The zone definition phase divides each sector into zones, and assigns a zone number to blocks belonging to each zone. The block definition phase assigns a block number to each block. In order to indicate the location of each block within a cell, 2-dimensional vector (d, a) is assigned to each block. After the completion of this phase each block has a set of block information.

The collection of block information is called the *block object*. The block object contains the following information: the sector number, the zone number, the block number, the vector data (d, a), the maximum and the minimum value of average PSS for the LOS block, the compensated value for the NLOS block and a bit for indicating "node" or "edge", etc.

Using MCDM and the block object which is constructed as described above, the estimator is started with a timer, and the estimation is performed sequentially in three steps: sector estimation, zone estimation, and finally block estimation.

3 Mobile Tracking Based on MCDM

3.1 Multi-Criteria Decision Parameters

In our study, the received signal strength, the distance between the mobile and the base station, the previous location, and the moving direction are considered as decision parameters. The received signal strength has been used in many schemes, but it has very irregular profiles due to the effects of radio environments. The distance is considered because it can explain the block allocation plan; however, it may also be inaccurate due to the effect of multi-path fading, etc. It is not sufficient by itself. We consider the previous location. It is normally expected that the estimated location should be near the previous one. Therefore, if the estimated location is too far from the previous one, the estimation may be regarded as inaccurate. We also consider the moving direction. Usually the mobile is most likely to move forward, less likely to move rightward or leftward, and least likely to move backward more than one block. The low-speed mobile (a pedestrian) has a smaller moving radius and a more complex moving pattern, while the high-speed mobile (a motor vehicle) has a larger radius and a simpler pattern.

In mobile tracking using MCDM, the Decision function D is defined by combining the degree of satisfaction for multiple evaluation parameters, and the decision is made on the basis of his function. The evaluation parameter can be seen as a proposition. A compound proposition is formed from multiple evaluation parameters with a connective operator, and the total evaluation is performed by totaling the values for the multiple parameters with connective operators. In this method errors in the evaluation parameters impose milder changes on the total evaluation value than in binary logics.

3.2 Membership Function

The membership function with a trapezoidal shape is used for determining the membership degree of the mobile because it provides a more versatile degree between the upper limit and the lower one than the membership function with a step-like shape. Let us define the membership functions for the pilot signal strengths from neighboring base stations.

The membership function of PSS_i, $\mu_R(PSS_i)$, is given by Figure 2. PSS_i is the signal strength received from the base station i, s_1 is the lower limit, and s_2 is the upper limit.

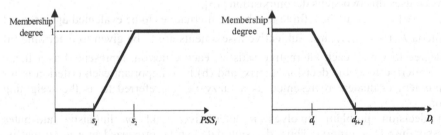

Fig. 2. The membership function of the PPS.

Fig. 3. The membership function of the distance

Now we define the membership function of the distance. The membership function of the distance, $\mu_R(D_i)$, is given by Figure 3, where D_i is the distance between the base station i and the mobile, d_1 is the upper limit, and d_2 is the lower limit.

630   J. Lee, S.-J. Yoo, and D.C. Lee

The membership function of the previous location of the mobile, $\mu_R(L_i)$, is given by Figure 4. Where L_i is the vector information of its current location, $E_1,\cdots,E_4$ is the vector information of the previous location, and g_i is the physical difference between them.

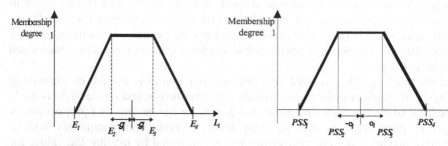

Fig. 4. The membership function of the location.

Fig. 5. The membership function of the direction.

The membership function of the moving direction, $\mu_R(C_i)$, is given by Figure 5. C_i is the vector information of the moving direction, $PSS_1,\cdots,PSS_4$ is the pilot signal strength and o_i the physical difference between the previous location and the current one

3.3 Location Estimation

Most of the MCDM approaches face the decision problem in two consecutive steps: aggregating all the judgments with respect to all the criteria and per decision alternative and ranking the alternatives according to the aggregated criterion. Also our approach uses this two-steps decomposition [13].

Let J_i ($i \in \{1, 2,\ldots, n\}$ be a finite number of alternatives to be evaluated against a set of criteria K_j (j=1, 2,\ldots, m). Subjective assessments are to be given to determine (a) the degree to which each alternative satisfies each criterion, represented as a fuzzy matrix referred to as the decision matrix, and (b) how important each criterion is for the problem evaluated, represented as a fuzzy vector referred to as the weighting vector.

Each decision problem involves n alternatives and m linguistic attributes corresponding to m criteria. Thus, decision data can be organized in a $m \times n$ matrix. The decision matrix for alternatives is given by Eq. (1):

$$\mu = \begin{bmatrix} \mu_R(PSS_{11}) & \mu_R(D_{12}) & \mu_R(L_{13}) & \mu_R(C_{14}) \\ \mu_R(PSS_{21}) & \mu_R(D_{12}) & \mu_R(L_{13}) & \mu_R(C_{14}) \\ \mu_R(PSS_{31}) & \mu_R(D_{12}) & \mu_R(L_{13}) & \mu_R(C_{14}) \\ \cdots & \cdots & \cdots & \cdots \\ \mu_R(PSS_{n1}) & \mu_R(D_{n2}) & \mu_R(L_{n3}) & \mu_R(C_{nm}) \end{bmatrix} \quad (1)$$

The weighting vector for evaluation criteria can be given by using linguistic terminology with fuzzy set theory [14]. It is a finite set of ordered symbols to represent the weights of the criteria using the following linear ordering: very high $\geq$ high $\geq$ medium $\geq$ low $\geq$ very low. Weighting vector W is represented as Eq. (2).

$$W = (w_i^{PSS}, w_i^{D}, w_i^{L}, w_i^{C}) \tag{2}$$

The fuzzification procedure leads to a performance matrix $\mu \in [0,1]^{n \times m}$ where each element μ_{nm} expresses how much the n-th alternative satisfies the m-th criterion. Therefore, each low of the performance matrix is a fuzzy set μ_m expressing the satisfaction of the m-th criterion in the universe of the available alternatives [13-14]. By multiplying the weighting vector by the decision matrix, the performance matrix is

$$\mu = \begin{bmatrix} \mu_R(PSS_{11}) \times w_1^{PSS} & \mu_R(D_{12}) \times w_1^{D} & \mu_R(L_{13}) \times w_1^{L} & \mu_R(C_{14}) \times w_1^{C} \\ \mu_R(PSS_{21}) \times w_2^{PSS} & \mu_R(D_{12}) \times w_2^{D} & \mu_R(L_{13}) \times w_2^{L} & \mu_R(C_{14}) \times w_2^{C} \\ \mu_R(PSS_{31}) \times w_3^{PSS} & \mu_R(D_{12}) \times w_3^{D} & \mu_R(L_{13}) \times w_3^{L} & \mu_R(C_{14}) \times w_3^{C} \\ \dots & \dots & \dots & \dots \\ \mu_R(PSS_{n1}) \times w_i^{PSS} & \mu_R(D_{n2}) \times w_i^{D} & \mu_R(L_{n3}) \times w_i^{L} & \mu_R(C_{nm}) \times w_i^{C} \end{bmatrix} \tag{3}$$

given by Eq. (3):
Given the decision matrix and the weighting vector, the decision making objective for the general fuzzy MCDM problem is to rank all alternatives by giving each of them an overall preference rating with respect to all criteria [14]. GMV (Generalized Mean Value) is used for ranking the alternatives according to the aggregated criterion. The GMV for alternatives is represented as Eq. (4).

$$m(\mu_n) = \frac{(C_i + D_i)^2 - (A_i + B_i)^2 + A_i \cdot B_i - C_i \cdot D_i}{3 \cdot [(C_i + D_i) - (A_i + B_i)]} \tag{4}$$

where $A_i = \mu_R(PSS_{n1}) \times w_i^{PSS}$, $B_i = \mu_R(D_{n2}) \times w_i^{D}$, and $C_i = \mu_R(L_{n3}) \times w_i^{L}$, $D_i = \mu_R(C_{nm}) \times w_i^{C}$, respectively.

4 Performance Analysis

The moving path and the mobile velocity are affected by the road topology. The moving pattern is described by the changes in moving direction and velocity. In our study we assume that low speed mobiles, pedestrians, occupy 60% of the total population in the cell and high-speed mobiles, vehicles, 40%. One half of the pedestrians are assumed to be still and another half moving. Also the private owned cars occupy 60% of the total vehicle, the taxi 10% and the public transportation 30%.

Vehicles move forward, leftward/rightward and U- Turn. The moving velocity is assumed to have a uniform distribution. The walking speed of pedestrians is 0~5 Km/hr, the speed of private cars and taxis 30~100 Km/hr, and buses 10~70 Km/hr. The speed is assumed to be constant during walking or driving. Figure 4 shows the road used in our simulation to consider traffic environments. The black circle indicates the branch of the road, and the shaded areas are blocks that the road passes through. Each block is a square and its side is assumed to have the length of 30 m. The time needed for a high speed mobile to pass through a block is calculated from $BT = r / \upsilon$ where r is the length of the road segment crossing at each block and v the mobile speed. As shown in Figure 4, BT is dependent on r. We can consider four different values - r, $n\sqrt{2}\ m$ (crossing diagonally), $\frac{3n}{4}\sqrt{2}\,m$ (3/4 crossing), $\frac{n}{2}\sqrt{2}\ m$ (2/4 crossing) and $\frac{n}{4}\sqrt{2}\ m$ (1/4 crossing) - according to which portion of a block each road segment crosses through. In order to reflect more realistic information into our simulation, it is assumed that the signal strength is sampled every 0.5 sec, 0.2 sec, 0.1 sec, 0.1 sec and 0.05 sec for the speed of ≤10km/h, ≤ 20km/h, ≤50km/h, ≤70km/h and ≤ 100km/h, respectively. If BT is too small, we cannot obtain enough samples to calculate the average signal strength. We consider the following simulation parameters regarding the received signal strength. The value of k_2, which indicates the changes in LOS/NLOS environments, is in the range of 20 through 50. The mean signal attenuation by the path-loss is proportional to 3.5 times the propagation distance, and the shadowing has a log-normal distribution with a standard deviation of $\sigma = 6dB$. A value of received signal strength less than −16 dB is regarded as an error, which is therefore excluded from the calculation.

To evaluate the error probability of our schemes in each estimation stage, the mobile population in the track boundary and sector boundary is generated according to a Poisson distribution. All the mobiles generated above are assumed to cross the sector boundary lines and track boundary lines. Also the curved path passes through the handoff area. Stationary mobiles appear at sector boundary areas and track boundary areas and remain still at those points. Pedestrian mobiles appear at sector and track boundary areas and move toward the neighboring sector or track.

Figure 6 shows the effect of the block size on the estimation performance of MCDM and the existing schemes. As the block size becomes smaller, the accuracies of the three schemes decrease. The accuracies of AOA and TOA decrease rapidly. On the other hand, the performance of MCDM is least affected by block size because it additionally utilizes the previous location and distance between the mobile and the base station for estimation.

Figure 7 shows the estimation rate or accuracy of our proposed scheme depending on the mobile speed. The accuracy of AOA and TOA becomes lower rapidly since the signal measurement error would be large as the mobile speed increases. The performance of MCDM is least affected by the mobile speed because the information such as moving direction and previous location are considered in MCDM and, therefore, errors during the signal evaluation step decrease. We compare our scheme, MCDM with VA [12], E-OTD and TDOA in Figure 8. In this figure the mobile maintains its y position at 1000m and traverse x axis from $x = 0$m to $x = 2000$m.

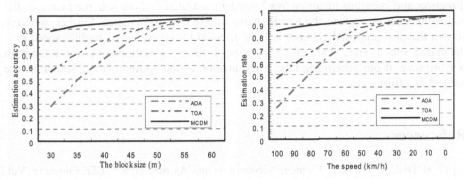

Fig. 6. The estimation accuracy versus the size

Fig. 7. The estimation accuracy versus the speed

Distance Root Mean Square stands for the root-mean-square value of the distances from the true location point of the position fixes in a collection of measurements. In order to get the estimated values for comparison we take an average of 20 values for each mobile position. We assume NLOS environment and the signal level of mobile may change abruptly due to shadowing. It shows that the performance of MCDM is least affected by abrupt change of signal level. MCDM has the most accurate result. This may well be attributed to the fact that it imposes less weight on the received signal strength in NLOS area and, instead, greater weights on other parameters such as the distance between mobile and base station, previous location, and moving direction are considered as decision parameters

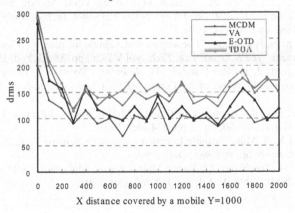

Fig. 8. Comparison of the estimation accuracy

5 Conclusions

In this study, we proposed a MCDM-based mobile tracking method for estimating more accurately the mobile location by considering multiple parameters, such the signal strength, the distance between the base station and mobile, the moving direction, and previous location. We have demonstrated that our scheme increases the estimation accuracy when the mobile moves along a boundary area. Further, we have shown that the proposed scheme is little affected by an increased mobile speed or a decreased block size. The effect of weight factor variations on the estimation performance of our scheme and the determination of the optimal weight should be the subject of a future study.

References

[1] G. M. Djuknic and R. E. Richton, "Geolocation and Assisted GPS," *IEEE Computer*, Vol. 34, No. 2, pp.123-125, Feb. 2001.
[2] W. G. Figel, N. H. Shepherd and W. F. Trammell, "Vehicle location by a signal attenuation method," *IEEE Trans. Veh. Technol.*, vol. VT-18, pp. 104-109, Nov. 1969.
[3] G. D. Ott, "Vehicle location in cellular mobile radio systems," *IEEE Trans. Veh. Tech.*, Vol. VT-26, pp. 43-46, Feb. 1977.
[4] Hatta M., Nagatsu T., "Mobile Location Using Signal Strength Measurements in a Cellular System", *IEEE Transactions on Vehicular Technology*, vol. VT29, pp245 - 252, May 1980.
[5] Song H.L., "Automatic Vehicle Location in Cellular Communication Systems", *IEEE Transactions on Vehicular Technology*, vol.43, pp902-908, Nov. 1994.
[6] Kennemann O., "Pattern Recognition by Hidden Markov Models for Supporting Handover Decisions in the GSM system", in *Proc. 6 th Nordic Seminar Dig. Mobile Radio Comm.*, Stockholm,Sweden, pp.195-202, 1994
[7] T. Nypan and O. Hallingstad, "Cellular Positioning by Database Comparison and Hidden Markov Models.," PWC2002:, pp. 277-284, Oct. 2002
[8] Kennemann O., "Continuous Location of Moving GSM Mobile Stations by Pattern Recognition Techniques", in *Proc. 5th Int. Symp. Personal, Indoor, Mobile, Radio Comm.*, denHaag, Holland, pp.630-634, 1994.
[9] H. Staras and S. N. Honikman, "The accuracy of vehicle location by trilateration in a dense urban environment," *IEEE Trans. Veh. Tech.*, vol VT-26, pp. 38-43, Feb. 1972.
[10] T. S. Rappaport, J. H. Reed and B. D. Woerner, "Position Location Using Wireless Communications on Highways of the Future," *IEEE Communications Magazine*, pp. 33-41, Oct.
[11] Y. A. Spirito, "On the Accuracy of Cellular Mobile Station Location Estimation," *IEEE Trans. Veh. Technol.*, vol. 50, no. 3, pp. 674-685, 2001.
[12] J. C. Lee and Y. S. Mun, "Mobile Location Estimation Scheme," SK telecommunications Review, Vol. 9, No. 6, pp. 968-983, Dec. 1999.
[13] C. Naso and B. Turchiano, "A Fuzzy Multi-Criteria Algorithm for Dynamic Routing in FMS," IEEE ICSMC'1998, Vol. 1, pp. 457-462, Oct. 1998.

A Host Protection Framework Against Unauthorized Access for Ensuring Network Survivability

Hyuncheol Kim[1], Sunghae Kim[3], Seongjin Ahn[2], and Jinwook Chung[1]

[1] Dept. of Electrical and Computer Engineering,Sungkyunkwan University,
300 Chunchun-Dong Jangan-Gu,Suwon, Korea, 440-746
{hckim,jwchung}@songgang.skku.ac.kr
[2] Dept. of Computer Education, Sungkyunkwan University,
53 Myungryun-Dong Jongro-Gu, Seoul, Korea, 110-745
sjahn@comedu.skku.ac.kr
[3] Electronics and Telecommunications Research Institutes, Daejon, Korea
shkim@etri.re.kr

Abstract. Currently, the major focus on the network security is securing individual components as well as preventing unauthorized access to network services. Ironically, Address Resolution Protocol (ARP) poisoning and spoofing techniques can be used to prohibit unauthorized network access and resource modifications. The protecting ARP which relies on hosts caching reply messages can be the primary method in obstructing the misuse of the network. This paper proposes a network service access control framework, which provides a comprehensive, host-by-host perspective on IP (Internet Protocol) over Ethernet networks security. We will also show how this framework can be applied to network elements including detecting, correcting, and preventing security vulnerabilities.

1 Introduction

Along with development of communication networks, the problem of network security has increasingly become a global challenge. Reflecting through these trends, the key focus on the network security is securing individual components as well as preventing unauthorized access to network services. Although IP over Ethernet networks are the most popular Local Area Networks (LANs) nowadays, an ignorance of the network security in designing TCP/IP (Transmission Control Protocol and Internet Protocol) has led important network resources to be wasted or damaged.

Among the network resources, IP address, a limited and important resource, is increasingly misused, which results from its inexperienced and malevolent purposes to cause a security problem or damage the entire networks. As an IP address is the only one to identify itself, the same IP address cannot be simultaneously used in other equipments. If IP addresses, which are respectively

H. Jin et al. (Eds.): NPC 2004, LNCS 3222, pp. 635–643, 2004.

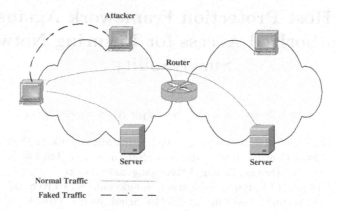

Fig. 1. ARP Spoofing and Poisoning Attack

set by hosts in the network, are misused for some inexperienced or malevolent purposes, the security problem could be triggered in the network.

IP over Ethernet networks use ARP to resolve IP addresses into hardware, or MAC (Media Access Control) addresses. All the hosts in the network maintain an ARP cache which includes the IP address and the resolved hardware or MAC addresses. ARP resolution is invoked when a new IP address has to be resolved or when an entry in the cache expires. As shown in Fig.1, the ARP poisoning and spoofing attack can easily occur when a malicious user tries to modify the association of an IP address and its corresponding hardware or MAC address by disguising himself of being an innocent host [1].

In this study, we propose an unauthorized network access control framework in IP over Ethernet networks that guarantees fast and continuous network protection. To this, we propose a network access control scheme based on ARP spoofing and demonstrate how this concept can be applied to network elements, services, and applications. In addition, we demonstrate how the security framework can be applied to all layers of the TCP/IP protocol suite.

The rest of this paper is organized as follows. The background relevant for ARP operations and details of proposed framework are described in section 2 and 3, respectively. Finally the paper concludes in Section 4.

2 Network Security and ARP Operations

2.1 Network Security

The network security technologies have been studied to prevent increasingly variable and sophisticated attacks on a network. Currently, they include an intrusion detection system that detects a sign of an attack, a firewall that mainly blocks the traffic of a detected attacker, a response system i.e., a packet filtering router to protect its domain, and many other systems to enhance network survivability.

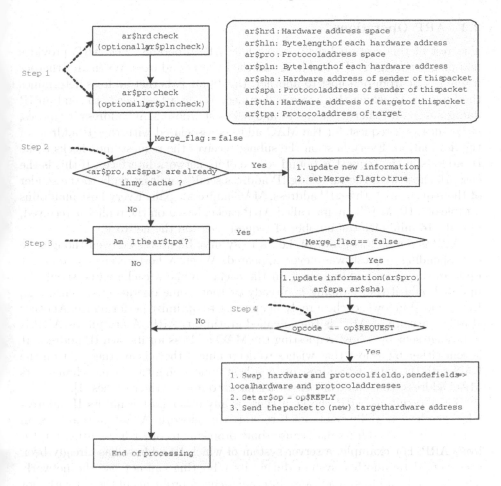

Fig. 2. ARP Mechanism

The network survivability refers to continuing the operation of a system to provide services even though it has been damaged by network attacks, system failures, and other overloads. While early security technologies mainly covered screening for a single computer attack, the contemporary security technologies have been developed to resolve and resist those network attacks. That is, the network survivability has focused on systematically managing the configuration of the network and its components.

The IP address management refers to securing the network survivability by monitoring and disabling the function of the host when a system detects the worms or other abnormal behaviors, as well as an intentional or malicious changes of the IP address. Thus, the IP management and blocking the misuse of IP address come to serve as a new concept in the security solution for controlling the network.

2.2 ARP Operations

The rest of this section briefly states how ARP operates. The ARP provides mapping between the IPv4 address and the Ethernet address. When an Ethernet frame is sent from one host to another, the 48 bit Ethernet address determines the interface to which the frame is destined. When a host needs to send an IP datagram as an Ethernet frame to another host whose MAC address it ignores, it broadcasts a request for the MAC address associated with the IP address of the destination. Every host on the subnet receives the request and checks if the IP address in the request is bound to one of its network interfaces. If this is the case, the host with the matching IP address sends a unicast reply to the sender of the request with the <IP address, MAC address> pair. Every host maintains a table of <IP, MAC> pairs, called ARP cache, based on the replies it received, in order to minimize the number of requests sent on the network.

ARP is a stateless protocol, i.e., a reply may be processed even though the corresponding request was never appeared. When a host receives a reply, it updates the corresponding entry in the cache. While a cache entry should be updated only if the mapping is already present, some operating systems, e.g., Linux and Windows, cache a reply in any case to optimize performance. Another stateless feature of ARP is the so called gratuitous ARP. A gratuitous ARP is a message sent by a host requesting the MAC address for its own IP address. It is sent either by a host that wishes to determine if there is another host on the LAN with the same IP address or by a host announcing that it has changed its MAC address, thus allowing the other hosts to update their caches [1].

The Gratuitous ARP checks if there is any other host using its IP address when the host initially boots itself to start the network. A system that uses an unauthorized IP address may cause some problems to other hosts using Gratuitous ARP. For example, a server system of which IP address has already been preoccupied by another system during its rebooting can-not use the network. That is, the IP address may cause internal security problems in the network, not from externally [2][3][4].

3 Proposed Network Access Control Framework

3.1 Gratuitous ARP

Using the gratuitous ARP, a host can check if the IP address is used by other hosts in order to avoid using duplicated IP address. Table 1, Table 2, Table 3, and Table 4 shows different types of collisions in using gratuitous ARP for each OS respectively. The ON (Offending Node) denotes a host which tries to use the IP, and the DN (Defending Node) denotes a host using the IP.

3.2 An Unauthorized Access Control Framework

Fig.2 illustrates an algorithm by the hosts in processing an ARP message. In processing the ARP algorithm, there can be many different types of attacks

Table 1. Windows (A) to Windows (B) Gratuitous ARP

Type	Sender	Receiver	Source IP	Source MAC	Target IP	Target MAC
Request	B's MAC	All	B	B's MAC	B	Ignored
Response	A's MAC	B's MAC	A	A's MAC	B	B's MAC
Request	A's MAC	All	A	A's MAC	A	Ignored

Table 2. Windows (A) to Linux (B) Gratuitous ARP

Type	Sender	Receiver	Source IP	Source MAC	Target IP	Target MAC
Request	B's MAC	All	B	B's MAC	B	Ignored

Table 3. Linux (A) to Windows (B) Gratuitous ARP

Type	Sender	Receiver	Source IP	Source MAC	Target IP	Target MAC
Request	B's MAC	All	0.0.0.0	B's MAC	B	Ignored
Response	A's MAC	B's MAC	A	A's MAC	0.0.0.0	B's MAC

Table 4. Linux (A) to Linux (B) Gratuitous ARP

Type	Sender	Receiver	Source IP	Source MAC	Target IP	Target MAC
Request	B's MAC	All	0.0.0.0	B's MAC	B	Ignored
Response	A's MAC	B's MAC	A	A's MAC	A	A's MAC

Table 5. Vulnerable Points of ARP

Number	Problems	Cause
1	Duplicated IP address	UNIX/Linux Server
2	ARP Cache Forgery	MAC address Forgery
3	Authorized IP Blocking	Malicious gratuitous ARP Response to authorized host
4	Unauthorized IP Misappropriation	IP address alteration of unauthorized host

such as ARP Spoofing, MAC Flooding, ARP Redirect, MAC Duplicating, etc. Different types of attack that can occur for each step is as follows.

- <Step 1> : <Step 1> is a stage that defines the types of hardware interface and upper layer protocol. The host needs to provide verification function to check if the protocol and the packet format have a valid MAC layer access protocol.
- <Step 2> : <Step 2> is a process that updates its current ARP cache based on ARP request message. If the hardware address and the protocol address is

already exists in the cache table, the host only needs to update the table. At this point, network security problem may occur if the third party broadcasts a packet with invalid MAC address. For example, if a host send an ARP request message with the invalid MAC address of A, the hosts that were communicating with the host A will change its cache with the invalid MAC address of host A. Thus, the host A would not be able to use the network. The attacker will continually generate the packet with the invalid MAC address. Thus, it can perform different forms of packet sniffing such as ARP table flooding, APR Spoofing, ARP Redirect, MAC Duplicating, etc [5].

- <Step 3> : <Step 3> is a process in which the host sends an ARP reply message for ARP request with its destination address. The problem of this step is that if the host is in hardware reboot status or if the host tries to change its non-used IP address, the host would be unable to use the network if a third-party deliberately sends a fake reply message.

Table 5 shows the security problems that can occur during the ARP operation. The two types of solution to the security problem 1 to 4 are modifying ARP process and managing IP and MAC addresses by monitoring ARP packets. The modifying method recognizes the fact that the IP and MAC address can always be changed by anyone thus it has no way of finding out who is privileged user. But, this method is not a perfect solution, due to the fact that the verification of gratuitous ARP is impossible and the ARP packet cannot be altered. But the security problem can be solved by managing IP and MAC addresses by monitoring ARP packets.

Just as IP spoofing, ARP spoofing also prevents a host in the network from functioning normal network processing by preventing it to perform ARP reply for ARP requests. If the host tries to perform ARP reply, the attacker uses the IP address of the incompetent host and configures it as a target host. When a victim host tries to communicate with the incompetent host, the attackers system will perform ARP reply to all the ARP broadcast request instead of the incompetent host. Thus, the MAC address of the victim system is stored in the attackers ARP cache, and the victim system will mistake the attacker as the incompetent system and perform normal communication with the attacker [1] [6] [7]. Ironically, techniques of preventing ARP poisoning and spoofing can be used to prohibit unauthorized network access and resource modifications.

The distributed network environment covered in this study includes manager and agent system. The agent is installed in each broadcast domain (including Virtual LAN) to collect packets generated within the domain. The manager enforces policies to block the unauthorized accesses detected by the agent in the network. The Agent uses the ARP spoofing technology to manage the network. It also creates the ARP packet under the order from the manager to confirm the up/down status of the network nodes and to obtain the MAC address, additionally shutting down the network against an unauthorized IP. Particularly, the ARP Request means an important message to define the ARP cache table of all hosts in the network through the ARP spoofing. Fig.3 shows the module struc-

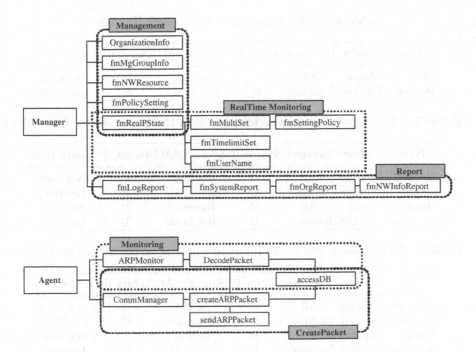

Fig. 3. The Module Architecture of Manager and Agent System

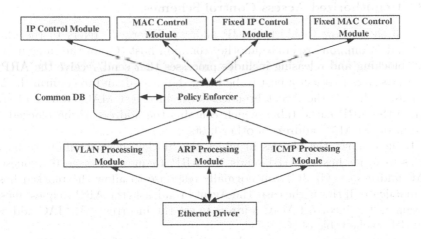

Fig. 4. The Process Module of Agent System

ture of the manager and agent system and Fig.3 shows the process architecture of the agent system, respectively.

Table 6. ARP message process to block IP address

Type	Sender	Receiver	Source IP	Source MAC	Target IP	Target MAC
Request	Agent	All	B	Incorrect	B	Not used
Response	Blocked	Incorrect	B	B's MAC	B	Incorrect

Table 7. ARP message process to interfere with the access of the blocked host

Type	Sender	Receiver	Source IP	Source MAC	Target IP	Target MAC
Request	Blocked	All	B	B's MAC	C	Not used
Response	Common	Blocked	C	C's MAC	B	Incorrect
Request	Agent	All	B	Incorrect	B	Not used
Response	Blocked	Incorrect	B	B's MAC	B	Incorrect

Table 8. ARP message process to interfere with the access to the common host

Type	Sender	Receiver	Source IP	Source MAC	Target IP	Target MAC
Request	Common	All	C	C's MAC	B	Not used
Response	Blocked	Common	B	B's MAC	C	C's MAC
Request	Agent	All	B	Incorrect	B	Not used
Response	Blocked	Incorrect	B	B's MAC	B	Incorrect

3.3 Unauthorized Access Control Schemes

Table 6 shows how to block the IP address. "Blocked" refers to the blocked host and "Common" refers to another common host (C) on the same network. Host blocking and releasing includes processes that send/receive the ARP Request messages to select a host to be blocked/released, and to confirm the MAC address. In line 1, the Agent broadcasts the incorrect MAC address of (B) to update the ARP cache table, which contains the address of the blocked host, with incorrect MAC address of other hosts.

Table 7 shows the process in which the blocked host attempts to have an access to other hosts. If (B) sends the ARP Request message to request the MAC address of (C), (C) will normally response to allow the blocked host to communicate. If this is the case, the Agent broadcasts the ARP Request message containing the incorrect MAC address to set the incorrect (B) MAC address in the ARP cache table of (C).

Table 8 shows the process where the Agent interferes with the access of other hosts to (B). If (C) sends the ARP Request message to request the MAC address of (B) in order to access (B), the (A) sends the ARP Response message containing the incorrect MAC address of the blocked host. Then, (C) will have the incorrect MAC address of (B) by updating the ARP cache table with the request message lately received from the Agent.

Table 9 shows how to release the blocked IP. The blocked IP will be released when (A) sends the gratuitous ARP packet for (B). Other hosts can obtain

Table 9. ARP message process to block IP address

Type	Sender	Receiver	Source IP	Source MAC	Target IP	Target MAC
Request	Agent	All	B	B's MAC	B	Not used
Response	Blocked	Agent	B	B's MAC	B	B's MAC

the correct MAC address of the blocked host, freely sending/receiving the ARP request/response message without future interferences from (A).

4 Conclusions

IP address which is a limited and important resource is increasingly misused, which results from its inexperienced and malevolent purposes to cause a security problem or damage the entire networks. Because a system that uses an unauthorized IP address may cause some problems to other hosts, the IP ad-dress may cause internal security problems in the network, not from externally.

In this paper, we propose an unauthorized network service access control framework focusing on the management and security of the IP, a network resource. This system consisting of agent and manager uses the network monitoring and the IP blocking algorithm to integrate the networks so as to effectively manage the IP resources. The agent can be expanded by installing Simple Network Management Protocol (SNMP) agent to the IP integration management.

This system also presents the possibility of developing the integration management system to protect the network from the external virus attacks. This study worked upon a system operating under the IPv4 environment, which will come to be needed under the IPv6 that is expected to get its popularity. The same network blocking mechanism as in the IPv4 network can optionally be operated on Internet Control Message Protocol version 6 (ICMPv6).

References

1. D. Bruschi, A. Ornaghi, et al.: S-ARP: a Secure Address Resolution Protocol, ACSAC '03 (2003) 66–74
2. WAndrew R. McGee, S. Rao Vasireddy, et al.: A Framework for Ensuring Network Security, Bell Labs Technical Journal, Vol. 8, (2004) 7–27
3. Anirban Chakrabarti, G. Manimaran: Internet Infrastructure Security: A Taxonomy, IEEE Network, Nov./Dec. (2002) 13–21
4. Soonchoul kim, Youngsu Choi, et al.: Study of Security Management System Based on Client Server Model, ICC, Vol 2. (1999) 1403–1408
5. Steven J. Templeton, Karl E. Levitt: Detecting Spoofed Packets, DISCEX03, Vol 1, (2003) 164–175
6. Bruce McDonald, Taieb Znati, et al.: Comparative Analysis of Neighbor Greeting Protocols: ARP versus ES-IS, SIMULATION '96, Apr. 1996 (71–80)
7. Ping Lin, Lin Lin: Security in Enterprise Networking: A Quick Tour, IEEE Communications Magazine, Jan. (1996) 56–61

A Design and Implementation of Network Traffic Monitoring System for PC-room Management

Yonghak Ahn, Oksam Chae

Dept. of Computer Engineering, Kyunghee University,
Sochen-ri, Giheung-eup, Yongin-si, Gyeonggi-do 449-701, Republic of Korea
yohan@vision.khu.ac.kr, oschae@khu.ac.kr

Abstract. This study proposes a network traffic monitoring system that will support the operation, management, expansion and design of a network system for its users through an analysis and diagnosis of the network-related equipments and lines in the PC-room. The proposed monitoring system is lightweight for its uses under the wireless environment and applies a web-based technology using JAVA to overcome the limits to managerial space, inconveniences and platform dependency and to raise its applicability to and usability on the real network based on performances, fault analyses and their calculation algorithm. The traffic monitoring system implemented in this study will allow users to effectively fulfill the network management including network diagnoses, fault detection, network configuration and design through the web, as well as to help users with their managements by presenting how to apply a simple network.

1 Introduction

With the surprising developments in Internet, the users on network have rapidly increased so that the traffic on network leads to an explosive increase in many companies, schools and public institutions. Along with the developments in network technologies and the uses of various applications, network traffic includes not only data but also voice, picture, image and multimedia traffic. Those increases in network users and traffic have raised a need for a massive network line and the resulting equipment investments and made network configuration more gigantic and complicated[1-2]. However, such trends escape the managerial scope of a manager, leading to a more need for managements of performance and fault on network. To help the managers with their managements, and accordingly, various management tools have been developed. Since those tools, however, had such fundamental limits as limited management functions, inconveniences, their insufficient expansion into large-scale network and problematic applications of analytic results, the managements of managers had to be restrictively fulfilled[3]. The solution to problems in the existing management technologies and tools is being pursued by applying such new Internet based technologies as web related technologies or JAVA to such fields as managements of networks, systems or applications[4-5]. This approach is called the web based management technology, by which the limits to managerial space and inconveniences can be overcome through their application to the web platform for an increase in effi-

H. Jin et al. (Eds.): NPC 2004, LNCS 3222, pp. 644-652, 2004.
© IFIP International Federation for Information Processing 2004

ciency. Web based network management products typically include MRTG (Multi Router Traffic Grapher) that collects management information through SNMP, stores traffic data into GIF and outputs the results in the form of HTML containing GIF files, N-Vision developed through JAVA interface of HP OpenView management platform, IntraSpection using JAVA SNMP-Applet, EnterprisePRO with WAN and LAN management functions, ANACAPA SOFTWARE tracking and providing user response time, and HP NetMetrix/UX Reporter[6-7]. Though an attempt to apply network management technology to the web using the platform has been made, many tools are for WAN management or monitor segments as well as the communications of all nodes within those segment for the management satisfying LAN environment, not including a function to analyze management information. On top of that, they carry problems with them that it is difficult to know the analytic result by providing static information without processing the extracted management information and that they do not provide the cumulative analysis function of long-term traffic statistics and trends through accumulation of management information [8-9].

In this study, RMON MIB, the extension of standard MIB-II together with web based management technology to solve these problems, is applied. It analyzes RMON MIB and MIB-II suitable for the network management, deriving relevant MIB objects and defining significant network performance and fault analyses in the position of the managers. It also attempts to apply JAVA and web related technology to the network management, and implements web based network traffic monitoring system to solve problems with the existing management tools, made it lightweight for its convenient use. Finally, it covers a simple application of network management to help managers optimize their managements.

2 Design and Implementation of Traffic Monitoring System

The whole structure of network traffic monitoring system proposed in this study is shown in Fig.1. The system consists of analysis server that will collect pieces of management information by monitoring network activities of systems managed on network to analyze their results and client system that will provide graphic data to raise an application of analysis result.

While the monitoring system comprises Internet server, intranet server and database existing on the web, HTML documents and JAVA bite codes on the web server are transferred to the client server for its operation. The client is implemented in applet, transferred to the server via new connection as requested by managers and answers the user in the graphic form. At this time is used a message form defined in MATP (Management Application Transfer Protocol) to receive and transfer message [10].

In the case of the real-time analyses subject to each analyzing item of its client, the server answers real-time requests to collect, analyze and show its response to information on a real-time base. In a cumulative analysis, the server polls the data on database to answer the request from the client.

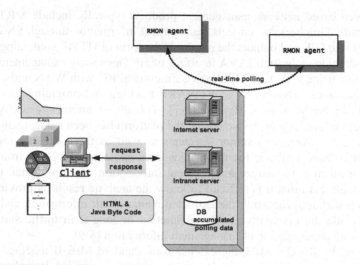

Fig. 1. The whole structure of network traffic monitoring system

2.1 Client System

The whole structure of client system is shown in Fig. 2. Client system is implemented on the web browser of its user client, which comprises such functions as user entry interface for the management request from user, real-time monitoring in which responses to the request are given, information collection requests/suspensions, accumulative analysis monitoring and graphic outputs of traffic results received from an analysis server and shows a simple application of network management.

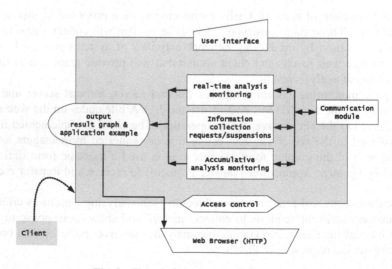

Fig. 2. The whole structure of client system

Function of real-time analysis monitoring. A user must enter the equipment name of the managed system, IP address, port number, community, network speed and polling time to analyze the conditions for the current traffic and fault of LAN. Specifically, such name and IP address are used to show the type of the analyzed equipment in output its results. The function of real-time monitoring is a user interface that receives a request to analyze the condition for the current traffic of LAN from a user, showing the analytic result via the graphic outputs, real-time. Table 1. shows items of analyzing the function of real-time monitoring:

Table 1. Items of analyzing real-time monitoring

type	analysis items	contents
internet	network utilization	rate of utilization of network per unit time
	input/output traffic	amount of input or output traffic
	network error	rate of error packet
	packet loss	rate of input and output error packet
	packet analysis	amount of broadcast packet
intranet	segment utilization	rate of segment utilization in use
	segment collision	rate of segment collision
	segment error	rate of segment error packet

Function of information collection requests/suspensions. It is required for a user to collect traffic statistics on segment and analyze its flows and trends to fulfill such managerial activities as for increasing its network performance & design and diagnosing a fault. In accordance with such collection requests from a user, traffic management information is periodically collected to save it on database up to the point of suspension requests.

Function of accumulative analysis monitoring. The function of accumulative analyses monitoring is required to enter Request ID, IP address and polling time to analyze the condition for traffic and faults during a specified period. Accumulative analyses show the analytic result of traffic data collected in response to a collection request to a user in the form of graph. The analyzing items of accumulative analyses monitoring are the same with that of real-time monitoring as shown in Table 1.

Function of outputting result graph & application example. In this function, the analytic results in response to a real-time monitoring request and accumulative analyses request are output to a user in the form of a graph. Graphic outputs include line graph, bar graph, and pie graph appropriate for the resulting outputs from an analysis of LAN performances & faults. And users make use of a simple application example on the result.

2.2 Analysis Server

Analysis server should go through daemon processes because it must provide services for a specific port to respond to the request from a client system. The server can be largely divided into Internet server and Intranet server.

Internet server. Internet server processes responses to the analysis request from the client, that is, the user interface and the connection setting for such process, message generation, or data processing and transferring by each item for their analyses. It is installed to operate in a place where the web server is installed. In receiving a message for the analysis request, the analysis module transfers it to the processor of analyzing items, acquires management information through the call from a SNMP user implemented in JAVA to poll the relevant management information according to each analyzing item, generates and transfers the analyzed information to the client system on a real-time base.

SNMP Manager. SNMP manager system performs the relevant MIB information polling so that the internet server can derive analysis information with respect to a message for real-time analysis request.

Message Processing Module. Message Processing Module processes the received message according to the mode requested by a user, analyzes the requested message and transfers the relevant processing module. The module interacting with this processing module provides a user with the processed results to the analyzing item requested by the analysis module and the graph generator module in the form of graph.

Analysis Module. It processes real-time responses to a request from a user to analyze the current internet status. This module calls SNMP manager system for the relevant MIB information polling to derive the request message from the client and the value of the current analyzing item from the data, delivers the obtained information to its processor and transfers the analysis information to the client every polls.

Analyzing Item Processor. It serves as a function that derives the analyzed results from the management information polled to each analyzing item by the analysis module. SNMP manager collects the polled management information form network devices in accordance with a request of the real-time analysis module, calculating the analyzed results at a specific point using different analysis methods according to the type of each analyzing item and delivering them to the real time analysis module.

Intranet server. Each module in intranet server has its own function form LAN analysis as user request control, RMON setting module, RMON check module, analysis management module.

User Request Control. It receives and analyzes a message transferred from the client and delivers it to process its appropriate requests. This system saves the message from the client in the message structure, and then analyzes its header to transfer a control to the relevant module corresponding to each analyzing item.

RMON Setting Module. This module is an RMON control module that sets RMON for its validity or invalidity, controlling RMON in a place where this module is required in accordance with the analyzing items.

RMON Check Module. This module inspects the managed system imported form a request of a user, that is, RMON, checks the function of RMON probe, and investigates whether there is no fault in collecting management information. It polls all the managed systems, respectively, imported from the requests of users for its identification of their functions and status.

Analysis Management Module. This module calculates the analyzed results by entering the managed information files real-time collected and accumulated to transfer them to the client module.

The proposed system comprises the client system and the analysis server. To give and receive a request from a user and its response within the system, each component requires a relevant message exchange procedure.

The client system that a user interfaces itself with sets TCP connection to the analysis server to transfer a requested message as a user requests a management, when the requested data may be transferred to the server together with the requested message, and the server transfers ACK to check the receipt. The server receiving the request from the client makes connection to RMON Agent to start polling. RMON Agent responds to the processed result to the server, which returns it to its client by using the responding message.

3   Results & Analysis

Network traffic monitoring system includes such functions as real-time analysis, collection request/suspension and accumulative analysis according to the request of user. To process these functions on the web, the client system and the analysis server contains their relevant processing module. Fig. 3 shows item setting required in conducting the function of tree structure interface and relevant processing of analyzing items as shown in the client system. In setting each item, the same interface structure is involved for the convenience of users, so that items alone requested in selecting the analyzing items could be set.

650   Y. Ahn and O. Chae

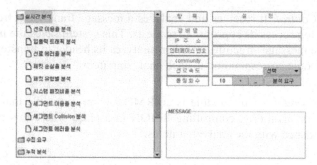

Fig. 3. user interface in client system

In the function of real-time analysis, the conditions for the current uses and fault of LAN are analyzed to provide a dynamic graphic view to help a user easily understand the network diagnosis. The result display of this real-time monitoring is shown in Fig. 4, which shows examples of graphs demonstrating line availability rate on LAN, real-time, and input and output traffic rate. Such setting helps optimize the management by presenting a simple application to the network management

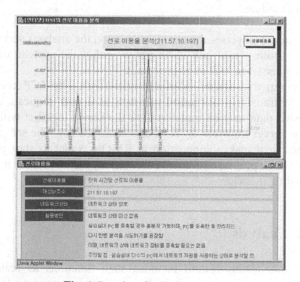

Fig. 4. Results of real-time analysis

In the function of collection request/suspension, LAN is monitored including its requests for the collection of management information to cumulate and analyze the management information of LAN. To fulfill this function, a user must enter RMON agent IP address, community, segment speed, management information of the managed segment, based on which the analysis server collects the management information. When such function of the collection request/suspension is fulfilled, the relevant message is displayed before a user.

The function of accumulative analysis involves analyzing the basic management considerations on the web. This function is implemented to facilitate the understanding of user by providing information about the analyzed results calculated on a basis of the cumulated information during a certain period through a graphic view of various types. During the collected period, a user can compare pieces of information such as line availability rate, error rate and collision rate through various graphic views to identify the abnormality of LAN. Fig. 5 shows the result of this function.

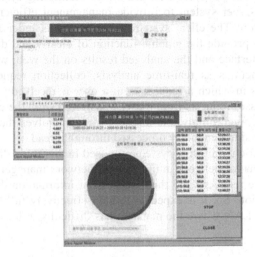

Fig. 5. Results of accumulative analysis

And the proposed system can manage to PC-room without an expert skill by offering a variety application example. That is, a manager can check a managing status showing currently information and a simple application on each items. Fig. 6 shows the result of internet information analyses, which can to help managers perform network management.

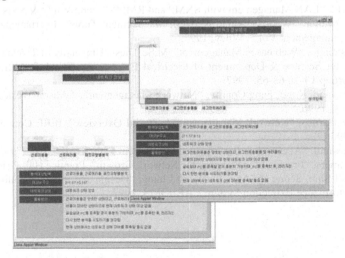

Fig. 6. Results of internet/intranet information analysis

4 Conclusions

In this study, we proposed the web-based network traffic monitoring system aimed to eliminate the constraints in managements, along with providing more user-friendly management tools. The proposed network traffic monitoring system is composed of client system and server system to provide management efficiency and distributed management function: The client system is implemented under JAVA and web related technology to provide the graphic function of clearly and dynamically demonstrating the user interface and the analyzed results on the web, while the client provides such the functions as real-time analysis, collection request/suspension, and cumulative analysis in which a request from a user is received. The analysis server analyzes and processes requests from a user transferred from the client to return their result to the client. Accordingly, the analysis server involves the function in which each request can be simultaneously processed through thread.

The network traffic monitoring system proposed in this study diagnoses the quality of and the conditions for network in the view of network manager to provide optimal performance, failure recovery and the management information that are measures of network configuration. So, it is expected to help effectively fulfill the managements on the complicated LAN where the manager has difficulty in handling such managements.

References

1. Nathan Kalowski,, "Applying the RMON Standard to Switched Environments", International Journal of Network Management Vol.7, Wiley, 1997.
2. Willian Stallings, "SNMP, SNMPv2 and RMON: Practical Network Management", Addison-Wesley Publishing Compan, 1996.
3. Gilbert Held, "LAN Management with SNMP and RMON", John Wildy & Sons Inc, 1996.
4. Nathan J. Muller, "Web-accessible Network Management Tools", International Journal of Network Management Vol.7, Wiley, 1997.
5. Wilco Kasteleijn, "Web based Management", M.Sc Thesis University of Twente Department of Computer Science & Department of Electrical Engineering Tele-Informatics and Open System Group 13-20 63-65, 1997.
6. Allan Leinwand, Karen Fang Conroy, "Network Management", Addison-Wesley Publishing Commpany, 1996.
7. Rechard E.Caruso, "Network Management: A Ttorial Overview", IEEE Comm. Magazine, March 1990.
8. Allan Leinwand, "Accomplish Performance Mangement with SNMP", INET'93, 1993.
9. John Blommers, "Practical for Planning for Network Growth", Prentice Hall PTR, 1996.
10. Snag-Chul Shin, Seong Jin Ahn, Jin Wook Chung, "Design and Implementation of SNMP-based Performance Extraction System", APNOMS, 1997.

A Vulnerability Assessment Tool Based on OVAL in Linux System

Youngmi Kwon[1], Hui Jae Lee[2], Geuk Lee[2]

[1] Dept. of InfoCom, Chungnam National University, Daejeon, South Korea
ymkwon@cnu.ac.kr
[2] Dept. of Computer Engineering, Hannam University, Daejeon, South Korea
lhuijae@ai.hannam.ac.kr, leegeuk@hannam.ac.kr

Abstract. Open Vulnerability Assessment Language (OVAL) is a standard language which is used to detect the vulnerability of local system based on the system characteristics and configurations. It is suggested by MITRE. OVAL consists of XML schema and SQL query statements. XML schema defines the vulnarable points and SQL query detects the vulnerable and weak points. This paper designed and implemented the vulnerability assesment tool with OVAL to detect the weak points in Linux System. It has more readability, reliability, scalability and simplicity than traditional tools.

1 Introduction

The vulnerability assessment tool is a security tool to diagnose the computer system and detect the weakness in advance to keep the system's status safe. The vulnerability assessment tools are broadly classified as host-based assessment tool, network-based assessment tool and application assessment tool to detect the specific applications' attack-ability. Existing vulnerability assessment tools detect the system's weakness by executing the attack code such as exploit scripts [1]. But, individual tools don't have common criteria with vulnerability detection and vulnerability assessment scripts are implemented with various programming languages. So it is difficult to know which tools provide more correct diagnoses, as well as the prices to develop and maintain the assessment script gets higher. MITRE suggested the OVAL (Open Vulnerability Assessment Language) to overcome these limitations. OVAL is a standard language to assess the fragility of the local system based on the information of the system's characteristics and the configurations. Basically OVAL defines the weakness of CVE with XML schema. Using these XML schemas, it constructs and executes the query statements to detect the weak points.

This paper designed the host-based vulnerability assessment tool in the RedHat Linux System with OVAL which has been proposed by MITRE. In the chapter two, related works, we analyzed and compared the existing assessment tools with OVAL.

H. Jin et al. (Eds.): NPC 2004, LNCS 3222, pp. 653–660, 2004.

2 Related Work

2.1 The Vulnerability Assessment Tool

The vulnerability assessment tool is a sort of security tool to keep the systems more safe by diagnosing the weak points in the computer systems in advance and providing the solutions and the proper patch information. It is also called as vulnerability scanner or security scanner. These scanners are classified as a host scanner and network scanner in accordance with the checking contents [2]. Host scanner is installed at each operator's platform. It searches the security problems which can be caused by the administrator's mistakes or mis-configurations [3]. The network scanner assesses the portable weak points which can be attacked by the external hackers.

The vulnerability scanner usually uses the detection scripts such as exploit to find weak points. But currently used commercial or free codes have a problem that the detection results are not reliable, because they apply some different criteria in the vulnerability assessment and the codes are made with different description languages with wide variety. Table 1 shows the free vulnerability assessment tools and their used languages in detection scripts.

Table.1. Free Vulnerability Assessment Tools and Their Languages

Name of Tools	Type	Used Languages
Tiger	Host scanner	C, Shell Script
COPS	Host scanner	C, Shell Script
Nessus	Network scanner	NASL
SARA	Network scanner	C, Perl
SAINT	Network scanner	C, Perl
Sscan	Network scanner	C
Vlad	Network scanner	Perl

2.2 OVAL

OVAL is the common language for security experts to discuss and agree upon technical details about how to check for the presence of vulnerabilities on a computer system. The end results of the discussions are OVAL queries, which perform the checks to identify the vulnerabilities [1, 4].

OVAL queries are written in SQL and use a collaboratively developed and standardized SQL schema as the basis for each query. OVAL queries detect the presence of software vulnerabilities in terms of system characteristics and configuration information, without requiring software exploit code. By specifying logical conditions on the values of system characteristics and configuration attributes, OVAL queries characterize exactly which systems are susceptible to a given vulnerability.

OVAL queries are based primarily on the known vulnerabilities identified in Common Vulnerabilities and Exposures (CVE), a dictionary of standardized names and descriptions for publicly known information security vulnerabilities and exposures developed by The MITRE Corporation in cooperation with the international security

security community. CVE common names make it easier to share data across separate network security databases and tools that are CVE-compatible. CVE also provides a baseline for evaluating the coverage of an organization's security tools, including the security advisories it receives. For each CVE name, there are one or more OVAL queries. Fig.1 shows the operational procedure of the assessment tool based on OVAL.

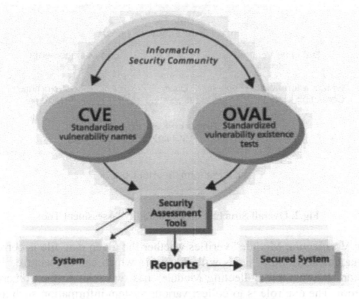

Fig. 1. Operational Procedures of OVAL

2.3 OVAL Schema

XML and SQL languages have a strong point of defining the vulnerable points most logically and clearly. Those languages can be understood by computer systems, and much readable to security experts. XML schema's purpose is to define vulnerabilities in the system and consists of the common schema and the per-platform schema. The common schema describes the fundamental information required to define vulner-abilities. And the per-platform schema describes operational elements to check on each platform.

3 Design of Vulnerabilities Assessment Tool

3.1 Overall Structure

In this paper, we designed the vulnerability assessment tool designed for RedHat Linux Platform with OVAL schema suggested by MITRE. Its overall structure is as in Fig. 2.

Data File consists of "INSERT DATA" part and "OVAL queries" part. In "INSERT DATA" part, the lists of data to be collected by the "System Information Collecting Module" are presented. In "OVAL queries" part, the conditions to detect the system's vulnerability based on the system information collected from input data using "query interpreter" module are described in the form of SQL query statements.

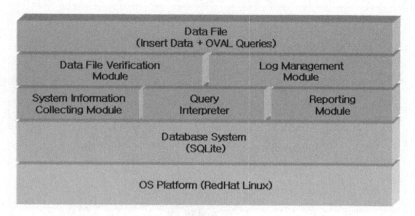

Fig.2. Overall Structure of Vulnerability Assessment Tool

"Data File Verification Module" verifies whether the given data file is correct or not. "Log Management Module" deals with the errors which can be occurred in the system. "System Information Collecting Module" has two roles in the vulnerability assessment tool. The one role is to collect various system information such as configuration setting information, software installation information, file information and process information based on "INSERT DATA." And the other role is to update database status based on the collected data. Because the "OVAL Queries" part is described with SQL language, OVAL-based vulnerability assessment system should contain DBMS (Database Management System). In our design, we used SQLite as DBMS. It operates in a file-base. We summarized the general characteristics of SQLite in table 2.

Table.2. Characteristics of SQLite

Characteristics	Description
SQL compatibility	Support almost syntax of SQL92
Speed	Two times faster than the conventional DBMS in general command processing
Size	About 25K lines C code. Very lightweight DBMS.
Database	All of Database is included in one file.
Operational Environment	Can be executed without the help of other libraries.

3.2 Database Design: Schema

System Data gathered by "System Information Collecting Module" is stored in database. OVAL Query statements are applied to this database to find corresponding vulnerabilities. Tables of database are constructed using OVAL schema of individual OS platform. In the RedHat-series Linux Platform, we designed the required schema; File Metadata Schema, Internet Server Daemon Schema, Passwd File Schema, Shadow File Schema, Process Information Schema, RPM Information Schema, Information for Comparison with Susceptible RPM Versions Schema and Operating Platform Information Schema. As an example, the File Metadata Schema is shown in Table 3.

Table.3. File Metadata Schema

Field	Description
FilePath	Absolute path of a file
FileType	Directory, normal file, device file, etc.
UserID	Owner ID of a file
GroupID	Group ID of a file
time	Access time (Atime), Status Change Time (Ctime), Data Update Time(Mtime)
MD5	MD5 hash for a file
Permission bits	SUID, SGID, STICKY, UREAD, UWRITE, UEXEC, GREAD, GWRITE, GEXEC, OREAD, OWRITE, OEXEC

3.3 Construction of System Information Base

"System Information Collecting Module" plays two roles; 1) collecting the required system information to assess the vulnerabilities in the system, 2) reflect that information to the database designed in subsection 3.2. The data list which this module should collect is listed up in "INSERT DATA" part in Fig. 2. OVAL uses this "INSERT DATA" part to reduce the time of collecting required system information. In other words, "INSERT DATA" part lists up not all the information of installed packages and files, but only the information items required to assess the vulnerability of the system. "System Information Collecting Module" consists of 8 sub-modules. Their names are taken after the corresponding schema. They are File Metadata Collecting Sub-module, Internet Server Daemon Information Collecting Sub-module, RPM Information Collecting Sub-module, RPM Version Comparison Sub-module, Password File Information Collecting Sub-module, Process Information Collecting Sub-module, Shadow File Information Collecting Sub-module and Operating Platform Information Collecting Sub-module.

Fig. 3 is the File Metadata Table which is one of the tables produced by the operation of "System Information Collecting Module." As same as this table, other information required to assess the system is collected in the form of SQLite Database Table.

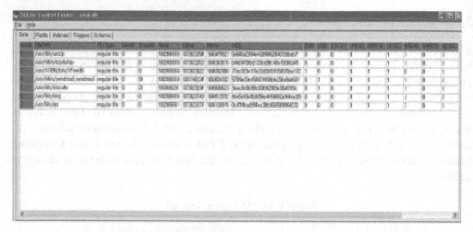

Fig.3. File Metadata Table produced by the "System Information Collecting Module"

3.4 Execution of Query Interpreter Module

"Query Interpreter" detects the existence of vulnerability of the system by applying the OVAL queries stored in "Data File" to the system information stored in SQLite Database. The return value of the OVAL query statement is CVE ID if the vulnerability is detected. In the case of detection, "Reporting Module" reports this susceptibility on the operator's screen. Fig. 4 is an example report output when "Query Interpreter" detects some vulnerability in the system. In this example, detected CVE IDs are CAN-2003-0165, CAN-2003-0547, and so on.

```
■ [ root@redhat9:/home/lhuijae/eclipse/workspace/oval_project ] RedHat9.0 - PineTerm v2.0.6     ▲  _□×
[root@redhat9 oval_project]# make run
java -Djava.library.path=. my.project.oval.Main
WARNING: using non-UTF SQLite engine
parsing data file
updating oval schema
updating insert data
creating probe vector
collect ps info.
collect inet listening servers.
collect uname info..
collect passwd info.
collect shadow info.
collect RPM info.
collect RPMVersionCompare info.
collect file attributes
    Vulnerability is found : CAN-2003-0165
    Vulnerability is found : CAN-2003-0547
    Vulnerability is found : CAN-2003-0548
    Vulnerability is found : CAN-2003-0549
    Vulnerability is found : CAN-2003-0354
    Vulnerability is found : CAN-2003-0187
    Vulnerability is found : CAN-2003-0244
    Vulnerability is found : CAN-2003-0246
    Vulnerability is found : CAN-2003-0247
    Vulnerability is found : CAN-2003-0248
```

Fig.4. Vulnerability report output when the vulnerabilities are detected in the system

4 Comparison with Previous Tools

We designed and implemented the OVAL-based vulnerability assessment tool operating on RedHat Linux Platform. There are some other existing tools used in UNIX-like platform such as Tiger or SATAN. They have specific scripts and specific goals. Our design follows the standard guideline suggested in the MITRE. So our tool is very general-purpose assessment tool and has as similar benefits as OVAL concept. They are following:

- A simple and straightforward way to determine if a vulnerability exists on a given system
- A standard, common schema of security-relevant configuration information
- For each CVE entry, one or more SQL queries precisely demonstrate that the vulnerability exists
- Reduces need for disclosure of exploit code as an assessment tool
- An open alternative to closed, proprietary, and replicated efforts
- A community effort of security experts, system administrators, software developers, and other experts
- Freely available vulnerability content for public review, comment, or download from the Internet
- Industry-endorsed via the OVAL Board and OVAL Community Forum

5 Conclusions

OVAL is the common language which has many benefits and capabilities of checking for the presence of vulnerabilities on a computer system by specifying logical conditions on the values of system characteristics and configuration attributes. The vulnerability assessment tool suggested in this paper is based on OVAL scheme, so it is more efficient and flexible. We designed the overall structure with five modules, one Data File and SQLite DBMS.

Existing assessment tools only check the existence of the vulnerabilities by checking the checklists mainly listed in [3]. But the suggested tool can not only check the weak points but also define new checklists in the form of XML and SQL syntax.

Traditional tools only check the mainly weak points which have been aimed to by the attackers. But the suggested tool can check all the weak points registered in CVE list at once.

In addition to them, because existing tools apply somewhat different description languages with wide variety each other, their detection results are not reliable. OVAL-based vulnerability methods are getting higher estimation by the security experts, so the tools on various OS platforms will be developed continuously in the future.

Acknowledgement

This work was supported by a grand No.R12-2003-004-02002-0 from Korea Ministry of Science and Technology.

References

1. Jung Hee Kim, "The Trends of International Standardization on Vulnerability Assessment of Computer Systems," The Trends in International Information Security, Korea Information Security Agency, June 2003
2. Ragi Guirguis, "Network and Host-based Vulnerability Assessments," http://www.sans.org, SANS Institute, February 2004.
3. UNIX Security Checklist v2, http://www.cert.org, AusCERT, October 2001
4. http://oval.mitre.org
5. M. Wojcik, T. Bergeron, T. Wittbold and R. Roberge, "Introduction to OVAL," http://oval.mitre.org/documents/, MITRE Corporation, November 2003.

Performance Analysis of Delay Estimation Models for Signalized Intersection Networks

Hyung Jin Kim[1], Bongsoo Son[1], Soobeom Lee[2]

[1]Dept. of Urban Planning and Eng. Yonsei Univ,, Seoul, Korea
{hyungkim, sbs}@yonsei.ac.kr
[2]Dept. of Transportation Engineering, Univ. of Seoul, Seoul, Korea
mendota@uos.ac.kr

Abstract. The primary purpose of this study is to examine the models' performance for estimating average delay experienced by the passing vehicles at signalized intersection network, and to improve the models' performance for Intelligent Transportation Systems (ITS) application in terms of actuated signal operation. Two major problems affected the models' performance have been defined by the empirical analyses in this paper. The first problem is related to the time period of delay estimation. The second problem is associated with the fact that the observed arrival flow patterns are so different from those applied for developing the existing models. This paper presents several methods to overcome the problems for estimating the delay by using the existing models.

1. Introduction

Many models have been developed for the purpose of delay estimation at signalized intersection network. It is known that the results of the existing models are very sensitive to the degree of saturation as well as the arrival flow pattern at the intersections during the time period of interest. This implies that the models' reliability seems to be highly dependent on whether the input variables of the model are adequate to describe the real traffic conditions [1, 2, 3, 4]. One main purpose of this study is to evaluate five major models for the feasibility of delay estimation for urban signalized intersection network. The five models are Webster, US Highway Capacity Manual (HCM), Transyt-7F, Akcelik, and Hurdle models. Another main purpose of this study is to improve the models' performances for the purpose of ITS application such as actuated signal operation. To accomplish the study purposes, the input variables of the five models were acquired from the traffic data collected from the field. The models' results were compared with the results obtained from the conventional queuing theory, cumulative arrival and departure technique, by using the field data. Two study sites in Seoul were selected, where traffic states of the two sites were different, one was saturated and another was non-saturated.

H. Jin et al. (Eds.): NPC 2004, LNCS 3222, pp. 661-669, 2004.
© IFIP International Federation for Information Processing 2004

2. Related Work

The operation of each intersection approach can be modeled as shown in Figure 1. In the figure, the y-axis is the cumulative vehicle count (N), and the x-axis is time (t). The curve labeled A(t) shows the cumulative number of arrivals by time t, and D(t) shows the cumulative number of departures. In fact, the A(t) curve does not indicate the number of actual arrivals at the stop line, but the number that would have arrived if the signal light had always remained green. The D(t) curve shows the actual departures from the stop line. When the signal light is red, there are no departures, so the D(t) curve is horizontal. The overall D(t) is the stair-step curve outlining the triangles. In reality, it would begin to curve upward as vehicles began to move after the start of green then after a few seconds become nearly straight with a slope equal to the saturation flow [5].

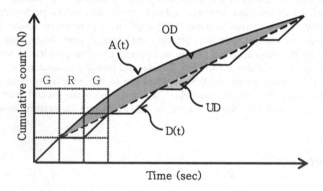

Figure 1. Typical cumulative arrival and departure curves

In Figure 1, the below area of the dashed line is associated with the traffic situation that all the arrivals within one signal phase can pass through the intersection during the same signal phase. This is called as non-overflow situation. In this case, A(t) curve will be the dashed line. The slope of A(t) curve is the arrival rate, and if this rate is constant over several signal cycles, the between the A(t) and D(t) curves is made up of a series of identical triangles. The total delay per cycle can be estimated as the area of any single triangle. Diving this area by the number of arrivals per cycle yields the average delay, that is denoted UD, which stands for average uniform delay, since it was derived under the assumption that vehicles arrive at a uniform rate throughout the signal cycle. It should be noted that, in making this assumption, we ignore both any random effects and any pattern imposed on the arrival stream by upstream intersections. In the same figure, the above area of the dashed line is related to the traffic situation that some of the arrivals within one signal phase cannot get through the intersection during the same signal phase. This is called as over-flow situation or over-saturation. The total overflow delay can be estimated as the area between the A(t) curve and the dashed line. Diving this area by the total number of arrivals during the time period which the arrival flows exceed the capacity yields the average overflow delay, that is denoted OD. The average delay of each signalized intersection approach is expressed by the sum of UD, OD, and a correction term which has a negative value typically. The correction term is generally obtained by simulation, but its value is relatively too small, so it is ignored for the practical purposes.

Figure 2 presents a good understanding of the relationship between the five models' performances and the degree of saturation, v/c, where v = arrival flow and c = capacity of intersection approach. Although this figure is an example, it provides very useful insights for the features of five models' performances. As the degree of saturation is close to 1.0, the discrepancies of the models' results are drastically increased. The discrepancies are serious in the range of v/c from 0.9 to 1.10. From the figure we can see that the results of the existing models are very sensitive to the degree of saturation as well as the arrival flow pattern at the intersection during the time period of interest. In the degree of saturation, c is a manageable variable, but the variable v is not, and thus v/c cannot be adjusted for the purpose of reducing the discrepancies between the five models' results.

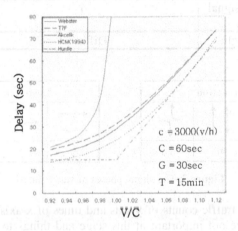

Figure 2. Comparison of the five models' results for the delay

It should be noted that US HCM recently presents new model which has improved the effects of the arrival flow variations by selecting an appropriate type of arrival flow pattern among several predetermined patterns for the analysis [6]. However, this is not the only way to improve the HCM model's performance, so this study has selected the model developed in 1994 for solving another problem involved in the model.

3. Evaluation of Existing Models' Performance

In order to evaluate the five models' performance, two study sites were selected. Table 1 summarizes traffic and signal conditions of the two study sites. Figure 3 shows the signal phases of the analysis intersection and the upstream intersections of the study site #1. The cycle length of the two intersections is 140 sec. and the roadway is 4-lane foe each direction. The travel time between the two intersections was 5-minute during the data collection period. Traffic volume and speed were collected at the 15-minute time interval during morning peak period between 7a.m. and 9a.m. Using the traffic data, the A(*t*) and D(*t*) curves were constructed as shown in Figure 4. In order to match the time of two curves, the travel time between the target and upstream intersections was estimated from the observed speed data.

Table 1. Traffic and signal conditions of two study sites

study sites		target Intersection	upstream intersection	distance
No.1	traffic state	Saturated	Saturated	600m
	number of signal phases	4		
	cycle length	Different		
No.2	traffic state	non-saturated	Saturated	500m
	number of signal phases	4		
	cycle length	Different		

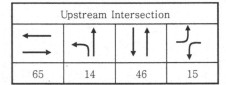

Target Intersection				Upstream Intersection			
58	21	46	15	65	14	46	15

Figure 3. The signal phases of study site #1

In Figure 4, specific traffic counts of y-axis and times of x-axis were not presented, since these values are not important at this stage and things to be discussed in this paper are related to shape of the two curves. The A(*t*) and D(*t*) curves are very similar. This result is quite different from that of Figure 1. The reader may be so confused to figure out which one is the reality, but Figure 4 is the case. At the study site #1, the target and upstream intersections were saturated. Under the traffic situation, all the vehicles passing the upstream intersection traveled at the same speed of the vehicles passing the target intersection, and the arrivals of the target intersection could not exceed the departures of the intersection. The reader should remember that the A(*t*) curve does not indicate the number of actual arrivals at the stop line, but the number that would have arrived if the signal light had always remained green. However, in the congested traffic condition, the A(*t*) curve will not be much changed from the D(*t*) curve of upstream intersection if the signal light had always remained green. As described in Section 1, the field delay can be obtained from Figure 4. From now, we have to review the problem caused by the length of evaluation time period in using the existing models. Figure 5 shows two settings of evaluation time periods, T1 and T2. In practice, it is reasonable that the evaluation time period does match with the congested time period of the intersection interested, but the evaluation time period has been typically defined as 15 minutes or 1 hour. In fact, the length of the evaluation time is not a big problem. The problem is the setting of the time period. T1 and T2 are the same length of evaluation time period, but the starting and ending times of the two time periods are different. The main difference between the two periods is that T1 starts at the beginning time of the first phase of signal and T2 terminates at the ending time of the final phase of signal. Depending on how to set the evaluation time period, the existing models' result for the delay will be changed significantly.

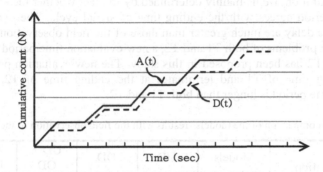

Figure 4. A(t) and D(t) curves of study site #1

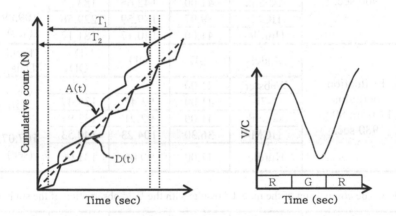

Figure 5. The relationship between delay evaluation period, signal phase, and v/c

As mentioned before, the signal cycle lengths of the intersections at the study site # 1 are 140seconds. If the evaluation time period, 15 minutes, is set as T1, then T1 will be from 0 to 900 seconds and will be terminated before the final phase of signal finished. For setting the evaluation time period as T2, we have to figure out the time not only matched with the ending time of the signal phase but also closed to the 15-minute evaluation period. This time is 980 seconds, so T2 is from 80 to 980 (i.e., 140 seconds x 7 cycles). Table 2 summarizes the models' results and the field delay obtained from the cumulative arrival and departure technique by using T1 and T2. In the table, the field delays obtained from the cumulative arrival and departure technique by using T1 and T2 are very similar. However, the models' results for overflow delay obtained by using the two periods are quite different, while the results for uniform delay of the two periods are identical with the exception of HCM model. Although the time

666   H.J. Kim, B, Son, and S. Lee

lengths of the two evaluation periods are equal, the overflow delays obtained by using T1 are much greater than those of T2. The evaluation period T1 terminates before the signal cycle finished so that v/c is definitely overestimated. From the results of Table 2, it is confirmed that the models' results are very sensitive to v/c and it is mainly dependent upon the ending time of evaluation time period. More specifically, the degree of saturation, v/c, is mainly determined by the fact whether the ending time of evaluation period agrees with the ending time of signal cycle. The overall models' results for the delay are much greater than those of the field observations. In order to overcome the problems of both T1 and T2, a new evaluation time period that includes both T1 and T2 has been proposed in this study. The new evaluation period starts at the beginning time of T1 and terminates at the ending time of T2, so the new evaluation time period is longer than both T1 and T2.

Table 2. The comparison of the models' results with the field observation of the study site #1

Evaluation period is T1 from 0 to 900 sec.	Models	UD	OD	UD + OD	Field Delay
	Webster	41.00	-	-	v/c = 1.31
	T-7F	41.00	142.61	183.61	
	Akcelik	41.00	142.65	183.65	
	HCM	39.97	189.59	229.56	109.09 (sec)
	Hurdle	41.00	140.17	181.17	
Evaluation period is T2 from 80 to 980 sec.	Models	UD	OD	UD + OD	Field Delay
	Webster	41.00	-	-	v/c = 1.20
	T-7F	41.00	93.47	134.47	
	Akcelik	41.00	92.91	133.91	
	HCM	36.30	104.23	140.53	107.07 (sec)
	Hurdle	41.00	90.06	131.06	

Table 3. The comparison of the models' results with the field observation of the study site #1

Evaluation period from 0 to 980 sec.	Models	UD	OD	UD + OD	Field Delay
	Webster	49.25	-	-	v/c = 1.24
	T-7F	49.25	109.56	158.81	
	Akcelik	49.25	109.26	158.51	
	HCM	37.44	129.27	167.11	107.55 (sec)
	Hurdle	41.00	106.57	147.57	

Comparing the results in Tables 2 and 3, it is very clear that T1 does overestimate the overflow delay, since the overflow delays obtained by using T1 are still much greater than those of the new period even though the new period is longer than T1. In general, the models' results are very fluctuated by the change of evaluation time period, while the field delays are consistently changed.

The models' overflow delays are persistently greater than the field observations. The reason for this can be found in Figure 6. The A(t) obtained from the field observation is stair step curve, while the A(t) of the existing models forms a smooth curve. It is interesting that the discrepancy of the overflow delay between the two curves is almost equal to the uniform delay, UD. Thus, if the uniform delay is subtracted from the total delay of the models, the models' results will be matched with the field values reasonably well.

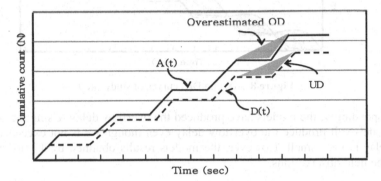

Figure 6. The discrepancy of A(t)

Figure 7 shows the signal phases of study site #2. The study site #2 is not saturated intersections. The travel time between the analysis intersection and the upstream intersection was 5.3-minute during the data collection period. Traffic volume and speed were collected at the 15-minute time interval during morning peak period between 7a.m. and 9a.m. Using the traffic data, the A(t) and D(t) curves were constructed as shown in Figure 8.

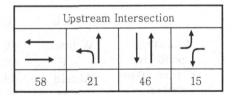

Target Intersection				Upstream Intersection			
27	25	47	41	58	21	46	15

Figure 7. The signal phases of study site #2.

In Figure 8, the shaded area marked by a solid line is the observed delay and the area represented by a dashed line is the estimated delay of the models. The two areas form the diamond shape that is quite different from the triangle as shown in Figure 1. Anyway, the shaded area is larger than the estimated area of model. The difference between two areas is gradually reduced over several signal cycles. Then, as the signal cycle runs over and over again, the two areas will be converged to the same size. The signal cycle lengths of the intersections at the study site # 2 are 140seconds. The delay of study site #2 has been estimated by the same procedures applied for the study site #1. Tables 4 and 5 summarize the models' results and the field delay obtained by using three different evaluation time periods. As shown in Table 4, the evaluation period T1 terminates before the signal cycle finished, so v/c is exceeded to 1.0 although the site is not saturated.

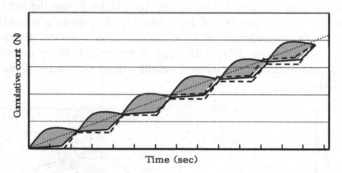

Figure 8. A(t) and D(t) curves of study site #2

Correspondingly, the models have produced the overflow delay. Using the period T2, the models still produce the overflow delay even though v/c is not exceeded 1.0, but the delay is very small. However, the models results obtained by T2 are much less than the field observations.

Table 4. The comparison of the models' results with the field observation of the study site #2

Evaluation period is T1 from 0 to 900 sec.	Models	UD	OD	UD + OD	Field Delay
	Webster	49.50	-	49.50	
	T-7F	49.50	38.10	87.60	v/c = 1.07
	Akcelik	49.50	34.95	84.45	
	HCM	38.77	33.94	72.71	58.99(sec)
	Hurdle	49.50	32.07	81.57	
Evaluation period is T2 from 80 to 980 sec.	Models	UD	OD	UD + OD	Field Delay
	Webster	49.50	-	49.50	
	T-7F	49.50	6.78	56.28	v/c = 0.95
	Akcelik	49.50	0.90	50.40	
	HCM	36..83	4.49	41.32	62.57(sec)
	Hurdle	49.50	-	49.50	

In Table 5, all the models with the exception of Transty-7F tend to underestimate the uniform delay of non-saturated intersection by using the evaluation time period proposed in this study. However, Transty-7F and Akcelik models produce the reasonable results that are very close to the field observation, so the two models seem to be good to estimate the delay of the non-saturated intersections.

Table 5. The comparison of the models' results with the field observation of the study site #2

Evaluation period from 0 to 980 sec.	Models	UD	OD	UD + OD	Field Delay
	Webster	49.71	-	49.71	v/c = 1.01
	T-7F	49.71	18.03	67.74	
	Akcelik	49.71	11.01	60.72	
	HCM	37.78	13.52	51.30	61.67(sec)
	Hurdle	49.50	4.93	54.43	

4. Conclusions

The primary purpose of this paper is to examine the models' performance for estimating average delay experienced by the passing vehicles at urban signalized intersection network, and to present the method for improving the models' performance. Two study sites in Seoul were selected, where traffic states of the two sites were different, one was saturated and another was non-saturated. From the empirical analyses, it was reconfirmed that the results of the existing models are very sensitive to the degree of saturation as well as the arrival flow pattern at the intersections during the time period of interest. Depending on how to set the evaluation time period, the existing models' results for the delay have been changed significantly. The field delays obtained from the cumulative arrival and departure technique by using T1 and T2 are very similar. However, the models' results for overflow delay obtained by using the two periods are quite different, while the results for uniform delay of the two periods are identical with the exception of HCM model. Although the time lengths of the two evaluation periods are equal, the overflow delays obtained by using T1 are much greater than those of T2. In order to improve the problem associated with the setting of evaluation time period, a new period that includes both T1 and T2 has been proposed in this study. The models performances have been somewhat improved by using the new period.

References

1. Transportation Research Board., Traffic Flow Theory, Traffic Flow at Signalized Intersection, Chapter 9, 1998
2. W.R. McShane and R. P. Roess, Traffic Engineering, second edition, Prentice Hall, 1998
3. S. Teply, Accuracy of delay Surveys at Signalized Intersections, Transportation Research Record 1225, 1989
4. S. Teply et al., Canadian Capacity Guide for Signalized Intersections, Institute of Transportation Engineers District7-Canada, 1996
5. V. F hurdle, Signalized Intersection Delay Model, TRR 841, 1984
6. Transportation Research Board, Highway Capacity Manual, Chapter16, 2000

Network Intrusion Protection System Using Rule-Based DB and RBAC Policy

Min Wook Kil [1], Si Jung Kim [2], Youngmi Kwon [3], Geuk Lee [4]

[1] Dept. of Computer & Image Information, Mun Kyung College, Mun Kyung, South Korea
mwkil@mkc.ac.kr

[2] Informatiom Technology Center, Chungju National University, Chungju, South Korea
kimsj@chungju.ac.kr

[3] Dept. of InfoCom, Chungnam National University, Daejeon, South Korea
ymkwon@cnu.ac.kr

[4] Security Engineering Research Center, Hannam Univ., DaeJeon, South Korea
leegeuk@hannam.ac.kr

Abstract. Role-Based Access Control (RBAC) is a method to manage and control a host in a distributed manner by applying the rules to the users on a host. This paper proposes a rule based intrusion protection system based on RBAC. It admits or rejects users to access the network resources by applying the rules to the users on a network. Proposed network intrusion protection system has been designed and implemented to have menu-based interface, so it is very convenient to users.

1 Introduction

The purpose of RBAC policy is to protect the computing and transmission resources from being updated, exhibited or destructed caused by the unprivileged access[1]. And the purpose of the intrusion protection system is to protect the network resources from the access of outside users and usually it is located on the local network server[2].

Basically the firewall operates closely related to the router program. It tests the network packets, decides whether it receives the packets or not, and filters some packets. The firewall works interactively with the proxy server whose role is to resolve the requests to the network on behalf of users, or it rather includes the role of proxy server in itself [2]. The firewalls are generally used in the corporation or the public organizations to filter the access from specific user(s) or host(s). But, it is not used in some specific purposed network such as proprietary PC room or Internet cafe.

Because buying a firewall of private security enterprise costs some price and needs some person to operate it. On the other hand, using the freeware based on Linux OS such as ipfwadm, ipchains and iptables [3] is too difficult for non-experts to configure the filtering-policies properly.

Intrusion Protection System (IPS) has mixed characteristics of firewall and Intrusion Detection System. This paper design and implement the IPS based on RBAC method.

H. Jin et al. (Eds.): NPC 2004, LNCS 3222, pp. 670–675, 2004.

It provides easy configuration interfaces to the operator. Additionally, it costs down the security tool and makes it easy for the operator to administrate the users on hosts.

In Section 2, we review the related works with RBAC method and network based Intrusion Protection System. And the efficiency of resource management is addressed under the condition that the RBAC is applied to the intrusion protection system. In Section 3, we designed the RBAC based Intrusion Protection System and in Section 4, we show the implementation-related items. Section 5 is the conclusion.

2 Related Works

2.1 RBAC Method

The basic concept of RBAC is to prohibit the information resources of company or organization from an unauthorized user. In RBAC, the access authority is given to the roles and each user is imposed on a proper role. If some user is imposed on some role, that user can access the minimum subset of total resources properly for that role [4]. This approach of authority management has some advantages: it simplifies an administration of a system security, and provides flexibility for a company to implement its specific security policy of its own.

Three DBs are necessary for the operation of RBAC. They are shown in Figure 1. In Operations-DB, the usage and execution authorities of the processes and resources are defined. They are used to decide whether a user or system daemon can use the resources or not. Roles-DB classifies the Operations-DB records according to the roles. And the third DB, Users-DB defines the roles permitted to each users.

The processes of ❶ from Operations-DB in Figure 1 are to add the combined and classified Operations-DB records to the Roles-DB. The processes of ❷ are to assign an authority based on Roles-DB to the system users. This process makes the management of user's authority very simple by distributing the responsibility of administrator management to each user.

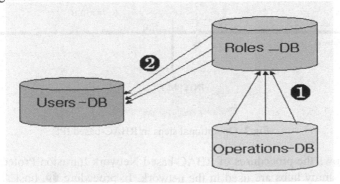

Fig.1. The necessary DBs in RBAC operation

2.2 The Definition of IPS

The IPS is one of the network components to protect the internal networks from the attacks initiated from the outside networks. The IPS uses policies to protect the internal information from incoming or updating by the unauthorized attack. It can be a type of software and/or hardware. It is an active protection process to prohibit from incoming of illegal traffics and permit only the authorized traffics [5]. The purpose of the IPS is an blocking of illegal external attack, preventing the loss, destroy and change of internal information from non-trusted user and hackers through Internet, and helping internal information to be provided to the outside safely.

IPS is located in the rear section of router generally. It permits or denies the forwarded packets to the router by analyzing and comparing with filter-rules.

3   The Design of RBAC-based IPS

3.1 Operational Steps

We made the operational steps of RBAC-based IPS as in Figure 2. The first operational step is to collect all the packets going through its own network by set the Network Interface Card to promiscuous mode.

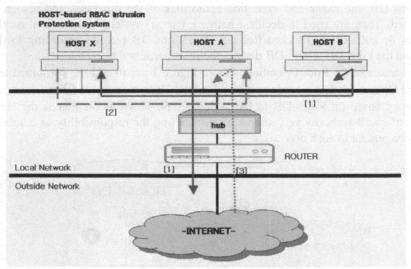

Fig.2. Operational steps in RBAC-based IPS

Figure 2 shows the procedures of RBAC-based Network Intrusion Protection System while the dummy hubs are used in the network. In procedure ❶, host A transmits a request packet to access to the illegal site or program. Or host A may transmit a packet to reply to backdoor client programs in the remote site. Anyway, transmitted packet from host A is forwarded to the hub and router to go to the external networks.

Simultaneously the transmitted packet is broadcasted to the other hosts in a internal network. When host B receives that packet, it discards it silently because it is not destined to MAC address of itself. But, host X is running a Intrusion Protection System with a promiscuous mode. So host X accepts all the packets going through the local network. In procedure ❷, RBAC-based Network Intrusion Protection System verifies the packets based on the predefined roles and sends an "ICMP Protocol Unreachable" message to the host A when the packets violate the Roles. These roles are stored in RBAC-based DBs in the form of rules. When host A receives an ICMP message, it conceives that there is some trouble or erroneous status at a host which has requested a connection. Therefore, host A notifies that situation the remote host. Procedure ❸ shows that host A ignores the request packets from the erroneous host afterwards.

And for the switch-based network environment, RBAC-based Intrusion Protection System uses an arp-spoofing capability to forward the packets that is going to the router to itself. Forwarded packets are verified based on the Roles, which was established in the IPS. If the verification is failed, IPS sends an "ICMP Protocol Unreachable" message to the host A. Then that host A processes an ICMP message as a normal response. The difference with dummy hub environment is that host A doesn't receive any remote packet from outside network because the reply packet transmitted from host A didn't go out to the outside world actually. Applying these procedures, RBAC-based Network Intrusion Protection Systems can restrict the usage of network resources based on the predefined Roles and assign a specific privilege to the hosts in the inner network.

3.2 Logging and Scheduling

The logs on the logging can be classified into three: site-log, program-log and backdoor-log. Site-log stores the list of illegal sites and domains. Program-log has information of non-permitted network programs. And backdoor-log is used as a backdoor protection log. The Log information filtered by RBAC in filtering module helps an network administrator find out the status of network resources.

4 Implementation of RBAC-based IPS

RBAC-based Intrusion Protection System is implemented on the Linux OS. Figure 3 and 4 shows the implemented command window of RBAC-based IPS. An administrator specifies the IP addresses of Managed Resources and the range of subnets for the managed ports in a file. Then the parsing module of IPS reads and parses the contents of a predefined file and filters all the packets by monitoring and capturing based on the policies of RBAC. Figure 3 is a window showing the definition of check items of packet filtering and Figure 4 is one of the active shots of RBAC-based Intrusion Protection System.

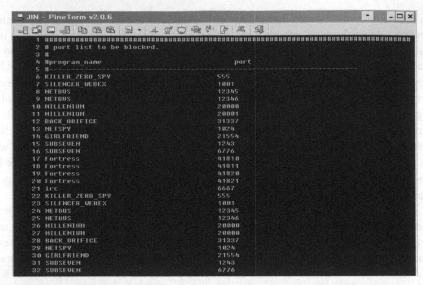

Fig.3. Managed Port Information Table of RBAC-based IPS

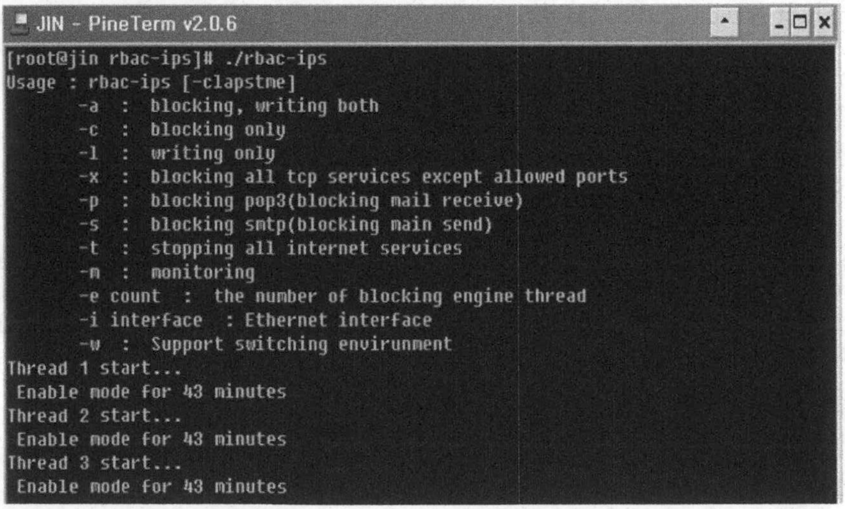

Fig.4. Menus and active shot of RBAC-base IPS

5 Conclusions

This paper designed and implemented an Intrusion Protection System, which manages hosts based on the predefined roles by applying the roles to the hosts in a network, not by applying the roles to the individual users. RBAC-based Intrusion Protection System has an advantage that it can be applied in one of the hosts as well as in the router in a network. Implemented IPS also includes the function of collecting the packets in a switched network using an arp-spoofing method. Additionally, proposed Intrusion Protection System has an effective filtering capability only by applying the predefined roles to the Hosts-DB instead of establishing the complex packet filtering rules by users.

Its application area is the companies, proprietary PC rooms or Internet café that requires security settings for the individual hosts to restrict the network resources.

Though we use an arp-spoofing technique to collect in the switched network environment, it can be a burden to the network. So the further study to lessen the load of arp packets would be required.

Acknowledgement

This work was supported by a grand No.R12-2003-004-02003-0 from Korea Ministry of Science and Technology.

References

1. Ravi S. Sandhu, et al, "Role-based Access Control Model," IEEE Computer, no.2, vol. 29, 1996.
2. Charlie Kaufman, et al, Network Security: Private Communication in a Public World, Prentice Hall PTR, 2002.
3. Olaf Kirch, et al, Linux Network Administrator's Guide, O'REILLY Press, 2000.
4. Suk Kyun Oh and Seong Ryeol Kim, " A Design of RBAC_Linux for the Linux Security System," The Journal of Korea Society Industrial Information Systems, no. 4, vol. 4, 1999.
5. http://www.terms.co.kr, Dictionary of Computer Terms.
6. Craig Hunt, TCP/IP Network Administration, O'REILLY Press, 2000.
7. David Ferrailo, et al, "Role-based Access Control," Proceedings of 15th National Computer Security Conference, 1992.
8. Jean Bacon, et al., "A Model of OASIS Role-based Access Control and its Supports for Active Security," ACM Transaction on ISS, no. 3, vol. 5, 2003.
9. Ravi S. Sandhu, et al, "Decentralized User-Role Assignment for Web-based Intranets," Proceedings of 3rd ACM Workshop on Role-based Access Control, 1998.

Effective FM Bandwidth Estimate Scheme with the DARC in Broadcasting Networks

Sang Woon Lee[1], Kyoo Jin Han[2], Keum Chan Whang[3]

[1] Senior Researcher, Technical R&D Center, MBC, Korea
lsw@mbc.co.kr
[2] Senior Researcher, CDMA System Lab. LG Electronics, Korea
[3] Dept. of Electrical and Electronics Eng. Yonsei Univ., Korea

Abstract. In this paper we propose the effect on the RF bandwidth when the DARC data signal is added to the ordinary FM broadcasting signal. Generally, the bandwidth of the commercial FM broadcasting signal is strictly restricted to 200KHz. Hence, even though the DARC data signal is added at the ordinary stereophonic FM signal, the required bandwidth should not exceed 200KHz. The simulation results show that even in the worst case, the required bandwidth is about 184 KHz, and the rest of 16 KHz bandwidth could be used for other FM data broadcasting services.

1. Introduction

After the service of the FM multiplex broadcasting called DARC was started at the mid of 1990, it has been much interested in the mobile data broadcasting service. By virtue of the broadcasting characteristics of the FM audio service, DARC system makes the information data broadcasting service to the many customers distributed in the wide area to be possible. Service area has been also widely extended from the traffic, DGPS (Differential Global Positioning System), weather, news to ITS (Intelligent Transportation System), Telematics [1, 2].

The detail specification of DARC system is known by ITU-R [3], and the performance analyses of the DARC system on the several constituent parts such as level-controlled MSK, the immunity on the multi-path fading environments, or error correction ability have been carried out at the papers [4,5].

RF bandwidth of the commercial FM broadcasting signals is usually set to 200KHz. Even though it is known that DARC service is possible within the bandwidth for the FM broadcasting service, there has been no work in which precise analysis on the RF bandwidth of the DARC system is treated. And this work is useful in the aspect of the efficient usage of the valuable frequency resources.

In this paper we analyze the effect on the RF bandwidth when DARC data signal is added to the ordinary FM broadcasting signals. It is performed by the computer simulation in which two systems are compared; one is ordinary FM broadcasting system and the other is the DARC system. Level controller and band-pass filter that are considered in this paper meet the requirement described in the DARC specification [3].

H. Jin et al. (Eds.): NPC 2004, LNCS 3222, pp. 676-683, 2004.
© IFIP International Federation for Information Processing 2004

2. DARC System Model

We fully follow the specification of the FM system and DARC system [3] in order to estimate precisely the RF bandwidth of the ordinary FM broadcasting system and the FM system including DARC data. Fig.1 shows the block diagram of the DARC system considered in this paper. The system consists of the stereophonic matrix containing L+R and L-R signals, 19 KHz pilot generator, frequency multiplier (X2 and X4), data signal generator, FM generator, and the modulation level is controlled according to the magnitude of the L-R signal.

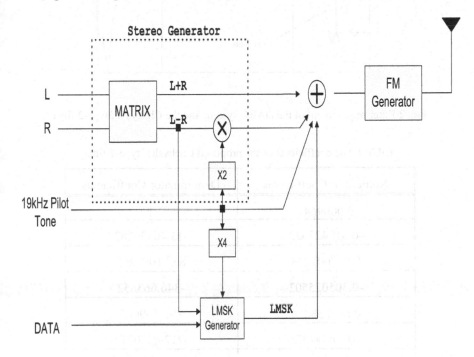

Fig. 1 The block diagram of the DARC system

The inputs of the stereo signal generator are L channel and R channel audio signals. At the matrix block, L+R signal that is sum of the two audio signals and L-R signal that is the difference between the two signals are generated. Then, L-R signal is frequency shifted by multiplying 38KHz single-tone carrier.

LMSK generator controls the magnitude of the DARC data signal according to the magnitude of the L-R signal. Its output is MSK modulated and band-pass filtered. The frequency of the sub-carrier for MSK modulation is 76KHz. In the specification of the DARC system [3], the upper bound and lower bound of the frequency response of the DARC data signals are described, which is shown at Fig. 2. To meet the requirement of the frequency response, we have adopted Chebyshef type-2 filter with order 8 [7], whose filter coefficients are chosen as shown in table 1.

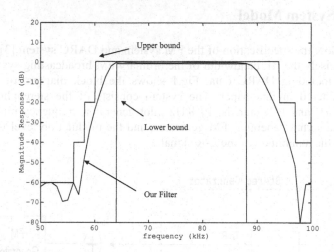

Fig. 2 Filter requirement of the DARC system and the Chebyshef type-2 filter

Table 1 The coefficients of the proposed Chebyshef type-2 filter

Numerator Coefficients	Denominator Coefficients
0.0009641	1
-0.012423622	-13.40536282
0.077007238	85.71009262
-0.305025502	-346.663852
0.865038284	992.139065
-1.8644737	-2129.490727
3.162690668	3544.666673
-4.310679576	-4666.626359
4.773804224	4910.109636
-4.310679576	-4142.52789
3.162690668	2793.189761
-1.8644737	-1489.580883
0.865038284	616.0639585
-0.305025502	-191.086542
0.0009641	0.38564381

3. Simulation and Results

3.1 The Characteristics of the Base Band Signal

We explore the effects on the frequency responses of the L+R and L-R signals according to the correlation of the L and R channel signals. The correlation coefficient cf of the input signals is defined as follows.

$$cf = \frac{\text{cov}(L, R)}{\sqrt{\text{cov}(L, L) \cdot \text{cov}(R, R)}}$$

Here, Cov is the covariance, and L and R is channel audio signals, respectively.

Because the DARC system adopts the LMSK modulation method, in which the injection level is controlled by the magnitude of the L-R signal, the level is adjusted according to the correlation coefficient of the L and R channel signals. Generally, the bandwidth of the L and R channel signals for FM broadcasting should not exceed 15KHz, so two stereophonic signals whose bandwidths are 15KHz are generated. Table 2 shows the relation between the correlation coefficients and the average injection level, where the following two input cases are considered. First, the correlation of the two stereophonic signals is 0.9, and second, the correlation is zero so that the two audio input signals are independent.

Fig. 3 shows, by base-band frequency spectrum, the relation between the magnitudes of the LMSK modulated DARC signals and the correlation coefficient between the L and R channel input signals. As the correlation coefficient is higher, the magnitude of the frequency spectrum of the L-R signals is also increased.

Table 2 The correlation coefficient and the average injection level of the DARC signals

cf	Average Injection Level for DARC
0.9	6.67 %
0	8.91 %

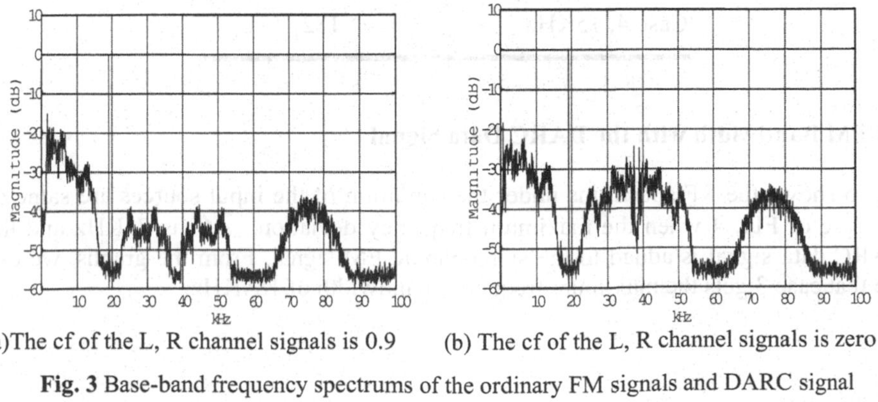

(a)The cf of the L, R channel signals is 0.9   (b) The cf of the L, R channel signals is zero

Fig. 3 Base-band frequency spectrums of the ordinary FM signals and DARC signal

3.2 FM Bandwidth in the Stereophonic Signals

The bandwidth of a signal can be defined that the bandwidth in which 99% of the total power spectrum of the signal is contained [8]. In this paper, 4 cases are considered and the detail simulation conditions are described as follows.
Case 1: the correlation coefficient of the L and R channel signals is 0.9.
Case 2: the correlation coefficient of the Land R channel signals is zero.
Case 3: L and R channel signals are independent of each other but their most powers are concentrated within the bandwidth between 10KHz and 15KHz.
Case 4: Both of the L and R channel signals are 15KHz single tones with random phase.
At Table 3, the estimated RF bandwidths according to the above four input conditions are present. From the results, it is known that the case 4 requires the largest bandwidth and the required bandwidth gets smaller as the correlation coefficient between L and R signals increases.
Fig. 4 shows the frequency spectrum when the maximum frequency deviation Δf is set to 75KHz and the stereophonic FM input signals fall under one of following three conditions; case 1, 2, and 4. The graphs show that among them the 4(c) requires largest bandwidth and 4(a) occupies minimum bandwidth.
As mentioned at the above section, because the magnitude of the L-R signal is frequency shifted by a 38KHz carrier, frequency shifted L-R signals put more effect on the FM modulated total bandwidth than L+R signals do. Hence FM modulated total bandwidth get larger as the magnitude of the L-R is larger.

Table 3 The required frequency bandwidths of the ordinary FM system

	Bandwidth (KHz)
Case 1, $cf = 0.9$	84.6
Case 2, $cf = 0$	93.8
Case 3, 10-15KHz	147
Case 4, 15KHz	182

3.3 FM Bandwidth with the DARC Data Signal

Fig. 5 shows the RF spectrums under the condition of the input sources are same as the case of FIg. 4 when the maximum frequency deviation, Δf, is 75KHz and the DARC data signal is added to the stereophonic FM signal. From the graphs, we can see that case 3 gets the maximum frequency bandwidth of 184KHz.

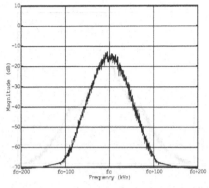 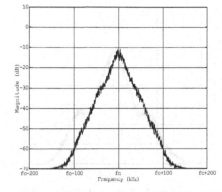

(a) The cf of the L,R channel signals is 0.9   (b)The cf of the L,R channel signals is zero

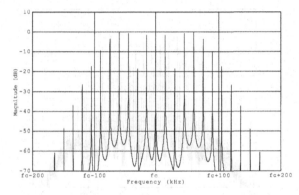

(c) Both of the L and R channel signals are 15KHz single tones

Fig. 4 Frequency spectrums of the ordinary FM systems

4. Conclusions

In this paper we analyze the effect on the RF bandwidth when the DARC data is added to FM broadcasting signals. As mentioned above, the FM broadcasting system and DARC data adding mechanism that is presented in this paper fully follows the ITU-R specification. Our research is on that how much the RF bandwidths of the ordinary FM broadcasting system and DARC system are affected by the statistics of the stereophonic input signals for FM broadcasting. The results show that, in the worst case, RF bandwidths of the ordinary FM broadcasting system and the DARC system are 182KHz and 184KHz, respectively. It means that in the ordinary FM broadcasting system there is still enough frequency space for the additional data services. Moreover the total RF bandwidth does not exceed 200KHz, that is the requirement of the FM broadcasting service, even though DARC data signal is added to the ordinary FM broadcasting signals. It can be useful baseline results for the efficient usage of the frequency resources such as additional data broadcasting service in the ordinary FM frequency band.

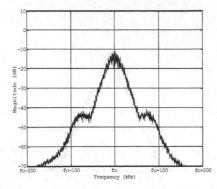

(a) The cf of the L, R channel signals is 0.9

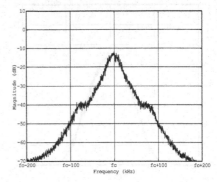

(b) The cf of the L, R channel signals is zero

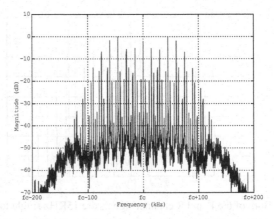

(c) Both of the L and R channel signals are 15KHz single tones

Fig. 5 Frequency spectrums when the DARC data signals are added at the ordinary FM signals

References

[1] Chen Wei and Shen-Weng Hong, An FM Sub-carrier Data Broadcasting System On Bus Transport Indication System, IEEE Transactions on Broadcasting, Vol. 47. No.1 Mar. 2001
[2] Jonguk Park, Jeongho Joh, Hyungchul Lim, Pilho Park and Sangwoon Lee, "THE DEVELOPMENT OF DGPS SERVICE SYSTEM USING FM DARC IN KOREA", Proceedings on the Federation of International Federation of Surveyors, May 2001
[3] ITU-R BS Recommendation DOC. 1194, 1995.
[4] Marion J. de Ridder-de Groote and Ramjee Prasad, Jan. H.Born, "Analysis of New Methods for Broadcasting Digital Data to Mobile Terminal over an FM-Channel", IEEE Transactions on Broadcasting, Vol. 40. No. 1. Mar. 1994
[5] K. Kuroda and M Takada, T. Isobe, "Transmission Scheme of of High-capacity FM Multiplex Broadcasting System", IEEE Transactions on Broadcasting, Vol. 42. No.3 Sep. 1996

[6] Papoulis, Probability, Random Variables, and Stochastic Processes. Third Edition, McGraw Hill, 1991.
[7] Michel C. Jeruchim, Philip Balaban, and K. Sam Shanmugan, Simulation of Communication Systems, Plenum Press, 1992.
[8] E B. Crutchfield, NAB Engineering Handbook 7th edition, NAB, 1985.
[9] ITU-R BS Recommendation DOC. 643, 1986
[10] Ferrel G. Stremler, Introduction to Communication Systems, Third Edition, Addison-Wesley, 1990.
[11] J. R. Carson, "Notes on the Theory of Modulation," Proceedings of the IEEE, Vol. 51 (1951) : pp 893-896.

Enhanced Algorithm of TCP Performance on Handover in Wireless Internet Networks

Dong Chun Lee[1], Hong-Jin Kim[2], and Jae Young Koh[3]

[1] Dept. of Computer Science Howon University, Korea
ldch@sunny.howon.ac.kr
[2] Dept. of Computer Information, KyungWon College, Korea
[3]Director, Principal Member of Eng. Staff, National Security Research Institute, Korea

Abstract. In the TCP over Wireless Internet Networks (WINs), TCP responds to losses such as high bit errors and handovers by invoking congestion control and avoidance algorithms. In this paper we propose new handover notification algorithm that is to send an explicit handover notification message to the source host from mobile host when occurring to handover. Upon receipt of explicit handover notification, the source host enters persist mode. This way, data transmissions at the source host during handover are frozen. In numerical result, proposed algorithm provides a little performance improvement compared with general TCP, and expects to greater performance improvements while having frequent handover in WINs.

1 Introduction

The existing Internet environment has been changed to single networks, integrated wire and wireless, due to appearance of wireless networks. The first issue we faced from this Internet integrated networks is terminal mobility. Accordingly, it has been studying very actively about mobile IP which can correspond to terminal mobility, through reinforce of addressing and routing. Except this network hierarchy issue, we still have issues such as validation of TCP efficiency to guarantee reliability of con-nection between End-to-End [2,3]. TCP dominated in communication environment is suitable to traditional network which is composed of wire network and fixed host. Application of TCP to wireless network which is different from wired network such as bandwidth, high delay, discrete, bit error, disconnection and handover will cause falling in efficiency of End-to -End throughout by unnecessary calling of mechanism [4, 7].

TCP treats packet loss caused by bit error rate in network as congestion control mechanism; because it considers that packet loss is from congestion. This mistreat-ment of TCP results in efficiency falling in throughout. If TCP sender finds packet loss, he lessens transport window size and resend lost packet. Disorder control or avoidance and packet loss in network caused by disconnection in handover high bit error rate. If the packet loss recovery mechanism mentioned in advance is applied to network, it causes unnecessary performance degradation. In addition, if you apply

H. Jin et al. (Eds.): NPC 2004, LNCS 3222, pp. 684-690, 2004.

TCP protocol to mobile host, it results in unnecessary decrease in terms of bandwidth usage and performance degradation through handling rate decrease and high delay. To make environment for mobile computing, we should find location of host which change its connection points, and keep connection with changeable connection during communication. The new revised activation method was invented and was studied. This activation isn't impacted to the existing TCP, however it considers character of wireless networks.

There are several methods to improve End-to-end throughput in wireless network in different perspectives. They are End-to-End protocol, Split connection protocol and link hierarchy protocol. End-to-End protocol is the protocol which sender knows existence of network, and it uses mainly Selective Acknowledge which can recover several packet in window not to depend on timeout while resending packet and ELN which can protect call of disorder control mechanism, by informing packet loss reason is not disorder but network characters. As we may guess the meaning of terms, Split-connection is the way to apply proper protocol after splitting the connection of wire and wireless network. In other words, it is split into wire network between mobile host and Base Station (BS) and wireless network between FH and BS, Link hierarchy protocol as providing local reliability, uses combination of ARQ (Automatic Repeat request) and FEC (Forward Error Correction) which bring TCP improvement by hiding loss related wireless network in network hierarchy such as TCP.

This paper proposes the way to improve TCP performance on handover in WINs. When handover happens, the Mobile Host (MH) which recognizes handover sends explicit handover notification packet formatted as ICMP to the fixed host and informs handover. Through this process, it protects not to happen retransmission timeout and over crowded control process on force.

2 Related Work

Fast retransmission algorithm is the way to take lesser time of handover by quick resending process of fixed host through process that MH sends three overlapped Acks allocated last received pack to Fixed Host (FH) after handover completion [5]. The existed solution for improvement of End-to-End efficiency is for transported protocol to re-start sending data after handover completion. By this, re-sender timer of fixed host can escape time out. The advantage of quick re-sending algorithm is to be requested a least change for software at end host. Mobile IP is revised to send available handover at the one layer in protocol hierarchy, and also be revised TCP to call quick re-sending procedure. It doesn't depend on other medium router in wireless network [7]. After fist resending, it goes through complicated control procedure by closing window and using slow start algorithms. Therefore both rest networks and mobile host can escape disorder of cell.

Probe [3] is the way to make resending quickly about related packet by mobiles sending three Negative Acks to the FH. Probe algorithms is the Split-connection protocol hiding MH movement from TCP to decrease impact of handover in TCP function.

686   D.C. Lee, H.-J. Kim, and J.Y. Koh

Probe chooses sign notifying handover in a layer of network as fast retransmission algorithms. This algorithm tries to solve disconnection over handover by using information from Mobile IP to find completion of handover.

Snoop protocol is the split connection way providing new routing protocol to decrease data loss on handover. If handover happens, it can skip the process forwarding data as new BS from primary BS, not like other protocol. In a result, it can remove data handover delay.

In previous handover algorithms, Fast Retransmission algorithm [4] as End-to-End protocol which fixed host, sender node, knows wireless existence reopens sending quickly to decrease stopping time over re-opening of communication in the network level after hand off completion, by measurement of impact from mobile movement over throughput and delay and recognition of reasons of function loss. In other words, it is the way to decrease time on hand off after completion of handover procedure. MH starts resending process of lost segment not waiting for re-sender timer after sending three overlapped Ack allocated in last receiving packet or for re-sender timer after sending to the FH. Because of fast retransmission call resending only when informed handover, it is only least change at software in existed FH. In addition, it doesn't depend on based network or medium router. However, it is only providing solution for packet loss due to disconnection in handover and disregards packet loss by high bit error rate of network in itself. Besides, after completion of handover, it takes round trip time to arrive completed bandwidth and it makes sending rate decrease by shrinking sending window size. Probe algorithms is the split connection protocol hiding movement of MH from TCP to decrease impact of handover in TCP function. It is the way to rise quick resending to corresponded packet by MH sending three Negative Acks to the FH after completion of handover. This algorithm has problems which it should always storage Ack packet and sends them and it cannot guarantee of transparency in hierarchy in the BS. Snoop protocol [2] is the split connection way to provide new routing protocol to decrease data loss on handover. This algorithm can remove delay over handover and improve efficiency in case of high bit error rate. However it has some deficits such as too much information related with handover process and heavy burden of unnecessary data and buffering,

The above algorithms to recover TCP efficiency decrease due to handover tried to improve End-to-End function through minimization of FH TCP timeout case and decrease delay time after completion of handover. However it still takes several round trip time to get completed bandwidth, and it has issue to resend lost data due to time out during sending data buffered in BS.

3 New Handover Algorithms

When the handover occur in a cell, MH send explicit handover notification packet with Internet control message protocol structure to FH and old BS, and indicate to handover start explicitly. Then it cannot be taken place the timeout of FH retransmission timer and the procedure of congestion control. The explicit handoff notification packet include the window size where window size mean to buffer size of received host and the address of new BS which it is after the handover in MH. This make sender FH to persist mode, and sending host cannot transmit all packets basically. Procedure of packet change in handover is the following figure 1.

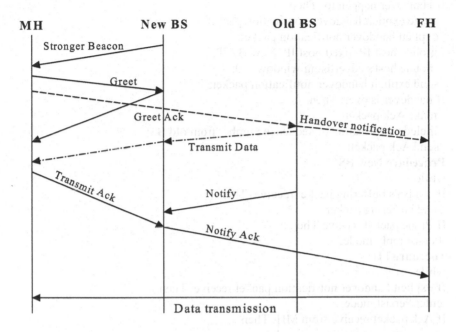

Fig. 1. Message changing procedure during the handover

In the handover process, the MH receive new beacon, and if it know handover start, new BS send Greet packet including IP address of FH with old BS and its IP address. FH send explicit handover notification packet with window information and address of new BS of MH. New BS send greet Ack packet to the MH, and old BS transmit buffering data to MH through new BS. If the handover is over, the MH sends information of the great sequence number that received from old BS, and the FH can be received packet data. When the FH receive explicit handover notification packet, it changes value of sending window size to 0, and waits for the Ack message of MH that handover will over after change to persist mode in itself. In persist mode, it halts to retransmission timer and states that is in FHs, and sends Probe packet period that inquire to increasing window size for sending packet to receiver node using the persist mode, which Probe packet process in the new BS. And when Ack message from MH send to new BS, FH change persist mode to normal mode, which have value advertising window before handover. Then the FH send packet as sending window size that use before handover. Explicit handover notification packet happens to one time during handover, and it has no much effect on traffic of the path. This algorithm is following

Algorithm Handover
  Procedure MH
  while
  If Handover happen to Then
    make explicit handover notification packet;
    explicit handover notification packet;
    mobile host IP, fixed host IP, New BS IP,
    mobile host's advertising window = 0;
    send explicit handover notification packet;
  If handover is over Then
    make Ack packet;
    include information of sequence number from old BS;
    send Ack packet;
  Procedure New BS
  while
  If old BS's buffering packet receive Then
   send buffering packet;
  If Probe packet receive Then
   Persist reply mode;
Procedure FH
  while
  If explicit handover notification packet receive Then
   enter Persist mode;
  If Ack packet receive from MH Then
   come out form the Persist mode;
   end FH;
   end New BS;
  end

4 Simulation and Analysis

The simulation was performed using NetSimulator and IBM compatible PCs with Pentium. For the purpose of this model, we have assumed that simulation is performed base on network model that configure switching system with linking to nodes. Fig. 2 shows that this network model consists of FH, MH, and BS in mobile environments. In this model, it assume that wire link has 56 Kbps, wireless link has 19.2Kbps, and maximum window size is 32, and packet size is 128 Bytes, and TCP in FH make use of Tahoe TCP protocol. In order to ensure proper packet processing, we applied the information used for actual simulations, which was computed using the Poisson distribution, equally to mobile networks. Simulation carried to 7 times handover by seconds during 100 seconds to compare to performance analysis.

Fig. 3 shows throughput that MH is in handover. The proposed algorithm has packet loss less than the general TCP. Because it transmits buffering packet to MH through old BS during the handover. The proposed method shows that the more handover time takes long, all throughput decrease, and staying time in cell take time more, the more throughput decrease. Also, the more holding time in cell and handover time take long, the more performance has difference.

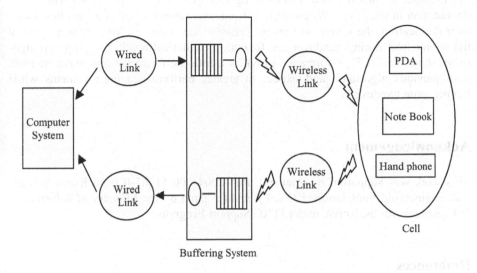

Fig. 2. Network model

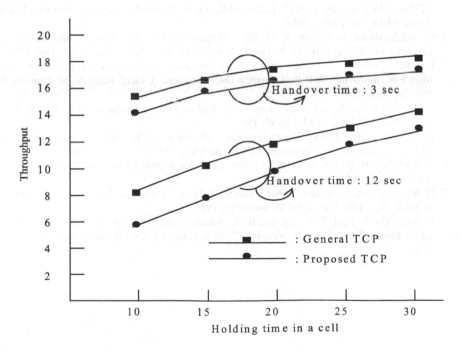

Fig. 3. Comparison of handover time

5 Conclusions

In this paper we propose new handover algorithm that improve the TCP performance degradation in handover. When starting handover, upon receipt of an explicit handover notification, the source host enters Persist mode. This way, data transmissions at the source host during handover are frozen. In numerical result, the proposed algorithm show that TCP performance provides a little performance improvement more than previous algorithm, and expect to greater performance improvements while having more handovers.

Acknowledgement

This work was supported by grant no. R05-2004-000-11267-0 from Korea Science and Engineering Foundation (KOSEF), and (in part) by the Ministry of Information & Communications, Korea, under ITRC Support Program..

References

1. Bikram S. Bakshi, P. Krishna, N. H. Vaidya, D. K. Pradhan, "Improving Performance of TCP over Wireless Networks", Technical Report # TR-01-014, Dept. of Computer Science, Texas A&M University., 2001.
2. H. Balakrishnan, S. Seshan, R. H. Katz, "Improving Reliable Transport and Handoff Performance in Cellular Wireless Networks," ACM Wireless Networks, Vol. 1, Dec. 1997.
3. H. Balakrishnan, V. N. Padmanabhan, S. Seshan, and R. H. Katz, "A Comparison of Mechanism For Improving TCP Performance Over Wireless Links," IEEE/ACM Tran. on Networking, Vol. 5, 1997.
4. R. Yavatkar and N. Bhagwat, "Improving End-to-End performance of TCP over Mobile Internetworks," Proc. of Moblie'94, 1994.
5. R. Caceres and L. Iftode, "Improving the Performance of Reliable Transport Protocols in Mobile Computing Environments," IEEE J.on SAC, Vol. 14, No. 5, 1996.
6. A. Bakre and B. Badrinath, "I-TCP: Indirect TCP for Mobile Hosts," Technical Report DCS-TR-614, Rutgers University, 1999.
7. H. Balakrishnan, S. Seshan, E. Amir and R. H. Katz, "Improving TCP/IP Performance over Wireless Networks," Proc. of Mobicom'95, 1995.
8. E. Ayanoglu, S. Paul, T. F. Laporta, K. K. Sabnani, and R. D. Gitlin, "AIRMAIL: A Link-Layer Protocol for Wireless Networks," ACM/Baltzer J. of Wireless Networks, Vol. 1, 1998.

Author Index

Ahn, Jong Suk, 473
Ahn, Seongjin, 635
Ahn, Yonghak, 644
An, Eung-Suk, 65
Attanasio, C. Richard, 5

Bianchini, Calebe P., 213
Bin, Cai, 252
Bouvry, Pascal, 411
Buczak, Anna L., 536

Cai, JiPing, 83
Cai, Xinxia, 522
Cao, Lei, 57
Chae, Oksam, 644
Chai, Xiaoyong, 584
Chen, Guo-liang, 261
Chen, Hao, 238
Chen, Huiqiong, 325
Chen, Jiming, 357
Chen, Ming, 133, 154, 481
Chen, Wei, 419
Chen, Yiqiang, 526, 584
Chen, Zhigang, 316
Cheng, Kuan-Wei, 92
Cheung, Shing-Chi, 568
Chi, Chi-Hung, 435
Cho, Young-Hoon, 374
Choi, Jong-Deok, 5
Chung, Jinwook, 635
Clifford, Gari, 65
Coddington, Paul, 73
Cooper, Jonathan M., 517
Crawford, John, 527
Cui, Dafu, 522
Cui, Li, 565
Cumming, David R.S., 517

Dai, Huaping, 333
Deng, Dafu, 238
Deng, Xiaoheng, 316
Deng, Yuhui, 489
Ding, Wenkui, 129
Dou, Wenhua, 167
Duato, José, 341

Dubey, Niteesh, 5
Dulman, Stefan, 592

Ekanadham, K., 5
Eom, Young Ik, 280
Esperidião, Marcelo D., 213

Feng, Dan, 248, 489
Feng, Yong, 256
Flich, Jose, 341
Fortes, José, 3
Fu, JianMing, 443
Fu, Wei, 30

Gao, Wen, 526, 559
Goel, Sushant, 22
Gómez, Maria Engracia, 341
Gong, Yili, 83
Guo, Xiaoxin, 502, 508
Gupta, Manish, 5

Hahn, GeneBeck, 451
Han, Kyoo Jin, 676
Havinga, Paul, 592
He, Bingsheng, 551, 576
He, Yanxiang, 419
Hruschka, Eduardo R., 213
Hsu, Ping-Yu, 230
Hu, Jinfeng, 154, 485
Huang, Joshua Zhexue, 57
Hwang, Il-Sun, 618
Hwang, Kai, 1, 9

Inagaki, Tatsushi, 5
Ishizaki, Kazuaki, 5

Jann, Joefon, 5
Jeong, Chang-Sung, 47
Jeong, Moon-Sang, 374
Jia, Rui-yong, 256
Jia, Yan, 141
Jiang, Hong, 248
Jiang, ShengYi, 459
Jin, Hai, 238
Jin, Hairong, 183
Jin, Hong, 536

Jin, Ren, 252
Jo, SungJae, 195
Johannessen, Erik A., 517
Johnson, Robert D., 5
Ju, Hailing, 565

Kang, Yong-hyeog, 280
Kil, Min Wook, 670
Kim, Byungsang, 65
Kim, HeeSook, 611
Kim, Hong-jin, 618, 684
Kim, Hyuncheol, 635
Kim, Hyung Jin, 661
Kim, Jung-hee, 280
Kim, Si Jung, 670
Kim, Sinkyu, 451
Kim, Su Myeon, 195
Kim, Sunghae, 635
Koh, JaeYoung, 684
Krishnamurthy, E.V., 272
Krishnamurthy, Vikram, 272
Kuhn, Bob, 4
Kwok, Yu-Kwong, 300
Kwon, Taekyoung, 205, 451
Kwon, Yong-Won, 47
Kwon, Youngmi, 653, 670

Lam, Kam-Yiu, 601
Le, Huy, 73
Lee, Bong-Hwan, 65
Lee, Dong Chun, 626, 684
Lee, Geuk, 653, 670
Lee, Gi-Sung, 618
Lee, Hui Jae, 653
Lee, Jinwon, 195
Lee, Jongchan, 626
Lee, JongHee, 611
Lee, KeunWang, 611
Lee, KwangHyoung, 611
Lee, Sang Woon, 676
Lee, Sang-Ho, 366
Lee, Soobeom, 661
Leung, K.C., 568
Li, Baosen, 536
Li, Dongsheng, 308
Li, Jianzhong, 528
Li, Jinbao, 528
Li, Keqiu, 187
Li, Kuan-Ching, 92
Li, Ming, 399, 403, 435

Li, Minglu, 57, 137, 175
Li, QingHua, 459
Li, Shanping, 183
Li, Shuangfeng, 544
Li, Tianpu, 565
Li, Yin, 175
Li, Zhi, 300
Liang, BiYu, 601
Liao, Huaming, 110
Liao, Xiaofei, 238
Lin, Chuang, 427
Liu, Bixin, 141
Liu, Dongxi, 435
Liu, Fei, 137
Liu, Jingao, 399
Liu, Junfa, 526
Liu, Xuezheng, 133, 154, 481
Liu, Yajie, 167
Liu, Yunhao, 146
Liu, Zhifeng, 167
Lo, Cindy, 568
Long, Dongyang, 399
López, Pedro, 341
Lu, Xicheng, 308
Luo, Haiyong, 565
Luo, Qiong, 544, 551, 576
Lysne, Olav , 341

Ma, Fanyuan, 137, 175
Ma, Tianchi, 183
Ma, Xiuli, 544
Macwan, Mikin, 9
Meng, Dan, 244
Min, Geyong, 284
Mukherjee, Nandini, 38

Najaf-abadi, H.H., 390
Nakatani, Toshio, 5
Nam, Dong Su, 65
Nam, Young Jin, 473
Ni, Lionel M., 146, 559, 576
Nordbotten, Nils Agne, 341

Ok, MinHwan, 221
Ould-Khaoua, Mohamed, 284
Ouyang, Kai, 493

Pang, Henry C.W., 601
Pang, Yunjie, 502, 508
Park, Chanik, 473

Park, Il, 5
Park, JaePyo, 611
Park, Jin-Sung, 47
Park, Jong-Tae, 374
Park, Myong-soon, 221
Pattnaik, Pratap, 5
Peng, Gang, 183
Peng, Wenling, 419
Pienkosz, Krzysztof, 411

Qu, Xiangli, 30

Robles, Antonio, 341
Roy, Sarbani, 38
Ryu, Junkil, 473
Ryu, So-Hyun, 47

Sarbazi-Azad, H., 390
Sato, Liria M., 213
Senger, Hermes, 213
Seredynski, Marcin, 411
Serrano, Mauricio, 5
Sharda, Hema, 22
Shen, Hong, 187
Shi, Bole, 325
Shi, Shengfei, 528
Shi, Wei, 292
Shim, Eun Bo, 65
Shin, Dong-Ryeol, 366
Shu, Ji-wu, 463
Shuf, Yefim, 5
Silva, Fabrício A.B., 213
Sim, Hyun-chul, 280
Skeie, Tor, 341
Smith, Stephen E., 5
Son, Bongsoo, 661
Son, Snag H., 601
Song, JooSeok, 451
Song, Junehwa, 195
Song, Sanghoon, 205
Song, Shanshan, 9
Song, Yeqiong, 357
Srimani, Pradip K., 292
Steiner, Ian, 5
Sterling, Thomas, 2
Su, Jinshu, 308
Sun, Weiwei, 325
Sun, Youxian, 333, 357
Sun, Yuzhong, 83, 110

Tajima, Keishi, 187
Takesue, Masaru, 382
Tan, Zhangxi, 427
Tang, Feilong, 57
Tang, Rongfeng, 244
Tang, Shiwei, 544
Tang, Yu, 498
Taniar, David, 22
Teo, Yong-Meng, 101
Ting, Ping-Ho, 230

Wang, Fang, 489
Wang, Fei, 565
Wang, Furong, 407
Wang, Hongan, 536
Wang, Hui, 459, 536
Wang, Ke, 513
Wang, Xianbing, 101
Wang, Yi, 57
Wang, YuFeng, 141
Wang, Zhengxuan, 502, 508
Wang, Zhi, 357
Wei, Jun, 568
Wen, Dongchan, 463
Wendelborn, Andrew L., 73
Whang, Keum Chan, 676
Wu, Hejun, 551, 576
Wu, Jian, 592
Wu, Xiaonian, 30
Wu, Ye, 407
Wu, Yongwei, 133, 154, 481

Xia, Tao, 493
Xiao, Li, 146
Xiao, Nong, 30, 498
Xie, Changsheng, 252
Xiong, Jin, 244
Xu, Chang, 568
Xu, Zhiwei, 559
Xu, Zhiwen, 502, 508
Xu, Zhuoqun, 129
Xue, Wenwei, 551

Yan, Fei, 443
Yan, Rui, 463
Yang, Baijian, 146
Yang, Chao-Tung, 92
Yang, Dongqing, 544
Yang, Guangwen, 133, 154, 481
Yang, Min, 419, 443

Yang, Qiang, 584
Yang, Xuejun, 498
Yao, Zhen, 261
Yi, FaLing, 252
Yin, Ai-Hua, 118
Yin, Hao, 427
Yin, Jie, 584
Yoo, Seung-Jae, 626
You, Ganmei, 110
Youn, Chan-Hyun, 65
Youn, Hee Yong, 366
Yu, Haiyan, 83
Yu, Huashan, 129
Yu, Shengsheng, 493
Yu, Shui, 137

Zha, Li, 83
Zhang, Dehui, 544

Zhang, Duan, 333
Zhang, HuanGuo, 443
Zhang, Li-bao, 513
Zhang, Lianming, 316
Zhang, Qing, 325
Zhang, Yan-yuan, 256
Zhang, Youhui, 485
Zheng, Pei, 576
Zheng, Qi-long, 261
Zheng, Weimin, 463, 485
Zhou, Bin, 141
Zhou, Haifang, 498
Zhou, Jingli, 493
Zhou, Ke, 489
Zhu, Guangxi, 427
Zhu, Yifeng, 248
Zou, Futai, 175

Lecture Notes in Computer Science

For information about Vols. 1–3159

please contact your bookseller or Springer

Vol. 3274: R. Guerraoui (Ed.), Distributed Computing. XIII, 465 pages. 2004.

Vol. 3273: T. Baar, A. Strohmeier, A. Moreira, S.J. Mellor (Eds.), <<UML>> 2004 - The Unified Modelling Language. XIII, 449 pages. 2004.

Vol. 3271: J. Vicente, D. Hutchison (Eds.), Management of Multimedia Networks and Services. XIII, 335 pages. 2004.

Vol. 3270: M. Jeckle, R. Kowalczyk, P. Braun (Eds.), Grid Services Engineering and Management. X, 165 pages. 2004.

Vol. 3266: J. Solé-Pareta, M. Smirnov, P.V. Mieghem, J. Domingo-Pascual, E. Monteiro, P. Reichl, B. Stiller, R.J. Gibbens (Eds.), Quality of Service in the Emerging Networking Panorama. XVI, 390 pages. 2004.

Vol. 3263: M. Weske, P. Liggesmeyer (Eds.), Object-Oriented and Internet-Based Technologies. XII, 239 pages. 2004.

Vol. 3260: I. Niemegeers, S.H. de Groot (Eds.), Personal Wireless Communications. XIV, 478 pages. 2004.

Vol. 3258: M. Wallace (Ed.), Principles and Practice of Constraint Programming – CP 2004. XVII, 822 pages. 2004.

Vol. 3256: H. Ehrig, G. Engels, F. Parisi-Presicce, G. Rozenberg (Eds.), Graph Transformations. XII, 451 pages. 2004.

Vol. 3255: A. Benczúr, J. Demetrovics, G. Gottlob (Eds.), Advances in Databases and Information Systems. XI, 423 pages. 2004.

Vol. 3254: E. Macii, V. Paliouras, O. Koufopavlou (Eds.), Integrated Circuit and System Design. XVI, 910 pages. 2004.

Vol. 3253: Y. Lakhnech, S. Yovine (Eds.), Formal Techniques, Modelling and Analysis of Timed and Fault-Tolerant Systems. X, 397 pages. 2004.

Vol. 3250: L.-J. (LJ) Zhang, M. Jeckle (Eds.), Web Services. X, 300 pages. 2004.

Vol. 3249: B. Buchberger, J.A. Campbell (Eds.), Artificial Intelligence and Symbolic Computation. X, 285 pages. 2004. (Subseries LNAI).

Vol. 3246: A. Apostolico, M. Melucci (Eds.), String Processing and Information Retrieval. XIV, 332 pages. 2004.

Vol. 3245: E. Suzuki, S. Arikawa (Eds.), Discovery Science. XIV, 430 pages. 2004. (Subseries LNAI).

Vol. 3244: S. Ben-David, J. Case, A. Maruoka (Eds.), Algorithmic Learning Theory. XIV, 505 pages. 2004. (Subseries LNAI).

Vol. 3242: X. Yao, E. Burke, J.A. Lozano, J. Smith, J.J. Merelo-Guervós, J.A. Bullinaria, J. Rowe, P. Tiňo, A. Kabán, H.-P. Schwefel (Eds.), Parallel Problem Solving from Nature - PPSN VIII. XX, 1185 pages. 2004.

Vol. 3241: D. Kranzlmüller, P. Kacsuk, J.J. Dongarra (Eds.), Recent Advances in Parallel Virtual Machine and Message Passing Interface. XIII, 452 pages. 2004.

Vol. 3240: I. Jonassen, J. Kim (Eds.), Algorithms in Bioinformatics. IX, 476 pages. 2004. (Subseries LNBI).

Vol. 3239: G. Nicosia, V. Cutello, P.J. Bentley, J. Timmis (Eds.), Artificial Immune Systems. XII, 444 pages. 2004.

Vol. 3238: S. Biundo, T. Frühwirth, G. Palm (Eds.), KI 2004: Advances in Artificial Intelligence. XI, 467 pages. 2004. (Subseries LNAI).

Vol. 3232: R. Heery, L. Lyon (Eds.), Research and Advanced Technology for Digital Libraries. XV, 528 pages. 2004.

Vol. 3229: J.J. Alferes, J. Leite (Eds.), Logics in Artificial Intelligence. XIV, 744 pages. 2004. (Subseries LNAI).

Vol. 3225: K. Zhang, Y. Zheng (Eds.), Information Security. XII, 442 pages. 2004.

Vol. 3224: E. Jonsson, A. Valdes, M. Almgren (Eds.), Recent Advances in Intrusion Detection. XII, 315 pages. 2004.

Vol. 3223: K. Slind, A. Bunker, G. Gopalakrishnan (Eds.), Theorem Proving in Higher Order Logics. VIII, 337 pages. 2004.

Vol. 3222: H. Jin, G.R. Gao, Z. Xu, H. Chen (Eds.), Network and Parallel Computing. XX, 694 pages. 2004.

Vol. 3221: S. Albers, T. Radzik (Eds.), Algorithms – ESA 2004. XVIII, 836 pages. 2004.

Vol. 3220: J.C. Lester, R.M. Vicari, F. Paraguaçu (Eds.), Intelligent Tutoring Systems. XXI, 920 pages. 2004.

Vol. 3219: M. Heisel, P. Liggesmeyer, S. Wittmann (Eds.), Computer Safety, Reliability, and Security. XI, 339 pages. 2004.

Vol. 3217: C. Barillot, D.R. Haynor, P. Hellier (Eds.), Medical Image Computing and Computer-Assisted Intervention – MICCAI 2004. XXXVIII, 1114 pages. 2004.

Vol. 3216: C. Barillot, D.R. Haynor, P. Hellier (Eds.), Medical Image Computing and Computer-Assisted Intervention – MICCAI 2004. XXXVIII, 930 pages. 2004.

Vol. 3215: M.G.. Negoita, R.J. Howlett, L.C. Jain (Eds.), Knowledge-Based Intelligent Information and Engineering Systems. LVII, 906 pages. 2004. (Subseries LNAI).

Vol. 3214: M.G.. Negoita, R.J. Howlett, L.C. Jain (Eds.), Knowledge-Based Intelligent Information and Engineering Systems. LVIII, 1302 pages. 2004. (Subseries LNAI).

Vol. 3213: M.G.. Negoita, R.J. Howlett, L.C. Jain (Eds.), Knowledge-Based Intelligent Information and Engineering Systems. LVIII, 1280 pages. 2004. (Subseries LNAI).

Vol. 3212: A. Campilho, M. Kamel (Eds.), Image Analysis and Recognition. XXIX, 862 pages. 2004.

Vol. 3211: A. Campilho, M. Kamel (Eds.), Image Analysis and Recognition. XXIX, 880 pages. 2004.

Vol. 3210: J. Marcinkowski, A. Tarlecki (Eds.), Computer Science Logic. XI, 520 pages. 2004.

Vol. 3209: B. Berendt, A. Hotho, D. Mladenic, M. van Someren, M. Spiliopoulou, G. Stumme (Eds.), Web Mining: From Web to Semantic Web. IX, 201 pages. 2004. (Subseries LNAI).

Vol. 3208: H.J. Ohlbach, S. Schaffert (Eds.), Principles and Practice of Semantic Web Reasoning. VII, 165 pages. 2004.

Vol. 3207: L.T. Yang, M. Guo, G.R. Gao, N.K. Jha (Eds.), Embedded and Ubiquitous Computing. XX, 1116 pages. 2004.

Vol. 3206: P. Sojka, I. Kopecek, K. Pala (Eds.), Text, Speech and Dialogue. XIII, 667 pages. 2004. (Subseries LNAI).

Vol. 3205: N. Davies, E. Mynatt, I. Siio (Eds.), UbiComp 2004: Ubiquitous Computing. XVI, 452 pages. 2004.

Vol. 3203: J. Becker, M. Platzner, S. Vernalde (Eds.), Field Programmable Logic and Application. XXX, 1198 pages. 2004.

Vol. 3202: J.-F. Boulicaut, F. Esposito, F. Giannotti, D. Pedreschi (Eds.), Knowledge Discovery in Databases: PKDD 2004. XIX, 560 pages. 2004. (Subseries LNAI).

Vol. 3201: J.-F. Boulicaut, F. Esposito, F. Giannotti, D. Pedreschi (Eds.), Machine Learning: ECML 2004. XVIII, 580 pages. 2004. (Subseries LNAI).

Vol. 3199: H. Schepers (Ed.), Software and Compilers for Embedded Systems. X, 259 pages. 2004.

Vol. 3198: G.-J. de Vreede, L.A. Guerrero, G. Marín Raventós (Eds.), Groupware: Design, Implementation and Use. XI, 378 pages. 2004.

Vol. 3195: C.G. Puntonet, A. Prieto (Eds.), Independent Component Analysis and Blind Signal Separation. XXIII, 1266 pages. 2004.

Vol. 3194: R. Camacho, R. King, A. Srinivasan (Eds.), Inductive Logic Programming. XI, 361 pages. 2004. (Subseries LNAI).

Vol. 3193: P. Samarati, P. Ryan, D. Gollmann, R. Molva (Eds.), Computer Security – ESORICS 2004. X, 457 pages. 2004.

Vol. 3192: C. Bussler, D. Fensel (Eds.), Artificial Intelligence: Methodology, Systems, and Applications. XIII, 522 pages. 2004. (Subseries LNAI).

Vol. 3191: M. Klusch, S. Ossowski, V. Kashyap, R. Unland (Eds.), Cooperative Information Agents VIII. XI, 303 pages. 2004. (Subseries LNAI).

Vol. 3190: Y. Luo (Ed.), Cooperative Design, Visualization, and Engineering. IX, 248 pages. 2004.

Vol. 3189: P.-C. Yew, J. Xue (Eds.), Advances in Computer Systems Architecture. XVII, 598 pages. 2004.

Vol. 3188: F.S. de Boer, M.M. Bonsangue, S. Graf, W.-P. de Roever (Eds.), Formal Methods for Components and Objects. VIII, 373 pages. 2004.

Vol. 3187: G. Lindemann, J. Denzinger, I.J. Timm, R. Unland (Eds.), Multiagent System Technologies. XIII, 341 pages. 2004. (Subseries LNAI).

Vol. 3186: Z. Bellahsène, T. Milo, M. Rys, D. Suciu, R. Unland (Eds.), Database and XML Technologies. X, 235 pages. 2004.

Vol. 3185: M. Bernardo, F. Corradini (Eds.), Formal Methods for the Design of Real-Time Systems. VII, 295 pages. 2004.

Vol. 3184: S. Katsikas, J. Lopez, G. Pernul (Eds.), Trust and Privacy in Digital Business. XI, 299 pages. 2004.

Vol. 3183: R. Traunmüller (Ed.), Electronic Government. XIX, 583 pages. 2004.

Vol. 3182: K. Bauknecht, M. Bichler, B. Pröll (Eds.), E-Commerce and Web Technologies. XI, 370 pages. 2004.

Vol. 3181: Y. Kambayashi, M. Mohania, W. Wöß (Eds.), Data Warehousing and Knowledge Discovery. XIV, 412 pages. 2004.

Vol. 3180: F. Galindo, M. Takizawa, R. Traunmüller (Eds.), Database and Expert Systems Applications. XXI, 972 pages. 2004.

Vol. 3179: F.J. Perales, B.A. Draper (Eds.), Articulated Motion and Deformable Objects. XI, 270 pages. 2004.

Vol. 3178: W. Jonker, M. Petkovic (Eds.), Secure Data Management. VIII, 219 pages. 2004.

Vol. 3177: Z.R. Yang, H. Yin, R. Everson (Eds.), Intelligent Data Engineering and Automated Learning – IDEAL 2004. XVIII, 852 pages. 2004.

Vol. 3176: O. Bousquet, U. von Luxburg, G. Rätsch (Eds.), Advanced Lectures on Machine Learning. IX, 241 pages. 2004. (Subseries LNAI).

Vol. 3175: C.E. Rasmussen, H.H. Bülthoff, B. Schölkopf, M.A. Giese (Eds.), Pattern Recognition. XVIII, 581 pages. 2004.

Vol. 3174: F. Yin, J. Wang, C. Guo (Eds.), Advances in Neural Networks - ISNN 2004. XXXV, 1021 pages. 2004.

Vol. 3173: F. Yin, J. Wang, C. Guo (Eds.), Advances in Neural Networks – ISNN 2004. XXXV, 1041 pages. 2004.

Vol. 3172: M. Dorigo, M. Birattari, C. Blum, L. M. Gambardella, F. Mondada, T. Stützle (Eds.), Ant Colony, Optimization and Swarm Intelligence. XII, 434 pages. 2004.

Vol. 3171: A.L.C. Bazzan, S. Labidi (Eds.), Advances in Artificial Intelligence – SBIA 2004. XVII, 548 pages. 2004. (Subseries LNAI).

Vol. 3170: P. Gardner, N. Yoshida (Eds.), CONCUR 2004 - Concurrency Theory. XIII, 529 pages. 2004.

Vol. 3166: M. Rauterberg (Ed.), Entertainment Computing – ICEC 2004. XXIII, 617 pages. 2004.

Vol. 3163: S. Marinai, A. Dengel (Eds.), Document Analysis Systems VI. XI, 564 pages. 2004.

Vol. 3162: R. Downey, M. Fellows, F. Dehne (Eds.), Parameterized and Exact Computation. X, 293 pages. 2004.

Vol. 3160: S. Brewster, M. Dunlop (Eds.), Mobile Human-Computer Interaction – MobileHCI 2004. XVII, 541 pages. 2004.